AF809789

Victims Before the International Criminal Court

Christoph Safferling • Gurgen Petrossian

Victims Before the International Criminal Court

Definition, Participation, Reparation

Springer

Christoph Safferling
School of Law
University of Erlangen-Nuremberg
Erlangen, Germany

Gurgen Petrossian
School of Law
University of Erlangen-Nuremberg
Erlangen, Germany

ISBN 978-3-030-80176-2 ISBN 978-3-030-80177-9 (eBook)
https://doi.org/10.1007/978-3-030-80177-9

© The Editor(s) (if applicable) and The Author(s), under exclusive license to Springer Nature Switzerland AG 2021
This work is subject to copyright. All rights are solely and exclusively licensed by the Publisher, whether the whole or part of the material is concerned, specifically the rights of translation, reprinting, reuse of illustrations, recitation, broadcasting, reproduction on microfilms or in any other physical way, and transmission or information storage and retrieval, electronic adaptation, computer software, or by similar or dissimilar methodology now known or hereafter developed.
The use of general descriptive names, registered names, trademarks, service marks, etc. in this publication does not imply, even in the absence of a specific statement, that such names are exempt from the relevant protective laws and regulations and therefore free for general use.
The publisher, the authors, and the editors are safe to assume that the advice and information in this book are believed to be true and accurate at the date of publication. Neither the publisher nor the authors or the editors give a warranty, expressed or implied, with respect to the material contained herein or for any errors or omissions that may have been made. The publisher remains neutral with regard to jurisdictional claims in published maps and institutional affiliations.

This Springer imprint is published by the registered company Springer Nature Switzerland AG.
The registered company address is: Gewerbestrasse 11, 6330 Cham, Switzerland

Preface

This book is based on DFG-funded research (DFG-Projekt SA 2269 4-1). The research was carried out between 2016 and 2019 and includes developments related to victims' participation. The research was drafted in 2014 and approved in 2015.

The participation of victims of genocide, crimes against humanity, war crimes, and the crime of aggression in international criminal trials have received growing attention since the foundation of the International Criminal Court (ICC). The participation of victims challenges the classical-liberal concept of criminal procedure and the recognition of the rights of the accused in criminal trials. Likewise, the question of which victim qualifies to participate in the prosecution of individual perpetrators bears considerable difficulties and poses the danger of producing injustices on the side of victims and victims' groups by a highly selective process. The ICC furthermore foresees a specific procedure to compensate the victims. The book first addresses the definition of the victim of international crimes and looks into the criteria relevant for the admission to participate in the criminal trial. The book will secondly question the implementation of the participation of victims in the criminal trial itself. The separate stages of the criminal process will be scrutinized to identify those parts of the trial, in which participation of the victim is possible. Furthermore, the structure of the process will be discussed and which influence victim participation has thereon. A comparative approach is necessary in this regard. Even if the Rome Statute created an autonomous procedural order in an international compromise, the most influential traditions of criminal procedure, namely the Anglo-American and the Continental European approach, need to be looked at in detail and how they relate to the participation of victims in the criminal process.

Thirdly, the issue will be taken with compensation of victims for the harm suffered. As before the question of inclusion and exclusion of victims' groups need to be looked at and how this is effectuated by the linking of the compensation issue with the criminal trial. The few cases in which the international courts addressed compensation will be analyzed.

We are very grateful for the support of Dr. Michaela Lissowsky in her contribution to this project. We are especially very thankful to Dr. Kevin Pikc for his support.

Without the help of Dr. Pike, this research would probably be linguistically unintelligible. We are also deeply thankful for the student support from Johannes Lechler, Kenan Bejtic, Georg Bugsch, Melanie Rosa, Martin Prokopek, and Deborah Weber.

Erlangen, Germany

Christoph Safferling
Gurgen Petrossian

Contents

Abbreviations

ABA	Amercian Bar Association
AHC	Ad hoc Committee
Art.	Article
ASP	Assembly of States Parties
B.C.E.	Before Common Era
CAR	Central African Republic
CCP	Code of Criminal Procedure
CETS	Council of Europe Treaty Series
Cf.	Compare
CICC	Coalition for an International Criminal Court
CLRV	Common Legal Representative of Victims
DER	Division for External Relations
DoJ	Department of Justice
DRC	Democratic Republic of Congo
ECCC	Extraordinary Chambers in the Courts of Cambodia
ECHR	European Convention on Human Rights
ECtHR	European Court of Human Rights
EFTA	European Free Trade Association
ELSA	European Law Students' Association
FCO	Foreign and Commonwealth Office of UK
IACHR	Inter-American Convention on Human Rights
IACPPT	Inter-American Convention to Prevent and Punish Torture
ICC	International Criminal Court
ICCPR	International Covenant on Civil and Political Rights
ICERD	International Convention on the Elimination of All Forms of Racial Discrimination
ICJ	International Commission of Jurists
ICRC	International Committee of the Red Cross
ICTR	International Criminal Tribunal for Rwanda
ICTY	International Criminal Tribunal for the former Yugoslavia

ILC	International Law Commission
IMT	International Military Tribunal
IRR	Internal Rules and Regulations
LRV	Legal Representative of Victims
N.	Number
NGO	Non-governmental Organisation
OAS	Organisation of American States
OAU	Organization of African Unity
OLG	Oberlandesgericht
OPCD	Office of Public Counsel for the Defence
OPCV	Office of Public Counsel for Victims
OTP	Office of the Prosecutor
OVC	Office of Victims of Crime
PIDS	Public Information and Documentation Section
PoW	Prisoner of War
PrepCom	Preparatory Committee
PTC	Pre-Trial Chamber
RoC	Regulations of the Court
RoP	Regulations of the Office of the Prosecutor
RoR	Regulations of the Registry
RoTFV	Regulations of the Trust Fund
RPE	Rules of Procedure and Evidence
RS	Rome Statute
SAARC	South Asian Association for Regional Cooperation
SADC	Southern African Development Community
SC	Security Council
SCSL	Special Court for Sierra Leone
STL	Special Tribunal for Lebanon
TFEU	Treaty on the Functioning of the European Union
UDHR	Universal Declaration of Human Rights
UK	United Kingdom
UN	United Nations
UNCAT	International Convention Against Torture and Other Cruel, Inhuman or Degrading Treatment or Punishment
UNCRC	UN Convention on the Rights of the Child
UNGA	United Nations General Assembly
US	United States
VPRS	Victims Participation and Reparation Section
VWS	Victims and Witnesses Section; Victims and Witnesses Unit/Victims and Witnesses Section

Chapter 1
Victims Before International Justice

1.1 Introduction

Both natural disasters and those created by humans provoke mass victimisation in the states affected. In comparison to human disasters, natural disasters are not attributable to any perpetrator[1] who could be held responsible for the damage caused. In the aftermath of the brutalities of World War II, the international community was forced to create new international rules for the protection of human rights and to attribute criminal responsibility for the damage caused by human beings. As Justice Robert H. Jackson, the US Chief Prosecutor, stated with regard to the alleged offences in his opening address for the United States prior to the International Military Tribunal in Nuremberg (IMT): "Civilisation cannot tolerate their being ignored because it cannot survive their being repeated".[2] Following a general trend in national criminal justice systems, as well as in international human rights law, and further developing from the experiences of Nuremberg, Tokyo, the UN ad hoc tribunals and the International Criminal Court (ICC), the aim is now to integrate victims into the criminal proceedings. Activating and empowering those persons who have suffered most from the atrocities is nowadays one of the principal aims of the criminal process.[3]

The relatively new system of victim participation at the ICC may be politically problematic under the legal framework of the Rome Statute. The problems are further intensified by the fact that a participation and compensation claim is open to registered victims only. Victim participation consists of the possibility of the victims exercising certain procedural rights during the judicial proceedings before the Court. These must be conducted in a manner that "is not prejudicial to or

[1] See Clark (1995), p. 184.

[2] Jackson RH (1946) Opening statement for the prosecution of the major war criminals case. IMT Trial http://avalon.law.yale.edu/imt/11-21-45.asp.

[3] Safferling (2011), p. 183.

© The Author(s), under exclusive license to Springer Nature Switzerland AG 2021
C. Safferling, G. Petrossian, *Victims Before the International Criminal Court*,
https://doi.org/10.1007/978-3-030-80177-9_1

inconsistent with the rights of the accused and a fair and impartial trial".[4] The compensation claim is a separate process against the convicted offender, in which the victim requests compensation for the damage suffered. Article 68 (3) RS in conjunction with Rule 85 of the ICC Rules of Procedure and Evidence (RPE) define those persons who might generally be recognised by the Court as a "victim".

Taking into consideration the possible victimisation of a large number of persons as a result of the macro-criminal context of international criminal law, and also taking into account the increasing number of victims interested in participating in ICC proceedings,[5] it is important to determine the particular crime that relates to the victims in order to be able to secure expeditious and objective criminal justice. At the same time, the broad definition of a victim, provided for in the RPE, enables the participation of hundreds of people who have directly or indirectly been victimised due to the macro-criminal context of the acts of the accused. In some cases, hundreds of victims' applications are submitted.[6] So many victims exercising their procedural rights[7] may lead to delays and protracted judicial proceedings which, in turn, could, from the accused's standpoint, undermine the principle of a fair trial in its classical perception.[8]

The victims' participation mechanism at the ICC provides a completely new system, one which had not been part of previous international tribunals which were responsible for prosecuting mass atrocities. This mechanism includes the active participation of the victims during both the truth-finding and the reparation processes. Neither the IMT, the ICTY nor the ICTR employed a similar mechanism during their procedures. The codification of the new mechanism in the Rome Statute attracted a great deal of criticism amongst practitioners as well as from academics. It is supposedly a politically *symbolic* mechanism[9] however, on the other hand, victim

[4] Olásolo (2008), p. 158; see ICC, *Prosecutor v. Bemba*, ICC-01/05-01/08-320, Fourth Decision on Victims' Participation (12 December 2008) paras. 87–94.

[5] ICC, Assembly of States Parties, Report on the Review of the System for Victims to Apply to Participate in Proceedings, ICC-ASP/11/22, 2012, Panel Report, Convened by REDRESS and Amnesty International, "Independent Panel of Experts Report on Victim Participation at the International Criminal Court", 22, and ASP Resolution ICCASP/ 11/Res.7, Victims and Reparations, Adopted at the 8th plenary meeting on 21 November 2012, by consensus, OP 5. Data as of April 2013, Registry Report to Diplomatic Briefing April 2013. The rate at which the Court receives applications has increased by 300%, from 187 applications received on average per month in 2010, to 564 in 2011. See ICC Assembly of States Parties, Report on the Review of the System for Victims to Apply to Participate in Proceedings, ICC-ASP/11/22, 2012, para. 5. *Prosecutor v. Lubanga*—120 victims, *Prosecutor v. Katanga*—365 victims, *Prosecutor v. Ruto and Sang*—628 victims, *Prosecutor v. Kenyatta*—725 victims, *Prosecutor v. Gbagbo and Blé Goudé*—728 victims, *Prosecutor v. Ntaganda*—2131 victims, *Prosecutor v. Bemba*—5229 victims, *Prosecutor v. Ongwen*—4100 victims.

[6] Van den Wyngaert (2011), p. 481.

[7] Albeit predominantly through legal representatives.

[8] Kuijer (2013), pp. 777–780.

[9] See van den Wyngaert (2011), p. 495; Kendall and Nouwen (2014), p. 255; Bottigliero (2004), pp. 2–3.

participation offers judicial possibilities within the truth-finding procedure. Through this, the victims may also claim compensation to help them recover from the harm[10] that was inflicted upon them.

The participation of the victim in the justice process is predominantly motivated by the fact that the victims want to see justice being done (*retributive justice*) whilst, at the same time, being compensated for the harm they have suffered (*restorative justice*). From other perspectives, the participation of the victim also plays a consultative role and is of great assistance during the truth-finding process. In many aspects, participation means objectivity and balance.

Within the framework mentioned, this book aims at understanding the victim participation system by analyzing three essential pillars thereof:

1. The first pillar is the recognition of the victims of a mass atrocity. This requirement means that the persons who are claiming to be victims enter the participation system. The authors of the Rome Statute have established standards by which those claiming victimhood can be recognised as such. The most difficult issue arises when attempting to establish a connection between the mass crime in question and the selection of the victims who participate. Participation as a victim depends not only upon the person who is accused, but also upon the charges preferred against this particular individual. This can lead to the exclusion of a considerable number of victims. Those victims who cannot prove that they have been harmed by the accused for the exact circumstances covered by the charges will not be invited to participate in the procedure. This book will address possibilities of widening the definition of the term 'victim' thereby proposing a more collective approach in order to include a larger number of affected persons within the class of victims in any given case.
2. The second pillar is the victims' actual participation. From the first reading of Article 68 (3) RS it appears that victims may directly participate in the proceedings at the ICC, however, this is not the case. Although they may be directly involved in the cases, their participation is in fact exercised vicariously through legal representatives. Another important feature of the participation system is the existence of different ranges of procedural rights. Although there is an international agreement and also established jurisprudence from the Court regarding judicial practice, there are still differences at the practical level which depend upon various matters which are subject to interpretation.
3. The third pillar is the outcome of the participation. This is the stage where victims are compensated for the suffering, injuries or damage that were caused. The reparation system at the ICC is another essential part of the Rome Statute. At the time of writing this book, only three reparation orders had been made by the ICC, one each in the cases of *Lubanga*, *Katanga* and *Al-Mahdi*. During this stage, the question arises with regard to the inclusion and exclusion of victims' groups

[10] Taylor (2014), p. 14; de Hemptinne (2010), p. 165.

as well as the link between the compensation stage and the procedural requirements that exist as part of a criminal trial.

The following text consists of three general parts. The first part of analyses the historical development in dealing with victims in civil society. It then proceeds to examine the existing international practice in judicial proceedings with regard to the recognition and participation of the victims of particular crimes. Furthermore, this part of the text compares how different national systems deal with victims' rights within their individual criminal justice systems, predominantly with regard to common law and civil law systems. The various types of participation victims have within criminal justice systems will be analysed accordingly and compared to the practice of international instruments.

The second part of this work delves deeper into the jurisprudence of the ICC in relation to the participating victims. It begins by dealing with the negotiations pertaining to the Rome Statute, with specific regard to victims, and analyses the cases heard and decisions made to date. Furthermore, this part aims at understanding and interpreting the definition of a 'victim' pursuant to the Rules of the Court and the established principles during both the application and participation stages and concludes by examining the different approaches to the victims by various stakeholders at the ICC.

The book concludes with a comprehensive analysis of the reparation process in comparison to the international practices of the ICC.

1.2 Methodology

The focus of this research rests primarily on the practices of the International Criminal Court. The methodology used at the research level is a historical and legal-doctrinal comparative review. It is based on a comparison of national and international approaches to victims' rights within judicial systems.

References

Bottigliero I (2004) Redress for victims of crimes under international law. Springer, Dordrecht

Clarke RS (1995) The United Nations Crime Prevention and Criminal Justice Program: formulation and standards and efforts at their implementation. University of Pennsylvania Press, Philadelphia

de Hemptinne J (2010) Challenges raised by victims' participation in the proceedings of the special tribunal for Lebanon. J Int Crim Justice 8(1):165–179

Kendall S, Nouwen S (2014) Representational practices at the international criminal court: the gap between juridified and abstract victimhood. Law Contemp Probl 76(3):235–262

Kuijer M (2013) The right to a fair trial and the Council of Europe's efforts to ensure effective remedies on a domestic level for excessively lengthy proceedings. Hum Rights Law Rev 13 (4):777–780

Olásolo H (2008) Essays on international criminal justice. Hart Publishing, London
Safferling C (2011) The role of the victim in the criminal process: a paradigm shift in national German and international Law? Int Crim Law Rev 11(2):183–215
Taylor D (2014) Victim participation in transitional justice mechanisms: real power or empty ritual. Impunity Watch 14
Van den Wyngaert C (2011) Victims before International Criminal Courts: some views and concerns of an ICC trial judge. Case West Reserve J Int Law 44(1):475–496

Chapter 2
International Practice of Victims' Rights

2.1 Short Historical Overview of the Victims' Role in Criminal Procedure

Due to the surge in victim-oriented movements around the world in the mid-1980s,[1] the Declaration of Basic Principles of Justice for Victims and Abuse of Power, hereinafter 'the Declaration', became known as the Magna Carta for the victims of crimes.[2] The Declaration began to change the offender-centric conception and to redress the victim-offender balance in criminal justice[3] and allowed victims to be internationally and effectively recognised for the loss, suffering, injury and trauma caused by crime. At the same time, the Declaration opened the doors for the victims to be involved in a criminal justice process. Prior to this, the main interaction in criminal proceedings had been between the accused and the state prosecutor, and the victims remained largely ignored, although this has not always been the case as victims have played a fundamental role in the formation of criminal law and criminal justice at both a procedural and a substantive level.[4]

The Code of Hammurabi, which is one of the oldest pieces of writing (dating from approx. 1700 B.C.E.) and was a compilation of almost three hundred laws on every aspect of life,[5] articulated the importance of state-administrated punishment for wrongdoings. Additionally, it highlighted the importance of the victims' role, and even considered appropriate compensation for the victims of crimes. Special

---

[1]See Garkawe (2007), pp. 54–55.

[2]Fernández de Casadevante Romani (2012), pp. 9–10; Waller (2010), pp. 45–46.

[3]Safferling (2011a, b), p. 299.

[4]Bottigliero (2004), p. 3.

[5]See the note of historian Christopher Oldstone-Moore and the Code of Hammurabi in http://www.wright.edu/~christopher.oldstone-moore/Hamm.htm, last visited on 14 December 2020.

© The Author(s), under exclusive license to Springer Nature Switzerland AG 2021
C. Safferling, G. Petrossian, *Victims Before the International Criminal Court*,
https://doi.org/10.1007/978-3-030-80177-9_2

attention was also paid to potential victims, such as widows, elderly parents and lesser officials, who were protected from those who may potentially disown them.[6]

§ 195 Code of Hammurabi: "*If a son strikes his father, they shall cut off his hand*".

With regard to aspects of retributive justice, the Code of Hammurabi considered the death penalty for those victims who brought an accusation against another man but were unable to prove it.

§ 1 Code of Hammurabi: "*If a man brings an accusation against another man, charging him with murder, but cannot prove it, the accuser shall be put to death*".

From the restorative perspectives, the Code considered special reparation processes for different situations: in cases of robbery, the city and the governor had to compensate the victim for the loss. Financial compensation was also considered for the heirs of the murdered man, or to the women who lost an unborn child as a consequence of the man's strike.

§ 23 Code of Hammurabi: "*If the robber is not caught, then shall he who was robbed claim under oath the amount of his loss; then shall the community, and … on whose ground and territory and in whose domain it was compensate him for the goods stolen*".[7]

A particular role was also given to the victims of crimes within the Roman legal system. The Laws of XII Tables from around 450 B.C.E. were designed by the commissioners to protect both societies in ancient Rome—patrician and plebeian—from different wrongdoings. The Laws of XII Tables foresaw retributive as well as restorative justice for wrongdoings. In particular, Table VIII considered material compensation for the victims. In some cases, the victims themselves were granted the right to sanction the "lawbreaker":

§ 14 VIII Table of XII Tables: "*In the case of all other … thieves caught in the act freemen shall be scourged and shall be adjudged as bondsmen to the person against whom the theft has been committed provided that they have done this by daylight and have not defended themselves with a weapon […]*".

Another important reference to victims' issues is found in the Code of Justinian, also known as the *Corpus Iuris Civilis*, issued from 529 to 534 in the Byzantine Empire. The Code of Justinian is the digest of XV books divided into public law and private law and contains elements which are still being employed by numerous legal

[6]Derene et al. (2007), p. 3.

[7]King (2017), p. 8.

systems today. Book IV makes an important remark concerning both the protection of victims from wrongdoings and restorative justice.

In the middle Ages, under the common law, the victim played a central role as a "private prosecutor" in criminal matters. The victim was mostly responsible for the allegations and the charges against the offender.[8] During the formation of the common law, crimes were mostly considered as personal wrongs rather than a violation of the state's interest. As a result, victims had to find their own solution for the personal wrongdoings. The exception to this was if the wrongdoing "disturbed" the King's peace or the interests of the Crown were somehow related to the case. The absence of restitution on the part of the wrongdoer sometimes culminated in a blood feud.[9] However, this state of affairs did not last long and the institution of the private prosecutor was abolished. This was due to the fact that vengeance exacted by the victims led, in numerous cases, to mayhem. In the twelfth and thirteenth centuries, the victims of crimes were slowly removed to the peripheries of criminal justice.

Firstly, a jury system known as the assize procedure was introduced. This meant that the noble personalities of the localities were responsible for charging the criminals; they gathered information and evidence, which was then presented to the Royal Justice.[10] The outcome of the proceedings led to the wrongdoer being compelled to pay compensation to the King, to the church or to the county. The victim was, however, not able to receive any compensation from this process. Secondly, with the centralisation of the administration of justice, the victims of crime were separated from penal law and the institution of the public prosecutor was developed. In continental Europe, this developed fast in the seventeenth century, in particular in the centralised kingdoms nurturing the absolute monarch's power. However, allegedly under Dutch influence, the US colonies followed this process which was cultivated not least by the highly influential writing of Cesare Beccaria.[11] Meanwhile, the victims were able to demand compensation from the wrongdoer in civil proceedings.

If there was a tendency under common law to minimise the role of the victim in criminal proceedings, French law, a civil law rather than a common law system, granted the victims far-reaching rights. With regard to the victims' status in criminal cases, the difference between the common law and the civil law systems lay in the fact that the common law system distinguished a crime as concerning the public interest, while a tort pertained to a personal interest.[12] In this regard, common law criminal procedure aimed to protect the public interest; civil law, in contrast, combined the protection of the public interest and redress for the victim.

---

[8] Kirchengast (2006), pp. 26–29.

[9] Hostettler (2009), pp. 16–17; Braun (2019), pp. 37 et seq.

[10] Kirchengast (2006), p. 39; Watkin (2012), 5–90 citation; Hostettler (2004), p. 17.

[11] A "prosecutor office" was established by statute in Connecticut in 1704, Virginia followed in 1711, Cardenas (1986), p. 369.

[12] Simons (2008), p. 720; Doak (2008), p. 7; Ochoa (2013), p. 134.

The *L'Ordonnance* from 1670, which was one of the first legal sources of French codified criminal procedural law,[13] granted victims the right to participate in criminal proceedings as a "*partie civile*". Accordingly, the victims had the opportunity to lodge a complaint (Article 1 titre III, Article 8 titre III *L'Ordonnance*). This would be at the expense of the victims if the accused were later acquitted (Article 6 titre première *L'Ordonnance*).[14] The participation of victims was limited to assisting the judicial authorities in the truth-finding process. Their role consisted of giving testimony (Article 18 titre XIV, Article 3 titre XI *L'Ordonnance*) as well as presenting evidence and witnesses (Article 22 titre XVI *L'Ordonnance*). However, the victims were not granted the right to examine the files compiled by the public prosecutor or to intervene in the trial in any other way.[15] During sentencing at the end of the trial, the victims were granted reparation for all the costs and any damage they had incurred (Article 16 titre XXV *L'Ordonnance*).

Parallel to the surge in humanist ideas and the French Revolution, the Napoleonic code of criminal procedure from 1808 (*Code d'instruction criminelle*) was confirmed and replaced the unsuccessful Code of 1791[16] in which victims' issues were considered far less. The Code from 1808, based upon *L'Ordonnance* from 1670, granted extensive rights to the victims of crime.[17]

Generally, it is safe to conclude that the role of the victims has always been unique, irrespective of all the social and cultural approaches towards them. Underlining the above-mentioned legal systems and comparing them with one other under the current social-cultural circumstances, it is possible to conclude that the Code of Hammurabi, as a sign of established society, stood for the protection of victims of wrongdoings.[18] During the feudal regime and in the dark ages, wrongdoings were considered to be related purely to personal interests and the victims were left without the monarch's protection. With this in mind, the victims themselves generally had to deal with their own "troubles".

The victims were usually deemed to be poor and weak and unable to defend themselves. At a political level, only the person who was "strong" and violent, was glorified. Such attention was not paid to the thousands of victims of colonial regimes or to the victims of mass destruction perpetrated during World War I.[19] However, this approach changed after World War II, and although the victims of Nazi-crimes did not directly participate in the Nuremberg Trials as victims, they were involved as

[13] See Andrews (1994), pp. 417–418; Delmas-Marty (2008), pp. 9–10.

[14] See Esmein et al. (1913), pp. 219–220.

[15] Monballyu (2014), p. 410.

[16] The new code was mostly oriented on the English law, see Esmein et al. (1913), pp. 408–410.

[17] E.g. The possibility of opposing the release orders of the accused, the presentation of a submission to the indictment, the request for referral of the case to a another judge in case of bias, requesting hearing of witnesses, requesting to accuse witness in case of false testimony etc., see more in Halpérin (2015), pp. 59 et seq.

[18] However, today it is not possible to argue how successful the law functioned in practice.

[19] Petrossian (2019), pp. 83–85.

witnesses. As a consequence, international attention increased and turned to focus on aspects appertaining to the protection and compensation of victims.

In order to analyse modern national approaches to victim participation within criminal justice systems, and to be able to compare them with the ICC victims' participation mechanism, it is necessary to examine the body of international documents relating to victims' issues which were drafted after World War II.

2.2 Historical Background of Victims' Rights[20]

The development of international law treaties is a political process involving numerous different actors. International law in general, and human rights law in particular, are both primarily addressed to states.[21] Although, at first glance, it might seem logical that states are responsible for the further development of international law, different international, transnational, national and non-governmental actors have had a huge impact on its development since the United Nations was founded in 1945 an all sovereign states have to agree to ratify international treaties, such as the Charter of the United Nations. However, before the eventual signing and ratification of such treaties, governments are actively involved in the drafting stage via their representatives. States are traditionally the most important actors in the norm-building process as well as for the subsequent implementation of these norms, both at the international and the national level.

The Rome Statute was adopted as an intergovernmental treaty on 17 July 1998, and it entered into force on 1 July 2002 following 60 state ratifications. This was the result of a number of years of developments and negotiations within the field of international criminal law. States participated in the drafting process both before and during the conference in Rome.[22] They submitted proposals on specific legal issues or took over the leading role in different working groups represented by diplomats or national experts. International actors, such as the International Law Commission, the UN Special Rapporteur on Drafting a Code of Offences against the Peace and Security of Mankind, the UN Legal Counsel and state representatives were involved in the political process of developing a treaty for an international criminal court.[23]

The lobbying efforts towards the norm-building processes by non-governmental organizations (NGOs) have increased during the time of the United Nations. The approach of these NGOs has shifted from a general demand for the enforcement of human rights and a role in monitoring human rights abuses, to more progressive action in further developing international (criminal) law norms.[24] It is hardly

---

[20]The authors would like to express their gratitude to Dr Michaela Lissowsky for her support in drafting this subsection.

[21]Egede and Sutch (2013), pp. 48–49.

[22]Kirsch (2002), pp. 451 et seq.; Cryer et al. (2014), pp. 121–127.

[23]Cryer (2008), pp. 118 et seq.

[24]Human Rights First, 'The Role of Human Rights NGOs in Relation to ICC Investigations: Discussion Paper' 2004 p. 11.

surprising that NGOs participated in the Rome Conference in 1998 after the international community had failed to prevent acts of genocide in Srebrenica and Rwanda. Many observers at the Rome Conference reported that the NGOs subsequently played an important role in the development of gender and victims' rights.[25]

The negotiations towards the inclusion of victims' rights within the Rome Statute can be considered a single political process, and several international, transnational, national and non-governmental actors played different roles at various stages of that process. As is the case in many political processes, individuals are responsible for propelling the dynamics. Too little attention is given to the research on the role of individuals in the norm-building processes, since individuals are not treated as actors at an international level and often act as representatives or as part of an international organisation. Through this section of the book, the key influences and developments in international law will be identified chronologically in order to provide a foundation from which victims' rights within the ICC emerged. Once this has been established, it will be possible to delve more deeply into the negotiations themselves and the influential actors involved in promoting victims' rights at the ICC with regard to both participation and reparation. In order to be able to fully understand the negotiations which led to the creation of the ICC, it is important to know how the rights of victims had previously been represented and developed prior to the Rome Statute, and the influence different actors had within this process. This establishes the platform from which the drafters were starting from. There will be a clear identification of the influential parties thereto, including states, NGOs, as well as individuals functioning within delegations or representing persuasive opinions relating to victims' rights within the Rome Statute.

2.2.1 The Geneva Conventions for the Protection of War Victims, 1949

A critical cornerstone for victims' rights in international criminal law was established by the four Geneva Conventions of 12 August 1949,[26] which aimed at protecting victims in armed conflicts. The Conventions' understanding of victims focused on persons who were not directly involved in hostilities anymore, but who were, for example, wounded or sick. The Conventions were developed by the International Committee of the Red Cross (ICRC) and government experts. The ICRC had a unique role in the adoption of the Geneva Conventions, which are intergovernmental treaties, despite its being an international NGO under the Swiss

[25] See Lohne (2018), pp. 109–127.

[26] See Convention (I) for the Amelioration of the Condition of the Wounded and Sick in Armed Forces in the Field. Geneva, 12 August 1949, Convention (II) for the Amelioration of the Condition of Wounded, Sick and Shipwrecked Members of Armed Forces at Sea, Geneva, 12 August 1949, Convention (III) relative to the Treatment of Prisoners of War. Geneva, 12 August 1949, Convention (IV) relative to the Protection of Civilian Persons in Time of War. Geneva, 12 August 1949.

Civil Code. Firstly, the ICRC describes its humanitarian mission as being "to protect the lives and dignity of victims of armed conflicts and other situations of violence [...]". Secondly, in its own words, the ICRC wants "to provide assistance" to the victims of armed conflicts. These are clear indications that the ICRC has always promoted the right to protection and has continued to this end. This emphasises the important role of NGOs in the development of victims' rights from the very outset.[27] In 1977, the additional protocols to the Geneva Conventions[28] broadened the concept of victims to "any persons affected by an armed conflict." Civilians and the civil population were thus integrated under the aegis of these additional protocols. As a consequence, strong legal norms were specifically established for the protection of victims.

2.2.2 *First Draft Code of Offences Against the Peace and Security of Mankind, 1954*

A year after the adoption of the Geneva Conventions in 1950, the UN General Assembly (UNGA), which at that time consisted of 60 Member States, agreed to work on the establishment of an international criminal court. In order to draft proposals and conventions, the UNGA decided to set up a committee, "composed of the representatives of seventeen Member States, namely, Australia, Brazil, China, Cuba, Denmark, Egypt, France, India, Iran, Israel, the Netherlands, Pakistan, Peru, Syria, the United Kingdom of Great Britain and Northern Ireland, the United States of America and Uruguay [...]." The first draft code of a statute for an international criminal court was developed by the committee and finally adopted by the International Law Commission (ILC) and submitted to the UNGA in 1954. That draft merely listed offences in four articles. In terms of the victims' rights, there was no further visible elaboration compared to other international criminal law documents such as the Nuremberg Principles. All seven Nuremberg Principles stand for fundamental international criminal law norms, rather than for an overall political aim such as "justice for victims". In fact, neither the Nuremberg Principles from 1950, the first Draft Code from 1954 nor the Genocide Convention from 1948 used the term "victims". Looking back at the first Draft Code of Offences against the Peace and Security of Mankind of 1954, a representative of the Soviet Union emphasised its close link to the London Charter of the Nuremberg Tribunal and the judgments of the Nuremberg Trials.[29] Nevertheless, while there appears to be no direct link to

---

[27]See Help of German war criminals after 1945 by Red Cross in Lewis (2014), pp. 238–241.

[28]Protocol Additional to the Geneva Conventions of 12 August 1949, and relating to the Protection of Victims of International Armed Conflicts (Protocol I), 8 June 1977, Protocol Additional to the Geneva Conventions of 12 August 1949, and relating to the Protection of Victims of Non-International Armed Conflicts (Protocol II), 8 June 1977.

[29]Schabas (2010), p. 145.

victims' rights, this first draft code did provide the basis for the future discussions of the International Law Commission.

2.2.3 *UNGA Resolution on the Prosecution of War Crimes and Crimes Against Humanity, 1970*

The UNGA and the International Law Commission became the main proponents for the establishment of a permanent international criminal court. The punishment of perpetrators was still of major concern during the Cold War, however, this dominant paradigm of punishment began to change very slowly towards a new understanding of justice for victims. Several UN Resolutions reminded the international community of the need to clarify the question of punishments for war criminals and persons who committed crimes against humanity. A small development can be seen at the UNGA meeting on 15 December 1970[30] when a Resolution endorsing the idea of a deterrent effect on future possible crimes through the prosecution of war crimes and crimes against humanity was adopted:

> Convinced that a thorough investigation of war crimes and crimes against humanity, as well as the arrest, extradition and punishment of persons guilty of such crimes—wherever they may have been committed—and the establishment of criteria for determining compensation to the victims of such crimes, are important elements in the prevention of similar crimes now and in the future, and also in the protection of human rights and fundamental freedoms, the strengthening of confidence and the development of cooperation between peoples and the safeguarding of international peace and security.[31]

For the first time in an official UN document, the UNGA had linked the principles of international criminal justice with a request for compensation for the victims.

2.2.4 *Mandate for the International Law Commission, 1981*

On 10 December 1981, the ILC received a mandate from the UNGA to continue its work on drafting a code of offences against the Peace and Security of Mankind.[32]

---

[30] See also Convention on the Non-Applicability of Statutory Limitations to War Crimes and Crimes Against Humanity, Adopted and opened for signature, ratification and accession by GA resolution 2391 (XXIII) of 26 November 1968, entry into force 11 November 1970, in accordance with Article VIII.

[31] UNGA A/RES/2712, Question of the Punishment of War Criminals and Persons who have committed Crimes against Humanity, 15 December 1970.

[32] UNGA A/RES/36/106, Draft Code of Offences against the Peace and Security of Mankind, 10 December 1981.

Hereby, the UNGA drew upon its Resolution from 21 November 1947 (Resolution 177)[33] and referred to the first draft of the ILC from 1954.

The motivation to continue the work on a draft code was clearly a result of the insecure times: the apartheid regime in South Africa, the war in Lebanon in 1982, as well as other potential conflicts and a general nuclear threat from both the superpowers, the USSR and the US. The representative from Afghanistan noted that "the peace and security of thousands of human beings had been disrupted and their most basic human rights had been violated through policies of colonialism, genocide, apartheid, racism and oppression."[34] However, there were positive motives for developing a draft for the establishment of an international criminal court too. The "work would have a positive effect on the rule of law in international relations by contributing to a greater respect for the norms of international law", as the representative from Trinidad and Tobago concluded.[35]

At its thirty-fourth session in July 1982, the ILC appointed Mr Doudou Thiam as the first UN Special Rapporteur on Drafting a Code of Offences against the Peace and Security of Mankind. The Special Rapporteur led the Working Group, which published several reports on the Draft Codes between 1982 and 1994. In those reports, victims are mentioned only in connection with charges. Regularly, victims are placed upon the same level as witnesses and their right to be protected by the courts' organs. The idea of broad victims' rights, in terms of the right to participate in international criminal trials and the right to reparation at a permanent international criminal court, had not been expressed by any UN body at this point.[36]

The Draft Code of Crimes against Peace and the Security of Mankind[37] was adopted by the UNGA on 23 March 1983. This version gave an overview of the different national arguments for and against a new code. The whole Draft Code is less a catalogue with articles for a statute, but rather a report of the governmental views on different legal questions. The states considered, for example, whether they should integrate the crime of aggression which was adopted by the UNGA in 1974.[38] Of further interest was the discussion surrounding the use of nuclear weapons as "the gravest crime against humanity." The representative of Algeria also felt that among the acts which should be defined as offences against the peace and security of mankind "the use of nuclear weapons in general and their use against non-nuclear-weapon states in particular" should be included.[39] The states also elaborated upon

[33]UNGA, A/RES/177 (II) Formulation of the Principles Recognised in the Charter of the Nurnberg Tribunal and in the Judgment of the Tribunal, 21 November 1947.

[34]UNGA A/C.6/36/SR.62, 23 March 1983, para. 30.

[35]UNGA A/C.6/37/SR.54, 23 March 1983.

[36]See, Reports by UN Special Rapporteur on Drafting a Code of offences against the Peace and Security of Mankind.

[37]UNGA A/CN.4/365, 23 March 1983.

[38]UNGA A/RES/3314 (XXIX) Definition of Aggression, 14 December 1974.

[39]UNGA A/CN.4/365, 23 March 1983, para. 83.

how to extend the charges and how to integrate existing human rights conventions into a new draft code.

Though the major concern of states can only be determined implicitly, they were clearly afraid of ceding their sovereignty. They even discussed a proposal by Syria for a so called "safeguard clause" which should protect the sovereignty of states and would emphasise the "right to self-determination and their struggle against occupation and all forms of colonialism".[40] Here, the clear primacy in the role of the states prevented the strengthening of victims' rights, particularly due to the focus on ensuring their right to sovereignty.

2.2.5 *Further Developments Towards Victims' Rights, 1992*

On 9 February 1992, the UNGA issued a statement in which it said it "[r]equests the International Law Commission to continue its work on this question by undertaking the project for the elaboration of a draft statute for an international criminal court as a matter of priority as from its next session [. . .]."[41] While the Working Group was drafting a statute, a major step towards the victims' rights was made with the study "Concerning the right to restitution, compensation and rehabilitation for victims of gross violations of human rights and fundamental freedoms" which was written by Theo Van Boven, the UN Special Rapporteur on the right to reparation to victims of gross violations of human rights. The study was published in 1993 and founded the "Basic principles and guidelines on the right to a remedy and reparation for victims of gross violations of international human rights law and serious violation of international humanitarian law". In its final report, the study recommended that "[t]he question of reparation for victims of gross violations of human rights and fundamental freedoms has received insufficient attention and should be addressed more consistently and more thoroughly both in the United Nations and other international organisations [. . .]".[42] In this case, it was clearly an individual functioning within an international role who was actively propelling the notion of victims' rights forward.[43]

Firstly, the idea that states or international organisations may act as civil parties had already been proposed in 1992 by the UN Special Rapporteur Doudou Thiam in order "[. . .] to obtain compensation for injury sustained as a result of a crime referred to the Court."[44] Secondly, it was discussed whether a state could bring a lawsuit on behalf of its nationals. The difficulties involved in integrating the right to reparation into international criminal law were evident within the Sixth Committee of the

[40] UNGA A/CN.4/365, 23 March 1983, para. 108.
[41] UNGA A/RES/47/33, 9 February 1992.
[42] E/CN.4/Sub.2/1993/8, 2 July 1993.
[43] van Boven (2013), pp. 18 et seq.
[44] A/CN.4/442,1992.

UNGA in 1993.[45] A number of representatives of delegations rejected the notion, while others emphasised the necessity to include reparation "as repression only cannot make justice when damage caused by the crime is not repaired."[46] Once again, these discussions were prompted by an individual, however, there is still clear reliance on the states themselves to further develop the right to reparation and participation for victims.

2.2.6 *Victims' Rights at the ICTY and the ICTR, 1993 and 1994*

In both corresponding statutes of the ad hoc tribunals for the former Yugoslavia and Rwanda, the term "victims" was not defined, although victims were recognised as witnesses.[47] Article 22 of the ICTY Statute and Article 21 of the ICTR Statute state: "The International Tribunal [. . .] shall provide in its rules of procedure and evidence for the protection of victims and witnesses. Such protection measures shall include, but shall not be limited to, the conduct of *in camera* proceedings and the protection of the victims' identity."[48]

Both the ICTY and the ICTR did not, however, allow victims to participate in the proceedings as civil parties[49] and were merely retributive tribunals. Hence, victims could not apply for compensation before these tribunals and restitution was treated as a penalty and victims were forced to then complain before the domestic courts "[. . .] or other competent body to obtain compensation."[50] Rule 106 (C) of the ICTY's Rules of Procedure and Evidence (RPE) bound national courts to the judgments of the tribunals regarding the criminal responsibility of the convicted person. Although both ad hoc tribunals were established by the UNSC, their jurisdiction did not recognise the "right to a judicial remedy". The decision not to include the right to remedy in the statutes of these ad hoc tribunals is somewhat surprising, given that a fund had previously been established as the UN Compensation Commission for Iraq. This fund was created by UNSC Resolution 687 in 1991 in order "[. . .] to pay compensation for claims [. . .]" to any "[. . .] direct loss, damage, including environmental damage, and the depletion of natural resources,

45 Bonneau et al. (2014), p. 154.

46 A/CN.4/446, §104–105, 25 January 1993.

47 Safferling (2003), p. 365.

48 ICTY Statute, Article 22; ICTR Statute, Article 21.

49 David Donat-Cattin, a key commentator on the Rome Statute as a main supporter of victims' rights, criticised comments which defended the common law system and argued that there would be only space for the prosecution case and the defence case in the trial. For more information see Donat-Cattin (2001), p. 191.

50 See, ICTY Rules of Procedure and Evidence, Rule 106 (B).

or injury to foreign nationals and corporations [...]" after Iraq's invasion of Kuwait.[51]

Despite its legal deficiencies in terms of the victims' rights in the statutes, Benedetti, Bonneau and Washburn came to the conclusion during the Preparatory Committee's negotiations in 1996 that Rule 106 of the ICTY's and the ICTR's Rules of Procedure and Evidence laid the foundation for a right to restitution and compensation for victims.[52] It has also been noted that both the ICTY and the ICTR, despite being averse to compensation claims being dealt with at their own tribunals due to efficiency issues, actually advocated the adoption of such claims by the ICC.[53]

2.3 Developed International Sources of Law for Victims' Issues

Victims of crime cannot be described in a broad sense; they are related to a specific wrongful act, which victimised the person and occasioned injury or damage. With regard to this matter, international multilateral treaties related to victims' rights cover contrasting territorial ranges[54] and are very different in nature. Therefore, the law pertaining to victims' rights can be subsumed under several headings with regard to international law:

- Victims of crime
- Victims of abuse of power
- Victims of gross violations of international human rights law
- Victims of serious violations of international humanitarian law
- Victims of enforced disappearance
- Victims of international criminal law
- Victims of trafficking
- Victims of terrorism

Victims' issues can be discussed on a multilateral/universal platform with a view to the European Union and the Council of Europe, the Inter-American Community and also the African Community.

[51] UN S/RES/687 (1991), 3 April 1991.

[52] Bonneau et al. (2014), p. 155.

[53] Zegveld (2019), p. 328.

[54] Universal or regional.

2.3.1 International Multilateral Treaties

There is still no international consensus between the states regarding victims' rights and their protection. It is left to regional and national regulations to define the victims' participation type within the domestic systems. Even where the states have agreed on declarations at the universal level, they are still not binding for the Member States.[55] The only binding instrument mentioned is the Rome Statute, which recognises the participation of the victims of certain crimes under its own jurisdiction. However, recognition at the ICC level triggers the Member States of the Rome Statute directly or indirectly to respect the victims' issues and to deal with them.

2.3.1.1 The Declaration of Basic Principles of Justice for Victims of Crime and Abuse of Power (UNGA Resolution 40/34 [1985])

The Declaration of Basic Principles of Justice for Victims of Crime and Abuse of Power was deemed to be the Magna Carta for victims, as it declared changes in the field of victimology. Due to this declaration, the person who was injured or suffered harm or damage was recognised as a victim, irrespective of whether the perpetrator was unknown or had been prosecuted or convicted. The Declaration recognised the need for victims to access justice, to be fairly treated and to be heard and informed before the judicial and administrative organs, so that they would not be victimised for a second time. The Declaration also underlined the forms of reparation for the victims. In the event of a lack of possibilities, it highlighted the need for state compensation in order to restitute the families of the victim.[56]

2.3.1.2 The Declaration on the Protection of All Persons from Enforced Disappearance (UNGA A/RES/47/133 (1992)) and International Convention for the Protection of All Persons from Enforced Disappearance (2006)

Acts of enforced disappearance are widely practiced in different parts of the world and are often accompanied by torture and unlawful detention.[57] Due to this fact, Member States of the UN afforded protection with regard to enforced disappearance by means of a declaration. Subsequently, this was transformed into a convention in

---

[55] Cf. Masol (2020), p. 12.

[56] Jaishankar (2014), p. 67.

[57] Human Rights Watch, 'Thailand: "it was like suddenly my son no longer existed": enforced disappearances in Thailand's southern border provinces' 2007, pp. 55–56, Human Rights Watch, 'Recurring Nightmare: State Responsibility for "Disappearances" and Abductions in Sri Lanka' 2008, p. 28.

2006, which came into force in 2010 and conferred enforced disappearance with the status of an international crime.[58] The Declaration, as well as the Convention, enable victims to claim for loss and harm owing to the responsibility of the government and to receive compensation. The documents specify and list the rights of those persons[59] who suffered and who were subjected to enforced disappearance.[60]

2.3.1.3 Rome Statute of International Criminal Court (1998)

As previously discussed, the role of the victims in supranational criminal justice was established by the Rome Statute in 1998. This furnished the Court with a restorative effect,[61] in contrast to the ad hoc tribunals where the main aim was retributive justice. These ad hoc tribunals had always afforded the victims and witnesses the same status whereas the Rome Statute grants victims the right of protection (Article 68 (2) RS), the right of participation (Article 68 (3) RS) and the right to compensation (Article 75 RS).[62]

2.3.1.4 Basic Principles and Guidelines of the Right to a Remedy and Reparation for Victims of Gross Violations of International Human Rights Law and Serious Violations of International Humanitarian Law (UNGA Resolution 60/147 [2005])

The Resolution on Basic Principles and Guidelines emphasises the importance of the state in acting if international human rights or the internationally recognised standards of international humanitarian law are violated. It demands that the state restore the losses of those individuals who suffered as a consequence of the violation. The Resolution indicates the types of restorative justice for the victims as well as the notion of 'victim' within the field of international humanitarian law, which is also partially illustrated in the Protocols of the Geneva conventions.[63]

---

[58] Crawshaw and Holmström (2008), pp. 187 et seq.

[59] Article 24 of the Convention explains the broad meaning of the definition of victim of enforced disappearance.

[60] Both declarations are non-binding, but they play the revolutionary role in establishing the principles for the rights of victims in the criminal procedure.

[61] See de Brouwer (2005), pp. 283–284.

[62] See Safferling (2012), pp. 171–179.

[63] Geneva Conventions for the Protection of War Victims of 12 August 1949 and Additional Protocols of 8 June 1977: Victims of International Armed Conflict (Protocol I) and Victims of Non-Internal Armed Conflict (Protocol II).

2.3.1.5 General Treaties with Relation to Victims' Issues

Parallel to the aforementioned documents, it is possible to find references to victims' rights in universal human rights treaties such as in:

General treaties related to victims' rights

- Article 8 Universal Declaration of Human Rights (UDHR)
- Articles 3 and 9 (5) International Covenant on Civil and Political Rights (ICCPR)
- Articles 13 and 14 International Convention Against Torture and Other Cruel, Inhuman or Degrading Treatment or Punishment (UNCAT)
- Article 6 International Convention on the Elimination of All Forms of Racial Discrimination (ICERD)
- Article 9 UN Convention on the Rights of the Child (UNCRC)

Other documents related to victims' issues

- ECOSOC[64] Resolution 1989/57 Implementation of the Declaration of Basic Principles of Justice for Victims of Crime and Abuse of Power
- ECOSOC Resolution 1990/22 Plan of Action for the Implementation of the Declaration of Basic Principles of Justice for Victims of Crime and Abuse of Power
- GA resolution 55/25 of 15 November 2000 United Nations Convention against Transnational Organised Crime and The Protocol to Prevent, Suppress and Punish Trafficking in Persons, Especially Women and Children
- GA resolution 58/4 of 31 October 2003 United Nations Convention against Corruption
- ECOSOC Resolution 2005/20 Guidelines on Justice in Matters involving Child Victims and Witnesses of Crime

As such, it is evident that the victims of crimes are, in general, still not fully recognised under international law.

2.3.2 Council of Europe

The Council of Europe (CoE) is a guarantor of human rights in the European region and has 47 European members. It was established after World War II and advocates the protection of victims.

[64] The UN Economic and Social Council.

2.3.2.1 Resolution (77) 27 on the Compensation of Victims of Crime (Adopted by the Committee of Ministers on 28 September 1977, at the 275th Meeting of the Ministers' Deputies)

In order to harmonise the CoE Member States' legislation and to increase the safeguards of the victims of crime, the CoE passed the Resolution for Member States which recommends the principles of possible compensation for victims. The Resolution provides compensation for the victims from the state, if there are no other possible existing resources which could be considered for compensating. Furthermore, the Resolution concretises the nature of the compensation. For example, compensation can be awarded for the loss of past and future earnings, an increase in expenses, medical expenses, medical and professional rehabilitation and funeral expenses.

2.3.2.2 European Convention on the Compensation of Victims of Violent Crimes 1983

The Convention, which is based on the CoE Resolution from 1977, secures the mechanism of compensation for victims who have suffered physical or mental injuries as a result of intentional crimes of violence. It also considers compensation for the relatives of victims who died as a consequence of the criminal conduct.[65] According to the Convention, compensation should be affirmed by the state should the offender not be able to compensate. The reason behind why the states should approve compensation is based upon the assumption that as the states were not able to prevent the crime, and were not able to introduce criminal policy measures, they should be liable.[66]

2.3.2.3 Recommendations of the Council of Europe

The recommendations of the CoE provide a common guidance for its Member States, which are not legally binding, however, they do serve an important role in the improved implementation of the binding principles.

[65] See Europe C.O 2006—Victims: support and assistance, p. 20, Gerry (2009), p. 451.

[66] See Explanatory Report to the European Convention on the Compensation of Victims of Violent Crimes, 24 November 1983.

2.3.2.3.1 Recommendation N. R (85) 11 of the Committee of Ministers to Member States on the Position of the Victim in the Framework of Criminal Law and Procedure (Adopted by the Committee of Ministers on 28 June 1985 at the 387th Meeting of the Ministers' Deputies)

This Recommendation directs national authorities to increase the awareness of public workers in relation to the assistance and protection of victims and their families.

2.3.2.3.2 Recommendation N. R (87) 21 of the Committee of Ministers to Member States on Assistance to Victims and the Prevention of Victimisation (Adopted by the Committee of Ministers on 17 September 1987 at the 410th Meeting of the Ministers' Deputies)

This Recommendation instructs the Member States to use the guidelines to extend the assistance for victims in order to meet the victims' needs in the most appropriate way and to increase public awareness of the victims' issues.

2.3.2.3.3 Guidelines on the Protection of Victims of Terrorist Acts (Adopted by the Committee of Ministers of the Council of Europe on 2 March 2005)

In contrast to the crimes of violence, the CoE passed a unique guideline for the victims of terrorist acts. The principles illustrated in the guideline enable the victims of such acts to receive compensation from the state irrespective of whether the perpetrator is identified, arrested or prosecuted. The principles internationally recognise the suffering of victims of terrorist acts and obligate the Member States to affirm the effective protection of the victims.[67]

2.3.2.3.4 Recommendation (2006) 8 of the Committee of Ministers to Member States on Assistance to Crime Victims (Adopted by the Committee of Ministers on 14 June 2006 at the 967th Meeting of the Ministers' Deputies)

This document replaces Recommendation N. R(87) 21 on the assistance to the victims and the prevention of victimisation. Considering the outcome of the Convention and the further agreements regarding victims, the CoE decided to extend

[67] Albrecht and Kilchling (2010), p. 224.

assistance to the victims of crimes and to combine it with the assistance to victims of terrorist acts.[68]

2.3.2.4 Other Documents

- CoE Convention the Prevention of Terrorism (CETS N. 196)
- CoE Convention on Action against Trafficking in Human Being (CETS N. 197)
- Recommendation N. R(83) 7 of the Committee of Ministers to Member States on participation of the public in the crime policy
- Recommendation N. R(91) 11 of the Committee of Ministers to Member States concerning sexual exploitation, pornography and prostitution of, and trafficking in children and young adults
- Recommendation N. R(96) 8 of the Committee of Ministers to Member States on crime policy in Europe in a time of change
- Recommendation N. R(97) of the Committee of Ministers to Member States concerning intimidation of witnesses and the rights of the defense
- Recommendation N. R(99) of the Committee of Ministers to Member States concerning mediation in penal matters
- Recommendation N. R(2000) 11 of the Committee of Ministers to Member States on action against trafficking in human beings for the purpose of sexual exploitation
- Recommendation N. R(2002) 5 of the Committee of Ministers to Member States on the protection of women against violence
- Recommendation N. R(2005) 9 of the Committee of Ministers to Member States on the protection of witnesses and collaborators of justice
- Resolution on the prevention of everyday violence in Europe (2004)
- Resolution N. 2 on the social mission of the criminal justice systems—restorative justice (2005)

From the examples of the resolutions and recommendations of the CoE, it is possible to ascertain how the need for assisting the victims of crime has increased, and since 1977 was politically greeted. How effectively the implementation of the resolutions and the recommendations has functioned at a national level is, however, another question.

2.3.3 European Union

Starting as an economic organisation after World War II, the EU no longer exists today for purely economic purposes. It also works towards cooperation on a criminal

[68]Letschert and Staiger (2010), p. 25; Peterson (2009), p. 141.

justice platform, an issue which has become one of the most important aspects of this union. In this regard, different directives and decisions have been passed in order to grant victims of crime different ranges of rights.

2.3.3.1 Council Framework Decision (2001/220/JHA) of 15 March 2001 on the Standing of Victims in Criminal Proceedings

This (hard law) decision was passed by the Council of the EU in order to harmonise national legislation in accordance with the Implementation Plan of the Treaty of Amsterdam and can be seen as a milestone in the field of victims' rights. The decision safeguards the active participation and the legal status of victims within national criminal proceedings and endorses the protection of and assistance given to victims. It also highlighted the expeditious implementation mechanism under national legislation with regard to the legal status of the victims of criminal conduct.[69]

2.3.3.2 Council Directive 2004/80/EC of 29 April 2004 Relating to Compensation to Crime Victims

Under Council Directive 2001/220/JHA—the declaration on combatting terrorism and the jurisprudence of the Court of Justice in the case of *Cowan*[70]—compensation for the victims was specified. Subsequently, the Council of the EU adopted a corresponding directive relating to compensation for the victims of crime. This directive allows the victims to apply for compensation from the Member State in which the crime was perpetrated, regardless of the victim's country of residence.

2.3.3.3 Directive 2012/29/EU of the European Parliament and of the Council of 25 October 2012 Establishing Minimum Standards on the Rights, Support and Protection of Victims of Crime, and Replacing Council Framework Decision 2001/220/JHA

The European Parliament passed this directive in the wake of a great deal of criticism concerning the decision of 2001,[71] and as a result of new agreements introduced at an international level. It was established on the basis of Article 82 (2) TFEU and was

[69] Pemberton and Rasquete (2010), pp. 99–112; van der Aa (2010), pp. 184–186.

[70] See ECJ, *Ian William Cowan v Trésor public*, Case 186/87, Judgment, 2 February 1989, para. 3.

[71] See Pemberton and Rasquete (2010), p. 110, Resolution of the Council of 10 June 2011 on a Roadmap for Strengthening the Rights and Protection of Victims, in particular in criminal proceedings, 2011/C 187/01, para. (7), Braun (2019), p. 7.

aimed at ensuring that victims of crime receive appropriate information, support and protection and are able to participate in criminal proceedings.[72] The directive replaces the Framework Decision on the standing of victims in criminal proceedings.

2.3.3.4 EU Strategy on Victims' Rights (2020–2025)

The global pandemic and the lockdowns have led to increase of domestic violence, hate speech, cybercrime and child sexual abuse. In this regard the EU considered a strategy plan on the victims' rights. In the plan the EU concentrated on the empowering victims of crimes, improving support and protection of the most vulnerable victims, facilitating victims' access to compensation, strengthening cooperation and coordination among all relevant actors and the international dimension of victims' rights.[73]

2.3.3.5 Other Documents

- Council Framework Decision of 13 June 2002 on combating terrorism
- Council Framework Decision of 19 July 2002 on combating trafficking in human beings 2002/629/JHA
- Directive 2011/36/EU of the European Parliament and of the Council of 5 April 2011 on preventing and combating trafficking in human beings and protecting its victims, and replacing Council Framework Decision 2002/629/JHA
- Resolution of the Council of 10 June 2011 on a roadmap for strengthening the rights and protection of victims, in particular in criminal proceedings from 28 June 2011
- Directive 2011/99/EU of the European Parliament and of the Council of 13 December 2011 on the European protection order
- Regulation (EU) N. 606/2013 of the European Parliament and of the Council of 12 June 2013 on mutual recognition of protection measures in civil matters

---

[72]See Klip (2016), p. 329; Alvaro and D'Andrea (2016), pp. 310–311, see also European Commission, Report from the Commission to the European Parliament and the Council on the implementation of Directive 2012/29/EU of the European Parliament and of the Council of 25 October 2012 establishing minimum standards on the rights, support and protection of victims of crime, and replacing Council Framework Decision 2001/220/JHA, 11 May 2020, see also Hoppe (2020), p. 148, see also EU, the DG justice guidance document related to the transposition and implementation of Directive 2012/29/EU of the European Parliament and of the Council of 25 October 2012 establishing minimum standards on the rights, support and protection of victims of crime, and replacing Council Framework Decision 2001/220/JHA, p. 10.

[73]European Commission, EU Strategy on victims' rights (2020–2025), European Commission, Report of the Special Adviser, J. Milquet, to the President of the European Commission, Jean-Claude Juncker, March 2019, Strengthening Victims' Rights: from compensation to reparation.

- DG justice guidance document related to the transposition and implementation of directive 2012/29/EU of the European Parliament and of the Council of 25 October 2012 establishing minimum standards on the rights, support and protection of victims of crime, and replacing council Framework Decision 2001/220/JHA from 12 December 2013.
- Council conclusions on victims' rights from 15 November 2019.

Compared to the common resolutions and recommendations of the CoE in regard to victims' issues, the EU specifies the rights and protection of the victims in criminal procedures through Directive 2012/29/EU.

2.3.4 Organisation of American States

As a guarantor of peace and security, the protection of human rights and of democracy, the Organisation of American States (OAS) has assumed a different approach to victims' issues. Compared to the European regional activity in promoting the rights of the victims, it is not possible to see the same enthusiasm on the part of the OAS with regard to strengthening or harmonising the issues concerning the victims of crime.

2.3.4.1 Inter-American Convention on Forced Disappearance of Persons

The agreement between the Member States refers indirectly to general victims' rights. Although the agreement does not consider the definition of victim *per se*, it still covers the concept of the specific rights of victims who have suffered forced disappearance. It allows the victims to access the national justice system for reparation matters.

2.3.4.2 Other Treaties

The same notions and references to the special victims of violations is underlined in the Inter-American Convention on Human Rights (IACHR) of 13 May 1969 (Article 63) and in the Inter-American Convention to Prevent and Punish Torture of 9 December 1985 (IACPPT) (Articles 2, 9 and 12).

2.3.5 *African Union*

The African Charter on Human and Peoples' Rights (the Banjul Charter) has been the result of long negotiations under the Organisation of African Unity. It exists, in a similar way to the aforementioned European and Inter-American conventions, for the protection of human rights and basic freedoms on the African continent. However, the rights, redress and rehabilitation of the victims of crime are left to national consideration.

2.4 Victim Under International Law

At the international level, there is no uniform definition regarding victims. The universal international documents classify victims according to several categories, dependent upon the specific crime: (a) victims of crime; (b) victims of abuse of power; (c) victims of gross violations of international human rights law; (d) victims of serious violations of humanitarian law; (e) victims of enforced disappearance; (f) victims of international criminal law; (g) victims of trafficking; and (h) victims of terrorism.

2.4.1 *Victims of Crime*

2.4.1.1 Universal

The terminology "victim of crime" is a general concept to define a person who has suffered as a consequence of an illegal act. The crime is a violation of the laws of a state and which is punishable by the state. Alternatively, a crime is a wrong perpetrated against society and the individual rights of the person, which is also punishable by the state.

Although the victims of crime are provided for under national human rights mechanisms, the internationalisation of the definition of "victims of crime" by the Declaration of Basic Principles of Justice for Victims of Crime and Abuse of Power 1985 enabled recognition of the fact that millions of people suffer harm as a result of crimes.[74] Before the role of victims was clarified under the Declaration, crime was, at the domestic level, not deemed to be against the individual, but rather against the sovereignty of the state. The Declaration provides the following explanation: 'A (1)' (1) victims are persons who, (2) individually or collectively, (3) have suffered harm, including physical or mental injury, emotional suffering, economic loss or substantial impairment of their fundamental rights, (4) through acts or omissions that are in

[74] Fattah (1997), p. 75; Jorge-Birol (2010), pp. 306–307; Ochoa (2013), p. 106; Doak (2008), p. 23.

violation of criminal laws operative within Member States including those laws proscribing criminal abuse of power.

1. Victims are persons [...]: it is important to mention that besides natural persons (human beings), legal persons (for example, organisations, institutions and entities) may also be considered as being classifiable as victims of crime.
2. [...] individually or collectively [...]: the notion of individuality with regard to victimisation prescribes the direct or indirect targeting of the person by the perpetrator. The collectivity of the victimisation may be interpreted in both broad and narrow aspects, including the direct targeting of the group of persons in the broad sense, or the direct targeting of the person, thereby indirectly harming the group of persons in the narrower sense.
3. [...] have suffered harm including (i) physical or mental injury (ii) emotional suffering, (iii) economic loss (iv) substantial impairment of their fundamental rights [...]: Harm emphasises the negative effect on the physical nature of the object as well as on the psychological balance of the person. According to the Declaration, the drafter included such harm which may victimise the person. Accordingly, (i) physical or mental injury refers to the health of the person; (ii) emotional suffering is the condition of the person, who experiences fear, anxiety, shock, grief, mental suffering, shame, embarrassment or emotional disturbance[75] as a result of the act or omission of the perpetrator; (iii) economic losses are the commercial profits which could have been gained had the act or omission of the perpetrator not taken place; and, finally, (iv) the substantial impairment of the fundamental rights means there is an obstacle to the possibility of enjoying the norms of *jus cogens* such as the right to life, the right to security of person etc., which will not occur, if the act or omission by the perpetrator is not carried out.
4. [...] through acts or omissions that are in violation of criminal law operative within Member States [...]. This highlights the activities or failures of the perpetrator, which are sanctioned under domestic law.

Parts 'A (2)' and 'A (3)' of the Declaration expand upon the definition of a victim embodied in 'A (1)', noting that a person may be considered a victim regardless of the legal situation of the perpetrator. The term victim also includes indirect victims such as the immediate family and dependents of the direct victim, as well as the persons who suffered harm while intervening to prevent the victimisation. 'A (3)' of the Declaration does not include any criteria for the classification of a victim on the grounds of political, racial, national, religious etc. criteria.

[75]Okrent and Buckley (2015), p. 109.

2.4.1.2 Regional

At a European regional level, the definition of the victims of crime had already been determined in 1977 by Resolution (77) 27 on the compensation of the victims of crimes. Although there is no clear and direct explanation for the victim's definition, it is, by analogy, possible to interpret the definition in the Resolution, particularly in I (1) (a) where it states that compensation should be contributed by the state to anyone who has sustained severe bodily injury as a result of a crime. Remarkably, this definition requires the victim to have bodily injury, which thus does not include mental injuries. With regard to the same matter, the dependents of any person who died as a result of crime were also deemed to be victims.

The European Convention on the Compensation of Victims of Violent Crimes from 1983, which is based upon Resolution (77) 27, expands upon the previous definition of a victim. The Convention states in Article 2 (1) (a): [The State shall contribute to compensate] those who have sustained serious bodily injury or impairment of health directly attributable to an intentional crime of violence. Including the wording "health" illustrates the progress in expanding the definition of victims as "health" then includes, in line with domestic law, mental as well as physical injury. This injury then has to be serious and directly attributable to the crime, that is, a relationship of cause and effect needs to be proven.

The Convention applies only to intentional offences as they are particularly serious and give rise to compensation less often than non-intentional offences. In addition, it excludes, for example, the extensive range of road traffic offences that are, in principle, covered by other schemes.[76] Although the Convention considers the compensation and reparation guarantees of the victims, it also protects the victims of offences against life, physical integrity and health. As such, this kind of wording obviously differs from the Declaration of Basic Principles of Justice for Victims of Crime and Abuse of Power from 1985. In this regard, it is possible to consider the idea that the definition of a victim is related to the natural person, other types of the persons are excluded (e.g. a moral person or a legal person). The compensation does not intend to cover the economic loss of the victim, however, Article 2 (1) (b) foresees compensation for the dependents of the persons who have died as a result of such a crime. By analogy, this may mean that the dependents could also be considered victims.

Within the field of the EU, The Council Framework Decision of 15 March 2001 on the standing of victims in criminal proceedings provides a new definition for the victims of crime. Article 1 (a) of the Decision explains that the term victim shall denote a natural person who has suffered harm, including physical or mental injury, emotional suffering or economic loss, directly caused by acts or omissions that are in violation of the criminal law of a Member State. As such, the decision stipulates that victims are natural persons, which means it definitively excludes legal persons which

[76]COE, Explanatory Report on the Convention on the Compensation of Victims of Violent Crimes 1983. Article 2 (17).

have suffered harm directly caused by acts or omissions that are in violation of the criminal law of a Member State.[77] While interpreting the legal definition, the European Court of Justice (ECJ) highlighted that victims of crimes are only natural persons. This is due to that fact that such persons are objectively in a situation which differs from that of legal persons by virtue of their greater vulnerability as a consequence of the nature of the interests which can be harmed by offences committable only against natural persons. This, for example, could include the victim's life or physical well-being.[78] The Framework Decision was replaced by Directive 2012/29/EU of the European Parliament and the CoE.

The Directive of the European Parliament and of the CoE of 25 October 2012, which established minimum standards with regard to the rights, support and protection of victims of a crime, was the result of the Stockholm Program and Action Plan.[79] This placed victims high on the EU agenda announcing in recital (19) that the recognition of victims is regardless of whether the accused is subsequently found guilty or not. This means that if the trial fails to prove beyond reasonable doubt that the accused is guilty, it does not necessarily mean that the victim did not suffer harm as a result of the offence. At the same time, the Directive provides under Article 2 (1) (a) the following description of the victims of crime: "victim means i) a natural person who has suffered harm, including physical, mental or emotional harm or economic loss which was directly caused by a criminal offence; and ii) family members of a person whose death was directly caused by a criminal offence and who have suffered harm as a result of that person's death". The same Article lit. (b) provides an explanation concerning family members, under which are included: the spouse, the person who is living with the victim in a committed intimate relationship, in a joint household and on a stable and continuous basis, the relatives in direct line and the siblings and dependents of the victim. This is the first time that a directive ensured that the family members of the victim can also be subsumed under the definition of a victim.[80] Furthermore, the limit of the number and priority of the family members who benefit from the rights set out in the Directive may be established by the procedures stated by the Member States (Article 2 (2)).

---

[77]ECJ, *Eredics, Vassné Sápi*, Case C-205/09, Judgment (21 October 2010), paras. 24–31.

[78]ECJ, *Eredics, Vassné Sápi*, Case C-205/09, Judgment (21 October 2010), para. 30, see also Hoppe (2020), p. 153.

[79]EU, OJ C 115, Information and Notices, 4 May 2010, p. 1, see also EC, Communication from Commission to the European Parliament, the Council, the European Economic and Social Committee and the Committee of the Regions, COM 2010, p. 171.

[80]See the Speech of Françoise Le Bail, Strengthening victims' rights in Europe, 26 November 2012, p. 2.

2.4.2 Victims of Abuse[81] of Power

The second part of the UN Declaration refers to victims who have suffered harm as a consequence of an abuse of authority. This manifests itself in different ways, but also includes the same acts stated in the first part of the Declaration. In contrast to the victims of crime, the Declaration considers the victims of an abuse of power, even if the acts do not constitute the violation of domestic criminal laws, to fall within the violation of internationally recognised norms relating to human rights. B (18) of the Declaration highlights that victims means persons who, individually or collectively, have suffered harm, including physical or mental injury, emotional suffering, economic loss or substantial impairment of their fundamental rights, through acts or omissions that do not yet constitute violations of national criminal law but of internationally recognised norms relating to human rights.

The Declaration emphasises the importance of states proscribing abuses of political and economic power under their domestic law and the importance of the consideration of redress for the victims of such circumstances. There is no codified definition of the term 'abuse of power', however it consists of different types of understandings and mechanisms of execution which have yet to be stipulated between states and could include political, economic power, social and religious power. There is no clear definition of what power is and what abuse is, nevertheless it may be determined as the ability of an individual or a group of individuals to act in such way so as to use the power as they prefer.[82] The concept of power should be understood in the manner of how it is executed and whether the access to such functions of its execution is legitimate or illegitimate. Illegitimate power is already a form of abuse by its very nature. Legitimate power, which is mostly based upon the position of the individual who exerts influence over his subordinates,[83] must be prescribed by law and an abuse thereof means the ill use, improper treatment and application for a wrong purpose. The operationalisation of the abuse of power requires the consideration of the three basic elements: (1) the goals for which the power is exercised; (2) the means by which the power is exercised; and (3) the limits within the power that should be exercised.[84] The definition for the victims of abuse of power prescribed by the Declaration points out that the exceeding one's power without violating national criminal law does not necessarily preclude victim status. This can be seen as a milestone in accepting the status victims in matters where there is a violation of internationally recognised norms relating to human rights (*jus cogens*) as the result of the abuse of power.[85]

---

[81]The word "*abuse*" comes from Latin word "*abusus*" which in the same time means the bad, excessive or unjust.

[82]Fattah (1989), p. 29.

[83]Raven (2001), p. 220.

[84]Fattah (1989), p. 30.

[85]See Article 2 (b) Draft UN Convention on Justice and Support for Victims of Crime and Abuse of Power from 8 February 2010, Fernández de Casadevante Romani (2012), pp. 43–44.

2.4.3 Victims of Gross Violations of International Human Rights Law and Victims of Humanitarian Law

Victims of gross violations of international human rights law are based upon UN Resolution 60/147 of 16 December 2005 on the Basic Principles and Guidelines on the Right to a Remedy and Reparation for Victims of Gross Violations of International Human Rights Law and Serious Violations of International Humanitarian Law. The Resolution defines victims in Section V N. 8 stating that:

> Victims are persons who individually or collectively suffered harm, including physical or mental injury, emotional suffering, economic loss or substantial impairment of their fundamental rights, through acts or omissions that constitute gross violations of international human rights law, or serious violations of international humanitarian law. Where appropriate, and in accordance with domestic law, the term "victim" also includes the immediate family or dependents of the direct victim and persons who have suffered harm in intervening to assist victims in distress or to prevent victimisation.

This expands upon the definition of a victim in three ways by including (1) victims of gross violations of international human rights law; (2) victims of serious violations of international humanitarian law; and (3) indirect victims. The separation of the victim's status into international humanitarian law and human rights law stems from the fact that the two fields of international law have evolved differently and are a distinct in nature and, therefore, require different sets of rights and obligations.[86] Although there is no clear understanding as to what a gross violation is, according to van Boven the wording was chosen for the purpose of indicating the seriousness of the violation. It is clear that the authors of the Resolution were convinced by the argument that the Resolution predominantly refers to the issue of reparation for the victims. Under violations of international human rights and humanitarian law, they described the elements[87] which had already been codified by the Rome Statute and other international multilateral documents pertaining to human rights. The relatively new aspect is the recognition of indirect victims as a class of victim and also the third party who intervenes in order to assist the victim or to prevent victimisation.

2.4.4 Victims of Enforced Disappearance

The concept of victims of enforced disappearance, although not included clearly in international treaty law, has been developed as customary law by the declarations of international institutions and by the jurisprudence of international courts. Before being internationally recognised, the necessity for international acceptance of the concept of victims of enforced disappearance was proclaimed several times by the

[86] van Boven (2013), p. 2.

[87] Condé (2004), p. 103.

Commission on Human Rights of the OAS, mostly in the Annual Report of 1977.[88] The Commission expressed its deep concern about the phenomena of disappearances, stating that:

> in various countries, there are numerous cases wherein the government systematically denies the detention of individuals, despite the convincing evidence that the claimants provide to verify their allegations that such persons have been detained by police or military authorities and, in some cases, that those persons are, or have been, confined in specified detention centers. This procedure is cruel and inhumane. As experience shows, a "disappearance" not only constitutes an arbitrary deprivation of freedom but also a serious danger to the personal integrity and safety and to even the very life of the victim. It is, moreover, a true form of torture for the victims' family and friends, because of the uncertainty they experience as to the fate of the victim and because they feel powerless to provide legal, moral and material assistance.[89]

To understand the definition of victims of enforced disappearance, it is first necessary to examine the definition of enforced disappearance which includes several violations of human rights. The disappearance, which constitutes the deprivation of liberty, may also imply the violation of personal integrity and safety.[90] Under those circumstances, a person is powerless to exercise their rights.[91] This particular status of the disappeared person is specific and it avoids the application of legal provisions established for the defense of personal integrity.[92] In 1992, enforced disappearances were internationally recognised in the sense that the systematic perpetration of such acts of the same nature constituted a crime against humanity. Such a crime undermines the deepest values of any society which is committed to respecting the rule of law, human rights and fundamental freedoms.[93] Under Article 1 (1), The Declaration on the Protection of All Persons from Enforced Disappearance affirms that enforced disappearance is an offence pertaining to human dignity.

The Declaration announces the relevance of compensation for the dependents of the victims. It ensures that within the meaning of the disappearance of the person,

---

[88] See also IACtHR, *Quinteros v. Uruguay, Bámaca Velásquez v. Guatemala*, 25 November 2000, para. 179, UN A/RES/33/179 of 20 December 1978, Disappeared persons, in relation to UN A/RES/43/173, of 9 December 1988, UN Economic and Social Council resolution 1989/65 of 24 May 1989 on Principles on the Effective Prevention and Investigation of Extra-legal, Arbitrary and Summary Executions, UN A/RES/44/162 of 15 December 1989 on Human rights in the administration of justice.

[89] IACtHR, Annual Report of the Inter-American Commission on Human Rights 1977, OEA/Ser.L/V/II.43, Doc. 21 corr. 1 April 20, 1978, Part, II.

[90] Inter alia: right to life, liberty and security of person, freedom from torture, freedom from arbitrary arrest and detention, and the right to a fair trial (Article 3, 5, 9, 10, 11).

[91] See OEA AG/RES. 443 (IX-0/79) of October 31, 1979; AG/RES 510 (X-0/80) of November 27, 1980; AG/RES. 618 (XII-0/82) of November 20, 1982; AG/RES. 666 (XIII-0/83) of November 18, 1983;AG/RES. 742 (XIV-0/84) of November 17, 1984 and AG/RES. 890 (XVII-0/87) of November 14, 1987.

[92] IACtHR, Ten Years of Activity 1971–1980, p. 319.

[93] Preamble of the Declaration on the Protection of All Persons from Enforced Disappearance.

consideration is given to the suffering of the family of the disappeared person, as per Article 1 (2). Although there is no clear definition of the victims of enforced disappearance, Article 19 of the Declaration considers the remedy issues to the victim of such an offence, and in the event of the death of the victim, the family may be compensated.[94] The provision for the compensation of the family merely in the event of the death of the victim was later changed by the jurisprudence of the Inter-American Court in the case of *Blake v. Guatemala*, where the relatives of the 'main' victim were considered autonomous victims.[95] It is also clear that the forced disappearance of a person may constitute a further violation of the rights of the victims, such as the right to truth,[96] the right to a fair trial or the right to humane treatment.

Article II of the Inter-American Convention on Enforced Disappearance from 1994, based upon the UN Declaration, describes enforced disappearance as the deprivation of the freedom of a person by agents acting in the interests of the state, which is also followed by the absence of information for relatives as to the whereabouts of the person. The Convention does not, however, mention the precise requirements for the recognition of the victim. Notwithstanding, it is possible to decipher by analogy the requirements for the definition of a victim within Article II of the Convention. This clarifies the victim as being (1) persons who is unable to execute his right to freedom (2) because of the will of the authorities, (3) who, as a consequence, are not willing to contribute to justice and to provide information on the whereabouts of the disappeared person.

The final aspect of the definition of victims of enforced disappearance can be found in Article 24 (1) of the International Convention for the Protection of All Persons from Enforced Disappearance from 2006. It qualifies the victim as a person who disappeared or who has suffered harm as the direct result of an enforced disappearance. This differs from the legal definitions mentioned above in the sense that the victim, according to the wording of this Article, is the direct victim, which may include the disappeared person and any person who has suffered harm as a direct consequence of an enforced disappearance. Consideration should be given to the indirect victims of enforced disappearance and they should be taken into account under such circumstances where the conduct is criminalised under domestic law.[97]

[94]See also Report of the Working Group on Enforced or Involuntary Disappearances 1997, UN, Economic and Social Council, Document E/CN.4/1998/43, Compilation of General Comments on the Declaration on the Protection of All Persons from Enforced Disappearance, p. 14.

[95]IACtHR, *Blake v. Guatemala*, 24 January 1998, para. 97, Scovazzi and Citroni (2007), p. 343, Sandoval-Villalba (2009), p. 257.

[96]Working Group on Enforced or Involuntary Disappearances, General Comment on the Right to the Truth in Relation to Enforced Disappearances.

[97]See Fernández de Casadevante Romani (2012), p. 56.

2.4.5 *Victims of Terrorism*

As a separate branch of international law pertaining to victims, conduct relating to terrorism differs from the other categories of offences. With this type of offence, there is an added degree of gravity and, by its very nature, the aim is to spread fear, apprehension and panic in society. Therefore, an act of terrorism impacts upon a large part of society. Accordingly, the damaged, injured or deceased victims are not the only direct victims of an act of terrorism. The secondary individuals, or so-called vicarious or tertiary victims,[98] who are not directly injured as a consequence of the act, may still be considered as direct victims of the particular conduct. Unfortunately, there is still no common and internationally recognised definition of terrorism which, in turn, does not allow for the development of a common agreement concerning the understanding of the concept of the victims of terrorism. Numerous international and regional agreements[99] have been drafted in order to develop the strategy against such

[98]See Pfefferbaum (2009), p. 176.

[99](1) Convention on the Prevention and Punishment of Crimes against Internationally Protected Persons, including Diplomatic Agents, adopted by the GA of the United Nations on 14 December 1973, (2) International Convention against the Taking of Hostages, adopted by the GA of the United Nations on 17 December 1979, (3) International Convention for the Suppression of Terrorist Bombings, adopted by the GA of the United Nations on 15 December 1997, (4) International Convention for the Suppression of the Financing of Terrorism, adopted by the GA of the United Nations on 9 December 1999, (5) International Convention for the Suppression of Acts of Nuclear Terrorism New York, adopted by the GA of the United Nations on 13 April 2005, (6) Convention on Offences and Certain Other Acts Committed on Board Aircraft, signed at Tokyo on 14 September 1963. (Deposited with the Secretary-General of the International Civil Aviation Organisation), (7) Convention for the Suppression of Unlawful Seizure of Aircraft, signed at the Hague on 16 December 1970. (Deposited with the Governments of the Russian Federation, the United Kingdom and the United States of America), (8) Convention for the Suppression of Unlawful Acts against the Safety of Civil Aviation, signed at Montreal on 23 September 1971. (Deposited with the Governments of the Russian Federation, the United Kingdom and the United States of America), (9) Convention on the Physical Protection of Nuclear Material, signed at Vienna on 3 March 1980. (Deposited with the Director-General of the International Atomic Energy Agency), (10) Protocol on the Suppression of Unlawful Acts of Violence at Airports Serving International Civil Aviation, supplementary to the Convention for the Suppression of Unlawful Acts against the Safety of Civil Aviation, signed at Montreal on 24 February 1988. (Deposited with the Governments of the Russian Federation, the United Kingdom and the United States of America and with the Secretary-General of the International Civil Aviation Organisation), (11) Convention for the Suppression of Unlawful Acts against the Safety of Maritime Navigation, done at Rome on 10 March 1988. (Deposited with the Secretary-General of the International Maritime Organisation), (12) Protocol for the Suppression of Unlawful Acts against the Safety of Fixed Platforms Located on the Continental Shelf, done at Rome on 10 March 1988. (Deposited with the Secretary-General of the International Maritime Organisation), (13) Convention on the Marking of Plastic Explosives for the Purpose of Detection, signed at Montreal on 1 March 1991. (Deposited with the Secretary-General of the International Civil Aviation Organisation), (14) Arab Convention on the Suppression of Terrorism, signed at a meeting held at the General Secretariat of the League of Arab States in Cairo on 22 April 1998. (Deposited with the Secretary-General of the League of Arab States), (15) Convention of the Organisation of the Islamic Conference on Combating International Terrorism, adopted at Ouagadougou on 1 July 1999. (Deposited with the Secretary-General of

acts, however none of them provides a definition of terrorism. There are still several ongoing attempts at drafting an international definition of terrorism, however, the discussions are currently deadlocked due to differing views regarding the elements of the offence. On the one hand, the acts are considered as a national struggle for liberation under anticolonial policies.[100] On the other hand, the acts are distinguished as a crime under national law in various iterations.

Particularly successful developments concerning the international disclosure of the definition of terrorism are to be found at European regional levels, especially by the CoE and the EU. In 1999, the Parliamentary Assembly of the CoE recommended[101] that terrorism be considered as any offence committed by individuals or groups resorting to violence or threatening to use violence against a country, its institutions, its population in general or specific individuals which, being motivated by separatist aspirations, extremist ideological conceptions fanaticism or irrational and subjective factors, is intended to create a climate of terror among official authorities, certain individuals or groups in society or the general public. In 2002, the definition of terror was consolidated by Article 1 EU Council Framework Decision. It considers that in regard to the Treaty establishing the EU, and in particular Articles 29, 31 (e) and 34 (2) (b) of the Treaty, the Member States of the EU should consider a terrorist act under national law as; the intimidation of the population, destabilisation of the fundamental political, constitutional, economic or social structures and values or the coercion of the government to act in other way, which is followed by attacks, upon a person, destruction of the governmental or public facilities, seizure of aircraft, ships or other means of public or goods transport,

---

the Organisation of the Islamic Conference), (16) European Convention on the Suppression of Terrorism, concluded at Strasbourg on 27 January 1977. (Deposited with the Secretary-General of the Council of Europe), (17) OAS Convention to Prevent and Punish Acts of Terrorism Taking the Form of Crimes against Persons and Related Extortion that are of International Significance, concluded at Washington, D.C. on 2 February 1971. (Deposited with the Secretary-General of the Organisation of American States), (18) OAU Convention on the Prevention and Combating of Terrorism, adopted at Algiers on 14 July 1999. (Deposited with the General Secretariat of the Organisation of African Unity), (19) SAARC Regional Convention on Suppression of Terrorism, signed at Kathmandu on 4 November 1987. (Deposited with the Secretary-General of the South Asian Association for Regional Cooperation), (20) Treaty on Cooperation among States Members of the Commonwealth of Independent States in Combating Terrorism, done at Minsk on 4 June 1999. (Deposited with the Secretariat of the Commonwealth of Independent States), (21) Inter-American convention against terrorism from 6 March 2002, (22) Council of Europe Convention on the Prevention of Terrorism from 16 May 2005, (23) International Convention for the Suppression of Acts of Nuclear Terrorism from 13 April 2005, (24) Beijing Convention on the Suppression of Unlawful Acts Relating to International Civil Aviation from 10 September 2010, (25) Protocol to Amend the Convention on Offences and Certain other Acts Committed on Board Aircraft from 4 April 2014, (26) Additional Protocol to the Council of Europe Convention on the Prevention of Terrorism from 22 October 2015.

[100]See Letschert and Staiger (2010), p. 10.

[101]CoE, Parliamentary Assembly Recommendation 1426 (1999) from 20 September 1999, European Democracies facing up to terrorism N. 5.

supply or use of different types of weapons, destruction of the natural resources and treatment of the commission of the offences mentioned.[102]

The first attempts to codify the definition of the victim of terrorism at the regional level was mainly based on the Guidelines on the Protection of Victims of Terrorist Acts adopted by the CoE in 2005, which tried to identify the victims of terrorist acts. Principle I of the Guidelines ensures that the victim is any person who has suffered direct physical or psychological harm as a result of a terrorist act. In appropriate circumstances, their close relatives can benefit from the services and measures prescribed under these Guidelines. These Guidelines paved the way towards the acceptance of the CoE's Convention on the Prevention of Terrorism, where solidarity with the victims of terrorism (preamble) and the protection, compensation and support (Article 13) of victims were emphasised. The aim of the principle is especially directed at the primary and secondary victims; under the principles, indirect victims are not protected, compensated or supported.[103] The lack of international regional instruments containing a definition for the victims of terrorism depends on several existing multilateral agreements on the victims of crime. As terrorism is prescribed as a crime under national law, the victims of terrorism are seen as victims of the crime. This is linked to the aforementioned international and regional multilateral agreements and also enables the states to investigate and prosecute the offence using the appropriate national organs.

In 2012, the UN Special Rapporteur on the promotion and protection of human rights and fundamental freedoms suggested, while considering measures to counter terrorism, the consideration of victims of terrorism in several categories:[104]

1. Direct victims of terrorism: Natural persons who have been killed or have suffered serious physical or psychological injury as a result of an act of terrorism.
2. Secondary victims of terrorism: Natural persons who are the next of kin dependent of a direct victim of terrorism.
3. Indirect victims of terrorism: Individuals who have suffered serious physical or psychological injury as the indirect result of an act of terrorism.
4. Potential victims of terrorism: They are the principal beneficiaries of the State's positive obligations under Article 6 of the Convention on Civil and Political Rights.

2.4.6 *Victims of Trafficking*

As with the category of victims of enforced disappearance and victims of terrorism, a consistent definition is lacking for the victims of trafficking. The internationally

[102] Argomaniz (2015), p. 127; Albrecht and Kilchling (2010), p. 224.

[103] Letschert and Groenhujsen (2011), p. 33, UNODC, The Criminal Justice Response to Support Victims of Acts of Terrorism, p. 9.

[104] UNGA, A/HRC/20/14, Human Rights Council, Ben Emmerson, Report of the Special Rapporteur on the promotion and protection of human rights and fundamental freedoms while countering terrorism, para. 16.

accepted document referring to the struggle against human trafficking is the United Nations Convention against Transnational Organised Crime and accordingly the Protocol to Prevent, Suppress and Punish Trafficking in Persons, especially Women and Children, both adopted by Resolution 55/25 GA in 2000.[105] There are, however, still no direct criteria for the definition of the victims of trafficking. Although in comparison to the definition of terrorism which, due to a lack of agreement between the different parties prevented the possibility of a consistent meaning of the definition, the crime of trafficking became internationally standardised as a consequence of the aforementioned documents. Article 3 (a) of the Protocol ensures that trafficking in persons includes; the recruitment, transportation, transfer, harboring or receipt of persons by means of the threat or use of force or the forms of coercion, of abduction, of fraud, of deception, of the abuse of power or of a position of vulnerability or of the giving or receiving of payments or benefits to achieve the consent of a person having control over another person, for the purpose of exploitation. This should also include, at a minimum, the exploitation of the prostitution of others or other forms of sexual exploitation, forced labor or services, slavery or practices similar to slavery, servitude or the removal of organs. As the Protocol does not mention any concept for the understanding of the victim of such crimes, it is possible to determine, by analogy, that the person who was targeted under the disposition of Article 3 (a) could be considered a victim of trafficking.

The CoE closed the existing gap between the definitions of the victim of trafficking in persons and the elements of the crime of trafficking. It proclaimed in the Convention on the Action against Trafficking in Human Beings that there must be consideration for those people who were subject to exploitation, as described in Article 4 (a) of the same Convention.[106]

2.4.7 Victims Under International Criminal Law

The category of victims under international criminal law accordingly envisages the crimes of genocide, crimes against humanity, war crimes and the crime of aggression. As previously mentioned, at the international criminal justice level, a victim participation system had not been used prior to the introduction of the Rome Statute. Neither the ICTY nor the ICTR[107]—and not even the IMT—recognised the victims

[105] See Goodey (2005), p. 232.

[106] See CoE, Guidance Note on the entitlement of victims of trafficking, and persons at risk of being trafficked, to international protection, June 2020.

[107] Despite to references to 'victims and witnesses' in the instruments and the jurisprudence of the ICTY, the ICTR and the SCSL, the victim as witness is the only substantial role that (s)he can formally play in those courts' proceedings. The status of victims as witnesses is of particular relevance to those courts as these forums rely much more on eyewitness testimony than their post Second World War predecessors, Pérez-León Acevedo (2014), p. 125.

as being independent parties in the justice process, as the ICC and the ECCC now partially do. Before the victims may participate in the proceedings or apply for reparations, the nature of their status must be recognised in accordance with Rule 85 RPE, which states that victims can be natural persons as well as legal persons. The wide-ranging concept of a victim described under Rule 85 RPE enables the coverage of almost all direct and indirect victims who have suffered harm. In comparison to the ICC, the ECCC considers using the term civil party, which is equivalent to a victim. The ECCC internal rules and regulations state that the term victim may refer to any person who has suffered harm caused by a crime within the jurisdiction of the ECCC. The differences in the interpretation of the concept of a victim under international criminal justice will be described in the following chapter.

Type of victim	International treaty	Definition of the victim	Right to participation	Right to compensation
Victims of crime	UN Declaration of Basic Principles of Justice for Victims of Crime and Abuse of Power 1985 A (1)	*Victims are persons* who, *individually or collectively*, have *suffered harm*, including *physical or mental injury, emotional suffering, economic loss* or *substantial impairment of their fundamental rights, through acts* or *omissions* that are *in violation of criminal laws operative within Member States including those laws proscribing criminal abuse of power.*	Yes	Yes
	EU Resolution (77) 27 on the compensation of the victims of crimes I (1) (a)	[The State shall contribute to compensate] *those who have sustained serious bodily injury or impairment of health directly attributable to an intentional crime of violence.*	No	Yes
	The European Convention on the Compensation of Victims of Violent	[The State shall contribute to compensate] *those who have sustained serious bodily injury or*	No	Yes

(continued)

Type of victim	International treaty	Definition of the victim	Right to participation	Right to compensation
	Crimes 1983 Article 2 (1) (a)	*impairment of health directly attributable to an intentional crime of violence.*		
	The Council Framework Decision of 15 March 2001 on the standing of victims in criminal proceedings Article 1 (a)	*Victim shall mean a natural person who has suffered harm, including physical or mental injury, emotional suffering or economic loss, directly caused by acts or omissions that are in violation of the criminal law of Member State.*	Yes	Yes
	Recommendation Rec (2006)8 of the Committee of Ministers to Member States on assistance to crime victims 1 (1.1)	*Victim means a natural person who has suffered harm, including physical or mental injury, emotional suffering or economic loss, caused by acts or omissions that are in violation of the criminal law of a member state. The term victim also includes, where appropriate, the immediate family or dependents of the direct victim.*	Yes	Yes
	Directive 2012/29/EU of the European Parliament and of the Council of 25 October 2012 establishing minimum standards on the rights, support and protection of victims of crime, and replacing Council Framework Decision 2001/220/	*Victim means a natural person who has suffered harm, including physical, mental or emotional harm or economic loss which was directly caused by a criminal offence; family members of a person whose death was directly caused by a criminal*	Yes	Yes

(continued)

Type of victim	International treaty	Definition of the victim	Right to participation	Right to compensation
	JHA Article 2 (1) (a) (i)	*offence and who have suffered harm as a result of that person's death;*		
Victims of abuse of power	UN Declaration of Basic Principles of Justice for Victims of Crime and Abuse of Power 1985 (B) 18	*Victim means persons who, individually or collectively, have suffered harm, including physical or mental injury, emotional suffering, economic loss or substantial impairment of their fundamental rights, through acts or omissions that do not yet constitute violations of national criminal law but of internationally recognised norms relating to human rights.*	Yes	Yes
Victims of the gross violations of international human rights law and serious violations of humanitarian law	UN Resolution 60/147 of 16 December 2005 on Basic Principles and Guidelines on the Rights to a Remedy and Reparation for Victims of Gross Violations of International Human Rights Law and Serious Violations of International Humanitarian Law V (8)	*Victims are persons who individually or collectively suffered harm, including physical or mental injury, emotional suffering, economic loss or substantial impairment of their fundamental rights, through acts or omissions that constitute gross violations of international human rights law, or serious violations of international humanitarian law. Where appropriate, and in accordance with domestic law, the term "victim" also includes the*	Yes	Yes

(continued)

Type of victim	International treaty	Definition of the victim	Right to participation	Right to compensation
		immediate family or dependents of the direct victim and persons who have suffered harm in intervening to assist victims in distress or to prevent victimisation.		
Victims of enforced disappearance	A/RES/47/133 18 December 1992 Declaration on the Protection of all Persons from Enforced Disappearance Article 19	*The victims of acts of enforced disappearance and their family shall obtain redress and shall have the right to adequate compensation, including the means for as complete rehabilitation as possible. In the event of the death of the victim as a result of an act of enforced disappearance, their dependents shall also be entitled to compensation.*	Yes	Yes
	Inter-American Convention on Enforced Disappearance 1994 Article II	For the purposes of this Convention, *forced disappearance is considered to be the act of depriving a person or persons of his or their freedom, in whatever way, perpetrated by agents of the state or by persons or groups of persons acting with the authorisation, support, or acquiescence of the state, followed by an absence of information or a refusal to acknowledge that*	No	No

(continued)

Type of victim	International treaty	Definition of the victim	Right to participation	Right to compensation
		deprivation of freedom or to give information on the whereabouts of that person, thereby impeding his or her recourse to the applicable legal remedies and procedural guarantees.		
	International Convention for the Protection of All Persons from Enforced Disappearance 2006 Article 24	*For the purpose of this Convention, "victim" means the disappeared person and any individual who has suffered harm as the direct result of an enforced disappearance.*	No	Yes
Victims of terrorism	COE Convention on the Prevention of Terrorism 2005 Article 13	*Each Party shall adopt such measures as may be necessary to protect and support the victims of terrorism that has been committed within its own territory. These measures may include, through the appropriate national schemes and subject to domestic legislation, inter alia, financial assistance and compensation for victims of terrorism and their close family members.*	Yes	Yes
	COE guidelines on the protection of victims of terrorist acts on 2 March 2005 Principle I	*States should ensure that any person who has suffered direct physical or psychological harm as a result of a terrorist act as well as, in*	Yes	Yes

(continued)

Type of victim	International treaty	Definition of the victim	Right to participation	Right to compensation
		appropriate circumstances, their close family can benefit from the services and measures prescribed by these Guidelines. These persons are considered victims for the purposes of these Guidelines.		
Victims of trafficking	Protocol to prevent, suppress and punish trafficking in persons, especially women and children 2000 Article 3 (a) (b)	*(a)"Trafficking in persons" shall mean the recruitment, transportation, transfer, harbouring or receipt of persons, by means of the threat or use of force or other forms of coercion, of abduction, of fraud, of deception, of the abuse of power or of a position of vulnerability or of the giving or receiving of payments or benefits to achieve the consent of a person having control over another person, for the purpose of exploitation. Exploitation shall include, at a minimum, the exploitation of the prostitution of others or other forms of sexual exploitation, forced labour or services, slavery or practices similar to slavery, servitude or the removal of organs;*	Yes	Yes

(continued)

Type of victim	International treaty	Definition of the victim	Right to participation	Right to compensation
		(b) The consent of a victim of trafficking in persons to the intended exploitation set forth in subparagraph (a) of this article shall be irrelevant where any of the means set forth in subparagraph (a) have been used;		
	Convention on Action against Trafficking in Human Beings from 2005 Article 4 (e)	*'Victim' shall mean any natural person who is subject to trafficking in human beings as defined in this article (Article 4 (a)).*	Yes	Yes
Victims of international criminal law	ICC Rules of Procedure and Evidence Rule 85	*(a) "Victims" means natural persons who have suffered harm as a result of the commission of any crime within the jurisdiction of the Court;* *(b) Victims may include organisations or institutions that have sustained direct harm to any of their property which is dedicated to religion, education, art or science or charitable purposes and to their historic monuments, hospitals and other places and objects for humanitarian purposes.*	Yes	Yes
	ECCC Internal Rules and Regulations Rev.9 Glossary	*Victim refers to a natural person or legal entity that has suffered harm as a result of the commission of any crime within the*	Yes	No

(continued)

Type of victim	International treaty	Definition of the victim	Right to participation	Right to compensation
		jurisdiction of the ECCC. Civil party refers to a victim whose application to Civil Party has been declared admissible by the Co-Investigating Judges or the PTC in accordance with these IRs.		
	STL Rules of Procedure and Evidence Rule 2	*Victim is a natural person who has suffered physical, material, or mental harm as a direct result of an attack within the Tribunal's jurisdiction.*	Yes	No
	SCSL Rules of Procedure and Evidence Rule 2	*Victim is a person against whom a crime over which the Special Court has jurisdiction has allegedly or has been found to have been committed.*	No	No
	UNTAET N. 2000/30 Regulation SPSC Transitional Rules of Criminal Procedure (x)	*Victim means a person who, individually or as a part of a collective, has suffered damage, including physical or mental injury, emotional suffering, economic loss or substantial impairment of his or her fundamental rights through acts or omissions in violation of criminal law. By way of illustration and not limitation, a victim may be the spouse, partner or immediate family member of a*	No	No

(continued)

Type of victim	International treaty	Definition of the victim	Right to participation	Right to compensation
		deceased person whose death was caused by criminal conduct; a shareholder of a corporation with respect to criminal fraud by the administrators or officers of the corporation; or an organisation or institution directly affected by a criminal act.		

2.4.8 Conclusion

The human rights movements have enabled the inclusion of victims of crime in the criminal justice process, allowing them to participate in the proceedings separately. The quantity of multilateral conventions and documents in international law which provide a definition of a victim pursuant to the elements of the respective crimes, establishes the relevance of victims' rights and, accordingly, their participation and compensation. Consequently, it is possible through international consensus to identify a role for victims within the justice system as a result of the violation of human rights which, in certain cases, constitutes a crime under national law. The definition of each victim is, however, strictly bound to the internationally recognised specific crimes and, due to the nature of the crimes, victims are included relating to internationally recognised specific crimes. This can be graphically represented in the following diagram:

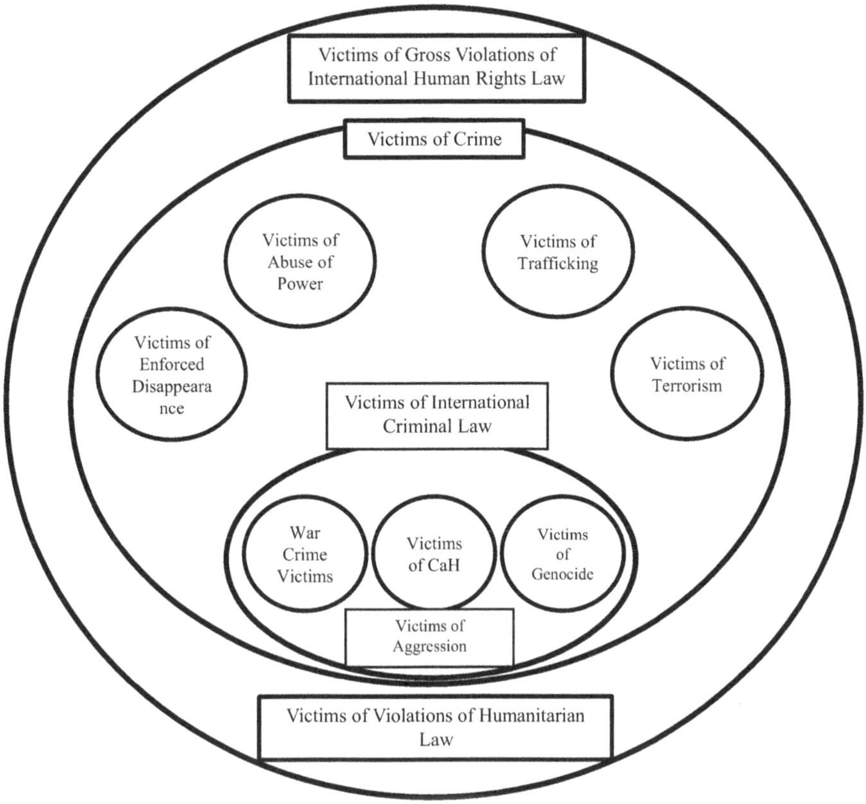

Although victims have now started to receive international attention, a state of affairs which did not previously exist, there is always a risk of violation of other general human rights principles, such as the equality of arms, the principle of a fair trial and other rights pertaining to the accused and the suspect. Generally, however, it is important to mention that this kind of attention focusing upon victims first occurred after World War II; the victims of World War I did not receive much attention. The international community began to discuss victimisation as being reality, not a weakness, thus rendering it a notion which could no longer be ignored or which should evoke shame. An essential advantage here is the recognition of victims as being independent of the case, which means that their status exists irrespective of whether the accused is identified or not.

Establishing and recognising the existence of restorative justice for victims as being parallel to retributive justice in order to compensate them for their harm and damage thus became a new feature.

A disadvantage to be mindful of is that the development of victims' rights was relatively slow compared to other human rights. Even the UN Declaration, which pays attention to the victims, does not have a legally binding role for them. The analysis of international documents shows that victims' rights are not universal, rather they have regional effect and are linked to specific types of crimes.

Advantages	Disadvantages
Victims received attention	Slow developments of victims' rights
Victims involved in the justice	Risk of losing the balance in criminal justice
UN Declaration on victims	The non-binding effect of the UN Declaration on victims
Victims are victims independent on other issues	The regional character of the victims' rights conventions
The regional character of the victims' rights conventions	
Victims of specific crimes receive more international attention	
Considering restorative justice	

2.5 National Comparison on Victims' Participation in Criminal Justice Systems

The judges serving at the international criminal tribunals each have their own national legal backgrounds. When faced with legal questions, the judges may have different opinions, and disagreements therefore arise between them. Since the victims' participation system at the ICC is a unique mechanism and differs from domestic systems, it is necessary to understand the different national approaches.

In the previous section, it was possible to identify the codified international treaties regarding victims' issues, treaties which confirm definitions as well as victims' recognition, participation and compensation and which also clarify the rights and responsibilities of the victims in the different stages of the justice system. In this section, it is important to look at the separate national legal systems and to ascertain how the victims' participation functions at a national level.

In order to underline the differences between the legal systems, the victims' participation mechanism will be analysed from three different perspectives: the definition and recognition of the victim; the participation type in the criminal justice procedures, such as the rights and responsibilities; and the compensation of the victims for injury and damage. It is important to note that the laws provided are bound to the temporal and linguistic ties at the time this research was composed.

In the following schematic overview, the following abbreviations will be used.

A: Definition and Recognition

A(1): Broad definition of a victim—mentioning only the existence of suffering as a consequence of the crime.

A(2): Narrow definition of a victim—including direct and indirect, natural, physical, legal persons who suffered harm, including physical or mental injury, emotional suffering, economic loss or substantial impairment of their fundamental rights, through acts or omissions that are in violation of criminal laws.

A(3): Partly broad, partly narrow definition of a victim, mentioning only one or two specific features in order to obtain the status of victimhood.

A(4): No specific definition: victim is mentioned as victim, injured person or damaged person.

A(5): Unique system.

B: Participation

B(x): No participation

B(1): Active participation, which includes such procedural rights as being represented during the trial, the right to file a complaint or a request, the right to point out the facts and to suggest evidence, the right to participate in evidentiary proceedings and to make statements, the right to file an appeal, etc.

B(2): Participation as (i) a private prosecutor,[108] (ii) a subsidiary prosecutor[109] or (iii) as a civil party,[110] which grants such rights as the right to submit evidence, to make notes and requests and to appeal the acts of the Court where their interests have been harmed.

B(3): Passive participation, which mostly includes the right to be informed and notified, the right to be present at the hearings, but no further participatory right.

C: Compensation

C(1): State compensation, which means general compensation without any specific features.

C(2): State compensation, which includes compensation for (1) loss of earnings, (2) medical and hospitalisation expenses, (3) funeral expenses, (4) loss of maintenance (5) counselling costs (6) reparation of damages, (7) etc.

C(3): No state compensation.

---

[108]In case of less serious crimes, the private person takes the responsibility for accusing the wrongdoer.

[109]In order to be a subsidiary prosecutor, the victim should be a civil claimant by the declaration.

[110]In order to become a civil claimant, the victim should file a declaration of estimated loss.

C(4): Private compensation by lodging a compensation claim either (1) at a criminal trial or, (2) separately in a civil trial.

2.5.1 States of the European Union

Even though the Member States of the EU are, at the same time, members of the CoE, there are, with regard to victims' issues, still a number of differences between the States in their respective codes of criminal procedure (CCPs).

Definition
The A(1) group represents the countries which mention only a broad concept of the victim. Sweden (*målsägande*), Finland (*asianomistaja*) and Norway (*fornærmede*), as an EFTA member, use only the wording "*injured person*".[111] The Slovenian, Croatian, Bulgarian and Romanian codes of criminal procedure also belong to this group in which the definition predominantly expresses a violation of the personal and property rights of the injured party (Article 144 Slovenian CCP and Article 202 (10–11) Croatian CCP) and the existence of harm (Article 79 Romanian CCP and Article 74 Bulgarian CCP).

The A(2) group includes almost 14 European countries which define victims in the narrower sense. The criminal codes in Austria, Czechia, Estonia, Hungary, Italy, Ireland, Latvia, Lithuania, Malta, the Netherlands, Poland, Portugal, Slovakia and Spain do not only mention the victim as a person who has suffered, they elaborate further. For example, they prescribe the type of harm, the connection to the offence and the indirect victims who may be considered as the successors of the direct victims for the further procedural stages.

The A(4) and A(5) codes of France, Germany and Denmark do not include any definition on victims.

Participation type of the victims
The B(x) category includes only Denmark, which does not recognise victims as being part of criminal procedure.

The B(1) group consists of 16 European states which grant victims a general right to participate actively within trials.

The B(2) group includes 17 European states which have systems parallel to the general victims' participation system, whereby they also consider special types of participation such as the victim as a private prosecutor, a subsidiary prosecutor or as a civil claimant. However, some states in this category do not accept the general participation mechanism for the victims. Only states such as Austria, Bulgaria and Hungary recognise all types of victim participation.

[111]See IVOR, implementing victim-oriented reform of the criminal justice system in the European Union, Sweden, Finland, under: https://www.apav.pt/ivor/images/ivor/PDFs/Fact_sheet_sweden.pdf and https://www.apav.pt/ivor/images/ivor/PDFs/Fact_sheet_finland.pdf, last visited on 8 December 2020, even if there is no victim definition in national procedural law, this may have been developed in case law.

Compensation type of the victims

Group C(1) includes the European states such as Denmark, Ireland, Italy and Lithuania which generally mention state compensation for victims. These states do not, however, specify what kind of state compensation should be provided to the victims.

Group C(2) consists of those EU states which have codified and harmonised state compensation to the victims of crimes in accordance with numerous Acts.

Group C(3) includes states which do not offer any state compensation to the victims of crimes.

Group C(4) represents all European states that consider compensation from the offender either in criminal or in civil trials.

State	(A) Definition	(B) Participation	(C) Compensation
Austria CCP	A(2) §65	B(1) (2)(i, ii, iii) §§66–72	C(2)[a] (4) §67
Belgium CCP	A(4) + A(5)	B(1) (2)(iii)	C(2)[b] (4)
Bulgaria CCP	A(1) Article 74	B(1) (2)(i, ii, iii) Article 75–78	C(2)[c] (4) Article 84
Croatia CCP	A(1) Article 202 (10–11)	B(1) (2) Article 47, 60–63	C(2)[d] Article 43 (2) Article 47
Czech Republic LVC[e]	A(2) §2 and Sec. 43 CCP	B(1) Sec. 43 CCP	C(2)[f] (4) Sec. 44 CCP
Denmark AJA[g]	A(4)	B(x)	C(1) (4) (ii)
Estonia CCP	A(2) §37 and §37[1]	B(1) §38	C(2)[h] §178 (4) (ii)
Finland CJP[i]	A(1) Sec.61	B(1) (2)(iii)	C(2) (4)
France CCP	A(4) + (A5)	B(1) (2)(iii)	C(2)[j] (4) Sec. 420-1
Germany CCP	A(4) + (A5)	B(1) (2)(ii) §§374–402	C(2)[k] (4)
Greece CCP	A(1)	B(2) (iii)	C(2) (4)
Hungary VSCA[l]	A(2) Sec. 1, Sec. 51 CCP	B(1) (2)(i,ii,iii) Sec. 51, 493–495	C(2)[m] (4) Sec. 54 CCP
Ireland CJB[n]	A(2) Head 2 (1)	B(2)(i)[o]	C(1) (4)[p]
Italy CCP	A(3) + (A5)	B(2)(iii) Article 74–81, 90–95	C(1) (4)[p] Sec. 76–82 CCP
Latvia CCP	A(2) Sec. 95	B(1) Sec. 97–101[q]	C(2)[r] (4) Sec. 97
Lithuania CCP	A(2) §28	B(1)	C(1) (4)[p]
Luxembourg CCP	A(4)	B(1) (2)(iii)	C(2)[s] C(4)
Malta VCA[t]	A(2) §2	B(2)(iii)	
Netherlands CCP	A(2) Sec. 51a	B(2)(iii) Sec. 51b to 51e	C(2)[u] (4) Sec. 51 f
Poland CCP	A(2) Article 49	B(2)(i, ii, iii) Article 49–70	C(2)[v] (4) Article 62
Portugal CCP	A(2) Article 67-A	B(2)(ii, iii) Article11 Law 130/15	C(2) (4) 67-A
Romania CCP	A(1) Article 79	B(1)(2)(iii) Article 22, 81	C (2)[w] (4) Article 9
Slovakia CCP	A(2) Sec. 43	B(1) Sec. 44–49	C(2)[x] (4) Sec. 46
Slovenia CCP	A(1) Article 144	B(1)	C(2)[y] (4) Article 110–112

(continued)

State	(A) Definition	(B) Participation	(C) Compensation
Spain LSVC[z]	A(2) Article 2	B(2)(i)	C(2)[aa] (4) Article 109
Sweden CJP	A(1) Sec. 8	B(2)(i, iii)	C(2)[bb](4)

[a]§2 Verbrechensopfergesetz of 20 March 2018; [b]The Law on State Compensation of 1 August 1985; [c]Crime Victim Assistance and Financial Compensation Act; [d]Victims of Crime Compensation Act of 1 July 2013; [e]See Law on Victims of Crime, see under: https://www.zakonyprolidi.cz/cs/2013-45, last visited on 8 December 2020; [f]Act N. 209/1997 Coll., on the Provision of Financial Support for the Victims of Criminal Acts; [g]Administration of Justice Act; [h]Victim Support Act of 17 December 2003, mediation also included; [i]Code of Judicial Procedure; [j]Commission on Compensation for Victims of Crime (CIVI) is responsible for the compensation by Act of 6 July 1990; [k]Opferentschädigungsgesetz of 7 January 1985. Mediation also included; [l]Victim Support and Compensation Act 2005; [m]Act CXXXV of 2005 on the Support of Victims of Crime and State Compensation; [n]Criminal Justice (Victims of Crime) Bill 2015; [o]Case Kelly & anor -v- Ryan ([2013] IEHC 321); [p]Mediation; [q]Definitively fewer rights than in other codes of criminal procedure; [r]Act on State Compensation to Victims; [s]Act of 12 March 1984 on compensation for certain victims of personal injury as the result of crime; [t]Victims of Crime Act 2015; [u]Act CXXXV of 2005 on the Support of Victims of Crime and State Compensation; [v]Act on State Compensation for the Victims of Certain Crimes of 5 October 2005, under: http://prawo.sejm.gov.pl/isap.nsf/download.xsp/WDU20051691415/T/D20051415L.pdf, last visited on 8 December 2020; [w]Act No 211/2004 on measures for the protection of crime victims; [x]Act No 215/2006; [y]Compensation to Crime Victims Act (ZOZKD) from 11 November 2005; [z]Law on Standing of Victims of Crime; [aa]Law 35/95 of 11 December 1995; [bb]Criminal Injuries Compensation Act

2.5.2 Balkan and Eastern European States

Definition

The A(2) group with its narrower definition of a victim includes all Eastern Europe states as well as North Macedonia. Some of the states consider a separate article on definitions, where the definition of a victim is described rather narrowly.

The A(4) group includes mainly the remainder of the Balkan states where the victim is mentioned merely as an injured person.

Participation type of the victims

Under the B(1) and B(2) categories, the majority of the states consider some form of participation for the victims. However, participation types differ from one other. Almost all Eastern European States, including North Macedonia and Serbia, consider general participation of the victims in the criminal trial. Meanwhile, all of the aforementioned states, including Albania and Montenegro, consider a certain type of participation of victims regarding private prosecution, subsidiary prosecution and a civil claim.

Under the B(x) category, the only state which does not consider victim participation in criminal procedure is Bosnia and Herzegovina. Before and during a criminal trial, a damaged person has the right to seek damages through the power of the prosecutor. If a person misses this deadline, they have 2 years to file a complaint before a civil court requesting damages, both material and non-material, once a conviction has been declared final. The problem is that the victim requests damages from the perpetrator directly and, more often than not, these are impossible to retrieve.

Within the B(3) category, Georgia only recognises the passive participation of the victim. The victims of crimes in Georgia are deprived of rights such as influencing the judicial procedure or examining the files. The victims in Georgia are afforded mostly passive rights, that is, the right to be informed and to be protected.

Compensation type of the victims

Under C(1), Bosnia and Herzegovina, Serbia, Azerbaijan, Moldova and Russia consider general compensation for the victims of crimes. The legislation of those states mention state compensation for the victim, however, they do not specify what may fall under that definition, such as initial medical first aid, legal assistance etc.

Under C(3), most of the Balkan and Eastern European states do not consider state compensation for the victims of crimes.

Under C(4), all states consider private compensation for the victims. Georgia, Moldova and Ukraine are states that only foresee compensation in a civil claim.

State	(A) Definition	(B) Participation	(C) Compensation
Albania CCP	A (4) Article 58	B (2) (i, iii) Article 59–64	C (3) (4) Article 65
Bosnia and Herzegovina CCP	A (4) Article 20 (h)	B (x)	C (1) (4) Article 195[a]
North Macedonia CCP	A (2) Article 21 (4–5)	B (1) (2) (i, iii) Article 53–68	C (3)[b] (4) Article 110–120
Montenegro CCP	A (4) Article 22 (5)	B (2) (i, ii, iii) Article 51–65	C (3)[c] (4) Article 234–245
Serbia CCP	A (4) Article 22 (6) CC	B (1) (2) (i, ii, iii) Article 50–67	C (1)[d] (4) Article 252–260

[a]Enforcement of damage compensation claims of victims of war crimes in criminal proceedings in Bosnia and Herzegovina—situation, challenges and perspectives, Trial, track impunity always, pp. 9 and 22; [b]Friscik et al. (2014, 2016); [c]See CoE, GRETA, 6th general report on GRETA'S activities, 2017, p. 59; [d]Ivana and Radovic (2017)

State	(A) Definition	(B) Participation	(C) Compensation
Armenia CCP	A (2) Article 58	B (1) (2) (iii) Article 60–62	C (3) (4) Article 159–164
Azerbaijan CCP	A (2) Article 87 (1)	B (1) (2) (i, iii) Article 88–89	C (1) (4) Article 191, (4) 189–190
Belarus CCP	A (2) Article 49	B (1) (2) (i, iii) Article 51–52	C (3) (4) Article 52
Georgia CCP	A (2) Article 3(22), 56	B (3) Article 57–58	C (3) (4) (ii)
Moldova CCP	A (2) Article 57, 59	B (1) Article 58, 60, (2) (iii)	C (1) (4) (ii)
Ukraine CCP	A (2) Article55	B (1) (2) (iii) Article 61	C (3) (4) (ii)
Russia CCP	A (2) Article 42	B (1) (2) (i, iii) Article 43–44	C (1) (4) Article 44

2.6 US Victims' Participation System

2.6.1 Introduction

US criminal procedure follows an adversarial structure, where—as is often claimed—the victim is largely marginalised, if not forgotten altogether:

> The adversary system is premised on the belief that the most effective was to arrive at just results in court is for each side of a controversy to present the evidence that is most favorable to its position and to let a neutral judge or jury sift through the conflicting evidence and decide where the truth lies. In other words, the truth emerges from the clash of opposing evidence.[112]

If this is the basic tenet, then of course there is no room for any form of victim participation. Logically, in most books on criminal procedure, the victim does not appear.[113] During law school the focus is directed exclusively towards an adversarial legal process—the State v. the Defendant—which leaves no room for victim participation and[114] criminal procedure has traditionally been taught without taking notice of the victim. This has strongly influenced forensic practice and the exclusion of the victim from the criminal trial is also claimed to be a product of law school curricula.[115]

Furthermore, it is often claimed that the constitution requires the victim to stay out of the courtroom.[116] Neither in the original text of the constitution, nor in the Amendments is the victim of crime mentioned, whereas all the attention is directed towards the defendant. The constitution has been extremely influential with regard to criminal trial procedures. This is true for the time starting with the "Warren Court" in the 1960s, which is said to have produced a "revolution" in criminal procedure,[117] nevertheless, how lasting the effects were and how revolutionary the Warren Court really was, is not the question here although[118] it does highlight the further concentration on the State v. Defendant view of the criminal justice process, leaving the victim aside. This state of affairs only began to change slowly with the emergence of the victim's movement in the 1970s; in 1975, the first victims association was founded, the National Organisation for Victim Assistance.[119]

---

[112]Myers (2016), p. 12.

[113]See e.g. Whitebread and Slobogin (2003) and Moskovitz (2014).

[114]Beloof et al. (2006), p. 3.

[115]Beloof et al. (2006), p. 16.

[116]LaFave (2009), § 24.4(d), p. 1122; Mosteller (1997), p. 1701.

[117]Israel and LaFave (2006), p. 1; Whitebread and Slobogin (2003), p. 1.

[118]Critically, e.g. Kamisar (1996), p. 119.

[119]Tobolowsky et al. (2016), p. 8.

If one looks for reasons for this belated interest in victims' issues in the last century, one finds a rather obscure bias against victims. For example, it is said that there is a mutual mistrust between the police and victims. The police often complain about the unwillingness of victims to report crimes, which paints an unreliable picture of them. Similarly, the police bemoan the lack of cooperation by victims during the investigation stage of the alleged crime. Inversely, victims claim they are left alone or even bullied by the police.[120]

It could be argued that one reason for this is that crime is often seen as flowing from social inequality. It is often members of the black community who are the victims of crime within the USA. Common theories also point to puritan or Darwinian attitudes. The Good will be commanded and the Evil will be punished. Therefore, subliminally, the victim is often considered to be responsible for the crime.[121]

In this section, a closer look will be taken at the present situation regarding the participation of the victims of crime in the USA. It must be taken into consideration that criminal prosecution takes place both at the federal and at state level. These levels sometimes vary to a dramatic extent and they do so in particular with a view to victim participation. Some states are more open, some are more reluctant to include the victim; some states even have provisions relating to the victims of crime in their constitution, some do not, as is the case at the federal level. In the following, the main focus will be placed on the situation at state level.

It is interesting to note that despite a general degree of scepticism towards state authority in the former colonies of North America and the early reluctance to establish public prosecution, the prosecutor today is entrusted with extremely far-reaching powers. "The prosecutor has more control over life, liberty and reputation than any other person in America," Justice Robert. H. Jackson, at that time as the US Attorney General, announced in his speech on April 1, 1940, at an assembly of Unites States Attorneys.[122] Indeed, the prosecutor here is vested with more powers than anywhere else in the world, despite being part of the executive branch, he can also act as legislator when deciding whether or not to try a case, and he can act as judge, when determining a sentence under a plea bargain.[123] The original intention of the separation of powers to monitor power appears to have gone missing.[124] It can also be argued that the American system has, in fact, turned out to be rather inquisitorial in nature as a consequence of this overall power on the part of the prosecutor.[125]

---

[120] Beloof et al. (2006), p. 21.

[121] Beloof et al. (2006), p. 16; Roach (1999), p. 281.

[122] Jackson (1940), p. 3.

[123] Lynch (2009), pp. 94 et sub.

[124] Indeed these prosecutorial powers are understood as an adequate tool not only to deal with the limited resources of the criminal justice system but also to rectify flaws in the criminal laws. This gives the prosecutor the power to overrule parliament; see also Green (1988), p. 490 with Fn. 11, who is otherwise rather critical and in favour of victim's rights.

[125] See Barkow (2006), pp. 1044–1045; McConkie (2015), p. 69.

As a result of this development, the exclusion of victims from criminal proceedings is sometimes referred to as an historic misunderstanding. The monopoly of district attorneys was not established by the law, however, the courts interpreted the power to prosecute as an exclusive right.[126] It is, at the very least, ironic that the system which started out by relying solely on the victims to find justice for themselves, but then ultimately took the authority to prosecute crimes step-by-step into its own hands, now seems to have forgotten the interests of the victim entirely.[127]

Yet the practice adopted by the prosecutor towards the victims—and towards the witnesses for that matter—is often described as an "administrative run-around".[128] Both are often required to make numerous trips to the courthouse in order to tell and re-tell their stories. In 1975, the Department of Justice declared: "At the present time the victim is the subject of fewer rights and fewer programs of service than any other group coming in contact with the criminal justice system".[129]

2.6.2 Crime Victim Reforms

In the 1960s, the victim returned to the sphere of public attention. In part, this was facilitated by criminologists who, in the 1950s, had begun to shift their focus to victims.[130] Yet the criminologists' interest was not so much about genuine victim-related issues, rather they expanded the classical criminological approach, i.e. to explain how the criminal became a criminal, they assessed the role of the victim in this process. Even if the development of victimology originated from this time, it was only later that interest turned to the victim directly. Nevertheless, criminologists certainly helped include the term victim into academic writing.

Institutional reform started with the victim assistance program in California in 1965. This served as an example which was replicated by many other states throughout the USA and was mainly due to the so-called Victims' Rights Movement. At the same time, development was fostered by the civil rights and anti-war movements, and mostly by the women's movement. The women's movement mainly addressed violence against women and entrusted public prosecutors with the reforms[131] whereas the victims movement sought to have individual rights for victims directly. President Lyndon Johnson established The President's Commission on Law Enforcement and Administration of Justice and its final report in 1967 also focused on victim-related issues like the need for services and provided suggestions

[126] Goldstein (1982), p. 52.

[127] McDonald (1976), pp. 663 et subs.

[128] McDonald (1976), p. 661; Beloof et al. (2006), p. 8; Kamisar (1996), p. 883.

[129] Quoted by McDonald (1976), p. 166.

[130] Von Hentig (1967).

[131] Tobolowsky et al. (2016), p. 8.

as how best to integrate victims into the criminal justice system.[132] The victim initiatives were, however, in conflict with police investigations and threatened to restrict their authority and so victims' rights were immediately interpreted as curtailing civil liberties.[133]

However, the greatest impact on the further development of victims' rights in the USA came from President Ronald Reagan. On April 23, 1982 he established the President's Task Force on Victims of Crime in 1982 which consisted of a panel of nine members who delivered their Final Report in December 1982.[134] He thereby "led the nation into a new era in the treatment of the victims of crime. Never before had any President recognised the plight of those forgotten by the criminal justice system - the innocent victims of crime", as is stated by the Commission in its report.[135]

This rather progressive report contained a thorough and rather distressing analysis of the current situation of the victim within the criminal justice process and delivered a multitude of proposed amendments which are still relevant for the continued development today. The report even pressed for a constitutional change to the Sixth Amendment: "Likewise, the victim in every criminal prosecution shall have the right to be present and to be heard at all critical stages of judicial proceedings". This, of course, has never became law, at least not yet, even though it was introduced into Congress in 1996, as it was never voted on.[136]

Nevertheless, the Report started a reform process in ordinary law which is still ongoing, starting with the Victim and Witness Protection Act 1982,[137] which famously introduced the victim impact statement. An important step towards the institutional recognition of the needs of the victims of crime was the Establishment of the Office for Victims of Crime within the Department of Justice (DoJ). The Victim of Crime Act 1983 established a fund to compensate the victims of crime, the Victims' Rights and Restitutions Act 1990 and further acts then followed. Further reform was enacted by the Crime Victims' Rights Act 2004 and the 2008 Amendment of the Federal Rules of Criminal Procedure, both of which were amended in 2015. This process has been described as the "third wave of victims' rights"[138] and the development has not yet come to a standstill. Vision 21 is the DoJ Office of Victims of Crime's program to set its Victim Services-Study from 2010 into practice. Essentially, this means more research into victim issues is required. At the same

[132]Tobolowsky et al. (2016), p. 7.

[133]Beloof et al. (2006), p. 29.

[134]President's Task Force on Victims of Crime. Final Report 1982 (available at: https://www.ovc.gov/publications/presdntstskforcrprt/welcome.html last visited 8 December 2020).

[135]President's Task Force on Victims of Crime. Final Report 1982, p. ii.

[136]Beloof et al. (2006), p. 12.

[137]Clevenger et al. (2018), p. 42.

[138]Beloof (2005), p. 255.

time, a push for a constitutional amendment continues, even if it is facing strong opposition for fear of creating an imbalance vis-á-vis the rights of the accused.[139]

In the following part of this section, it is important to describe the current state of the law concerning victim participation within the separate steps of a criminal prosecution.

2.6.3 Participation of Victims

As previously stated above, the victim of crime is nowadays present in several stages of the prosecution process, however, predominantly as a witness. Yet there are different stages of the investigation and prosecution process at which the victim could participate and it will be discussed in which ways they are indeed made part of the process. The federal rules of criminal prosecution today foresee a rather extensive list of victims' rights. Title 18 of the U.S. Code § 3771 reads as follows:

Rights of Crime Victims

A victim of crime has the following rights:

1. The right to be reasonably protected from the accused.
2. The right to reasonable, accurate, and timely notice of any public court proceeding, or any parole proceeding, involving the crime or of any release or escape of the accused.
3. The right not to be excluded from any such public court proceeding, unless the court, after receiving clear and convincing evidence, determines that testimony by the victim would be materially altered if the victim heard other testimony at that proceeding.
4. The right to be reasonably heard at any public proceeding in the district court involving release, plea, sentencing, or any parole proceeding.
5. The reasonable right to confer with the attorney for the Government in the case.
6. The right to full and timely restitution as provided in law.
7. The right to proceedings free from unreasonable delay.
8. The right to be treated with fairness and with respect for the victim's dignity and privacy.
9. The right to be informed in a timely manner of any plea bargain or deferred prosecution agreement.
10. The right to be informed of the rights under this section and the services described in section 503(c) of the Victims' Rights and Restitution Act of 1990 (42 U.S.C. 10607 (c)) [1] and provided contact information for the Office of the Victims' Rights Ombudsman of the Department of Justice

These victim rights apply to any "public court proceeding" throughout the criminal prosecution process. This is, of course, less radical than it looks, as the victim, who is a member of the general public, would be allowed to take part in the hearings anyway. This chapter is therefore directed more towards the prior practice of explicitly excluding the victim from the proceedings. In the following, a close look shall be taken at the individual steps of the proceedings.

[139]Tobolowsky et al. (2016), pp. 257 et subs.

2.6.3.1 Definition of Victim

Before looking at the different procedural steps, it is first necessary to clarify who has participatory rights. The Crime Victims' Rights Act foresees a definition for federal cases,[140] which can be found at 18 USC 3771(e), and reads:

> (e) Definitions. – For the purposes of this chapter, the term
>
> 'crime victim' means a person directly and proximately harmed as a result of the commission of a Federal offense or an offense in the District of Columbia. In the case of a crime victim who is under 18 years of age, incompetent, incapacitated, or deceased, the legal guardians of the crime victim or the representatives of the crime victim's estate, family members, or any other persons appointed as suitable by the court, may assume the crime victim's rights under this chapter, but in no event shall the defendant be named as such guardian or representative.

Obviously, this definition comprises only the "direct" victim. Similar definitions can be found in state laws, where jurisprudence is mostly concerned with the causal link between victim and harm, i.e. the interpretation of the words "as a result of" as an indicator for the "direct" victim.[141]

Questions are rightly raised as to the dependency of the victimhood to the actual crime. This is connected to the question of which point in time a victim can in legal terms be referred to as a victim.[142] Both questions—first, what crime has been committed and, second, has it really been committed—depend on a legally valid decision. Thus, the answer to the question of who the victim of the crime is, is actually very similar to the question as to who the culprit is. Nevertheless, even if such a harmonisation of these two mutually dependent questions were consistent, it would also be impractical. A number of states therefore grant victim status from the moment the crime occurred, whereas other states make victimhood dependent upon the first contact of the victim with the police, in order to have some formal requirement.

To date, there has been only one case decided by the Supreme Court on a related question. In *Hughey v. US*[143] it was held that restitution for harm suffered for a crime can only be claimed by those who really have been the victim of a crime that has actually been committed.[144] Procedurally, this question is also related to one of the following sections of this chapter and to bail proceedings, as can be seen in the case of *Littlefield v. Williams*.[145] Williams was suspected of having committed several white-collar crimes.[146] The prosecutor only charged Williams with a part of these crimes and dropped the other charges in the course of a plea agreement with the defendant. Littlefield complained about this deal pointing to his status as a victim of

140 Tobolowsky et al. (2016), p. 49.

141 Tobolowsky et al. (2016), p. 18.

142 Beloof et al. (2006), p. 52.

143 US Supreme Court, *Hughey v. U.S.*, 495 U.S. 411 (1990).

144 Beloof et al. (2006), p. 56.

145 US Supreme Court, *Littlefield v. Williams*, 540 S.E. 2d 81 (2000).

146 Beloof et al. (2006), p. 53.

crime, however the court ultimately denied Littlefield the status of victimhood. Instead, the court prompted the victims to take action before the civil courts.

2.6.3.2 Bail Proceedings

When a suspect of crime is arrested and brought before a judge, the judge will have to decide whether to detain the suspect or to bail him. The arrest can be considered as the first official recognition of victimhood as an investigation is underway at this point. Therefore, the question arises as to whether to involve the victim at the bail hearing. Federal law indeed foresees not only the right of the victim to be present, but also the right to be heard at the bail hearing, see 18 U.S.C.A. § 3771(a) (4).

It is unclear, however, what the precise reasons for victims presenting statements in court at this stage of the proceedings actually are.[147] These statements have little, if any, legal effect and, of course, the defendant has a right to be bailed (at least in non-capital crimes),[148] the purpose of the bail being solely to secure the appearance of the defendant at trial.[149] Furthermore, how many times should the victim be summonsed and allowed to the relate their story for therapeutic value?[150] It is not surprising that the necessary reforms of pre-trial detention are not discussed here regarding victim participation at this stage.[151]

2.6.3.3 Decision to Prosecute

A far more important, if not the most important, decision in the course of the criminal justice process is the prosecutor's decision to prosecute. Obviously, this decision has dramatic effects on the position of the victim and their struggle for justice. It has already been seen that the role of the prosecutor at this crucial part of the proceedings is rather dominant. This being so, the question arises of whether there is room for victim participation at this stage at all. Referring to the Federal Rules will also not help. The decision to prosecute is not taken in open court in a public hearing; it is a decision which lies purely at the discretion of the prosecutor. The President's Task Force recommended in 1982 that the prosecutor consult with victims before dismissing a case.[152] However, not even half of the states foresee a constitutional or legal right of the victim to confer, consult or communicate with prosecutors before they decide to either press or to drop charges. Quite the opposite is found in 18 U.S.

[147]Henderson (1999), pp. 406 and 414; Kamisar et al. (2015), p. 883.

[148]Duker (1977), p. 33.

[149]US Supreme Court, *Ex Parte Milburn*, 34 U.S. (9 Pet.) 704 (1835).

[150]Henderson (1999), p. 406.

[151]See e.g. the very critical analysis of pre-trial detention by Appleman (2012), 297. Her proposal for reform do also not mention the crime victim.

[152]Tobolowsky et al. (2016), p. 70.

C.A. § 3771 (d) (6), where the law states that, despite victims' rights, the power of the prosecutor must prevail; nothing shall impair prosecutorial discretion.[153] While it has been said that under a "victim participation model" of the criminal procedure victims should have a veto power over whether a charge is brought, and they should be able to challenge the prosecutor's decision not to charge, reformers have been unwilling (or unable) to bring about such a monumental shift regarding the victims' rights pendulum.[154]

One could propose an "equal protection" challenge to the prosecutor's decision on the charge. However, in *Linda R.S. v. Richard D.*, the Supreme Court held that "a private citizen lacks a judicially recognizable interest in the prosecution or non-prosecution of another".[155] This stern denial of any interest in prosecution by a victim is not tenable. Should the victim not at least be entitled to seek "*a declaratory judgment that a prosecutor has abused his discretion not to prosecute*", as has been proposed—*de lege ferenda*—by Stuart Green?[156]

2.6.3.4 Plea Bargaining

As mentioned previously, the question of plea bargaining and the role of the victim of crime is thereby related to the question concerning the decision to prosecute. A plea agreement is between the prosecutor and the defendant, whereby the prosecutor "runs the show". The plea agreement needs to be brought before a judge who ensures that the plea presented is "knowing" and "voluntary", however judges essentially tend to "rubberstamp most plea agreements".[157] As such, there is an official hearing at court before a judge at which the crime victim is allowed to participate and must be informed in advance of such a hearing. Victims of crime are supposed to be heard by the prosecutor and judges can allow the use of victims' statements. This also holds true with regard to the sentencing decision, which will be discussed below. The victim statement represents the moment of the victim's greatest influence. However, given the conflict described above with the unchallenged powers of the prosecutor, the participation of the victim at this stage need not necessarily lead to a *de facto* veto power.[158] The prosecutor must, at all times, maintain control of the proceedings. "At the very least, such a practice gives the appearance that the resolution of criminal charges could turn on the whims of victims rather than the equities of each case".[159]

---

[153]Tobolowsky et al. (2016), p. 71.

[154]Kamisar et al. (2015), p. 914.

[155]US Supreme Court, *Linda R.S. v. Richard*, D. 410 U.S. 614 (1973), these were of course very particular circumstances and the question in substance was rather whether the Texas Penal Code provided an inequality between a "legitimate" and an "illegitimate" child.

[156]Green (1988), p. 490.

[157]McConkie (2015), p. 66.

[158]Tobolowsky et al. (2016), p. 97.

[159]Kamisar et al. (2015), p. 1240.

In addition, the victim's intervention usually comes at a time where an agreement between the parties, the prosecutor and the defendant has already been reached. Therefore, it does not help to guide either the court or the parties involved.[160]

This is the situation for most cases given that, at a federal level, 97% of criminal cases are terminated by plea bargaining. Despite victims rights being accepted by law, the legal practice reduces victims to mere bystanders in what is an obscure bargaining process between the prosecutor and the defence counsel.

2.6.3.5 Trial

The majority of literature pertaining to criminal procedure is based upon the assumption that a jury trial takes place. In practice, however, the US-American criminal justice system seldom relies on a "trial by jury", notwithstanding Article 3 Sec. 2 and the 6th Amendment of the US Constitution.[161] It has even been declared that "One of the greatest cultural achievements" of American legal history is dying,[162] though not without cause. In 2014 only 2.6% of cases at federal level actually went to court, either to a bench or a jury trial.[163] Yet the jury was introduced originally to limit the uncontrolled power held by prosecutors and judges, which casts American scepticism upon all government power.[164] The US Supreme Court has even expanded the right to jury trial onto the state level by interpreting the 14th Amendment as encompassing jury trials.[165]

Juries also have the power to exercise control over the legislation by what is called jury nullification. This is based on the maxim that if the jury concludes that the defendant is not guilty and acquits, there can be no appeal. If it considers the criminal norm to be irrelevant, a jury can acquit despite there being proof of guilt beyond reasonable doubt. Accordingly, jury nullification acts declare a criminal norm null and void. It gives the jury the power to monitor the legislator by holding a criminal norm inapplicable in the case, although it is questionable whether the judge may instruct the jury in this regard.[166] In any event, where the jury declares that there has been no crime at all, then this power vested in the jury does not work in favour of the victim who has suffered harm and expects the offender to be prosecuted. This is, of course, a very unusual situation and rarely occurs.

---

[160] McConkie (2015), p. 72, who proposes a reform of the plea bargaining with the laudable purpose to add transparency to the entirely obscure decision-making process in place. This would also allow for victim participation which could actually have an impact.

[161] As to the reasons, see Fisher (2004), pp. 175 et subs.

[162] Burns (2009), p. 1.

[163] See U.S. Department of Justice, Federal Justice Statistics 2014 Table 4.1 and Map 4.1 (published in 2017 at: https://www.bjs.gov/content/pub/pdf/fjs14st.pdf last visited on 8 December 2020).

[164] Kamisar et al. (2015), p. 1269.

[165] US Supreme Court, *Duncan v. Louisiana*, 391 U.S. 145 (1968).

[166] Kamisar et al. (2015), p. 1269.

In the rare event of a full-scale jury trial, victims are not welcomed either. There are several reasons for this. Firstly, it is often claimed that the constitution requires the victims to stay out of the courtroom,[167] as their presence would conflict with the rights of the defendant.[168] Secondly, the victims' presence, in particular before having testified as witness for the prosecution, could induce them to construct their testimony according to the evidence which has already been adduced. Thirdly, the presence of the victim would open the door to potential emotional reactions which might, in turn, prejudice the defence and influence the jury.[169] Fourthly, it is critical that in modern times lay jurors are fit for the complicated evaluation of evidence.[170]

The rule of exclusion, also referred to as the "rule on witnesses", has dominated the discussion for decades.[171] Not permitting witnesses to be present in the courtroom, save for when they are testifying, does have its benefits. It enhances the reliability of the witness if the testimony is not influenced by what has previously been discussed in the courtroom. That being said, however, police officers are usually allowed into the court hearing before and after their testimony.[172] In many cases this problem could be solved by simply hearing the victim witnesses first.[173] Originally, the exclusionary rule also applied to opening and closing statements. An exception was possible if the presence of a witness' was deemed "essential". However, the victim's presence was usually not considered to be relevant.

Nevertheless, the opposite case can also be made; the presence of victims does in fact assist in the truth-finding process. A stressed prosecutor might not remember all the facts at a complex hearing and the victim will almost certainly remember this with a greater degree of clarity. Indeed, it can be argued that no one knows more about the case than the victim.[174] This knowledge can help during cross-examination, and the victim could, in effect, support the prosecutor in ascertaining the truth.[175]

The President's Task Force recommended interpreting the law to the contrary in order to allow victims to be present at the hearing on a general basis. In 2004 and 2008, the legislator followed suit and granted victims the right to be present unless there was clear and convincing evidence that testimony by the victim would be

---

[167] Kamisar et al. (2015), p. 1122; and Mosteller (1997), p. 1701.

[168] As explained by Beloof et al. (2006), p. 14.

[169] Beloof and Cassell (2005), p. 538 refute this argument by claiming this to be a general problem of order in the courtroom which to uphold is the duty of the judge.

[170] Kamisar et al. (2015), p. 1264.

[171] Tobolowsky et al. (2016), p. 52. Similar discussions have been going on in Germany, where the same rule applied, Safferling (2011a, b), pp. 199–200, see also §243 II German CCP, Beulke and Swoboda (2018), § 371.

[172] This pointed out by Beloof and Cassell (2005), p. 526.

[173] Suggested already by Wigmore (1901).

[174] As is argued by Beloof and Cassell (2005), p. 544.

[175] This has also been stressed by DoJ OVC, for the twenty-first century, p. 15.

materially altered.[176] Thus, even if the rule-exception dynamic has been reversed, the presence of the victim is still dependent upon the assumed value of their testimony. It appears that the lack of participation at the trial stage of the proceedings is aligned to an enhanced influence during the sentencing stage, something which will be discussed in the following.

2.6.3.6 Sentencing

The separation of the trial, when the jury decides upon the guilt of the defendant, and the sentencing hearing for those who have been found guilty, opens the door for the victim to participate at this latter stage. At this stage, the testimony is no longer required in order to establish the facts of the case. It is no longer about evidence; it is now about punishment. This is also the stage where victimhood has been established by the jury. At the same time, the presumption of innocence has been negated by a guilty verdict and the victim has been officially declared a victim.

It is at this stage that the so-called victim impact statement comes into play. These provisions typically grant victims the right to make an oral statement during sentencing or allow for the victim's written statement to appear in the pre-sentencing report, or both. The function of the victim impact statement is to provide information about the effects of the crime on the victim and the victim's family.[177] It is highly questionable whether or not the judge should, or even must, take into account the victim's view. It is also questionable whether the effects of the crime, and how they are in the personal view of the victim, can be seen as aggravating circumstances. There are instances of discomfort, in particular within reports like Steve Bogira's statement. He claims that Judge Locallo had a strange way of evaluating the social harm stemming from the crime: "When a victim is productive and going to school and has potential, that's a greater loss to society than if he's some goof who's involved in gangs".[178] This being an exceptional misunderstanding of the value of human life, the impact of the victim on sentencing is a delicate question. One could claim that taking the victim statement into account could enhance the acceptance of the judgment on the part of the victim. In contrast, one could argue that this would be overstressing one purpose of criminal prosecution and, at the same time, disregarding other aims. Furthermore, other groups could also be encouraged to try to influence the sentencing decision.[179]

The right of the victim to be heard at the sentencing stage, however, enjoyed early recognition. Victim impact statements were introduced at state level even prior to the Task Force in 1982.[180] Prosecutors were supposed to ensure that victims have the

[176] Tobolowsky et al. (2016), p. 55.
[177] Kamisar et al. (2015), p. 1419.
[178] Bogira (2006), pp. 261–262.
[179] Beloof et al. (2006), p. 19.
[180] Tobolowsky et al. (2016), p. 99.

opportunity to appear and to be heard by the court at the time of sentencing. The President's Task Force claimed that a victim's life is profoundly affected by the sentence imposed and pressed very strongly for the victims to be present at the sentencing hearing. Victims are no less entitled to their day in court than the defendant is.[181]

The Supreme Court was initially undecided. In 1987, the Supreme Court held in *Booth v. Maryland* that victim impact statements violate the provision against cruel and unusual punishment.[182] Two years later, the Court followed these lines in *South Carolina v. Gathers*, stating that there was no mandatory consideration of victims' impact evidence as the 8th amendment stood against this.[183] A further 2 years later, however, in 1991, the Court in *Payne v. Tennessee* overruled *Booth* by saying that victim impact statements were merely a piece of information on the actual harm done, which traditionally has to be taken into account by the judge at the sentencing stage.[184] This time, the Court did not see the 8th Amendment as being affected. Victim impact statements would only be excluded if they were to be contrary to the fair trial principle set down in the 14th Amendment.[185]

Special attention is required in the case of capital punishment. With regard to the death penalty, critical voices have been raised in the face of a personalisation of the criminal trial and the sentencing process.[186] It has also been said that arbitrariness will influence the decisions as some families are against the death penalty as a matter of principle, while others favor the death penalty as the only acceptable punishment in a murder case.[187]

Today, victim impact statements are commonly made at the sentencing stage. However, there is neither clear evidence as to the impact of victim participation on the outcome of the sentence nor on victim satisfaction.[188]

2.6.3.7 Parole

The final stage of the criminal justice process is the parole decision. This questions whether the detainee is eligible to be released early. Prior to the Task Force Report on Victims' Rights, parole hearings were held exclusively behind closed doors. Now the right for the victim to be heard has been significantly expanded. The Federal Code clearly considers the information and the statements of the victim at a parole

---

[181] Tobolowsky et al. (2016), p. 100.

[182] US Supreme Court, *Booth v. Maryland*, 107 US 2529 (1987).

[183] US Supreme Court, *Caroline v. Gathers*, 490 US 805 (1989) see also Tobolowsky et al. (2016), p. 104.

[184] US Supreme Court, *Payne v. Tennessee*, 501 SC 808 (1991).

[185] Tobolowsky et al. (2016), p. 106.

[186] Logan (1999), p. 517.

[187] Alschuler (2009), p. 699.

[188] Tobolowsky et al. (2016), p. 129.

hearing, and empirical evidence suggests that the victims' participation at this stage has the potential to have a more significant impact on the parole decision outcome.[189] It does, however, seem odd that victims are able to influence the question of eligibility for parole. At the sentencing stage of the criminal trial, the main focus should lie on the rehabilitation and the resocialisation of the offender. Criteria for a release include the behaviour of the offenders in detention and maybe evidence of remorse. It will also be relevant whether the detainees are still considered a danger to the public and whether there is a likelihood that they will re-offend. The victim is not in a position to be able to add anything of value to these criteria.

2.6.4 Reparation

A criminal conviction can play a major role in the healing process for the victim. The public trial establishes an official declaration of victimhood; however, this is only one aspect. The victims also require financial support and compensation for their loss. Whereas public law has taken over the criminal law element of the conflict between the victim and offender, the private law element has been left to the person who was harmed. Civil litigation was available, however it was seldom used before the victims' movement in the 1970s. Even today, only a relatively small proportion of the victims of crime will actually litigate. It nevertheless represents an important option for crime victims seeking to be compensated for their crime-related losses.[190]

Since the Task Force Report in 1982, legislation has been adopted to expand restitution. At the same time, crime victim compensation schemes have been adopted extensively. Notwithstanding, it is a limited remedy and provides restricted funds for otherwise uncompensated expenses for those who suffer personal injury or death as a result of a crime.[191]

2.7 Participation Types of Victims in Criminal Procedure

The participation of a victim in criminal procedure assumes the existence of certain rights and obligations which the victims have to consider when expressing their willingness to be a part of this process. Besides the accused and the public prosecutor, different approaches have been established in criminal justice for how to deal with the "third party". A number of different terms are used: victim, injured or damaged person or aggravated person.

---

[189]Tobolowsky et al. (2016), p. 140.

[190]Tobolowsky et al. (2016), p. 221.

[191]Tobolowsky et al. (2016), p. 197; Clevenger et al. (2018), p. 41.

As it was mentioned above, during the formation of the common law, crimes were mostly considered as personal wrongs rather than interests of the state.[192] As a result, the victim had to find his or her own solution for the personal wrongdoings, unless it "disturbed" the king's peace or the interests of the Crown were somehow related to the case.[193] The victim in common law held a crucial position acting as a "private prosecutor" in criminal matters. Over time, the justice administration system was centralised, and a public prosecutor was established; as a consequence, the victim became detached from criminal law.[194]

If, in the common law, the tendency was to minimise the role of the victim in the criminal proceedings, French law granted the victims rather wide rights within the criminal process.[195] The difference between both systems in relation to the victims' status in criminal cases was connected to the fact that the common law system differentiated between a crime as affecting the interests of the public and torts affecting a personal interest. In this regard, criminal procedure solely aims at the protection of the public interest. French civil law, in contrast, combines the protection of public interest with redress for the victim.

However, several types of victim participation systems have developed through the decades, granting victims of crimes different ranges of rights and different legal positions within their respective criminal justice systems. Analyzing the practice of the European states and the states of the common law family, it is possible to divide the victims' participation mechanism into four types: (1) general victim participation; (2) private prosecutor; (3) subsidiary prosecutor; and (4) civil plaintiff. A comparison between these different types of participation will help understand the problems with the victim participation mechanism at an international level of criminal justice.

2.7.1 General Provisions

Traditional criminal justice depersonalised the victims of crime; they were treated as an "*item of evidence*"[196] or as a "*non-person*".[197] In this way, victims were ranked as witnesses who had the obligation to support public interests by delivering statements and evidence.[198] The situation partly changed in the United States after the establishment of the Victims of Crime Act 1984. This Act demanded procedural rights for the victims as well as assistance. In the European Community, the establishment of

[192] Hostettler (2004), p. 17; Kirchengast (2006), pp. 4 and 26–29.

[193] Safferling (2007), p. 9; Hostettler (2004), pp. 16–17.

[194] Hostettler (2004), pp. 18–19.

[195] See Andrews (1994), pp. 417–418; Delmas-Marty (2008), pp. 9–10; Braun (2019), p. 31.

[196] Rössner and Wulf (1984), p. 8.

[197] Shapland et al. (1985), p. 20; Dubber (2006), p. 229.

[198] Dearin (2017), p. 10.

several guidelines for the involvement of victims within the criminal justice system, such as the European Convention on Compensation of Victims of Violent Crimes 1983, began to develop.[199] Since the 1980s, there has been a tendency to enhance the sphere of activity for the victims of crime during criminal justice proceedings. In this regard, a particular peak was reached with the adoption of the victim participation scheme in the Rome Statute. On the one hand, this has been a revolutionary change in the conservative field of law and politics and,[200] on the other hand, it leads to further rather serious disputes between common and civil law systems. Before Article 68(3) RS, which grants victims an opportunity to participate in the international proceedings, can be analysed, it is important to classify the scope of rights and obligations which are granted to the victims of crime under national legislation if they participate in the criminal procedure.

Although there is still no generally binding rule with regard to involving the victims of crime in the proceedings as an independent party,[201] an increasing number of European states, including the Member States of the CoE, have now codified the general principle of involvement of victims in their respective criminal justice systems. On this basis, it is possible to divide the participation of victims into two generally adopted forms, one being a passive form of participation and one being active. The passive form of participation can be summarised under a general right to information,[202] whereas active participation expresses itself first in the right to be heard and, second, in the right to be compensated. The passive form of participation, or the general right to be informed, includes such rights as the right to access to the dossier or the disclosure of evidence, the right to legal representation and legal aid, the right to interpretation and translation and the general right to understand the case.[203] The active participation of the victim, or the right to be heard, encompasses all active measures of the victim in positively contributing to finding justice, such as the right to lead evidence, the right to give explanations, the right to present materials, the right to declare challenges or motions, the right to object against the actions of bodies of criminal prosecution, the right to participate in court sessions and the right to review them, as well as the right to appeal against the decisions of the body at the level of inquiry, investigator, prosecutor and the court.

The right to be informed by the criminal justice system: If a person who is affected is not informed about an official proceeding, that person will feel insecure and stranded in an aura of uncertainty.[204] This is not only true in terms of the

[199] See van Dijk (1988), p. 120.

[200] Baumgartner (2008), p. 414.

[201] Only Directive 2012/29/EU of the European Parliament and of the Council of 25 October 2012 Establishing Minimum Standards on the Rights, Support and Protection of Victims of Crime, and Replacing Council Framework Decision 2001/220/JHA establishes a general rule of participation by Article 10–12, see Klip (2016), p. 327.

[202] Cf. Shapland et al. (2011), p. 37.

[203] Cf. Wemmers (1996), p. 87; Wolhuter et al. (2009), p. 175.

[204] Sharma (2003), p. 33.

accused, but also for the victim who has suffered as a consequence of the crime perpetrated by the accused. Parallel to the frustration, despair and the emotional stress and anguish after the crime,[205] for the victims a lack of information about their situation is another psychological constraint. Informing the victim of their position within the criminal proceedings, of the charges brought against the accused and giving the victim the possibility to become familiar with the evidence makes the victim feel at least a little more secure. The kind of information that would be useful to relay to the victims also includes the procedures which will follow and the victim's role within these procedures, including how, and in what circumstances, the victim may obtain protection and compensation from the offender, as well as possibilities for legal aid and the right to receive translations.[206] However, this is only the passive form of participation for the victims within the criminal justice system, which is accompanied either by their attendance at criminal trials or their being informed by the court, prosecutor or investigative bodies.

Another general participatory right is the right to be heard. The active participation model may also be considered in two forms, namely as the right to make a statement during and at the closing of the proceedings, and the right to be involved in the proceedings as a third party. The right to be heard, or active participation, also includes the right to be informed. However, making statements and being involved means that the victims have specific rights and obligations.[207] The general difference between the two forms is based upon the possibility to actively influence the course of the proceedings. The right to make a statement, either orally or in writing, may not change the outcome of the proceedings in a radical way. In contrast, the right to be involved in the proceeding may well influence the course of criminal justice.

The right to make statements as a general right to be heard means giving the victim a chance to state their position during the public proceedings. While making a statement, the victim may, during the proceedings and at the time of sentencing, point to several aspects of the crime and the trial that are of concern to them.[208] This allows the court to hear the victim's side of the story and rebalance the offender-victim relationship during the criminal trial. However, the statement of the victim is not binding upon the court, although it can help within the truth-finding process.

Being actively involved in the criminal justice system as a third party means the existence of a wide scope of rights which may be used at the criminal trial by the victim. By having the rights to appeal, to object, to challenge and to provide explanations, the victim gains powers resembling those of the offender and the

[205]Fattah (1989), p. 51; Gerry (2009), p. 468; Wemmers (1996), p. 208; Edmunds et al. (2003), p. 188.

[206]Council of Europe, Victims: Support and assistance 2008, p. 76, see notification types to the victim in United States in Edmunds and Underwood (2003), p. 233, see also P. 6 (a) of the Declaration of Basic Principles of Justice for Victims of Crime and Abuse of Power from 29 November 1985.

[207]Cf. Roche (2013), p.79.

[208]Beloof (2012), p. 222; Doyle (2008), pp. 19–20; Klip (2016), p. 327.

public prosecutor. These rights may impact upon the outcome of the proceedings, both in its economic and prosecutorial aspects (restorative and retributive justice).

An additional right of victims is the right to be compensated.[209] This, however, does not provide the victims with *locus standi* for active participation in the criminal trial, but rather serves mostly as an additional claim on the part of the victim. It may help the victim by virtue of the fact that no separate tort proceedings need be taken. As such, the legal conflict can be settled in the course of one single trial.

Analyzing the different participatory rights mentioned above, it is possible to formulate the following graphic in order to show the expansion of the rights of victims in criminal proceedings according to their status:

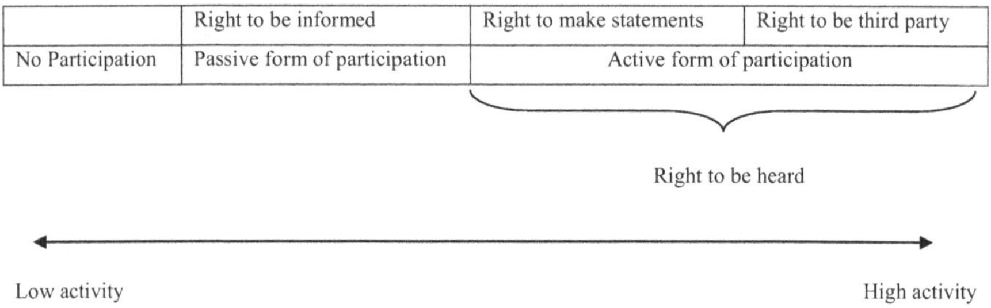

The general participation of victims itself may be interpreted from broad perspectives as well as from narrower ones. In that sense, even the mere consideration of the victims and the inclusion of the victims in the criminal justice process can already be deemed as participation for them within the criminal procedure. However, under political pressure, the established atmosphere for political reform has enabled victims to gain more rights than they previously possessed. At the same time, even the distinction of the victim from the witnesses can be considered as being a distinct form of victim participation. The states which are not bound by the minimum standards for the participation of victims of crime still practise a general participation of victims in their domestic jurisdictions. The general participation of victims, without extended features, such as private prosecutors', subsidiary prosecutor's and civil plaintiff's rights, is also well practiced in a number of European criminal justice systems.

2.7.2 *Private Prosecution*

Private prosecution is a form of active victim participation. This legal status allows the victim to actively prosecute without the public prosecutor being involved in the investigation and the trial. Private prosecutors demand justice for their own rights

[209]Dignan (2004), p. 53.

that have been violated and are interested in accusing the defendant and in the outcome of the trial. From the accused's point of view, this clashes with the principle of the right to be prosecuted by a neutral party.[210]

While the public prosecutor with no particular personal interest in the outcome of the trial seeks to reach equitable justice,[211] private prosecutors are under no particular public constraint in pursuing their personal interests. On the other hand, from the victims point of view, as a private prosecutor it becomes possible to prove in their own way the damage caused by the defendant, whereas the public prosecutor may ignore certain aspects of victimisation, especially the wishes and needs of the victim. As a result of that, the victim may not feel satisfied and well represented within the criminal justice procedures. The difference between the public and private prosecutor is illustrated by the fact that the public prosecutor is interested in the punishment of the crime, whereas the private prosecutor is interested not only in punishment, but also in dispute resolution.[212]

In practice, national legislations consider minor offences, such as assault, invasion of privacy, violation of secrecy of correspondence or defamation, to be eligible for private prosecution. Prosecutions of these offences are generally not in the public interest and, as a result of that, the prosecution can be referred to the victim.[213] A number of European jurisdictions use private prosecutions in those circumstances, either when there have been no criminal proceedings initiated by the public prosecutor or the public prosecutor drops the case.

Even if the private prosecution process is similar to civil proceedings, the aim still remains the imposition of a criminal sanction. In comparison to criminal procedures, where the public prosecutor is involved, there is no investigation before trial and the victims, by lodging a complaint, have to prove all the facts. By lodging the complaint as a private prosecutor, the victim receives similar procedural rights to those held by the public prosecutor, such as the right to review the files and to substantiate the charge.[214] However, the private prosecutor stands alone within the criminal justice system. The burden of proof lies with the private prosecutor who may not collaborate with the public police authorities in order to obtain evidential material. A victim who acts as a private prosecutor bears all the material risks and the consequences of the case, including possible criminal investigations against themselves, for example, for an abuse of process, malicious prosecution or defamation.[215]

International criminal justice, however, does not recognise the institute of the private prosecutor. The victims at the ICC, or at similar institutions such as the ECCC, do not have the right to directly accuse the perpetrator who committed an

---

[210] Cf. Davis (1989), p. 380; Doak (2008), pp. 124–126; Braun (2019), p. 110.

[211] Meier (1992), p. 108.

[212] Cf. Howse (2013), p. 136; Dubber (2006), p. 168.

[213] Schroth and Schroth (2018), p. 246; Brian (2019), § 374, Rn. 6–10; Lothar (2019), § 374, Rn. 6–6j.

[214] Brienen and Hoegen (2000), pp.78–79.

[215] Spencer (2012), p. 145.

international crime against them. The victim may report the crimes committed by the perpetrator to the prosecutor (e.g. Article 15 (2) RS),[216] but not directly to the Court. At the same time, the use of a private prosecution may still be employed at a national level in order to accuse people of international crimes. For example, all Australian criminal procedure legislations recognise private prosecutions for minor offences as well as for serious crimes.[217] On March 16, 2018, after the arrival of the first chancellor of Myanmar Aung San Suu Kyi to Australia for the summit in Sydney, the Rohingya community in Australia filed a private case on charges of crimes against humanity, specifically the crime of deportation and the forced transportation of people.[218] It was mostly alleged that the Aung San Suu Kyi had failed to use her power to stop the crimes against the Rohingya Muslim community in Myanmar. However, the application was rejected on the issues of immunity as head of state.[219]

2.7.3 Subsidiary Prosecution

The institution of the subsidiary or auxiliary prosecutor is another active form of victim participation within a criminal justice system. If private prosecutors accuse the defendant based upon their own authority, the subsidiary prosecutor will act adjacently to the public prosecutor. The participation of the subsidiary prosecutor allows the victim, in the event of a withdrawal by the public prosecutor, to continue the accusation on their own. They have procedural rights similar to those of the public prosecutor, except those that are granted to the public prosecutor possess an official authority. Practice, however, reveals that the involvement of victims within the criminal prosecution by way of active participation alongside the public prosecutor leads to the fact that the victims feel more connected to the trial and more satisfied after the judgment, irrespective of the severity of the sentence meted out to the defendant.[220]

The presence of the subsidiary prosecutor in criminal prosecutions can be considered a control mechanism for the public prosecutor. In cases where the public prosecutor is unwilling to prefer charges at all or remains largely inactive during the trial process,[221] subsidiary prosecutors have the power during the proceedings to challenge the decisions of the public prosecutor and to make their own contributions at the trial stage. At the same time, this kind of involvement of the victim in criminal

---

[216] *Notitia Criminis*, Petrossian (2020), p. 139.

[217] Gans (2017), pp. 68–69.

[218] See Doherty (2018b) and Stubley (2018).

[219] See Doherty (2018a).

[220] See Edna and Bienkowska (1993), pp. 220–224; Goodrum (2017), pp. 306–307.

[221] Cf. Michel (2018), pp. 22–23.

justice must be effective[222] and not counterproductive and it must be determined that the public prosecutor is far better "equipped"[223] with regard to investigations and accusations. The aim of the subsidiary prosecutor is not merely a repetition of the public prosecutor, as the judges and the public prosecutor have a duty to protect the interests of the victims.[224]

Distinguishing the scope of the rights and obligations of the victims under the Rome Statute and established jurisprudence, it is possible to determine that although the ICC does not fully recognise the victims as a subsidiary prosecutor, the victims' participation system has some features similar to those of the subsidiary prosecutor. An example of this is the fact that victims may "intervene" in the proceedings by way of written or oral submissions. The exercise of this right is, however, dependent upon the personal interests and the specific situation during the proceedings.[225] As the procedural rights of the victims are not determined by the Rome Statute, the Court needs to fill this gap by taking into account the modalities of victims' participation. The Court has found that the modalities of participation must be determined by the competent Chamber at each stage of the proceedings, in a manner not prejudicial to the rights of the person under investigation or the accused, and in no way antagonistic to a fair and impartial trial.[226] At the investigation stage, where the active participation of the victims could be much more effective, the Court has two obligations. On the one hand, it must allow the victims to present their views and concerns and, on the other hand, it must then examine them.[227] Nevertheless, the judges have found that the victims do not have the general right to participate at this, the investigatory stage, although the victims still have the chance to participate in discrete hearings.[228] If the Prosecutor is unwilling to press charges, the victims are not entitled to take over and draft charges. At the same time, the victims may

[222]See Schroth and Schroth (2018), p. 144, cmp, ECtHR, *Remetin v. Croatia* (2), 7446/12, Judgement (24 July 2014), para. 112, ECtHR, *M.S. v. Croatia 2*, 75450/12, Judgment (19 February 2015), para. 75–76.

[223]See ECtHR, *Butolen v. Slovenia*, 41356/08, Judgement (9 January 2009), para. 70.

[224]Doak (2008), p. 271.

[225]ICC, *Prosecutor v. Lubanga*, ICC-01/04-01/06-1119, Decision on victims' participation (18 January 2008), para. 102.

[226]ICC, *Situation in Darfur*, ICC-01/04-556, Appeals Judgement on victim participation in the investigation stage of the proceedings in the appeal of the OPCD against the decision of PTC I of 3 December 2007 and in the appeals of the OPCD and the Prosecutor against the decision of PTC I of 6 December 2007 (2 February 2009), para. 45.

[227]ICC, *Situation in the DRC*, ICC-01/04-101-tEN-Corr, Decision on the Applications for Participation in the Proceedings of VPRS 1 VPRS 2, VPRS 3, VPRS 4, VPRS 5 and VPRS, 5 (17 January 2006), para. 71, see also Tochilovsky (2008), p. 521.

[228]Ferstman (2012), p. 411, ICC, *Situation in the DRC*, ICC-01/04-556, Appeals Judgment on victim participation in the investigation stage of the proceedings in the appeal of the OPCD against the decision of PTC I of 7 December 2007 and in the appeals of the OPCD and the Prosecutor against the decision of PTC I of 24 December 2007 (19 December 2008), para. 59.

participate in the investigation by presenting their views and concerns about specific activities, filing documents and requesting that the Court order specific measures.[229]

At the pre-trial stage victims gain further rights of participation. Bearing in mind that the victims are not party to the case, they may still have access to all the documents and evidence filed either by the prosecutor or the defence, providing they are not *ex parte* documents. Furthermore, victims may make submissions relating to all issues, they may examine the witnesses and make oral motions, responses and submissions, they may attend all public and closed hearings and they have still the option to make written submissions.[230] At the same time, the Court may limit or grant new procedural rights at this stage.[231]

Compared to the pre-trial stage, the victims have a more extensive set of rights during the trial stage. Nevertheless, for each activity the victim is obliged to file an application to request participation, where their genuine contribution to the ascertainment of the truth must be appropriately explained.[232]

During the appeal stage, the victims have the right again to present their views and concerns regarding the issues under review, if these are connected to their personal interests. However, at the appeal stage, they once again have the obligation to explain the reasons for their participation and to prove the importance of their application.[233]

Even if there are similarities between the victims' participation system at the ICC and the institute of the subsidiary prosecutor, the role and powers of the victims are still less than that of the subsidiary prosecutor's. For each activity, the victim has to request leave from the Court, while the subsidiary prosecutors are not bound by that obligation, which makes them a relatively strong party in the proceedings. In contrast, the victims at the ICC are, to some extent, restricted to the role of the observer.

2.7.4 Civil Claim

Prosecution, be it public or private, aims at the criminal punishment of the accused. In contrast to that, the civil claimant is interested in compensation for the damage

---

[229] See ICC, *Situation in the Republic of Kenya*, ICC-01/09-159, Decision on the "Victims' request for review of Prosecution's decision to cease active investigation" (5 November 2015), para. 28.

[230] ICC, *Prosecutor v. Katanga, Chui*, ICC-01/04-01/07-474, Decision on the Set of Procedural Rights Attached to Procedural Status of Victim at the PTC Stage of the Case (13 May 2008), paras. 127–145.

[231] ICC, *Prosecutor v. Katanga, Chui*, ICC-01/04-01/07-474, Decision on the Set of Procedural Rights Attached to Procedural Status of Victim at the PTC Stage of the Case (13 May 2008), para. 147.

[232] See de Brouwer and Heikkilä (2013), p. 1324, e.g. the conditions of testimonies of the victims in ICC, *Prosecutor v. Katanga, Chui,* TC, Directions for the conduct of the proceedings and testimony in accordance with rule 140 (20 November 2009), paras. 19–32.

[233] Eckelmans (2013), pp. 218–219.

caused by the accused, i.e. their aim is financial or material retribution for the harm suffered. There are two ways in which the victim may claim compensation before a court: either in separate civil proceedings or in a combined fashion with contiguous criminal proceedings. By joining in criminal proceedings, the victim gains full participatory status and may access all the documents related to the case. On the other hand, the victim is not questioned as a witness but rather as a party, by giving testimony.[234] If and when the accused is found guilty, the convicted person is obliged to pay damages for the harm done to the victims who have been identified by the Court.[235] Joining the criminal case with the civil claim makes it easier for the victims as they do not need to initiate civil litigation against the defendant separately before a civil court.[236]

The definition of "civil claimant"[237] mainly refers to the financial interests of victims within the criminal proceedings, which is also a part of international criminal law. The definition is used within the ECCC where the victims of the atrocities of Khmer Rouge have the possibility of joining the criminal proceedings as a third party. At the ICC, the definition of civil claimant is not used as the definition refers to the nature of a unique and independent party which is not the case at the ICC. Article 75 RS, however, states that victims have the possibility of claiming restitution, compensation and rehabilitation. Accordingly, the victims at the ICC also have the same feature as the civil claimant: claiming regarding their financial and material interests.

The participation of the victims at the ECCC trials as a civil claimant aims at supporting the prosecution and at seeking collective and moral reparations (Rule 23 (1) IRR).[238] Victims may provide information to the Office of the Co-Prosecutors, however, this information may not stipulate an opening of the proceedings; the victims may apply for the status of civil claimant as soon as the case is under investigation by the Co-Investigating Judges.[239] In gaining the status of civil claimant, the victims have, in contrast to the victims at the ICC, full party status. The main difference between both institutions is that the victims at the ECCC do not have to provide reasons for their personal interests in the respective matter.[240]

Unlike the ICC, the ECCC Rules consider the rights of civil claimants during the stages of prosecution. At the different judicial stages, the civil claimants have the right to access documents, the right to question the person charged, the right to request the Co-Investigative Judges to carry out specific investigations, the right to request witnesses and experts, the right to attend via written or oral interventions,

[234]See e.g. van Camp (2016), p. 49.

[235]Schroth and Schroth (2018), p. 229.

[236]See Pérez-León Acevedo (2014), p. 58.

[237]Civil party.

[238]See detailed in Killean (2019), pp. 160–192; Elander (2018), pp. 104–144.

[239]See ECCC, Practice Direction on Victim Participation, Practice Direction 02/2007/Rev. 1 (amended on 27 October 2008), Article 3 (3).

[240]See also Studzinsky (2013), pp. 179–180; Bachvarova (2017), p. 214; Zhang (2016), p. 518.

and the right to support the Co-Prosecutors.[241] The civil claimant is, however, restricted when appealing on sentencing issues.

In summarising, it is possible to note that even if the main aim of civil claimants is material compensation, in doing so they attain similar rights to those of the subsidiary prosecutor.

2.8 International Criminal Justice System Dealing with Victims' Issues

In the following, a brief overview of the different international approaches to the international victims' participation scheme will be provided.

2.8.1 ICC

Article 68(3) RS establishes a platform for victims to be heard before the ICC, but only if their interests are affected.[242] This obviously does not mean that the victims participate in the international trial as an independent party. The way the victims participate at the International Criminal Court's proceedings is unique. Even if they are participants, they take part in the proceedings vicariously through their legal representatives. As such, the rights attached to the victims are executed by the legal representatives of victims (LRV) or by the common legal representatives of victims (CLRV). The jurisprudence of the ICC has determined several general rights and procedural modalities regarding the participation of victims during the different stages of the international criminal judicial system. Before each judicial stage, the Chambers decide how actively the victims may be involved in the proceedings.[243] These general rights are:

---

[241]See detailed in Pérez-León Acevedo (2014), pp. 393–404 and 455–470.

[242]Cf. Sergii (2020), pp. 10 et seq.

[243]ICC, *Prosecutor v. Kenyatta, Muthaura, Ali,* ICC-01/09-01/11-249, Decision on Victims' Participation at the Confirmation of Charges Hearing and in the Related Proceedings (26 August 2011), paras. 103–118, ICC, *Prosecutor v. Kenyatta, Muthaura,* ICC-01/09-02/11-503, Decision on victims' representation and participation (3 October 2012), paras. 63–76, ICC, *Prosecutor v. Ruto, Kosgey, Sang,* ICC-01/09-01/11-249, Decision on Victims' Participation at the Confirmation of Charges Hearing and in the Related Proceedings (8 August 2011), paras. 86–101, ICC, *Prosecutor v. Ruto, Sang,* ICC-01/09-01/11-460, Decision on victims' representation and participation (3 October 2012), paras. 64–77, Petrossian (2020), p. 139.

Attendance and participation at the hearings[244]

Rule 91(2) RPE allows LRVs to attend the proceedings; however, the Court may still limit the attendance of LRVs on a case-by-case basis. In connection with Rule 89 (1) RPE, the LRV is also entitled to making opening and closing statements. In certain cases, only the LRV or the CLRVs may attend the closed session with the agreement not to disclose to their clients any of the information that is covered by protective measures ordered by the Chamber.[245]

Access to the records of the case[246]

The victims may have access to the public documents through the LRV. Rule 121 (10) RPE limits, on a case-by-case basis, the access of victims to confidential material. The general right to access the files may be interpreted differently by the Court. On the one hand, the Court may decide to grant the LRVs access to all documents, even to confidential ones.[247] On the other hand, the Chamber may instruct the LRVs not to communicate the confidential information to their clients until the Court has given permission for them to do so.[248]

Submissions[249]

This right may include not only written but also oral submissions by LRVs or CLRVs. However, the LRV or CLRV has to demonstrate the nexus between the submissions and the interests of the victims pursuant to Article 68(3) RS.[250] The

[244]ICC, *Prosecutor v. Bemba*, ICC-01/05-01/08-320, Fourth Decision on Victims' Participation (12 December 2008), para. 101, ICC, *Prosecutor v. Mbarushimana*, ICC-01/04-01/10-166, Decision on the 138 applications for victims' participation in the proceedings (11 August 2011), paras. 41–42, ICC, *Prosecutor v. Katanga, Chui*, ICC-01/04-01/07-474, Decision on the Set of Procedural Rights Attached to Procedural Status of Victim at the PTC Stage of the Case (13 May 2008), para. 140, ICC, *Prosecutor v. Ruto, Sang*, ICC-01/09-01/11-460, Decision on victims' representation and participation (3 October 2012), paras. 70–72.

[245]ICC, *Prosecutor v. Banda*, ICC-02/05-03/09-545, Decision on the participation of victims in the trial proceedings (20 March 2014), para. 41.

[246]ICC, *Prosecutor v. Ruto, Sang*, ICC-01/09-01/11-460, Decision on victims' representation and participation (3 October 2012), paras. 90–92, ICC, *Prosecutor v. Katanga, Chui*, ICC-01/04-01/07-474, Decision on the Set of Procedural Rights Attached to Procedural Status of Victim at the PTC Stage of the Case (13 May 2008), paras. 128–130.

[247]ICC, *Prosecutor v. Katanga, Chui*, ICC-01/04-01/07-1788-tENG, Decision on Modalities of Victim Participation at Trial (22 January 2010), paras. 121–123.

[248]ICC, *Prosecutor v. Bemba*, ICC-01/05-01/08-807-Corr-Anx, Corrigendum to Decision on the participation of victims in the trial and on 86 applications by victims to participate in the proceedings (12 July 2010), para. 47, compare with ICC, *Prosecutor v. Ongwen*, ICC-02/04-01/15-350, Decision on contested victims' applications for participation, legal representation of victims and their procedural rights (27 November 2015), para. 31.

[249]ICC, *Prosecutor v. Ble Goude*, ICC-02/11-02/11-69, Decision on victims' participation in the pre-trial proceedings and related issues (11 June 2014), paras. 37–38, ICC, *Prosecutor v. Muthaura, Kenyatta, Ali*, ICC-01/09-01/11-249, Decision on Victims' Participation at the Confirmation of Charges Hearing and in the Related Proceedings (26 August 2011) para. 71.

[250]ICC, *Prosecutor v. Ble Goude*, ICC-02/11-02/11-69, Decision on victims' participation in the pre-trial proceedings and related issues (11 June 2014), para. 40, ICC, *Prosecutor v. Bemba*, ICC-01/05-01/08-320, Fourth Decision on Victims' Participation (12 December 2008), para. 108.

victims are also entitled to submit evidence if the Court considers it necessary for the determination of the truth, and if the Chamber decides to exercise its discretionary power to use Article 69(3) RS.[251]

Request to call witnesses and question the witnesses or the accused[252]
The LRVs and CLRVs have the possibility of calling witnesses, in which case the Court has to consider how the testimony may affect the personal interest of the victims, whether that testimony is relevant to the issues of the case, whether it contributes to the determination of the truth and whether the testimony would be consistent with the rights of the accused.[253] For the examination of witnesses, the Court has established different procedures for the LRVs and CLRVs, who are not entitled to examine witnesses on behalf of anonymous victims.[254] In order to question the witnesses in accordance with Rule 91 (3), LRVs and CLRVs must file an application demonstrating a connection to the personal interests of their clients.[255] The subsequent questioning may only be permitted after completion of the prosecution's questioning in the limited time set by the Court.[256]

Further rights for the victims may be granted by the Court following an appropriate request by the victims.

2.8.2 ECCC

Article 23 of the Law on the Establishment of the ECCC, pertaining the prosecution of crimes committed during the period of Democratic Kampuchea, provides for the

[251]ICC, *Prosecutor v. Banda*, ICC-02/05-03/09-545, Decision on the participation of victims in the trial proceedings (20 March 2014), para. 27, ICC, *Prosecutor v. Katanga, Chui*, ICC-01/04-01/07-2288, Appeals Judgement on the Appeal of Mr Katanga Against the Decision of Trial Chamber II of 22 January 2010 Entitled "Decision on the Modalities of Victim Participation at Trial" (16 July 2010), para. 40.

[252]ICC, *Prosecutor v. Banda*, ICC-02/05-03/09-545, Decision on the participation of victims in the trial proceedings (20 March 2014), paras. 24, 31, ICC, *Prosecutor v. Ruto, Sang*, ICC-01/09-01/11-460, Decision on victims' representation and participation (3 October 2012), para. 74, ICC, *Prosecutor v. Katanga, Chui*, ICC-01/04-01/07-1788-tENG, Decision on Modalities of Victim Participation at Trial (22 January 2010), paras. 94–97.

[253]ICC, *Prosecutor v. Banda*, ICC-02/05-03/09-545, Decision on the participation of victims in the trial proceedings (20 March 2014), para. 25, cf. with para.109.

[254]ICC, *Prosecutor v. Abu Garda*, ICC-02/05-02/09-136, Decision on victims' modalities of participation at the Pre-trial Stage of the Case (6 October 2009), para. 22.

[255]ICC, *Prosecutor v. Muthaura, Kenyatta, Ali*, ICC-01/09-01/11-249, Decision on Victims' Participation at the Confirmation of Charges Hearing and in the Related Proceedings (26 August 2011), paras. 116–117.

[256]ICC, *Prosecutor v. Banda*, ICC-02/05-03/09-545, Decision on the participation of victims in the trial proceedings (20 March 2014), paras. 32–33, ICC, *Prosecutor v. Lubanga*, ICC-01/04-01/06-1119, Decision on victims' participation (18 January 2008), para. 103.

Co-Investigating Judge to have the power to question victims. Article 33 of the Law enshrines the obligation for the Extraordinary Chambers of the trial Court to fully respect the rights of the accused and the protection of the victims. It stipulates that such protection measures shall include, but are not be limited to, the conduct during *in camera* proceedings and the protection of the victims' identity.

Article 36 of the same law grants the victims the right to lodge an appeal against the decision of the Extraordinary Chamber at the trial court. The Internal Rules and Regulations (IRR) of the ECCC enshrine the existence of a Victims Support Section, established by the Office of the Administration (Rule 12 IRR). Rule 12bis IRR then specifies the role of the Victims Support Section stating that it shall, *inter alia*:

- assist victims in lodging complaints under the supervision of the Co-Prosecutors;
- assist victims in submitting Civil Party applications under the supervision of the Co-Investigating Judge;
- provide general information to the victims; and
- be entrusted with the development and implementation of non-judicial programs and measures addressing the broader interests of the victims. Such programs may, where appropriate, be developed and implemented in collaboration with governmental and non-governmental organisations external to the ECCC.

Rule 21 IRR enshrines as a fundamental principle the necessity for an interpretation of the ECCC Law, Internal Rule, Practice Directions and Administrative Regulations that safeguard the interests of victims. This includes the fact that the ECCC ensures that victims are kept informed and that their rights are respected throughout the proceedings.

Rule 23 IRR deals with the General Principles of Victims Participation as Civil Parties. It details the fact that the purpose of a Civil Party action before the ECCC is to participate in criminal proceedings against those responsible for the crimes within the jurisdiction of the ECCC. It does so by supporting the prosecution and seeking collective and moral reparations. Rules 23bis to 23 IRR provide further details concerning the participation of Civil Parties. Rule 23 IRR stipulates that if an accused is convicted, the Chambers may award only collective and moral reparations to Civil Parties. Collective and moral reparations for the purpose of the Rules are measures that acknowledge the harm suffered by Civil Parties as a result of the commission of the crimes for which an accused is convicted and provide benefits to the Civil Parties which address this harm.

Rule 29 IRR envisages that the ECCC shall ensure the protection of victims who participate in the proceedings. When the Co-Investigating Judge or the Chambers issue an order, or when other offices within the ECCC fulfil their duties, they shall take into account the needs of the victims and witnesses. The Co-Investigating Judges and the Chambers may, on their own motion or upon request, and after having consulted with the Victims Support Section or the Witnesses/Experts Support Unit, order appropriate measures to protect victims and witnesses whose appearance before them is likely to place their life or health, or that of their family members or close relatives, in serious danger. Concerning the exercise of Public Action, Rule 49 (2) IRR details how victims can lodge complaints for information concerning the commission of crimes within the jurisdiction of the ECCC with the Co-Prosecutors.

Rule 55 IRR regulates the general provisions concerning investigations. It provides details of how the Co-Investigating Judges may interview witnesses and record their statements.

2.8.3 STL

Pursuant to Article 12 (4) of the Statute of the Lebanon Tribunal, the Registrar shall set up a Victims and Witnesses Unit within the Registry. This Unit shall provide, in consultation with the Office of the Prosecutor, measures to protect the safety, physical and psychological well-being, dignity and privacy of victims and witnesses. Additionally, such other appropriate assistance is available to witnesses who appear before the Special Tribunal and also others who are at risk on account of any testimony given by such witnesses.

Article 17 of the Statute of Lebanon Tribunal then focuses more precisely on the rights of victims by specifying that where the personal interests of the victims are affected, the Special Tribunal shall permit their views and concerns to be presented and considered at stages of the proceedings. This is only where they are determined to be appropriate by the Pre-Trial Judge or the Chamber, and in a manner that is not prejudicial to or inconsistent with the rights of the accused and a fair and impartial trial. Such views and concerns may be presented by the legal representatives of the victims where the Pre-Trial Judge or the Chamber considers it appropriate.

Article 25 of the Statute deals with the compensation of victims. In accordance with this Article, The Special Tribunal may identify victims who have suffered harm as a result of the commission of crimes by an accused convicted by the Tribunal. The Registrar shall convey to the competent authorities of the state concerned the judgment finding the accused guilty of a crime that has caused harm to a victim. Based upon the decision of the Special Tribunal, and pursuant to the relevant national legislation, a victim, or persons claiming to be victims, whether or not such victims had been identified as such by the Tribunal under paragraph 1 of Article 25, may bring an action in a national court or other competent body to obtain compensation. For that purpose, the judgment of the Special Tribunal shall be final and binding as to the criminal responsibility of the convicted person.

Rule 2 RPE defines a victim as a natural person who has suffered physical, material, or mental harm as a direct result of an attack within the Tribunal's jurisdiction. Rule 50 RPE regulates that The Registrar shall set up a unit responsible for protecting witnesses, victims who participate in the proceedings and, where appropriate, others at risk on account of their interaction with the Tribunal (Victims and Witnesses Unit). It specifies that the Unit shall exercise the following functions:

- to formulate strategies and provide adequate protective and security measures for victims and witnesses in conjunction with the relevant Party, States, intergovernmental and non-governmental organisations where appropriate;
- to provide all necessary administrative and logistical assistance to witnesses appearing before the Tribunal, including informing witnesses about: (1) any matter relating to their security and safety; (2) the nature of the courtroom proceedings; (3) the courtroom layout and the participants; and (4) the role, rights and obligations of witnesses in the proceedings;
- to assist victims and witnesses in obtaining the medical, psychological and other appropriate support necessary for them to testify before the Tribunal; and
- to provide any additional assistance as ordered by a Judge or Chamber as is consistent with the mandate and responsibilities of the Unit.

At the request of the Registrar, a Party, a victim participating in the proceedings or its legal representative, or, *proprio motu*, where the interests of justice so require, a Judge or Chamber may grant the person in charge of the Unit, or a person designated by them, the right of audience in relation to matters of interest to the protection of victims and witnesses in the proceedings.

Rule 51 PRE regulates that the Registrar shall set up a unit within the Registry responsible in order to assist the victims in participating in the proceedings pursuant to the Statute and the Rules (Victims' Participation Unit). It specifies that the Unit shall exercise the following functions:

- to formulate long- and short-term strategies in this regard;
- to inform the victims of their rights under the Statute and the Rules and of the existence and functions of the Unit;
- to receive applications from victims seeking to participate in the proceedings in accordance with Rule 87, to verify that these applications are complete and, once this has been done, to convey them to the Pre-Trial Judge;
- to ensure that the victims or their legal representatives receive documents filed by the Parties and the files submitted by the Pre-Trial Judge, subject to any restrictions due to confidentiality or the interests of justice, in accordance with Rule 87;
- to inform, in a timely manner, the victims of relevant decisions of the Tribunal that might have an impact on their rights or specific interests, subject to any confidentiality restrictions;
- to provide all necessary administrative and logistical assistance to victims participating in the proceedings or to their legal representatives; and
- to provide any additional assistance as ordered by the Pre-Trial Judge or a Chamber as is consistent with the mandate and responsibilities of the Unit.

The Rules of Procedure and Evidence dedicate Part 5, Section 3 to the Participation of Victims in Proceedings. Rule 86 RPE regulates the granting of victim status for participating in the proceedings and Rule 87 RPE then deals with the different modes of participation in the proceedings. As a general rule, a victim participating in the proceedings is entitled to receive documents filed by the parties, insofar as they have been disclosed by one party to the other as well as the file, excluding any confidential and *ex parte* material, handed over by the Pre-Trial Judge to the Trial Chamber before the commencement of the trial pursuant to Rule 95 RPE.

At the trial stage, victims participating in the proceedings may request that the Trial Chamber, after hearing the Parties, call witnesses and authorise them to tender other evidence. They may also, subject to the authorisation by, and under the control of, the Trial Chamber after hearing the Parties, examine or cross-examine witnesses and file motions and briefs.

At the sentencing stage, subject to the authorisation by the Trial Chamber, a victim participating in the proceedings may be heard by the Trial Chamber or file written submissions relating to the personal impact of the crimes.

At the appeal stage, subject to the authorisation of the Appeals Chamber after hearing the Parties, a victim participating in proceedings may participate in a manner deemed appropriate by the Appeals Chamber.

In accordance with Rule 93 RPE, at the request of the parties the Pre-Trial Judge shall question the witness in the absence of the Parties or any legal representative of a victim participating in the proceedings where at any stage of the proceedings there is:

- a serious risk that a witness or a person close to the witness would lose his life or suffer grave physical or mental harm as a result of his identity being revealed, and measures for the protection of witnesses as provided for in Rule 133 would be insufficient to prevent such danger; or
- a serious risk that imperative national security interests might be jeopardised should the witness's identity or affiliation be revealed.

Rule 133 RPE sets out a lengthy catalogue of measures for the protection of victims and witnesses such as measures aimed at preventing disclosure to the public or the media of the identity or whereabouts of a victim or a witness, or of persons related to or associated with a victim or a witness, by means such as:

- expunging names and identifying information from the Tribunal's public records;
- not disclosing to the public any records identifying the victim or witness;
- applying image- or voice-altering devices;
- giving testimony through closed circuit television or video-conferencing links;
- assigning pseudonyms;
- having closed sessions; and
- implementing appropriate measures to facilitate the testimony of vulnerable victims and witnesses, such as one-way closed-circuit television or shielding the accused from the direct view of the witness.

Pursuant to Rule 171 (E) RPE, the sentence shall be pronounced in the presence of the victims participating in the proceedings.

2.8.4 SCSL

In accordance with Article 15(2) of the Statute of the Special Court for Sierra Leone, victims can be questioned by the Office of the Prosecutor. By virtue of the nature of the crimes committed and the particular sensitivities of girls, young women and child victims of rape, sexual assault, abduction and slavery of all kinds, due consideration should be given in the appointment of staff to the employment of prosecutors and investigators experienced in gender-related crimes and juvenile justice.

The Registrar established a Victims and Witnesses Unit within the Registry, and Article 16(4) provides protective measures and security arrangements as well as counseling and other appropriate assistance for witnesses, victims who appear before the Court and others who are at risk on account of testimony given by such witnesses.

The presence of victims has an influence on the rights of the accused as the latter must be entitled to a fair and public hearing subject to measures ordered by the Special Court for the protection of victims and witnesses pursuant to Article 17(2). Rule 2 RPE defines the victim as a person against whom a crime over which the Special Court has jurisdiction has allegedly been committed or has been found to have been committed.

Rule 26bis RPE requests that the trial be conducted in a fair and expeditious way with full respect for the rights of the accused and due regard for the protection of victims and witnesses. Rule 34 RPE concerns the obligation of the Registrar to set up a Witnesses and Victims Section which shall, amongst other things, perform the following functions with respect to all witnesses, victims who appear before the Special Court and others who are at risk on account of testimony given by such witnesses, in accordance with their particular needs and circumstances:

- recommend that the Special Court adopt protective and security measures;
- provide them with adequate protective measures and security arrangements and develop long- and short-term plans for their protection and support; and
- ensure that they receive relevant support, counselling and other appropriate assistance, including medical assistance, physical and psychological rehabilitation, especially in cases of rape, sexual assault and crimes against children.

Rule 34 RPE regulates the need for experts, particularly in cases of trauma.

In accordance with Rule 39 RPE, victims may be questioned by the Prosecutor. Pursuant to Rule 40 (A) (iii) RPE, the Prosecutor may, in urgent cases, request any State to take all necessary measures to prevent the escape of a suspect or an accused, injury to or intimidation of a victim or witness or the destruction of evidence.

Rule 69 RPE—Protection of Victims and Witnesses—as amended on 29 May 2004 governs the possibility of the parties applying to a Judge of the Trial Chamber or the Trial Chamber itself to order the non-disclosure of the identity of a victim or witness who may be in danger or at risk, until the Judge or Chamber decides otherwise, 69(A). Furthermore, in the determination of protective measures for victims or witnesses, the Judge or Trial chamber may consult the Witnesses and

Victims Section, as set down in Article 69(B). Furthermore, subject to Rule 75, the identity of the victim or witness shall be disclosed in sufficient time before a witness is to be called in order to allow adequate time for the prosecution and the defense to prepare.

Rule 75 RPE regulates the measures for the Protection of Victims and Witnesses. Rule 75(A) RPE allows a Judge or a Chamber to order—and the parties, the victim or witness concerned, or the Witnesses and Victims Section to request—appropriate measures to safeguard the privacy and security of victims and witnesses, provided that the measures are consistent with the rights of the accused. Measures can, for example, consist of preventing disclosure to the public or the media of the identity or whereabouts of victims or witnesses, or of persons related to or associated with them, ordering a closed session in accordance with Rule 79 RPE, or taking appropriate measures to facilitate the testimony of vulnerable victims and witnesses, such as one-way closed-circuit television.

Rule 105 RPE regulates the compensation of victims and provides that the Registrar shall convey to the competent authorities of the States concerned the judgment finding the accused guilty of a crime which has caused injury to a victim. Sub-Rule (B) then states that, pursuant to the relevant national legislation, a victim or persons claiming through a convicted person may bring an action in a national court or other competent body to obtain compensation. For the purposes of a claim made under Sub-Rule (B), the judgment of the Special Court shall be final and binding as to the criminal responsibility of the person convicted of having occasioned such harm or injury.

2.8.5 KSC

Article 22(1) of the Law on Kosovo Specialist Chamber and Specialist Prosecutor's Office defines a victim as "a natural person who has personally suffered harm, including physical, mental or material harm, as a direct result of a crime within the jurisdiction of the Specialist Chambers. Participation as a victim at the Specialist Chambers shall not be a bar to providing testimony as a witness before the Specialist Chambers.

Article 22 (3) specifies the interest and rights a victim has before the Specialist Chambers as being notification, acknowledgment and reparation. Article 22 (2) grants the victim the right to seek reparation through other reparation mechanisms, even if the victim did not participate in the proceedings before the Specialist Chambers.

Pursuant to Article 22 (5), the victims are assisted and represented by a Victims' Counsel provided through the Registry's Victims Participation Office. Self-representation is not permitted. The Specialist Chambers may permit the Victims' Counsel to represent victims during the pre-trial and the trial proceedings within the limits of the rights of the accused, in accordance with Article 22 (6) of the Law. Pursuant to Article 22 (7), a Trial Panel may, either upon request or on its own motion, in exceptional circumstances include a decision on the scope and extent of any damage, loss and injury to or in respect of the victims.

In the event that a Trial Panel or Court of Appeals Panel of the Specialist Chambers convicts an accused of a crime, it may make an order directly against that accused specifying appropriate reparation to, or in respect of victims collectively or individually, in line with Article 22 (8).

Pursuant to Article 22 (9), the Specialist Chambers may refer the victims to civil litigation in the other courts of Kosovo. Before making any decision under Article 22, a Trial Panel may invite and shall take account of representations on behalf of the accused, victims, other interested persons and/or interested States, as per Article 22 (11). Article 23 regulates the protection of the victims and witnesses.

Article 23 (2) enshrines the necessity of special provisions to be included in the Rules of Procedure and Evidence in order to ensure the protection of vulnerable witnesses such as victims of sexual and gender-based violence and also children. Article 23 (3) renders it possible for the Witness Protection and Support Office to make representations to a Pre-Trial Judge, a Panel or the Specialist Prosecutor on appropriate protective measures, security arrangements, counselling and assistance for a witness before, during and after testimony before the Specialist Chambers. The Rules of Procedure and Evidence before the Kosovo Specialist Chambers defines a victim as being a natural person who has suffered physical, material, or mental harm as a direct result of a crime alleged in an indictment confirmed by the Pre-Trial Chamber (PTC). Rule 27 deals with the responsibilities of the Registrar for Witness Protection and Support and states its main responsibility as being the protection of witnesses, victims participating in the proceedings and, where appropriate, others at risk on account of testimony given by witnesses.

Chapter 8 of the Rules of Procedure and Evidence is dedicated to the participation of victims in the proceedings, with Rule 113 pertaining to the admission of victims for participation in the proceedings and Rule 114 dealing with the modalities of participation in the proceedings.

2.9 Conclusion

A number of states in Europe—29 in all—have, within their national jurisdiction, included the institution of the civil claim into their criminal justice system. In contrast, only a few states provide the institution of the private prosecution (18) and the subsidiary prosecution (11). This demonstrates the fact that the material compensation of victims is more widely used and accepted nowadays.

Irrespective of the status of the victims and the procedural issues, the victim has a general right to be informed about the details of the trial, including where the trial will take place and when. Alongside the general right to be informed about the location, the victim still has the possibility of attending the public trial and being present at trial. However, the presence of the victim at trial may be limited due to witness status.

The criminal justice process in the U.S. has developed considerably in an attempt to include the victims of crime. In particular, since the 1982 influential report of the President's Task Force on victims' rights, the victim's role in the entire criminal process, as well as with regard to reparation and compensation, has been enhanced. It is thus untenable to say that victim participation is alien to the US-American system of criminal justice. What is more, this development has not come to an end; on the contrary, the "victim participation model", as a "third model of criminal process" after the "crime control" and the "due process" models, which has been announced, has not yet been attained.[257] Within the US criminal justice system, one can observe a worrying imbalance in victim participation. Whereas the victim's influence is discomfortingly low at the outset of the prosecution—and, in particular, with regard to the discretionary powers of the prosecutor whether or not to prosecute—the influence is remarkably high at the sentencing stage and at the parole hearings.

For the further development and positioning of the victim within a criminal prosecution, it would certainly be valuable if "fairness to the victim" were explicitly mentioned in the US Bill of Rights. As a constitutional amendment is a long-lasting political process, it should not be considered a necessary condition for any further development. Any criminal prosecution should be critically evaluated under two specifically victim-driven criteria: Firstly, to avoid secondary victimisation and, secondly, to prevent victim alienation.[258]

Even under restrictions and limited access to justice for the victims at the ICC, it is possible to determine that victims gain the ability to be informed, to be heard and to be compensated, as provided for by Article 75 RS. However, each involvement within the proceedings is bound by the decision of the Court which, in many cases is not satisfactory for the victims who participate at the proceedings indirectly through their legal representatives among hundreds of other victims. The victims at the ICC, as was shown above, are not the initiators of proceedings, as is the case with a private prosecutor. The only thing that they may do is to report the crimes to the OTP at the ICC. However, it is still up to the Prosecutor to decide whether the investigations will be commenced or not, or whether there will be any charges. At the same time, the victims have, under Article 54 (1) (b) RS, the possibility of challenging the Prosecutor's failure to take appropriate measures to ensure the effective investigation and the prosecution of crimes within the jurisdiction of the Court, and only then if they are recognised as victims in the given situation.[259]

On the other hand, even if the victims' rights may be similar to the subsidiary prosecutor's, they are again bound to the personal interests of the victims and to the decision of the Court. The victims at the ICC have to prove the harm they have suffered due to the alleged crime in order to fall under the definition of a victim in

[257] Beloof (2005), p. 289; Roach (1999), pp. 20 et seq.

[258] Beloof et al. (2006), p. 19; Beloof and Cassell (2005), p. 538.

[259] See e.g. ICC, *Situation in the Republic of Kenya*, ICC-01/09-159, Decision on the "Victims' request for review of Prosecution's decision to cease active investigation" (5 November 2015), para. 28.

accordance with Rule 85 RPE, and in order to be able to make a claim for reparations. Thus, not every victim can be certain that they will receive financial compensation as in the case of civil claimants, as this is considered at the national level.

Alongside these aspects, it is very important to determine that not every victim among those thousands of victims registered and recognised by the ICC may have the chance to act directly at the ICC; their participatory rights are executed remotely. Bearing in mind that victims want to be informed, to be heard and to be compensated, the ICC victim participation mechanism allows these wishes only indirectly. Such circumstances will tend thus to leave the victims less satisfied than they could be on the national level. At the same time, the difference between the national and international judicial systems has to be ascertained, something which is not always comprehensible for the victims of such crimes.

The system of how victims are involved in the ICC victims' participation mechanism is neither active, such as an independent third party, nor passive, such as the victims at the IMT, the ICTY or the ICTR (as they were considered merely as witnesses). These provisions may be deemed a compromise—giving the victims a limited platform so that they can be informed, be heard and be compensated.

Today, there is a clear tendency towards involving victims not only at the national level in the criminal justice systems, but also within the international criminal justice framework. The "newcomers", such as the Kosovo Chambers or the STL, have included victim participation in their system in a timely manner. It now just remains to be seen how meaningful or helpful this will actually be.

References

Albrecht H, Kilchling M (2010) Victims of terrorism policies: should victims of terrorism be treated differently. In: Wade M, Maljevic A (eds) A war on terror? The European stance on a new threat, changing laws and human rights implications. Springer Science Business Media LLC, Berlin, pp 221–244

Alschuler AW (2009) Plea bargaining and the death penalty. De Paul Law Rev 58:671–680

Alvaro G, D'Andrea A (2016) The impact of directive 2012/29/EU on the Italian system for protecting victims of crime in criminal proceedings. In: Ruggeri S (ed) Human rights in European criminal law: new developments in European Legislation and case law after the Lisbon Treaty. Springer, Berlin, pp 307–317

Andrews RM (1994) Law, magistracy, and crime in Old Regime Paris: 1735–1789. Cambridge University Press, Cambridge

Appleman LI (2012) Justice in the shadowlands: pretrial detention, punishment & the sixth amendment. Wash Lee Law Rev 69:1297–1369

Argomaniz J (2015) European instruments concerning the rights of victims of terrorism: meeting needs? In: Lynch O, Argomaniz J (eds) Victims of terrorism: a comparative and interdisciplinary study political violence. Routledge, London, pp 122–138

Bachvarova T (2017) The standing of victims in the procedural design of the International Criminal Court. Brill Nijhoff, Leiden

Barkow RE (2006) Separation of powers and the criminal law. Stanford Law Rev 58:989–1052

Baumgartner E (2008) Aspects of victim participation in the proceedings of the International Criminal Court. Int Rev Red Cross 90(870):409–440
Beloof DE (2005) The third wave of victims' rights: standing, remedy and review. Brigham Young Univ Law Rev: 255–365
Beloof DE (2012) Victims' rights: a documentary and reference guide. Documentary and reference guides, Greenwood
Beloof DE, Cassell G (2005) The crime victim's right to attend the trial: the reascendant national consensus. Lewis Clark Law Rev 9:481–546
Beloof DE, Cassell P, Twist S (2006) Victims in criminal procedure. Carolina Academic Press, Carolina
Beulke W, Swoboda S (2018) Strafprozessrecht. C.F. Müller, München
Bogira S (2006) Courtroom 302: a year behind the scenes in an American criminal courthouse, 1st Vintage Books edn. Vintage Books
Bonneau K, Benedetti F, Washburn JL (2014) Preliminary material. In: Bonneau K, Benedetti F, Washburn JL (eds) Negotiating the International Criminal Court: New York to Rome, 1994–1998. Brill, Leiden, pp 145–168
Bottigliero I (2004) Redress for victims of crimes under international law. Springer Netherlands, Dordrecht
Braun K (2019) Victim participation rights: variation across criminal justice systems. Palgrave Macmillan
Brian V (2019) §374. In: Knauer C et al (eds) Münchener Kommentar zur Strafprozessordnung. 1. Auflage. C.H. Beck, München
Brienen MIE, Hoegen EH (2000) Victims of crime in 22 European criminal justice systems: the implements of recommendations (85) 11 of the Council of Europe on the position of the victim in the framework of criminal law and procedure; Proegschrift. Wolf Legal Productions
Burns R (2009) The death of the American trial. University of Chicago Press
Cardenas J (1986) The crime victim. Harv J Law Pub Policy 9
Clevenger S, Navarro JN, Marcum CD, Higgins GE (2018) Understanding victimology: an active-learning approach. Routledge, New York City
Condé V (2004) A handbook on international human rights terminology. University of Nebraska Press, Nebraska
Crawshaw R, Holmström L (2008) International convention for the protection of all persons from enforced disappearance. In: Crawshaw R, Holmström L (eds) Essential texts on human rights for the police: a compilation of international instruments. Martinus Nijhoff, Leiden, pp 187–210
Cryer R (2008) The doctrinal foundations of international criminalisation. In: Bassiouni CM (ed) International criminal law, vol I: Sources, subjects and contents. Martinus Nijhoff, Leiden, pp 107–128
Cryer R et al (2014) An introduction to international criminal law and procedure. Cambridge University Press
Davis P (1989) The crime victim's "right" to a criminal prosecution: a proposed model statute for the governance of private criminal prosecutions. DePaul Law Rev 38:329–409
de Brouwer A (2005) Supranational criminal prosecution of sexual violence: the ICC and the practice of the ICTY and the ICTR. Intersentia, Mortsel
de Brouwer A, Heikkilä M (2013) Victim issues: participation, protection, reparation and assistance. In: Sluiter G (ed) International criminal procedure: principles and rules. Oxford University Press, Oxford, pp 1299–1374
Dearin A (2017) Justice for victims of crime: human dignity as the foundation of criminal justice in Europe. Springer
Delmas-Marty M (2008) European criminal procedures. Cambridge University Press, Cambridge
Derene S, Walker S, Stein J (2007) History of the crime victims' rights movement in the United States National Victim Assistance Academy
Dignan J (2004) Understanding victims and restorative justice (crime and justice). Open University Press, Glasgow

Doak J (2008) Victims' rights, Human rights and criminal justice: reconceiving the role of third parties. Hart, Oxford
Doherty B (2018a) Aung San Suu Kyi cannot be prosecuted in Australia, Christian Porter says. The Guardian, 17 March
Doherty B (2018b) Aung San Suu Kyi: lawyers seek prosecution for crimes against humanity. The Guardian, 16 March
Donat-Cattin D (2001) The rights of victims and International Criminal Justice. In: Fischer H, Ipsen K, Wolf J, ELSA International (eds) International law as we enter the 21st century. Berlin Verlag Arno Spitz, Berlin, pp 181–200
Doyle C (2008) Crime victims' rights act. Nova Science
Dubber MD (2006) Victims in the war on crime: the use and abuse of victims' rights. NYU Press, New York City
Duker WF (1977) The right to bail: a historical inquiry. Albany Law Rev 42:33–120
Eckelmans F (2013) ICC's practice on victim participation. In: Bonacker T, Safferling C (eds) Victims of international crimes: an interdisciplinary discourse. T.M.C. Asser Press, pp 189–222
Edmunds C, Underwood T (2003) Victim advocacy and public policy. In: Underwood T, Edmunds C (eds) Victim assistance: exploring individual practice, organisational policy, and societal responses. Springer, Berlin
Edmunds C, Petersen D, Underwood T (2003) Victims of criminal death. In: Underwood T, Edmunds C (eds) Victim assistance: exploring individual practice, organisational policy, and societal responses. Springer, Berlin
Edna E, Bienkowska E (1993) Victim participation in proceedings and satisfaction with justice in the continental systems: the case of Poland. J Crim Just 21(1):47–60
Egede E, Sutch P (2013) The politics of international law and international justice. Edinburgh University Press, Edinburgh
Elander M (2018) Figuring victims in International Criminal Justice: the case of the Khmer Rouge Tribunal. Routledge, New York City
Esmein A, Garraud R, Mittermaier CJA (1913) A history of continental criminal procedure: with special reference to France. Little Brown and Company, New York City
Fattah EA (1989) Victims of abuse of power: the David/Goliath Syndrome. In: Fattah EA (ed) Plight of crime victims in modern society. Palgrave Macmillan, London, pp 29–73
Fattah EA (1997) From crime policy to victim policy, the need for a fundamental policy change. In: Marilyn McShane DM, Williams PF (eds) Victims of crime and the victimisation process. Routledge, New York City, pp 75–93
Fernández de Casadevante Romani C (2012) International law of victims. Springer, Berlin
Ferstman C (2012) International criminal law and victims' right. In: Schabas WA (ed) Routledge handbook of international criminal law. Routledge, New York, pp 407–418
Fisher G (2004) Plea bargaining's triumph: a history of plea bargaining in America. Stanford University Press
Friscik J, Antik D, Mihov S (2014) Compensation of victims of violent crimes in the Republic of Macedonia
Friscik J, Antik D, Mihov S (2016) Compensation of victims of violent crimes in the Republic of Macedonia
Gans J (2017) Modern criminal law of Australia. Cambridge University Press, Cambridge
Garkawe S (2007) The (human) rights of crime victims do not necessarily infringe the rights of accused and convicted persons. In: Chan W (ed) Support for victims of crime in Asia. Routledge, London, pp 51–80
Gerry A (2009) Victims of crime and the criminal justice system. In: Colvin M, Cooper J (eds) Human rights in the investigation and prosecution of crime. Oxford University Press, pp 447–468
Goldstein A (1982) Defining the role of the victim in criminal prosecution. Mississippi Law J 52:515–561

Goodey J (2005) Victims and victimology: research, policy and practice. Longman criminology series. Pearson Longman

Goodrum S (2017) Expecting an ally and getting prosecutor. In: Copes H, Pogrebin M (eds) Voices from criminal justice: insider perspectives, outsider experiences. Routledge, Abingdon, pp 305–320

Green SP (1988) Private challenges to prosecutorial inaction: a model declaratory judgment statute. Yale Law J 97:490–507

Halpérin J-L (2015) Benoît Garnot Les victimes, des oubliées de l'histoire ? Pu, Rennes

Henderson L (1999) Revisiting victim's rights. Utah Law Rev:383–442

Hoppe A (2020) In: Abraham M et al (eds) Verletzte im Strafrecht. Nomos, Hamburg

Hostettler J (2004) The criminal jury old and new: jury power from early times to the present day. Waterside Press, Sherfield Gables

Hostettler J (2009) A history of criminal justice in England and Wales. Waterside Press, Sherfield Gables

Howse T (2013) England. In: Ligeti K (ed) Toward a prosecutor for the European Union: a comparative analysis, vol 1. Hart, Portland, pp 133–178

Israel JH, LaFave RW (2006) Criminal procedure, constitutional limitations in a nutshell. West nutshell series, 5th edn. West Publ. Co

Jackson R (1940) The federal prosecutor. J Am Jud Soc J Crim Law 31:3

Jaishankar K (2014) Implementing victim rights in newly industrialised countries: reflections on major challenges and recommendations for the future. In: Vanfraechem I, Pemberton A, Ndahinda F (eds) Justice for victims: perspectives on rights, transition and reconciliation. Taylor and Francis, Abingdon, pp 66–88

Jorge-Birol PA (2010) Victims' participation in the criminal justice system and its impact on peace-building. In: Benedek W et al (eds) Transnational terrorism, organised crime and peace-building. Palgrave Macmillan, London, pp 305–328

Kamisar Y (1996) The Warren Court and Criminal Justice. In: Schwartz B (ed) The Warren Court, a retrospective. Oxford University Press, Oxford

Kamisar Y et al (2015) Modern criminal procedure, cases, comments, and questions. American casebook series, 14th edn. West Academic Publishing

Killean R (2019) Victims, atrocity and international criminal justice: lessons from Cambodia. Routledge, New York City

King LW (2017) The code of Hammurabi. Independent Publishing Platform

Kirchengast T (2006) The victim in criminal law and justice. Palgrave Macmillan, London

Kirsch P (2002) The development of the Rome Statute. In: Lee RS (ed) The International Criminal Court: the making of the Rome Statute; issues, negotiations, results. Kluwer Law International, Alphen aan den Rijn

Klip A (2016) European criminal law: an integrative approach. Intersentia, Mortsel

LaFave W (2009) Criminal procedure. Hornbook series, 5th edn. West/Thomson Reuters

Letschert R, Groenhujsen M (2011) Global governance and global crime: do victims fall in between? In: Letschert R, van Dijk J (eds) The new faces of victimhood: globalisation, transnational crimes and victim rights. Studies in global justice, vol 8. Springer Science Business Media, Berlin, pp 15–40

Letschert R, Staiger I (2010) Compensation and reparation for victims of terrorism. In: Letschert R, Pemberton A, Staiger I (eds) Assisting victims of terrorism: towards a European standard of justice. Springer Science Business Media B.V., pp 1–30

Lewis M (2014) The birth of the new justice: the internationalisation of crime and punishment, 1919–1950. Oxford University Press, Oxford

Logan WA (1999) Opining on death: witness sentence recommendations in capital trials. Boston College Law Rev 41:517–540

Lohne K (2018) NGOs for international justice: criminal or victims' justice. In: Føllesdal A, Ulfstein G (eds) The judicialisation of international law: a mixed blessing? Oxford University Press, pp 109–127

Lothar S (2019) § 374. In: Hannich R, Appl E, Bader M (eds) Karlsruher Kommentar zur Strafprozessordnung: Mit GVG, EGGVG und EMRK. 8. Auflage Beck, München
Lynch D (2009) Inside the criminal courts, 2nd edn. Carolina Academic Press, Durham
Masol S (2020) The content of internationally recognised human rights under the Rome Statute of the International Criminal Court. In: Pérez-León-Acevedo JB, Nicholson J (eds) Defendants and victims in international criminal justice. Routledge, London, pp 10–32
McConkie DS (2015) Judges as framers of plea bargaining. Stanford Law Policy Rev 26:61–118
McDonald WF (1976) Towards a bicentennial revolution in criminal justice: the return of the victim. Am Crim Law Rev 13:649–673
Meier J (1992) The "Right" to a disinterested prosecutor of criminal contempt: unpacking public and private interests. Wash Univ Law Rev 70:85–129
Michel V (2018) Prosecutorial accountability and victims' rights in Latin America. Cambridge University Press, Cambridge
Monballyu J (2014) Six centuries of criminal law: history of criminal law in the Southern Netherlands and Belgium (1400–2000). Brill Nijhoff, Leiden
Moskovitz M (2014) Cases & problems in criminal procedure: the courtroom. LexisNexis, New York
Mosteller RP (1997) Unnecessary amendment. Geo Law J 85:1691–1716
Myers JEB (2016) Legal issues in clinical practice with victims of violence. Guilford Publications, New York City
Ochoa JC (2013) The rights of victims in criminal justice proceedings for serious human rights violations. Brill Nijhoff
Okrent JC, Buckley RW (2015) Torts and personal injury law, 5th edn. Cengage Learning, 2015
Pemberton A, Rasquete C (2010) Victims in Europe: assessment of the implementation of the framework decision on the standing of victims in criminal proceedings: preliminary results. In: Hartmann J, Arbeitskreis der Opferhilfen (eds) Perspektiven professioneller Opferhilfe: Theorie und Praxis eines interdisziplinären Handlungsfelds. Springer, Berlin, pp 99–112
Pérez-León Acevedo JP (2014) Victims' status at international and hybrid criminal courts: victims' status as witnesses, victim participants/civil parties and reparations claimants. Åbo Akademi Förlag
Peterson N (2009) Developing a framework for legal rights of victims and witnesses: what can European institutions & the International Criminal Court learn from each other? In: Cools M, de Kimpe S, de Ruyver B (eds) Readings on criminal justice, criminal law & policing. Maklu, Antwerpen, pp 125–157
Petrossian G (2019) Staatenverantwortlichkeit für Völkermord. Duncker & Humblot, Berlin
Petrossian G (2020) Opferbeteiligung auf internationaler Ebene. In: Abraham M et al (eds) Verletzte im Strafrecht. Nomos, Hamburg
Pfefferbaum B (2009) Victims of terrorism and the media. In: Silke A (ed) Terrorists, victims and society: psychological perspectives on terrorism and its consequences. Wiley, Chichester, pp 176–187
Radovic I (2017) Access to compensation of victims of human trafficking. Astra, Belgrade
Raven BH (2001) Power/interaction and interpersonal influence: experimental investigations and case studies. In: Lee-Chai A, Bargh J (eds) The use and abuse of power. Taylor and Francis, New York, pp 217–240
Roach K (1999) Due process and victims' rights: the new law and politics of criminal justice. University of Toronto Press, Toronto
Roche D (2013) Retribution and restorative justice. In: Johnstone G, Van Ness D (eds) Handbook of restorative justice. Routledge, New York City
Rössner D, Wulf R (1984) Opferbezogene Strafrechtspflege: Leitgedanken u. Handlungsvorschläge für Praxis u. Gesetzgebung. Dt. Bewährungshilfe
Safferling C (2003) Das Opfer völkerrechtlicher Verbrechen. Zeitschrift für die gesamte Strafrechtswissenschaft:352–365
Safferling C (2007) Towards an international criminal procedure. Oxford University Press, Oxford

Safferling C (2011a) Internationales Strafrecht, Strafanwendungsrecht - Völkerstrafrecht - Europäisches Strafrecht. Springer, Heidelberg
Safferling C (2011b) The role of the victim in the criminal process. ICLR 11:183–215
Safferling C (2012) International criminal procedure. Oxford University Press, Oxford
Sandoval-Villalba C (2009) The concepts of 'Injured Party' and 'Victim' of gross human rights violations in the jurisprudence of the Inter-American Court of Human Rights: a commentary on their implications for reparations'. In: Ferstman C, Goetz M, Stephens A (eds) Reparations for victims of genocide, war crimes and crimes against humanity: systems in place and systems in the making. Martinus Nijhoff, Leiden, pp 243–282
Schabas W (2010) The International Criminal Court: a commentary on the Rome Statute. Oxford University Press, Oxford
Schroth K, Schroth M (2018) Die Rechte des Opfers im Strafprozess. Praxis der Strafverteidigung, vol 26. C.F. Müller, Heidelberg
Scovazzi T, Citroni G (2007) The struggle against enforced disappearance and the 2007 United Nations Convention. Martinus Nijhoff, Leiden
Sergii M (2020) The content of internationally recognised human rights under the Rome Statute of the International Criminal Court. In: Perez-Leon-Acevedo JP, Nicolson J (eds) Defendants and victims in international criminal justice: ensuring and balancing their rights. Routledge, New York City, pp 10–31
Shapland J, Willmore J, Duff P (1985) Victims in the criminal justice system. Gower
Shapland J, Robinson G, Sorsby A (2011) Restorative justice in practice: evaluating what works for victims and offenders. Taylor & Francis, New York City
Sharma DP (2003) Victims of terrorism. A. P. H. Publ. Corp
Simons KW (2008) The crime/tort distinction: legal doctrine and normative principles. Widener Law J 17:719–732
Spencer J (2012) The victim and the prosecutor. In: Bottoms A, Roberts J (eds) Hearing the victim: adversarial justice, crime victims and the state. Routledge, Abingdon, pp 145–167
Stubley P (2018) Lawyers for Rohingya community want to prosecute Myanmar leader Aung San Suu Kyi for crimes against humanity. Independent, 17 March
Studzinsky S (2013) Participation rights of victims as civil parties and the challenges of their implementation before the extraordinary chambers in the Courts of Cambodia. In: Bonacker T, Safferling C (eds) Victims of international crimes: an interdisciplinary discourse. T.M.C. Asser Press, The Hague, pp 175–188
Tobolowsky PM et al (2016) Crime victim rights and remedies, 3rd edn. Carolina Academic Press, Durham
Tochilovsky V (2008) Jurisprudence of the International Criminal Courts and the European Court of Human Rights: procedure and evidence. Martinus Nijhoff, Leiden
van Boven T (2013) Victim-oriented perspectives: rights and realities. In: Bonacker T, Safferling C (eds) Victims of international crimes: an interdisciplinary discourse. T.M.C. Asser Press, pp 17–27
van Camp T (2016) Victims of violence and restorative justice: finding a voice. Routledge, New York
van der Aa S (2010) Stalking in the Netherlands: nature and prevalence of the problem and the effectiveness of anti-stalking measures. Maklu, Antwerpen
van Dijk J (1988) Ideological trends within the victims movements. In: Maguire M (ed) Victims of crime: a new deal? Open University Press, pp 115–126
von Hentig H (1967) Criminal and his victim. Shoe String Press Inc., Brooklyn
Waller I (2010) Rights for victims of crime: rebalancing justice. Rowman & Littlefield, Lanham
Watkin TG (2012) The legal history of wales, 2nd edn. University of Wales Press
Wemmers MJA (1996) Victims in the criminal justice system. Studies on crime and justice, WODC Ministry of Justice
Whitebread CH, Slobogin C (2003) Criminal procedure: an analysis of cases and concepts. Foundation Press, New York

Wigmore J (1901) Sequestration of witnesses. Harv Law Rev 14:475–495
Wolhuter L, Denham D, Olley N (2009) Victimology: victimisation and victims' rights. Routledge, Cavendish
Zegveld L (2019) Victims as a third party: empowerment of victims? Int Crim Law Rev 19 (2):321–328
Zhang B (2016) Recognising the limits of victims participation: a comparative examination of the victim participation schemes at the ECCC and the ICC. In: Meisenberg SM, Stegmiller I (eds) The extraordinary chambers in the Courts of Cambodia: assessing their contribution to international criminal law. T.M.C. Asser Press, The Hague, pp 515–534

Chapter 3
Victims' Participation Under the Rome Statute

3.1 Historical Overview of Drafting the Victims' Institute at the Rome Conference[1]

In 1993, the Working Group[2] for the draft statute for an international criminal court was established by the UNGA within the International Criminal Law Commission.[3] The first report[4] of the Working Group focused on the right to protection of the victims only. All the lists of the target groups to be protected by the Court always start with the accused, followed by the victims and subsequently the witnesses. At that stage, the drafters of the closed Working Group focused on the rights of the accused, and the paradigm of punishment prevailed in the debate. Consequently, all articles guarantee the rights of the accused first before they continue with the necessary protection for the victims and the witnesses. The new draft further emphasised the rights of the accused, as unlawfully arrested people were also referred to as "victims". Conversely, the new draft did turn over a new leaf in the development of the whole drafting process and in terms of victims' rights.

---

[1]The authors would like to express their gratitude to Dr. Michaela Lissowsky for her support in drafting this subsection.

[2]Members of the Working Group: Mr. Crawford, Chairman, Mr. Thiam, ex officio member as Special Rapporteur on the Draft Code of Crimes against the Peace and Security of Mankind, Mr. Kabatsi, ex officio as General Rapporteur, Mr. Al-Baharna, Mr. Al-Khasawneh, Mr. Arangio-Ruiz, Mr. Bennouna, Mr. Bowett, Mr. de Saram, Mr. Eiriksson, Mr. Elaraby, Mr. Fomba, Mr. Guney, Mr. He, Mr. Idris, Mr. Rao, Mr. Razafindralambo, Mr. Robinson, Mr. Rosenstock, Mr. Tomuschat, Mr. Vereshchetin, Mr. Villagran-Kramer, Mr. Yankov.

[3]UNGA, A/RES/48/31, Report of the International Law Commission on the work ofits forty-fifth session 9 December 1993.

[4]ILC, A/CN.4/L.491/Rev2 14 July 1994, Commentary Article 25 to 47 in A/CN.4/L.491/Rev.2/Add.2 18 July 1994.

© The Author(s), under exclusive license to Springer Nature Switzerland AG 2021
C. Safferling, G. Petrossian, *Victims Before the International Criminal Court*,
https://doi.org/10.1007/978-3-030-80177-9_3

3.1.1 Drafting Process

After the "Draft Code of Crimes against the Peace and Security of Mankind" was submitted in 1994, the UNGA expressed "its appreciation for the progress achieved by the International Law Commission in its elaboration of a draft statute for an international criminal court." Additionally, the UNGA invited states to submit written comments on the draft articles proposed by the Working Group on a draft statute for an international criminal court to the Secretary General by 15 February 1994, as requested by the International Law Commission.[5] Several governments followed that invitation and made commented on the draft statute.[6]

Slovenia pointed out that "the procedural standards as laid down in Article 14 of the ICCPR must be respected." Article 14 of the ICCPR guarantees equality before the Court and the right to be innocent until proven guilty. Article 14 ICCPR also contained the accused's guaranteed human rights which are the rights to be informed in comprehensible language, to be defended and to be tried without delay, to have the witnesses against him examined, to have free access to an interpreter and the right to not have to testify against himself. This particular article protects accused juveniles and guarantees everybody the right to a review of their own conviction by a higher tribunal, the right to be compensated in, for example, cases of a miscarriage of justice and finally the right not to be tried again for an offence for which they have already been convicted or acquitted.[7] Additionally, "the Republic of Slovenia suggested that more care should be devoted to victims and witnesses at the court."[8]

Referring to Article 46 draft statute—the protection of the accused, victims and witnesses—Hungary added that "only one objection can be raised to Article 46 draft statute[9] and that is the principle of direct evidence. It is a limit to the accused's rights if evidence such as electronically recorded testimony is introduced, since it may deny the accused of the right to cross-examination or the opportunity to practice other rights of defence. For this reason, Hungary considered that Article 43 should be reworded in order to fully protect the rights of both the accused and the victim".[10]

On 9 December 1994, the UNGA established an *ad hoc* Committee (AHC) in order to review "the major substantive and administrative issues" of the draft by the

[5] A/RES/48/31, 9 December 1993.

[6] Comments and observations received from Governments Extract from the Yearbook of the International Law Commission:-1993 Document:-vol. II(1) Topic: Draft code of crimes against the peace and security of mankind (Part II)- including the draft statute for an international criminal court.

[7] International Covenant for Civil and Political Rights, Article 14.

[8] A/CN.4/458 and Add.1-8 Observations of Governments on the report of the Working Group on a draft statute for an international criminal court Extract from the Yearbook of the International Law Commission:- 1994 Document:vol. II(1).

[9] Article 46 – Protection of the accused, victims and witnesses.

[10] A/CN.4/458 and Add.1-8 Observations of Governments on the report of the Working Group on a draft statute for an international criminal court Extract from the Yearbook of the International Law Commission:- 1994 Document:vol. II(1).

ILC and all Member States were invited to send their written comments on the draft statute by March 1995.

3.1.1.1 Ad hoc Committee Meetings, 1995

The two meetings of the AHC took place at the UN Headquarters in New York from 3 to 13 April 1995 and from 14 to 25 August 1995. The first session was opened by Hans Correll, Under-Secretary-General and UN Legal Counsel. During that first meeting, the AHC elected its Bureau. Adriaan Bos from The Netherlands (representing Western Europe) became the Chairman, as Vice-Chairpersons Cherif Bassiouni from Egypt (representing the African Group), Marek Madej from Poland (representing Eastern Europe) and Silvia Fernández de Gurmendi from Argentina (representing the Latin American and Caribbean Group) were elected. Kuniko Saeki from Japan (representing the Asian Group) was appointed Rapporteur. Around 75 delegations participated in the meetings of the AHC, including the P5. The AHC identified the main substantive and administrative issues in the draft statute.

A working group was established under the aegis of Austrian Professor, Gerhard Hafner, in order to prepare an informal paper on the methods of proceedings. That paper became significantly influential and added to the AHC report. Subsequently, the Working Group was asked to develop guidelines for the relationship between the ICC and state parties and non-state parties and general rules of criminal law. The AHC considered the arrangements for a conference of plenipotentiaries.[11]

Unfortunately, there are no verbatim records of statements made by the governments available as based upon the report of the AHC, it is not possible to identify the states that spoke and supported victims' rights in the report. There are only indications of how much support governments had expressed for a particular position. The report does not name those delegations that suggested the idea of a trigger mechanism for victims. The adoption of that proposal would have enabled the victims and their relatives to trigger the jurisdiction of the Court, provided that firstly the crime was in the scope of the jurisdiction, secondly, the state had accepted the jurisdiction of the Court and thirdly, the "Court was entitled to initiate an investigation or prosecution in conformity with the principle of complementarity." It was furthermore suggested that individual complaints should be reviewed by a special commission within the Court.[12]

In its third position paper from August 1995, the NGO International Commission of Jurists (ICJ), which became an observer at the AHC, summarised the different

[11] Report of the Ad hoc Committee on the Establishment of an International Criminal Court, A/50/22, New York, 1995.

[12] Report of the Ad hoc Committee on the Establishment of an International Criminal Court, A/50/22, New York, 1995 para. 117.

views of state delegations during the meetings of the AHC.[13] The ICJ reported that the Czech Republic and Chile requested a complaint mechanism in the statute. Compared to the ECtHR, the Czech Republic saw a right to bring in complaints before the ICC as being especially important for victims and their relatives. Though again comparable to the ECtHR, all domestic legal remedies must have been exhausted beforehand. At the same time, other delegations such as Denmark, Russia, France, UK and Thailand opposed an individual complaint mechanism due to the fear of over-burdening the Court with too many cases.[14]

3.1.1.2 Preparatory Committee, 1996–1998

Adriaan Bos was also Chairman during the meetings of the Preparatory Committee which "was an early example of the importance of the continuity of persons as well as procedures and concepts throughout the ICC negotiations."[15] At its first session, from 25 March to 12 April 1996, the members of the Committee discussed the definitions of the crimes. At the second meeting, from 12 to 30 August 1996, the main discussion revolved around the question of cooperation and how cases would be tried before the ICC. Victims' rights never appeared on the agenda and were never treated as a core issue in the negotiations.

Article 68 in the Report of the Preparatory Committee on the Establishment of an International Criminal Court (1) obliged the Court to "[. . .] take the necessary measures available to it to protect the accused, victims and witnesses." Although the article is entitled "Protection of the [accused], victims and witnesses [and their participation in the proceedings]", the rights of the accused are strongly emphasised. The focus of the victims' rights is again on the right to be protected and the ensuing paragraphs did not highlight the right to participate in the trials. Only paragraph 4, although as a draft version in brackets, would permit the Court to "present and consider the views and concerns of the victims at appropriate stages of the proceedings."[16]

The victims' rights were institutionally strengthened by Article 44 of the Preparatory Committee Report which suggested establishing a "Victims and Witnesses Unit" within the Registry. The Unit "[. . .] shall provide counselling and other assistance to victims [. . .] and their family members [. . .] and "[. . .] advice the organs of the Court on appropriate measures of protection [. . .]."

New Zealand was the first country that suggested that victims participate in the proceedings of the ICC in its proposal submitted to the Preparatory Committee in

---

[13]International Commission of Jurists: The International Criminal Court, Third ICJ Position Paper, August 1995.

[14]International Commission of Jurists: The International Criminal Court, Third ICJ Position Paper, August 1995.

[15]Bonneau et al. (2014), p. 39.

[16]A/CONF.183/2/Add.1, 14 April 1998.

August 1997. At that time, Article 43 (3) recommended to the Court to "enable victims of the crimes charged and/or their legal representatives to participate in the proceedings in order to 'allow the views and concern of the victims to be presented and considered at appropriate stages of the proceedings where their personal interests are affected,' [...]".[17]

During the negotiations for the Rome Statute, NGOs played an influential role in promoting victims' rights. They coordinated their objections in the Coalition for an International Criminal Court (CICC). The CICC was founded on 10 February 1995 as a broad network of NGOs with the purpose of establishing an effective and independent international criminal court. During the negotiations of the Preparatory Committee, the CICC published the missing issues in the draft statute and began their lobbying work with the states.[18] Additionally, a network of experts was established. Even as early as 1998, the CICC had more than 800 members from which 236 representatives were sent to participate in the Rome conference.[19] In order to be as efficient as possible, the CICC was split into three groups at the Rome conference, focusing on thematic issues such as, firstly, gender and victims, secondly on regional issues, lobbied by state representatives, and thirdly on working groups which dealt with several articles of the Statute. The greatest achievement of the lobby work by the NGOs was the integration of gender crimes and victims' rights into the Rome Statute.[20]

While they were organising their lobby work in the CICC, a number of NGOs published valuable working and position papers on victims' rights. In addition, daily publications were submitted by NGOs (Terra Viva, On the Record and CICC Monitor) and kept the diplomats and experts informed of the results of the working groups. These publications contributed to assuring that the discussions regarding victims' rights continued. Since 1953, the ICJ has dedicated its work to ending impunity and promoting the rule of law and human rights. In the aforementioned third position paper, the ICJ did not only summarise the different governmental positions during the AHC meetings, but also its own arguments towards the ILC revised draft statute for the ICC.[21] The ICJ supported the initiative for a complaint mechanism stating that "the ICJ believes that such a procedure should be included in the Statute of the ICC. At the minimum, victims who are nationals of State Parties to the Statute should be capable of bringing complaints to the Court."[22]

---

[17]Non-Paper/WG.4/N. 19, 13 August 1997, see Annex A, Compilation of the Preparatory Works for the Drafting of Article 43/6) and Article 68 of the Rome Statute, https://www.icc-cpi.int/RelatedRecords/CR2007_04932.PDF, last visited on 12 December 2020.

[18]Kristie (2004), pp. 15–16.

[19]Glasius (2006), p. 27.

[20]Pace and Thieroff (2002), p. 394.

[21]International Commission of Jurists: The International Criminal Court, Third ICJ Position Paper, August 1995.

[22]International Commission of Jurists: The International Criminal Court, Third ICJ Position Paper, August 1995.

Additionally, Human Rights Watch (HRW) recommended in its position paper from 1996 "to accept petitions from individuals concerning the most severe human rights violations."[23] Furthermore, the right to be protected by the Court was the primary request of all the NGOs. HRW "strongly recommend(ed) that the Court establish a service for victims and witnesses to ensure the safety of the accused, victims and witness, as well as that of their families, from intimidation and retaliation, before, during and after the trial."[24] The Women's Caucus for Gender Justice in the International Criminal Court endorsed this view by recommending "A Victims and Witnesses Unit (VWU) should be established as an autonomous unit within the Registry under the supervision of the Presidency" and describing the role as protective and possibly rehabilitative.[25]

3.1.1.3 Rome Diplomatic Conference, June–July 1998

The United Nations Diplomatic Conference of Plenipotentiaries on the Establishment of the ICC began on 15 June 1998. The draft statute by the Preparatory Committee[26] was the main basis for the forthcoming negotiations. Even a cursory glance at that draft with its numerous articles, texts in brackets and alternative versions suffices to be able to say that many questions remained open at that stage and still had to be discussed. Additionally, the rights of victims were still under consideration.

Article 68 (4) of the draft statute of the Preparatory Committee, albeit as a draft version in brackets, permitted the Court to present and consider the views and concerns of the victims at the appropriate stages of the proceedings. The victims' right to participate in the trials was discussed very late in Rome. Primarily, NGOs managed to include the right to participate in the proceedings. In the late nineties, David Donat-Cattin, a member of the European Law Students' Association (ELSA), drafted several proposals for victims' rights and became the NGOs' team leader on Parts VI and VIII of the Rome Statute during the negotiations in Rome.

Benedetti, Bonneau and Washburn reported that from interviews with persons present during the debates of the working groups that some delegations complained about the attendance of representatives of victims' organisations. As a result, Argentina suggested adopting the Rules of Procedure and Evidence at a later stage when only one representative for all victims' groups would be present. Argentina, like other countries with a civil law system, e.g. France, South Africa and Colombia,

---

[23]Human Rights Watch, Commentary for the Preparatory Committee on the Establishment of an International Criminal Court, August 1996, Article 25.

[24]Human Rights Watch, Commentary for the Preparatory Committee on the Establishment of an International Criminal Court, August 1996, Article 43.

[25]Women's Caucus for Gender Justice in the International Criminal Court 'Summary of Recommendations Composition & Administration of the Court Crimes Against Humanity' (1998), p. 3.

[26]Report of the Preparatory Committee on the Establishment of an International Criminal Court.

strongly supported the NGOs in terms of the right of victims to participate in the proceedings. The supporting states favoured the possibility of victims presenting their views before the Court. Those supporting states were even concerned that "[...] victims would be victimised again by the criminal proceedings if they had to follow those proceedings without any possibility to express their views and concerns".[27]

The legal but also the cultural differences between the states were apparent at that stage of the discussions regarding victims' rights. While some delegations were in favour, other delegations were opposed to including the UN Victims Declaration from 1985. The Arab states even rejected the mention of the terms "gender" and "sexual violence against women".[28] Despite these different positions towards the right to participate in the proceedings, Cherif Bassiouni concludes that "there is nothing in the legislative history of the Rome Statute to assume that the victim was to be anything more than a participant."[29]

France, in particular, wanted a balanced relationship between the Prosecutor and the PTC, and between the Prosecutor and powerful states. The head of the French delegation, Beatrice le Fraper du Hellen, presented a proposal on Article 15, the trigger mechanism *proprio motu* which allows the Prosecutor to "[...] initiate investigations [...] on the basis of information on crimes within the jurisdiction of the Court". This provision guarantees victims direct participation and access to justice.[30]

The culmination of these negotiations and this work resulted in the inclusion within the Rome Statute of the following Articles relating to the protection and the participation of victims:

Article 68: Protection of the victims and witnesses and their participation in the proceedings

1) The Court shall take appropriate measures to protect the safety, physical and psychological well-being, dignity and privacy of victims and witnesses. In so doing, the Court shall have regard to all relevant factors, including age, gender as defined in Article 7 (3), and health, and the nature of the crime, in particular, but not limited to, where the crime involves sexual or gender violence or violence against children. The Prosecutor shall take such measures particularly during the investigation and prosecution of such crimes. These measures shall not be prejudicial to or inconsistent with the rights of the accused and a fair and impartial trial.
2) As an exception to the principle of public hearings provided for in Article 67 draft statute, the Chambers of the Court may, to protect victims and witnesses or an accused, conduct any part of the proceedings in camera or allow the presentation of evidence by electronic or other special means. In particular, such measures shall be implemented in the case of a victim of sexual violence or a child who is a victim or a witness, unless otherwise ordered by the Court, having regard to all the circumstances, particularly the views of the victim or witness.
3) Where the personal interests of the victims are affected, the Court shall permit their views and concerns to be presented and considered at stages of the proceedings determined to

[27]Bonneau et al. (2014), p. 153.

[28]Bonneau et al. (2014), p. 153.

[29]Bassiouni (2006), p. 244.

[30]Bonneau et al. (2014), p. 111.

be appropriate by the Court and in a manner which is not prejudicial to or inconsistent with the rights of the accused and a fair and impartial trial. Such views and concerns may be presented by the legal representatives of the victims where the Court considers it appropriate, in accordance with the Rules of Procedure and Evidence.

4) The Victims and Witnesses Unit may advise the Prosecutor and the Court on appropriate protective measures, security arrangements, counselling and assistance as referred to in Article 43(6) draft statute.
5) Where the disclosure of evidence or information pursuant to this Statute may lead to the grave endangerment of the security of a witness or his or her family, the Prosecutor may, for the purposes of any proceedings conducted prior to the commencement of the trial, withhold such evidence or information and instead submit a summary thereof. Such measures shall be exercised in a manner which is not prejudicial to or inconsistent with the rights of the accused and a fair and impartial trial. A State may make an application for necessary measures to be taken in respect of the protection of its servants or agents and the protection of confidential or sensitive information.

3.1.2 Towards a Reparation Mandate for Victims Within the ICC

The comments on the draft statute were not limited to those relating to protection or participation, but also referred to the right to reparation. Belgium proposed that "It should also be noted that inclusion of State responsibility in the Code would make it possible to provide a sound juridical basis for the granting of compensation to the victims of crimes and other eligible parties."[31] Denmark, Finland, Iceland and Italy demanded that the "Court must impose penalties and determine where the sentences will be executed. At the same time, if the Court is given authority to decide on compensation for the victims of crimes and the victim's right to compensation is recognised by the Court, other mechanisms (resulting, for example, from the establishment of special funds) may also come into play to resolve issues such as the amount of compensation, the identification of the debtor and the implementation of the Court's decision."[32] Additionally, Denmark, Finland and Germany "(. . .) felt that there is good reason, partly with a view to Article 40 (fair trial), to specify in the statute the interests of victims and witnesses, and especially their need for protection."[33]

The Nordic countries demanded that in Article 46 (Protection of the accused, victims and witnesses) "[. . .] rules regarding the protection and assistance of victims of the crimes (should be included), in accordance with certain basic principles set

[31] A/CN.4/448 and Add.1.

[32] A/CN.4/452 and Add.1-3 Comments of Governments on the report of the Working Group on the question of an international criminal jurisdiction Extract from the Yearbook of the International Law Commission:-1993 Document:- , vol. II(1).

[33] A/CN.4/458 and Add.1-8 Observations of Governments on the report of the Working Group on a draft statute for an international criminal court Extract from the Yearbook of the International Law Commission:- 1994 Document:- , vol. II(1).

forth in the Declaration of Basic Principles of Justice for Victims of Crime and Abuse of Power." The Nordic countries made the proposal to "[...] delete the possibility of judgment of fines." They stated that with "the magnitude of the crimes in question, it is difficult to imagine how fines would be applicable. Furthermore, it should be noted here that the penalty of confiscation/seizure is a punishment for criminal activity which should be included in the statute, as it is in fact related to criminal punishment. This should be possible in order to provide a compensatory remedy for victims of certain crimes, such as victims of stolen property."

The United Kingdom requested the Commission "to consider whether the Court should be directed to the order in which fines or confiscated property should be paid out. [...] It is doubtful whether a trust fund is needed at all, and it may be that the tribunal should itself have the power to pay sums of money directly to the victims or to the State of their nationality expressly for their benefit."[34]

The United States emphasised that Article 53, as drafted, "appears to permit the tribunal to exercise jurisdiction over and attach individual and even government property located within States. This is likely to require subsequent enforcement actions in national courts. Such litigation can be complex." On the other hand, they "[...] strongly support remedies of forfeiture and restoration of property to victims, this has proved one of the more difficult areas in international assistance. Thus, the statute may need to be revised to reflect the fact that court orders involving execution in States with respect to property may be subject to review by national courts under national law."[35]

3.1.2.1 Ad hoc Committee Meetings, 1995

There were limited records of these meetings, however, the AHC did provide a report as an overview. In terms of the election of the judges, the AHC report emphasised the need for an equitable geographical representation at the ICC from across the world as well as a representation of the principal legal systems. During the discussion about the penalties, "proposals were also made that the statute should provide for confiscation, restitution of property and compensation for victims."[36] The victims' rights were not extended upon in the report of the two Ad hoc committee meetings when compared to the draft by the ILC from 1994. The

[34]A/CN.4/458 and Add.1-8 Observations of Governments on the report of the Working Group on a draft statute for an international criminal court Extract from the Yearbook of the International Law Commission:- 1994 Document:- , vol. II(1).

[35]A/CN.4/458 and Add.1-8 Observations of Governments on the report of the Working Group on a draft statute for an international criminal court Extract from the Yearbook of the International Law Commission:- 1994 Document:- , vol. II(1).

[36]Report of the Ad hoc Committee on the Establishment of an International Criminal Court, A/50/22, New York, 1995, 188.

UNGA decided to continue the work of the AHC in two meetings of the Preparatory Committee in 1996.[37]

3.1.2.2 Preparatory Committee, 1996–1998

A number of governments had noticed a kind of competition between civil and common law approaches. From France's point of view, both statutes of the ICTY and the ICTR drew too strongly on the common law system. In order to avoid an overbalance of the common law tradition at the ICC, France drafted its own version of a statute.[38] The French working paper of a draft statute included its own Article 50 for the "Rights of victims". Victims "[. . .] may inform the Registrar of the Court in writing of the acts having caused injury to him and the nature and amount of the losses which he has sustained."[39] The right to compensate the victims was emphasised. Paragraph 3 of that draft allows the Preliminary Investigation Chamber to "[. . .] order the provisional seizure of all or part of the property of the person committed for trial, if it believes that such a measure is necessary to compensate the victims [. . .]".[40]

Silvia Fernández de Gurmendi, who would later become the ICC president from 2015 to 2018, stated that French and other national proposals "made discussions extremely difficult".[41] On the other hand, those proposals were bridging gaps between the common law and the civil law system, especially in terms of victims' rights. France strongly promoted the rights of the victims. During a meeting of the Preparatory Committee in August 1997, the French delegation wanted the Trial Chamber "(. . .) to determine the scope and extent of the victimisation and establish principles relating to compensation for damage caused to the victims and to restitution of property unlawfully acquired by the person convicted, in order to allow victims to rely on that judgement for the pursuit of civil remedies, including compensation, either in national courts or through their governments, in accordance with national law."[42]

In February 1998, France modified that paragraph and drafted its own definition of "reparation" that included "restitution", "compensation" and "rehabilitation" as different forms of reparations:

> Where necessary, the Trial Chamber shall also determine the scope and extent of the victimisation and establish principles relating to compensation for damage caused to the victims and to restitution of property unlawfully acquired by the person convicted, in order

[37] UNGA A/RES/50/46, Establishment of an international criminal court, 18 December 1995.

[38] Working Paper, submitted by France, UN Doc. A/AC.249/L.3 (6 August 1996), http://www.un.org/en/ga/search/view_doc.asp?symbol=A/AC.249/L.3, last visited on 12 December 2020.

[39] Working Paper, submitted by France, UN Doc. A/AC.249/L.3 (6 August 1996), Article 50 (1).

[40] Working Paper, submitted by France, UN Doc. A/AC.249/L.3 (6 August 1996), Article 50 (3).

[41] Fernández de Gurmendi (2002), p. 221.

[42] A/AC.249/1997/WG.4/DP.3.

> to allow victims to rely on that judgement for the pursuit of appropriate forms of reparation, such as restitution, compensation and rehabilitation, either in national courts or through their governments, in accordance with national law.[43]

That version enabled the Court was to act directly. In the second part of its proposal, France regarded the principle of complementarity at the ICC: "If the national competent authorities are no longer able, due to their total or partial collapse or unavailability, to proceed upon the judgment, the Court shall do so directly."[44] France had launched an initiative on its own several times before. Neither in reports submitted by observers later, nor in the official reports by the Preparatory Committee were there any signs that France was interested in close cooperation with other states or groups, for example, with the group of like-minded states.

The group of the like-minded states[45] was formed in 1994 when "An informal group of states"[46] grew slowly from year to year and began as early as 1995, pushing for a conference in order to establish an independent international criminal court. Originally, states from the UNGA's sixth committee formed a group of friends, consisting of Argentina, Canada, Norway and the Netherlands. During the Rome Conference, several authors counted more than sixty Member States within the "like-minded group".[47] Besides the group of the European states—except France and the UK—the group of the Southern African Development Community (SADC), led by South Africa, became an important sub-group in the negotiations. The Caribbean states were represented by Trinidad and Tobago. Jordan was the only representative from the Arab region within the "like-minded group". A huge advantage of the group of like-minded states was their close relationship to the chair of the negotiations. While the Preparatory Committee was chaired by the Dutch Adriaan Bos, the like-minded group was led by the Canadian, Philippe Kirsch, who would later chair the Rome conference and indeed become the first President of the ICC, after Adriaan Bos became seriously ill.[48]

Despite the strong influence of the like-minded states on different elements of the later Statute, France and the UK persistently followed their own policy. They neither joined the group of like-minded states nor did they support the second important group of states with the other permanent members of the UNSC. The US, China and Russia favoured a strong role of the UNSC and the exclusion of nuclear weapons

---

[43] A/AC.249/1998/L.13, 4 February 1998, 123.

[44] A/AC.249/1998/L.13, 4 February 1998, 123.

[45] Australia, Austria, Argentina, Belgium, Canada, Chile, Croatia, Denmark, Egypt, Finland, Germany, Greece, Guatemala, Hungary, Ireland, Italy, Lesotho, the Netherlands, New Zealand, Norway, Portugal, Samoa, Slovakia, South Africa, Sweden, Switzerland, Trinidad and Tobago (representing 12 Caricom states), Uruguay, Venezuela. See, Bassiouni (1999), pp. 443–468, 455.

[46] Glasius (2006), p. 22.

[47] Schabas (2007), p. 15.

[48] Glasius (2006), pp. 22–26.

from the prohibited weapons under the Rome Statute. From their point of view, a jurisdiction over armed conflict was to be the main focus of the Court's work.[49]

After France's solo run in terms of victims' rights, the UK also submitted a proposal for an article on the right to reparation. That British draft did not include the principle of rehabilitation in the definition of reparation and focused instead on punitive awards and included broader measures related to protection and enforcement. The biggest difference compared to the French proposal was that the UK's draft directed such punitive awards at the persons convicted of crimes and not against a state.[50]

REDRESS, as the main NGO promoting redress for victims, was interested in finding consensus on the question of reparation. Therefore, REDRESS arranged a meeting with the delegations from France and the UK.[51] The different approaches to reparations can also be seen in the Preparatory Committee's Report from meetings in Zutphen, also known as the Zutphen Draft, in which there were three different proposals for articles on reparations.[52]

Eventually, in March 1998, a joint draft was submitted by France and the UK following what the CICC described as "extensive consultations" which also included NGOs.[53] The CICC indicated the positive nature of the discussions regarding reparations, which meant that the common draft led to the version of Article 73 in the report of the Preparatory Committee. Based upon this draft, it was possible for further discussions to be held as to how such reparations were to be funded.[54] In the draft statute for the International Criminal Court of 14 April 1998, in Article 73, paragraph 1, a footnote was added in order to guarantee that reparation "shall be granted not only to victims but also to others such as the victims' families and successors."[55] That footnote referred to the definitions of "victims" and "reparation" in the "Declaration of Basic Principles of Justice for Victims of Crime and the Abuse of Power" from 1985 and the Van Boven Principles from 1993. In the Rome Statute that was later enacted, that footnote had been deleted. Hence, the Basic Principles and the Van Boven Principles are not mentioned as a source within the Rome Statute.[56]

---

[49] Glasius (2006), pp. 22–26.

[50] Muttukumaru (2002), p. 266.

[51] In May 1998 REDRESS published a booklet including the main principles for reparation and recommendations to the Rome Diplomatic Conference. REDRESS, Reparation for Victims in the International Criminal Court: Principles, Commentary, and Recommendations for the Rome Diplomatic Conference. London, June 1998.

[52] A/AC.249/1998/L.13 4 February 1998.

[53] CICC Report 'Report on the March-April 1998 Session of the Preparatory Committee on the Establishment of an International Criminal Court' March 16–April 3, 1998.

[54] CICC Report 'Report on the March-April 1998 Session of the Preparatory Committee on the Establishment of an International Criminal Court' March 16–April 3, 1998.

[55] A/CONF.183/2.

[56] A/CONF.183/C.1/WGPM/L.63/Rev.1, 11 July 1998, n1.

This was a result of Japan's vote against a direct referral to the UN Declaration of Principles of Justice. Japan feared a possible violation of the principle of sovereignty. Principle 11 was, in Japan's view, contradictory to the principle of individual criminal responsibility since it would allow victims of crimes committed by public officials to apply for restitution from that state.[57] Principle 11 stated:

> Where public officials or other agents acting in an official or quasi-official capacity have violated national criminal laws, the victims should receive restitution from the State whose officials or agents were responsible for the harm inflicted. In cases where the Government under whose authority the victimising act or omission occurred is no longer in existence, the State or Government successor in title should provide restitution to the victims.[58]

Considering Japan's handling of the judgments by the Military Tribunal for the Far East, often referred to as the "Tokyo Tribunal", subsequent Japanese governments' attitudes towards victims' rights in the statute for the ICC are not surprising. In the mid- and late-1990s, Japan still denied any obligation to redress with regard to victims of the Japanese military actions in countries like South-Korea or the Philippines.[59]

The U.S. delegation wanted the scope of reparation to be narrow. Again, REDRESS arranged a meeting with U.S. delegates and after this meeting, the U.S. representatives agreed not to limit the article on the reparation of victims. Thus, REDRESS was extremely successful in lobbying for victims.[60] Benjamin Ferencz, former American Prosecutor at the Nuremberg *Einsatzgruppen* trials, strongly promoted the right to compensation for victims at the International Criminal Court: "*Of course, victims of crimes against humanity, wherever they may be, should – as far as possible – be entitled to appropriate compensation from those who caused the injury.*"[61]

On a number of occasions, the drafters included several alternatives for one article. Three different proposals were considered for an article on compensation for victims during the inter-sessional meeting in Zutphen, the Netherlands, from 19 to 30 January 1998.[62] Finally, the Preparatory Committee Report to the Rome Diplomatic Conference contained Article 73 dealing with reparation, however, the whole text was in brackets and each set of brackets was to be read as disagreement by certain states:

---

[57] Bonneau et al. (2014), pp. 157–158.

[58] A/RES/40/34.

[59] For the first time in December 2015 Japan agreed to pay one-time 8.3 million US-Dollars for common projects with South Korea. Not only survivors, mainly the so called comfort women, criticised that agreement, also UN authorities, see the statement by the UN Human Rights Office of the High Commissioner.

[60] Bonneau et al. (2014), pp. 157–158.

[61] Ferencz (1998), p. 203 et seq.

[62] Article 75 had previously different numbers during the negotiation process: Article 45 G (1996 PrepCom Report, Vol. II), Article 45 bis (December 1997), Article 66 (after December 1997), Article 66 in Zutphen Draft Statute, Article 73 in PrepCom Draft Statute.

> [Article 73 Reparations to victims. The Court [shall] [may] establish principles relating to reparations to, or in respect of, victims, including restitution, compensation and [compensation for the purposes of] rehabilitation. The Court may, upon request, [or upon its own motion if the interests of justice so require,] determine, in its judgement, the scope and extent of any damage, loss and injury to, or in respect of, victims. (. . .)[63]

Nevertheless, this article became the basis for Article 75 RS.

Furthermore, REDRESS developed materials on the ICC and hosted a number of events in order to find consensus on the question of reparation. REDRESS and the victims' participation group[64] canvassed for the inclusion of an article on reparation in the Rome Statute. During the negotiations in Rome, the delegations followed the broader definition of "reparation" instead of the lesser term of "compensation" made by REDRESS in accordance with the Van Boven principles from 1993.[65]

Other reports by NGOs also influenced the right to reparation in the Rome Statute.[66] Amnesty International and Human Rights Watch published their recommendations during the Preparatory Committee meetings in 1997 and early 1998, along with smaller NGOs such as Justice in the Balance and International Society for Traumatic Stress Studies. Amnesty International, for example, asserted that "The court itself should have the power to award such reparations since it is unlikely that national courts, which were unable or unwilling to bring the person responsible to justice, will be able or willing to award reparations or to enforce the award."

The Women's Caucus for Gender Justice cooperated with the academic Roger Clark who promoted a strong gender focus. As a representative of the delegation of Samoa, Roger Clark participated in the negotiations in Rome and managed to include rape as a war crime and persecution as a gender crime in the Statute. Samoa was supported by delegates from Australia, Bosnia, Canada, Costa Rica, Mexico, the Netherlands, South Africa, Sweden and the UK.[67]

During these negotiations there were NGOs that opposed the inclusion of reparations for victims within the Rome Statute. The Amercian Bar Association (ABA), for example, explicitly stated in its recommendations on 2 February 1998 that "The ICC may impose sentences of imprisonment or fines, but neither the death penalty nor reparations for victims may be ordered."[68]

It is important to note that there was no agreement on the funding of the ICC in the last Preparatory Committee's draft, hence, it comes as no surprise that the tricky

[63]PrepCom Report A/CONF.183/2/Add.1, 14 April 1998.

[64]Fiona McKay and Michael O'Flaherty from REDRESS and the victims' rights working group were supported by Dr. Yael Daniele, victimologist and director of the group project for holocaust survivors and their children, as well as David Donat-Cattin from ELSA.

[65]Bonneau et al. (2014), p. 156.

[66]NGOs accredited to participate in the Rome Conference, see UN A/CONF.183/INF3, 5 June 1998, see also: Bassiouni (1999), pp. 443–468, 455.

[67]Gender crimes and victims' participation were mainly drafted by NGOs, see Petrossian (2019b), p. 85.

[68]ABA Resolution, recommendation on the International Criminal Court was passed by the American Bar Association's House of Delegates on February 2, 1998, p. 6.

question of funding reparations had not even been touched upon.[69] Furthermore, they advised that "Also heavily bracketed is language concerning reparation to victims."[70] It is clear that both these points had been left for the last leg of negotiations.

3.1.2.3 Dakar Declaration, 6 February 1998

During the multilateral negotiations of the AHC and the Preparatory Committee, representations by the African states contributed to the establishment of a permanent international criminal court. In a similar fashion to the like-minded group, the African states coordinated and advocated a common position during several independent meetings. Regional conferences were hosted by African states and the Southern African Development Community (SADC).

An important conference took place in Dakar, the capital of Senegal, in February 1998. That conference led to the drafting and adoption of a declaration, the Dakar Declaration, "affirming our commitment to the establishment of the ICC and underline the importance that the accomplishment of this Court implies for Africa and the world community as a whole." Victims' rights were strongly emphasised in the Dakar Declaration. The African states requested the Preparatory Committee to work "on the question of victim compensation"[71] and NGOs like REDRESS and No Peace without Justice participated in the meeting of the African states.

The Declaration went on to state: "That the Statute of the Court must ensure respect for Human Rights in all phases of the procedure, namely the rights of the suspects, the accused, the victims and the witnesses, and consequently that the Preparatory Committee should intensify its efforts to establish a consensus on the question of victim compensation."[72] Following the Declaration, Amnesty International additionally proposed a way in which the assets of convicted persons could be used for the purposes of reparations: "Any money or other property confiscated from convicted persons should go to victims or their families directly as reparations or, when they cannot be identified, to a general fund for the benefit of all victims."[73]

---

[69] 'Preparatory committee on establishment of International Criminal Court concludes work by adopting draft Statute' (19980403) press release L/2864 3 April 1998.

[70] 'Preparatory committee on establishment of International Criminal Court concludes work by adopting draft Statute' (19980403) press release L/2864 3 April 1998.

[71] Dakar Declaration for the establishment of an International Criminal Court, 6 February 1998.

[72] Dakar Declaration for the establishment of an International Criminal Court, 6 February 1998.

[73] Amnesty International "The international criminal court: Making the right choices - Part IV", IOR 40/04/98 March 1998.

3.1.2.4 Rome Diplomatic Conference, June–July 1998

Article 75, "reparations to victims", is the successful outcome of the cooperation between single state parties, predominantly France, the UK and several NGOs. Despite the differences in their legal systems, France and the UK formed a strong alliance for the right to reparation.[74] During the negotiations for the enactment of the Rome Statute, other delegations disagreed on that right for fear that "addressing and defining reparations would be too complex for a criminal court with members from such different legal traditions and that implementation would be particularly problematic in states that do not have reparations proceedings in their domestic legislation."[75]

Secondly, some delegations were afraid that the Court could award reparations against states. Others thought that a right to reparation would shift the Court's main responsibilities in prosecuting and punishing. Hereby, it was argued that the Court would already recognise victims.[76] Article 75 on "reparations to victims" was finally adopted on 13 July 1998. For the first time in the history of international criminal justice, a criminal court provided the right to reparation for victims. The procedure for reparations to victims was later defined in Rules 94 to 99 RPE. Reparations would be granted upon request or upon a motion of the Court.[77] The Court was thus able to consider the victims, the convicted persons and their defence lawyers at reparation hearings. In addition, interested persons and interested state parties could also be affected by the rulings.

Article 79 describes the establishment of a Trust Fund by the Assembly of States Parties. Even though the Trust Fund is mentioned in the Rome Statute, it was seen as an independent institution of the Court. Both Article 75 and 79 improved not only the legal status of victims at the international level, but also resulted in a higher recognition within the international criminal justice system. During the negotiations, supporters and opponents balanced the victims' rights, on the one hand, and the rights of the defendants on the other. The biggest opponents of the Court—India, China, Pakistan, Israel, the Arab States and the United States—were, of course, also not in favour of victims' rights. In fact, only a small number of governments supported the inclusion of victims' rights into the Rome Statute at all.

The resultant article that provides for the reparation mandate for the ICC within the RS is as follows:

> Article 75 Reparations to victims
>
> 1) The Court shall establish principles relating to reparations to, or in respect of, victims, including restitution, compensation and rehabilitation. On this basis, in its decision the Court may, either upon request or on its own motion in exceptional circumstances, determine the scope and extent of any damage, loss and injury to, or in respect of, victims and will state the principles on which it is acting.

---

[74] Bottigliero (2004), pp. 213 et seq.

[75] Bottigliero (2004), p. 213.

[76] Muttukumaru (2002), pp. 262–270.

[77] ICC, Rules of Procedure and Evidence, 2013, Rule 94–99.

2) The Court may make an order directly against a convicted person specifying appropriate reparations to, or in respect of, victims, including restitution, compensation and rehabilitation. Where appropriate, the Court may order that the award for reparations be made through the Trust Fund provided for in Article 79.
3) Before making an order under this article, the Court may invite and shall take account of representations from or on behalf of the convicted person, victims, other interested persons or interested States.
4) In exercising its power under this Article, the Court may, after a person is convicted of a crime within the jurisdiction of the Court, determine whether, in order to give effect to an order which it may make under this article, it is necessary to seek measures under Article 93 (1).
5) A State Party shall give effect to a decision under this article as if the provisions of Article 109 were applicable to this article.
6) Nothing in this article shall be interpreted as prejudicing the rights of victims under national or international law.

3.2 ICC Procedural History in Relation to Victims' Participation

In order to understand the decisions related to victims and the established jurisprudence for victims' participation, a closer look at the background of the judges is relevant. As mentioned above, there are differences in national legislation regarding victims' participation in criminal procedures. This information concerning victims considers, in alphabetic order, the number of victims who have participated in the proceedings at the ICC (Number of victims: Stand December 2020).

3.2.1 Afghanistan

Conflict Background

After the attacks on 11 September 2001 in Washington D.C. and New York City, the U.S. authorities led a coalition against the Taliban government and Al-Qaeda and launched military operations in Afghanistan in October 2001. In December 2001, the Agreement on Provisional Arrangements in Afghanistan Pending the Re-Establishment of Permanent Government Institutions, otherwise known as the Bonn Agreement, was signed and resulted in the establishment of an interim government for a 6-month period. However, the security situation continued to deteriorate parallel to the establishment of the governing institutions.[78] On 20 November 2017, the OTP requested that the Court authorise an investigation *propriu motu* in the Islamic Republic of Afghanistan in relation to crimes committed

[78]ICC, *Situation in the Islamic Republic of Afghanistan*, ICC-02/17-7-Red, Public redacted version of "Request for authorisation of an investigation pursuant to Article 15", 20 November 2017, ICC-02/17-7-Conf-Exp (20 November 2017) paras. 16–18.

by members of the Taliban and its affiliated groups, members of the ANSF, members of the US armed forces and of the CIA and members of international armed forces since 1 May 2003.[79] The request by the OTP also related to the crimes that took place in the context of the armed conflict in Afghanistan since 1 July 2002 in Poland and Romania, as well as since 1 August 2002 in Lithuania.

Victims of the Conflict

On 9 November 2017, the Chamber extended the time limit from the 30-day deadline pursuant to Regulation 50 (1) RoC ICC for the submission of representations to 31 January 2018.[80] By 9 February 2018, 699 transmitted representations—165 individual and 534 collective ones—had been transferred to the Chamber, which included representations for over 10 million victims (approximately one third of the entire population of Afghanistan). It should be noted that if there had been a longer time limit, the number of victims represented would have been considerably higher.[81] Accordingly, it is almost impossible to assess the precise number of potential victims.

Situation in Afghanistan		
Chamber	PTC III	Antoine Kesia-Mbe Mindua (DRC) Chang-ho Chung (South Korea) Raul C. Pangalangan (Philippines)
Crimes		Imprisonment, persecution, murder, torture, outrages upon personal dignity, intentionally directing attacks against protected objects and civilians, entlisting children, sexual violence
Victims representations according to Article 15 (3) RS	Men	146 (165 individual representations)
	Women	10 (165)
	Children	9 (165)
	Organisation	–
	Total	6385 (individual victims) 1.163.950 and 26 villages (12 collective representations) and 7 to 9 million victims (1 collective representation)
	Victim representation	699
Harm		Economic, mental, physical
Demands/wishes		Security issues

[79] The date the Rome Statute entered into force for Afghanistan.

[80] ICC, *Situation in the Islamic Republic of Afghanistan*, ICC-01/17, Public redacted version of "Registry's Request for Extention of Notice Period and Submissions on Aspects Related to the Article 15(3) Process" (7 November 2017) paras. 13–14, ICC, *Situation in the Islamic Republic of Afghanistan*, ICC-02/17, Order to the Victims Participation and Reparation Section Concerning Victims' Representations (9 November 2017) para. 12.

[81] ICC, *Situation in the Islamic Republic of Afghanistan*, ICC-02/17, Final Consolidated Registry Report on Victims' Representations Pursuant to the PTC's Order ICC-02/17-6 of 9 November 2017 (20 February 2018) para. 29.

On 12 April 2019, the investigation into the Islamic Republic of Afghanistan was rejected by the ICC's PTC II as it would not serve the interests of justice.[82] On 5 March 2020 the Appeals Chamber amended the decision of the PTC II and authorised the Prosecutor to commence investigations.[83]

3.2.2 *Georgia*

Conflict Background

In 2008, a war broke out between Georgia and Russia. The roots of the conflict were a result of the dismantling of the Soviet Union. Shortly after the independence of Georgia in 1991, the autonomous region of South Ossetia declared its independence from Georgia on 29 May 1992.[84] The armed conflict ended with the signing of the Sochi Agreement and by making South Ossetia a semi-autonomous area governed by a *de facto* government which was not recognised by the Georgian authorities.[85] In 2008, the tensions between South Ossetia and Georgia began to escalate and reached the status of an active internal armed conflict. Shortly thereafter, as soon as Russia became involved, the internal armed conflict became an international armed conflict causing significant civil casualties and destruction.[86] On 15 and 16 August 2008, a ceasefire agreement was signed between Georgia and Russia.[87] On 27 January 2016, PTC I authorised the request of Prosecutors *proprio motu* to proceed with an investigation of crimes under the jurisdiction of the Court, committed in and around South Ossetia, Georgia between 1 July and 10 October 2008.

Victims of the Conflict

After the 30-day deadline for the submissions for victimhood, the VPRS received representations from 6335 victims in accordance with Article 15 (3)[88] RS and Rule

[82]ICC, *Situation in the Islamic Republic of Afghanistan*, ICC-02/17, Decision Pursuant to Article 15 of the Rome Statute on the Authorisation of an Investigation into the Situation in the Islamic Republic of Afghanistan (12 April 2019).

[83]ICC, *Situation in the Islamic Republic of Afghanistan*, ICC-02/17OA4, Judgment on the appeal againstthe decision on the authorisation of an investigation into the situation in the Islamic Republic ofAfghanistan (5 March 2020).

[84]Potier (2001), pp. 13–14; Companjen and Polese (2012), pp. 88–89.

[85]ICC, *Situation in Georgia*, ICC-01/15, Request for authorisation of an investigation pursuant to Article 15 (13 October 2015) paras. 22–23.

[86]Leach (2012), pp. 328–329, ICC, *Situation in Georgia*, ICC-01/15, Decision on the Prosecutor's request for authorisation of an investigation (27 January 2016) paras. 12–13, 22–24.

[87]Ian Traynor, Luke Harding, Helen Womack, Georgia and Russia declare ceasefire, The Guardian, 16 August 2008, https://www.theguardian.com/world/2008/aug/16/georgia.russia2, visited on 12 December 2020.

[88]The victims are not the participants but important source of information at the stage of preliminary examination, see Bergsmo et al. (2016), p. 735.

50 (1) RPE.[89] The information given by the victims played a significant role in authorising the Prosecutor to start the investigations. According to the report of the Registry,[90] significant efforts were required to assist victims in understanding the nature and purpose of their representations, which were only for purposes of information at this point in time and were not a guarantee for the future participation or reparation during the proceedings.[91]

Situation in Georgia		
Chamber	PTC I	Judge Joyce Aluoch (Kenya) Judge Cuno Tarfusser (Italy) Péter Kovács (Hungary)
Crimes		Destruction of the property, forcible transfer, murder, pillage applications of enforced disappearance, deprivation of liberty, other inhuman acts, mutilation, outrages upon personal dignity, torture, rape, crimes against members of armed forces
Victims representations according to Article 15 (3) RS	Rejected representations[a]	95
	Men	3141
	Women	3169
	Children	24
	Organisation	1
	Total	6335
	Victim representation	69
Harm		Economic, mental, physical
Demands/wishes		Punishment for those found guilty of crimes, reparations from persons convicted, uncover the truth, arrest of suspects

[a]Not in accordance with Rule 85 RPE of ICC

There is still no case and there have been no further developments in the case of Georgia.

[89]See ICC, *Situation in Georgia*, ICC-01/15, Report on the Victims' Representations Received Pursuant to Article15(3) of the Rome Statute, (4 December 2015).

[90]See ICC, *Situation in Georgia*, ICC-01/15, Report on the Victims' Representations Received Pursuant to Article15(3) of the Rome Statute, (4 December 2015) para. 4.

[91]Cf. ICC, *Situation in the Republic of Cote D'Ivoire*, ICC-02/11, Report on Victims' Representations (29 August 2011) para. 94.

3.2.3 Central African Republic (CAR)

3.2.3.1 Background

The situation in the Central African Republic is related to the former accused DRC politician, Jean-Pierre Bemba Gombo, who was accused of being responsible as the superior for different crimes committed by his subordinates in the conflict in the CAR. The ICC's investigation focused on alleged war crimes and crimes against humanity which had occurred since 1 July 2002. The case was based on the referral of the government of the CAR on 22 December 2004 pursuant to Article 14 RS. On 23 May 2008, and then on 10 June 2008, a replacing arrest warrant was issued against Mr. Bemba accusing him of rape, torture, pillage and outrage upon personal dignity.[92] On 15 June 2009, the PTC confirmed that Mr. Bemba was criminally responsible within the meaning of Article 28 (a) RS for the charges of murder and rape as war crimes and crimes against humanity and pillaging as a war crime.[93] On 21 March 2016, the Trial Chamber found Mr. Bemba guilty of the charges.[94] With the Appeals Chamber's decision of June 8 2018, Mr. Bemba was, however, acquitted of the charges. In 2014, CAR referred to the situation on its territory since August 1, 2012 (CAR II) in connection with the conflict between Muslim Séléka and Christian anti-balaka groups.[95] In this context, the former militia leaders Alfred Yekatom and Patrice-Edouard Ngaïssona were extradited to The Hague in 2018. On 11 December 2019, PTC partially confirmed the charges of war crimes and crimes against humanity against them.[96]

Situation in the CAR
Case: Jean-Pierre Bemba Gombo

Crimes:		War Crime: murder, rape, pillage Crimes against humanity: murder, rape	
PTC III Ekaterina Trendafilova (BU) Hans-Peter Kaul (GE) Cuno Tarfusser (IT)	Recognised victims	Rejected	3
		Men	30
		Women	25
		Children	–

(continued)

[92] ICC, *Prosecutor v. Bemba*, ICC-01/05-01/08, Warrant of Arrest for Jean-Pier Bemba Gombo replacing the Warrant of Arrest issued on 23 May 2008 (10 June 2008).

[93] ICC, *Prosecutor v. Bemba*, ICC-01/05-01/08, Decision Pursuant to Article 61 (7) (a) and (b) of the Rome Statute on the Charges of the Prosecutor Against Jean-Pierre Bemba Gombo (15 June 2009).

[94] ICC, *Prosecutor v. Bemba*, ICC-01/05-01/08, Judgment pursuant to Article 74 of the Statute (21 March 2018).

[95] ICC, *Situation in the Central African Republic II*, ICC-01/14, Public, with public annex Decision Assigning the Situation in the Central African Republic II to Pre-Trial Chamber II (18 June 2014).

[96] ICC, *Prosecutor v. Yekatom and Ngaïssona*, ICC-01/14-01/18-403-Red-CorrCorrected version of Public Redacted Version of 'Decision on the confirmation of charges against Alfred Yekatom and Patrice-Edouard Ngaïssona' (14 May 2020).

Situation in the CAR Case: Jean-Pierre Bemba Gombo			
		Organisation	–
		Total	55
		Victim representation as LRV and CLRV	CLRV
Trial Chamber III Sylvia Steiner (AR) Joyce Aluoch (KE) Kuniko Ozaki (JA)	Recognised victims	Rejected	471
		Men	2692[a]
		Women	2526
		Children	–
		Organisation	11
		Total	5229
		Victim representation as LRV and CLRV	LRV, OPCV
		Victims permitted to present views and concerns	3
Appeals Chamber Christine Van den Wyngaert (BE) Chile Eboe-Osujie (NGA) Sanji Mmasenono Monageng (BWA) Howard Morrison (UK) Piotr Hofmański (PO)	Recognised victims	Rejected	
		Men	2692
		Women	2526
		Children	–
		Organisation	11
		Total	5229[b]
		Victim representation as LRV and CLRV	LRV–OPCV

[a]ICC, *Prosecutor v. Bemba*, ICC-01/05-01/08, Decision on the participation of victims in the trial and on 86 applications by victims to participate in the proceedings (30 June 2010), ICC, *Prosecutor v. Bemba*, ICC-01/05-01/08, Decision on 653 applications by victims to participate in the proceedings (23 December 2010), ICC, *Prosecutor v. Bemba*, ICC-01/05-01/08, Decision on 401 applications by victims to participate in the proceedings and setting a final deadline for the submission of new victims' applications to the Registry (8 July 2011), ICC, *Prosecutor v. Bemba*, ICC-01/05-01/08, Decision on 270 Applications by Victims to participate in the Proceedings (25 October 2011), ICC, *Prosecutor v. Bemba*, ICC-01/05-01/08, Decision on 418 applications by victims to participate in the proceedings (15 December 2011), ICC, *Prosecutor v. Bemba*, ICC-01/05-01/08, Decision on 1400 applications by victims to participate in the proceedings (21 May 2012), ICC, *Prosecutor v. Bemba*, ICC-01/05-01/08, Decision on 799 applications by victims to participate in the proceedings (5 November 2012)
[b]ICC, *Prosecutor v. Bemba*, ICC-01/05-01/08 A2 A3, Decision on the participation of victims in the appeals against Trial Chamber III's "Decision on Sentence pursuant to Article 76 of the Statute" (1 September 2016)

Situation in the CAR II Case: Alfred Yekatom and Patrice-Edouard Ngaïssona	
Crimes:	War Crime: directing attacks against the civilian population, murder, displacement, directing an attack against a building dedicated to religion, cruel treatment, torture, conscription, enlistment and use of children under the age of 15 years to participate actively in hostilities, destruction of the adversary's property, rape, pillaging

(continued)

Situation in the CAR II Case: Alfred Yekatom and Patrice-Edouard Ngaïssona			
		Crimes against humanity: murder, forcible transfer and deportation, other inhumane acts, torture, imprisonment and other forms of severe deprivation of physical liberty, persecution, rape	
PTC II Antoine Kesia-Mbe Mindua (DRC) Tomoko Akane (JA) Rosario Salvatore Aitala (IT)	Recognised victims	Rejected	14
		Men	
		Women	
		Children	
		Organisation	
		Total	1085
		Victim representation as LRV and CLRV	2 CLRV for former child soldiers and for victims of other crimes[a]
Trial Chamber III Bertram Schmitt (GE) Péter Kovács (HU) Chang-ho Chung (SK)	Recognised victims	Rejected	12
		Men	
		Women	
		Children	
		Organisation	
		Total	1186+[b]
		Victim representation as LRV and CLRV	2 CLRV for former child soldiers and for victims of other crimes

[a]ICC, *Prosecutor v. Yekatom and Ngaïssona*, ICC-01/14-01/18-205, Decision on the Legal Representation of Victims (23 May 2019), ICC, *Prosecutor v. Yekatom and Ngaïssona*, ICC-01/14-01/18-227-Red Decision regarding the Registry's First Assessment Report on Applications for Victim Participation, the Registry's First Transmission of Group C Applications, the appointment of counsel for Victims of Other Crimes, and the victims' procedural position (23 November 2020)
[b]ICC, *Prosecutor v. Yekatom and Ngaïssona,* ICC-01/14-01/18-765, Second Decision on Victims' Participationin Trial Proceedings (Group A) (11 December 2020)

3.2.4 Côte d'Ivore

Conflict Background

The aftermath of the post-election violence in Côte d'Ivore in December 2010 led to mass crimes throughout the country. This resulted in the intervention of the international community, which backed the elected president of Côte d'Ivore, Alassane Ouattara, and the arrest of his opponent, Laurent Gbagbo, on 11 April 2011.[97] On 23 June 2011, the Prosecutor requested that the Chamber authorise an investigation into the situation in the Republic of Côte d'Ivore from 28 November 2010 pursuant to Article 15 RS. On 3 October 2011, PTC III authorised the request of the

[97]See ICC, *Situation in the Republic of Cote d'Ivore*, ICC-02/11, Request of authorisation of an investigation pursuant to Article 15 (23 June 2011) paras. 10–15.

Prosecutor in respect to future potential crimes.[98] On 22 February 2012, PTC III decided to expand its authorisation for the investigation in Côte d'Ivoire to include crimes within the jurisdiction of the Court allegedly committed between 19 September 2002 and 28 November 2010.

Victims of the Conflict

The 30-day deadline in accordance with Regulation 50 (1) RoC ICC was extended until 29 August 2011 upon a request of the VPRS on 28 July 2011.[99] In its report, the Registry noted the high interest among citizens of the Republic and considered that submissions of the representations were delivered in a very short timeframe.[100]

Situation in Côte d'Ivore		
Chamber	PTC III	Silvia Fernandez de Gurmendi (AR) Elizabeth Odio Benito (Costa Rica) Adrian Fulford (UK)
Crimes		Murder, rape, other inhumane acts, attempted murder, and persecution
Victims representations according to Article 15 (3) RS	Rejected representations	359
	Men	423 (655 individual)
	Women	179 (655)
	Children	–
	Organisation	–
	Total	1481
	Victim representation	679 (655 individual and 26 collective, representing 826 persons)
Harm		Economic, mental, physical
Demands/wishes		To punish the perpetrators, justice to be done, justice will bring them compensation

[98]ICC, *Situation in the Republic of Cote d'Ivore*, ICC-02/11, Corrigendum to "Decision Pursuant to Article 15 of the Rome Statute on the Authorisation of an Investigation into the Situation in the Republic of Côted'Ivoire", (15 November 2011) paras. 179, 212.

[99]ICC, *Situation in the Republic of Cote d'Ivore*, ICC-02/11, Decision on the VPRS request for an extension of time to report on victims' representations pursuant to Regulation 35 of the Regulations of the Court (28, July 2011) para. 6.

[100]ICC, *Situation in the Republic of Côte d'Ivore*, ICC-02/11, Report on Victims' Representations (29 August 2011) para. 72.

3.2.4.1 Laurent Gbagbo and Blé Goudé

On 23 November 2011, the PTC issued a warrant for the arrest of Laurent Gbagbo.[101] On 12 June 2014, the charges against Mr. Ggabgo[102] were confirmed and on 11 March 2015 the Trial Chamber joined the cases of Mr. Gbagbo and Mr. Blé Goudé. On 15 January 2019, Trial Chamber I, acquitted Mr Gbagbo and Mr Blé Goudé of all charges.

Situation in Côte d'Ivore **Case: Laurent Gbagbo**			
PTC III Silvia Fernandez de Gurmendi (AR) Elizabeth Odio Benito (Costa Rica) Adrian Fulford (UK)	Recognised victims	Rejected	+38
		Men	205[a]
		Women	264
		Children	–
		Organisation	–
		Total	469
		Victim representation as LRV and CLRV	CLRV–OPCV
Situation in Côte d'Ivore **Case: Blé Goudé**			
PTC III Silvia Fernandez de Gurmendi (AR) Elizabeth Odio Benito (Costa Rica) Adrian Fulford (UK)	Recognised victims	Rejected	–
		Men	205[b]
		Women	264
		Children	
		Organisation	0
		Total	469
		Victim representation as LRV and CLRV	CLRV–OPCV
Situation in Côte d'Ivore **Case: Laurent Gbagbo and Blé Goudé**			
Crimes		Crimes against humanity: murder, rape, and other inhumane acts, attempted murder and persecution.	
Trial Chamber I Cuno Tarfusser (IT) Olga Herrera Carbuccia (Dom. Republic) Geoffrey Henderson (Trinidad &Tobago)	Recognised victims	Rejected	91
		Men	332
		Women	393
		Children	
		Organisation	1

(continued)

[101] ICC, *Situation in the Republic of Côte d'Ivore*, ICC-02/11, Warrant of Arrest for Laurent Koudou Gbagbo (23 November 2011).

[102] ICC, *Prosecutor v. Gbagbo*, ICC-02/11-01/11, Decision on the confirmation of charges against Laurent Gbagbo (12 June 2014).

		Total	726[c]
		Victim representation as LRV and CLRV	CLRV–OPCV, LRVs

[a]See ICC, *Prosecutor v. Gbagbo*, ICC-02/11-01/11-138, Decision on victims' participation and victims' common legal representation at the Confirmation of Charges Hearing and in the Related Proceedings (4 June 2012) 139 victims, ICC, *Prosecutor v. Gbagbo*, ICC-02/11-01/11-384-Corr, Corrigendum to the second decision on victims' participation at the confirmation of charges hearing and in the related proceedings (6 February 2013) 60 victims
[b]See, ICC, *Prosecutor v. Ble Goude*, ICC-02/11-02/11, Decision on victims' participation in the pre-trial proceedings and related issues (11 July 2014) 199 victims ICC, *Prosecutor v. Ble Goude*, ICC-02/11-02/11, Second Decision on victims' participation in the pre-trial proceedings and related issues (1 August 2014) 271 victims
[c]ICC, *Prosecutor v. Gbagbo*, ICC-02/11-01/11, Decision on victim participation (6 March 2015), ICC, *Prosecutor v. Gbagbo, Goude*, ICC-02/11-01/15, Decision on victims' participation status (7 January 2016)

3.2.4.2 Simone Gbagbo

On 29 February 2012, the warrant for arrest was issued against Simone Gbagbo. Simone Gbagbo has not surrendered to the ICC to date (December 2020).

3.2.5 Democratic Republic of the Congo (DRC)

Conflict Background

In March 2004, the government of the DRC made a referral to the Prosecutor in accordance with Article 14 RS to investigate the ongoing conflict in the territory of the DRC. The roots of the conflict in the DRC are related to the Rwandan Genocide and the First and Second Congolese wars. On 21 June 2004, the OTP opened an investigation, focusing on crimes which had been committed in the Ituri and Kivu regions since 1 July 2002. The economic dispute in the Ituri region evolved into the ethnic conflict between two ethnic groups fuelled by their desire to control the region's rich mineral resources.[103] South of Ituri in the Kivu region, the "genocidaries", along with former Hutu Power government figures who had fled from Rwanda to the DRC, organised themselves as the FDLR (*Forces Démocratiques de Libération du Rwanda*)[104] and began to oppose the new

[103]Kambale and Rotman (2004), p. 3.

[104]See Justice in the Democratic Republic of Congo: A background, Following the commencement of the second trial at the ICC concerning the situation in the DRC, the Hague Justice Portal looks at the background to the country's troubled history, 17 December 2009, http://www.haguejusticeportal.net/index.php?id=11284, Autesserre (2006), p. 7; Moffett (2014), p. 240, see

government in Rwanda. To date, six arrest warrants have been issued in relation to the Ituri and Kivu conflicts.

Victims of the Conflict

On 14 June 2005, the Registry registered six victims represented by legal representative for the victims. In response to that, the PTC of the ICC issued a decision on 17 January 2006, raising the question as to whether the victims may participate during the investigation stage and afforded six applicants the status of victim.[105] On 31 July 2006, the PTC granted a further three applicants victim status, whilst the Prosecutor's and OPCD's appeal on the PTC's decision was pending.[106] Until the appeal judgment on 19 December 2008, the PTC furnished further applicants with victim status.[107] On 19 December 2008, the Appeals Chamber reversed the decision of the PTC which had granted the victims victim status at the investigation stage.[108] Accordingly, all decisions granting the victims participatory rights at the investigation stage were reversed.

Situation in the DRC		
Chamber	PTC I	Cuno Tarfusser (IT) Sylvia Steiner (BR) Sanji Mmasenono Monageng (BWA)
Crimes		Enlisting and conscripting child soldiers, murder and attempted murder, willful

(continued)

also Human Rights Watch, Ituri, "Covered In Blood" Ethnically Targeted Violence In Northeastern DR Congo, July, 2003.

[105]ICC, *Siuation in the DRC*, ICC-01/04-101-tEN-Corr, Decision on the Applications for Participation in the Proceedings of VPRS 1 VPRS 2, VPRS 3, VPRS 4, VPRS 5 and VPRS, 5 (17 January 2006) paras. 28–46.

[106]ICC, *Prosecutor v. Lubanga*, ICC-01/04-01/06-228-tEN, Decision on the Applications for Participation in the Proceedings of a/0001/06, a/0002/06 and a/0003/06 in the case of the Prosecutor v. Thomas Lubanga Dyilo and of the investigation in the Democratic Republic of the Congo (28 July 2006), see also ICC, *Situation in the DRC*, ICC-01/04-103, Prosecution's Application for Leave to Appeal PTC I's Decision on the Applications for Participation in the Proceedings of VPRS 1, VPRS 2, VPRS 3, VPRS 4, VPRS 5 and VPRS 6, ICC-01/04, 23 January 2006 (23 January 2006).

[107]ICC, *Situation in the DRC*, ICC-01/04, Décision sur les demandes de participation à la procédure déposées dans le cadre del'enquête en République démocratique du Congo par a/0004/06 à a/0009/06, a/0016/06à a/0063/06, a/0071/06 à a/0080/06 et a/0105/06 à a/0110/06, a/0188/06, a/0128/06 à a/0162/06, a/0199/06, a/0203/06, a/0209/06, a/0214/06, a/0220/06 à a/0222/06, a/0224/06,a/0227/06 à a/0230/06, a/0234/06 à a/0236/06, a/0240/06, a/0225/06, a/0226/06, a/0231/06 à a/0233/06, a/0237/06 à a/0239/06 et a/0241/06 à a/0250/06 (24 December 2007), ICC, *Situation in DRC*, ICC-01/04-505, Decision on the applications for participation filed in connection with the investigation in the Democratic Republic of Congo by Applicants a/0047/06 to a/0052/06, a/0163/06 to a/0187/06, a/0221/06, a/0225/06, a/0226/06, a/0231/06 to a/0233/06 (4 July 2008).

[108]See ICC, *Situation in the DRC*, ICC-01/04-556, Appeals Judgment on victim participation in the investigation stage of the proceedings in the appeal of the OPCD against the decision of PTC I of 7 December 2007 and in the appeals of the OPCD and the Prosecutor against the decision of PTC I of 24 December 2007 (19 December 2008).

Situation in the DRC		
		killing, attacking civilians, rape; sexual slavery of civilians, pillaging, displacing civilians, attacking protected objects, destroying property, rape, sexual slavery, mutilation, cruel treatment, torture, destruction of property, pillaging
Recognised victims before the appeals judgement of 19 December 2008	Rejected	16+
	Men	88
	Women	46
	Children	–
	Organisation	1
	Total	132[a]
	Victim representation	12 LRV, OPCV
Harm		Economic, mental, physical
Demands/wishes		Justice and reparation

[a]The gender of 13 victims was unknown

3.2.5.1 Thomas Lubanga Dylio

On 10 February 2003, the arrest warrant was issued against Mr. Lubanga and on 29 January 2007, the PTC confirmed the charges against him.[109] On 14 March 2012, the Trial Chamber found Mr. Lubanga guilty as a co-perpetrator of war crimes, of conscripting and enlisting children under the age of fifteen and of using them to participate actively in hostilities.[110] On 1 December 2014, the Appeals Chamber confirmed the decision, sentencing Mr. Lubanga to 14 years' imprisonment.

Situation in the DRC Case: Thomas Lubanga Dylio			
Crimes	War crimes: conscripting, enlisting, and using child soldiers		
PTC I Claude Jorde (FR) Akua Kuenyehia (JA) Sylvia Steiner (BR)	Recognised victims	Rejected	–
		Men	6
		Women	1
		Children	–
		Organisation	0
		Total	**7**[a]

(continued)

[109]ICC, *Prosecutor v. Lubanga*, ICC-01/04-01/06, Decision on Confirmation of Charges (29 January 2007).

[110]ICC, *Prosecutor v. Lubanga*, ICC-01/04-01/06, Judgment pursuant to Article 74 of the Statute (14 March 2012).

Situation in the DRC Case: Thomas Lubanga Dylio			
		Victim representation as LRV and CLRV	2
Trial Chamber I Adrian Fulford (UK) Elizabeth Odio Benito (Costa R) René Blattmann (Bolivia)	Recognised victims	Rejected	60+
		Men	87
		Women	33
		Children	–
		Organisation	–
		Total	120[b]
		Victim representation as LRV and CLRV	5 LRV + OPCV
Appeals Chamber Erkki Kourula (FI) Sang-Hyun Song (KO) Sanji Mmasenono Monageng (BWA) Anita Ušacka (LA) Ekaterina Trendafilova (BU)	Recognised victims	Rejected	–
		Men	94
		Women	57
		Children	–
		Organisation	0
		Total	151
		Victim representation as LRV and CLRV	5 LRV
		Victims permitted to present views and concerns	3
Reparation Trial Chamber II Marc Perrin de Brichambaut (FR) Olga Herrera Carbuccia (Dom R.) Péter Kovács (HU)	Recognised victims	Rejected	–
		Men	343
		Women	82
		Children	–
		Organisation	–
		Total	425
		Victim representation as LRV and CLRV	

[a]*Prosecutor v. Lubanga* (n 404), ICC, *Prosecutor v. Lubanga*, ICC-01/04-01/06, Decision on applications for participation in proceedings a/0004/06 to a/0009/06, a/0016/06, a/0063/06, a/0071/06 to a/0080/06 and a/0105/06 in the case of The Prosecutor v.Thomas Lubanga Dyilo (20 October 2006)

[b]*Prosecutor v. Lubanga* (n 409), ICC, *Prosecuto v. Lubanga*, ICC-01/04-01/06, Decision on the applications by 7 victims to participate in the proceedings (10 July 2009), ICC, *Prosecutor v. Lubanga*, ICC-01/04-01/07, Decision on the applications by 2 victims to participate in the proceedings (10 September 2009), ICC, *Prosecutor v. Lubanga,* ICC-01/04-01/06, Redacted version of the Corrigendum of Decision on the applications by 15victims to participate in the proceedings (8 February 2011), ICC, *Prosecutor v. Lubanga*, ICC-01/04-01/06, Redacted version of the Decision on the applications by 7 victims to participate inthe proceedings (25 July 2011)

3.2.5.2 Germain Katanga

On 2 July 2007, the PTC issued the arrest warrant against Mr. Katanga, considering there to be reasonable grounds to believe that he had committed crimes against humanity and war crimes.[111] On 10 March 2008, the PTC merged the cases of Katanga and Chui and on 26 September 2008 confirmed the charges against them.[112] On 21 November 2012, the Trial Chamber severed the charges against Mr. Chui and on 18 December 2012 he was acquitted. On 7 March 2014, Mr. Katanga was found guilty of the charges.[113]

Situation in the DRC
Case: Germain Katanga

Crimes	Crimes against humanity: murder, rape War crimes: murder, rape, pillage, attack against civil population, conscripting, enlisting, and using child soldiers, destruction of enemy property		
PTC II Akua Kuenyehia (JA) Anita Usacka (LI) Sylvia Steiner (BR)	Recognised victims	Rejected	47
		Men	48
		Women	9
		Children	–
		Organisation	1
		Total	58[a]
		Victim representation as LRV and CLRV	3 LRV
Trial Chamber II Bruno Cotte (FR) Fatoumata Dembele Diarra (Mali) Christine Van den Wyngaert (BE)	Recognised victims	Rejected	12+
		Men	245
		Women	118
		Children	–
		Organisation	1
		Total	364[b]
		Victim representation as LRV and CLRV	2 LRV
Reparation Trial Chamber II Marc Perrin de Brichambaut (FR) Olga Herrera Carbuccia (Dom R.) Péter Kovács (HU)	Recognised victims	Rejected	–
		Men	203
		Women	94
		Children	–
		Organisation	–

(continued)

[111]ICC, *Prosecutor v. Katanga*, ICC-01/04-01/07, Warrant of Arrest (2 July 2007).

[112]ICC, *Prosecutor v. Katanga*, ICC-01/04-01/07, Warrant of Arrest (30 September 2008).

[113]ICC, *Prosecutor v. Katanga*, ICC-01/04-01/07, Judgment pursuant to Article 74 of the Statute (7 March 2014).

Situation in the DRC
Case: Germain Katanga

		Total	297
		Victim representation as LRV and CLRV	

[a]ICC, *Prosecutor v. Katanga*, ICC-01/04-01/07, Decision on the Applications for Participation in the Proceedings of Applicantsa/0327/07 to a/0337/07 and a/0001/08 (2 April 2008), ICC, *Prosecutor v. Katanga*, ICC-01/04-01/07-712, Public Redacted Version of the "Decision on the 97 Applications for Participationat the Pre-Trial Stage of the Case (10 June 2008)

[b]ICC, *Prosecutor v. Katanga*, ICC-01/04-01/07-1349, Dispositif de la décision relative aux 345 demandes de participationde victimes à la procedure (31 July 2009), ICC, *Prosecutor v. Katanga*, ICC-01/04-01/07-1349, Operative Part of the Second Decision on the Applications by Victims for Participation in the Proceedings (23 November 2009), ICC, *Prosecutor v. Katanga*, Fourth decision on two applications for victims' participation in the proceedings (8 November 2010)

3.2.5.3 Bosco Ntaganda

On 22 August 2006, the ICC issued a warrant for Bosco Ntaganda's arrest, considering there to be reasonable grounds to believe that Mr. Ntaganda had committed war crimes by enlistment, conscription and using children under the age of fifteen to participate actively in hostilities.[114] On 13 July 2012, the second arrest warrant was issued against Mr. Ntaganda considering that there were reasonable grounds to believe that Mr. Ntaganga committed murder, rape and persecution as crimes against humanity and murder, rape and attack against civilian population by way of pillage as war crimes.[115] On June 9 2014, the PTC confirmed the charges against Mr. Ntaganda.[116] Mr. Ntaganda was convicted on 8 July 2019 on counts of war crimes and crimes against humanity.

Situation in the DRC
Case: Bosco Ntaganda

Crimes	Crimes against humanity: murder, rape, persecution War crimes: murder, rape, pillage, attack against civil population, conscripting, enlisting, and using child soldiers		
PTC II Ekaterina Trendafilova (BU) Hans-Peter Kaul (GE) Cuno Tarfusser (IT)	Recognised victims	Rejected	52
		Men	701 (victims of attacks of child soldiers)
		Women	418

(continued)

[114]ICC, *Prosecutor v. Ntaganda*, ICC-01/04-02/06, Warrant of Arrest (22 August 2006).

[115]ICC, *Prosecutor v. Ntaganda*, ICC-01/04-02/06, Decision on the Prosecutor's Application under Article 58 (13 July 2012).

[116]ICC, *Prosecutor v. Ntaganda*, ICC-01/04-02/06, Decision Pursuant to Article 61(7)(a) and (b) of the Rome Statuteon the Charges of the Prosecutor Against Bosco Ntaganda (9 June 2014).

Situation in the DRC Case: Bosco Ntaganda			
		Children	140 (former child soldiers)
		Organisation	0
		Total	1119[a]
		Victim representation as LRV and CLRV	2 CLRV
Trial Chamber VI Robert Fremr (CzR) Kuniko Ozaki (JA) Chang-ho Chung (SK)	Recognised victims	Rejected	70+
		Men	1289 (victims of attacks of child soldiers)
		Women	840
		Children	285 (former child soldiers)
		Organisation	0
		Total	2129[b]
		Victim Representation as LRV and CLRV	2 CLRV
		Participating victims	6

[a]ICC, *Prosecutor v. Ntaganda*, ICC-01/04-02/06, Decision on Victims' Participation at the Confirmation of Charges Hearing and inthe Related Proceedings (15 January 2014), ICC, *Prosecutor v. Ntaganda*, ICC-01/04-02/06, Second Decision on Victims' Participation at the Confirmation of Charges Hearing and in the Related Proceedings (7 February 2014)

[b]ICC, *Prosecutor v. Ntaganda*, Decision on Prosecution requests relating to victims applications (30 January 2015), ICC, *Prosecutor v. Ntaganda*, ICC-01/04-02/06-650, Second decision on victims' participation in trial proceedings (16 June 2015), ICC, *Prosecutor v. Ntaganda*, ICC-01/04-02/06-449, Third decision on victims' participation in trial proceedings (2 July 2015), ICC, *Prosecutor v. Ntaganda*, Fourth decision on victims' participation in trial proceedings (1 September 2015), ICC, *Prosecutor v. Ntaganda*, ICC-01/04-02/06-449, Fifth decision on victims' participation in trial proceedings (16 November 2015) ICC, *Prosecutor v. Ntaganda*, ICC-01/04-02/06-449, Decision on victims' participation in trial proceedings (6 February 2015), ICC, *Prosecutor v. Ntaganda*, ICC-01/04-02/06-1427, Seventh decision on victims' participation in trial proceedings (1 July 2016), ICC, *Prosecutor v. Ntaganda*, ICC-01/04-02/06-1597, Eighth decision on victims' participation in trial proceedings (27 October 2016)

3.2.5.4 Callixte Mbarushimana

On 28 September 2010, the PTC issued the arrest warrant against Callixte Mbarushimana, considering there to be reasonable grounds to believe that Mr. Mbarushimana had committed crimes against humanity and war crimes.[117] On

[117]ICC, *Prosecutor v. Mbarisheima*, ICC-01/04-01/10-1, Decision on the Prosecutor's Application for a Warrant of Arrest (28 September 2010).

23 September 2011, the PTC did not confirm the charges and Mr. Mbarushimana was acquitted.

Situation in the DRC
Case: Callixte Mbarushimana

Crimes	Crimes against humanity: murder, rape, torture War crimes: murder, rape, pillage, attack against civil population, destruction of property		
PTC I Sanji Mmasenono (Botswana) Sylvia Steiner (BR) Cuno Tarfusser (IT)	Recognised victims	Rejected	4
		Men	47
		Women	85
		Children	–
		Organisation	–
		Total	132
		Victim representation as LRV and CLRV	OPCV

3.2.6 Kenya

Conflict Background
On 26 November 2009, the Office of the Prosecutor of the ICC requested authorisation for an investigation pursuant to Article 15 RS, in view of the violence that had erupted as a result of the presidential elections on 27 December 2007 which had enabled the ruling party to remain in power.[118] On 31 March 2010, the PTC authorised the request for the Prosecutor to investigate the alleged crimes committed between 1 June 2005 and 26 November 2009 in the territory of the Republic of Kenya.[119]

Victims of the Conflict
On 10 December 2009, the PTC ordered the VPRS to identify the community leaders of the affected groups and to receive the victims' representations pursuant to Article 15 (3) RS and to summarise them in a consolidated report.[120] In response to that, within the 30-day time limit, 406 representations were received by the VPRS. On 3 November 2010, the PTC issued a decision allowing the victims to participate

[118]ICC, *Situation in the Republic of Kenya*, ICC-01/09, Request for authorisation of an investigation pursuant to Article 15 (26 November 2009), paras. 4–6, due to the international mediation efforts a power-sharing agreement was signed between the government and the opposition.

[119]ICC, *Situation in the Republic of Kenya*, ICC-01/09-19, Decision Pursuant to Article 15 of the Rome Statute on the Authorisation of an Investigation into the Situation in the Republic of Kenya (31 March 2010).

[120]ICC, *Situation in the Republic of Kenya*, ICC-01/09-4, Order to the Victims Participation and Reparation Section concerning Victims' Representations Pursuant to Article 15 (3) of the Statute (10 December 2009) para. 9.

in proceedings related to the situation and ordered the VPRS to implement this decision in accordance with the established jurisprudence.[121] Up until 2016, 5807 applications for participation had been received by the VPRS.

Situation in the Republic of Kenya		
Chamber	PTC II	Ekaterina Trendafilova (BU) Hans-Peter Kaul (GE) Cuno Tarfusser (IT)
Crimes		Crimes against humanity: murder, deportation or forcible transfer of population, persecution, rape, and other inhumane acts
Victims representations according to Article 15 (3) RS	Rejected	10
	Men	192
	Women	128
	Children	–
	Organisation	–
	Total	396 (320 individual applications and 76 community applications)
	Victim representation	
Harm		Economic, mental, physical
Demands/wishes		If no steps are taken, then this conflict will not come to an end; to make sure it does not happen again; For the sake of justice

3.2.6.1 William Samoel Ruto, Joshua Arap Sang

On 15 December 2010, the OTP requested the appearance of the suspects accusing them of having committed murder, deportation, persecution and other inhuman acts as crimes against humanity. After the voluntary appearance of the suspects, the PTC confirmed the charges on 23 January 2012.[122] On 5 April 2016, the Trial Chamber decided to terminate the case against Mr. Ruto and Mr. Sang.[123] On 3 October 2012, the Trial Chamber decided to separate the victims into those who wanted to express their views individually and those who did not want to express them individually but rather through the common LRV. Accordingly, the victims not willing to directly

[121] ICC, *Situation in the Republic of Kenya*, ICC-01/09-24, Decision on Victims' Participation in Proceedings Related to the Situation in the Republic of Kenya (3 November 2010) paras. 18–23.

[122] ICC, *Prosecutor v. Ruto, Kosgey, Sang*, ICC-01/09-01/11, Decision on the Confirmation of Charges Pursuant to Article 61(7)(a) and (b) of the Rome Statute (23 January 2012).

[123] ICC, *Prosecutor v. Ruto, Sang*, ICC-01/09-01/11, Public redacted version of Decision on Defence Applications for Judgments of Acquittal (5 April 2016).

participate were not bound by Rule 89 RPE and they were only able to register with the Registry and give their names and contact details.[124]

Situation in the Republic of Kenya Case: Ruto & Sang			
Crimes		Crimes against humanity: murder, deportation or forcible transfer of population, persecution, rape, and other inhumane acts	
PTC II Ekaterina Trendafilova (BU) Hans-Peter Kaul (GE) Cuno Tarfusser (IT)	Recognised victims	Rejected	67
		Men	175
		Women	152
		Children	–
		Organisation	0
		Total	327[a]
		Victim representation as LRV and CLRV	1 CLRV
Trial Chamber V (A) Chile Eboe-Osuji (NI) Olga Herrera-Carbuccia (Dom.R) Robert Fremr (CzR)	Recognised victims	Rejected	
		Men	–
		Women	–
		Children	0
		Organisation	
		Total	628
		Victim representation as LRV and CLRV	1 CLRV

[a]ICC, *Prosecutor v. Ruto, Kosgey, Sang*, ICC-01/09-01/11, Decision on Victims' Participation at the Confirmation of Charges Hearing and inthe Related Proceedings (5 August 2011)

3.2.6.2 Uhuru Muigai Kenyatta

On 15 December 2010, the OTP requested the appearance of the suspects, accusing them of having committed murder, deportation, persecution and other inhuman acts as crimes against humanity. After the voluntary appearance of the suspects, the PTC confirmed the charges on 23 January 2012, however, on 5 December 2014, the Prosecutor withdrew the charges.

[124]ICC, *Prosecutor v. Ruto, Kosgey, Sang*, ICC-01/09-01/11-460, Decision on victims' representation and participation (3 October 2012) paras. 25–30.

Situation in the Republic of Kenya Case: Uhuru Muigai Kenyatta			
Crimes		Crimes against humanity: murder, deportation or forcible transfer of population, persecution, rape, and other inhumane acts	
PTC II Ekaterina Trendafilova (BU) Hans-Peter Kaul (GE) Cuno Tarfusser (IT)	Recognised victims	Rejected	16
		Men	98
		Women	135
		Children	–
		Organisation	0
		Total	233[a]
		Victim representation as LRV and CLRV	1 LRV–OPCV
Trial Chamber V Chile Eboe-Osuji (NI) Olga Herrera-Carbuccia (Dom.R) Robert Fremr (CzR)	Recognised victims	Rejected	–
		Men	378
		Women	461
		Children	0
		Organisation	0
		Total	839[b]
		Victim representation as LRV and CLRV	1 LRV–OPCV

[a]ICC, *Prosecutor v. Muthaura, Kenyatta, Ali,* ICC-01/09-01/11-249, Decision on Victims' Participation at the Confirmation of Charges Hearing and in the Related Proceedings (26 August 2011)
[b]ICC, *Prosecutor v. Muthuara, Kenyatta*, ICC-01/09-02/11, Decision on victims' representation and participation (3 October 2012), some victims were deceased

3.2.7 Mali

Conflict Background

Mali gained independence from France in 1960 and faced difficult times of instability until Alpha Oumar Konaré was elected President in 1992 in the first democratic election in Malian history. His successor, President Amadou Toumani Touré, was ousted on 21 March 2012 by mutinying soldiers dissatisfied with the handling of the Tuareg rebellion taking place in the Northern parts of the country.[125]

The rebellion in 2012 was only one in a series of many violent conflicts between the Malian government and the Tuareg people. The conflicts concerned the request of

[125]Mark Tran, Mali: a guide to the conflict, The Guardian, 16 January 2013, see below, https://www.theguardian.com/world/2013/jan/16/mali-guide-to-the-conflict#102, visited on 12 Decemer 2020.

the Tuareg people for the recognition of the Tuareg culture and their demand for an independent Berber state.[126]

Instability, war and civil war-like conditions existing in the aftermath of the rebellion and the coup d'état in Mali led to the intervention of foreign military powers. During the uprising, the deliberate damaging of shrines of Muslim saints in the city of Timbuktu occurred, as well as attacks on the military bases in Gao, Kidal and Timbuktu. Furthermore, executions of detainees and incidents of looting and rape occurred during the ensuing conflict.

On 18 July 2012, the Malian Government referred the situation in Mali from January 2012 to the ICC.[127] The Prosecutor alleged that there were reasonable grounds to believe that war crimes had been committed, including murder, mutilation, cruel treatment and torture as well as intentionally directing attacks against protected objects, the passing of sentences and the carrying out of executions without previous judgement pronounced by a regularly constituted court and pillaging.

3.2.7.1 Ahmad Al Faqi Al Mahdi

On 26 September 2015, Mr. Al Mahdi was surrendered to the ICC. On 1 March 2016, the charges against Mr. Al Mahdi were confirmed by the PTC[128] and on 27 September 2016, the Trial Chamber found Al Mahdi guilty of the charges.[129]

Situation in Mali Case: Ahmad Al Faqi Al Mahdi			
Crimes		War Crimes: Intentionally directing attacks against buildings dedicated to religion, education, art, science or charitable purposes, historic monuments	
PTC I Joyce Aluoch (KE) Cuno Tarfusser (IT) Péter Kovács (HU)	Recognised victims	Rejected	
		Men	–
		Women	
		Children	
		Organisation	
		Total	
		Victim representation as LRV and CLRV	

(continued)

[126] Alexander Göbel, Mali: Der lange Weg in die Krise, tagesschau.de, 1 November 2012, see below https://www.tagesschau.de/ausland/mali-hintergrund100.html, visited on 12 December 2020.

[127] ICC, *Situation in Mali*, Article 53(1) Report (16 January 2013) para. 2.

[128] ICC, *Prosecutor v. Al Mahdi*, ICC-01/12-01/15, Decision on the confirmation of charges against Ahmad Al Faqi Al Mahdi (24 March 2016).

[129] ICC, *Prosecutor v. Al Mahdi*, ICC-01/12-01/15, Judgement and Sentence (27 September 2016).

Situation in Mali Case: Ahmad Al Faqi Al Mahdi			
Trial Chamber VIII Raul C. Pangalangan (PH) Antoine Kesia-Mbe Mindua (DRC) Bertram Schmitt (GE)	Recognised victims	Rejected	–
		Men	8[a]
		Women	0
		Children	
		Organisation	0
		Total	8
		Victim representation as LRV and CLRV	1 LRV and OPCV
Reparation Trial Chamber VIII Raul C. Pangalangan (Philipinnes) Antoine Kesia-Mbe Mindua (DRC) Bertram Schmitt (GE)	Recognised victims	Rejected	
		Men	46
		Women	91
		Children	0
		Organisation	2
		Total	139

[a]ICC, *Prosecutor v. Al Mahdi*, ICC-01/12-01/15, Public redacted version of Decision on Victim Participation at Trial and on Common Legal Representation (8 June 2016) ICC, *Prosecutor v. Al Mahdi*, TC Public redacted version of 'Second Decision on Victim Participation at Trial', 12 August 2016, 12 August 2016

3.2.7.2 Al Hassan Ag Abdoul Aziz Ag Mohamed Ag Mahmoud

The warrant of arrest was issued against Mr. Al Hassan on 27 March 2018 considering there to be reasonable grounds to believe that Mr. Al Hassan had committed crimes against humanity including torture, rape, persecution, other inhuman acts and war crimes including violence to persons and outrages upon personal dignity, the passing of sentences without previous judgment pronounced by a regularly constituted court, intentionally directing attacks against buildings dedicated to religion and historic monuments, rape and sexual slavery.[130] On 31 March 2018, he was surrendered to the ICC. On 24 May 2018, the PTC issued a joint formal application process for the victims applying for participation.[131] On 30 September 2019, PTC confirmed the charges of war crimes and crimes against humanity.[132]

[130]ICC, *Prosecutor v. Al Hassan*, ICC-01/12-01/18, Warrant of Arrest for Al Hassan Ag Abdoul Aziz Ag Mohamed Ag Mahmoud (27 March 2018).

[131]ICC, *Prosecutor v. Al Hassan*, ICC-01/12-01/18, Decision Establishing the Principles Applicable to Victims' Applications for Participation (24 May 2018).

[132]ICC, *Prosecutor v. Al Hassan*, ICC-01/12-01/18-761-Corr-Red, Rectificatif à la Décision relative à la confirmation des charges portées contre Al Hassan Ag Abdoul Aziz Ag Mohamed Ag Mahmoud (13 November 2019).

Situation in Mali
Case: Al Hassan Ag Abdoul Aziz Ag Mohamed Ag Mahmoud

Crimes		Crimes against humanity: torture, rape and sexual slavery, persecution, other inhumane acts War crimes: torture, outrages upon personal dignity, passing of sentences without previous judgement by a regularly constituted court affording all judicial guarantees, intentionally directing attacks against buildings dedicated to religion and historic monuments, rape and sexual slavery	
PTC I Peter Kovacs (HU) Marc Perrin de Brichambaut (FR) Reine Adelaide Sophie Alapini-Gansou (Benin)	Recognised victims	Rejected	4
		Men	
		Women	
		Children	
		Organisation	
		Total	882[a]
		Victim representation as LRV and CLRV	LRVs
Trial Chamber X Antoine Kesia-Mbe Mindua (DRC) Tomoko Akane (JA) Kimberly Prost (KA)	Recognised victims	Rejected	47
		Men	
		Women	
		Children	
		Organisation	
		Total	1280+
		Victim representation as LRV and CLRV	LRVs

[a]ICC, *Prosecutor v. Al Hassan*, ICC-01/12-01/18-563-Anx-Red2, Public redacted version of "Annex to the Registry Report on the implementation of Trial Chamber X's Decision of 20 December 2019 (ICC-01/12-01/18-536)" (27 January 2020)

3.2.8 *Sudan*

Conflict Background

On 31 March 2005, the UNSC referred the situation in Sudan to the ICC in order to investigate the reports of human rights' violations in Darfur. The roots of the conflict were bound to the independence movement of the local tribes from the Khartoum government in the course of 2001 and 2002. The conflict in the Darfur region of Sudan emerged in early 2003 when rebel groups of the Sudan Liberation Army (SLA) and the Justice and Equality Movement (JEM) started to attack government targets in the region. The rebellion was based on the accusation that the government in Khartoum oppressed black Africans in favor of Arabs and due to the alleged marginalisation and underdevelopment of the region of Darfur.

The government mobilised militias following rebel attacks which allegedly killed non-Arab villagers in Darfur as a counter-insurgency campaign. The International Commission of Inquiry on Darfur was established by the former UN Secretary, Kofi Annan, pursuant to the UNSC Resolution 1564. In January 2005, the Commission reported that there was reason to believe that crimes against humanity and war crimes had been committed. On 31 March 2005, the UNSC referred the situation to the Prosecutor of the ICC in Resolution 1593. On 6 June 2005, the Prosecutor decided to open an investigation as all required statutory requirements had been satisfied. On 4 March 2009, the first warrant for the arrest of President Omar Al Bashir was issued on charges of war crimes and crimes against humanity in Dafur. The second warrant for arrest for President Al Bashir was issued on 12 July 2010 on the charge of genocide. Despite the arrest warrants, President Al Bashir still remains at large.

Victims of Conflict

Situation in Sudan		
Chamber	PTC II	Akua Kuenyehia (JA) Anita Usacka (LI) Sylvia Steiner (BR)
Crimes		Genocide: genocide by killing; genocide by causing serious bodily or mental harm; and genocide by deliberately inflicting on each target group conditions of life calculated to bring about the group's physical destruction; war crimes: murder; attacks against the civilian population; destruction of property; rape; pillaging; and outrage upon personal dignity; violence to life and person; intentionally directing attacks against personnel, installations, material, units or vehicles involved in a peacekeeping mission; and crimes against humanity: murder; persecution; forcible transfer of population; rape; inhumane acts; imprisonment or severe deprivation of liberty; torture; extermination; and torture.
Recognised victims	Rejected	10
	Men	8
	Women	3
	Children	0
	Organisation	0
	Total	11[a]
	Victim representation	2 LRV
Harm		Economic, mental, physical

[a]ICC, *Situation in Sudan*, ICC-02/05, Decision on the Applications for Participation in the Proceedings of Applicantsa/0011/06 to a/0015/06, a/0021/07, a/0023/07 to a/0033/07 and a/0035/07 to a/0038/07 (6 December 2007)

3.2.8.1 Ahmad Muhammad Harun and Ali Muhammad Ali Abd-Al-Rahman

On 27 April 2007, the arrest warrant for Mr. Harun and Mr. Kushayb was issued, considering the fact that there are reasonable grounds to believe that crimes against humanity and war crimes had been committed in Darfur, Sudan.[133] Ali Muhammad Ali Abd-Al-Rahman was transferred to the ICC's custody on 9 June 2020, after surrendering himself voluntarily in the Central African Republic.

Situation in Sudan Case: Ahmad Muhammad Harun and Ali Muhammad Ali Abd-Al-Rahman			
Crimes	Crimes against humanity: persecution, murder, forcible transfer, rape, inhuman acts, imprisonment or severe deprivation of liberty, torture War crimes: attacks against the civilian population, destruction of property, murder, pillage, rape		
PTC I Sanji Mmasenono (Botswana) Sylvia Steiner (BR) Cuno Tarfusser (IT)	Recognised victims	Rejected	
		Men	6
		Women	0
		Children	
		Organisation	0
		Total	6[a]
		Victim representation as LRV and CLRV	OPCV

[a]ICC, *Prosecutor v. Harun, Ali Kushayb*, ICC-02/05-01/07, Decision on 6 Applications for Victims' Participation in the Proceedings (17 June 2010), ICC, *Prosecutor v. Ali Muhammad Ali Abd-Al-Rahman* ("Ali Kushayb"), ICC-02/05-01/20-203, Registry Observations on Aspects Related to the Admission of Victims for Participation in Proceedings (17 November 2020)

3.2.8.2 Omar Al Bashir

On 4 March 2009, the PTC issued a warrant of arrest against the President of Sudan considering the Prosecution's application under Article 58 filed on 14 July 2009, considering the fact there were reasonable grounds to believe that in Darfur, Sudan war crimes and crimes against humanity had been committed. At the same time, the PTC dropped the charges on genocide. After the appeal on 3 February 2010, the PTC issued a new warrant of arrest on 12 July 2010 which also included charges of genocide.[134] The suspect is still at large.

---

[133]ICC, *Prosecutor v. Harun, Ali Kushayb*, ICC-02/05-01/07, warrant of arrest for Ahmad Harun (27 April 2007).

[134]ICC, *Prosecutor v. Al Bashir*, ICC-02/05-01/09, Second Decision on the Prosecution's Application for a Warrant of Arrest (12 July 2010).

Situation in Sudan Case: Omar Al Bashir			
Crimes	Crimes against humanity: persecution, murder, forcible transfer, rape, torture War crimes: attacks against the civilian population, destruction of property, murder, pillage Genocide: by killing, by causing serious bodily or mental harm, by deliberately inflicting conditions of life calculated to bring about physical destruction		
PTC I Sanji Mmasenono (Botswana) Sylvia Steiner (BR) Cuno Tarfusser (IT)	Recognised victims	Rejected	–
		Men	12
		Women	–
		Children	–
		Organisation	–
		Total	4[a]
		Victim representation as LRV and CLRV	1 LRV

[a]ICC, *Prosecutor v. Al Bashir*, ICC-02/05-01/09, Decision on Applications a/0011/06 to a/0013/06, a/0015/06 and a/0443/09 toa/0450/09 for Participation in the Proceedings at the Pre-Trial Stage of the Case (10 December 2009), ICC, *Prosecutor v. Al Bashir*, ICC-02/05-01/09, Victims' notification of withdrawal from the case against Omar Hassan Ahmed al-Bashir (19 November 2015)

3.2.8.3 Bahar Idriss Abu Garda

On 20 November 2008, the Prosecution requested the warrant of arrest for Mr. Abu Garda. On 7 May 2009, the PTC issued a summons for him to appear. On 30 October 2009, the PTC did not confirm the charges against Mr. Abu Garda.

Situation in Sudan Case: Bahar Idriss Abu Garda			
Crimes	War crimes: directing attacks against personnel, installations		
PTC I Sanji Mmasenono (Botswana) Sylvia Steiner (BR) Cuno Tarfusser (IT)	Recognised victims	Rejected	19
		Men	45
		Women	42
		Children	33
		Organisation	–
		Total	87[a]
		Victim representation as LRV and CLRV	4 LRV

[a]ICC, *Prosecutor v. Abu Garda*, ICC-02/05-02/09, Decision on the 34 Applications for Participation at the Pre-Trial Stage of the Case (25 September 2009), ICC, *Prosecutor v. Abu Garda*, ICC-02/05-02/09, Public Redacted Version of "Decision on the 52 Applicationsthe Pre-Trial Stage of the Case" for Participation (9 October 2009)

3.2.8.4 Abdallah Banda Abakaer Nourain

On 20 November 2008, the OTP requested a warrant of arrest for Mr. Banda, accusing him of having committed war crimes. The charges against Mr. Banda were confirmed on 7 March 2011.[135] The suspect is still at large.

Situation in Sudan Case: Abdallah Banda Abakaer Nourain			
Crimes	War crimes: murder, directing attacks against personnel, installations, pillaging		
PTC I Sanji Mmasenono (Botswana) Sylvia Steiner (BR) Cuno Tarfusser (IT)	Recognised victims	Rejected	11
		Men	47
		Women	42
		Children	33
		Organisation	0
		Total	89[a]
		Victim representation as LRV and CLRV	6 LRV 2 CLRV
Trial Chamber V Joyce Aluoch (KE), Chile Eboe-Osuji (NI) Silvia Fernandez de Gurmendi (AR)	Recognised victims	Rejected	–
		Men	54
		Women	49
		Children	35
		Organisation	0
		Total	103[b]
		Victim representation as LRV and CLRV	

[a]ICC, *Prosecutor v. Banda*, ICC-02/05-03/09, Decision on Victims' Participation at the Hearing on the Confirmation of the Charges (29 October 2010)
[b]ICC, *Prosecutor v. Banda*, ICC-02/05-03/09, Decision on 19 applications to participate in the proceedings (12 December 2013)

3.2.9 Uganda

Conflict Background

Between 2002 and 2004, the Lord Resistance Army (LRA), a group operating mainly in northern Uganda, carried out insurgencies against national authorities. The leader of the LRA is Joseph Kony, who claims to be God's messenger and aims to establish a theocratic state. The targets of the attacks were the government and its army, also known as the Uganda People's Defence Force, local defence units and civilian populations. Furthermore, the LRA is accused of having abducted and forcibly recruited civilians, including children, as fighters and sex slaves. On

[135]ICC, *Prosecutor v. Banda*, ICC-02/05-03/09, Corrigendum of the "Decision on the Confirmation of Charges" (7 March 2011).

16 December 2013, the Government of Uganda referred the situation concerning northern Uganda to the ICC and on 29 July 2004, the Prosecutor established a reasonable basis to be able to open an investigation thereupon.

The alleged crimes in this situation include the charges of war crimes and crimes against humanity. A warrant of arrest against the most senior members of the LRA was issued in 2005. After a decade without any successful arrest of a suspect, Dominic Ongwen surrendered himself in January 2015, however, other top members of the LRA, including Joseph Kony, remain at large.

Victims of Conflict

Situation in Uganda		
Chamber	PTC II	Mauro Politi (IT) Fatoumata Dembele Diarra (Mali) Ekaterina Trendafilovaa (BU)
Crimes		War crimes: murder; cruel treatment of civilians; intentionally directing an attack against a civilian population; pillaging; inducing rape; and forced enlistment of children; Crimes against humanity: murder; enslavement; sexual enslavement; rape; and inhumane acts of inflicting serious bodily injury and suffering
Recognised victims	Rejected	27+
	Men	15
	Women	6
	Children	
	Organisation	0
	Total	21[a]
	Victim representation	1 LRV, OPCV
Harm		Economical, mental, physical

[a]ICC, *Situation in Uganda*, ICC-02/04-01/05, Decision on victims' applications for participation a/0010/06, a/0064/06 to a/0070/06,a/0081/06 to a/0104/06 and a/0111/06 to a/0127/06 (7 March 2011), ICC, *Situation in Uganda*, ICC-02/04-01/05, Decision on victims' applications for participation a/0010/06, a/0064/06 to a/0070/06,a/0081/06, a/0082/06, a/0084/06 to a/0089/06, a/0091/06 to a/0097/06, a/0099/06,a/0100/06, a/0102/06 to a/0104/06, a/0111/06, a/0113/06 to a/0117/06, a/0120/06,a/0121/06 and a/0123/06 to a/0127/06 (14 March 2008)

3.2.9.1 Domonic Ongwen

On 6 May 2005, the OTP submitted a request for the warrants of arrest for Dominic Ongwen and four other individuals. The request was amended and supplemented on 13 May 2005 and 18 May 2005. On 8 July 2005, PTC II issued warrants of arrest under seal against the five individuals concerned for the commission of crimes against humanity and war crimes. It also requested the Republic of Uganda to search for and arrest the suspects and to surrender them to the Court.[136] On 21 January 2015, Dominic Ongwen surrendered and was transferred to the ICC.[137] He made his initial appearance before the single Judge of the PTC II on 26 January 2015. On 6 February 2015, the PTC II decided to separate the proceedings against Dominic Ongwen from the case of The Prosecutor v. Joseph Kony, Vincent Otti, Okot Odhiambo and Dominic Ongwen as the other suspects have not appeared before the Court or have not been apprehended yet. On 23 March 2016, The PTC II confirmed the charges against Dominic Ongwen.[138]

Situation in Uganda Case: Dominic Ongwen			
Crimes		Crimes against humanity: murder, enslavement, inhuman acts War crimes: treatment of civilians, intentionally directing an attack against a civilian population, and pillaging.	
PTC II Cuno Tarfusser (IT) Marc Perrin de Brichambaut (FR) Chang-ho Chung (SK)	Recognised victims	Rejected	22
		Men	902
		Women	1124
		Children	
		Organisation	0
		Total	2026
		Victim representation as LRV and CLRV	
Trial Chamber IX Bertram Schmitt (GE), Péter Kovács (HU), Raul C. Pangalangan (PH)	Recognised victims	Rejected	6
		Men	2009
		Women	2090
		Children	
		Organisation	1
		Total	4100[a]
		Victim representation as LRV and CLRV	
		Victims presenting their views and concerns	3

[a]ICC, *Prosecutor v. Ongwen*, ICC-02/04-01/15-1746, Updated Consolidated List of Participating Victims (29 June 2020)

[136]ICC, *Situation in Uganda*, ICC-02/04, Warrant of Arrest for Dominic Ongwen (8 July 2005).

[137]ICC, *Prosecutor v. Joseph Kony, Vincent Otti, Okot Odhiambo, Dominic Ongwen*, PTC II, Report of the Registry on the voluntary surrender of Dominic Ongwen and his transfer to the Court.

[138]ICC, *Prosecutor v. Dominic Ongwen*, ICC-02/04-01/15, Decision on the confirmation of charges against Dominic Ongwen (23 March 2016).

3.2.9.2 Joseph Kony

On 6 May 2005, the OTP submitted a request for the warrants of arrest for Joseph Kony and four other individuals, including Dominic Ongwen. The request was amended and supplemented on 13 May 2005 and 18 May 2005. On 8 July 2005, the PTC II issued warrants of arrest under seal against the five individuals concerned for the commission of crimes against humanity and war crimes.[139] After an "Application for Unsealing of Warrants of Arrest Issued on 8 July 2005"[140] by the OTP, the PTC II unsealed the arrest warrants on 13 October 2005.[141]

Even though arrest warrants were issued, and the Republic of Uganda was instructed to search for, arrest, detain and surrender Joseph Kony to the Court, he remains at large, more than 10 years after the issue of the warrant of arrest.

Based upon Article 19(1) RS, the PTC II decided on 21 October 2008 to initiate proceedings with a view to determining the admissibility of the case.[142] Based upon the submissions of the OTP, the Counsel for the Defence, the Government of Uganda and also the Office of the Public Counsel for Victims, the PTC II reached the decision on 10 March 2009 that the case was deemed admissible under Article 17 RS.[143]

The Counsel for the Defence then lodged an appeal against that decision of 10 March 2009 and on 16 September 2009, the Appeal Chamber confirmed the decision taken by the PTC II.[144]

Situation in Uganda Case: Joseph Kony			
Crimes		Crimes against humanity: murder, deportation or forcible transfer of population, persecution, rape, and other inhumane acts War crimes: murder	
PTC II Ekaterina Trendafilova (BU)	Recognised victims	Rejected	27+
		Men	21
		Women	19

(continued)

[139]ICC, *Situation in Uganda*, ICC-02/04-01/05, Warrant of Arrest for Joseph Kony issued on 8 July 2005 as amended on 27 September 2005 (27 September 2005).

[140]ICC, *Situation in Uganda*, ICC-02/04-01/05, Application for Unsealing of Warrants of Arrest Issued on 8 July 2005, and Other Related Relief (9 September 2005).

[141]ICC, *Situation in Uganda*, ICC-02/04-01/05, Decision on the Prosecutor's Application for unsealing of the warrants of arrest (13 October 2005).

[142]ICC, *Prosecutor v. Joseph Kony, Vincent Otti, Okot Odhiambo, Dominic Ongwen*, ICC-02/04-01/05, Decision initiating proceedings under Article 19, requesting observations and appointing counsel for the Defence (21 October 2008).

[143]ICC, *Prosecutor v. Joseph Kony, Vincent Otti, Okot Odhiambo, Dominic Ongwen*, ICC-02/04-01/05, Decision on the admissibility of the case under Article 19(1) of the Statute (10 March 2009).

[144]ICC, *Prosecutor v. Joseph Kony, Vincent Otti, Okot Odhiambo, Dominic Ongwen*, ICC-02/04-01/05 OA 3, Judgement on the appeal of the Defence against the "Decision on the admissibility of the case under Article 19(1) of the Statute" of 10 March 2009 (16 September 2009).

Situation in Uganda Case: Joseph Kony			
Hans-Peter Kaul (GE) Cuno Tarfusser (IT)		Children	1
		Organisation	0
		Total	41
		Victim representation as LRV and CLRV	OPCV

3.3 Victims' Participation

The unique participation system of victims at the ICC depends on the jurisdiction of the Court. This means that there are several conditions under which the Court may be accessible to victims. As soon as the question of jurisdiction is solved, the victims of the crimes enter a common and standardised system, which still has some unique features regarding their participation. Whereas the ECtHR is accessible to the persons[145] under the jurisdiction of the Member States of the CoE, and whereas in the Extraordinary Chambers at the Courts of Cambodia the victims may have contact to the Court because of the crimes committed in the different temporal and territorial borders, the accessibility of the victims to the ICC is flexible and may change from case to case. Articles 11–15 RS provide the scenarios of how the victims of the crimes under Article 5 (1) RS may be attained by the Court. According to the Rome Statute, one of those scenarios where the victims may be involved in the Court's system is if the crimes, enumarated under Article 5 (1) RS, were committed within the territory of the State Party. Another way for the victims to reach the Court could be in cases where certain nationals of the Member State committed the crimes described in Article 5 (1) RS or if the Non-Member State accepts the jurisdiction of the Court pursuant to Article 12 (3) RS.[146] In order to enable the victims to be a part of the Court's procedures, there are four ways the jurisdiction of the Court may be exercised:

- By a referral of a situation by a State Party to the Prosecutor (Article 13 (a) RS);
- By a declaration to the Registrar of acceptance of jurisdiction of the Court by a Non-Member State (Article 12(3) RS);
- By a referral to the Prosecutor by the UNSC (Article 13 (b) RS); or
- By an initiation of investigation in respect of a crime by the Prosecutor (Article 15 RS)

---

[145]Not only the citizens or residents, but also for foreigners dealing with the justice or administration system of the Member States.

[146]Bassiouni and Schabas (2016), p. 133; Bassiouni (2013), p. 659; Kaul (2014), p. 63.

It is important to note that the victims who have suffered as a result of macro-crimes have to go through a long process before their participation in certain judicial proceedings against accused persons. This process means that all requisites pertaining to jurisdiction, admissibility, the interest of justice and also political decisions regarding the selection of the perpetrators have been met. In the ECtHR, every so-called victim may reach the Court by lodging a complaint against the State. The decision about the exact or possible participation of the victims in the judicial proceedings before the ICC depends on other stakeholders, such as the Prosecutor, the UNSC or individual States. At the same time, parallel to the question of jurisdiction, and even to the case where the suspect/accused is already known, the victims are confronted with another barrier to the admissibility question of the case pursuant to Article 17 RS. This means that before their actual involvement in the judicial proceedings and being recognised as victims, the victims have to wait to exercise their participatory rights until the preconditions for the jurisdiction are met and exercised and there is no issue of admissibility.

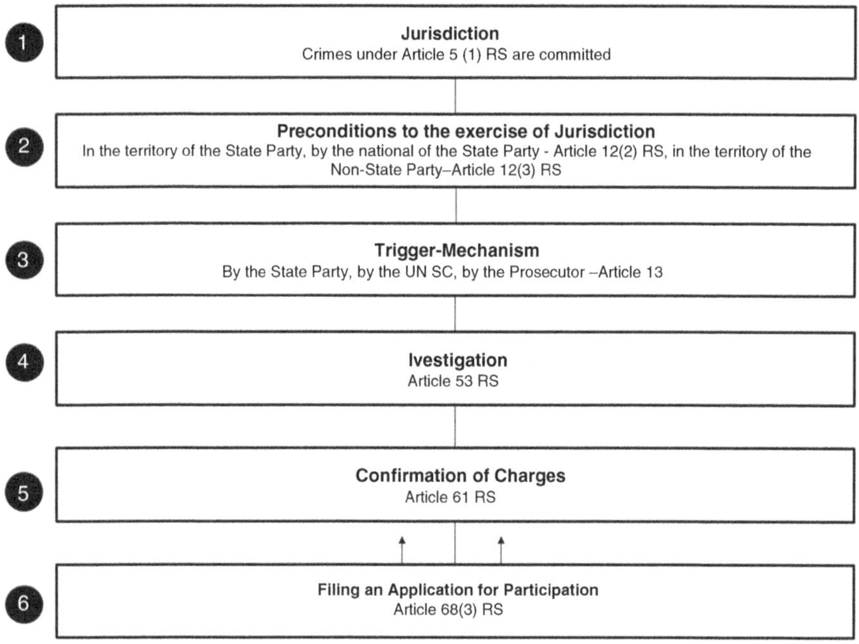

In order to move the situation from the preliminary examination to the investigation of the situation in accordance with Article 53 (1) RS, the OTP has established a filtering process comprising four phases. Phase 1 consists of the assessment of information based upon communications with victim representations, reports of NGOs and ends with the decision to open a preliminary examination. In phase 2, the factual and legal analysis takes place to ascertain whether the preconditions of Article 12 RS are satisfied and whether there is a reasonable basis to believe that the alleged crimes fall within the jurisdiction of the Court. In phase 3, the OTP focuses on the admissibility issues of potential cases in terms of complementarity and gravity. Before initiating an investigation, phase 4 is completed with the examination of the interests of justice.[147] Only after initiating the investigation and issuing a warrant of arrest pursuant to Article 58 RS may the victims be called to apply for participation against the suspect relating to the charges brought against them.

Victims may be contacted by the Prosecutor under Article 15 (3) RS in order to collect evidence and information about the alleged crimes under the investigation, however, they are not able to exercise participatory rights at that stage. They will first receive these rights during the judicial proceedings before the Court, starting with the confirmation of charges against the accused pursuant to Article 61 RS. At the same time, the Rome Statute, the Rules and Regulations of the Court as well as the jurisprudence of the Court do not restrict the victims from not participating in the preliminary examination or investigation by filing submissions or reports, or victims' groups in order to support and complement the Prosecutor in his or her examinations.

	Preliminary examination stage	Investigation stage
Prosecutor *proprio motu* investigations according to Article 15 RS	Situation in Colombia Situation in Guinea Situation in Iraq/UK Situation in Nigeria Situation in the Philippines	Situation in Afghanistan Situation in Bangladesh/Myanmar Situation in Burundi Situation in Cote D'Ivore Situation in Georgia Situation in Kenya
Referral by the State Party pursuant to Article 14 RS	Situation in Comoros Situation in Gabon	Situation in Central African Republic I Situation in Central African Republic II Situation in Democratic Republic of Congo Situation in Mali, Situation in Uganda
Acceptance of Jurisdiction of the Court pursuant to Article 12 (3) RS	Situation in Palestine Situation in Ukraine	Situation in Côte D'Ivore
Referral by the SC pursuant to 13 (b) RS		Situation in Libya Situation in Sudan

[147] See ICC, Policy Paper on Preliminary Examinations, pp. 18–21.

3.3.1 Application Process

The actual participation of the victims in the judicial proceedings starts with the submission of the written application for participation pursuant to Rule 89 (1) RPE. Firstly, this gives the victim the opportunity of being recognised as a victim and, secondly, the victim will receive participatory rights in the different stages of the court proceedings in accordance with Article 68 (3) RS. With the application, the victim and the crimes committed against them are identified. The standardised application form has been changed several times (Regulation 86 (1) RoC), in order to make the information in the application editable. However, the use of a form, approved by the Presidency, is not compulsory.[148] The victims may also submit an application in a different form. Rule 102 RPE allows applications in audio, video or other electronic form. At the same time, the Court encourages the use of the standardised application forms,[149] which also simplifies the work of the VPRS for submission to the Chamber. In the case of *Al Hassan*, the Registry requested a redesign of the application form from one page to five pages with the explanation that the specific circumstances in the case mentioned requested additional details.[150] The information in the application must be in English or French. The Court does not cover the translation costs of applications completed in other languages.[151] The victims submitting their application should indicate several important points in order to have the application completed pursuant to Regulation 86 (2) RoC including information such as: the identification and the address of the applicant; evidence of consent if the applicant is represented by other person; description of the harm; description of the incident; documentation of any witnesses or other supportive material; information about the personal interests of participation; information on the stage of the proceedings in which the victim wishes to participate; and information on legal representation.

The timing of the application is open throughout the whole judicial process from the initiation of proceedings to the reparation order.[152] However, the Chambers in various cases have set different deadlines for the victims in particular phases of the proceedings,[153] nevertheless, it still does not mean that the victim will not have a

[148]See FIDH, Victims' Rights before the ICC, p. 8.

[149]One for natural persons and one for the legal persons.

[150]See ICC, *Prosecutor v. Al Hassan*, ICC-01/12-01/18, Registry Observations on Aspects Related to the Admission of Victims for Participation in the Proceedings (9 May 2018) paras. 5–7.

[151]Fardel and Olarra (2017), p. 17.

[152]In Contrast the victims at the ECCC may apply by five pages long application only until the conclusion of judicial investigation pursuant to Rule 23 bis (2) Internal Rules and in STL the deadline for submitting the nine pages long applications for the participation by the Judges in the Pre-Trial pursuant to Rule 51(B)(iii) STL RPE.

[153]ICC, *Prosecutor v. Katanga*, Chui, ICC-01/04-01/07-933, Décision relative au traitement des demandes de participation (26 February 2009) para 27, ICC, *Prosecutor v. Bemba*, ICC-01/05-01/08-875, Decision Setting a Time-Limit for the Submission of New Victims' Applications for Participation (7 September 2010) para 9, ICC, *Prosecutor v. Bemba*, ICC-01/05-01/08-1590-

chance to apply afterwards. Deadlines are mostly set in relation to the Registry in order to transmit and to report on the victims' applications.[154] Another important feature for the victims lies in the fact that after an application of certain victims has been rejected, they still have the chance to apply for victim status again and again.

The applications received are then transmitted to the Chamber for the decision on participation on a rolling basis. The rejection of an application may be related to the fact that either the application was incomplete[155] and after the communication with the victims by the VPRS the missing information was still not delivered or the requirements set by Rule 85 RPE were not fulfilled (Rule 89 (2) RPE). The applicant does not, however, have standing for an appeal against the decision on rejection,[156] however, the applicant is allowed to apply again (Rule 89 (3) RPE). The Registry is encouraged by the Court to assist the victims during the application period via reliable intermediaries *in situ*.[157]

The growing interest in the ICC demands a developing approach to victims. Since the establishment of the Court, and in order to examine the victims' applications, different approaches have been adopted by the Judges. This was aimed at making victims' participation as meaningful as possible and to avoid more symbolic contributions as much as possible (Rule 89 (4) RPE).

Lubanga case	Two-Step application process: Firstly, the Court analysed if the victims fall under the definition prescribed in Rule 85 RPE. Secondly, they determined if the personal interests of the victim have been affected.[a]
Gbagbo case	Partly collective application process: The Court encouraged the victims to join others and to make group applications for the participation under Rule 89 (3) RPE.[b] Two types of forms were therefore developed; a group form describing elements common to certain individuals as a

(continued)

Corr, Corrigendum to the Decision on 401 Applications by Victims to Participate in the Proceedings and Setting a Final Deadline for the Submission of New Victims' Applications to the Registry (21 July 2011) para 25.

[154]See e.g. Fardel and Olarra (2017), p. 21, ICC, *Prosecutor v. Katanga, Chui*, ICC-01/04-01/07-474, Decision on the Set of Procedural Rights Attached to Procedural Status of Victim at the PTC Stage of the Case (13 May 2008) para 189, ICC, *Prosecutor v. Bemba*, ICC-01/05-01/08-103-tEN-Corr, Decision on Victim Participation (12 September 2008) p. 5, ICC, *Prosecutor v. Bemba*, ICC-01/05-01/08-305, Decision Concerning the Time Limit for the Submission of New Victim Applications (2 December 2008) para 1, ICC, *Prosecutor v. Katanga*, Chui, ICC-01/04-01/07-933, Décision relative au traitement des demandes de participation (26 February 2009) para 27, ICC, *Prosecutor v. Abu Garda*, ICC-02/05-02/09-55-RSC, Decision on the Designation of a Single Judge on Victims' Issues and on the Deadline for the Filing of Applications for Participation (19 August 2009) p. 6.

[155]This means that the requirements of Regulation 86 (2) RoC were not sufficiently elaborated.

[156]ICC, *Situation in the DRC*, ICC-01/04-418, Decision on the Requests of the OPCV (10 December 2007) para 16.

[157]ICC, *Prosecutor v. Al Hassan*, ICC-01/12-01/18, Decision Establishing the Principles Applicable to Victims' Applications for Participation (24 May 2018) paras. 36–40.

	group and an individual declaration which connects the individual application to the information provided in the Group form.
Kenyan cases	Remote Participation through common legal representative: The Court considered parallel to the victims who applied for the participation also those victims who did not wish to present their views and concern directly before the Chamber but solely through common legal representative, they had the possibility to send their registration solely without the statutorily requirements.[c]
Ntaganda case Ongwen case	Simplified Application Process: The Court emphasised the special circumstances of the specific case and were satisfied with the proposal of the Registry to use one-page application form for determining the victims pursuant to Rule 85 RPE.[d]
Al Hassan case	Individual and Partly Collective Dual Application: Bearing in mind the situation in Mali the Court set a new five-page application form either for the participation or reparation or both and allowed the victim families to apply collectively and electronically.[e]

[a]Catani (2012), p. 905 et seq
[b]ICC, *Prosecutor v. Gbagbo*, ICC-02/11-01/11, Decision on issues related to the victims' application process (6 February 2012) paras. 9–11
[c]ICC, *Prosecutor v. Muthaura, Kenyatta, Ali*, ICC-01/09-01/11-249, Decision on Victims' Participation at the Confirmation of Charges Hearing and in the Related Proceedings (26 August 2011) *Prosecutor v. Kenyatta, Muthaura* (n 275) paras 47–54, Zago (2014), p. 7
[d]ICC, *Prosecutor v. Ntaganda*, ICC-01/04-02/06-67, Decision Establishing Principleson the Victims' Application Process (28 May 2013) para 21, ICC, *Prosecutor v. Ongwen*, ICC-02/04-01/15-205, Decision Establishing Principles on the Victims'Application Process (4 March 2015) paras 14
[e]ICC, *Prosecutor v. Al Hassan*, ICC-01/12-01/18, Decision Establishing the Principles Applicable to Victims' Applications for Participation (24 May 2018) paras. 18–29

In the recent case of *Al Hassan*, the Court accepted the Registry's request to use the five-page standardised application form for natural and legal persons with specific guidelines for the application procedure. The Court accepted the possibility of allowing victims to create associations or apply jointly as a family.[158]

Generally, it is possible to determine the decisions on victims' application process based upon several important aspects. The Court is a platform for the victims to present their views, general rules to that end were statutorily established, however, those rules may be developed in different ways. The key aspect in this development and those playing important roles are:

- General rule of participation and established practice of other judges (jurisprudence);
- the judges themselves; their legal background, their philosophy and their approach to the victims' participation system;
- the case; different aspects of the case, subject matter of the case;
- the victims; their application, the facts, the motivation; and
- prosecutor or defense lawyer; their argumentations and strategy for the present case.

[158]ICC, *Prosecutor v. Al Hassan*, ICC-01/12-01/18, Decision Establishing the Principles Applicable to Victims' Applications for Participation (24 May 2018) paras. 34–36.

Since 2010, the ASP has started to discuss the growing interest of the victims and the challenges of the Court in order to review the participation system of victims. The ASP stated in its Resolution from 21 December 2011 that bearing in mind the continued backlogs in the application system of the victims, there is a need for review with a view to ensuring the sustainability, effectiveness and efficiency of the victims' participation system.[159] This was a milestone where the Judges started to use different approaches in order to make the application system more effective for the victims.

3.3.1.1 Victims' Individual Application

The core concept of participation is a submission by an individual application for participation pursuant to Rule 89 (1) RPE. In all cases, this method of application was an essential element during the application process.[160] In order to make the application complete, the victim has to provide the necessary documentation of self-identification and further supporting documentation. Bearing in mind the purpose of the application system,[161] the Court decided to simplify the application process reducing the form from seven pages to a one-page application form starting with the case of *Ntaganda*. In the Court's view, this method encourages victims to participate in the case at hand.[162] This method helps the victims to bring forward the important elements of the events and the nature of the alleged crime[163] and leads to significant savings in terms of paperwork, the time required by the applicants to fill it in, the time and resources employed by the VPRS to process and transmit the forms to the parties and the time and resources used by Chamber in its final determination of each application.[164] In the case of *Al Hassan*, the challenging situation in Mali required the Court to change the simplified method used before and to use a new approach where a maximum of victim-related information could be secured with a minimum impact on victims' personal safety and security.[165] The new approach also allowed the victims to apply electronically by sending online application forms directly to the VPRS.

---

[159] Resolution ICC-ASP/10/Res.5, para. 49.

[160] See e.g. ICC, *Prosecutor v. Gbagbo*, ICC-02/11-01/11-86, Second decision on issues related to the victims' application process (5 April 2012) para. 16.

[161] Determination whether the applicant can be qualified as a victim under the Rule 85 RPE.

[162] ICC, *Prosecutor v. Ntaganda*, ICC-01/04-02/06-67, Decision Establishing Principleson the Victims' Application Process (28 May 2013) paras. 17–25.

[163] ICC, *Prosecutor v. Ntaganda*, ICC-01/04-02/06-67, Decision Establishing Principleson the Victims' Application Process (28 May 2013) para. 22.

[164] ICC, *Prosecutor v. Ongwen*, ICC-02/04-01/15-205, Decision Establishing Principles on the Victims'Application Process (4 March 2015) para. 16.

[165] ICC, *Prosecutor v. Al Hassan*, ICC-01/12-01/18, Decision Establishing the Principles Applicable to Victims' Applications for Participation (24 May 2018) para. 22.

3.3.1.2 Victims' Group Application

The collective application process is aimed at reducing the time and resources needed for the Court to process the victims' applications. In the case of *Gbagbo*, the Registry proposed a unique system by which the victims had the possibility to apply for the participation as a group, filling out a group application form first. They were then able to submit an individual declaration which connected the individual application to the information provided in the group form and included the information necessary under the statutory provisions.[166] In the collective application, the grouped victims still have the possibility of consenting to one person acting on their behalf under Rule 89 (3) RPE or of appointing a contact person for the communication between the Court and the group.[167] Therefore, a collective form was designed which might be used by groups of victims to file a single application, to which individual statements from victims constituting the group are appended.[168] Although the parties and the OPCV were against collective applications, it is a way of reducing the collection of information and in cases where additional information would be needed, the individual victim had to be summonsed to give testimony. Another unique type of collective application can be considered in the Court's approach to the Kenyan cases, where the victims who were not willing to participate directly before the Chamber in person or via video-link are given a chance to present their views through a common legal representative. In order to do so, the victims had to be registered by the Registry.[169]

In the case of *Al Hassan*, the Court also distinguished the possibility for the victim to make associations while applying for participation. The Court encouraged the Registry to make consultations with the affected victims if the group applications were in the interest of the victims. However, those applications should include such information as the names of victims and proof of their identity, a description of the personal harm done to each victim and further supporting documentation of the alleged harm.[170]

---

[166] ICC, *Prosecutor v. Gbagbo*, ICC-02/11-01/11, Decision on issues related to the victims' application process (6 February 2012), ICC, *Prosecutor v. Gbagbo*, ICC-02/11-01/11-86, Second decision on issues related to the victims' application process (5 April 2012) para. 17.

[167] ICC, *Prosecutor v. Gbagbo*, ICC-02/11-01/11, Decision on issues related to the victims' application process (6 February 2012), ICC, *Prosecutor v. Gbagbo*, ICC-02/11-01/11-86, Second decision on issues related to the victims' application process (5 April 2012) para. 18.

[168] Redress (2015), p. 41.

[169] ICC, *Prosecutor v. Kenyatta, Muthaura, Ali*, ICC-01/09-01/11-249, Decision on Victims' Participation at the Confirmation of Charges Hearing and in the Related Proceedings (26 August 2011) para. 24, ICC, *Prosecutor v. Ruto, Kosgey, Sang*, ICC-01/09-01/11-249, Decision on Victims' Participation at the Confirmation of Charges Hearing and in the Related Proceedings (8 August 2011) para. 25.

[170] ICC, *Prosecutor v. Al Hassan*, ICC-01/12-01/18, Decision Establishing the Principles Applicable to Victims' Applications for Participation (24 May 2018) paras. 34–36, see also ICC, *Prosecutor v. Al Hassan*, ICC-01/12-01/18-119-Red-tENG, Decision on the Registry's Reports concerning Victim Participation (11 September 2018) paras. 29–31.

3.3.1.3 Victims' Application Through Representative

There are different cases where a third party may make an application for participation on behalf of the applicant. One of those cases is where the victim is unable to apply for victim status at the Court due to different disabilities; they are than allowed to apply via another person representing them who has to prove the consent given. Another case of representation of this kind is in cases where children are involved. However, at the same time the group of victims may give consent to one person who will represent their interests by applying for the participation pursuant to Rule 89 (3) RPE.

3.3.2 Determination of Victims

Taking into consideration the large number of victims of international crimes and their demands, and due to the globally active, victim-oriented movements, the parties at the Rome Conference agreed to codify the victim participation scheme in criminal proceedings before the ICC by virtue of Article 68 (3) RS.

As already mentioned, international crime is by its very nature a collective experience.[171] However, in order to participate in international criminal proceedings, the victims are forced to individually apply pursuant to Rule 89 RPE in order for their status as victims to be recognised.

Pursuant to Rule 85 RPE, the general requisites for the recognition and identification of victims are fourfold:

i) the legal personality of the victim;
ii) the harm sustained;
iii) a crime within the jurisdiction of Rome Statute;
iv) the causality of the crime within the jurisdiction of the Rome Statute and the harm sustained

The norm reads as follows:

> 'Victims' means natural persons who have suffered harm as a result of the commission of any crime within the jurisdiction of the Court. Rule 85 (a) RPE.

Another additional criterion for victim participation is the link to "personal interests" set forth under Article 68 (3) RS. This means that it is not sufficient to have suffered harm as a result of the criminal conduct; victims can only apply for participation, if they can claim that their "personal interests" are affected during that particular stage of the proceedings.[172]

---

[171] Safferling (2012), p. 165.
[172] Safferling (2011a), p. 206.

The ICC definition on victims accordingly encompassed four types of victimhood:

- Those individuals, who directly suffered harm;
- Dependents or family of a direct victim, who suffered indirectly because of the primary victimisation;
- Individuals injured while intervening to prevent violations; and
- "Collective" victims such as organisations and entities.[173]

The wording of the victim definition embodied in the RPE does not include the limitation to direct and indirect harm for a natural person.[174] On this matter, the ICC Appeals Chamber emphasised that in order to be recognised as a victim, the harm sustained should be *personal* harm, which also encompasses direct as well as indirect victims.[175] Harm suffered by one victim[176] as a result of the commission of a crime can give rise to harm experienced by other victims.[177] Accordingly, indirect victims are also those who suffered harm as a result of the (later) criminal conduct of the direct victims.[178]

The direct "perpetrators" who acted under duress, under coercive circumstances (*Nötigungsnotstand*) such as, for example, under threats or force or were not able to understand what he or she was doing was wrong (insanity defence) may still be regarded as as direct victims and not as direct perpetrators.[179]

This establishes a "chain of victims", which can be described as follows:

[173]Bassiouni (2013), p. 123.

[174]Moffet (2016), p. 91.

[175]ICC, *Prosecutor v. Lubanga*, ICC-01/04-01/06-1432, Judgment on the appeals of The Prosecutor and The Defence against Trial Chamber's Decision on Victims' Participation of 18 January 2008 (11 July 2008) paras. 1, 32.

[176]Cp. ECtHR, *Tanase v. Moldova*, 7/08, GC, Judgment (27 April 2010) para. 104, ECtHR, *Burden v. U.K.* GC, Judgment (29 April 2008) para. 33.

[177]ECtHR, *Burden v. U.K.* GC, Judgment (29 April 2008) para. 32, see also STL, *Prosecutor v. Ayyash et al*, STL-1101/PT/PTJ, Decision on Victims' Participation in the Proceedings (8 May 2012) para. 45.

[178]The Trial Chamber noticed in the "Decision on 'indirect victims'" from 8 April 2009 that this category of victims should be excluded: *"The charges confirmed against the accused in this case are confined to the conscription, enlistment or use of children to participate actively in hostilities. Indirect victims, therefore, are restricted to those whose harm is linked to the harm of the affected children when the confirmed offences were committed, not those whose harm is linked to any subsequent conduct by the children, criminal or otherwise. Although a factual overlap may exist between the use of the child actively to participate in hostilities and an attack by the child on another, the person attacked by a child soldier is not an indirect victim for these purposes because his or her loss is not linked to the harm inflicted on the child when the offence was committed"*, para. 52, ICC, *Prosecutor v. Lubanga*, ICC-01/04-01/06-1813, Decision on Indirect Victims (8 April 2009) para. 50.

[179]Cp. indirect perpetration (mittelbare Täterschaft) in Brammsen, Apel (2008), p. 256.

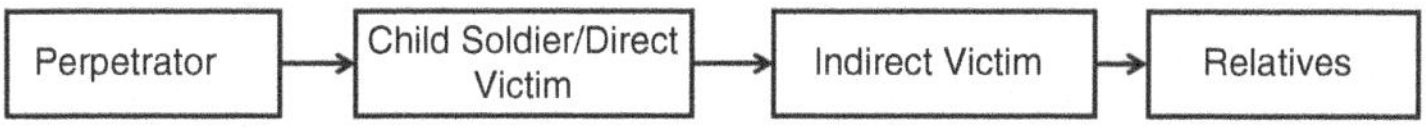

The term "indirect victim" encompasses persons who actually suffered psychological injury, for example, because of injury to their loved ones, whether temporary or permanent.[180] This could be a close relative of the direct victim,[181] someone who suffered harm when attempting to avert harm from the direct victim or someone who suffered harm as a result of the subsequent (criminal) conduct by direct victims.[182] At the same time, the damage or injury should be the direct consequence of the crime.[183] The harm may be seen as damage or injury due to the crime, which may be physical, psychological/mental or material/economic. The most important of the aforementioned requirements is the causality between the crime committed and the harm suffered. This essentially means that the harm suffered was a result of the commission of the crime.

On the international level, there are different institutions, such as criminal tribunals or human rights bodies, striving either to punish the perpetrator or to compensate the victim(s) for a human rights violation. In each case, it is necessary to establish "victim status". The following table describes the specific violations which can give rise to victimhood under the jurisdiction of certain international instruments.

Violations of international law				
International human rights courts[a]		International criminal court	Hybrid international criminal court	
IACtHR	ECtHR	ICC	ECCC[b]	STL[c]
Violation of human rights prescribed by the special conventions		• The crime of genocide • Crimes against humanity • War crimes • The crime of aggression	• National criminal law • The crime of genocide • Crimes against humanity • War crimes • Destruction of cultural property	• The attack of 14th February 2005 against Rafiq Hariri • Other attacks that occurred in Lebanon between 1st October 2004 and 12th December 2005

(continued)

[180]ECCC, *Case of Kamg Guek Eav (Case 001)*, 001/18-07-2007-ECCC/SC, Appeal Judgment, Supreme Court Chamber (3 February 2012) para. 417.

[181]The Indirect victims should proof *prima facie* the close relationship with the direct victim.

[182]Olásolo (2012), Edna and Bienkowska (1993), p. 155, see also Bassiouni (2013), p. 123, if the primary income earner is disappeared or unable to work because of injuries sustained, then certainly the family suffers loss as well, or individuals who are injured trying to pull a victim from harm's way, loss of employment, or imprisonment for challenging authorities for persecuting a targeted group.

[183]ECCC, *Case of Kamg Guek Eav (Case 001)*, 001/18-07-2007-ECCC/SC, Appeal Judgment, Supreme Court Chamber (3 February 2012) para. 417.

Violations of international law			
International human rights courts[a]	International criminal court	Hybrid international criminal court	
		• Crimes against internationally protected persons	

[a]The American Convention on Human Rights and the European Convention on Human Rights respectively

[b]The crimes are considered under time limitation—from 17 April 1975 to 6 January 1979, see Arts. 3–8 of Law on ECCC

[c]The crime is considered under time limitation from 1 October 2004 to 12 December 2005, see Article 1of Statute of Special Tribunal for Lebanon

In the international human rights courts, complainants need to demonstrate their harm for the admissibility of the case, harm which is sustained as a consequence of the violation of human rights as found in the relevant conventions.[184] In addition, the complainant must, however, meet the temporal, territorial and personal requirements for each case.

The same mechanism of identification is also required at the international criminal law level.[185] The ICC exercises jurisdiction over international crimes, namely the crime of genocide, crimes against humanity, war crimes and, theoretically, also the crime of aggression.[186] The victims of the aforementioned crimes should furthermore fulfil the requirements set by the court. In determining victim status, the ICC examines the temporal, territorial and personal requirements on a case-by-case basis.

If the human rights courts and the ICC have broader jurisdiction for the determination of the victims, the hybrid international criminal courts, such as the ECCC and the STL, have a narrower jurisdiction which allows a narrower determination of victims. Therefore, the purpose of the ECCC is to bring to trial the senior leaders of the Democratic Kampuchea, who were most responsible for the crimes and serious violations in the territory of Cambodia in the time period from 17 April 1975 to 6 January 1979. The victims are those persons who were targeted during this period

---

[184]See ECtHR, *Shesti Mai Engineering OOD and Others v. Bulgaria*, 17854/04, Judgment (20 September 2011), para. 114, ECtHR, *Andrejeva v. Latvia*, 55707/00, Judgment (18 February 2009) para. 111, ECtHR, *Nikolova and Verlichkova v. Bulgaria*, 7888/03, Judgment (20 December 2007) para. 82, ECtHR, *Kadikis v. Latvia*, 62393/00, Jugdment (4 August 2006) para. 67, ECtHR, *Van Geyseghem v. Belgium*, 26103/95, Judgment (21 January 1999) para. 40, ECtHR, *Podkolzina v. Latvia*, 46726/99, Judgment (9 July 2002) para. 49, see also Altwicker et al. (2016), pp. 14–15; Ichim (2015), pp. 25–26, IACtHR, *Aloeboetoe et al. v. Suriname*, Judgment (10 September 1993) paras. 96–97, IACtHR, *Heliodoro Portugal v. Panama*, Judgment (12 August 2008) para. 180, Rivier (2010), p. 757.

[185]ICC, *Situation in Uganda*, ICC-02/04-101, Decision on Victims' Applications for participation a/0010/06, a/0064/06 to a/0070/06, a/0081/06 to a/0104/06 and a/0111/06 to a/0127/06 (10 August 2007) para. 14.

[186]Since 1 January 2017.

for the violations under Cambodian penal law, international humanitarian law and customary and international conventions recognised by Cambodia. The STL has a very limited jurisdiction, namely the attack of 14 February 2005 against Rafiq Hariri and the other attacks that occurred in Lebanon between 1 October 2004 and 12 December 2005.[187]

This accordingly means that for the identification of the victim and victim's participation there are several aspects to examine which will allow a determination of the victims.

The use of the wording, such as *"interests"* in Article 68 (3) RS, as well as *"any crime" "indirect harm", "psychological harm"* embodied in Rule 85 RPE establishes a rather broad concept and enables a large number of victims willing to participate in the ICC proceedings.

If the wording *"any crime", "indirect harm"* and *"psychological harm"* may be seen as exact conditions for the participation, the *personal interest*, which serves two interrelated purposes,[188] must be interpreted during the different stages of the ICC proceedings on a case-by-case basis.

The ICC employs special terminology in order to divide victims within two separate participatory stages: *situation*-victims and *case*-victims. From a chronological procedural perspective, a situation relates to the preliminary examination stage, which is the initial phase of all prosecutorial activities, including those that result from referral by the UNSC or by a State Party.[189] The Office of the Prosecutor (OTP) searches for individuals who may be charged for specific crimes. The involvement of the situation-victims in the investigations enables the OTP to ascertain what crimes might indeed have been committed by certain individuals. The next stage (case) is the phase where, following the issuing of an arrest warrant, specific allegations of crimes subject to the ICC's jurisdiction are lodged against individual defendant (s).[190] Therefore, certain victims are chosen among the situation-victims in order to participate in the case against a specific individual (case-victims).

3.3.2.1 Natural Person

Natural person means an individual (a human being)[191] who has both rights and obligations. The doctrine of the natural person as the subject of the international law

[187]Possibly, also additional cases, see STL, Public Redacted Version Of "Decision On The Prosecutor's Connected Case Submission Of 30 June 2011" Of 5 August 2011, 16 September 2019.

[188]In the negative, it excludes victims' participation in proceedings the outcome of which does not affect their interests; in the positive, it grounds the right of the victims to participate before the Court once the other criteria have been met, see in Rojo (2017), p. 520.

[189]Schabas (2010), p. 401.

[190]Moore (2008), p. 186.

[191]So far as legal theory is concerned, a person is any human being whom the law regards as capable of rights and duties. Any being that is capable is a person, whether a human being or not and not being that is not so capable is a person, even though he be a man. Persons are the substances of

is controversial.[192] If traditional international law does not commonly accept the individual as a subject of international law, international organisations have established a possibility, whereby the individual has obtained rights and obligations in the field of international law. The identification of the individual is a precondition for the exercise of participatory rights in international organisations. For the determination of the status of the *natural person* before the given international organisation, the individual must demonstrate *prima facie* proof of their identity.

The identification of the natural person in international law

International human rights court		International criminal court	Hybrid international criminal court	
IACtHR	ECtHR	ICC	ECCC	STL
• Birth Certificate • Identity Card • Marriage Certificate • Another Document issued by a Competent Authority which refers to one of the Victims, such as a Death Certificate[a]	Rule 47 Rules of ECtHR	• National Identity Card • Birth Certificate • Voting Card • Passport • Driver's License • Student or Employee Card • Letter from a Local Authority • Camp Registration Card	• Identity card (also student or employee card) • Voting card • Letter from Local Authority • Driver's license • Passport • Camp registration card • Card from humanitarian agency (such as UNHCR, WFP • Other • None[c]	• Identity cards • Extracts from individual record books • Passports, Special Passports • Residence cards • Driving licenses[d]

(continued)

which rights and duties are the attributes. It is only in this respect that persons possess juridical significance, and this is the exclusive point of view from which personality receives the legal recognition; see Garner (2011), p. 654.

[192]Some authors in the field of international law are not agree with the thesis that the individuals are the principal subjects of the international law. See Kelsen (1952), p. 97; Boczek (2005), p. 75; Lauterpacht and Lauterpacht (1975), p. 487; Aust (2009), pp. 12–13.

The identification of the natural person in international law				
International human rights court		International criminal court	Hybrid international criminal court	
		• Card from a Humanitarian Agency • Tax Document • Other Document identifying the Person[b]		

[a]Based on the Article 50 ACHR in conjunction with Article 33(1) Court's Rules of Procedure and mostly specified in the IACtHR, *Case of Plan de Sánchez Massacre*, Judgment, Reparations (19 November 2004) para. 63, IACtHR, *Case of the Moiwana Community*, Judgment (15 June 2005) para. 178, IACtHR, *Case of the "Mapiripán Massacre" v. Colombia*, Judgment (15 September 2005) para. 257

[b]Based on the Regulation 23 (2) and Regulation 86 (2) (a) of the RoC, ICC, *Situation in the DRC*, ICC-01/04-374, Decision on the Requests of the Legal Representative of Applicants on application process for victims' participation and legal representation (17 August 2007) para, 12, ICC, *Prosecutor v. Bemba*, ICC-01/05-01/08-320, Fourth Decision on Victims' Participation (12 December 2008) para. 81, further identification documents were enabled by the Decision on the Registry Report on Six Applications to participate in the Proceedings, ICC, *Prosecutor v. Banda*, ICC-02/05-03/09-231-Corr, Corrigendum to Decision on the Registry Report on six applications to participate in the proceedings (29 October 2011) para. 22, acceptance of the further documents was the result of the situation, in which the applicants were not able to provide national identity card and passport because of the lack of access to civil records in the areas of the conflict, ICC, *Prosecutor v. Lubanga*, ICC-01/04-01/06-1119, Decision on victims' participation (18 January 2008) para. 87

[c]Based on Rule 3.5 (a) and Rule 23(2), Rule 23bis (1) of Internal Rules of the Practice Direction 02/2007, ECCC, *Case of Kamg Guek Eav (Case 001)*, 001/18-07-2007/ECCC/TC, Decision of the Trial Chamber Concerning Proof of Identity for Civil Party Applications (26 February 2009) para. 6, see also Eckelmans (2013), p. 194; de Brouwer and Heikkilä (2013), p. 1301

[d]Where the documents cannot be provided, other reliable documents whose primary purpose is not to be used as identification documents, but which nonetheless contain information identifying the applicant. Examples include, but are not limited to, documents relating to medical treatment, work identification documents, letters from the local authorities and membership cards. The probative value of these other documents will be assessed on a case by case basis, see the Decision on Victims' Participation in the Proceedings, ICC, *Prosecutor v. Bemba*, ICC-01/05-01/08-320, Fourth Decision on Victims' Participation (12 December 2008) para. 33 (ii). Based on Rule 86 (B) (i), Rule 2 of the Rules of Procedure and Evidence, STL, see also Morisson and Pountney (2014), p. 162

3.3.2.2 Deceased Persons

International law established conditions for the recognition of the victim. One of the most important aspects of these conditions is that the person should suffer harm. In practice, this kind of wording has led to difficulties in case law. The international courts were presented with applications sent on behalf of deceased persons.

The jurisprudence of the Inter-American Court is clear on the issue of the deceased person. The issue of the participation of deceased persons was never discussed while the work of the Preparatory Commission for the ICC was in progress.[193] The Inter-American Court recognises the participation of the deceased person through their heirs by succession.[194] The successors of a deceased person hereby exercise the rights of the deceased person during the proceedings in order to safeguard claims for any future reparation. The Chambers of the ICC failed to establish common provisions for the applications on behalf of deceased persons. Certain Chambers found that only the natural and living person may apply to participate in the ICC proceedings.[195] This is embodied by the argument that a deceased person is not able to express consent as Rule 89 (3) RPE stipulates and, accordingly, the nature of the deceased person does not fall within the scope of Rule 85 (a) RPE. On the other hand, in the case of *Bemba*, the Single Judge found that the deceased person's right may be represented during the proceedings by the successor, as long as the successor is also a victim.[196] At the same time, Trial Chamber I established that the representation of the deceased person does not have to be a relative or legal guardian, as in Rule 89 (3) RPE the definition of the person acting is unrestricted.[197]

The rules and the established case law of the ECCC demonstrate that in the event of the death of a civil party, the successor must submit that the applicant filed a civil party application before his/her death, otherwise the successor should act in their own capacity.[198] The same conditions for deceased persons are considered for the STL.

---

[193]Laucci (2014), p. 524.

[194]IACtHR, *Aloeboetoe et al. v. Suriname*, Judgment (10 September 1993) para. 54, IACtHR, *Case of Garrido and Baigoma v Argentina*, Judgement (27 August 1998) para. 50.

[195]ICC, *Situation in Darfur*, ICC-02/05-111-Corr, Corrigendum to Decision on the Applications for Participation in the Proceedings of Applicants a/0011/06 to a/0015/06, a/0021/07, a/0023/07 to a/0033/07 and a/0035/07 to a/0038/07 (6 December 2007); ICC, *Situation in the DRC*, ICC-01/04-423-Corr-tENG, Corrigendum to the "Decision on the Applications for Participation Filed in Connection with the Investigation in the Democratic Republic of the Congo by a/0004/06 to a/0009/06, a/0016/06 to a/0063/06, a/0071/06 to a/0080/06 and a/0105/06 to a/0110/06 (1 February 2008) para 24–25, ICC, *Prosecutor v. Kenyatta, Muthaura, Ali*, ICC-01/09-01/11-249, Decision on Victims' Participation at the Confirmation of Charges Hearing and in the Related Proceedings (26 August 2011) para. 47.

[196]ICC, *Prosecutor v. Bemba*, ICC-01/05-01/08-320, Fourth Decision on Victims' Participation (12 December 2008) paras. 39–52.

[197]ICC, *Prosecutor v. Lubanga*, ICC-01/04-01/06-2065-Anx2-RSC, Order issuing confidential and public redacted versions of Annex A to the "Decision on the applications by 7 victims to participate in the proceedings" of 10 July 2009 (23 July 2009) p. 15 annex 2, the participation of the person, who has already filed an application may be continued after the death of the applicant by the appointed family member, ICC, *Prosecutor v. Katanga*, Chui, ICC-01/04-01/07-1737, Motifs de la deuxième décision relative aux demandes de participation de victimes à la procédure (22 December 2009), paras. 30–32.

[198]ECCC, *Case of Kamg Guek Eav (Case 001)*, 001/18-07-2007/ECCC/TC, Judgment (26 July 2010) para. 641, ECCC, *Case of Kamg Guek Eav (Case 001)*, 001/18-07-2007/ECCCffC, Decision

Participation by succession in case of death	
IACtHR	✓
ECtHR	✓
ICC	○
ECCC	○
STL	○

3.3.2.3 Children and Disabled Persons

The preamble of the Rome Statute articulates the fact that in the history of mankind men, women and children have been the target of mass crimes and atrocities. Regarding this issue, specific groups of victims such as children, elderly persons, persons with disabilities and victims of sexual and gender-based violence are taken into special consideration under Rule 86 RPE. This expresses the need for special measures for the protection of the most vulnerable groups.[199]

Practice shows that during hostilities, the involvement of children in crimes as perpetrators or as victims is widespread. Therefore, a problematic issue was the determination of the age limitations regarding children.[200] Pursuant to Article 8 (2) (b) (xxvi) RS, the participation of children *(child soldiers)* under the age of fifteen in crimes as perpetrators is seen as the victimisation of children. In contrast to that, Article 26 RS prescribes the prohibition of the prosecution of perpetrators under the age of eighteen. This establishes a gap of 3 years during which children from the age of fifteen to seventeen are considered neither victims nor perpetrators.[201] In comparison to the practice of the Special Court of Sierra Leone, the Statute of the SCSL does not consider this gap of 3 years and therefore child soldiers not older than fifteen were seen as victims. In this regard, special attention must be given to the practice of the Special Panels for Serious Crimes in East Timor where the punishment of the child soldier started at the age of twelve. In comparison to the statutory provisions of international criminal law in regard to child soldiers and child perpetrators, there are still discussions as to whether children younger than eighteen should be considered victims of war crimes and not perpetrators.[202] The dispute on the determination of the victim status of child soldiers based on their age is still undetermined due to the special circumstances and the differences between the

on Motion Regarding Deceased Civil Party, E2/5/3 (13 March 2009) paras. 10–12, ECCC, *Case of Kamg Guek Eav (Case 001)*, 001/18-07-2007-ECCC/SC, Appeal Judgement (3 February 2012) paras. 410–413.

[199]See also IACtHR, *Gomez-Paquiyauri Brothers v. Peru*, Judgment (8 July 2004), Gal (2011), p. 117.

[200]See also Leveau (2013), p. 39.

[201]Chaikel (2015), see also Drumbl (2012), p. 127; Rikhof (2011), pp. 180–181.

[202]See Amann (2016), pp. 269–271; Amann (2013), p. 422; Rikhof (2011), p. 180; Seyfarth (2013), p. 123.

established case law.[203] On the issue of victims and witnesses who are minors, the Office of the Prosecutor of the ICC published a draft policy on children which determined the strict child-sensitive approach to children during the proceedings at the ICC.[204]

Culpability of children

	International human rights court		International criminal court	Hybrid international criminal court			
	IACtHR	ECtHR	ICC	ECCC[a]	STL[b]	SCSL	SPSCET[c]
Child Soldier **Victim**			<15 years[d]			<15 years[e]	<12 years[f]
Child Soldier **Perpetrator**			>18 years[g]			>15 years[h]	>12 years

[a]The ECCC has no special provisions regarding the victim children. The reason for not including the special regulations on the matter of children lies on several aspects: 1) The ECCC has his main aim to prosecute the senior leaders of Khmer Rouge, pursuant to Article 1 of the ECCC Law 2) As the jurisdiction of ECCC covers the events in 1975–79 in Cambodia, there cannot be any other children seen as perpetrator or victim. The indirect victims of the events are considered under standardised regulations and on the case law. There are 381 children (they were children during the Khmer Rouge Era) being considered by office of co-investigating judges as indirect victims. 226 out of 381 are girls and 155 boys)

[b]STL has no jurisdiction on child soldiers and on the participation issues of the children as victims in STL proceedings

[c]Special Panels for Serious Crimes in East Timor

[d]Article 8 (2) (b) (xxvi) of the Rome Statute

[e]Article 4 (c) of the Statute of the Special Court for Sierra Leone

[f]UN, UNTEAT Regulation 2001/25 on the Amendment of UNTAET Regulation N. 2000/11 on the Organisation of Courts in East Timor and UNTAET Regulation N. 2000/30 on the Transitional Rules of Criminal Procedure, Sec. 45

[g]Article 26 of the Rome Statute

[h]Article 7 of the Statute of the Special Court for Sierra Leone

Rule 89 (3) RPE establishes the possibility, whereas the application for participation pursuant to Rule 89 (1) RPE may be made by a person acting with the consent of the victim, or a person acting on behalf of children and disabled persons. The wording of the rule envisages the possibility, but not the necessity, of the applications made on someone's behalf.[205] As already mentioned above, the rules do not determine the nature of the person acting on behalf or with consent, therefore it is not an obligation for victims who are minors to be represented by their parents or legal

[203]See Birchall et al. (2011), pp. 10–12; Nilsson (2013), p. 1153.

[204]See Fatou Bensouda, a Draft Policy on Children, ICC-CPI-20160622-PR1224, this was mostly based on the existing codifications in internationally law, especially UN Convention on the Rights of the Child, UN Resolution, 2005/20 Guidelines on Justice in Matters involving Child Victims and Witnesses of Crime.

[205]See also Olásolo (2008), p. 149, *Prosecutor v. Ruto, Kosgey and Sang,* ICC-01/09-01/11, Decision on Victims' Participation at the Confirmation of Charges Hearing and in the Related Proceedings, (5 August 2011) para. 43.

guardians.[206] This approach is strengthened by the argumentation that during the atrocities and the recruitment of child soldiers, children are separated from their families, parents and relatives.[207] As such, they are not able to be represented by their next of kin or even identify themselves due to the lack of documents and access to institutions. On the issue of the representation of child victims and disabled persons, the ECCC links to Article 15 of the Cambodian Criminal Procedure Code where it is stated that a civil action can be filed on behalf of a victim by their guardian if the victim is a minor or an adult under legal guardianship.[208] A similar provision for minors and disabled persons was established by the case law of the STL.[209] The pre-trial judge of the STL in the case of *Ayyash et al* pointed out that for the application for victim status, the applicant has to possess legal capacity, otherwise the application can be brought by a person acting on the applicant's behalf.[210]

3.3.2.4 Legal Person

The protection of the fundamental rights of the entities is not considered by the ICCPR, for the simple reason that the Covenant asserts that human rights derive from the inherent dignity of the human person.[211] On the one hand, Article 34 ECHR enables corporations and other legal persons to claim their victimhood under the articles of the Convention.[212] In contrast to the ECtHR, the Inter-American Institute does not afford full protection to the legal persons under the IACHR. In accordance with Article 1(2) IACHR, protection under the Convention is only granted to *human beings*. At the same time, Article 44 IACHR allows non-governmental organisations to lodge a complaint to the Inter-American Commission but not to the Court in terms

[206]See ICC, *Prosecutor v. Lubanga*, ICC-01/04-01/06, Decision on the applications by victims to participate in the proceedings (15 December 2008) para. 67–68.

[207]Committee on the Rights of the Child, General Comment N. 6 (2005), 1 September 2005, CRC/GC/2005/6, paras. 3, 7 and 8. Although this General Comment applies to children who have crossed an international border, the Committee has acknowledged that there are many similar challenges related to internally displaced unaccompanied and separated children and encourages States Parties to adopt the relevant aspects of the General Comment in relation to internally displaced unaccompanied and separated children para. 5.

[208]Pérez-León Acevedo (2014), p. 341

[209]This was not considered by the RPE of STL.

[210]STL, *Prosecutor v. Ayyash et al*, STL-1101/PT/PTJ, Decision on Victims' Participation in the Proceedings (8 May 2012) para. 31.

[211]See the Preamble of ICCPR.

[212]ECtHR, *Ernewein v. Germany*, 14849/08, Decision (12 May 2009) para. 2(a), the Court has submitted in the decision that the legal person may invoke a violation only of its own rights but may not complain about a violation of its members' rights since Article 35 does not provide for individuals to institute a kind of *actio popularis* for the interpretation of the Convention, see also van Kempen (2010), p. 3.

of representing the groups of natural persons who have suffered the violation of human rights.[213]

> [. . .], the person protected by the Convention is "every human being"–in Spanish "to do ser humano", in French "tout être humain". Consequently, the Commission considers that the Convention grants its protection to physical or natural persons, excluding juridical or ideal persons from its field of application, inasmuch as the latter are legal fiction and do not enjoy real existence in the material order. This interpretation is confirmed on verifying the true significance attributed to the phrase "person is every human being" with the text of the Preamble to the Convention which recognises that the essential rights of man are "based on attributes of his human personality" and reiterates the necessity of creating conditions which permit every individual to "achieve the ideal of free human beings enjoying freedom from fear and want"[214]

Although Rule 85 (b) RPE considers the participation of legal persons as victims, there are still a number of strict limitations to the legal person in comparison to human beings[215] and not every legal person may be recognised as a victim. The ICC accepts victimhood only for those legal persons who have sustained direct harm to their property which is dedicated to religion, education, art or science or charitable purposes and to their historic monuments, hospitals and other places and objects employed for humanitarian purposes. Meanwhile, with regard to legal persons, the ICC differentiates between the organisations and institutions. Under this wording, it is possible to determine that the private organisations or entities as well as the non-governmental or governmental legal persons are also included within the definition. The most important features for the recognition of the victimhood of the legal person are the existence of the property and the dedication of that property. Pursuant to Rule 85 (b) RPE, in order to gain the status of a victim before the Court, i) the quality of the organisation/institution must be established, ii) the individual acting on behalf of the organisation/institution must demonstrate his or her capacity to represent the organisation, iii) the individual acting on behalf of the organisation/institution must establish his/her identity, iv) the organisation/institution has suffered direct harm, and v) the harm suffered is a result of an incident falling within the parameters of the confirmed charges.[216] The quality of the organisation is conditioned by any document which endorses the establishment, creation or registration of the legal person under domestic law. Furthermore, the natural person acting on behalf of that organisation must prove their capacity to represent the legal person

[213]See IACoHR, *Metropolitan Nature Reserve v. Panama*, Report 88/03 (22 October 2003) para. 29–30, IACoHR, *Janet Espinoza Feria et al. v. Peru*, Annual Report (10 October 2002) para. 35, IACoHR, *Bendeck-Cohdinsa v. Honduras*, Report N 106/99 (27 September 1999), para. 17.

[214]IACoHR, *Mevopal S.A. v. Argentina*, Report 39/99 (11 March 1999) para. 17.

[215]See Ambos (2016), p. 174; Safferling (2012), p. 169.

[216]ICC, *Prosecutor v. Al Mahdi*, ICC-01/12-01/15, Public redacted version of Decision on Victim Participation at Trial and on Common Legal Representation (8 June 2016) para. 23.

(*locus standi*).[217] This will require determining in what way the person is authorised to act on behalf of that organisation. The identification should follow the same regulation considered for the natural persons.[218] Finally, applicants must prove the causal link between the actions of the suspect/accused and the harm they have suffered.[219]

In comparison to the ICC, where different provisions for gaining victim status during the proceedings are given to natural and legal persons, the ECCC has enlarged the victim definition so that natural persons as well as legal persons require the same features in order to be recognised as victims (civil party) before the Court.

In its jurisprudence, the STL does not accept legal persons as victims and, therefore, legal persons are excluded from participating in the Tribunal's proceedings.[220]

Participation access of victims in international law

		Limited/full access	Natural person	Legal person
International human rights court	IACtHR	Full	✓	○
	ECtHR	Full	✓	✓
International criminal court	ICC	Full	✓	✓
Ad hoc tribunal	ICTY	Limited[a]	✓	○
	ICTR	Limited	✓	○
Hybrid international criminal court	ECCC	Full	✓	✓
	STL	Full*[b]	✓	○
	SCSL	Limited	✓	○
	SPSCET	Full[c]	✓	✓

[a]ICTR/ICTY/SCSL statutes do not include independent victims' institute; victims have the same status as witnesses

[b]Through legal representatives, para. 19

[c]In practice, they were considered but as witnesses

[217]ICC, *Prosecutor v. Bemba*, ICC-01/05-01/08-320, Fourth Decision on Victims' Participation (12 December 2008) paras. 53–56, ICC, *Prosecutor v. Al Mahdi*, ICC-01/12-01/15, Public redacted version of Decision on Victim Participation at Trial and on Common Legal Representation (8 June 2016) para. 2, ICC, *Prosecutor v. Lubanga*, ICC-01/04-01/06-1119, Decision on victims' participation (18 January 2008) para. 89, ICC, *Prosecutor v. Banda*, ICC-02/05-03/09, Decision on Victims' Participation at the Hearing on the Confirmation of the Charges (29 October 2010) paras. 44–49.

[218]See also Eckelmans (2013), p. 199; de Brouwer and Heikkilä (2013), p. 1301.

[219]See also Novic (2016), p. 204.

[220]Rules of Procedure and Evidence, Explanatory Memorandum by the Tribunal's President, 12 April 2012, para. 19 ("President's Explanatory Memorandum"), STL, *Prosecutor v. Ayyash et al*, STL-1101/PT/PTJ, Decision on Victims' Participation in the Proceedings (8 May 2012) para. 30.

3.3.2.5 Forms of Harm

International human rights courts consider the violation of the individual human right[221] to be one of the main criteria for the admissibility of a claim whereas international criminal tribunals emphasise the existence of harm to the applicant for the status of victimhood. The ICC and the ECCC[222] Statutes and Rules do not endorse the notion of harm.[223] In this regard, the interpretation was left to the courts to decide on a case-by-case basis. Article 21 (3) RS and Article 12 (1) of the ECCC Agreement refer this interpretation to the UN Declaration of Basic Principles of Justice for Victims of Crime and Abuse of Power (1985), the UN Basic Principles and Guidelines on the Right to Remedy and Reparation for Victims of Gross Violations of International Humanitarian Law (2005) and to the international human rights courts.

As Rule 85 RPE considers two types of harm—one to the natural person and another to the legal person[224]—it is necessary to separate the clarifications accordingly.

The Appeals Chamber of the ICC indicated the harm as hurt, injury and damage and it carries the same meaning in legal texts, denoting injury, loss or damage within the meaning of harm in Rule 85 (a) RPE.[225] Under the wording 'harm', the Court emphasises material, physical and psychological harm.[226]

Type of harm	Meaning
Material Harm	*Economic Loss*, for example, as a result of the pillaging of the victims' personal belongings, destruction of household items, cattle, goats and sheep or the destruction of the victims' home.
Physical Harm	Rape, sexual enslavement, assaults and battery and other similar acts.

(continued)

[221]Rights-focused.

[222]Injury-focused.

[223]ICC, *Siuation in the DRC*, ICC-01/04-101-tEN-Corr, Decision on the Applications for Participation in the Proceedings of VPRS 1 VPRS 2, VPRS 3, VPRS 4, VPRS 5 and VPRS, 5 (17 January 2006) para. 81.

[224]In contrast the ECCC does not distinguish the notion of harm between natural and legal persons.

[225]ICC, *Prosecutor v. Lubanga*, ICC-01/04-01/06-1432, Judgment on the appeals of The Prosecutor and The Defence against Trial Chamber's Decision on Victims' Participation of 18 January 2008 (11 July 2008) para. 31.

[226]ICC, *Prosecutor v. Lubanga*, ICC-01/04-01/06-1432, Judgment on the appeals of The Prosecutor and The Defence against Trial Chamber's Decision on Victims' Participation of 18 January 2008 (11 July 2008) para. 32.

Type of harm	Meaning
Psychological/Mental Harm	*Emotional harm* suffered, for example, as result of the militia killing a family, or making death threats, witnessing events of an exceedingly violent and shocking nature, such as a militia person's sexual abuse and torture of an applicant's mother or the mutilation of a child, or abducting a victim's child and forcing that child to participate in armed fighting.[a]

[a]Funk (2015), p. 101, see also the Regulation 48 of the Trust Fund, ICC, *Prosecutor v. Lubanga*, ICC-01/04-01/06-1432, Judgment on the appeals of The Prosecutor and The Defence against Trial Chamber's Decision on Victims' Participation of 18 January 2008 (11 July 2008) para. 31–32 ECCC, *Case of Kamg Guek Eav (Case 001)*, 001/18-07-2007-ECCC/SC, Appeal Judgement (3 February 2012) para. 415, see also Donat-Cattin (2016), p. 1705

On the international level, there are two broad meanings of the term 'harm' which are accepted. Firstly, Article 31 (2) of the Draft Articles on Responsibility of States for Internationally Wrongful Acts classifies moral and material harm. In this regard, material harm means damage to property or other interests which is assessable in financial terms. On the other hand, moral harm includes individual pain and suffering, loss of loved ones or personal affront associated with an intrusion on one's home or private life.[227]

3.3.2.5.1 Material Harm

Article 8 (2) RS specifies the offences that include loss of property or damage to or destruction of the victims' property. This also means that the deprivation of property constitutes an element of the establishment of the offence. "Property" is defined as those material objects that may be appropriated, and also any right that may form part of a person's patrimony; this concept includes all moveable and immovable property, corporal and incorporeal elements, and any other intangible objects of any value.[228] Material harm would only occur as a direct result of a qualifying attack and thus comprises damage to property, vehicles or buildings owned by the applicant.[229] Under the broad definition of harm, the ICC distinguishes under material harm between the burning of the houses,[230] which is also based on the judgment of the ECtHR in the case of *Ayder and Others v. Turkey,*[231] looting and the destruction of

[227]ILC Commentary to the Articles on the Responsibility of the States for Internationally Wrongful Acts, p. 92.

[228]IACtHR, *Ivcher-Bronstein v. Peru*, Judgment (6 February 2001) para. 122, IACtHR, *Indigenous Community Yakye Axa v. Paraguay*, Judgment (17 June 2005) para. 174.

[229]STL, *Prosecutor v. Ayyash et al*, STL-1101/PT/PTJ, Decision on Victims' Participation in the Proceedings (8 May 2012) para. 69.

[230]ICC, Situation in the DRC, ICC-01/04-101-tEN-Corr, Decision on the Applications for Participation in the Proceedings of VPRS 1 VPRS 2, VPRS 3, VPRS 4, VPRS 5 and VPRS, 5 (17 January 2006) para. 132.

[231]ECtHR, *Ayder and Others v. Turkey*, 23656/94, Judgment (8 January 2004) paras. 141–146.

property as an economic loss.[232] Parallel to this approach, one can also say that economic loss may encompass the loss of employment[233] and any associated income.[234] Accordingly, a direct victim's relatives, especially those who depend financially upon the person who has lost their income as a direct result of an attack, may claim to have suffered material harm as a result of that attack.[235] The ECCC, in contrast, characterises material harm as any injury which refers to a material object's loss of value, such as the complete or partial destruction of personal property or the loss of income.[236]

Rule 85 (2) RPE separates the common elements for the determination of a legal person as a victim. Predominantly, the most significant role for applying victim status to a legal person is the determination of the damage sustained to the property, property which is classified as being dedicated to religion, education, art or science or charitable purposes and to their historic monuments, hospitals and other places and objects for humanitarian purposes.

Property dedicated to Religion—Article 1 (a) of the Hague Convention for the Protection of Cultural Property in the Event of Armed Conflict from 1954 establishes the necessity for the protection of moveable and immoveable religious monuments of architecture, art and history, archaeological sites; groups of buildings which, as a whole, are of historical or artistic interest; works of art; manuscripts, books and other objects of artistic, historical or archaeological interest; as well as scientific collections and important collections of books or archives or of reproductions of the property. Similar protection regarding this kind of property is also considered in Article 27 of the Hague Convention of 1907 and in Article 53 Add. Pro. I. Property dedicated to religion may also be classified as cultural as well as of spiritual value. In general, the adjective 'cultural' applies to historic monuments and works of art, whereas the adjective 'spiritual' applies to places of worship. Notwithstanding, this should not prevent a temple from being assigned cultural value, or a historic monument or work of art from acquiring spiritual value.[237] At the same time, the

---

[232] ICC, *Situation in Darfur*, ICC-02/05-111-Corr, Corrigendum to Decision on the Applications for Participation in the Proceedings of Applicants a/0011/06 to a/0015/06, a/0021/07, a/0023/07 to a/0033/07 and a/0035/07 to a/0038/07 (6 December 2007) paras. 40–48.

[233] See Bassiouni (2013), p. 123.

[234] ICC, *Prosecutor v. Banda*, ICC-02/05-03/09, Decision on Victims' Participation at the Hearing on the Confirmation of the Charges (29 October 2010) para. 28, ICC, *Prosecutor v. Abu Garda*, ICC-02/05-02/09, Public Redacted Version of "Decision on the 52 Applicationsthe Pre-Trial Stage of the Case" for Participation (9 October 2009) paras 93–96.

[235] STL, *Prosecutor v. Ayyash* et al, STL-11-01/PT/PTJ, VPU Submission on legal issues pursuant to the Pre-Trial Judge's Decision of 5 April 2012 (23 April 2012) paras 18–20. The Victim Participation Unit of the STL is the opinion that economic loss may also arise due to a) physical injuries sustained during the attack, psychological harm incurred as a result of the attack or c) damage or destruction of real property as well as personal property.

[236] ECCC, *Case of Kamg Guek Eav (Case 001)*, 001/18-07-2007-ECCC/SC, Appeal Judgement (3 February 2012) para. 415, ECCC, *Case of Kamg Guek Eav (Case 001)*, 001/18-07-2007/ECCC/TC, Judgment (26 July 2010) para. 641.

[237] Pilloud et al. (1987), p. 646, para. 2065, see also Lenzerini (2013), pp. 41–42.

ICC's OTP stated in the Mali Report of 16th January 2013 that cultural or spiritual heritage covers objects whose value transcends geographical boundaries, and which are unique in character and are intimately associated with the history and culture of the people. In its view, the religious and historical buildings in Timbuktu, which had been designated UNESCO World Heritage sites since 23 December 1988, clearly fall within this category.[238]

Property dedicated to Education—In the case of *Prosecutor v. Kordic and Cerkez*, the TC noted that educational institutions are certainly civilian objects[239] and are undoubtedly immovable property of great importance to the cultural heritage of peoples in that they are, without exception, centres of learning, arts and sciences, with their valuable collections of books and works of art and science.[240]

Property dedicated to art or science—The same provisions mentioned for religion and education have to be considered for art and science.

Property dedicated to charitable purposes—The legal meaning of the term 'charitable purpose' is wide and it incorporates those objects which are of service to the community[241] or, in other words, the community may benefit therefrom (*gemeinnützig*). Although there is no strict international interpretation of the jurisprudence on the clarification of what constitutes a charitable purpose, it is possible to describe a charitable purpose in accordance with national legislation and interpretation. The UK Charities Act 2011 describes a charity as an institution which is established for charitable purposes and accordingly a charitable purpose constitutes a purpose which is for the benefit of the public (Section 2 (2) of Charities Act 2011) or if the purpose falls under any of the following descriptions: the prevention or relief of poverty, the advancement of education, religion, health or saving lives, citizenship, or community development, arts, culture, heritage or science, amateur sport, human rights, conflict resolution, reconciliation, harmony, equality and diversity, environmental protection or improvement, animal welfare, the relief of those in need because of youth, age, ill-health, etc. (see Section 3 (1) Charities Act 2011). Section 52 of the German Fiscal Code (*Abgabeordnung*) also provides a description of charitable purposes.

Property dedicated to Historic Monuments—The same provisions mentioned for religion and education also have to be considered for historic monuments.[242]

[238]ICC OTP, Situation in Mali, Article 53(1) Report, 16 January 2013, p. 31, para. 155.

[239]ICTY, *Prosecutor v. Kordic and Cerkez*, IT-95-14/2-T, Judgment (26 February 2001) para. 361.

[240]ICTY, *Prosecutor v. Kordic and Cerkez*, IT-95-14/2-T, Judgment (26 February 2001) para. 360, see also ICTY, *Prosecutor v. Kordic and Cerkez*, IT-95-14/2-T, Appeal Judgment (26 January 2005) paras. 86–92.

[241]See Nuzhat (2008).

[242]See also ICTY, *Prosecutor v. Strugar*, IT-01-42-T, Judgement (31 January 2005) paras. 277–281.

Property dedicated to Hospitals—Hospitals and medical units are afforded special protection under international humanitarian law.[243] Here is important to note that the definition of a hospital incorporates the narrow understanding of a medical unit. It is possible to define hospitals as civil or military establishments[244] or institutions which are responsible for the medical treatment,[245] reception and care of sick or wounded persons.[246]

Property dedicated to Other Places and Objects for Humanitarian Purposes—Despite the broad definition, it is still possible to describe limitations based upon the meaning of 'humanitarian purposes'. The notion of humanitarian assistance/purpose, which predominantly means aid and action designed to save lives, alleviate suffering and maintain and protect human dignity during and in the aftermath of man-made crises or natural disasters,[247] limits other legal persons and those who are attempting to gain economic benefit are excluded from being determined as a victim.

3.3.2.5.2 Physical Harm

Physical harm, which is embodied in almost every offence under international criminal law, means any physical injury to the body, including an injury that caused, either temporarily or permanently, partial or total physical disability, incapacity or disfigurement.[248] The ICC adopts a broad definition of physical harm also encompassing enslavement, detention and torture,[249] beatings, denial of medical treatment, limited access to food[250] and injuries caused by gunshot.[251] Physical harm

[243]Boothby (2012), pp. 233–235, See also Lane (1999), pp. 174–175.

[244]International Committee of the Red Cross, Draft Additional Protocols to the Geneva Conventions of August 12, 1949, Commentary, p. 22.

[245]Cp. Pilloud et al. (1987), p. 114.

[246]Black's Law Dictionary, Hospital.

[247]See the definition designed by Global Humanitarian Assistance, A Development Initiative, in: http://www.globalhumanitarianassistance.org/data-guides/defining-humanitarian-aid/, last visited on 12 December 2020.

[248]See US Legal Definitions at http://definitions.uslegal.com/p/physical-harm/, last visited on 12 December 2020.

[249]ICC, *Siuation in the DRC*, ICC-01/04-101-tEN-Corr, Decision on the Applications for Participation in the Proceedings of VPRS 1 VPRS 2, VPRS 3, VPRS 4, VPRS 5 and VPRS, 5 (17 January 2006) para. 147, basing on the judgment ECtHR, *Selmouni v. France*, 25803/94, Judgment (28 July 1999) para. 123.

[250]ICC, *Situation in Darfur*, ICC-02/05-111-Corr, Corrigendum to Decision on the Applications for Participation in the Proceedings of Applicants a/0011/06 to a/0015/06, a/0021/07, a/0023/07 to a/0033/07 and a/0035/07 to a/0038/07 (6 December 2007) para. 40.

[251]ICC, *Prosecutor v. Katanga*, ICC-01/04-01/07-712, Public Redacted Version of the "Decision on the 97 Applications for Participationat the Pre-Trial Stage of the Case (10 June 2008) paras. 71, 115.

is also considered as substantial bodily injury, ordinarily requiring a degree of medical treatment for the victim.[252] The ECCC describes physical harm as biological, anatomical and functional injuries such as wounds, mutilation, disfiguration, disease and the loss or dysfunction of organs or death.[253]

3.3.2.5.3 Mental Harm

Mental harm, which is also equivalent to psychological and emotional trauma or harm, refers to the psychological negative condition of the person which has resulted from a crime. In terms of psychology, trauma is a narrative fracture, on the one hand, and a traumatic event is, on the other hand, defined by its inability to fit within a person's linear meaning structure. In contrast, neuroscience teaches that memories of traumatic events are actually stored in a different part of the brain from regular, narrative memories.[254] The harm is not limited to the physical sense, but can also include psychological harm[255] and, in certain cases, even serious forms of intimidation such as death threats.[256] This must also be considered under such circumstances where the psychological harm may lead to physical harm. The ECCC also characterised mental harm as the result of the uncertainty and fear regarding the direct victim's fate, the knowledge of their suffering and the loss of the sense of safety and moral integrity.[257] This psychological condition sometimes leads to physical injury by inducing various ailments.[258] As the term psychological injury may cover many victims under international criminal law, the ICC established a strict precondition for the status of victimhood on the basis of psychological pain/suffering in its decision on indirect victims[259] i.e. there is a close personal relationship,[260] such as those between parents and children. This kind of psychological

[252]STL, *Prosecutor v. Ayyash et al*, STL-1101/PT/PTJ, Decision on Victims' Participation in the Proceedings (8 May 2012) para. 66. It mostly upheld that physical harm does not have to be life-threating or permanent, but on the same time must be of such nature and gravity as to interfere with the health, well-being or comfort of the victim, see also Morisson Pountney (2014), pp. 163–164.

[253]ECCC, *Case of Kamg Guek Eav (Case 001)*, 001/18-07-2007-ECCC/SC, Appeal Judgement (3 February 2012) para. 415.

[254]Sandick (2012), p. 105.

[255]Below mental disorders, psychiatric trauma, such as post-traumatic stress-disorder, see ECCC, *Case of Kamg Guek Eav (Case 001)*, 001/18-07-2007-ECCC/SC, Appeal Judgement (3 February 2012) para. 415.

[256]Moffett (2014), p. 137.

[257]ECCC, *Case of Kamg Guek Eav (Case 001)*, 001/18-07-2007-ECCC/SC, Appeal Judgement (3 February 2012) para. 417.

[258]ECCC, *Case of Kamg Guek Eav (Case 001)*, 001/18-07-2007-ECCC/SC, Appeal Judgement (3 February 2012) para. 417.

[259]ICC, *Prosecutor v. Lubanga*, ICC-01/04-01/06-1813, Decision on Indirect Victims (8 April 2009) para. 50.

[260]Basing on ICC, *Prosecutor v. Lubanga*, ICC-01/04-01/06-1432, Judgement on the appeals of The Prosecutor and The Defence against Trial Chamber's Decision on Victims' Participation of

injury is expressed by the sudden loss of a family member or the material deprivation that accompanies the loss of their contributions.[261] Additionally, the STL determined that psychological harm encompasses harm of an emotional, psychological and psychiatric nature which should be sufficiently serious for the determination of the victim status.[262]

3.4 Individual and Collective Victimisation Concepts

The concept of individual and collective victimisation is directly included within the meaning of the term victim adopted by the UN Declaration of Basic Principles of Justice for Victims of Crime and Abuse of Power and by the UN Resolution on Basic Principles and Guidelines on the Rights to a Remedy and Reparation for Victims of Gross Violations of International Human Rights Law and Serious Violations of International Humanitarian Law. Both the ICC and the ECCC indirectly mention this concept in their respective Statutes.[263] International criminal law deals with macro-crimes, which results in the victimisation of multiple persons and thus international crime is a collective experience.[264] If individual victimisation may be prescribed to a single person who has experienced a victimising event or suffered all the consequences of victimisation, then collective victimisation refers to a certain group. This group can be identified by its specific group affiliation and because of this affiliation the members of that group have become the targets of victimisation.[265] In accordance with the Statutes of the ICC and the ECCC, the concept of the collectivity of victims is encompassed in a limited sense, as already mentioned above, by organisations and entities.[266] This does not mean that the victim status may be also gained

18 January 2008 para. 32, see also broader interpretation by the ECCC considering the siblings and also spouses as the close personal relationship, ECCC, *Case of Nuon Chea (Case 002)*, 002119-09-2007-ECCC-OCIJ, Order On Admissibility of Civil Party Applicants From Current Residents Of Kratie Province (9 September 2010) para. 15, referring also to Declaration of Basic Principles of Justice for Victims of Crime and Abuse of Power, Basic Principles and Guidelines on the Right to a Remedy and Reparation for Victims of Gross Violations of International Human Rights Law and Serious Violations of International Humanitarian Law para. 8, *Prosecutor v. Lubanga* (n 498) para. 32, IACtHR, *Villagrán Morales et al. v. Guatemala*, Judgment (26 May 2001) para. 68, IACtHR, *Myrna Mack Chang v. Guatemala*, Judgment (25 November 2003) paras. 232, 244.

[261]ICC, *Prosecutor v. Lubanga*, ICC-01/04-01/06-1813, Decision on Indirect Victims (8 April 2009) para. 50.

[262]STL, *Prosecutor v. Ayyash et al*, STL-1101/PT/PTJ, Decision on Victims' Participation in the Proceedings (8 May 2012) para. 78.

[263]See Safferling (2003), p. 368.

[264]Safferling (2012), p. 165.

[265]Kiza (2006), p. 82.

[266]As it was already explained above, not every legal person may claim for the victimhood, cf. Elander (2018), p. 51.

on a collective basis. Each victimised person should apply individually in order to gain the requisite participatory and reparation rights.

3.4.1 Five Categories of Victims

In order to establish a better link between the victims and their form of participation, it is helpful to divide victims into categories using the deduction-induction methodology. The methodology of deduction explains the reasoning process from a wider and more general approach to a very specific case and the induction conversely from the specific to wider approaches.

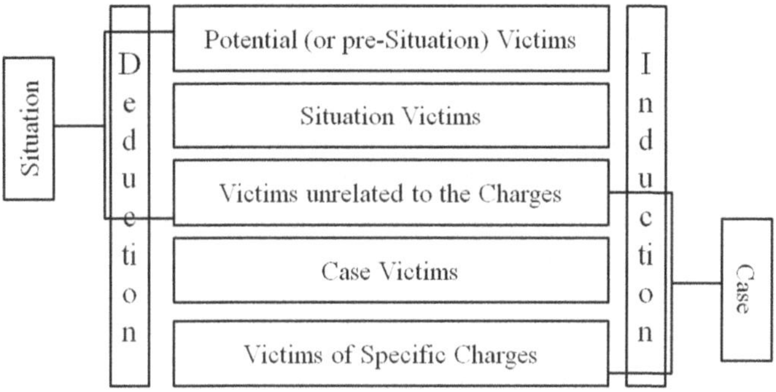

The use of this methodology allows for the possibility of determining the specific victims at different stages of international criminal procedure in order to individualise the victims and relate them to a specific crime. This, of course, runs contrary to the collective nature of the crime and minimises the number of victims who participate in the proceedings. In a way, this process inversely proportionally matches the identification of the actor who is being put on trial. International crimes, in general, have several perpetrators on different hierarchical levels. The OTP individualises and decides who will actually be prosecuted out of the many persons responsible. This selection process can depend either on political considerations or on the strength of the evidence available and both adhere to the appearance of arbitrariness.

As soon as the temporal, territorial, personal and material requirements are met, the victims gain different statuses and we have identified five different victim statuses: the most general is the pre-situation victim, who might develop into a situation-victim, who can prove to be unrelated to the charges or turn into a case-victim or, even more specifically, a victim of a certain charge.

3.4.1.1 Potential Victims

The commission of an international crime assumes the existence of hundreds, sometimes even thousands, of victims. Throughout the preamble of the Rome Statute, the ICC indicates that the focus of justice lies primarily on ensuring peace and security for victims and potential victims.[267] Accordingly, if an international crime is perpetrated within a limited geographical area, there is also an assumption that the community living inside and outside of the aforementioned geographical area is affected as a result of the crime committed. Therefore, it is possible to distinguish between the potential victims in two separate sub-categories: *those who have already been directly/indirectly victimised because of the crime committed* and *those who might be victimised if the commission of the crime continues.*[268] From the perspective of international criminal law direct/indirect victims fall within the category of potential victims as long as they are not included in the ICC proceedings. This is based upon Article 9 of the Basic Principles and Guidelines on the Right to a Remedy and Reparation for Victims of Gross Violations of International Human Rights Law and Serious Violations of International Humanitarian Law.[269] This endorses the fact that the person shall be considered a victim, regardless of whether the perpetrator of the violation is identified, apprehended, prosecuted or convicted. This consequently means that victims who are not recognised as victims by the ICC or by other international instruments are not precluded from being referred to as victims. At the same time, the ECtHR developed the idea that the established situation may violate the rights of so-called potential victims.[270] This, however, indicates that potential victims may not claim victimhood by direct violation.[271] Despite this kind of classification and the acknowledgment of the existence of victimhood, the ICC does not recognise victimhood in the event of a continuation of the commission of a crime due to a potential violation of Rule 85 RPE. This is endorsed by the wording of "[...] who have suffered harm as a result of the commission of any crime [...]". At the same time, the ICC automatically considers close family members of the direct victims to be potential victims.[272] On the other

[267]Findlay (2013), p. 308.

[268]ICTY, *Prosecutor v. Msksic, Radic, Sljivancanin*, IT-95-13/1, Review of the Indictment Pursuant to Rule 61 of the Rules of Procedure and Evidence (3 April 1996) para. 32, Swaak-Goldman (2000), p. 155.

[269]UN,GA A/RES/60/147, 21 March 2006.

[270]See ECtHR, *Klass and Others v. Germany*, 5029/71, Judgment (6 September 1978) paras 37–38, ECtHR, *Marckx v. Belgium*, 6833/74, Judgment (13 June 1979) paras. 27–28, ECtHR, *Vijayanathan and Pusparajah v. France*, 17550/90 17825/91, Judgment (27 August 1992) para. 46, ECtHR, *Open Door and Dublin Well Woman v. Ireland*, 14234/88 14235/88, Judgement (29 October 1992) para. 44.

[271]de Casadevante Romani (2012), p. 93.

[272]See Peters (2016), p. 271; Funk (2015), pp. 119–121.

hand, direct and indirect victims are potential victims as long as the temporal and territorial requisites are not met or identified:[273]

> Example: the political dissident group X is targeted for elimination by the government of State A. The possible acts of crimes against humanity are taking place in State A. However, it is still not clear in which regions of state A the possible acts of crimes against humanity are taking place. This accordingly means that since the affected geographical area and the time period of the acts are not determined, the members of the political group X may be considered potential victims.

3.4.1.2 Situation Victims

The specific term "situation" used by the Rome Statute describes both a geographical area under investigation and a temporal period of the investigation pursuant to Articles 12 to 15 RS owing to a possible occurrence of an international crime.[274] For this purpose, the OTP investigates incriminating and exonerating circumstances and dispatches investigators to local areas to gather evidence. In its first decision on victim participation of 17 January 2006, the ICC PTC found that in order to be involved in the investigation stage pursuant to Article 68 (3) RS which, according to the findings of the Court, is the part of the judicial proceedings,[275] during which the victims must demonstrate the conditions set out in Rule 85 of the RPE.[276] For the recognition of the situation of a victim's status, the PTC still has to clarify whether

1) the victim applicant is a natural person or an organisation or institution;
2) a crime within the jurisdiction of the Court appears to have been committed;
3) the victim applicant has suffered harm; and
4) such harm arose "as a result" of the alleged crime.

This, however, does not mean that in order to participate in the trial proceedings the victim should apply twice, i.e. once for recognition as a situation-victim and once for recognition as a case-victim. The transfer from situation to case depends on the decision of the Court and the "personal interests" of certain victims pursuant to Article 68 (3) RS. Within the framework of Article 54 RS, an involvement of

[273]See the first stages of the investigations in Groome (2014), pp. 117–118.

[274]Safferling (2011b), pp. 82–83.

[275]ICC, *Siuation in the DRC*, ICC-01/04-101-tEN-Corr, Decision on the Applications for Participation in the Proceedings of VPRS 1 VPRS 2, VPRS 3, VPRS 4, VPRS 5 and VPRS, 5 (17 January 2006) para. 63 ICC, *Situation in DRC*, ICC-01/04OA4 OA5 OA6, Judgment on victim participation in the investigation stage of the proceedings in the appeal of the OPCD against the decision of Pre-Trial Chamber I of 7 December 2007 and in the appeals of the OPCD and the Prosecutor against the decision of Pre-Trial Chamber I of 24 December 2007 (19 December 2008) para. 56, ICC, PTC, *Situation in Kenya*, ICC-01/09, Decision on Victims' Participation in Proceedings Related to the Situation in the Republic of Kenya, (10 November 2010) para. 9.

[276]ICC, *Siuation in the DRC*, ICC-01/04-101-tEN-Corr, Decision on the Applications for Participation in the Proceedings of VPRS 1 VPRS 2, VPRS 3, VPRS 4, VPRS 5 and VPRS, 5 (17 January 2006) paras. 66–68.

situation-victims in the investigation stage may assist in the selection of an person to be charged and the clarification of the facts.[277] At the same time, the subsequent decisions on victims in Northern Uganda and Darfur took a view which grants a general right to victims of situations to participate in the investigations.[278] The Rome Statute and the Rules of Procedure and Evidence foresee different scenarios for judicial proceedings related to the situation stage where victims' personal interests may be affected and where judicial scrutiny is required, such as articles 53, 56 (3) and 57 (3) (c) RS and Rule 93 RPE.[279] Despite the critical approach of the OTP in recognising victims' status during the investigation stage, the PTC considers several scenarios which may arise during the investigation stage. However, with its decision on victims of 18 January 2008, the Trial Chamber in the *Lubanga* case came to the conclusion that the status of a victim should be granted only to those victims who are victims of the crimes mentioned in the arrest warrant.[280] Thereby, the status of a victim may not be granted at the investigation stage but, at the same time, the participation of those persons is not excluded at the investigation stage. The Appeals Chamber noted that it is not in a position to advise the PTC as to how applications for participation in judicial proceedings, at the investigation stage of a situation, should generally be dealt with in the absence of specific facts. It is for the PTC to determine how best to rule upon applications for participation in compliance with the relevant provisions of the Court.[281] The PTC must do so bearing in mind that participatory rights can only be granted under Article 68 (3) of the Statute once the requirements of that provision have been fulfilled.[282] On 3 November 2010, the PTC, based upon the decision of the Appeals Chamber,[283] came to the conclusion that three different hypotheses should be taken into account in order to consider the victim application at the situation stage on its merits:

a) the Chamber is seised of a request that is not submitted by victims of the situation;

[277]Zegveld (2009), p. 375, see also ICC, *Situation in Uganda*, ICC-02/04, Public Redacted Version Decision on victims' applications for participation a/0010/06, a/0064/06 to a/0070/06, a/0081/06 to a/0104/06 and a/0111/06 to a/0127/06, (10 August 2007) para. 84.

[278]Chung (2008), p. 471.

[279]ICC, *Situation in Uganda*, ICC-02/04, Decision on Victim's Participation in Proceedings Related to the Situation in Uganda (9 March 2012) para. 12.

[280]ICC, *Prosecutor v. Lubanga,* Decision on victims' participation, ICC-01/04-01/06-1119, (18 January 2008), paras. 92–95.

[281]E.g. If the crime alleged meets the jurisdictional requirements and the PTC determines that a harm has occurred, then the PTC has to determine that the harm has a causal connection to the alleged crime before the Court, see Kelly (2013), p. 51.

[282]ICC, *Situation in Darfur,* ICC-02/05-177, Judgment on victim participation in the investigation stage of the proceedings in the appeal of the OPCD against the decision of Pre-Trial Chamber I of 3 December 2007 and in the appeals of the OPCD and the Prosecutor against the decision of Pre-Trial Chamber I of 6 December 2007 (2 February 2009) para. 57.

[283]ICC, *Prosecutor v. Lubanga,* ICC-01/04-01/06-1119, Decision on victims' participation (18 January 2008) para. 95.

b) the Chamber decides to act *proprio motu*; and
c) the Chamber is seised of a request emanating from victims of the situation who have filed an application for participation in the proceedings with the Registry.[284]

Accordingly, the Chamber should determine within the scope of the first and third hypotheses whether the issue raised could lead to, or be linked to, judicial proceedings. Based upon the second hypothesis, the judicial proceedings will take place as the Chamber has decided to act of its own accord.[285] Firstly, however, the requirements of Rule 85 RPE have to be identified in order to prove the interest of victims pursuant to Article 68 (3) RS in order to ascertain whether they are affected in the particular situation. A distinction should be made between those applying for participation in the proceedings and those applying solely for the purposes of reparations. If the wishes of the victims are not mentioned, the applications must be considered as a desire for reparations only.

Generally, it is possible to conclude that situation-victims are those who have already suffered harm as a consequence of a possible international crime within a determined geographical area and temporal period.[286]

Example: After the conclusion of preliminary investigations by the OTP, it was estimated that region B of State A was mainly affected during N time, where the political group X was mostly active. Accordingly, the "situation victims" are those members of political group X, who were targeted in region B of State A in N time period.

3.4.1.3 Victims Unrelated to the Charges

The Trial Chamber in the case of *Lubanga* came to the conclusion that Rule 85 RPE requires the alleged harm to be the result of *any* crime within the jurisdiction of the Court. Thus, there is no requirement for a link between the crimes alleged against the defendant and the harm suffered by those who apply for participation as victims.[287] This means that as soon as the suspect/accused is identified, the victim who demonstrates their interest in accordance with Article 68 (3) RS may attend the proceedings, assuming they meet the requirements set by Rule 85 RPE. In comparison to the potential and situation victims, where the territorial and temporal param-

[284] ICC, *Situation in Kenya*, ICC-01/09-24, Decision on Victims' Participation in Proceedings Related to the Situation in the Republic of Kenya, (3 November 2010) para. 15.

[285] ICC, *Situation in Kenya*, ICC-01/09-24, Decision on Victims' Participation in Proceedings Related to the Situation in the Republic of Kenya, (3 November 2010) para. 16.

[286] ICC, *Situation on the Registered Vessels of the Union of the Comoros, the Hellenic Republic and the Kingdom of Cambodia*, ICC-01/13-18, Decision on the Victims' Participation (24 April 2015) para. 12.

[287] ICC, *Prosecutor v. Lubanga,* ICC-01/04-01/06-1119, Decision on victims' participation (18 January 2008) paras. 92–95, Olásolo (2008), p. 148.

eters have already been identified, this stage presumes the requirement *ratione personae* that the suspect/accused is already known. At this stage, two different victim categorisations may arise: first, the victims who are related to the alleged crimes but not the defendant and, secondly, the victims who suffered harm as a result of other crimes committed by the defendant which are not considered as part of the charges. This provision for the general participation of victims at the proceedings in a given case of there not being any causality between the harm, the alleged crime and the defendant, was later rejected by the Appeals Chamber on the basis that only the victims of the crimes indicted may demonstrate that the trial affects their personal interests.[288]

However, the personal interest of the victims (Article 68 (3) RS) may still be directly or indirectly connected to the criminal allegations levelled against the defendant as a consequence of the gravity of the crime in its macro-context. If the PTC held the opinion that the causal link "is satisfied if the spatial and temporal circumstances surrounding the appearance of the harm and the occurrence of the incident seem to overlap, or at least appear compatible",[289] the Appeals Chamber estimated that all the requirements must be met in order to grant the procedural rights to the victims. Accordingly, the victims may not participate in further stages if the causality between them and the defendant is determined only by the circumstances of the alleged crime or only by the person of the defendant. Therefore, for the purpose of participation in the trial proceedings, the harm alleged by a victim and the concept of personal interests under Article 68 (3) RS must be linked to the specific charges confirmed against the accused.[290]

Example: The OTP accuses defendant K, member of a special police force of State A, of committing crimes against humanity, more specifically the murder of members of political group X. Accordingly, those victims who were robbed and raped by defendant K may not gain the procedural rights in the case against defendant K. At the same time, those indirect victims, whose relatives were killed as members of X not by defendant K but by other policemen, may not participate in the case against defendant K.

[288] ICC, *Prosecutor v. Lubanga*, ICC-01/04-01/06-1432, Judgment on the appeals of The Prosecutor and The Defence against Trial Chamber's Decision on Victims' Participation of 18 January 2008 (11 July 2008) paras. 62, 65–66.

[289] Kelly (2013), p. 51, ICC, *Situation in Uganda*, ICC-02/04, Public Redacted Version Decision on victims' applications for participation a/0010/06, a/0064/06 to a/0070/06, a/0081/06 to a/0104/06 and a/0111/06 to a/0127/06, (10 August 2007) paras. 11–12,

[290] ICC, *Prosecutor v. Lubanga*, ICC-01/04-01/06-1432, Judgment on the appeals of The Prosecutor and The Defence against Trial Chamber's Decision on Victims' Participation of 18 January 2008 (11 July 2008) para. 65, ICC, *Prosecutor v. Kenyatta*, ICC-01/09-02/11-267, Decision on Victims' Participation at the Confirmation of Charges Hearing and in the Related Proceedings (28 August 2011) para. 60, Eckelmans (2013), p. 201.

3.4.1.4 Case Victims

After distinguishing the victims unrelated to the charges as victims of the case, Judge René Blattmann considered this approach to be contrary to the principles of criminal law, such as the principle of legality, where the status of victim and subsequent rights of participation are not linked to the charges confirmed against the accused.[291] Therefore, the Appeals Chamber rejected the idea of a broad determination of the victims and stated that harm alleged by the victim and the concept of personal interests under Article 68 (3) RS must be linked to the charges confirmed against the accused.[292] This, however, resulted in another critical approach regarding victims. In particular, the determination of the victim depends upon the charges and, therefore, if the Prosecution chooses to present a narrow, streamlined selection of charges against an accused for whatever reason, the victims' rights to participate will effectively be curtailed.[293]

Case victims represent all those victims who are determined as victims under the specific charges that have been confirmed. Accordingly, it is possible to conclude that at this stage, after determination of temporal, territorial and personal elements, the material element comes into question which enables classification of the victims of macro-crime from the narrow perspectives.

Example: The OTP accused Defendant K of multiple acts of genocide, acts of crimes against humanity and acts of war crimes: therefore, all victims who have suffered harm because of the acts committed by the Defendant against them as members of the respectively protected groups are to be considered case victims.

3.4.1.5 Victims of Specific Charges

Even if the case victims and the victims of specific charges may share similarities, it is important to distinguish the two categories from each other in order to articulate the fact that victims must be chosen according to the charges brought against the accused. This will also enable to allocate the victims of reparations. As soon as the guilt of the accused is confirmed by the specific charge, the victims of the specific charge may receive reparations in the future. The category of victims of specific charges represents, from the methodology of deduction, the narrowest group of victims who are affected as a result of the commission of specific crimes under the

---

[291] ICC, *Prosecutor v. Lubanga*, ICC-01/04-01/06-1119, Decision on victims' participation (18 January 2008) Judge Blattmann's dissenting opinion, para. 21, ICC, *Prosecutor v. Mbarushimana,* ICC-01/04-01/10-351, Decision on the 138 Applications for Victims' Participation in the Proceedings (11 August 2011) paras. 21–22.

[292] ICC, *Prosecutor v. Lubanga*, ICC-01/04-01/06-1432, Judgment on the appeals of The Prosecutor and The Defence against Trial Chamber's Decision on Victims' Participation of 18 January 2008 (11 July 2008) para. 65, see also Baumgartner (2008), p. 423.

[293] Gillett (2009), p. 38.

jurisdiction of the ICC. At this stage, all requirements, particularly territorial, temporal, personal and material ones, are met.

Example: The OTP accuses Defendant K of acts of rape as crimes against humanity. Therefore, the victims of specific charges are those victims who as members of a civilian population have suffered harm because of rape committed by Defendant K.

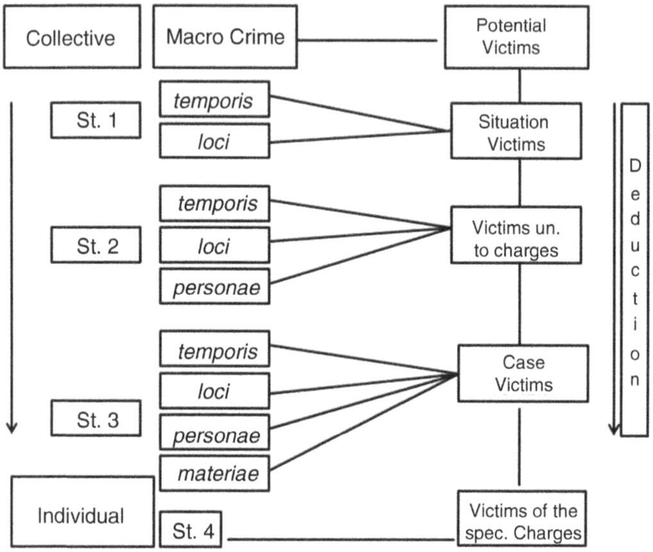

3.4.2 Victims of Genocide

Article 6 RS and Article 4 of the ECCC Agreement include the crime of genocide, which is similar to Article II of the Genocide Convention. The main difference between the crime of Genocide and national crime is that the victim of the crime of genocide is targeted not as an individual, but as a member of a specific group.[294] It is firmly entrenched that the crime of genocide is the crime of crimes.[295] This invokes the fact that for being victimised as the member of the group, the perpetrator should

[294]Boas et al. (2008), p. 139.

[295]ICTR, *Prosecutor v. Niyitegeka*, ICTR-96-14, Appeal Judgement (9 July 2004) para. 53, ICTY, *Prosecutor v. Krstić*, IT-98-33-A, Appeal Judgment (19 April 2004) Partial Dissenting Opinion of Judge Shahabuddeen, para. 95, ICTY, *Prosecutor v. Jelisić*, IT-95-10, Appeals Judgement (14 December 1999) Partial Dissenting Opinion of Judge Wald, para. 2, ICTY, *Prosecutor v. Stakić*, IT-97-24, Judgement (31 July 2003) para. 502, ICTR, *Prosecutor v. Musema*, ICTR-96-13-T, Judgement and Sentence (27 January 2000) para. 981.

intend the mass destruction of that specific group. This intent is known as the *dolus specialis*. Accordingly, the Rome Statute states that the crime of genocide is any act committed with the intent to destroy, in whole or in part, a national, ethnic, racial or religious group as such. Each of the underlying offences in Article 6 RS contains an element by which the victim must have belonged to a particular group. This enables the Court to preclude the liability for genocide, where the victim was distinguished as being a part of the group mentioned.[296] Pursuant to the jurisprudence of the *ad hoc* Tribunals for the determination of the group, a substantial feature of the group is its stability and permanency (*ejusdem generis*).[297] This approach is also used in that sense if the accused or the physical perpetrator believed that victim belonged to certain group.[298]

The main problem in this field is the fact that as the victim is not targeted as an individual, but rather as a group, it is not logical to consider a single victim as the only person who was targeted by the crime. If the special intent of the perpetrator is proven beyond reasonable doubt, the victim is therefore the whole group to which victimised persons belong, as they were targeted for their identity.[299]

> The term 'as such' clarifies the specific intent requirement. It does not prohibit a conviction for genocide in a case in which the perpetrator was also driven by other motivations that are legally irrelevant in this context. Thus the Trial Chamber was correct in interpreting 'as such' to mean that the proscribed acts were committed against the victims because of their membership in the protected group, but not solely because of such membership[300]

In practice, as well as in theory, the ICC already recognises that the victims of genocide are not simply individuals who suffered certain harm but are rather groups. At the same time, genocide victims are not simply a loose, arbitrary collection of individuals but the specified groups against whom killings are directed.[301]

Concluding, victims of genocide are protected groups whose members were targeted for their identity by the acts of genocide.[302] According to this view, it is more appropriate in genocide cases to identify not the individual as a single victim but rather the whole group as collective victims[303] which will be represented as a community in the case. A possible analogy in this matter is the Jewish Claims

---

[296]Boas et al. (2008), p. 201.

[297]See Safferling (2011b), p. 165, the political groups are excluded as they are classified as a mobile groups, Schabas (2016), p. 135, ICTR, *Prosecutor v. Musema*, ICTR-96-13-T, Judgement and Sentence (27 January 2000) para. 162, see also Petrossian (2019b), p. 106.

[298]ICTR, *Prosecutor v. Semanza*, ICTR-97-20-T, Judgment (15 May 2003) para. 317, ICTR, *Prosecutor v. Kajelijeli*, ICTR-98-44A, Judgment (1 December 2003) para. 811, ICTY, *Prosecutor v Brđanin*, IT-99-36, Judgment (1 September 2004) para. 684.

[299]ICTR, *Prosecutor v. Niyitegeka*, ICTR-96-14, Judgment (16 May 2003), para. 410, Prosecutor v Brđanin (n 640) para. 700.

[300]ICTR, *Prosecutor v. Niyitegeka*, ICTR-96-14, Appeal Judgment (9 July 2004) para. 53.

[301]Simon (2007), p. 37.

[302]Cp. The approaches of Lemkin and Lauterpacht about the Genocide and Crimes against Humanity in Sands 2018.

[303]Cf. Barth (2013), p. 260.

Commission which represents the interests of the whole group and community as the victimisation was not directed against a single person, but against the whole group. Genocide cases stand out amongst other criminal cases, as they have more a specific and political nature being directed against groups.

3.4.3 Victims of Crimes Against Humanity

From the perspectives of victims who suffered as a result of crimes against humanity as prescribed in Article 7 RS, there are similarities and differences between the victims of crimes against humanity and the victims of genocide. If the main victim of an act of genocide is the group itself (as a type of collective victimisation), the elements of crimes against humanity ensure the individuality of the victimisation.[304] At the same time, the similarity is that a crime against humanity as an international crime aims at defending the whole of humanity from barbaric acts. This is endorsed by the wording "systematic or widespread attack". This is, however, an abstract protected interest.[305] Indeed, during the acts of crimes against humanity, the selection of victims is irrelevant and optional, but the cornerstone of the crime is based upon the elimination or persecution of "undesirable" individuals. Even if the chapeau of the elements of crimes against humanity and the jurisprudence on this matter prescribe a widespread or systematic attack against a multiplicity of victims,[306] one must nevertheless consider the single victimisation of the individual dependent upon the crime committed.[307] The Trial Chamber in the case against *Akayesu* stated that in order to commit any act of crimes against humanity a) it must be perpetrated as a part of widespread or systematic attack; b) the attack must be against a civilian population; and c) the attack must be lunched on discriminatory grounds, such as racial, religious, national, political, ethnic grounds.[308] The discriminatory intent was, however, later rejected.[309] Accordingly, the victims of crimes against humanity are

---

[304]Kirsch (2009), p. 119.

[305]Cp. Safferling (2011a), pp. 183–184; Neubacher (2005), p. 113; de Guzman (2010), p. 129.

[306]ICTR, *Prosecutor v. Baglishema*, ICTR-95-lA-T, Judgment (7 June 2001) para. 77, ICTR, *Prosecutor v. Rutanganda*, ICTR-96-3, Judgment (6 December 1999) para. 69.

[307]Cp. Werle and Jeßberger (2014), para. 880, some crimes consider the group victimisation, others such as rape or murder are directed against an individual.

[308]ICTR, *Prosecutor v. Akayesu*, ICTR-96-4, Judgment (2 September 1998) para. 595, ICTR, *Prosecutor v. Semanza*, ICTR-97-20-T, Judgment (15 May 2003) para. 326, see also Robinson (1999), p. 46.

[309]Only with regard to those crimes for which this is expressly required, that is, for Article 5(h), concerning various types of persecution, siehe ICTY, *Prosecutor v. Tadic*, IT-94-1, Appeal Judgment (15 July 1999) paras. 283, 292, 305, in Hall and Stahn (2016), p. 173, see also ICTY, *Prosecutor v. Kordic and Cerkez*, IT-95-14/2-T, Appeal Judgment (26 January 2005) para. 186, ICTY, *Prosecutor v. Blaskic*, IT-95-14, Judgement (3 March 2000) paras. 244, 260 see Hall & Ambos (2016), p. 173.

those civilians[310] who have suffered harm because of the acts enumerated under Article 7 (1) RS, which were conducted as part of a widespread or systematic attack.[311] The approaches to determining the victims of international crimes identify whole groups of people which means that each crime, whether national or international, effects the whole of society which suffers indirectly as a consequence of the commission of a crime.

3.4.3.1 Murder

In order for murder to occur, the victim has to be dead and the death must result from the act of murder which may be committed by action or omission.[312] Due to the existence of mass killings, the ICC PTC found that there is no need to identify the precise number of victims or to determine the corpse of the victims or the direct perpetrators of each killing. In the ICC PTC's view, it is impractical to insist on the high degree of specificity.[313] In this case, the victimisation is directed against the specific individual victim.

3.4.3.2 Extermination

Although there are many similarities between extermination and murder, the main difference between the two crimes is based upon the killing of a group of individuals who do not share any common characteristics.[314] The intent here is the killing of not only one person but to commit mass destruction. This must be distinguished from genocide since the group specificities are not only based on religious, ethnic, racial and national grounds but may also include the political beliefs, social placement, sexual orientations, philosophy of life, cultural traditions, etc.[315] It also includes the imposition of slow-death measures. The act of extermination must be collective in

[310]See also de Guzman (2010), p. 132.

[311]As a policy or plan, see ICTR, *Prosecutor v. Kayishema and Ruzindana*, ICTR-95-1, Judgment (21 May 1999) para. 122–123, ICTR, *Prosecutor v. Akayesu*, ICTR-96-4, Judgment (2 September 1998) para. 580.

[312]ICC, *Prosecutor v. Bemba*, ICC-01/05-01/08-424, Decision Pursuant to Article 61(7)(a) and (b) of the Rome Statute on the Charges of the Prosecutor Against Jean-Pierre Bemba Gombo (15 June 2009) para. 132.

[313]ICC, *Prosecutor v. Bemba*, ICC-01/05-01/08-424, Decision Pursuant to Article 61(7)(a) and (b) of the Rome Statute on the Charges of the Prosecutor Against Jean-Pierre Bemba Gombo (15 June 2009) para. 134.

[314]ILC, Draft Code of Crimes against the Peace and Security of Mankind with commentaries, 1996, para. (8), p. 48.

[315]See also Boot (2002), p. 497, Safferling (2011b), p. 96, ICTY, *Prosecutor v. Krstić*, IT-98-33-A, Appeal Judgment (19 April 2004) para. 500, cp also Boas et al. (2008), p. 65.

nature rather than directed towards singled-out individuals.[316] Therefore, the victims of extermination are not only those who were exterminated, but also the families of the direct victims as well as the others who share the same characteristics as the direct victims in a geographically limited area.

3.4.3.3 Enslavement

Enslavement is the intentional exercise of any or all of the powers attached to the rights of ownership over a victim.[317] In this matter, there is no possibility of defining the act as a collective victimisation; it is rather individual victimisation.

3.4.3.4 Deportation or Forcible Transfer of Population

The right to homeland ensures the fact that people living in their communities or in limited geographical areas may not be deported or forcibly transferred from their territory. This differs from the situations where people are evacuated on humanitarian grounds.[318] Therefore, the deportation or forcible transfer of a population as part of a widespread or systematic attack implies the victimisation of the whole deported or transferred population, insofar a collective victimisation.

3.4.3.5 Imprisonment or Other Severe Deprivation of Physical Liberty in Violation of the Fundamental Rules of International Law

According to the jurisprudence of the ICTY and the ICTR, imprisonment refers to the arbitrary or otherwise unlawful detention or deprivation of liberty of an individual without due process of law.[319] This excludes collective victimisation, as in the case of extermination where the group itself is targeted. Therefore, the target of the imprisonment is an individual.

3.4.3.6 Torture

The prohibition on torture is recognised in various international human rights instruments. The multiplicity of the documents which declare the importance of

---

[316] ICTY, *Prosecutor v. Vasiljevic*, IT-98-32, Judgement (29 November 2002) para. 227.

[317] ICTY, *Prosecutor v. Kunarac et al.*, IT-96-23 & 23/1, Appeal Judgement (12 June 2002) para. 116.

[318] See Safferling (2011a), p. 198.

[319] ICTY, *Prosecutor v. Kordic and Cerkez*, IT-95-14/2-T, Appeal Judgment (26 January 2005) para. 302–303, in Bassiouni (2011), p. 444.

the prohibition of torture has led to the recognition of the crime as a *jus cogens* prohibition.[320] As a crime against humanity it does, indeed, possess individual character, as it is directed against an individual.

3.4.3.7 Rape, Sexual Slavery, Enforced Prostitution, Forced Pregnancy, Enforced Sterilisation, or Any Other Form of Sexual Violence of Comparable Gravity

Sexual violence is a 'weapon' of war and tool of terror and torture during armed conflict based on political and strategic motives in order to repress and to punish the opponents.[321] In sexual violence cases, it is difficult to ascertain the collective nature of victimisation.

In patriarchal societies, the membership of the group is determined by the identity of the father. Consequently, the child will not belong to its mother's group if the woman was impregnated by a man from another group.[322] On the other hand, sexual violence is aimed at oppressing and humiliating opponents as they are not able to protect themselves and "*their*" women.[323] Accordingly, sexual violence as a method of humiliation of the whole group can be described as group victimisation rather than an act aimed at singled-out individuals.[324] Therefore, the type of victimisation depends on the situation, whereby it may be classified as an act against a whole group of individuals or against a single victim.

3.4.3.8 Persecution

The act of persecution by its very nature is directed towards a group of victims who share the same characteristics as the other members of a group. Therefore, the act of persecution is aimed at spreading fear in order to disorganise a group. Various proposals have nevertheless suggested that this crime covers conduct against both individuals and groups, whereby emphasis is placed upon the notion that groups consist of individual members.[325] However, the structure of the act has similarities with the act of genocide where the main basis for discrimination and persecution is the identity[326] of membership of a victim.[327]

---

[320]See Hall and Stahn (2016), p. 204.

[321]Kieler (2003), p. 22.

[322]Flores (2006), p. 49.

[323]Petrossian (2019a), p. 143.

[324]See d Brouwer (2005), p. 57.

[325]The Commentary of 1991 ILC Draft Code, 2 YbILC (1991) 104, which refers to both individuals and groups of individuals, p. 268, Hall and Stahn (2016), p. 220.

[326]de Guzman (2010), p. 134.

[327]Safferling (2011a), p. 203.

3.4.3.9 Enforced Disappearance of Persons

The central element of the act of enforced disappearance of persons is the deprivation of liberty of a victim without any knowledge of the victim's fate and whereabouts. It is also used to spread fear and insecurity within the group of people, mostly political dissident groups and family members. Accordingly, this is by its very nature directed not only against a group of individuals but against the individual victim.

3.4.3.10 The Crime of Apartheid

The crime of apartheid, as an act of racial discrimination, targets by its very nature the entire racial group. In its elements, the crime of apartheid shares similarities with the crimes of persecution and genocide, and it is even possible to determine both individuals as well as the whole racial group as victims of the conduct. The main basis of the crime is a discriminatory feature on the grounds of race.

3.4.3.11 Other Inhumane Acts of a Similar Character Intentionally Causing Great Suffering, or Serious Injury to Body or to Mental or Physical Health

The inhumane acts which are directed against victims causing them great suffering, injury to body or to mental health cannot be distinguished as a group/collective victimisation and, therefore, have to be classified as an act towards a single victim.

Acts of crimes against humanity	Victimisation type
Murder	Individual
Extermination	Group
Enslavement	Individual
Deportation or forcible transfer of population	Group
Imprisonment or other severe deprivation of physical liberty in violation of fundamental rules of international law	Individual
Torture	Individual
Sexual violence	Individual
Persecution	Group
Enforced disappearance of persons	Individual/ Group
The crime of apartheid	Group
Other inhumane acts of a similar character intentionally causing great suffering, or serious injury to body or to mental or physical health	Individual

3.4.4 *Victims of War Crimes*

In comparison to crimes against humanity, it is considerably easier to determine the protected values regarding war crimes. Although there are still a number of disputes regarding the determination of the protected interests—for example, whether it should be seen as a collective value of a plurality of persons or the protection of individuals during the armed conflict—[328] it is clear that individuals are protected in different situations during the armed conflict, such as prisoners of war, civilians being bombed, etc. At the same time, some types of war crimes may, however, lead to collective victimisation or may include individual as well as collective victimisation (mostly under Hague Law).[329] Accordingly, it depends on the nature of the war crime itself.

Acts of war crimes	Victimisation type
(a) Grave breaches of the Geneva Conventions of 12 August 1949, namely, any of the following acts against persons or property protected under the provisions of the relevant Geneva Convention:	
Willful killing;	Individual
Torture or inhuman treatment, including biological experiments;	Individual
Willfully causing great suffering, or serious injury to body or health;	Individual
Extensive destruction and appropriation of property, not justified by military necessity and carried out unlawfully and wantonly;	Individual
Compelling a prisoner of war or other protected person to serve in the forces of a hostile Power;	Individual
Willfully depriving a prisoner of war or other protected person of the rights of fair and regular trial;	Individual
Unlawful deportation or transfer or unlawful confinement;	Individual/ Group
Taking of hostages.	Individual
(b) Other serious violations of the laws and customs applicable in international armed conflict, within the established framework of international law, namely, any of the following acts:	
Intentionally directing attacks against the civilian population as such or against individual civilians not taking direct part in hostilities;	Individual
Intentionally directing attacks against civilian objects, that is, objects which are not military objectives;	Group
Intentionally directing attacks against personnel, installations, material, units or vehicles involved in a humanitarian assistance or peacekeeping mission in accordance with the Charter of the United Nations, as long as they are entitled to the protection given to civilians or civilian objects under the international law of armed conflict;	Individual/ Group

(continued)

[328] Safferling (2011b), p. 222, cp. Werle, Jeßberger (2014), p. 409, cp. Bock (2013), p. 270.

[329] Several offenses overlap with or are even largely identical to another offense. Cottier (2016), p. 317.

Acts of war crimes	Victimisation type
Intentionally launching an attack in the knowledge that such attack will cause incidental loss of life or injury to civilians or damage to civilian objects or widespread, long-term and severe damage to the natural environment which would be clearly excessive in relation to the concrete and direct overall military advantage anticipated;	Individual/ Group
Attacking or bombarding, by whatever means, towns, villages, dwellings or buildings which are undefended and which are not military objectives;	Group
Killing or wounding a combatant who, having laid down his arms or having no longer means of defense, has surrendered at discretion;	Individual
Making improper use of a flag of truce, of the flag or of the military insignia and uniform of the enemy or of the United Nations, as well as of the distinctive emblems of the Geneva Conventions, resulting in death or serious personal injury;	Individual
The transfer, directly or indirectly, by the Occupying Power of parts of its own civilian population into the territory it occupies, or the deportation or transfer of all or parts of the population of the occupied territory within or outside this territory;	Group
Intentionally directing attacks against buildings dedicated to religion, education, art, science or charitable purposes, historic monuments, hospitals and places where the sick and wounded are collected, provided they are not military objectives;	Group
Subjecting persons who are in the power of an adverse party to physical mutilation or to medical or scientific experiments of any kind which are neither justified by the medical, dental or hospital treatment of the person concerned nor carried out in his or her interest, and which cause death to or seriously endanger the health of such person or persons;	Individual
Killing or wounding treacherously individuals belonging to the hostile nation or army;	Individual
Declaring that no quarter will be given;	Group
Destroying or seising the enemy's property unless such destruction or seizure be imperatively demanded by the necessities of war;	Individual/ Group
Declaring abolished, suspended or inadmissible in a court of law the rights and actions of the nationals of the hostile party;	Group
Compelling the nationals of the hostile party to take part in the operations of war directed against their own country, even if they were in the belligerent's service before the commencement of the war;	Individual
Pillaging a town or place, even when taken by assault;	Group
Employing poison or poisoned weapons;	Group
Employing asphyxiating, poisonous or other gases, and all analogous liquids, materials or devices;	Group
Employing bullets which expand or flatten easily in the human body, such as bullets with a hard envelope which does not entirely cover the core or is pierced with incisions;	Individual/ Group
Employing weapons, projectiles and material and methods of warfare which are of a nature to cause superfluous injury or unnecessary suffering or which are inherently indiscriminate in violation of the international law of armed conflict, provided that such weapons, projectiles and material and methods of warfare are	Group

(continued)

Acts of war crimes	Victimisation type
the subject of a comprehensive prohibition and are included in an annex to this Statute, by an amendment in accordance with the relevant provisions set forth in Articles 121 and 123;	
Committing outrages upon personal dignity, in particular humiliating and degrading treatment;	Individual
Committing rape, sexual slavery, enforced prostitution, forced pregnancy, as defined in Article 7(2) (f), enforced sterilisation, or any other form of sexual violence also constituting a grave breach of the Geneva Conventions;	Individual/ Group
Utilising the presence of a civilian or other protected person to render certain points, areas or military forces immune from military operations;	Individual
Intentionally directing attacks against buildings, material, medical units and transport, and personnel using the distinctive emblems of the Geneva Conventions in conformity with international law;	Individual/ Group
Intentionally using starvation of civilians as a method of warfare by depriving them of objects indispensable to their survival, including willfully impeding relief supplies as provided for under the Geneva Conventions;	Individual/ Group
Conscripting or enlisting children under the age of 15 years into the national armed forces or using them to participate actively in hostilities.	Individual

3.4.5 *Victims of Crime of Aggression*

Since 1 January 2017, the ICC has been able to exercise its jurisdiction over the crime of aggression.[330] This is, however, still the most problematic political and legal issue under the aims of the ICC. Although the state itself may not be criminalised for the warfare, the main purpose of the crime is to prevent the aggressive conduct of war, based upon Article 2 (4) UN-Charter. The protected interest in this sense is not only an individual or group of individuals, as is the case in other macro-crimes, but the general prohibition of the use of force by states aims at protecting the sovereignty of each state as well as international peace and security. The victim in this case is the state, the sovereignty of which is at risk. Accordingly, individual victimisation is excluded for all types of acts pertaining to crimes of aggression,[331] as the whole population may suffer under the aggressive war.

[330]ICC Resolution RC/Res. 6 on 11 June 2010.

[331]Such as; a) invasion or attack by the armed forces of a State of the territory of another State, or any military occupation, however temporary, resulting from such invasion or attack, or any annexation by the use of force of the territory of another State or part thereof; b) Bombardment by the armed forces of a State against the territory of another State or the use of any weapons by a State against the territory of another State; c) The blockade of the ports or coasts of a State by the armed forces of another State; d) An attack by the armed forces of a State on the land, sea or air forces, or marine and air fleets of another State; e) The use of armed forces of one State which are within the territory of another State with the agreement of the receiving State, in contravention of

Therefore, including the crime of aggression in the victimhood scheme under international criminal law is among the most problematic issues.

3.5 Article 68 (3) RS

Article 68 RS is the basis of the victims' participation system. It establishes the general provision for victims to be involved at the different levels before the Court and to be protected as victims. The core provision enabling victims to present their views and concerns lies in Article 68 (3) RS. However, it lies within the discretion of the Court to develop the further mechanisms of the involvement of the victims in the proceedings and to limit or to grant the victims a different range of rights. For this reason, the process of victims' participation differs from case to case. In the decisions of the Court regarding victims, the ICC judges are statutorily obligated to determine whether the interests of the victims are affected and to respect the fact that such participation is appropriate and is not prejudicial to or inconsistent with the rights of the accused and a fair and impartial trial.

Article 68 (3) RS reads as follows:

> Where the personal interests of the victims are affected, the Court shall permit their views and concerns to be presented and considered at stages of the proceedings determined to be appropriate by the Court and in a manner which is not prejudicial to or inconsistent with the rights of the accused and a fair and impartial trial. [...]

The wording used in the Article such as "personal interests", "views and concerns", "stages of the proceedings", "[...] is not prejudicial to or inconsistent with the rights of the accused" and "fair and impartial trial" requires further interpretation as it has often been construed differently by the Court.

3.5.1 Personal Interests

The most difficult element to interpret lies in the wording of the "personal interests" of the victims. From the first and general point of view, the personal interests of the victims is a precondition for their participation. This means that the victims may have been affected by the alleged crime or situation, which will enable them to be

the conditions provided for in the agreement or any extension of their presence in such territory beyond the termination of the agreement; f) The action of a State in allowing its territory, which it has placed at the disposal of another State, to be used by that other State for perpetrating an act of aggression against a third State; g) The sending by or on behalf of a State of armed bands, groups, irregulars or mercenaries, which carry out acts of armed force against another State of such gravity as to amount to the acts listed above, or its substantial involvement therein.

involved in various ways in the entire process,[332] starting with the recognition and participation. On the other hand, the personal interests of the victim could be considered the second step for participation.[333] As soon as the status of the victim is recognised by the Court pursuant to Rule 85 RPE,[334] the victim may exercise the right to participate directly at every stage at the Court, provided that their interests are somehow affected and they have previously made a request for participation to the Court.[335] If the Court finds a connection between the affected interests and the specific situation, it may allow the victims to present their views.[336] Thus, in general terms, the interpretation of the term "personal interests" depends how this is going to be interpreted from the broad (systematic) or narrow (casuistic) perspectives.[337] Another question which arises under these provisions is that if victims are already recognised as victims before the Court, their interests are potentially affected during the different stages of the proceedings. There should, therefore, be no limits imposed upon lodging a request to present particular views and concerns on each matter.[338] However, as it was already mentioned above, the Court has to balance the victims' participation with the rights of the accused and thus the victims may not express their views on the matter where their interests are not affected or considered. To determine

[332]ICC, *Prosecutor v. Katanga, Chui*, ICC-01/04-01/07-933, Decision on the treatment of applications for participation (26 February 2009) para. 10, "*in the interest of the proper administration of justice, victims authorised to participate in the proceedings at the pre-trial stage must, in principle, and subject to the considerations set forth below, automatically be authorised to participate in the proceedings at the trial stage, without the need for their applications to be registered and assessed a second time*".

[333]ICC, *Prosecutor v. Lubanga*, Prosecutor's 25 August Observations on the Application for Participation of Applicants a/0047/06 – a/0052/06 (6 September 2006) para. 10, ICC, *Prosecutor v. Lubanga*, ICC-01/04-01/06-824, Judgment on the appeal of Mr. Thomas Lubanga Dyilo against the decision of PTC I entitled "Décision sur la demande de mise en liberté provisoire de Thomas Lubanga Dyilo" (13 February 2007) ICC, *Prosecutor v. Bemba*, ICC-01/05-01/08-623, Decision on the Participation of Victims in the Appeal against the "Decision on theInterim Release of Jean-Pierre Bemba Gombo and Convening Hearings with the Kingdom of Belgium, the Republic of Portugal, the Republic of France (27 November 2009) Dissenting Opinion of Judge Sang-Hyun Song, see also Donat-Cattin (2016), p. 1695, para. 22.

[334]ICC, *Prosecutor v. Ruto, Kosgey, Sang*, ICC-01/09-01/11-249, Decision on Victims' Participation at the Confirmation of Charges Hearing and in the Related Proceedings (8 August 2011) para. 101.

[335]See e.g. ICC, *Prosecutor v. Ongwen*, ICC-02/04-01/15-1199-Red, Decision on the Legal Representatives forVictims Requests to Present Evidence and Views and Concerns and related requests (6 March 2018) paras. 17–25.

[336]ICC, *Prosecutor v. Lubanga*, ICC-01/04-01/06-1119, Decision on victims' participation (18 January 2008) para. 96, see also Bock (2010), pp. 449–451.

[337]In case of casuistic approach the victims are forced to apply for the participation in each judicial procedural activity, which will lead to ineffective and to inefficient operation of the Court, ICC, *Situation in Darfur*, ICC-02/05-121, Decision on the Requests for Leave to Appeal the Decision on the Application for Participation of Victims in the Proceedings in the Situation (5 February 2008) p. 6, compare with ICC, ICC, *Prosecutor v. Lubanga*, ICC-01/04-01/06-1119, Decision on victims' participation (18 January 2008) paras. 94–100.

[338]See Vasiliev (2008), p. 636 et seq.

the limits of where the victims' interests may not be affected is, however, difficult.[339] At this point, it is again important to mention that the victims are not party to the proceedings, but merely participants.[340] In the case of *Katanga*, the Chamber found that the personal interests of the victims to participate in the proceedings flow from: (1) the desire to have a declaration of truth by a competent body (right to truth); (2) the wish to have those who victimised them identified and prosecuted (right to justice); and (3) the wish to be compensated for the harm suffered (right to reparation).[341]

Due to the lack of guidance both in Article 68 (3) RS and the Rules, it is within the discretion of the Court to decide how the interests of victims should be analysed. This might be considered from stage to stage, or from procedural activity to procedural activity. The selection of the approaches mentioned depends on the situation, subject matter and upcoming procedural activities.[342] Although, on the one hand, the wording of "personal interests" is designed to abut the "chaotic" victims' participation at all stages, it is, at the same time, left to the Court to decide in each specific case how the victims' participation will function during the process and how it will be balanced against the rights of the accused.[343] Victims' intervention should not introduce notions based merely on a legal interpretation but also needs to be linked to actual consultations with the victims. It should also focus on matters from their personal perspectives.[344]

3.5.2 Views and Concerns

In comparison to "personal interests", the interpretation of "views and concerns" is less complex. This is the fundamental point which enables victims to be a participant in or "potential-party"[345] to the proceedings. Secondly, it allows them to express

---

[339]See e.g. ICC, *Prosecutor v. Lubanga*, ICC-01/04-01/06-1119, Decision on victims' participation (18 January 2008) para. 97, Kelly (2013), p. 54.

[340]See e.g. ICC, *Prosecutor v. Katanga, Chui*, ICC-01/04-01/07-1788, Decision on the Modalities of Victim Participation at Trial (22 January 2010) para. 58.

[341]ICC, *Prosecutor v. Katanga, Chui,* ICC-01/04-01/07-474 Decision on the Set of Procedural Rights Attached to Procedural Status of Victim at the Pre-Trial Stage of the Case (15 May 2008) paras. 31–44, ICC, *Prosecutor v. Abu Garda*, ICC-02/05-02/09, Decision on the 34 Applications for Participation at the Pre-Trial Stage of the Case (25 September 2009) para. 3.

[342]ICC, *Situation in Darfur*, ICC-02/05-113, Decision on the Requests for Leave to Appeal the Decision on the Application for Participation of Victims in the Proceedings in the Situation (5 February 2008) pp. 6–7, ICC, *Prosecutor v. Katanga, Chui,* ICC-01/04-01/07-474 Decision on the Set of Procedural Rights Attached to Procedural Status of Victim at the Pre-Trial Stage of the Case (15 May 2008) paras. 45–46.

[343]Cf. Trumbull (2008), pp. 800–801; Bachvarova (2017), pp. 110–115.

[344]FIDH, Five Myths about Victim Participation in ICC Proceedings, p. 11.

[345]Donat-Cattin (2016), p. 1696, para. 23.

their presentations, opinions, stances and positions on the subject[346] and their concerns about the case, so that this can guide the Chamber in making a decision. In this way, the victims are able to express themselves and to point out their concerns. However, the main problem arises with regard to the method of expressing those views and concerns. The high number of victims in different cases, which will almost certainly grow in the future, makes it difficult for the victims to express their concerns directly. Given this difficulty, a legal representative for the victims is deemed to be voicing those views and concerns pursuant to Rule 91 RPE. This is where the practical difficulties of effectiveness and meaningfulness of participation come to the fore. The legal representatives, regardless of the fact of how professional they might be, are unable to represent every single victim in this complex process. This is due to the fact that a group of victims is not a homogenous entity; the victims have a variety of views and perspectives.[347] Only in specific matters may selected victims be invited to present their views and concerns on their own behalf before the Chamber. However, the selection of those victims who will be present in the proceedings could be randomised and, therefore, case-relevant information from other victims may be overshadowed. The legal representatives have the discretion to select the victim who is to appear before the Chamber based upon strategical aspects of the case.[348]

3.5.3 Stages of the Proceedings

If the terminology "personal interests" and "presenting views and concerns" form the core of developing jurisprudence regarding the victims' participation system and are still very much in the process of being modernised and developed, the Court has given strict clarification with regard to interpreting the stages of the proceedings. In the early period of the Court's existence, with regard to the situation in the DRC, the Chamber allowed victims to participate in the investigations considering it an appropriate stage of the proceedings.[349] Later on, the Appeals Chamber curtailed the decision on participation in early investigations noting that the participation of victims was to be confined to proceedings before the Court, with the aim of affording victims an opportunity to voice their views and concerns on matters affecting their

[346]See. Bachvarova (2017), p. 142.

[347]Rombouts (2004), p. 188.

[348]See e.g. ICC, *Prosecutor v. Bemba,* ICC-01/05-01/08-2138, Decision on the supplemented applications by the legal representatives of victims to present evidence and the views and concerns of victims (22 February 2012) para. 55, ICC, *Prosecutor v. Bemba*, ICC-01/05-01/08-2220, Decision on the presentation of views and concerns by victims/0542/08,a/0394/08anda/0511/08 (24 May 2012), see also The Victims' Court, Human Rights Center, 2015, p. 21.

[349]ICC, Siuation in the DRC, ICC-01/04-101-tEN-Corr, Decision on the Applications for Participation in the Proceedings of VPRS 1 VPRS 2, VPRS 3, VPRS 4, VPRS 5 and VPRS, 5 (17 January 2006) paras. 57–60.

personal interests within the judicial proceedings.[350] Therefore, the investigation may not be considered a stage of the proceedings with regard to victims' participation. Generally, one might say that enabling the victim to participate in the investigation may give false hope and inflate their role in the proceedings.[351]

3.5.4 Rights of the Accused

Originally, criminal justice predominantly concentrated on the accused. Starting with the human rights movements in the 1980s, an agreement was reached to include victims in criminal justice. The involvement of the victim in the proceedings may endanger and jeopardise the delicate balance of the equality of arms. This means that if the balance before was maintained between the prosecutor and the defence, the balance now needs to be secured between three players, including the victim. Article 68 (3) RS mentions two important preconditions for the participation of victims in relation to the accused, and the judges should limit the participation of the victim if it may be prejudicial to or inconsistent with the rights of the accused.

The provision on prejudice is linked to the principle of the presumption of innocence of the accused. Each and every procedural activity by the victims which could be considered prejudicial has to be rejected by the ICC judges.[352] Indeed, from the outset the participation of the victims in the proceedings could be seen as a violation of the principle of the presumption of innocence. This is because their participation *per se* presupposes the commission of a crime and the ensuing harm suffered. The burden of proof still rests only on the prosecution pursuant to Article 66 (2) RS to identify the disputed perpetrator.[353]

Regarding any inconsistency with the rights of the accused, the provision assumes that the participation of the victim is not incompatible with Article 67 RS if certain requirements are met. These include, *inter alia*, the fact that the accused:

- must be given adequate time and facilities to prepare the defense;
- must be tried without undue delay;
- must be able to examine the witnesses against him or her;[354]

[350]ICC, *Situation in DRC*, ICC-01/04OA4 OA5 OA6, Judgment on victim participation in the investigation stage of the proceedings in the appeal of the OPCD against the decision of Pre-Trial Chamber I of 7 December 2007 and in the appeals of the OPCD and the Prosecutor against the decision of Pre-Trial Chamber I of 24 December 2007 (19 December 2008) paras. 55–57.

[351]Kelly (2013), p. 55.

[352]Inadmissible evidence, prejudicial or sensationalist statements of the victims etc, see Dué (1966), pp. 821–822.

[353]See Zagar (2018), p. 306; Zappala (2010), p. 146; McAsey (2011), p. 118.

[354]See also Rule 140 (2) (d) RPE and Donat-Cattin (2016), p. 1698, para. 27.

- must obtain the attendance and examination of witnesses on his or her behalf under the same conditions as the witnesses against him or her; and
- must not to be accused by an anonymous victim.[355]

3.5.5 *Fair and Impartial Trial*

Although the fair trial principle is an internationally recognised principle under European and Inter-American Human Rights Law, and is also bound within Articles 9 (3) and 14 ICCPR which stipulate the minimum standards and guarantees for the accused in criminal cases, the use of the principle of a fair trial at the ICC is broad and implies not only a fair trial with minimal standards and guarantees for the accused, but also for victims and witnesses, as well as for the Prosecutor pursuant to Article 64 (2) RS. The Court interprets the fair trial principle as being respect for the procedural rights of the Prosecutor, the defense and the victims as guaranteed by the relevant status under the principle of equality.[356] One could therefore say that, on the one hand, the fair trial principle under the provisions of the ICC secures the exercising of the rights of the accused and the existence of minimum standards and guarantees for the accused, such as an impartial trial, the presumption of innocence and a trial within reasonable time,[357] whilst, on the other hand, providing a whole set of duties for the well-being of the victims and the witnesses and enabling the Prosecutors to fulfil their respective mandates independently and without influence, which further allows the Court to make its decisions.[358]

From the perspective of the victims, even in cases where it is disputed that the victims have the right to a fair trial, this provision is aimed at protecting the defendant from the victims, the participation of whom may violate the very principle of a fair trial for the accused. This means that where the victim pushes hard to prove the guilt of the defendant, this will be considered a violation of the equality of arms principle as it is not the task of the victims to prove the guilt of the defendant.

Another important aspect of marginalising victims' participation is the impartiality and judicial independence of the Court itself, whereby the question of

---

[355]ICC, *Prosecutor v. Lubanga*, ICC-01/04-01/06-462-tEN, Decision on the arrangements for participation of victims a/001/06m 1/0002/06 and 1/0003/06 at the confirmation hearing (22 September 2006) p. 7.

[356]ICC, *Situation in the DRC*, ICC-01/04-135-tEN, Decision on the Prosecutor's Application for Leave to Appeal the Chamber's Decision of 17 January 2006 on the Application for Participation in the Proceedings of VPRS1,VPRS 2, VPRS 3, VPRS 4, VPRS5 and VPRS6, (31 March 2006) para. 38.

[357]ICC, *Prosecutor v. Bemba*, ICC-01/05-01/08-2027, Second order regarding the applications of the legal representatives of victimsto present evidence and the views and concerns of victims (21 December 2011) para. 11.

[358]See Stewart (2014), p. 2.

disqualifying a Judge may be considered under the provision set out in Article 41 (2) (a) RS in conjunction with Rule 34 RPE.

3.5.6 *Types of Participation for Victims*

Under the provisions of Article 68 (3) RS, two possible victim participation types may be considered in the proceedings: direct and indirect participation. Indirect participation, which is meant more often than the direct participation of the victims at the Court, can be exercised in three forms; indirect participation or representative participation through legal representative, indirect participation through common legal representative and indirect participation through the OPCV. The choice of which form of participation is more appropriate depends on the situation, specific case matters, the wishes of the victims and also objective circumstances.

3.5.6.1 Direct Participation

The participation of victims in criminal justice procedures assumes the direct participation of the victim during different procedural activities, standing as a victim and exercising a different range of procedural rights and obligations. This type of participation is rarely seen in international criminal procedure. Direct participation at the Court is interpreted as the physical or remote[359] appearance of the victim before the Chamber solely in order to present his or her views and concerns, not as a witness.[360] This type of participation includes engaging with justice processes, such as personal contribution for the determination of the truth.[361] Bearing in mind that the physical presence of victims before the Chamber in order to present the views and concerns increases the length of the trial, and given that the victims' common views and concerns may, on occasions, be better presented by a common legal representative,[362] not every victim is able to present his or her position during the trial. In order to authorise the exercise of the direct participation of the victims upon the request of legal representative, the Court has established a guideline based upon

[359]Through video-link, or in writing.

[360]ICC, *Prosecutor v. Bemba,* ICC-01/05-01/08-2138, Decision on the supplemented applications by the legal representatives of victims to present evidence and the views and concerns of victims (22 February 2012), ICC, *Prosecutor v. Ntaganda*, ICC-01/04-02/06-449, decision on victims' participation in trial proceedings (2 February 2015) para. 39, compare with ICC, *Prosecutor v. Banda*, ICC-02/05-03/09-545, Decision on the participation of victims in the trial proceedings (20 March 2014) para. 20.

[361]See Garbett (2017), p. 201.

[362]ICC, *Prosecutor v. Bemba*, ICC-01/05-01/08-807-Corr-Anx, Corrigendum to Decision on the participation of victims in the trial and on 86 applications by victims to participate in the proceedings (12 July 2010) para. 27.

the general principles pertaining to the presentation of evidence by victims or the expression of views and concerns in person, upon the requirements applicable to the presentation of evidence and the expressing of views and concerns in person and upon a victim-by-victim assessment as to whether the requirements are met.[363]

The Chamber has also established criteria for legal representatives in order to shorten the list of victims willing to participate directly and to find the most relevant victims for the determination of the truth. Those victims have to be best placed to assist the Chamber in the determination of the truth of the particular case and the testimony presented should not be cumulative and repetitive. Furthermore, the victims must be willing to disclose their identity.[364] This is the only practical way for the victims to be allowed to participate at the proceedings directly before the Chamber, expressing their views and concerns or contributing by providing evidence. Although the victims are equipped with further participatory rights, they are not able to exercise them in person. Those rights, such as calling witnesses or cross-examining witnesses, are exercised by their legal representatives. It is important to mention that the appearance of a high number of victims before the Chamber may not be effective for the determination of the truth as it may lead to repetition. However, at the same time each victim has an interest in his or her own presentation, view and concern which cannot be ignored. Nevertheless, in high-profile cases, for example, in the proceedings against *Bemba*, only three victims from 5229 participating were ultimately permitted to express their concerns before the judges and the parties, and even then not physically, but remotely by video-link.[365] This must, of course, be distinguished from those victims who are called to testify before the Court as witnesses.[366]

3.5.6.2 Indirect Participation

The most common form of participation at the Court is through a legal representative, which is referred to as indirect participation or representative participation. Indirect participation does not position the victims as central agents within the justice system;[367] they are rather passive or remote observers who communicate with the Court through their chosen legal representative. As mentioned previously, this type

[363]ICC, *Prosecutor v. Bemba*, ICC-01/05-01/08-2138, Decision on the supplemented applications by the legal representatives of victims to present evidence and the views and concerns of victims (22 February 2012) para. 12.

[364]ICC, *Prosecutor v. Bemba*, ICC-01/05-01/08-2027, Second order regarding the applications of the legal representatives of victimsto present evidence and the views and concerns of victims (21 December 2011) para. 12.

[365]ICC, *Prosecutor v. Bemba*, ICC-01/05-01/08-2220, Decision on the presentation of views and concerns by victims /0542/08,a/0394/08 and a/0511/08 (24 May 2012) para. 13 and only after long "negotiations" with the Court was the direct participation of the victims possible.

[366]See the dual status of the victim.

[367]Garbett (2017), p. 201.

of participation may begin during the application process, i.e. as soon as the applicant mentions in their application the lawyer who is representing their interests. Under the system operating at the Court, there are three types of representative participation:

- Representation through Legal Representative (LRV)
- Representation through Common Legal Representative (CLRV)
- Representation through the Office of Public Council for Victims (OPCV)

In accordance with Rule 90 (1) RPE, victims are, in principle, free to choose a legal representative. This should give assurances to the victims that their views and concerns will be represented in Court once they have been granted victim status in a case. Given the number of persons that could be granted victim status in any given case, Rule 90 (2) RPE states that the Chamber has the ability to "request" that the victims or groups of victims select a common legal representative or representatives. This can be facilitated by the Registry in order to ensure the "effectiveness of the proceedings".[368]

When it comes to the freedom of the victims to choose their legal representatives, the Trial Chamber clarified that "although victims are free to choose a Legal Representative, this right is subject to the important practical, financial, infrastructural and logistical constraints faced by the Court. Common legal representation is the primary procedural mechanism for reconciling the conflicting requirements of having fair and expeditious proceedings".[369] As a result, the Chamber concluded that "the freedom to choose a personal Legal Representative, set out in Rule 90 (1) RPE is qualified by Rule 90(2) RPE and subject to the inherent and express powers of the Chamber to take all measures necessary if the interests of justice so require."[370] Here, it is possible to identify how the practical implications of victim participation in international criminal justice manifest themselves resulting a number of restrictions on the right of the victim to choose their legal representative.

It is also possible for the Registrar to choose the common legal representative (s) on behalf of the victims if the Chamber so requests. This will occur in the event of the lapsing of a time limit provided to the victims to select the representative (s) themselves in accordance with Rule 90 (3) RPE. Furthermore, it falls within the responsibility of the Chamber and the Registrar to take all reasonable steps to ensure that in selecting common legal representatives, the distinct interests of the victims, in particular as provided for in Article 68 (1) RS, are represented, and that any conflict of interest is avoided (Rule 90 (4) RPE). There is a possibility for victims to request the Chamber to review the Registrar's choice of common legal

[368]Rule 90 (2) RPE ICC, cf. Magsam (2014), p. 187.

[369]See ICC, *Prosecutor v. Katanga, Chui,* ICC-01/04-01/07-1328, Order on the organisation of common legal representation of victims (22 July 2009) paras. 10–18.

[370]ICC, *Prosecutor v. Katanga, Chui,* ICC-01/04-01/07-1328, Order on the organisation of common legal representation of victims (22 July 2009) paras. 10–18.

representative pursuant to Regulation 79 (3) RoC. In practice, there is limited opportunity for the victims to review the choice of common legal representative.[371]

It should be noted that where the Chamber appoints legal representatives in accordance with the Regulations of the Court, such an appointment may be made by the counsel of the OPCV pursuant to Regulation 80 (2) RoC.[372] As a result, the LRV is not the only section of the ICC that may represent victims throughout the trial proceedings. It is, however, the LRV's primary mandate and role. This highlights the fact that the composition of the institutional framework for victims at the ICC can be somewhat confusing for the victims. In a report by the Registry on consultations with victims, the common legal representative was seen as a 'complex and abstract concept for many victims' and there was little understanding regarding the different actors of the Court and how participation for victims fitted into this.[373]

Should the victims not be in a position to pay for a common legal representative, financial assistance is provided through the Registry in accordance with Rule 90 (5) RPE. Importantly, there is no equivalent provision relating to financial assistance for a single victim and their chosen legal representative. The Regulations of the Court determine that the scope of legal assistance paid by the Court regarding victims shall be determined by the Registrar in consultation with the Chamber, where appropriate (Regulation 83 (2) RoC). Pursuant to Rule 90 (6) RPE, the LRVs must have the same qualifications as the defence counsel. These are prescribed in Rule 22 (1) RPE. Such qualifications include at least 10 years' experience in relevant criminal proceedings, fluency in English or French and no convictions or disciplinary offences incompatible with the office of counsel. In fact, the list enumerating all the possible LRVs is the same list that the defense can choose their counsel from and is purely entitled 'List of Counsel'.[374]

The distinction between three types of representative participation is because the Legal Representative is a lawyer who has been directly chosen by the victims to represent their views before the Court. Distinguishing the fact that during the proceedings more victims apply for participation via their own representatives, a situation arises where numerous representatives are involved in the process. Therefore, in order to make the representation meaningful and to simplify the communication between the Court and the victims, a common legal representative among the legal representatives might be appointed or chosen. Another type of representative participation is through the OPCV. In contrast to LRVs and CLRVs where the victims are aware of their lawyer or representative before the Court, those victims

---

[371]Hirst (2017), p. 145; Kelly (2013), p. 52.

[372]ICC, *Prosecutor v. Katanga, Chui,* ICC-01/04-01/07-1328, Order on the organisation of common legal representation of victims (22 July 2009) para. 11, ICC, Prosecutor v. Lubanga, ICC-01/04-01/06-1211, Decision on the role of the Office of Public Counsel for Victims and its request for access to documents (6 March 2008) para. 30.

[373]ICC, *Prosecutor v. Ntaganda*, ICC-01/04-02/06-513, Registry's Report on Consultations with Victims Pursuant to Decision ICC-01/04-02/06-449 (16 March 2015).

[374]*Legal Professionals,* International Criminal Court, see at https://www.icc-cpi.int/get-involved/Pages/legal-professionals.aspx, last visited on 12 December 2020.

who applied for participation on their own or without legal representative are, in principle, represented by the OPCV. However, there might be different scenarios for how the representation of victims is organised. This depends on several aspects including the situation of the conflict, the existing groups of victims and their wishes, the alleged crimes, the suspect and other objective circumstances. At the same time, the OPCV stands as assistance for the LRVs.

Where the victims are not satisfied with the activities of their legal representative, the Chamber is in a position to be able to appoint a common legal representative, if the interests of justice so require.[375] However, the statutory appointment of the CLRV may also lead to further disappointment and frustration among the victims.

Nevertheless, the whole weight of the participation of victims is attributed to their legal representation as this institution is aimed at exercising the victims' rights before the Court. This means that the participation depends on the professionalism of the counsel representing the victims. At the same time, the legal representative is responsible for the argumentation of how the personal interests of the victims could be affected at the various stages during which they wish to present their views and concerns. Based upon that argumentation, the victims could be allowed by the Chamber to do so.[376]

The legal representative has to keep the victims informed and must respond to their enquiries, receive instruction and guidelines from them, maintain files related to the victims, obtain qualified support and store and process confidential materials accessible to him or her.[377] Additionally, the legal representative may essentially have more rights in comparison to the victims as they are, upon application, entitled to have access to confidential documents. Only upon a further application can the victims be informed of the details of such confidential documents.[378]

---

[375]See in this regard different approaches to appointment of CLRVs or OPCVs in different cases in Human Rights Watch, Who Will Stand for Us, Victims' Legal Representation at the ICC in the Ongwen Case and Beyond, 2017, pp. 14–20, Vasiliev (2015), p. 1182, ICC, *Prosecutor v. Bemba*, ICC-01/05-01/08-1005, Decision on common legal representation of victims for the purpose of trial (12 November 2010) paras. 11–13, ICC, *Prosecutor v. Ruto, Sang*, ICC-01/09-01/11-330, Decision on the "Motion from Victims a/0041/10, a/0045/10, a/0051/10 and a/0056/10 requesting the PTC to Reconsider the Appointment of Common Legal Representative Sureta Chana for All Victims" (9 September 2011) paras. 9–12, ICC, *Prosecutor v. Banda*, ICC-02/05-03/09-337, Decision on common legal representation (25 May 2012).

[376]See e.g. ICC, *Prosecutor v. Ruto, Sang*, ICC-01/09-01/11-1930, Decision on the Common Legal Representative for Victims' Request for viva voce Presentation of Views and Concerns by the Victims (20 July 2015) para. 7.

[377]ICC, *Prosecutor v. Gbagbo*, ICC-02/11-01/11-138, Decision on victims' participation and victims' common legal representation at the Confirmation of Charges Hearing and in the Related Proceedings (4 June 2012) para. 38.

[378]ICC, *Prosecutor v. Gbagbo*, ICC-02/11-01/11-749, Decision on the Legal Representative of Victims' access to certain confidential filings and to the case record (19 January 2015) para. 15, ICC, *Prosecutor v. Ongwen*, ICC-02/04-01/15-369, Decision on issues concerning victims' participation (15 December 2015) para. 3.

3.5.7 *Participatory Rights of the Victims*

As mentioned above, the Chambers have decided differently on victims' participation. Various types of participatory rights for victims have been developed in the course of different cases. At the same time, the victims' specific and participatory rights have to be defined according to general principles, as set down in Article 68 (3) RS. In contrast, the rights of the accused are statutorily established and may not be changed (Article 67 RS).[379] The participatory rights of the victims are based upon five statutory general rights of victims: (1) the right to participate (Article 68 (3) RS); (2) the right to be protected (Article 68 (1) RS); (3) the right to be informed deriving from Article 15 (6) RS in conjunction with Article 43 RS, and Rule 16 RPE; (4) the right to provide observations in relation to jurisdiction and admissibility challenges (Article 19 (3) RS); and (5) the right to seek reparations pursuant to Article 75 RS and Rules 94 and 97 RPE.

In order to analyse the participatory rights and possibilities of the victims which were composed by the Chambers, these have to be considered in four stages of the proceedings: the pre-trial phase—which includes three sub-stages, namely the pre-situation or preliminary examination, the stage of investigation and the confirmation of charges—the trial phase, the appeals phase and finally the reparation phase.

3.5.7.1 Pre-trial Phase

At the early stages of the proceedings before the Chamber, at the stage where the "potential" victims are, as such, not registered or and have not been granted victim status, they are still entitled to make intial communications regarding the crimes committed by informing the Prosecutor and making representations to the PTC in accordance with Article 15(2) RS and Rule 50 RPE. Taking into account the possibility of being able to challenge the jurisdiction of the Court in a particular situation or the admissibility of the case, the Court is in a position to invite victims, or groups of victims, and their legal representatives who have previously made communication with the Court to submit observations in this regard pursuant to Article 19 (3) RS and Rule 59 RPE.[380] Victims are entitled to make further

---

[379] See Peters (2016), pp. 273–275; Evans (2012), p. 86, compare the rights of victims in Bohacik (2010); Moffett (2015), p. 266.

[380] ICC, *Prosecutor v. Katanga, Chui*, ICC-01/04-01/07-1497, Judgment on the Appeal of Mr. Germain Katanga against the Oral Decision of Trial Chamber II of 12 June 2009 on the Admissibility of the Case (25 September 2009) para. 12, ICC, ICC-RoC46(3)-01/18, Observations on behalf of victims from Tula Toli, 18 June 2018 in regard to Situation in *Myanmar-Bangladesh* (18 June 2018), ICC, *Prosecutor v. Gadaffi*, Observations on behalf of victims on the "Admissibility Challenge by Dr. Saif Al-Islam Gadafi pursuant to Articles 17(1)(c), 19 and 20(3) of the Rome Statute" (28 September 2018), ICC, *Prosecutor v Muthuara, Kenyatta, Ali*, Observations on the "Directions on the submission of observations pursuant to Article 19 (3) of the Rome Statute and

observations in cases where the Prosecutor is not willing to initiate proceedings due to a lack of reasonable basis pursuant to Article 53 RS and Rule 92 (2), 93 RPE.[381] The same may be considered in the case of a decision by the Prosecutor not to prosecute. The victims further have the possibility to provide views and concerns, if permitted, in relation to a decision to hold a confirmation hearing in the absence of the person concerned (Rule 125 RPE), or to amend the charges (Rule 128 RPE).

At the confirmation of charges stage, the PTC has ascertained three further common and essential participatory rights: (1) attendance; (2) participation at the confirmation of charges hearing, which arises from Rule 91 (2) RPE; and (3) enabling the LRV to have access to any public transcripts and documents.[382] In the event of an *ex parte* or *in camera* hearing, the Chamber has to decide on a case-by-case basis whether the presence of the LRV is possible. Pursuant to Rule 89 (1) RPE, the victims are also entitled to make opening and closing statements through their LRV and, if the interests of the victims are affected, they might be permitted by the Chamber to present their views and concerns during the actual confirmation hearing.[383]

Another participatory right consists of the access to public records. This means that the LRV has the possibility to have access to the records pursuant to Rule 121 (10) PRE and to be notified of any motion, submission or statement provided by the parties. In the case of confidential documents, the Chamber may decide on a case-by-case basis whether to grant access to the LRV.[384] Addi-

rule 59 (3) of the Rules of Procedure and Evidence" (3 February 2012) paras. 6–9, Schabas (2016), pp. 492–493; de Brouwer and Heikkilä (2013), p. 1321.

[381] See ICC, *Situation on the Registered Vessels of the Union of the Comoros, the Hellenic Republic and the Kingdom of Cambodia*, ICC-01/13-18, Decision on the Victims' Participation (24 April 2015) paras. 10–13, ICC, *Situation on Registered Vessels of Comoros, Greece and Cambodia*, ICC-01/13-27-Red, Observations on behalf of victims in the proceedings for the review of the Prosecutor's decision not to initiate an investigation (23 June 2015).

[382] Accessible to everyone.

[383] ICC, *Prosecutor v. Gbagbo*, ICC-02/11-01/11-384-Corr, Corrigendum to the second decision on victims' participation at the confirmation of charges hearing and in the related proceedings (6 February 2013) paras. 49–52, ICC, *Prosecutor v. Katanga, Chui,* ICC-01/04-01/07-474 Decision on the Set of Procedural Rights Attached to Procedural Status of Victim at the Pre-Trial Stage of the Case (15 May 2008) paras. 127–133, 140, ICC, *Prosecutor v. Ntaganda*, ICC-01/04-02/06-211 Decision on Victims' Participation at the Confirmation of Charges Hearing and in the Related Proceedings (15 January 2014) paras. 85–87.

[384] ICC, *Prosecutor v. Gbagbo*, ICC-02/11-01/11-384-Corr, Corrigendum to the second decision on victims' participation at the confirmation of charges hearing and in the related proceedings (6 February 2013) paras. 53–58, ICC, *Prosecutor v. Katanga, Chui,* ICC-01/04-01/07-474 Decision on the Set of Procedural Rights Attached to Procedural Status of Victim at the Pre-Trial Stage of the Case (15 May 2008) para. 140, ICC, *Prosecutor v. Ntaganda*, ICC-01/04-02/06-211 Decision on Victims' Participation at the Confirmation of Charges Hearing and in the Related Proceedings (15 January 2014) para. 88, ICC, *Prosecutor v. Ongwen*, ICC-02/04-01/15-369, Decision on issues concerning victims' participation (15 December 2015).

tionally, written submissions on law or fact may be filed by the LRV, if permitted by the Court.[385]

The examination of witnesses is an additional procedural right for the victims which is not granted in every case.[386] The examination of witnesses by the victims or the respective LRV may only take place after the examination of the prosecution and defense and upon the authorisation of the questions.[387] Taking into account that the pre-trial phase is not a truth-finding stage, it is important to mention that the victims are not entitled to adduce any additional evidence at the confirmation hearing and cannot be part of the disclosure process at the pre-trial phase.[388]

3.5.7.2 Trial Phase

As soon as the charges brought against the accused are confirmed, the case proceeds to the trial phase. At this stage, the Chamber can recognise the victims in connection with the confirmed charges, if they were participating at the pre-trial phase, as well as accept new applications and grant new victims procedural status. In comparison to the pre-trial phase, the victims have, relatively speaking, a wider range of rights during the proceedings. The victims are allowed to present evidence and call witnesses, provided they are able to show that their personal interests are affected. Bearing in mind the fact that the right to adduce evidence pertaining to the guilt or innocence of the accused and to challenge the admissibility or relevance lies primarily with the parties, the Rules and the Statute do not preclude victims from

[385]ICC, *Prosecutor v. Gbagbo*, ICC-02/11-01/11-384-Corr, Corrigendum to the second decision on victims' participation at the confirmation of charges hearing and in the related proceedings (6 February 2013) paras. 59–60, ICC, *Prosecutor v. Katanga, Chui,* ICC-01/04-01/07-474 Decision on the Set of Procedural Rights Attached to Procedural Status of Victim at the Pre-Trial Stage of the Case (15 May 2008) para. 134, 142, ICC, *Prosecutor v. Ntaganda*, ICC-01/04-02/06-211 Decision on Victims' Participation at the Confirmation of Charges Hearing and in the Related Proceedings (15 January 2014) para. 96.

[386]In compare to Gbagbo case the PTC issued in the Decision about the modalities at the stage of confirmation of Hearing in the case of Katanga a more substantial role to the victims in the proceedings, see also Moffett (2015), p. 264.

[387]ICC, *Prosecutor v. Katanga, Chui,* ICC-01/04-01/07-474 Decision on the Set of Procedural Rights Attached to Procedural Status of Victim at the Pre-Trial Stage of the Case (15 May 2008) para. 139, taking into account the manner of questioning, see ICC, *Prosecutor v. Lubanga*, ICC-01/04-01/06-2127, Decision on the Manner of Questioning Witnesses by the Legal Representatives of Victims (16 September 2009) paras. 26–30.

[388]ICC, *Prosecutor v. Katanga, Chui,* ICC-01/04-01/07-474 Decision on the Set of Procedural Rights Attached to Procedural Status of Victim at the Pre-Trial Stage of the Case (15 May 2008) paras. 107–114, the Chamber also noted that according to Article 61 (7) RS the power of PTC is confined to "requesting the consideration by the Prosecutor of the opportunity to provide additional evidence, in contrast to Article 69(3) RS which gives the competent Chamber "the authority to request the submission of all evidence that considers necessary for the determination of the truth, see ICC, Policy Paper on Victims' Participation, p. 17.

adducing evidence in order to support the determination of the truth.[389] In order to permit the evidence adduced by the victims, the Chamber has to examine a discrete application, notice to the parties, the demonstration of personal interests, compliance with disclosure obligations and protection orders and the determination of appropriateness and consistency with the rights of the accused to a fair trial.[390]

Parallel to the rights and possibilities generally granted to the victims at the pre-trial phase,[391] the victims at the trial phase may be entitled to call witnesses under strict conditions set by the Chamber. In the case of *Katanga*, the Chamber decided that, in principle, the legal representative may not call witnesses other than the victims they represent, however, the legal representative may seize the initiative to bring to the attention of the Chamber the fact that calling the witness may provide a genuine contribution to the ascertainment of the truth pursuant to Article 69 (3) RS.[392] In order to analyse the application of legal representatives to call a witness, the Chamber will consider whether the testimony affects the victims' personal interests, is relevant to the issues of the case, contributes to the determination of the truth and whether the testimony would be consistent with the rights of the accused.[393]

---

[389]ICC, *Prosecutor v. Lubanga*, ICC-01/04-01/06-1432, Judgment on the appeals of The Prosecutor and The Defence against Trial Chamber's Decision on Victims' Participation of 18 January 2008 (11 July 2008) paras. 3–5, see also Gosnell (2016), p. 125.

[390]ICC, *Prosecutor v. Lubanga*, ICC-01/04-01/06-1432, Judgment on the appeals of The Prosecutor and The Defence against Trial Chamber's Decision on Victims' Participation of 18 January 2008 (11 July 2008) para. 4, ICC, Prosecutor v. Lubanga, ICC-01/04-01/06-1119, Decision on victims' participation (18 January 2008) paras 108–110, ICC, *Prosecutor v. Lubanga*, ICC-01/04-01/06-2032, Order issuing public redacted version of the "Decision on the request by victims a/0225/06, a/0229/06 and a/0270/07 to express their views and concerns in person and to present evidence during the trial" (9 July 2009) cf. with ICC, *Prosecutor v. Ntaganda*, ICC-01/04-02/06-1780-Conf, Public redacted version of 'Decision on the request by the Legal Representative of the Victims of the Attacks for leave to present evidence and victims' views and concerns' (15 February 2017).

[391]Almost the same activities for the legal representative may be granted also at the trial stage to the legal representative under the criteria if the personal interests of the victim may be affected, see e.g. access by victims to confidential documents in the record in ICC, *Prosecutor v. Lubanga*, ICC-01/04-01/06-1119, Decision on victims' participation (18 January 2008) paras. 105–107, ICC, *Prosecutor v. Bemba*, ICC-01/05-01/08-807-Corr-Anx, Corrigendum to Decision on the participation of victims in the trial and on 86 applications by victims to participate in the proceedings (12 July 2010) para. 41, *Prosecutor v. Banda*, ICC-02/05-03/09-545, Decision on the participation of victims in the trial proceedings (20 March 2014) paras. 34–39.

[392]See ICC, *Prosecutor v. Katanga, Chui*, ICC-01/04-01/07, Directions for the conduct of the proceedings and testimony in accordance with rule 140 (1 December 2009) paras. 45–48, ICC, *Prosecutor v. Katanga, Chui*, ICC-01/04-01/07-2288, Judgment on the Appeal of Mr Katanga Against the Decision of Trial Chamber II of 22 January 2010 Entitled "Decision on the Modalities of Victim Participation at Trial" (16 July 2010) paras. 111–114, ICC, *Prosecutor v. Ongwen*, Decision on the Legal Representatives for Victims Requests to Present Evidence and Views and Concerns and related requests (6 March 2018) paras. 17–19.

[393]*Prosecutor v. Banda*, ICC-02/05-03/09-545, Decision on the participation of victims in the trial proceedings (20 March 2014) para. 25, ICC, *Prosecutor v. Bemba*, ICC-01/05-01/08-807-Corr-

Granting procedural rights to the victims participating at the trial phase may depend on various circumstances. Even though the victims will be granted a broad range of different procedural rights, the exercising thereof will still depend on a case-by-case analysis and on how the Chamber determines the personal interests of the victims affected by the exercise of these procedural rights.

3.5.7.3 Appeal Phase

The participation of victims at the appeal stage depends both on the subject matter of the appeal and the personal interests of the victims affected by the appeal. At this level, it is possible to categorise participation according to the subject matter of the appeal. Generally, victims may participate in an appeal against a conviction or against a sentence (Article 81 (1) and (2) RS) by submitting a response pursuant to Rule 150 RPE and Regulation 59 (1) RoC. Participation is also possible in the event of an appeal against an acquittal (Article 83 (3 (c) (ii) RS) by submitting a response pursuant to Rule 154 (1) RPE and Regulation 64 (4) RoC).[394]

Furthermore, general participation in the appeal process for the victims is possible in matters of jurisdiction or admissibility (Article 19 (3) RS) or in respect of the decision granting or denying the release of the person concerned (Article 82(1) (b) and (c) RS). In the appeal against other decisions of the Pre-Trial or the Trial Chamber, the victims must prove their personal interests in the case.

Bearing in mind that the victims are not a party to the proceedings, they are not entitled to appeal against any decision of the Court. Only the prosecutor and the defendant are allowed to appeal against such decisions.[395]

3.5.7.4 Reparation Phase

The general right of the victims afforded by the Rome Statute enables them to seek reparations for the harm suffered, including restitution, compensation and rehabilitation pursuant to Article 75 RS. At the reparation phase, the victims are actively involved and are entitled to file submissions prior to the reparation order pursuant to Article 75 (3) RS.[396] Victims are given the possibility to determine the damage they

Anx, Corrigendum to Decision on the participation of victims in the trial and on 86 applications by victims to participate in the proceedings (12 July 2010) para. 33.

[394]ASP, Court's Revised strategy in relation to victims, 14–22 November 2012, p. 11, See also Eckelmans (2013), p. 217.

[395]See Klamberg (2017), pp. 606–607.

[396]ICC, *Prosecutor v. Al Mahdi*, ICC-01/12-01/15-190-Conf, Public redacted version of "Submissions of the Legal Representative of Victims on the principles and forms of the right to reparation" dated 2 December 2016 (3 January 2017), ICC, *Prosecutor v. Katanga*, ICC-01/04-01/07-3702, Observations des victimes sur la valeur monétaire des préjudices allégués? (30 September 2016).

have suffered and they may also request help from an expert who will than assist them in the determination of the scope or extent of any damage loss or injury and who will be able to give advice on the modalities of reparation matters. In any event, if the expert is requested on behalf of the victims or is appointed by the Chamber on its own motion, the legal representative is allowed to provide observation on the expert's report[397] pursuant to Rule 97 (2) RPE. Within the scope of Rule 91 (4) RPE, the victims may question the witnesses, experts and the accused in the course of the reparation proceedings, taking into account the procedures set for questioning.

In exceptional circumstances, the victims are allowed to submit a motion to postpone a hearing on matters relating to reparations pursuant to Rule 143 RPE.

The victims have the right to appeal against an order of reparation in accordance with Article 82 (4) RS in conjunction with Rule 150 (1) RPE and Regulation 58 RoC.[398] At the appeal phase of the reparations, Regulations 59 and 60 RoC enable the victims to actively participate by submitting a response or reply.

3.5.8 Dual Status

The victims invited to testify as witnesses on the matters receive dual status. Although the notion of such a "dual status" is not enshrined explicitly in the Rome Statue, the latter supposes the existence of so-called 'victim-witnesses', as it generally regulates the questioning of victims (Article 54(3)(b) RS), more specifically of victims of sexual violence (Article 72(2) RS). This implies that the legal framework of the ICC assumes the aforementioned dual status. Contrasting opinions—implying that an individual cannot combine the status of victim and the status of witness in one—do not enjoy a great deal of support, either among academics or in practice. The abovementioned provisions, as well as the fact that a victim's testimony can be a valuable contribution of evidence, argue the converse.[399] It is apparent that victims are the closest one can be to the alleged crimes and that their participation can help to establish the facts of a case.[400] The legal framework of the ICC does not stipulate any restrictions with regard to the probative value of the evidence provided by a person with the dual status as a victim-witness and, therefore, the dual-status does not affect the probative value of witnesses' statements. The dual status can be acquired by being admitted as a witness after having been recognised as a victim before or vice versa. The participation both as a victim and as a witness does, however, raise security and protection concerns. Since the *Lubanga* case—the first ICC case to go

[397]See e.g. ICC, *Prosecutor v. Al Mahdi*, Annex 1 to the Transmission of the Public Version of one Expert's Report pursuant to the Trial Chamber's Order of 11 July 2017 (27 April 2017).

[398]See ICC, *Prosecutor v. Al Mahdi*, ICC-01/12-01-/15-236, Judgment on the appeal of the victims against the "Reparations Order" (8 March 2018).

[399]Bachvarova (2017), p. 146 et seq.

[400]Cohen (2009), p. 351.

to trial—the Court has had to deal with these issues. In its decision of 5 June 2008, the Trial Chamber established three general principles[401] that have largely been upheld until today.[402]

Should victims wish to testify before the Chamber, their legal representative must file an application containing a comprehensive summary of the testimony that is to be given by the victim.[403] With regard to the security and protection of victim-witnesses, the provisions regulating this issue in respect of single-status victims or witnesses can be applied. Nevertheless, doubts remain as the legal documents of the ICC, for example, do not specify how the different organs of the Court, parties and participants are supposed to contact victim-witnesses. The decision in the *Lubanga* case refers to the Victims and Witnesses Unit/Victims and Witnesses Section and the obligation to facilitate contact.[404]

3.5.9 Victim Protection

The protection of victims is a crucial part of the work of the Court as it is needed in order to encourage them to participate or to testify without putting their own safety and security at risk (Article 68 (1) and (2) RS). The protective measures must always be in accordance with the rights of the suspect or the accused and the right to a fair and impartial trial.[405] The Victims and Witnesses Unit/Victims and Witnesses Section enshrined in Article 43 (6) RS provides assistance on protective measures and advice for victims and witnesses, as well as for the Chambers. Rules 87 and 88 RPE regulate the possibility for the Chambers to order protective measures or special measures.

Rules 16 and 17 RPE regulate the Victims and Witnesses Unit provision of support, assistance and protection to all victims appearing before the Court. The Trial Chamber in the *Lubanga* case held that the obligation of protection under Article 43 (6) RS begins as early as when an application for victim participation reaches the Court.[406] It has also been held that the non-disclosure of the identity of an

---

[401](1) Security measures, (2) no additional rights, (3) communication between the Registry and victim-witnesses should be neutral, direct and continuous.

[402]ICC, *Prosecutor v. Lubanga*, ICC-01/04-01/06-1379, Decision on certain practicalities regarding individuals who have the dual status of witness and victim (6 June 2008) paras. 52–78.

[403]ICC, *Prosecutor v. Katanga, Chui*, ICC-01/04-01/07, Directions for the conduct of the proceedings and testimony in accordance with rule 140 (1 December 2009) paras 25–28.

[404]Bachvarova (2017), p. 191 et seq., see also ICC, *Prosecutor v. Bemba*, ICC-01/05-01/08-807-Corr-Anx, Corrigendum to Decision on the participation of victims in the trial and on 86 applications by victims to participate in the proceedings (12 July 2010) paras. 50, 54.

[405]ICC, Representing Victims before the International Criminal Court, A manual for legal representatives, p. 31.

[406]ICC, *Prosecutor v. Lubanga*, ICC-01/04-01/06-1119, Decision on victims' participation (18 January 2008) para. 137.

applicant to the defence is not constitutive of an infringement of the presumption of innocence, but rather a protective measure allowing the applicants to make an application without endangering their safety or well-being.[407] In addition, the Prosecution is mandated with an active role in the protection of victims and witnesses under Articles 54 (3) (f) and 68 (1) RS. Therefore, it can take protective measures during both the investigation and prosecution stage.

3.6 ICC Organs Dealing with Victims

The ICC, as a judicial body created on the basis of a multinational treaty, consists of four general organs: The Presidency, the Judicial Divisions, the Office of the Prosecutor and the Registry. There are, however, more than twenty sections and divisions dealing with different types of tasks in order to keep the Court functioning, but very few institutions within the ICC have direct contact to the victims. The OTP and the Registry have contact:

- via the Victims Participation and Reparation Section (VPRS);
- in cooperation with the Public Information and Documentation Section (PIDS)/ nowadays called the Public Information and Outreach Section (PIOS);
- through the Victims and Witnesses Section (VWS), previously called the Victims and Witnesses Unit (VWU); and
- through Office of the Public Counsel for Victims (OPCV).

The role of the Registry with regard to victims is more an indirect representative one. In 2013, the ASP authorised the restructuring of the Registry in order to avoid duplicating its functions, to help reduce the costs and to increase the efficiency of the organ in view of growing capacities. Since then, several structural changes have been undertaken by the Registry's project "ReVision" with regard to victims.

The Structure of the ICC before ReVision

[407] ICC, *Situation in the DRC*, ICC-10/04, Decision on the Defence request for leave to appeal regarding the transmission of applications for victim participation (6 Novmber 2006) para. 4.

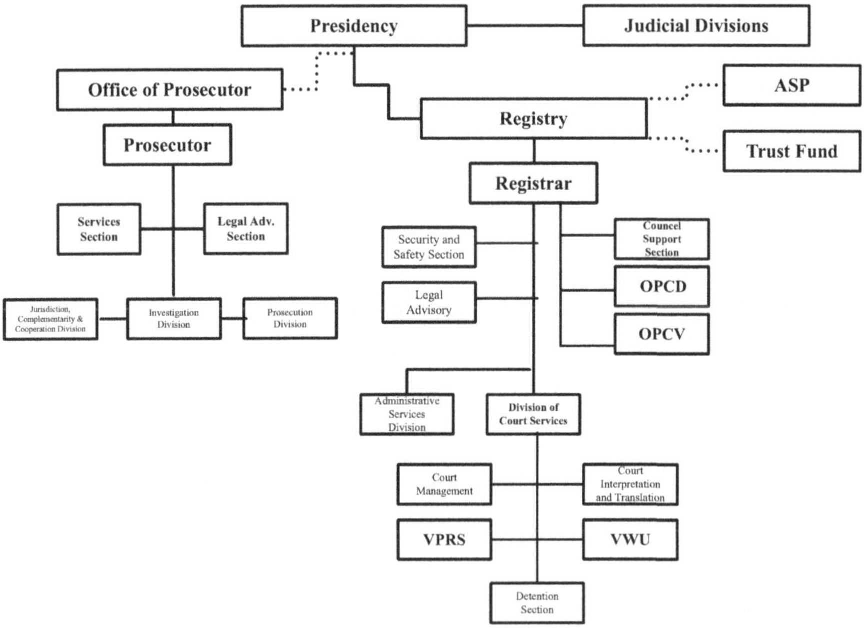

The Structure of the ICC after ReVision

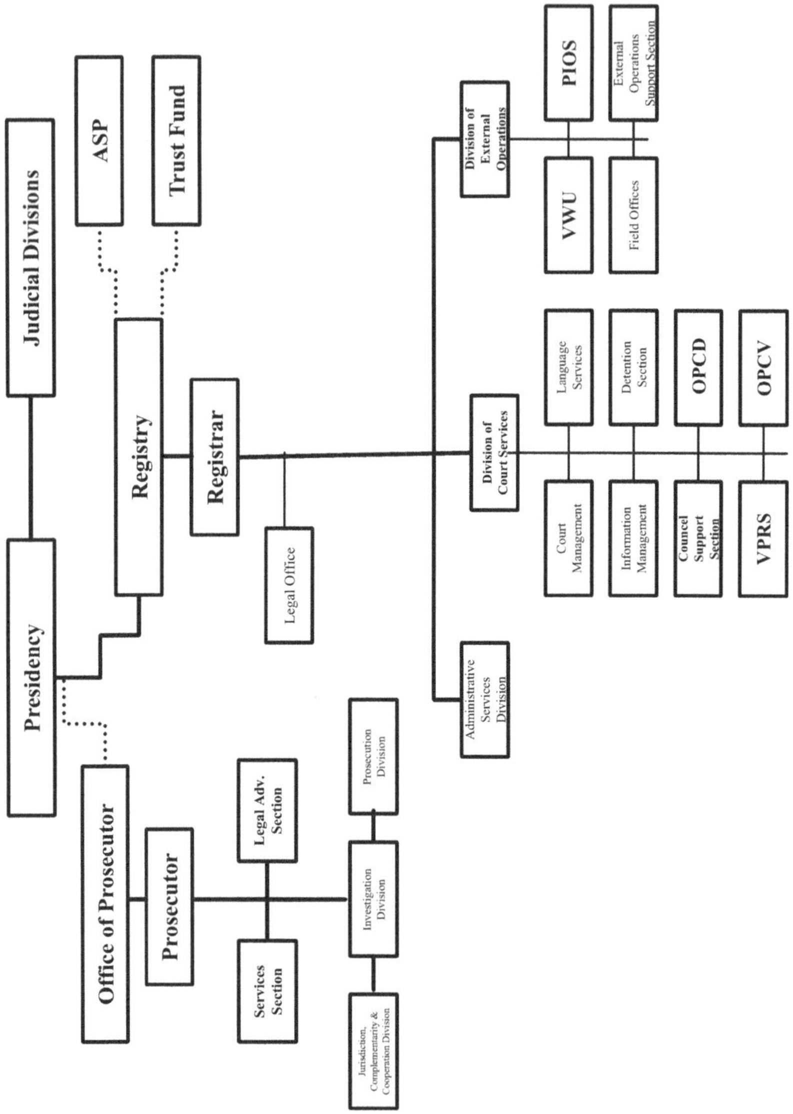
Judicial Divisions
Presidency
ASP
Trust Fund
Registry
Registrar
Legal Office
Office of Prosecutor
Prosecutor
Legal Adv. Section
Services Section
Investigation Division
Prosecution Division
Jurisdiction, Complementarity & Cooperation Division
Administrative Services Division
Division of Court Services
Division of External Operations
Court Management
Language Services
Information Management
Detention Section
Councel Support Section
OPCD
VPRS
OPCV
VWU
PIOS
Field Offices
External Operations Support Section

There are different scenarios as to how victims may attain international criminal justice through the ICC. This interaction may begin with the victims themselves submitting information concerning the crime to the Prosecutor or as soon as they are identified by the outreach campaign of the VPRS. In the following, the different sections of the Court dealing with victim related matters will be looked at in greater depth. This will include:

- The Office of the Prosecutor
- The Office of the Public Counsel for Defense and Defense Counsels
- The Chambers
- The Registry
- The Victims Participation and Reparation Section
- The Victims and Witnesses Section
- The Office of the Public Council for Victims
- The Trust Fund for Victims

3.6.1 *The Office of the Prosecutor (OTP)*

The Office of the Prosecutor (OTP) is an independent organ of the ICC which is responsible for the examination of situations under the jurisdiction of the Court where international crimes appear have to be committed. In accordance with Article 42 (1) RS, it is also responsible for the prosecution of the individuals who have committed these crimes. The Prosecutor investigates information in order to establish whether there is a reasonable basis to proceed with an investigation and, as such, the Prosecutor has the earliest contact with the victims. The OTP plays a role in raising awareness and in giving victims the opportunity to participate in the proceedings. It also carries responsibility for the safety and well-being of the victims while preparing all necessary security plans pursuant to Regulations 8 and 35 (3) of the Regulations of the Office of the Prosecutor (RoP).[408]Furthermore, it takes into account the interests of the victims during all stages of the proceedings, in accordance with Regulation 16 RoP.[409]

There are two general scenarios where the victims may interact with the Office of the Prosecutor. The first of these is based upon the Article 15 RS, which considers the *proprio motu* initiation of the investigations. The second is based upon Article 19 RS, where the interaction between the Prosecution and the victims may arise in further judicial proceedings.

The first communication with the victim may arise from the situation where the victims approach the Prosecutor pursuant to Article 15 (1) RS in order to report information regarding the crimes committed. The victims who are contacted are then

---

[408]Reyes (2017), p. 182.

[409]See also Article 53 (1)(c) RS.

informed by the OTP of all possible activities and instructed on how to forward their personal data to the VPRS in accordance with Regulation 37 RoP. The information gathered from the victims will enable Prosecutors to initiate the investigations of their own accord (*proprio motu*) and to conclude that there is reasonable basis to proceed with an investigation. While requesting authorisation for an investigation pursuant to Article 15 (3) RS, the Prosecutor should, pursuant to the Rules 50 (1) and 92 (2) RPE, inform any victims known to them about the request to the PTC. The victims will then gain the chance to make representations to the PTC.

As already mentioned above, the victims are not entitled to participate during the investigation of a situation,[410] as one must bear in mind that the investigation of a situation does not constitute judicial proceedings before the Court.

The interaction between the Prosecutor and the victim has to be conducted in a safe and agreeable environment, which stipulates the consideration of the personal circumstances of the victim and their interests pursuant to Article 54 (1) (b) RS and, if necessary, the presence of an accompanying victim worker pursuant to Regulation 39 RoP. The rights of the accompanying worker are, however, limited. They are not allowed to interfere with the interaction of the OTP and the victims themselves. In order to protect the victim from secondary victimisation, and in order to guarantee the security of the victim during this interaction, the Prosecutor has to consult with the Victims and Witnesses Unit/Victims and Witnesses Section (VWS) within the Registry, as stipulated under Article 43 (6) RS and Regulation 47 RoP.

As soon as the Prosecutor presses charges against the suspect, the victims may apply for participation at the confirmation hearing. The applications for victimhood and participation are then transferred from the Registry to the Chamber assigned to the case. The OTP then has time, pursuant to Rule 89 RPE and Article 68 (3) RS, to file observations regarding the recognition of the victims who have applied.

The recognised victims are then automatically acknowledged as participants during the trial stage, unless the charges are confirmed in the pre-trial stage. During the pre-trial, trial and appeal stages, the Prosecutor engages with the legal representatives of the victims and may file observations on the motions of the legal representatives. At the confirmation hearing, the participating victims may add any point of any fact or any evidence to the Prosecution's casefile by their opening and closing statements. Notwithstanding, the principle of anonymous accusation prohibits anonymous victims from doing this.[411] The role of the Prosecutor at the reparation stage is passive, however, the Rome Statute does not limit the Prosecutor's active participation by submitting the observations, motions etc.

[410]ICC, *Situation in DRC*, ICC-01/04-556, Judgement on victim participation in the investigation stage of the proceedings in a the appeal of the OPCD against the decision of Pre-Trial Chamber I of 7 December 2007 and in the appeals of the OPCD and the Prosecutor against the Decision of Pre Trial Chamber I of 24 December 2007 (19 December 2008) paras. 48, 58.

[411]ICC, *Prosecutor v. Lubanga*, ICC-01/04-01/06-462-tEN, Decision on the arrangements for participation of victims a/001/06m 1/0002/06 and 1/0003/06 at the confirmation hearing (22 September 2006) p. 7.

3.6.2 OPCD, Defense

At the national level, the ICC also grants the suspect/accused the right to be represented by counsel pursuant to Articles 9 and 14 ICCPR. There are two types of defense included in the mechanism of the ICC. On the one hand, the Office of the Public Counsel for the Defense (OPCD) and, on the other hand, the defense counsel selected by the suspect/accused. The functions of the OPCD, as established by Regulation 77 of the RoC, are similar to those of the defense counsel. However, the OPCD is aimed at protecting the rights of the suspect/accused during the initial stages of the investigation and at supporting the defense team as an independent office of the Court.[412] Bearing in mind that the defense team is not a permanent institution as the OTP is, it lacks the "institutional memory", which is a disadvantage for the suspect/accused. In order to close that gap, the OPCD's role as such is very important for the defense team. The defense team, which includes the OPCD as well as the defense counsel and the defendant, is dedicated to defending the rights of the suspect/accused. In most scenarios it is, however, the most "victim-unfriendly" party in the process dealing with the victims in the whole course of the proceedings. The defense team is not a party; it first comes into contact with the victims when they are shown the case of the Prosecutor by invoking Article 15 (1) RS. The defense deals with the victims in the further stages of judicial proceedings, beginning with the confirmation of charges. From a strategical point of view, the defense may oppose all victim participation applications, requesting the rejection of their participation or requesting limitation of the participation of the victims by submitting observations set by the Court in accordance with Rule 89 (2) RPE.[413] However, at the same time, victim participation may also play an important role for the defense team, which may differ from case to case. The tendency is, however, to request rejection of at least some applications. The defense is also entitled to make observations regarding different ranges of issues of the victims' participation such as, *inter alia*, the interpretation of Rule 85 RPE and Article 68 (3) RS, the interpretation of the modalities of the participation and the range of rights of the victims.[414] At the same time, the defense counsel is bound by Article 29 of the Code of Professional Conduct for the Council to refrain from intimidating, harassing or humiliating victims during the course of any interaction with them. The strategy of the defense team towards the victims may change from stage to stage of the proceedings. Thus, it

[412]See Khan (2016), p. 1202, OPCD is not an organ of the Court.

[413]See e.g. ICC, *Prosecutor v. Katanga*, ICC-01/04-01/07, Defence observation of the 12 applications for participation as victims (7 March 2008), ICC, *Prosecutor v. Katanga, Chui*, Defence Observations regarding victims' participation and scope thereof (29 January 2009), ICC, *Prosecutor v. Ongwen*, Defence's Observations on 336 Victims' Applications for Participation (11 November 2015).

[414]See Fardel and Olarra (2017), p. 28 and compare with Jacobs (2017), p. 573.

means that the defense team may still agree with the participation where it finds it useful for its own strategy.[415]

The main problem which arises between the defense team and the victims relates to the personal interests of the victims, on the one hand, and to the fair trial principle and the presumption of innocence of the accused on the other. The interaction with victims during different procedural issues may also be a reason which could delay the entire judicial process and may be considered a disadvantage for the accused. This kind of mediation between the principles is left to the discretion of the Court on a case-by-case basis.[416]

Further interaction between the defense and the victims arises during the reparation phase of the proceedings, where the defense has the possibility to submit observations regarding victim applications[417] for reparation by refuting the damage suffered by certain victims or by appealing against the reparation order so as to minimise or deny any kind of reparation.[418] This is yet another part of the proceedings during which the victims may be psychologically affected.

3.6.3 Judicial Division, Chamber, Judge

The most important organs of the Court are the Judicial Divisions. Article 34 RS divides this organ into the Appeal, Trial and Pre-Trial Divisions. The judicial functions of the Court are, pursuant to Article 39 (2) RS, carried out in each Division by a Chamber consisting up to five Judges. The Chambers are the most important players in the development of the victim participation mechanism which creates further rules for the victims under specific circumstances. The Chambers express the collective agreement of the Judges when interpreting Rule 85 RPE and Article 68 (3) RS and the modalities of the participation of the victims in the pre-trial, trial, appeal and reparation stages. As decision makers, the Chambers are located at the centre of the communication between different institutions of the Court regarding victims' issues. There are different ways and scenarios as to how the decisions regarding the victims are made, decisions which depend on the specific situation. At

[415]E.g. the defence team may use the participation of the victims which is related to the charges brought against the accused, but the participation of those victims may verify that the committed crimes are not related to the accused himself in the course of proceedings.

[416]Hafetz (2018), p. 87.

[417]ICC, *Prosecutor v. Katanga*, ICC-01/04-01/07-3660-Red 08-03-2016, Defence Observations on the Victims Applications for Reparation (8 March 2016) paras. 13–20, e.g. the Defence argued on that the convicted may not expected to provide a house build of significantly different and more expensive material than that of original straw home lost or damaged in the couse of the attack.

[418]E.g. ICC, *Prosecutor v. Al Mahdi*, ICC-01/12-01/15-192-Red, General Defence observations on reparations (2 December 2016) para. 41, ICC, *Prosecutor v. Katanga*, ICC-01/04-01/07-3711, Defence Observations on the Monetary Value of the Alleged Harm (30 September 2016) paras 12–13.

the same time, it is interesting to distinguish the legal background of the judges who are making the decisions regarding the victims. One must bear in mind the "legal baggage" of the judges who have their own views on different matters depending on where they come from. In particular, those who stem from common law countries may have very different opinions concerning victim participation within the criminal justice system than those with a civil law background.[419]

The interaction between the Chambers and victims may be considered direct as well as indirect. However, the communication between the Chambers and the victims is mostly indirect, through the offices of the Registry. If the proceedings are initiated by the OTP pursuant to Article 15 (3) RS, the victims gain the possibility of making representations to the PTC, however, this communication goes through the VPRS office.[420] On the basis of Article 19 (3) RS, the victims may submit the observations in relation to jurisdiction and admissibility of a case directly to the Chamber.[421]

Pursuant to Regulation 80 RoC, the Chamber has the power to appoint a legal representative for the victim, if the interests of justice so require.

At the stage of the confirmation of the charges, the PTC has an essential role in authorising and ordering the Registry to contact known victims for them to participate in the pre-trial. As soon as the victims apply for victim status in the proceedings, the Registry transmits those applications to the Chamber for it to decide on protective measures and then they are sent to the parties for observations pursuant to Regulation 86 RoC. After the observations of the defense and OTP, the Chamber has to make individual decisions based upon the *prima facie* assessment of the victim status of the person or organisation in relation to Rule 85 RPE.[422] By having their participation authorised, the victims gain the right to participate in the proceedings in accordance with the established modalities of participation. Apart from the situation when the victims communicate with the Judges via the LRV, the only direct interaction occurs when the victims are invited to testify before the Court. On the other hand, the Chambers are in a position to be able to leave or to reject the motions or requests of the victims unless the interests of the victims are affected. The participation of the victims in the trial stage depends on the confirmation of the charges. The Chamber then decides that the victims who participated at the pre-trial stage may automatically participate in the trial,[423] as soon as the all charges against the accused are confirmed. The Trial Chamber, however, may still decide on the

---

[419]ICC, *Prosecutor v. Bemba*, 8 June 2018 (Judgment on the appeal of Mr Jean-Pierre Bemba Gombo against Trial Chamber III's "Judgment pursuant to Article 74 of the Statute) Separate opinion Judge Christine Van den Wyngaert and Judge Howard Morrison, para. 30, van den Wyngaert (2011), p. 495.

[420]Moffett (2014), p. 97.

[421]Moffett (2014), p. 97, see ICC, ICC-RoC46(3)-01/18-9, Submissions on Behalf of the Victims Pursuant to Article 19(3) of the Statute (30 May 2018).

[422]Van den Wyngaert (2011), p. 481.

[423]ICC, *Prosecutor v. Katanga, Chui*, ICC-01/04-01/07-933, Decision on the treatment of applications for participation (26 February 2009) para. 10.

authorisation of the participation of new victims and on the modalities of participation in the trial stage, pursuant to Regulation 54 (o) RoC. At the appeal stage, participation is limited to the personal interests affected by the issues on appeal.[424] In the course of the judicial or investigative proceedings, the Chambers have to take all appropriate measures to protect the victims in cooperation with the VWU/VWS pursuant to Articles 68 (1) and (4) RS. Pursuant to Regulation 21 (8) RoC, the Chamber may, upon a request of the Registry, order not to publish any information regarding the public hearing if the safety or security of the victims could be affected.

At the reparation stage the Chamber is dedicated to setting the type of reparation and the amount of reparation for the victims who have applied for reparation in accordance with Article 75 RS in cooperation with Trust Fund.

3.6.4 Registry

As an organ of the ICC described in Article 34 (d) RS, the Registry is responsible for the administrative tasks and services of the Court pursuant to Article 43 (1) RS. The Registry plays an essential role in coordinating the communication between the chambers and the victims. The Registry,[425] which has three important offices with a different set of tasks, organises the contacting, the registration of applicant victims and the participation of the victims in the proceedings, as soon the chamber authorises their participation. Those offices supporting the Registry for the accomplishment of diverse administrative tasks are the VWU/VWS which is responsible for the safety of the victims, the OPCV which is responsible for the representation of the victims in the event of there being no legal representative for the victims and the VPRS which is responsible for the outreach and communication with the victims directly and the victims' application process.

The Registry is mandated with implementing the E-Court system designed by Regulation 26 RoC and is responsible for the updating of the lists of victims of the situation and of the case, pursuant to Regulations 10 and 21 (i) and (j) of RoR.[426]

The functions of the Registry are executed pursuant to the Regulations of the Registry. With the growth of the Court, structural and reorganisational issues have arisen within the system of the Registry.[427] As a result of overlaps in the administration of the Registry, the Assembly of State Parties (ASP) was authorised in its

[424]ICC, *Prosecutor v. Katanga*, Decision on the Participation of Victims in the Appeal of Mr Katanga Against the "Decision on the Modalities of Victim Participation at Trial" (24 May 2010) para. 5, see also Eckelmans (2013), p. 219.

[425]The Registry was reorganised in 2016, see ICC, Comprehensive Report on the Reorganisation of the Registry of the International Criminal Court, August 2016.

[426]See e-Court System, ICC, *Prosecutor v. Mbarushimana*, ICC-01/04-01/10-118, Annex 1 to the Registry Report on the eCourt Protocol (21 April 2011) para. 30.

[427]ICC, Comprehensive Report on the Reorganisation of the Registry of the International Criminal Court, August 2016, pp. 35–38, ICC, ASP Audit report of the ReVision project of the International

twelfth session to restructure the Registry in order to avoid the duplication of the functions of the Offices.[428] The proposals for creating the Victims Office,[429] which would include victim-related sections in one general office, is still pending. This is due to the fact that Regulations of the Court must be amended.[430] In the course of restructuring, the Registry Victims and Witnesses Unit was transferred from the Division of the Court Services to the Division for External Relations (DER) and was renamed the Victim and Witness Section.[431] At the same time, even though the Regulations of the Registry were amended on 1 August 2018, it is still not clear which Office is responsible for which functions of the Registry and this will still undoubtedly lead to overlaps between the Offices, unless the Regulations include the division of functions between the Offices. The strict responsibilities of the VWU/VWS are regulated by Rules 16–21 RPE and Regulations 79–96 bis RoR or OPCV by Regulation 81 RoC. This makes it possible to understand clearly the objectives of the section under the Registry. The discussions concerning the reorganisation of the VPRS and the OPCV compared to the VWS are bound to the outcome of the discussions on the possible creation of a Victims Office. On that basis, no structural changes have been considered for the VPRS and OPCV to date. According to the proposal for the new combined Victims Office, the new Office would be responsible for the management in regard to victims' participation and for giving effect to decisions by the Judges, as well as having direct access to all other Registry support services.[432] Those responsibilities would include the outreach and first communication with the victims, the administration of the application process and the representation of the victims at the proceedings. Currently, the existing system of assistance for the victim via the Registry creates overlaps between the Offices. As a consequence, victims and affected communities and intermediaries communicate with different sections of the Court during the application process and even after the assignment of the LRV the victims are still obliged to deal with the different methods of the Court.[433]

Criminal Court's Registry, fifteenth session, 16–24 November 2016, p. 2, *J. Eesterday*, Major Changes at the ICC: the Registry's ReVision, 24 August 2015, ijmonitor.org.

[428]See ASP, Resolution ICC-ASP/12/Res.1, 27 November 2013, H, para. 3.

[429]See the comments of FIDH to the Registrar, FIDH Comments on the ICC Registrar'sReVision proposals in relation to victims 18 November 2014, Fardel and Olarra (2017), p. 14.

[430]ICC, ASP Report on the review of the organisational structure of the Registry Outcomesof Phase 4of the ReVision Project, Decisions on the structure of the Registry, ICC-ASP/14/18, 4 May 2015, para. 6.

[431]ICC, ASP Report on the review of the organisational structure of the Registry Outcomesof Phase 4of the ReVision Project, Decisions on the structure of the Registry, ICC-ASP/14/18, 4 May 2015, para. 4 (i).

[432]ICC, Registry ReVision Project, Basic Outline of Proposals to Establish Defence and Victims Offices, pp. 4–5.

[433]ICC, Registry ReVision Project, Basic Outline of Proposals to Establish Defence and Victims Offices, p. 3.

Another problematic issue arises from the separated regulations of each Organ. The official journal includes 13 regulations on the different spheres of functions of the Court (Regulation 7 RoC). On the one hand, it is dedicated to the independent establishment and development of its own agenda and regulations of the given Organ but, in the case of the Registry which interacts with all the Organs of the Court, the responsibilities are split among all regulations and rules.

3.6.5 *The Victims Participation and Reparations Section (VPRS)*

The Victims Participation and Reparations Section (VPRS) is the main actor during the initial contact with the victims of crimes under the ICC's jurisdiction and is responsible for the outreach campaigns and for assisting the victims during the participation period. The Section designs an application and processing system for the victims in order to precede the victims' claims.[434] In contrast to the OPCV and the VWU/VWS, the VPRS is not explicitly mentioned in any foundational documents of the Court.[435] The Regulations pertaining to the exact responsibilities of the VPRS towards victims are not strict. Although the VPRS is mentioned several times in the Regulations,[436] it is difficult to distinguish the responsibilities of the Registry and the VPRS from each other in Chapter 3 RoR.

Generally, the responsibilities of the VPRS may be divided into four parts:

i) Outreach to the victims;
ii) Application process;
iii) Participation process; and
iv) Reparation process.

At the early stage, the VPRS implements its outreach programs in tight cooperation with the Public Information and Documentation Section (PIDS) which is today called the Public Information and Outreach Section (PIOS). The VPRS designs the manuals and strategies for the outreach programs and distributes them through the PIOS. The informational materials prepared by the VPRS include strategies on how

---

[434] ICC, ASP, Report on participation of and reparations to victims, ICC-ASP/3/21, 25 August 2004, paras. 3, 8–10.

[435] ICC, Review Committee Response in Relation to the OPCV Interlocutor, Women's Initiative for Gender Justice, p. 8.

[436] E.g. Regulation 37 (RoP), *"Victims questioned by the Office shall be informed of the procedures for participation andaccess to reparations under the Statute, and of the existence and role of the Victims Participationand Reparations Section of the Registry"*, Regulation 86 (9) RoC, *"There shall be a specialised unitdealing with victims' participation andreparations under the authority of the Registrar. This unit shall be responsible forassisting victims and groups of victims"*.

the victims may contact the VPRS and participate in the proceedings.[437] In relation to the outreach programs, the PIOS' functions[438] are based on the communication with the intermediaries, local NGOs and legal representatives in order to establish initial contact with the victims. The VPRS holds meetings and seminars in the field in accordance with Regulation 103 (1) RoR in order to reach the victims and to assist them with information for their possible participation and reparation, bearing in mind the specific circumstances of the local region such as tradition, dialects and culture. The content of the information has to include such features as the meaning of the ICC and what the institution stands for, how the proceedings are held at the Court, the role and the meaning of the victims in the particular cases and how they are able to express their views and concerns regarding their specific matters. It also includes details as to what their participation may look like, the parameters of the specific case, where the victims may be included—such as temporal, geographical and material parameters—how the victims may receive any financial assistance from the Court for their participation and an explanation of the institution of the OPCV.

At the application stage, the VPRS is responsible for the design and preparation of the application form for participation and reparation, in accordance with Regulation 86 RoC and for making this available in the language spoken by the victims (Regulation 104 RoR).[439] During the different situations and cases, different application forms were designed by the VPRS. As a result of the high number of applications, the form was redesigned and reduced several times until the Presidency of the ICC decided to simplify and to shorten the application form to one page in accordance with Regulation 23 (2) RoC.[440] On a case-by-case basis, the VPRS still has the possibility of requesting a redesigning of the application form under specific circumstances or in order to be able to collect more information from the victims.[441] For specific matters, the Court may set a time limit for the VPRS to collect the victims' applications (Regulation 107 (3) RoR), however, the further applications may still be considered in further proceedings.[442] The regulations are, however, silent with regard to any deadline for the collection and transmission of the victims' applications to the Court, which enables the victims to send their applications at any

---

[437]See narrow in ASP, Report on participation of and reparations to victims, ICC-ASP/3/21, 25 August 2004, p. 2.

[438]See the critics and identified problems of the PIDS/PIOS at ICC, ICC, Comprehensive Report on the Reorganisation of the Registry of the International Criminal Court, paras. 515–516.

[439]See McKay (2008), pp. 1–2.

[440]ICC, Chamber Practice Manual, May 2017, p. 20 (i).

[441]See ICC, *Prosecutor v. Al Hassan*, ICC-01/12-01/18, Registry Observations on Aspects Related to the Admission of Victims for Participation in the Proceedings (9 May 2018) para. 5.

[442]See e.g. ICC, *Prosecutor v. Bemba*, ICC-01/05-01/08, Decision setting a time-limit for the submission of new victims' applications for participation (7 September 2010) para. 8, ICC, *Prosecutor v. Ongwen*, 3 September 2015, Decision concerning the procedure for admission of victims to participate in the proceedings in the present case for the participation in the confirmation hearings (ICC-02/04-01/15) para. 4, in the *Al Hassan* case the victims had to apply until 24 August 2018.

time during the proceedings. This is combined with the fact that the victims may be reached out during the course of the proceedings and in order not to leave them behind, the victims are given a chance to contact the VPRS even during the proceedings. Before the VPRS transmits the applications to the Chamber on a rolling basis, it categorises the applications into three groups. These are (1) those who meet the requirements set by the Rule 89 RPE; (2) those who do not meet the requirements set; and (3) those for whom the VPRS is not able to provide any conclusion. Furthermore, the VPRS still has to encourage the victim to complete the application if the application received is incomplete (Regulation 107 (2) RoR).

The VPRS is further responsible for the reports to the Chambers regarding any further applications received, be they for participation, reparations,[443] withdrawals or other matters pertaining to the victims (Regulation 101, 109, 110 (1) RoR). Information about the victims' applications is then stored in the electronic system in accordance with Regulation 10 RoR and is accessible to the Chambers. Applications may also still be received at the participation stage. Thus, the main responsibility of the VPRS during the participation and reparation stages is the coordination work between the other Court's Sections and the victims for the meaningful participation of the latter. This refers mostly to the safety and security measures surrounding their participation, transportation and accommodation pursuant to Regulations 79–96 RoR. In close cooperation with the PIOS, the VPRS enables participating victims to gain access to the judicial proceedings via the web-streaming of the hearings *in situ*.

Although the staff of this Section does tremendous work in making the highly critisied participation of the victims in the international criminal justice a reality, the drafters of the ICC could never have imagined the practical capacities of the victims' participation in these proceedings. Realistically, such a small team is physically unable to deal with thousands of applications in different cases, a fact which ultimately makes communication with and assistance for the victims far from individual but instead rather indirect and remote.[444]

3.6.6 VWU/VWS

The Victims and Witnesses Section (VWS)[445] (previously known as the Victims and Witnesses Unit (VWU)) was established in line with Article 43 (6) RS as part of the

---

[443] See e.g. ICC, *Prosecutor v. Al Mahdi*, ICC-01/12-01/15-275, First Registry Report on Applications for Individual Reparations (10 August 2018), ICC, *Prosecutor v. Lubanga*, Seventh Transmission to Trial Chamber II of Confidential Applications for Reparations and the Report Thereon (15 June 2017), ICC, *Situation in Uganda*, Eighteenth Periodic Report of the Registry on the Applications Received by the Victims Participation and Reparations Section in the Situation in Uganda (11 May 2018).

[444] See narrower in Vasiliev (2015), p. 1151.

[445] Since 2015 the Victims and Witness Unit was restructured to Victim and Witness Section under External Division of External Operations, see ICC, Comprehensive Report on the Reorganisation of

Registry. The purpose of this Office is to provide, in consultation with the Office of the Prosecutor and the VPRS, protective measures and security arrangements in order to protect the physical and psychological well-being of the victims who appear before the Court pursuant to Rule 16 RPE. These arrangements are organised in close cooperation with the Member States, relevant actors and field intermediaries.

This office also has an advisory role regarding the security, protection and measures that victims may need, and provides advice to the Prosecutor and to the Court on these matters.

Regulation 41 RoC states that the Victims and Witness Unit may, pursuant to Article 68 (4) RS, draw any matter to the attention of a Chamber where protective or special measures under Rules 87 und 88 RPE require its consideration. In order to facilitate the services for the travel of the victims to the Court, the Council or the Prosecutor has to request the protection measures and services of the VWS (Regulation 80 RoR). The VWS conducts vulnerability assessments and helps victims throughout their experience at the ICC. It also provides medical and psychological assistance (Regulation 83 RoR). Although invisible, it fulfils an essential task on behalf of the Registry including handling requests for victims, preparing orientation materials (Regulation 83 RoR) organising travel (Regulation 81 RoR), housing (Regulations 82, 84 RoR) or ensuring the application of protection measures and the availability of psychological support (Rule 17 RPE). The victims are allowed to be accompanied by any person whose costs are, once again, covered by the Registry and the VWS (Regulation 91 RoR). For these reasons, it has been described as the "engine room" of the Registry[446] as it accompanies the victims through all the relevant phases of their travel through the ICC.

The interaction between the VWS and the victims comprises six steps. The first of these is the initial contact with the VWS which takes place after the victims have been selected by the party calling them and the approval of a list of victims for appearance by the Chamber. The VWS then contacts the victim. The second step is the pre-trial familiarisation during which the victims receive information concerning the Court and all that lies ahead of them. Before initiating the travel, the victims may obtain a pseudonym in order to protect their identity pursuant to Rule 87 RPE and Regulation 94 RoR. In the third step, the VWS takes care of the logistical issues of the victims' travel and accommodation issues. This step ends with their arrival in The Hague. In a fourth step, there is a short waiting period before the victims actually participate in the trial. Prior to the actual testimony, the VWS may use protection measures to render the person unrecognisable. These include facial and voice distortion or a request for private or closed sessions pursuant to Regulations 94–96

the Registryof the International Criminal Court, p. 151. Reyes (2017), p. 174, ASP, Report on activities and programme performance of the International Criminal Court for the year 2015, 14 September 2016, para. 181, ASP Report on activities and programme performance of the International Criminal Court for the year 2014, 4 May 2015, para, 172, see also Schabas (2016), p. 357.

[446] Cody (2016), p. 304.

RoR. After the actual testimony has been given, the victim enters a cooling-off phase. Further security assessments are made in order to determine whether it is safe for the victim to travel home.[447] It is also the responsibility of the VWS to secure persons who could be targeted after the victims' or witnesses' testimonies, including further victims.

The reorganisation of the Victims and Witnesses Unit to the Section under the Division of External Operations from the Division of Judicial Services dramatically reduced the travel costs incurred by the staff and enabled day-to-day decision-making on case management to be carried out *in situ*. This now means faster and better-considered assistance and protection is provided to the victims.[448] Hence, only nine victims were invited to be heard before the Chamber in 2017 in contrast to 134 witnesses.[449]

3.6.7 The Office of the Public Council for Victims (OPCV)

The Office of the Public Council for Victims (OPCV) was set up in accordance with Regulation 81 RoC for administrative purposes within the remit of the Registrar, however beyond this it is also an independent Office. As the VPRS is not mandated to represent the victims before the Court, and is predominantly there to provide them with initial assistance in approaching the Court, the OPCV already assumes the role of officially representing and assisting the victims before the Chambers. Members of this office may also include those who fulfil the criteria for counsel for the defence in line with Rule 22 RPE, similarly to the LRV, and are bound by the Code of Professional Conduct for Counsel.

The mandate of the OPCV is to provide support and assistance to the legal representatives for victims and the victims as a legal advisor or as a representative before a Chamber in respect of specific issues (Regulation 81 (4) RoC). This was further extended by the PTC in 2008 as the Single Judge ruled that the OPCV must provide support and assistance to victims allowed to participate in the proceedings until such victims choose a legal representative or a legal representative is appointed by the Court.[450] This role therefore extends, where necessary, beyond a supportive role for the LRV to a supportive role for the victims themselves.

---

[447] Cody (2016), pp. 305–310.

[448] ICC, Comprehensive Report on the Reorganisation of the Registry of the International Criminal Court, p. 151.

[449] ASP, Report on activities and programme performance of the International Criminal Court for the year 2017, para. 148.

[450] ICC, *Situation in the DRC*, ICC-01/04-423-Corr-tENG, Corrigendum to the "Decision on the Applications for Participation Filed in Connection with the Investigation in the Democratic Republic of the Congo by a/0004/06 to a/0009/06, a/0016/06 to a/0063/06, a/0071/06 to a/0080/06 and a/0105/06 to a/0110/06 (1 February 2008) p. 52.

There are clear similarities and crossovers between the roles of the LRV/CLRV and the OPCV, especially in view of the aforementioned Regulation allowing the Chamber to appoint Counsel for the victims from the OPCV rather than just the LRV. At the same the victims are free to choose their own legal representative pursuant to Rule 90 (1) RPE, and for the purposes of ensuring the effectiveness of the proceedings the Court may request the victims to choose a common LRV. Regulation 80 RoC enables the Court to appoint the CLRV where the interests of justice so require. There is, however, no general separation of the responsibilities of the CLRV and the OPCV as to when and where exactly the counsels have to act. This is mostly solved on a case-by-case basis. Various Chambers have developed different approaches in appointing the CLRV and the OPCV:

i) in the cases of *Lubanga*, *Katanga/Chui* and *Bemba*, an external legal representative was appointed to represent the victims, while the OPCV was ordered to assist the legal representatives and to represent those victims who were willing to be represented by the appointed LRV.[451]
ii) in the cases of *Kenyatta and Muthaura* and *Ruto and Sang*, the Chamber divided the responsibilities of the legal representatives and the OPCV, appointing a common representative *in situ* and the OPCV to act before the Court.[452] A similar approach, with minor differences, was adopted in the cases of *Gbagbo and Ble Goude* and *Ntaganda,* where the OPCV was appointed as a common legal representative and was assisted by the legal group *in situ.*[453]
iii) in the case of *Ongwen*, the Chamber appointed as a representative of the victims an external counsel chosen by the victims and the OPCV representing as CLRV of other victims.[454]
iv) in the case of *Al Mahdi*, the role of the OPCV was limited to general assistance to the CLRV.[455]

The division of the responsibilities between these two institutions depends on the situation, the case, the applicant victims and the wishes of the victims. This further illustrates the overlapping roles that the two Offices have and helps in understanding

---

[451] ICC, *Prosecutor v. Bemba*, ICC-01/05-01/0, Fifth Decision on Victims' Issues Concerning Common Legal Representation of Victims (16 December 2008) paras. 13–16, ICC, *Prosecutor v. Katanga, Chui*, ICC-01/04-01/07-1328, Order on the organisation of common legal representation of victims (22 July 2009) para. 17.

[452] ICC, *Prosecutor v. Kenyatta, Muthaura*, ICC-01/09-02/11, Decision appointing a common legal representative of victims (20 November 2012) paras. 5–8.

[453] ICC, *Prosecutor v. Gbagbo*, ICC-02/11-01/11-384-Corr, Corrigendum to the second decision on victims' participation at the confirmation of charges hearing and in the related proceedings (6 February 2013) para. 61 ICC, *Prosecutor v. Ntaganda*, ICC-01/04-02/06, Decision Concerning the Organisation of Common Legal Representation of Victims (2 December 2013) para. 26.

[454] ICC, *Prosecutor v. Ongwen*, ICC-02/04-01/15-350, Decision on contested victims' applications for participation, legal representation of victims and their procedural rights (27 November 2015) paras. 21–23.

[455] ICC, *Prosecutor v. Al Mahdi*, ICC-01/12-01/15, Public redacted version of 'Decision on Victim Participation at Trial and on Common Legal Representation of Victims' (8 June 2016) para. 30.

why there can be confusion for victims with regard to the institutional framework. This office's position still appears to be under development as the Registry's "ReVision" project appears to advocate the OPCV becoming the counsel for the victims, which would require a change in the Regulations of the Court and its primary mandate.[456] However, the main difference between the LRV and the OPCV is that the members of the OPCV are not able to distribute an application on behalf of the victims for further participation *proprio motu*. Only once the application has been filed by the victims can the OPCV represent those victims.

Another overlap of functions arises between the VPRS and the OPCV. While the VPRS is responsible for reaching out to the victims and for the application process, in the situation in the Central African Republic, the OPCV seized the initiative to reach out to the communities which were subsequently represented by the OPCV.[457]

3.6.8 The Trust Fund for Victims (TFV)

The establishment of the ICC resulted in the creation of the Trust Fund for Victims (TFV) as provided for in Article 79 RS. As a separate and independent institution within the Court, the TFV was established by the Resolution of 9 September 2002 of the Assembly of States Parties for the benefit of victims of crimes and of the families of such victims, Regulation 42 RoTVF.[458] Additionally, the Rules of Procedure and Evidence provide more details about the two mandates of the TVF, the Reparations Mandate and the Assistance Mandate. Rule 98 (1–4) RPE deals with the reparations that can be awarded by the Court against a convicted person, whereas Rule 98 (5) RPE specifies the task of the Trust Fund in providing assistance for the benefit of victims. Furthermore, the Regulations of the Trust Fund adopted by the Assembly of States Parties clarify that all resources of the Trust Fund shall be for the benefit of victims and/or their families. In order to put into practice its mandates, it is firstly implementing Court-ordered reparations and, secondly, providing physical and psychosocial rehabilitation or material support to victims of crimes that fall within the jurisdiction of the Court.[459] The grant-making process is, amongst other principles, also strongly based upon the participation of victims in program planning and the accessibility for applicants that would otherwise lack access to funding. The first mandate of the TFV is based upon the conviction of the accused (Regulation 59 RoTFV), which leads to the reparation of the victims who have suffered as a result of the crimes for which the accused has been convicted. In order to receive

[456]Hirst (2017), p. 152.

[457]See ICC, Review Committee Response in Relation to the OPCV Interlocutor, Women's Initiative for Gender Justice, p. 12.

[458]See Resolution ICC-ASP/1/Res.6.

[459]See Peschke (2013), p. 319.

reparations, the victims have to apply for them under Article 75 RS and Rule 94 (1) RPE.

3.7 Conclusion

"It is our collective responsibility to keep in mind the raison d'être of the Court, which is the protection of victims, and to ensure its success," Philippe Kirsch said at the end of the conference in Rome in 1998.[460] A case can therefore be considered successful in terms of this aim when the trial ends with a conviction, a reparation order and the implementation of this order.

The Rome Statute codifies the participation of the victims of international crimes at the international criminal proceedings. The universal human rights approach to victims' rights in international criminal justice is strengthened by the Rome Statute. While the Rome Statute regulates international cooperation on international criminal justice matters between states, a change of the international political framework was necessary in order to induce more actors into participating in the drafting of the Rome Statute and, eventually, into enshrining the rights of the victims in international criminal law.

The required scope of action was opened for NGOs and, in particular, victims rights NGOs and human rights NGOs promoted victims' rights in the Rome Statute. NGOs had the necessary expertise to be able to submit proposals for Article 68 (protection of victims and witnesses and their participation in the proceedings) and Article 75 (reparations to victims). Three NGOs that were identified had a crucial influence on the victims' rights at the ICC: The Coalition for the ICC, ELSA and REDRESS.

On the other hand, only a couple of states actually played a significant role. France contributed significantly to ensure the right to reparation as did the UK. Chile and the Czech Republic even supported, albeit unsuccessfully, an individual trigger mechanism for victims at the ICC. New Zealand proposed the right of victims participating in the proceedings. The legal tradition in terms of victims' rights might be one reason why some states strongly endorsed victims' rights and others not. However, the example of France also points out that political decisions were important for supporting victims' rights.

It is possible to clearly identify the influence that the NGOs as well as the individuals representing governments or official UN positions had on the development and overall negotiations in the run-up to the Rome Statute and subsequent victims' rights that are enshrined in this treaty. Moving forward, states are still part of the decision-making processes and, therefore, it will be important to see how the ICC and the Trust Fund for Victims will ensure that victims' rights are successful.

---

[460]Kirsch and Holmes (1999), p. 12.

The distinction between the victims participating at the different cases before the Court depends on various circumstantial grounds. In the cases of Sudan, the low participation rate amongst the victims is due to the lack of national cooperation with the Court. Only those victims who were outside of Sudan applied to participate.

In the cases of the Central African Republic and Uganda, the participation of a high number of victims stemmed from successful outreach programs. The case of *Bemba*, who was accused of committing war crimes under command responsibility, included more affected regions and victims and thus a high level of participation was expected. The broader the alleged crimes are, the higher the number of victims participating in the proceedings is. The distinction between males and females also plays an essential role regarding participation.

At the same time, even with a high number of participating victims, unfortunately only few of them were allowed to act on their own before the Chamber.

On the other hand, the decision-making in regard to victims is another important aspect at the Court. The decisions depend, of course, on the subject matter and must be seen on a case-by-case basis. However, it is important to note that these decisions affect the length of the proceedings. The content of the decisions depends not only on the subject matter, but also on the legal basis of the judges as to how strongly they want the involvement of the victims in the proceedings.

Is indirect participation actually participation by the victim? This is a question which stands as a core question regarding the meaningfulness of the participation system at the Court. Is the remote and abstract involvement of victim participation meaningful or symbolic? The presence of thousands of individuals who suffered in a direct or indirect way but who are not able to air their real concerns and views about the case, about the issues. The legal representatives who stand far away, even though they have a team with them *in situ*, may not be able to illustrate the pain, views, opinion and positions with regard to the different matters in the proceedings. This cannot be considered as a participation system but rather a representation system.

References

Altwicker TH, Altwicker A, Peters A (2016) Measuring violations of human rights: an empirical analysis of awards in respect of non-pecuniary damage under the European Convention on Human Rights. Heidelberg J Int Law. ZaöRV 76:1–51

Amann DM (2013) Children and the first verdict of the international criminal court. Wash Univ Global Stud Law Rev 12:411–430

Amann DM (2016) Children. In: Schabas W (ed) The Cambridge companion to international criminal law. Cambridge University Press, Cambridge, pp 253–274

Ambos K (2016) Treatise on international criminal law, 1st edn. Oxford University Press, Oxford

Aust A (2009) Handbook of international law. Cambridge University Press, Cambridge

Autesserre S (2006) Local violence, national peace? Postwar 'settlement' in the eastern D.R. Congo (2003–2006). Afr Stud Rev 49(3):1–29

Bachvarova T (2017) The standing of victims in the procedural design of the international criminal court. Brill Nijhoff, Leiden

Barth B (2013) Victims of genocide and crimes against humanity. In: Bonacker T, Safferling C (eds) Victims of international crimes: an interdisciplinary discourse. T.M.C. Asser Press, The Hague, pp 253–262
Bassiouni CM (1999) Negotiating the Treaty of Rome. Cornell Int Law J 32:443–468
Bassiouni CM (2006) International recognition of victims' rights. Hum Rights Law Rev 6:203–279
Bassiouni MC (2011) Crimes against humanity: historical evolution and contemporary application. Cambridge Univ. Press, Cambridge
Bassiouni CM (2013) Introduction to international criminal law. Brill Nijhoff, Leiden
Bassiouni CM, Schabas W (2016) The legislative history of the international criminal court: second revised and expanded edition. Brill Nijhoff, Leiden
Baumgartner E (2008) Aspects of victim participation in the proceedings of the International Criminal Court. Int Rev Red Cross 90(870):409–440
Bergsmo M, Pejic J, Zhu D (2016) Article 15. In: Triffterer O, Ambos K (eds) Rome Statute of the international criminal court: a commentary. Beck, München
Birchall E, Francq E, Pijnenburg A (2011) The international criminal court and reparations for child victims of armed conflict. Reparations Unit, Briefing Paper 4
Boas G, Bischoff JL, Reid NL (2008) International criminal law practitioner library. Cambridge University Press, Cambridge
Bock S (2010) Das Opfer vor dem Internationalen Strafgerichtshof. Duncker & Humblot, Berlin
Bock S (2013) Victims of civil wars. In: Bonacker T, Safferling C (eds) Victims of international crimes: an interdisciplinary discourse. T. M. C. Asser Press, The Hague, pp 263–277
Boczek BA (2005) International law: a dictionary. Scarecrow Press, Lanham
Bohacik B (2010) Report on the standing and rights of victims in criminal proceedings. European Committee on Crime Problems
Bonneau K, Benedetti F, Washburn JL (2014) Preliminary material. In: Bonneau K, Benedetti F, Washburn JL (eds) Negotiating the international criminal court: New York to Rome, 1994-1998. Brill, Leiden, pp 145–168
Boot M (2002) Genocide, crimes against humanity, war crimes: Nullum crimen sine lege and the subject matter jurisdiction of the international criminal court. Intersentia, Anwerpen
Boothby WH (2012) The law of targeting. Oxford University Press, Oxford
Bottigliero I (2004) Redress for victims of crimes under international law. Springer Netherlands, Dordrecht
Brammsen J, Apel S (2008) Anstiftung oder Täterschaft?: "Organisationsherrschaft" in Wirtschaftsunternehmen. ZJS 3:256–265
Catani L (2012) Victims at the international criminal court: some lessons learned from the Lubanga Case. J Int Crim Just 10(4):905–922
Chaikel D (2015) The ICC's child soldier provisions: time to close the three-year gap. ijmonitororg
Chung C (2008) Victims' participation at the internatinal criminalcourt: are concessions of the court clouding the promise? J Int Hum Rights:459–545
Cody S, Koenig A, Stover E (2016) Witness testimony, support, and protection at the ICC. In: Clarke, Knottnerus AS, de Volder E (eds) Africa and the ICC. Cambridge University Press, Cambridge, pp 301–322
Cohen M (2009) Victims' participation rights within the international criminal court: a critical overview. Denv J Int Law Policy 37:351–377
Companjen F, Polese A (2012) Subtle line between self-defence and war. In: Mahapatra DA (ed) Conflict and peace in Eurasia. Routledge, Abingdon, pp 88–102
Cottier M (2016) Article 8. In: Triffterer O, Ambos K (eds) Rome Statute of the international criminal court: a commentary. Beck, München
de Brouwer A-M (2005) Supranational criminal prosecution of sexual violence: The ICC and the practice of the ICTY and the ICTR, School of human rights research series, vol 20. Intersentia, Antwerpen

de Brouwer A, Heikkilä M (2013) Victim issues: participation, protection, reparation and assistance. In: Sluiter G (ed) International criminal procedure: principles and rules. Oxford University Press, Oxford, pp 1299–1374
de Casadevante Romani CF (2012) International law of victims. Springer, London
de Guzman M (2010) Crimes against humanity. In: Schabas W (ed) Routledge handbook of international criminal law. Routledge, London, pp 121–138
Donat-Cattin D (2016) Article 68. In: Triffterer O, Ambos K (eds) Rome Statute of the International Criminal Court: a commentary. Beck, Munich
Drumbl MA (2012) Reimagining child soldiers in international law and policy. Oxford University Press, Oxford
Dué P (1966) Prejudicial publicity versus the rights of the accused. La Law Rev 26:818–847
Eckelmans F (2013) ICC's practice on victim participation. In: Bonacker T, Safferling C (eds) Victims of international crimes: an interdisciplinary discourse. T. M. C. Asser Press, pp 189–222
Edna E, Bienkowska E (1993) Victim participation in proceedings and satisfaction with justice in the continental systems: the case of Poland. J Crim Just 21(1):47–60
Elander M (2018) Figuring victims in international criminal justice: the case of the Khmer Rouge tribunal. Routledge, London
Evans C (2012) The right to reparation in international law for victims of armed conflict. Cambridge Univ. Press, Cambridge
Fardel M, Olarra NV (2017) The application process: procedure and players. In: Tibori-Szabó K, Hirst M (eds) Victim participation in international criminal justice. International criminal justice series, vol 11. T.M.C. Asser Press, The Hague, pp 11–43
Ferencz B (1998) International criminal courts: the legacy of Nuremberg. Pace Int Law Rev 10 (1):203–235
Fernández de Gurmendi S (2002) International criminal procedures. In: Lee LR (ed) The international criminal court: the making of the Rome Statute; issues, negotiations, results. Kluwer Law International, The Hague, pp 175–188
Findlay M (2013) Enunciating genocide: crime, rights and the impact of judicial intervention. In: Rothe DL, Meernik JM, Ingadóttir T (eds) The realities of international criminal justice. BRILL, Leiden
Flores A (2006) The Rome Statute's sexual related crimes: an appraisal under the light of international humanitarian law. Humanitäres Völkerrecht 19:39–51
Funk TM (2015) Victims' rights and advocacy at the international criminal court. Oxford Universtiy Press, Oxford
Gal T (2011) Child victims and restorative justice: a needs-rights model, interpersonal violence. Oxford University Press, Oxford
Garbett C (2017) The international criminal court and restorative justice: victims, participation and the processes of justice. Restorative Just 5(2):198–220
Garner BA (2011) Garner's dictionary of legal usage, 3rd edn. Oxford University Press, Oxford
Gillett M (2009) Victim participation at the international criminal court. Aust Int Law J 16:29–46
Glasius M (2006) The international criminal court: a global civil society achievement. Routledge, London
Gosnell C (2016) Damned if you don't: liability for omission in international criminal law. In: McDermott Y, Schabas W, Hayes N (eds) The Ashgate research companion to international criminal law: critical perspectives. Routledge, Abingdon, New York, pp 101–132
Groome D (2014) Evidence in cases of mass criminality. In: Mylonaki E, Bantekas I (eds) Criminological approaches to international criminal law. Cambridge University Press, Cambridge, pp 117–158
Hafetz J (2018) Punishing atrocities through a fair trial: international criminal law from Nuremberg to the age of global terrorism. Cambridge University Press, Cambridge
Hall C, Ambos K (2016) Article 7. In: Triffterer O, Ambos K (eds) Rome Statute of the international criminal court: a commentary. Beck, München

Hall CK, Stahn C (2016) Article 7. In: Triffterer O, Ambos K (eds) Rome Statute of the International Criminal Court: a commentary. Beck, Munich
Hirst M (2017) Legal representation of participating victims. In: Tibori-Szabó K, Hirst M (eds) Victim participation in international criminal justice. International criminal justice series, vol 11. T.M.C. Asser Press, The Hague, pp 111–170
Ichim O (2015) Just satisfaction under the European Convention on Human Rights. Cambridge University Press, Cambridge
Jacobs D (2017) A tale of four illusions: the right of the defense before international criminal tribunals. In: Rohan CM, Zyberi G (eds) Defense perspectives in international criminal justice. Cambridge University Press, Cambridge, pp 561–586
Kambale P, Rotman A (2004) The international criminal court and Congo
Kaul HP (2014) Der Beitrag Deutschlands zum Völkerstrafrecht. In: Safferling C, Kirsch S (eds) Völkerstrafrechtspolitik: Praxis des Völkerstrafrechts. Springer, Berlin, Heidelberg, pp 51–84
Kelly M (2013) The status of victims under the Rome Statute of the international criminal court. In: Bonacker T, Safferling C (eds) Victims of international crimes: an interdisciplinary discourse. T. M. C. Asser Press, The Hague, pp 47–66
Kelsen H (1952) Principles of international law. Originally published: New York: Rinehart & Company, Inc Reprinted 2003, 2012 by The Lawbook Exchange, Clark
Khan K (2016) Article 32. In: Triffterer O, Ambos K (eds) Rome Statute of the international criminal court: a commentary. Beck, München
Kieler M (2003) Tatbestandsprobleme der sexuellen Nötigung, Vergewaltigung sowie des sexuellen Mißbrauchs widerstandsunfähiger Personen, vol 52. Tenea-Verlag, Berlin
Kirsch P, Holmes JT (1999) The Rome conference on an international criminal court: the negotiating process. Am J Int Law 93:2–12
Kirsch S (2009) Der Begehungszusammenhang der Verbrechen gegen die Menschlichkeit. Frankfurter kriminalwissenschaftliche Studien, vol 115. Peter Lang, Frankfurt
Kiza E (2006) Victimisation in wars: a framework for further inquiry. In: Turković K, Ewald U (eds) Large-scale victimisation as a potential source of terrorist activities: importance of regaining security in post-conflict societies. IOS Press, pp 72–88
Klamberg M (2017) Article 81. In: Klamberg M (ed) Commentary on the law of the international criminal court. FICHL publication series N. 29, Torkel Opsahl Academic
Kristie B (2004) The role of NGOs in the establishment of the international criminal court. Dialogue: Acad Soc Sci Aust 2(1):11–22
Lane C (1999) Hospitals. In: Gutman R (ed) Crimes of war. Norton
Laucci C (2014) The annotated digest of the international criminal court. Nijhoff Publishers, Leiden
Lauterpacht H, Lauterpacht E (1975) International law: being the collected papers of Hersch Lauterpacht. Cambridge University Press, Cambridge
Leach P (2012) South Ossetia. In: Wilmshurst E (ed) International law and the classification of conflicts. Oxford University Press, Oxford, pp 317–355
Lenzerini F (2013) The role of international and mixed criminal courts in the enforcement of international norms on the protection of cultural heritage. In: Francioni F, Gordley J (eds) Enforcing international cultural heritage law. Oxford University Press, Oxford, pp 40–64
Leveau F (2013) Liability of child soldiers under international law. Osgoode Hall Rev Law Policy 4:36–66
Magsam D (2014) Die Opfer in völkerstrafrechtlichen Prozessen in Deutschland. In: Safferling C, Kirsch S (eds) Völkerstrafrechtspolitik: Praxis des Völkerstrafrechts. Springer, Berlin, Heidelberg, pp 181–189
McAsey B (2011) Victim participation at the international criminal court and its impact on procedural fairness. Aust Int Law J 5:105–125
McKay F (2008) Victim participation in proceedings before the international criminal court. Hum Rights Brief 15(3):2–5
Moffett L (2014) Justice for victims before the international criminal court. Routledge, Abingdon, New York

Moffett L (2015) Meaningful and effective? Considering victims' interests through participation at the international criminal court. Crim Law Forum 26(2):255–289

Moffett L (2016) Justice for victims before the International Criminal Court. In: Routledge research in international law. Routledge Taylor & Francis Group, London

Moore B (2008) Courting history: the landmark international criminal court's first years. HRW

Morisson H, Pountney E (2014) Victim participation at the special tribunal for Lebanon. In: Alamuddin A (ed) The special tribunal for Lebanon: law and practice (Oxford monographs in international humanitarian and criminal law). Oxford University Press, Oxford, pp 153–176

Muttukumaru C (2002) Reparation to victims. In: Lee LR (ed) The international criminal court: the making of the Rome Statute; issues, negotiations, results. Kluwer Law International, The Hague, pp 262–270

Neubacher F (2005) Kriminologische Grundlagen einer internationalen Strafgerichtsbarkeit: Politische Ideen- und Dogmengeschichte, kriminalwissenschaftliche Legitimation, strafrechtliche Perspektiven. Mohr Siebeck, Tübingen

Nilsson A (2013) Children and youth in armed conflict. The Raoul Wallenberg Institute human rights library volume 43/I-43/II. Martinus Nijhoff Publishers, Leiden

Novic E (2016) The concept of cultural genocide: an international law perspective. Oxford University Press, Oxford

Nuzhat M (2008) Defining "charity" and "charitable purposes" United Kingdom. Int J Not-for Profit Law 11

Olásolo H (2008) Essays on international criminal justice. Hart Publishing, London

Pace WR, Thieroff M (2002) Participation of non-governmental organisations. In: Lee LR (ed) The international criminal court: the making of the Rome Statute; issues, negotiations, results. Kluwer Law International, The Hague, pp 391–399

Pérez-León Acevedo J P (2014) Victims' Status at International and Hybrid Criminal Courts

Peschke K (2013) The role and mandates of the ICC trust fund for victims. In: Bonacker T, Safferling C (eds) Victims of international crimes: an interdisciplinary discourse. T.M.C. Asser Press, The Hague, pp 317–327

Peters A (2016) Beyond human rights: the legal status of the individual in international law. Cambridge University Press, Cambridge

Petrossian G (2019a) Elements of superior responsibility for sexual violence by subordinates. Manitoba Law J 42:123–152

Petrossian G (2019b) Staatenverantwortlichkeit für Völkermord. Duncker & Humblot, Berlin

Pilloud C et al (1987) Commentary on the Additional protocols of 8 June 1977 to the Geneva Conventions of 12 August 1949. Nijhoff, Leiden

Potier T (2001) Conflict in Nagorno-Karabakh, Abkhazia and South Ossetia: a legal appraisal. Kluwer Law International, Alphen aan den Rijn

Redress (2015) Victim participation in criminal law proceedings. Redress, The Hague

Reyes YA (2017) The protection of victims participating in international criminal justice. In: Tibori-Szabó K, Hirst M (eds) Victim participation in international criminal justice. International criminal justice series, vol 11. T.M.C. Asser Press, The Hague, pp 171–204

Rikhof J (2011) Child soldiers: protection or responsibility. In: Cook DT, Wall J (eds) Children and armed conflict: cross-disciplinary investigations. Studies in childhood and youth. Palgrave Macmillan, London, pp 171–189

Rivier R (2010) Inter-American mechanisms. In: Crawford J et al (eds) The law of international responsibility. Oxford University Press, Oxford, pp 739–762

Robinson D (1999) Defining "Crimes Against Humanity" at the Rome Conference. Am J Int Law 93:43–57

Rojo EC (2017) Personal interests of victims. In: Klamberg M (ed) Commentary on the law of the international criminal court. FICHL publication series N. 29, Torkel Opsahl Academic

Rombouts H (2004) Victim organisations and the politics of reparation: a case-study on Rwanda. Intersentia, Mortsel

Safferling C (2003) Das Opfer völkerrechtlicher Verbrechen. Zeitschrift für die gesamte Strafrechtswissenschaft:352–384
Safferling C (2011a) The role of the victim in the criminal process. ICLR 11:183–215
Safferling C (2011b) Internationales Strafrecht, Strafanwendungsrecht - Völkerstrafrecht - Europäisches Strafrecht. Springer, Berlin, Heidelberg
Safferling C (2012) International criminal procedure. Oxford University Press, Oxford
Sandick PA (2012) Speechlessness and trauma: why the international criminal court needs a public interviewing guide. Northwest J Int Hum Rights 11:105–125
Schabas W (2007) An introduction to the international criminal court, 3rd edn. Cambridge University Press, Cambridge
Schabas W (2010) The international criminal court: a commentary on the Rome Statute. Oxford University Press, Oxford
Schabas W (2016) Article 6. In: Triffterer O, Ambos K (eds) Rome Statute of the international criminal court: a commentary. Beck, München
Seyfarth L (2013) Child soldiers to war criminals: trauma and the case for personal mitigation. Chi-Kent J Int Comp Law 14:1–30
Simon TW (2007) The laws of genocide: prescriptions for a just world. Praeger Security International
Stewart J (2014) Fair trial rights under the Rome Statute from a prosecution perspective: ICTR Symposium
Swaak-Goldman O (2000) Crimes against humanity. In: McDonald GK, Swaak-Goldman O (eds) Substantive and procedural aspects of international criminal law. The experience of international and national courts. Kluwer Law International, Leiden
Trumbull CP (2008) The victims of victim participation in international criminal proceedings. Mich J Int Law 23:777–826
van den Wyngaert C (2011) Victims before international criminal courts: some views and concerns of an ICC trial judge. Case West Reserve J Int Law 44(1):475–496
van Kempen PH (2010) Human rights and criminal justice applied to legal persons. Protection and liability of private and public juristic entities under the ICCPR, ECHR, ACHR and AfChHPR. Electron J Comp Law 14:1–32
Vasiliev S (2008) Article 68 (3) and personal interests of victims in the emerging practice of the ICC. In: Sluiter G, Stahn C (eds) The emerging practice of the international criminal court. BRILL, Leiden, pp 635–690
Vasiliev S (2015) Victim participation revised: what the ICC is learning about itself. In: Stahn C (ed) Law and practice of the international criminal court. Oxford University Press, Oxford, pp 1133–1201
Werle G, Jeßberger F (2014) Principles of international criminal law. Oxford University Press
Zagar M (2018) A defendant's right to a fair trial and improvement of the victim's status in the proceedings before international criminal jurisdictions. In: Lorenzmeier S, Sancin V (eds) Contemporary issues of human rights protection in international and national settings. Nomos, Hart Publishing, Baden-Baden, Oxford, pp 289–308
Zago G (2014) The role of victims at the international criminal court, legal chalanges from the tension between restorative and retributive justice. Diritto Penale Contemporaneo, Milan
Zappala S (2010) The rights of victims v. the rights of the accused. J Int Crim Just 1:137–164
Zegveld L (2009) Compensation for the victims of chemical warfare in Iraq and Iran. In: Ferstman C, Goetz M, Stephens A (eds) Reparations for victims of genocide, war crimes and crimes against humanity: systems in place and systems in the making. Martinus Nijhoff Publishers, Leiden, pp 369–384

Chapter 4
Reparation for Victims

Ubi ius, ibi remedium.

4.1 General Principle of Reparation

Article 231 of the Treaty of Versailles opened up the possibility for reparations stemming from the war initiated by the German Empire in World War I. It was not until 2010, 91 years later, that the Federal Republic of Germany was able to pay its final debts for the ravages of World War I.[1] After World War II, reparations for the two wars were regulated in the Treaty of London of 27 February 1953. Furthermore, the reparations for the damage caused by the Holocaust were enshrined in the Agreement of Luxembourg of 10 September 1952.[2] These are the best examples of how reparations for international crimes, such as war crimes, crimes against humanity, genocide and crimes of aggression, function in practice on an international level. States were responsible for reparations for damage and for repairing the damage suffered by individuals as a result of macro-violations.

The starting point for the reparations for victims of macro-crimes is parallel to state responsibility in tort law. In this context, if the state commits an internationally wrongful act, violating an international obligation by act or omission, it is furthermore responsible for reparations for that damage.[3] The reparations themselves may be practiced in a very broad manner. They may include not only material compensation for the harm or damage suffered, but also include several political and moral actions which will be required for the psychological and moral satisfaction of those who have suffered. It is true to say that international harm which is not recognised

[1]See Spiegel.de (online) 2010 (1. October) Deutschland begleicht letzte Schulden, see http://www.spiegel.de/wirtschaft/soziales/erster-weltkrieg-deutschland-begleichtletzte-schulden-a-720672.html, last visited on 17 December 2020.

[2]Rombeck-Jaschinski (2011), pp. 442–444.

[3]See Petrossian (2019), pp. 157–158.

© The Author(s), under exclusive license to Springer Nature Switzerland AG 2021

C. Safferling, G. Petrossian, *Victims Before the International Criminal Court*,
https://doi.org/10.1007/978-3-030-80177-9_4

leads to further frustration and even to secondary victimisation.[4] This is more so in cases of mass violations of people's fundamental rights. The resolutions, conventions and international agreements which have been adopted by the states in order to punish acts causing damage are examples of such satisfaction or recognition of existing victimisation. As a result of widespread practice regarding enforced disappearance in Latin America, the Inter-American Convention on Forced Disappearance of Persons was adopted in 1994. In this way, the harm inflicted upon those victims who suffered as a result of that particular crime is recognized throughout that particular continent. This is a form of reparation where the international community takes action so as to be responsible for the damage to individuals by making their own contributions to prevent or to punish those acts. Accordingly, reparations may be considered on three different levels: firstly, on the grounds of tort law—the wrongdoers (tortfeasors) are responsible for the reparations; secondly, on the grounds of state responsibility—the states are responsible for making their own contribution to the victims; and, on the third level, the international community is responsible. Every subject is then individually and in their own capacity involved in the reparation process for the victims. These three levels of reparation are also considered in the reparation system of the ICC, however, before the system of reparation under international criminal justice can be analysed, it is important to discuss each level of reparation individually.

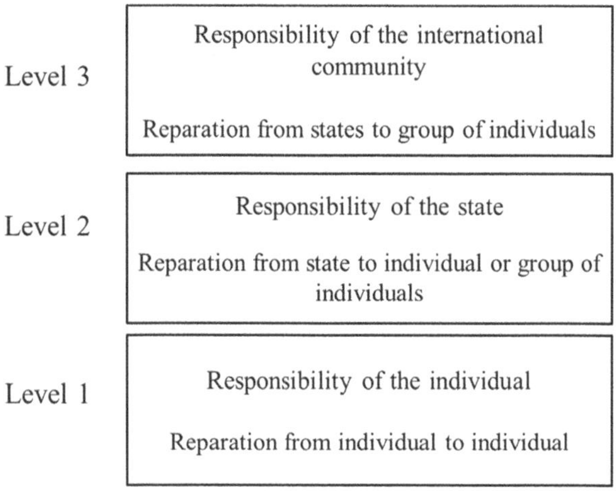

[4]There are three types of secondary victimisation: (a) as a result of victimisation or the consequences of victimisation extending to another party, (b) as a result of further victimisation because of processes and responses to the victim's feelings of victimisation, (c) as a result of a social reaction to a primary victim's status, see Condry (2010), pp. 220–228, cf. also Underwood and Palmer (2003), pp. 30–38.

4.1.1 *Responsibility of the Individual*

In Roman law, the person who committed a civil wrong[5] was obligated to recover or to repair the damage.[6] This system is a fundamental pillar of civil law and is known under the terms *obligationes ex contractu* (obligation arising from contracts) and *obligationes ex delicto* (obligations arising from torts).[7] Compared to a criminal offence, which is directed not only against the personal rights of another person but also against the community itself and is punished by the state, a tort, which is a breach of duty of care,[8] is a recovery for the harm caused as a consequence of the tort. Accordingly, it is possible to ascertain that one incident may raise two sets of judicial proceedings. On the one hand, criminal or administrative proceedings and, on the other hand, civil proceedings. However, it is not in every case that a tort is connected to the crime. In cases of mass violation of human rights, crimes are linked to torts. As already discussed above, there are several states which combine both systems into one.[9] Section 823 (1) of the German Civil Code (*Bürgerliches Gesetzbuch*; BGB) gives the best overview of how the obligation to compensate arises as a result of the tort. It states that "a person who, intentionally or negligently, unlawfully injures the life, body, health, freedom, property or another right of another person is liable to make compensation to the other party for the damage arising from this". In almost every case where mass atrocities take place, there is a huge risk that the protected interests mentioned might be breached and, therefore, an obligation for compensation may arise. However, not every breach is recoverable. At the same time, the compensation for damage does not cover or replace the object damaged, it is rather a new and further influence on the object, in order to relieve the sustained harm.[10]

4.1.1.1 Wrongful Death

In the event of death, compensation arises not because of the claims of the deceased person, since they do not have legal capacity anymore, but from the claims of indirect victims, i.e. the relatives of the deceased.[11] These compensation claims cover a wide range of different expenses for the funeral costs and loss of earnings, especially in cases where the deceased person was the only person responsible for

---

[5]Zimmermann (1996), pp. 902–903.

[6]See Twelve Tables mentioned in the first Chapter.

[7]McGinn (2013), p. 272.

[8]McBride and Bagshaw (2018), p. 47, Owen (2003), p. 31, cf. Harke (2010), p. 253.

[9]Such as Germany or Spain, see the first chapter and comparison of the European states, see also Findlay and Chuah Hui Ying (2018).

[10]Cf. Herraclitus, "it is not possible to step into the same river twice", cf. Cane and Goudkamp (2018), p. 4.

[11]Fuchs (2003), p. 10.

maintaining the family.[12] At the same time, the more distant relatives have the possibility to claim for compensation for the psychological harm sustained as a consequence of the loss of a loved one.[13] The latter is, however, not common in national legal systems and it is hard to quantify. It is true to say that the pain and hurt experienced by the victims as a result of crime is not easily possible to transfer into material compensation.

Within common law systems, damages for wrongful death were previously not recoverable, however, today it is possible to determine that almost every jurisdiction permits compensation for pecuniary losses and suffering arising from the tortious conduct of others.[14] There are discussions within the common law systems which maintain that there are further damages arising from wrongful death, such as damages arising from pre-impact fear, anxiety and emotional distress and pain and suffering before the death, all of which are known as ante-mortem injuries.[15] At the same time, due to the instantaneousness of the death, there cannot be compensation for the pain and suffering which is conscious. To that effect even if the person survived for a short period of time, the common law does not recognise it as pre-mortem damage until there is expert testimony about the period of suffering and pain of the person after the incident.[16] Furthermore, there are post-mortem injuries arising from wrongful death, for instance:

- the expenses of lasting illness;
- including the transportation, nursing, hospitalisation etc.;
- funeral expenses, lost earnings or accumulations, lost gifts and contributions;
- lost services, lost advice, counsel and guidance;
- lost society companionship or consortium;
- loss of enjoyment of life or hedonic damages; and
- punitive or exemplary damages.[17]

The civil law does not recognise the common law's discussions on compensation of pre-mortem injuries and mostly concentrates on the post-mortem injuries,[18] as is shown, for example, in Section 844 BGB. Firstly, one analyses the funeral expenses which arise, bearing in mind that such costs differ from state to state and depend on further features of the funeral. Pursuant to German jurisprudence, the funeral costs may include not only the deployment of the hearse and the preparation of the grave or rent of the morgue and the possible transfer of the corpse, but also a moderate

[12] Gschnitzer (1963), pp. 175–176, Goldberg et al. (2016), p. 403.

[13] Cf. Section 844 (3) German BGB since 2017.

[14] *Alexander v. Whitman*, 114 F, 3d 1392–1398, 1996.

[15] This includes also conscious awareness of approaching death, see Schramm (2010), pp. 59–61, Vesper (2010), pp. 956–958.

[16] Vesper (2010), p. 957.

[17] Vesper (2010), pp. 957–960.

[18] Including economic and non economic losses, see Ward (2015), p. 39.

customary wake, clothes and further arrangements related to the mourning.[19] In addition, German jurisprudence has determined that such costs related to the travel of funeral guests, the care of the grave and religious ceremonies in honor of a deceased person may not be considered as compensation.[20]

While the funeral costs are relatively fixed, a problematic issue arises in the event of a wrongful death and the loss of earnings of the deceased person. This is a common issue where relatives may claim for the loss of income due to the death. However, the calculation of those earnings is not as easily conceivable as it appears to be at first sight. Every national jurisdiction considers its own calculation mechanism for compensation. The settlement for economic losses and the damages award in the U.S. tort law system is placed in the hands of the jury, though the plaintiff has to prove any loss of earnings using the testimony of expert reports, witnesses, life-care planners or economists and further experts.[21] In the UK, a unique method of calculation for the loss of earnings—known as the *Ogden Tables*—was developed in 1999.[22] These 28 tables provide a multiplier for calculating the loss of earnings bearing in mind the gender, age and loss of earnings or pension up to various retirement ages.[23] German jurisprudence categorises three main groups, where the calculations of loss of incomes may differ. The first group includes cases involving the death of the sole-earner in the family, where the calculation of the loss of income is carried out in eight steps.[24] The second group calculation is considered in the event of the death of the household spouse and the third group in the event of the death of a member of a dual-earner marriage.

The most difficult aspect of compensation for wrongful death is the calculation of non-pecuniary damages. The value of life is unquantifiable. However, national legislations, as well as international jurisprudence, have attempted to establish rates of compensation for non-pecuniary damages, which predominantly include

---

[19]Wagner (2019a), Rn. 20–23, Drees (1994), p. 7, cf. RGZ 139, 393, 394, BGHZ 32, 72, 75, NJW 60 910 911. Lange et al. (2003), pp. 319–320.

[20]Boujong (1989), p. 87, including transportation to hospital, fees for the notary and lawyer.

[21]Ward (2015), p. 41, cf. Posner and Landes (1980), p. 851 et seq., Ireland (2016), pp. 13–14.

[22]See the last version of Ogden Tables https://assets.publishing.service.gov.uk/government/uploads/system/uploads/attachment_data/file/930494/Actuarial_tables_for_use_in_personal_injury_and_fatal_accident_cases_7th_edition_Supplementary_Tables__July_2019_.cleaned__4_.pdf, last visited 17 December 2020.

[23]See Korn and Sethi (2011), p. 138.

[24]See Wagner (2019b), 'Section 844' Rn. 48–51, cf. Drees (1994), p. 109 sub. seq, in order to calculate the damage award the following steps has to be done, firstly the hypothetical future income of the deceased person should be determined, secondly from this amount should be deducted those expenses which were related to capital formation, thirdly fix costs have to excluded, fourthly individual quota of the family member should be determined, the fix costs have to be recouped per rata. These five steps lead to provisional result and in order to have the final result of loss of earnings further three steps should be considered namely the liability of wrongdoer according to Section 846, secondary the violation of obligation to mitigate the damage and thirdly partial compensation of the damage caused by the incident, cf. OLG Hamm, Judgment 19-12-1995 – 27 U 117/95.

the psychological harm of the indirect victim. German legislation determines indirect victimisation in connection with psychological distress due to the wrongful death of a loved one. Obviously, it does not have to be a relative of the descendant, but a person who stands close to the deceased person.[25] The burden of proof for the psychological harm still rests with the indirect victim and their special and very close relationship[26] to the deceased person.[27] Legal liability insurance policies in Europe usually consider anywhere from between 2000 and 5000 EUR and from between 10,000 and 20,000 EUR compensation for psychological distress, pain and suffering as a result of the loss of a loved one.[28] The compensation in this matter equalises and balances the harm sustained. National jurisprudence of individual countries is, however, critical to the practice of compensation for pain and suffering. Therefore, national legislations have established strict criteria for settlement awards for pain and suffering, whereby others are considered in the common law system.[29]

4.1.1.2 Wrongful Injury to Body or Health

If, in the event of death, the deceased person is unable to claim damages due to a lack of legal capacity, the indirect victims, i.e. the relatives, become the main claimants. In the event of injuries to the direct victim, the victim themselves evidently remains the main claimant. The broad definition of injury to body or health means any wrongful action as a consequence of which the victim will suffer bodily or psychological harm or ill-health. Under these circumstances, tort law also foresees compensation in cases of damage arising, bearing in mind the inability of the victim to proceed with their further activities, including their inability to work.[30] In such cases, the victim may receive a pension for life from the wrongdoer because of damage (*cf.* Section 843 BGB). At the same time, not every injury might be considered wrongful. Medical procedures or consent injuries like tattoos, hair loss[31] etc. are not injuries for which compensation might be claimed, unless it refers to a medical error or medical malpractice. As mentioned above, the UK and Germany have developed lists of compensation for different injuries, which serve as a guide when claiming compensation for injuries. The range of compensation in the event of wrongful injuries to body and health for which the direct victims may claim are considerably broader

[25]Biela and Tomson (2017), p. 300.

[26]Devaney (2009), p. 4.

[27]Cf. Sections 253 and 844 (3) German BGB, cf. Jahnke (2018b), Rn. 214–220.

[28]Emmerich (2012), p. 829, cf. Stellungnahme des Gesamtverbandes der Deutschen Versicherungswirtschaft, 16 Januar 2017, Steele (2014), p. 521, Section 253 German BGB and Schmerzensgeld Katalog 775 EUR - 250.000 EUR beim Tod, see Zwißler (2016).

[29]Hulsebosch and Bernstein (2013), p. 244, Goldberg and Zipursky (2010), Damages.

[30]See Cane (1997), p. 103.

[31]Cf. Wagner (2019a), Rn. 173–176.

than in cases involving death.[32] The award for compensation depends on the matter and the circumstances of the case, and the established jurisprudence in Germany and the UK individually provide a clear guide through the compensation claims. However, these lists show how differently jurisdictions assess compensation with regard to different matters. Examining the lists, it is possible to admit that the German jurisprudence gives lesser awards compared to the UK compensation system. In Germany, higher awards[33] are given for malpractice and are not paid by the wrongdoers themselves but by the insurer.

General overview of compensation rates for injuries in UK and Germany				
	UK £		Germany €	
Injuries	Low	High	Low	High
Head	1700	342,000	100	750,000
Teeth	850	32,000	300	15,000
Nose	1200	19,000	300	15,000
Eyes	1700	214,000	300	230,000
Arm	5300	111,000[34]	260	17,000[35]
Hand	700	170,000[36]	100	15,000
Shoulder	3500	40,000	800	50,000
Leg	23,000	125,000	600	70,000
Ankle	4390	61,000	100	45,000
Body	750	136,000	1.000	250,000
Hips and pelvis	100	111,000	500	160,000

4.1.1.3 Wrongful Damage to Property

Damage to property is a common reality in everyday life. Compensation awards for economic loss are, however, easier to calculate compared to the immaterial compensation for bodily or psychological harm. Property has its market price and any compensation for it may differ, bearing in mind objective circumstances surrounding the property.[37] Pursuant to Section 249(2) BGB, the plaintiff may request not to seek restitution of the damaged property, but rather financial compensation.

[32]There are mostly three possible post mortem compensation rates, funeral costs, loss of earnings and compensation for non-pecuniary damages.

[33]Cf. DAWR-Schmerzensgeldtabelle 2018, Ausgabe 2, cf. also Sugarman (2005), pp. 405–434.

[34]Amputation £250,000.

[35]Amputation €50,000.

[36]Amputation £115,000.

[37]See Lange et al. (2003), p. 51.

4.1.1.4 Wrongful Violation of Personal Rights

A breach of personal rights, such as the deprivation of liberty, or the violation of other personal rights are rare in tort law compared to the above-mentioned cases and rather fall within the framework of the remedial system under administrative law. However, a compensation award for the violation of personal rights by a wrongdoer is calculated on the basis of objective and subjective circumstances.

4.1.1.5 Inability of the Perpetrator to Pay Damages

A situation often arises in which the damage outweighs the financial situation of the perpetrator who is then not in a position to be able to compensate the victim for the damage caused. This can frequently lead to frustration and, mostly in the cases where the compensation awards exceeds five-digit sums, it becomes yet more difficult to enforce the judgment. National jurisdictions have therefore established legal mechanisms for collecting the judgment sums from the wrongdoers as soon as the wrondoers receive any income, bearing in mind future circumstances. At the same time, reparation for the injured parties still remains a problematic issue, as they have to be actively involved in the collection process of the judgment sums and in seeking possibilities for compensation. There are different schemes and mechanisms which exist to assist victims in collecting damages from the wrongdoer. Even in cases where the wrongdoer is not able to pay the damages, the judgment does not disappear, as the wrongdoer will not always remain unable to pay. However, the injured party should be actively involved in order to be able to follow the process and to receive the damages owed.

4.1.2 Responsibility of the State

In order to avoid secondary victimisation through the inability of a perpetrator to pay damages, the Europe established a mechanism for compensation for victims of crimes through state compensation.

The European Convention on the Compensation of Victims of Violent Crimes from 1983 provides a platform for the Member States to implement a state compensation mechanism within their national jurisdiction. This enables the victims of violent crimes to claim minimal compensation if there is no other source available to cover those expenses (Articles 3 and 4 Convention on Compensation 1983). It mostly includes such expenses which relate to the loss of earnings, funerals costs, medical and hospitalisation costs and loss of maintenance. However, this does not preclude the victims from claiming compensation before the civil courts for torts committed under the crime. Further international agreement within the EU is illustrated by Directive 2004/80/EC—relating to compensation for the victims of crime—which requires the EU states to have a compensation scheme for the victims of intentional violent crimes. Even though the Convention on Compensation establishes minimal standards for state compensation for the victims, these sources of compensation are not always easily available to the victims. The victims still have to prove their victimhood and their inability to cover the costs, which have arisen as a consequence of the crime, from other sources. Accordingly, there is always an assumption that the injured person may continue to suffer due to their search for compensation.

The Convention on Compensation is based on the principle of state responsibility, where the state should be held responsible for its failure to prevent the crime as a result of which the victim suffered harm.[38] The result of the aforementioned Convention is the implementation of national legislation for the compensation of victims of violent crimes, such as the 1985 Victims Compensation Act (*Opferentschädigungsgesetz*; OEG)[39] in Germany and the Criminal Injuries Compensation Act 1995[40] in the UK. These laws not only consider payments to the victims who have suffered harm within the territory of the state as a result of a crime under national legislation, but also contain further criteria for the compensation of the violent crimes which are not solely bound to the victims inability to cover the costs. For example, the German OEG does not grant compensation awards to victims who provoked the commission of crime, or who are involved in criminal gangs or other criminal activities (Section 2 OEG).[41]

However, the question arises as to how the state should be held responsible in criminal cases. The answer to this question may be dealt with from two perspectives, on the one hand, from the perspectives of the national crime and, on the other hand, from the perspective of international crime. The theory of state responsibility relates to the aspect of the internationally wrongful act.

4.1.2.1 State Responsibility Under International Law

A wrongful act or omission by the state which violates the interests of other domestic law subjects may give rise to state responsibility. State responsibility is, however, a new phenomenon and although, in theory, it is not generally accepted, in practice state responsibility includes different forms of actions which follow the breach of international obligations.[42] While attempts have been made to develop and codify standards of state responsibility, and to establish inter-state agreements for state responsibility due to violations of international standards, the UN International Law Commission has failed to draft a document accepted by all states. The doctrine of

[38]Cf. BSG, Judgment 7 November 1979, Az. 9 RVg 2/78; BVBl. 6/1980, p. 1.

[39]Schroth and Schroth (2018), p. 299, see also Jahnke (2018a).

[40]Cf. Ashworth (2010), p. 298.

[41]Cf. Schroth and Schroth (2018), p. 303, Haupt et al. (2003), Rn. 358.

[42]Cf. Cohen (2020a), p. 27 et seq.

state responsibility is, at least, anchored in customary law and is practiced by the International Court of Justice.[43] At first sight, it appears that state responsibility is attributable towards and among states. Although traditionally state responsibility was accepted as a legal issue between state relationships, Article 33 (2) of the ILC Draft Articles on State Responsibility acknowledges that state responsibility may accrue directly to any person or entity.[44] Before discussing how state responsibility is attributable to an individual, it is first important to understand how state responsibility arises within international law.

As mentioned above, should the state breach an international obligation then that state may be held responsible for the damage caused. In cases concerning an individual's criminal conduct, state responsibility may also arise.[45] This is the case if the state has failed to prevent the individual's criminal conduct, as it is in the general duty of a state to prevent crimes from occurring. If a crime has nevertheless been committed, the state is obligated to punish the perpetrator and to rectify the damage. In this way, the actions of the individual are attributed to the state indirectly, even if the individual was not a subject of international law or acting on behalf of the state.[46] Hugo Grotius did not recognise the doctrine of state responsibility, however, he did consider a breach of an obligation to imply a new obligation to repair the damage.[47] For example, in accordance with the Westphalia Peace Treaty of 1648, states were obligated to provide restitution for the damage of property caused by the preceding war. It is possible to ascertain that the use of the doctrine of state responsibility after World War I,[48] by making the German Empire pay for the damage caused by the war, is the first step towards conceptualising and "codifying" the doctrine within customary international law.[49] The next attempt to codify the doctrine of state responsibility was then demonstrated after World War II in various treaties which considered reparations for the damage caused by the war.[50] However, the attempt by the UN to request codification of the law on state responsibility in 1953 played a significant role.[51] Although the efforts by the International Law Commission to codify were illustrated in the draft articles on state responsibility, they were, nevertheless, not accepted by the majority of states.

---

[43]See Petrossian (2019), p. 139.

[44]Peters (2018), p. 545.

[45]Siehe Nollkaemper (2003), p. 617, Bonafè (2009), p. 44.

[46]Siehe Kelsen (2009), p. 97, Boczek (2005), p. 75, Aust (2010), pp. 12–13, Shaw (2014), p.258, Bonafè (2009), pp. 52–53, 64, see also ECtHR, *Streletz, Kessler, Krenz v. Germany*, Judgment (22 March 2001) para. 86, ECtHR, *Jordan v. U.K. Judgment* (4 May 2001) para. 107, ECtHR, *Ekinci v. Turkey*, Judgment (18 July 2000) para. 78, Safferling (2011), pp. 548–549, 552, Krajewski (2017), pp. 292–293.

[47]Grotius and Tuck (2005), p. 884.

[48]Articles 231–232 Versailles Peace Treaty 1920.

[49]Trapp (2011), p. 231.

[50]See e.g. London Agreement on German External Debts 1953.

[51]UN/GA, Resolution 799 (VIII), 7 December 1953, Request for the Codification of the principles of International Law governing State Responsibility.

The main actors in international law are the states and international organisations, and like any legal entity they exercise their rights and obligations through their organs. Hence, any natural or legal person acting in the name of the organ,[52] or in the name of the state and only for the state and not for private interests, may constitute state responsibility.[53] The breach of obligation by the state may occur in two forms: either by specific positive action or by omission.[54] At the same time, international obligations of a state arise from customary norms as well as from treaties, agreements or from decisions of international organisations or the International Arbitral Tribunal, as well as the ICJ. Despite the existence of sources for state obligations, neither the international legal doctrine nor the case law of the ICJ provide a distinction between obligations raising from a contract (*ex contractu*) or as a result of the torts (*ex delicto*).[55] Accordingly, irrespective of the reason for the breach of either universal or local obligations,[56] the breach constitutes a duty to repair or to compensate for the damage.[57] The ILC Draft Articles also considers cases where the breach of obligation does not, under certain circumstances, constitute responsibility. These are consent,[58] self-defence, counter-measures in respect of an internationally wrongful act,[59] *force majeure*, distress and necessity.[60] If responsibility cannot be

---

[52]Cf. ICJ, *Certain German Interests in Polish Upper Silesia Case* (1926), p. 19, CJ, *Treatment of Polish Nationals and other Persons of Polish Origins in the Danzig Territory Case* (1932), pp. 24–25 and ICJ, *Phosphates in Marocco Case* (1938), p. 25, Reports of International Arbitral Awards, *U.S. (Roper). vs. Mexico, General Claims Commission* (1923), p. 159, *U.S. (Boldwin) vs. Panama (1933)*, p. 331, Pike (2014), p. 274, see Reports of International Arbitral Awards, *Antoine Fabiani Case* (1905), pp. 84–85 and Paulsson (2005), pp. 57, 84–87.

[53]Petrossian (2019), pp. 155–157.

[54]See Article 2 of ICL Draft Articles, see also Shelton (2015), p. 13.

[55]Reports of International Arbitral Awards, *Case concerning the difference between New Zealand and France* (Rainbow Warrior Affair), Decision (30 April 1990), para. 75, "[...] *The reason is that the general principles of International Law concerning State responsibility are equally applicable in the case of breach of treaty obligation, since in the international law field there is no distinction between contractual and tortious responsibility, so that any violation by a State of any obligation, of whatever origin, gives rise to State responsibility and consequently, to the duty of reparation. The particular treaty itself might of course limit or extend the general Law of State Responsibility, for instance by establishing a system of remedies for it* [. . .]".

[56]See Draft Articles of State for Internationally Wrongful Acts, with Commentaries, 2001, Article 48, para. 6, Crawford (2000), Regulation 106 (a), ICJ, *Barcelona Traction Case*, Judgment (5 February 1970), para. 34.

[57]ICJ, *Portugal vs. Australia, Case Concerning East Timor*, Judgment (30 June 1995), para. 29 ICJ, *Barcelona Traction Case*, Judgment (5 February 1970), para. 33.

[58]Aust 2014, 180, Report of the International Law Commission on the work of its fifty-third session 2001, Article 20 (6),

[59]See Declaration on Principles of International Law concerning Friendly Relations and Cooperation among States in accordance with the Charter of the United Nations, 1970, UN A/RES/25/2625, "*States have a duty to refrain from acts of reprisal involving the use of force.*"

[60]Petrossian (2019), pp. 162–164.

excluded by any of the aforementioned, then the wrongdoer must consider further consequences.[61]

4.1.2.1.1 Crime as an International Wrongful Act

Not every crime committed by the state can be distinguished as a breach of an international obligation. In order for the crime to qualify as an internationally wrongful act, it has to be internationally recognised as such either by international customary law, by any treaty or agreement or by any decision of international organisations. The ICJ uses different terms for the determination of an internationally wrongful act. In the case of *U.S.A. vs. Iran* from 1980, the Court described the violation as "incompatibility with the obligations" of a state,[62] in the case of *Nicaragua vs. U.S.A.* from 1986 as being "contradictory" to the customary norms[63] and in the case of the *Gabčíkovo-Nagymaros project* of 1997 as a "breach of contract".[64] It is therefore noteworthy that the ILC was able to agree on the legal notion of a violation of international obligations enshrined in Article 12 ILC Draft Articles. Moreover, the doctrine of state responsibility has not established the distinction between "merely wrongful" acts or "punishable" acts. They both constituted a breach of an obligation not to commit the conduct.[65] Under the term 'universal internationally wrongful acts' one can identify offences such as genocide, crimes against humanity, war crimes, torture, apartheid, piracy, slavery and terrorism which are deemed to be *jus cogens*.[66] Further crimes can be distinguished under various violations of human rights. Accordingly, if the states are obligated to protect the population on their territory, and if the rights of its citizens or foreigners are violated within the territory of the state, then the state can be held responsible for the internationally wrongful act.

---

[61]PICJ, *Factory at Chorzów Case*, Judgment (26 July 1927) A, p. 21, ICJ, *LeGrand Brothers Case*, Judgment (27 June 2001), para. 48.

[62]ICJ, *U.S.A. v. Iran, Case concerning U.S. Diplomatic and Consular Staff in Teheran*, Judgemnet (24 May 1980), para. 56, "[...] *it must consider their compatibility or incompatibility with the obligations of Iran under treaties in force or under any other rules of international law that may be applicable* [...]".

[63]ICJ, *Nicaragua v. U.S.A. Case concerning Military and Paramilitary Activities in and against Nicaragua*, Judgment (27 June 1986), para. 186, "[...] *the Court deems it sufficient that the conduct of States should, in general, be consistent with such rules, and that instances of State conduct inconsistent with a given rule should generally have been treated as breaches of that rule, not as indications of the recognition of a new rule* [...]".

[64]ICJ, *Hungary/Slovakia, Case concerning the Gabcikovo-Nagymaros Project*, Judgment (25 September 1997) para. 87, "[...] *a state of necessity linked to the performance of the 1977 Treaty, Hungary would not have been permitted to rely upon that state of necessity in order to justify its failure to comply with its treaty obligations, as it had helped, by act or omission to bring it about* [...]".

[65]Cf. Spinedi (1989), p. 12.

[66]Kleinlein (2017), p. 307.

4.1.2.1.2 The State as an Active Wrongdoer

In the majority of cases involving mass violations of human rights, the states themselves are actively involved. However, the doctrine of state responsibility does not recognise the criminal liability of the state in view of international crimes. At the same time, for example, the crime of genocide automatically constitutes two types of responsibility; on the one hand, the responsibility of the individual[67] and, on the other, the responsibility of the state for committing genocide or for its failure to prevent genocide. In order to determine the involvement of the state in the mass violation of human rights, one first needs to prove the link between the state organs and the individuals committing the crimes. After the Genocide in Rwanda, tensions between the ethnic groups continued. For this reason, the DRC brought a case before the ICJ against neighboring states,[68] holding them responsible for the atrocities committed in the DRC.[69] The Court held in its judgment that as Uganda occupied the territories of the DRC in the region of Ituri, it was responsible for the violation of international humanitarian law and human rights committed by its forces within that region.[70] Therefore, Uganda was obligated to guarantee the non-repetition of the acts and to make reparation for any injuries caused by the violation of the obligations imposed under international law.[71] The Court even established an amount for the reparations paid by Uganda to the DRC. However, to date no war reparations have been paid by Uganda to the DRC in order to compensate for the damage determined by the Court.

4.1.2.1.3 The State as a Passive Wrongdoer

Another type of state responsibility arises in cases where the state does not take any action or fails in its duty and commits an internationally wrongful act. However, difficulties arise when one asks what the state was supposed to do in order *not* to violate an international obligation. This depends from case to case and the objective circumstances under which the state officials should have acted. However, in cases of mass violations of human rights or serious breaches of international law, the main objective of the state is the duty in its capacity to prevent such acts from happening and, should they not be able to be prevented, to take measures to punish the perpetrators. Accordingly, it first has to be established whether the state has effective

---

[67]Here, the responsibility lies either with the national courts in the implementation of the harmonisation measures or as a complementary solution with the International Criminal Court.

[68]Uganda, Burundi, Rwanda, last two cases however were respectfully discontinued and dismissed.

[69]ICJ, *Case Concerning Armed Activities on The Territory of The Congo, (Democratic Republic Of The Congo v. Uganda)*, Judgment (19 December 2005) paras. 168–171.

[70]ICJ, *Case Concerning Armed Activities on The Territory of The Congo, (Democratic Republic of the Congo v. Uganda)*, Judgment (19 December 2005), paras. 178–180.

[71]ICJ, *Case Concerning Armed Activities on The Territory of The Congo, (Democratic Republic of the Congo v. Uganda)*, Judgment (19 December 2005), para. 252.

control with regard to the conduct, whether the conduct is committed by a state official and, furthermore, whether the state was obligated to take measures to prevent the conduct.[72] For example, in the case of *U.S.A. vs. Iran*, the Court found that Iran was in a position to take measures to protect the diplomats who were attacked by non-state actors.[73] The reparations for the breach could, however, not be determined by the Court, as the breach of the obligation was ongoing at the time of the judgment.[74] In the *Genocide* case, the Court firstly tried to establish the connection between the forces of *Republika Srpska* and the military of the Federal Republic of Yugoslavia (FRY). As it was not possible to confirm the participation of the state military forces in the Genocide of Srebrenica, the Court was not able to identify any state responsibility for the genocide.[75] Hence the Court found that the FRY was in a position to exert influence on the military forces of the *Republika Srpska* and to prevent the atrocities. The FRY neither prevented nor punished the perpetrations. The Court held that the only available reparation for the failure to prevent the genocide in Srebrenica was the satisfactory and close cooperation of the FRY with the ICTY, namely by transferring the wanted alleged criminals to the Tribunal.[76]

4.1.2.2 State Responsibility at the Domestic Level

As mentioned above, state responsibility does not only function towards other states and the populations of other states. The question of responsibility may also arise internationally in cases of a violation of human rights where a state's own population is concerned. In contrast to situations where a case might be brought against one state by another state, there are fewer tools available in order to be able to recall the responsibility in cases of violations against one's own citizens. It may be dealt with on the political level by sanctioning the state through various methods, or by the involvement of international political institutions recalling compliance of the state with its obligation to protect its own citizens in a specific case, which rarely happens and when it does, only indirectly. Another possibility exists where the individuals may bring cases against their states before international human rights courts. This is the first time in the history of international law that individuals are seen partly as subjects of international law.[77] The thesis of the natural person as a subject of

[72]Cf. Christenson (1991), pp. 323–324.

[73]ICJ, *U.S.A. v. Iran, Case concerning U.S. Diplomatic and Consular Staff in Teheran*, Judgemnet (24 May 1980), para. 67, cf. ICJ, *Corfu Channel Case Great Britain and Northern Ireland v. Albania*, Judgment (9 April 1949), pp. 21–23, the Albanian Government refused to pay reparations and compensation, it even refused on demand of apology.

[74]ICJ, *U.S.A. v. Iran, Case concerning U.S. Diplomatic and Consular Staff in Teheran*, Judgemnet (24 May 1980), para. 90, Schweigman (2001), p. 235.

[75]ICJ, *Bosnia and Herzogowina v. Yugoslavia (Serbia and Montenegro) Application for Revision*, Judgment (26 February 2007) para. 376.

[76]See Petrossian (2019), pp. 179–187, such as transferring Radovan Karadžić, Ratko Mladić.

[77]Cf. Kelsen (2004), p. 97, Boczek (2005), p. 75, Aust (2016), pp. 10–13.

international law is controversial and is denied by traditional international law. Although natural persons may not influence international law, the new international instruments provide a place for natural persons to access international law and claim state responsibility.[78] In cases, where a violation of breach is confirmed by international human right courts, such as the ECtHR and the IACtHR, this may establish the responsibility of the state and determine the type of reparation for the breach of their obligation.[79] State responsibility at a domestic level may be distinguished in two ways. On the one hand, the doctrine may be used by internationalising a specific case as soon as the individuals exhaust the national remedies and bring the case before the International Human Rights Court and, on the other hand, state responsibility may arise within the domestic jurisdiction.

4.1.2.2.1 International Human Rights Courts

The establishment of state responsibility by an international court in a particular case is a common issue. Therefore, the court determines reparation if it finds that there has been a violation of human rights. Setting a reparation order for the state creates a new obligation[80] for that state which should be implemented in good faith (*pacta sunt servanda*). However, the execution and enforcement of the judgment is left to other institutions, which monitor on a political level. This is bound to the fact that, internationally, there are no other possible mechanisms for ensuring that the judgment is enforced. The fact that a judgment is not sufficiently enforced, for whatever reasons, can lead to frustration on the part of the victims.[81] Analyzing the jurisprudence of European and Inter-American Human Rights Courts, it is possible to ascertain that the Inter-American Court has developed a strict policy in cases of state responsibility and reparation.[82] This is not only the conventional provision which enables the Court to use a wide range of remedy measures, but also the result of the historical cases brought by the victims of gross violations of human rights against the dictatorships in the Central and South Americas.[83] Article 63 (1) IACHR considers the consequences of the determination of a breach of human rights, namely the remedial measures.

---

[78]Cf. Soto Velásquez (2015).

[79]Shelton (1996), p. 338.

[80]Kunz (2020), p. 26 et seq.

[81]Issaeva et al. (2011), pp. 67–68, Pérez-León-Acevedo (2016) see also Lambert-Abdelgawad (2008), pp. 12–19.

[82]Cf. Kunz (2020), p. 61 et seq.

[83]Sandoval-Villalba (2009), p. 243.

Among satisfaction and restitution at the IACtHR,[84] the Inter-American human rights system accepts compensatory reparations. In a similar manner to the ECtHR, the IACtHR accepts two types of damages: pecuniary[85] and non-pecuniary damages. Traditional compensation of *lucrum cessans* (future, expected loss) and *damnum emergens* (actual loss) is familiar to both Courts.[86]

As previously mentioned, the conventional provision in the ECHR does not elaborate upon a broad reparation system for the European Court as it does in cases of the Inter-American Court. Article 41 ECHR states that in the case of a determination of a violation, the Court may afford just satisfaction, if the domestic law of the member state allows only partial reparation for the victims. The restricted reparation[87] is bound according to the domestic law of the member state, if it does not have the capacity to fully redress the violation.[88] Just satisfaction to the victim would only then be possible, if the Court firstly determines a violation by the state, if the violating state does not have the capacity to fully redress the victim, if the victim has, pursuant to Rule 60 (1) of the Rules of the Court, claimed for just satisfaction, if the violation and damages are connected by a causal link and if the Court finds that just satisfaction is necessary. Although it is not clear on what grounds the calculation and reduction of the requested amount is made by the Court, there are still some general principles in the determination of the amount of just satisfaction to consider.[89] Generally, it considers that the main principle in reparation at the ECtHR is that the just satisfaction will not exceed the amount that has been requested and proven by the applicant. At the same time, there should be a causal link between the violation of human rights and the damage caused.[90]

Compensation for loss of earnings[91] is an essential part of the reparation process in the Inter-American human rights system. However, it very often faces practical difficulties. This is due to the fact that the people affected by the gross violation of human rights in Central and South America were engaged in seasonal employment

---

[84] Full restitution is not possible in the case of extrajudicial execution or a disappearance, as the state is not in a position anymore to right to life, see Pasqualucci (1996), IACtHR, *Velásquez-Rodríguez v. Guatemala*, Judgment, Merits (29 July 1988) paras. 96 191–92.

[85] IACHR considers pecuniary damage as loss or detriment to the victims' income, the expenses incurred as a result of the facts, and consequences of a monetary nature that have a causal connection to the facts of the case, IACtHR, *Bámaca-Velásquez v. Guatemala*, Judgment, Reparation and Costs (22 February 2002) para. 43.

[86] Burgorgue-Larsen et al. (2011), p. 229.

[87] Even by the convention a redress for the victims of human rights violations was considered, the Court was rather conservative in granting the victims the compensations at the beginning of its work, see narrow in White (2000), pp. 196–198, Altwicker et al. (2016), p. 4 et seq., Sandoval (2020), p. 222 et seq.

[88] ECtHR, *Guzzardi v. Italy*, 7367/76, Judgment (6 November 1980) para. 114, White (2000), pp. 196–198.

[89] Büyüksagis (2009).

[90] ECtHR, *Aktaş V. Turkey*, 24351/94, Judgment (24 April 2003) para. 352.

[91] It equals the sum of victims' income for the labor life if a human rights violations would not have occurred, see IACtHR, Aloeboetoe et al. v. Suriname, Judgment (10 September 1993) para. 50.

or did not even have employment. In the *Aloeboetoe* case, the population affected was the Saramakas tribe in Suriname, which was not literate and lived in the jungles.[92] As such, it was not an easy task for the Court to make a reasonable calculation of the loss of earnings. For this reason, the Court preferred compensation for moral damage, the damage which might not be proven due to a lack of written documents.[93] In cases where written evidence was possible to be able to gain proof of the earnings, taxation and other information regarding the employment of the victims, the Court established more strict criteria for the reasonable calculation of the loss of earnings. This was established in the *El Amparo* case:

> the Court calculated that the indemnity to be granted to each of the victims or their next of kin depended on their age at the time of death and the years remaining before they would have reached the age at which normal life expectancy is estimated in Venezuela, or the time during which the two survivors remained unemployed. In its calculations, the Court used as the base salary an amount not less than the cost of the basic food basket, which is higher than the minimum rural wage at the time of the events. Once the calculation was made, 25 percent was deducted for personal expenses, as in other cases. To this amount was added the interest accruing from the date of the events up to the present.[94]

Accordingly, it was determined by the Court that in order to ascertain compensation for the loss of earnings, the Court has to base its calculations upon the victim's age and life expectancy at the time of death and the victim's actual wage.[95] In the event of no reliable evidence being provided with regard to the actual financial status of the victims, the Court established calculations based upon the principles of equity and the current economic and social situation at that time. However, the Court found that 25% of the total sum of the projected income has to be subtracted.[96] In the case of survivors, the Court only estimated the calculation for the loss of earnings for the period of unemployment of the victims.[97] The Court is also of the opinion that the deceased, who at the time were unemployed, would later have been in position to earn wages. Accordingly, it calculated the wages according to the salary earned by the deceased persons' colleagues who were employed after the war.[98] This proves that while the general principle for the calculation of the loss of earnings was established, it is still down to the objective circumstances of the case to determine the actual amount of compensation given to the victims for their loss of earnings. In

---

[92]IACtHR, Aloeboetoe et al. v. Suriname, Judgment (10 September 1993) para. 17, see also Carrillo (2006), pp. 514–520, Cançado Trindade (2018), p. 288.

[93]Shelton (1998) p. 205.

[94]IACtHR, *El Amparo v. Venezuela*, Judgment, Reparation and Costs (14 September 1996) paras. 28, 88–89.

[95]See also IACtHR, *Neira Alegria v. Peru*, Judgment, Reparations (19 September 1996) para. 49.

[96]IACtHR, *El Amparo v. Venezuela*, Judgment, Reparation and Costs (14 September 1996) paras. 28.

[97]IACtHR, *Castillo-Páez v. Peru*, Judgement, Reparation and Costs (27 November 1998) para. 72, Pasqualucci (1996), p. 235.

[98]IACtHR, *Bámaca-Velásquez v. Guatemala*, Judgment, Reparation and Costs (22 February 2002) para.44, see also Saul (2003), p. 553.

most cases, this amount may exceed hundreds of thousands of dollars/euros,[99] which makes it impossible for the state to pay, or, for of various reasons, creates difficulties for the payment of the entire amount.[100] At the same time, this causes frustration on the part of the victims. Accordingly, the question arises regarding how reasonable the calculation of the loss of earnings is if, hypothetically, it is not possible to calculate the exact amount of compensation for the loss of earnings in the future.[101]

The European reparation system does not employ a standardised approach. It differs from case to case bearing in mind the inherently speculative effect of the future earnings of the victims.[102] In the case of *Aktas v. Turkey*, the Court took into account the Government's non-response to the amount requested by the applicants and awarded the applicant the entire sum claimed.[103] It stated:

> An award may still be made notwithstanding the large number of imponderables involved in the assessment of future losses, though the greater the lapse of time involved the more uncertain the link between the breach and the damage becomes. The question to be decided in such cases is the level of just satisfaction, in respect of either past and future pecuniary loss, which it is necessary to award to an applicant, the matter to be determined by the Court at its discretion, having regard to what is equitable.[104]

In contrast to the compensation for loss of earnings, it is much easier for the Court to estimate the compensation for other pecuniary actual damage such as lost property and other types of economic loss. However, the victim has to prove the connection between the loss of property or other costs[105] and the human rights violation. If the evidence is not reliable or insufficient, the Court is in a position to reject the compensation for the loss of property or other costs.[106] In the event of there being

---

[99]Cf. the estimated reparation amount e.g. IACtHR, *Bámaca-Velásquez v. Guatemala*, Judgment, Reparation and Costs (22 February 2002) para.106 (5).

[100]Cf. also damages to life plan (proyecto de vida) and social damages, IACtHR, *Loayza Tamayo v. Peru*, Judgment, Reparations and Costs (27 November 1998) para. 147, Schneider (2015), pp. 117–118.

[101]Cf, there are still 195 judgments pending for the implementation, only 31 judgments were implemented to date see official statistics of IACHR, visited (December 2020) see also, Inter-American Court of Human Rights, Annual Report 2017, González-Salzberg (2010), pp. 115–142, González-Salzberg (2014), pp. 97.

[102]Ichim (2015), p. 110.

[103]ECtHR, *Aktaş V. Turkey*, 24,351/94, Judgment (24 April 2003) paras. 349–355.

[104]ECtHR, *Aktaş V. Turkey*, 24,351/94, Judgment (24 April 2003) para. 353, ECtHR, *Sunday Times v. the United Kingdom*, 6538/74, Judgment (6 November 1989) para. 15, ECtHR, *Lustig-Prean and Beckett v. the United Kingdom*, 31417/96 32377/96, Judgment (27 December 1999) paras. 22–23, 431.

[105]Erdal and Bakirci (2006), p. 190.

[106]IACtHR, *Radilla-Pacheco v. Mexico*, Judgment, Merits, Reparation and Costs (23 November 2009) para. 368, Erdal and Bakirci (2006), p. 185, the jurisprudence of ECHR is however on this matter not standard, in case *Dizman v. Turkey* the Court awarded compensation even in case the applicant could not provide any medical bills, which were arisen because of the violation of the human rights, see ECtHR, *Dizman v. Turkey*, 27309/95, Judgment (20 September 2005) paras. 105–107.

no other possibility of restituting the property, the Court may order just compensation, though not necessarily based on the market value of what was lost.[107] Other pecuniary costs may include very broad expenses which were a result of the violation of human rights.

Even though there are some difficulties in calculating compensation for the victims' pecuniary damages, it is even more difficult to determine the compensation for non-pecuniary damages, also referred to as moral damages. If it is possible to establish a precise formula for calculation of loss of income, moral suffering is indeterminable. It includes suffering caused to the direct victim as well as emotional distress to the family of the victim. In its groundbreaking case of *Velásquez Rodríguez*, the Inter-American Court found that reparations for moral damage should be based upon the principle of equity[108] and must recall the particular circumstances of the case[109] in order to set the amount for non-pecuniary damages.[110] However, even recalling the principles for reparations, the Court estimated the amount of compensation without providing any explanations, and awarded each of the victims the same amount, irrespective of the fact that there were varying circumstances for each victim.[111] In its first judgment and first granting of just satisfaction for non-pecuniary damages, the ECtHR found there had been a case of injustice for the victims who were unlawfully detained.[112] This was the first time that the Court referred to the principle of just satisfaction for moral damages. The judgments of the ECtHR included not only the merits of the case, but also considered just satisfaction. In contrast, the Inter-American Court separates the merits and the reparation. The ECtHR often does not mention the grounds which were taken into account for the estimation of just satisfaction. It is no longer a secret that the European judges use internal standards for the establishment of compensation for moral damages for of breaches of human rights dependent upon the Member State. These tables are, however, not revealed to the public.[113] In theory, they are only used to analyse the cases and one can assume that they are also used to understand the logic of the internal principles for the estimation of the amount of moral damages.

Besides the monetary awards of the ECtHR and the IACtHR, there is an important difference between the two human rights courts in their reparation processes. The only function of the ECtHR is to determine a violation and to estimate the level of just satisfaction if the requirements for reparation are met. It is not in a position to

[107] IACtHR, *Salvador Chiriboga v. Ecuador*, Judgment, Reparation and Costs (3 March 2011) paras. 98–100.

[108] IACtHR, *Velásquez-Rodríguez v. Guatemala*, Judgment, Merits (29 July 1988) para. 27.

[109] IACtHR, *El Amparo v. Venezuela*, Judgment, Reparation and Costs (14 September 1996) para. 37.

[110] 20.000$ for deceased and survived.

[111] See Pasqualucci (1996), p. 35 cf. IACtHR, *Pueblo Bello v. Colombia*, Judgment (31 January 2006) para. 483, Marfn and Sandoval (2011), p. 33, Human Rights Quarterly, p. 1086.

[112] ECtHR, De Wilde, *Ooms and Versyp v. Belgium*, 2832/66 2835/66 2899/66, Decision (Article 50) (10 March 1972) para. 24.

[113] Ichim (2015), pp. 122–126.

be able to guide the responsible state on how it should act, besides compensation, regarding the violation. The Court may not order the case to be reopened or to declare the applicant innocent. At the same time, the Court may not use further mechanisms of reparation, e.g. satisfaction. In contrast, the Inter-American Court may use further mechanisms of reparations such as rehabilitation, guarantees of non-repetition, satisfaction etc. However, the only control mechanism for the implementation of judgment for the Inter-American Court is the supervision of the judgment. The AOS does not possess any political tool in order to be able to put the responsible state under political pressure to ensure implementation of the judgment.

The Inter-American Court has established a broad set of case law on the various types of satisfaction. Despite the fact that monetary awards play a relevant role for the victims in the rehabilitation process, the implementation of the satisfaction has a wider impact not only on the victims, but on the society as a whole,[114] even if the satisfaction is attributed to an individual. The jurisprudence of the IACtHR established various types of satisfaction depending on the specific cases. So-called "illustration within the State" is a type of satisfaction whereby the state takes several important steps to reveal the victims' fate and to locate the remains[115] and, furthermore, to identify and punish the perpetrators.[116] A further important aspect of satisfaction was determined by the participation of the victims in the criminal proceedings against the perpetrators pursuant to national laws.[117] Taking into account the sensitivity of the cases, an important role is played through the involvement of symbolic measures of satisfaction such as naming the streets, boulevards or parks after victims or building memorials or organising public ceremonies.[118] The Inter-American Court has also established a practice of state apology towards the individuals, something which was not common before.[119] Another important feature of satisfaction was established by the Court in determining the need and support for legal and social reforms in the state where the civilian society has to be actively involved.

---

[114]See Petrossian (2019), p. 226.

[115]IACtHR, *Aloeboetoe* et al. *v. Suriname*, Judgment (10 September 1993) para. 109.

[116]IACtHR, *Godínez Cruz v. Honduras*, Judgment, Compensatory Damages (20 January 1989) para. 32, Pasqualucci (1996), p. 39.

[117]IACtHR, *Bámaca-Velásquez v. Guatemala*, Judgment, Reparation and Costs (22 February 2002) para. 106.2, IACtHR, Caracazo v. Venezuela, Judgment, Reparations and Costs (29 August 2002) para. 143.1.

[118]IACtHR, *Velásquez-Rodríguez v. Guatemala*, Judgment, Merits (29 July 1988) para. 123.7, IACtHR, *Plan de Sánchez Massacre v. Guatemala*, Judgment, Reparation (19 November 2004) para. 125.6, IACtHR, *Merchants v. Colombia*, Judgment, Reparation (5 July 2004) para. 295.7.

[119]IACtHR, *Cantoral-Benavides v. Peru*, Judgment, Reparation and Costs (3 December 2001) para. 280.12, IACtHR, *Durand and Ugarte v. Peru*, Judgment, Reparation and Costs (3 December 2001) para. 45.4.

4.1.2.3 State Responsibility Inside the Domestic Jurisdiction

State responsibility may be established by the decision of the international courts and is widely used within the national jurisdiction towards individuals within the field of administrative law and this is comparable to state liability. Bearing in mind the pluralism of state liability in various situations,[120] it is firstly important to concentrate on the perspectives of the victims of various crimes. Irrespective of any international agreements and obligations, the state binds itself in various situations to the obligation for a certain action which arises by any law or any decision entered into force pursuant to national legislation. Going back to the *raison d'être* of criminal law, the criminalisation of certain conduct is *in situ* to protect citizens from being victimised. Accordingly, it means that the criminal law does not only have a punitive character, but is also preventive in nature.[121] In that sense, it is possible to determine that criminal law is only a tool of the state which guarantees to protect its subjects from being victimised. As a result, if the state fails to protect its subjects, it is furthermore responsible for the consequences arising from the criminal conduct. Taking into account the internationally growing attention focused upon the issues of victims, states are starting to develop legal mechanisms to protect the victims and to take partial responsibility for the conduct by initiating various actions and compensating victims for the damage suffered. Under the doctrine of state responsibility for not preventing the crime, one must consider the further investigative and judicial activities which follow the criminal conduct. Afterwards, the rehabilitative support of the state, parallel to the punishment of the criminal, should be considered under state responsibility. The granting monetary awards to the victims by states is still a problematical practice in many countries. However, the state might also have taken on the duty to protect the victims from further victimisation or so-called double victimisation. In conclusion, one can say that the state is responsible for its individuals. If a crime is committed, the state is then responsible for the victims in order to protect them from further criminal conduct and to rehabilitate them.

4.1.2.4 Reparations Under International Law

The breach of an international obligation establishes a new legal relationship between the state and the victim.[122] The new relationship is based on Article 28 ILC Draft Articles, which consider legal consequences for internationally wrongful acts. This was also established by the judgment of the Permanent International Court of Justice in its *Chorzów* case and later confirmed by the ICJ, stating that this

[120]Cf. Marboe (2010), pp. 379–390.

[121]Gardner (2011), p. 213, Günther (2016), p. 79, Mühl (2015), p. 26.

[122]Eichhorst (2011), pp. 81–82, siehe die Definitionen der Reparation in Seifert (1971), pp. 31–35.

legal consequence is the duty to repair.[123] In customary international law, compensation is considered as a redress of the injury caused as a result of the internationally wrongful act. Pursuant to Article 31 (2) ILC Draft Articles, injury includes material as well as moral damage. In another case, the ICJ found that even such damage as the reputation and prestige of the state may still be repaired. Thus, the nature of the damage is not limited only to material and non-material, but also includes disadvantages of a political, legal and economic nature.[124] Full reparation generally occurs in the form of restitution, compensation and satisfaction. The reparation mechanisms can also be used in combination. The reparation process can be divided into three levels. When the restitution of the damage is not possible, the reparation process enters the compensation level. The third level includes satisfaction. It is, however, possible to distinguish satisfaction in combination with either restitution or compensation.

4.1.2.4.1 Restitution

If a breach of international law which should not have occurred did occur, then the state is firstly obligated to eliminate all measures, mechanisms and activities which aid or support the breach of international law. Restitution is the primary remedy under international law. *Restitutio in integrum*, or a restoration of the original state, means the re-establishment of the situation which existed prior to the breach.[125] Article 35 ILC Draft Articles considers two types of restitution. On the one hand, material restitution, where the injuring party must restore the material condition and, on the other hand, immaterial restitution, e.g. the termination of the occupation, derogation of the judicial, executive, legislative and administrative legal norms and the dismissal of detainees.[126] Restitution has a great deal of influence on the first stage of the reparations process.[127] The difficulties, however, are that in the majority of cases, it is not possible to prove or to restore the previous state of affairs. In the event of impossibility or uncertainty, which may well result in a new violation of international law, the injured party may claim compensation. The state cannot refuse restitution on the grounds that these are subject to national regulations, and the same applies to the existence of political or administrative factors aimed at preventing a restoration obligation.

[123]PICJ, *Factory at Chorzów Case*, Judgment (26 July 1927) A, p. 21, ICJ, *LeGrand Brothers Case*, Judgment (27 June 2001), para. 48.

[124]Reports of International Arbitral Awards, *Case concerning the difference between New Zealand and France* (Rainbow Warrior Affair), Decision (30 April 1990) paras. 107–110, See Report of the International Law Commission on the work of its fifty-third session 2001, Article 31 (5).

[125]Grey (2010), p. 589, Marschik (1997), p. 281.

[126]Aust (2016), p. 387.

[127]See PICJ, *Factory at Chorzów Case*, Judgment (26 July 1927) A, p. 48.

4.1.2.4.2 Compensation

Damages include any financially measurable loss, including loss of profits.[128] The system of compensation, which is deeply rooted in customary international law, is one of the general principles of international law.[129] The question of compensation arises either as a consequence of the impossibility of restitution or in combination with the duty to restitute. However, the compensation for damage can be considered only as damage of a financial character.[130] Compensation is used in combination with restitution to fill the gaps that cannot be covered by restitution as, pursuant to Article 31 ILC Draft Articles, full redress must be made for the loss and damage.

Compensation does not seek to punish the state for its wrongful act, but rather represents the financial recovery for the actual loss.[131] Compensation became more prevalent immediately after the Second World War.

4.1.2.4.3 Satisfaction

In addition to material compensation, moral compensation in the form of satisfaction is to be paid in serious cases. This consists of an outward declaration of honor towards the injured party.[132] If the moral damage lies in the impairment of the honor of an injured party and its rights under international law, satisfaction often takes the form of symbolic acts, such as formal apologies, flagship honors, expressions of atonement, the punishment and/or removal from office of the persons responsible or also an expression of regret.[133] The doctrine of satisfaction is divided into two parts. On the one hand, satisfaction may be part of other forms of reparation, which means that, for example, symbolic acts in addition to restitution and damages are made by the injuring party. On the other hand, satisfaction can occur as a form of compensation if the above-mentioned forms are, for whatever reason, not sufficient. An important part of satisfaction is legislative and judicial reform. Another form of satisfaction may consist of guarantees that exclude repetition. The list of typical forms of satisfaction is not exhaustive.[134] This confirms the fact that most political compensation is made as compensation in the form of state responsibility.

---

[128] von Arnauld (2012), p. 179, Rn. 430.

[129] ICJ, *Hungary/Slovakia, Case concerning the Gabcikovo-Nagymaros Project*, Judgment (25 September 1997) para. 152.

[130] Seegers (2005), p. 72.

[131] Aust (2016), p. 387.

[132] Fleischmann and von Liszt (1925), p. 287.

[133] Wengler (2014), p. 515.

[134] von Arnauld (2012), p. 170, Rn. 430.

4.1.3 Responsibility of the Community

One might be tempted to place the international community on the third level of remedies for the victims of gross human rights violations. However, the responsibility of the international community is not as distinct as in the case of state responsibility on the second level. Before it is possible to analyse what part the international community might play in this regard, one must first clarify what is understood by the term "international community".

The anti-Hitler coalition, formed in the wake of the Second World War, is a clear example of the cooperation of states in maintaining international security. Later, the Organisation of the United Nations was founded as both a symbol and an institution for that matter.[135] Analogically, it is possible to determine any multilateral cooperation of states as an "international community", even if the influence of this community could be deemed political rather than legal. Nevertheless, at the same time, political will may still create the capacity for implementing legal instruments. In its judgment in *Barcelona Traction*, the ICJ confirmed the existence of the *erga omnes* principle in international law and in international relations, and even strengthened the principle, stating that:

> An essential distinction should be drawn between the obligations of a State towards the international community as a whole, and those arising vis-à-vis another State in the field of diplomatic protection. By their very nature the former are the concern of all States. In view of the importance of the rights involved, all States can be held to have a legal interest in their protection; they are obligations erga omnes.[136]

Accordingly, the "international community" might be understood not only as a group of states which are in cooperation with each other, but may also be referred to as a wider group of existing, like-minded governments in the world, which share common values in various matters.[137] The "international community" *(Völkergemeinschaft)* plays an important role in condemning atrocities. This was the case when the UN, acting as or on behalf of the international community, agreed to establish international ad hoc tribunals, in order to overcome the situation in Rwanda and the former Yugoslavia.[138] This condemnation by states, even on a

---

[135]See Petrossian (2019), p. 151, anti-Hitler coalition was called as "United Nations" not in the sence of modern understanding of UN but in form of linkminded governments which are aiming at achieving common liberal and peaceful goals.

[136]ICJ, *Barcelona Traction Case*, Judgment (5 February 1970) p. 32, para. 33.

[137]Cf. Lauterpacht (2012), p. 76, cf. Verdross (1926), p. 9, quoted in Pfeffer (2012), p. 87.

[138]As an clear example of the condemnation of the atrocities is the Joint Declaration of 1915 of France, Great Britain and Russian in relation to the atrocities in Ottoman Empire "*For about a month the Kurd and Turkish populations of Armenia has been massacring killing Armenians with the connivance approval and often assistance of Ottoman authorities.[...] In view of those new crimes of Turkey against humanity and civilisation, the Allied governments announce publicly to the Sublime-Porte that they will hold personally responsible for these crimes all members of the Ottoman government and those of their agents who are implicated involved in such massacres*" Grenville and Wasserstein (2013), p. 66.

political level, may in itself be considered as an action expressing responsibility as the international community thereby creates a common standpoint on a specific matter. At the same time, there is no alternative in the fight against the ignorance of the international community in relation to various atrocities committed in different parts of the world. The condemnation of this very ignorance may be considered only at a moral level, not a political or a legal one. The international community is the last resort in order to create space for responsibility. Chapter IV of the ILC Draft Articles provides for the liability of third states. Pursuant to Article 16 ILC Draft Articles, a third state may be held responsible for its aid and assistance to other states in the commission of an internationally wrongful act. However, the ILC Draft Articles do not establish responsibility of the third states for an omission, unlike cases of direct responsibility.[139]

International crimes or gross violations of human rights are contrary to the principles of any society, those societies that were referred to as "civilised" during and after World War II. Resultantly, the international community is bound by good faith to prevent such acts from occurring. If the international community fails to prevent them, its further actions to condemn and punish the perpetrators can be considered as reparations in the form of satisfaction, and must express responsibility of the international community.[140] The foundation of the Trust Fund for the Victims (TFV) at the ICC is a clear example of this responsibility on the part of the international community. The voluntary donations by individual states to the TFV express the willingness of this group of states to bear the responsibility for not preventing international crimes from being committed. The victims who receive reparations from the TFV indirectly actually receive it from the international community which donated the money to the TFV.

4.1.4 International Practice of Reparation

The system of reparations may be practiced at different levels and under various conditions. As already described above, the process of reparation may be initiated not only because of the decision of international institutions but may arise from national or international agreements. There are dozens of examples of how states have practiced redress towards victims as a consequence of unlawful acts and redress can be either collective or individual in nature. The collectivity of reparations includes a number of actions which are aimed at healing society and repairing the damage caused by the destructive occurrence. As such, reparation might be considered instrumental in the establishment of truth and reconciliation commissions, funds for compensation, justice reforms and further satisfactory activities, the

[139]Cf. Lanovoy (2016), p. 248, Klein (1981), p. 427.

[140]Another type of responsibility of international community consists in political statements of condemnation towards various matters—as a form of satisfaction.

range of which may depend on the specific cases and matters. The individual reparations are in most cases used parallel to the collective reparations based on material compensation of the damage caused.

4.1.4.1 Post-World War I Reparations

After the defeat of the Central Powers in the Paris Peace Conference, the Allied Powers claimed reparations for the damage caused by the Great War. Each of the defeated powers was required to make not only payments, but also to take into account further satisfactory activities and territorial changes. These included, in the case of defeated Germany: interrelated state recognition of establishment of power or protectorate over other territories proclaimed by the Allied Powers (Articles 31–153 Treaty of Versailles); the prosecution of war criminals,[141] also including Kaiser Wilhelm II[142] (Articles 227–230 Treaty of Versailles) and the establishment of a commission for the material reparation of war damage (Articles 231–244 Treaty of Versailles). The commission which was established in 1921 estimated Germany's total liability for material reparation at 132 billion gold marks. Bearing in mind that it was impossible for the German economy to pay the material reparations estimated by the commission, it was subsequently reduced to 50 billion gold marks. In the summer of 1921, the German government made its first cash payment from the London Schedule of Payment presented to Germany on 5 May 1921.[143] These provisions were almost identically included in the treaties with separate members of the Central Powers.[144] In practice, however, the Allied Powers were predominantly concentrating on the territorial changes of the defeated powers, rather than the prosecution of the war criminals.

In the case of the Ottoman Empire, despite its partition[145] and the establishment of power over it, the Allied governments sought the prosecution of the Ottoman war criminals (Articles 226–230 Treaty of Sèvres).[146] The trials were therefore held in Istanbul, but the judgments were later declared null and void by the new Turkish government. The Treaty of Sèvres, with which the Ottoman Empire was abolished, was later replaced by the Treaty of Lausanne from 1923, which did not contain any

---

[141]Known as Leipzig Trials, see narrower in Horne and Kramer (2001), p. 345.

[142]However the Kaiser was not prosecuted because of the refusal of the Dutch authorities to extradite the former German Emperor, see Schabas (2018), p. 27, Klinkert (2017), p. 37.

[143]See narrow in Marks (2003), p. 45, Mierzejewski (2000), p. 59.

[144]Treaty of Treaty of Neuilly-sur-Seine 1919 in regard to Bulgaria, Saint-Germain-en-Laye 1919 in regard to Austria, Treaty of Sèvres 1920 in regard to Ottoman Empire, Treaty of Trianon 1920 in regard to Hungary.

[145]Similar monetary demands were raised against the Ottoman Government, see Petrossian (2019), p. 221.

[146]Known as Istanbul Trials, see narrow in Petrossian (2019), p. 70.

provision on the punishment of war criminals. Similarly, Bulgaria,[147] Austria[148] and Hungary[149] were forced to take measures in order to punish, before national military tribunals and in accordance with the treaties, those who were involved in the violations of customs of war, but in practice this was not highly motivated. The same ignorance was practiced towards the material compensation of the other members of the Central Powers, and the Allied Powers were aware of the fact that those states were not in a position to be able to make such material contributions for war damage. As a consequence, Austrian and Turkish material reparations were halted.[150] Hungary was given a moratorium on small coal deliveries.[151] The Reparation Commission estimated the amount of 550 million gold francs for Bulgaria's liability.[152]

This development illustrates how reparations were not aimed at repairing the damage suffered by individuals who were victimised by the destructive war as the individuals were not considered as beneficiaries of the redress. Even the satisfactory reparations, such as the criminal prosecution of war criminals, were not meant to be for the better good of the people, but rather for the political interests of the victorious states.

4.1.4.2 Post World War II Reparations

In contrast to the reparations of World War I, where the redress had a collective character, the defeated states after World War II were forced to make contributions not only on a collective basis, but also to repair the damage suffered by individual victims. The concept of reparations after World War II was enlarged and the methods of repairing innovated.[153] The principle of claiming reparation from Germany was bound to the Potsdam Agreement of 1945,[154] pursuant to which each victorious state was able to claim reparations from the zone under its control.[155] The Germans had

[147] Articles 118–120 Treaty of Neuilly-sur-Seine 1919, later on the Bulgarian government organised successful referendum 1922 whether the war criminals of World War should be tried, afterwards the members of old cabinet were arrested, see narrower in Rothschild, 1974 p. 339, see also in El Zeidy (2008), p. 22, Borchard and Wynne (2000), pp. 551–553.

[148] Articles 173–176 Treaty of Saint-Germain-en-Laye 1919.

[149] Articles 157–160 Treaty of Trianon 1920.

[150] Cottrell (2013), p. 64.

[151] Lojkó (2006), pp. 85–88.

[152] Marks (2003), p. 63.

[153] See "Operation Paperclip" and "Operation Osoaviakhim" the forced recruitment of German scientists in the U.S. and USSR scientific projects, forced labour of PoWs in the reconstruction in USSR and eastern part of Europe, etc., see also Maddrell (2005), p. 186.

[154] The Berlin (Potsdam) Conference, July 17–August 2, 1945(a) Protocol of the Proceedings, August l, 1945.

[155] In Yalta conference 1945 the allied powers were agree on the fact that the reparations should only to be exacted in kind of Germany, rather than paid in cash over lengthy period of time, see Roberts (2019), p. 127.

actually stopped paying for the damage caused in World War I prior to and during World War II, and after their surrender, they were forced to pay for the damage of both destructive wars. After World War II, Germany was obligated to make different collective and individual reparations towards various states and communities. Despite bilateral[156] and multilateral[157] agreements of material compensation between Germany and beneficiary states, not only under the provisions of the treaty of Luxembourg,[158] the German Government was obligated to pay individual compensation to the individuals who suffered damage as a result of the Nazi perpetrations. The Control Council had already adopted law Nr. 59 for the restitution of confiscated and identifiable property during the occupation.[159] The national legislation on reparation was formed after the establishment of West Germany.[160] This was the first time that individuals were supposed to be beneficiaries of reparations. Besides the fact that citizens of West Germany were targeted for reparations, after the Reunification of East and West Germany, several foundations in Belarus, Ukraine, the Czech Republic, Poland, Latvia and Lithuania received reparations in order to compensate individuals who had suffered as a result of Nazi crimes. German national legislation considered individual reparation in cases where the victims had

---

[156]Cf. *Treaty between Germany and Kingdom of Greece 18 March 1960, Vertrag. v. 18. März 1960 zwischen der Bundesrepublik Deutschland und dem Königreich Griechenland über die Leistungen zugunsten griechischer Staatsangehöriger, die von nationalistischen Verfolgungsmaßnahmen betroffen worden sind*, Germany was obligated to pay 115 million Deutschmark for the Nazi occupation in Greece. *Treaty of Zgorzelec* 6 July 1950 Poland rejected reparations from East Germany under the Pressure of USSR but in turn the eastern territories of Germany were given to Poland and Russia, no further reparations were paid to Poland, see also Bundestag, Völkerrechtliche Grundlagen und Grenzen kriegsbedingter Reparationen unter besonderer Berücksichtigung derdeutsch-polnischen Situation, 28 August 2017, Treaty of Settlement with Kingdom of Netherlands 8. April 1960, *Vertrag vom 8. April 1960 zwischen der Bundesrepublik Deutschland und dem Königreich der Niederlande zur Regelung von Grenzfragen und anderen zwischen beiden Ländern bestehenden Problemen (Ausgleichsvertrag),* Germany paid Dutch autorities 280 million Deutschmark as reparation, in return Dutch government was obligated to return the occupied territories, see further state reparations in *Bundesministerium der Finanzen*, Entschädigung von NS-Unrecht, Regelungen zur Wiedergutmachung, 2012, p. 37.

[157]Cf. Potsdam Agreement 1945, London Agreement on German External Debts 27 February 1953, see Rombeck-Jaschinski (2011), pp. 442–443, Treaty on the Final Settlement with Respect to Germany 1990.

[158]Both the Versailles Treaty and the London Agreement referred exclusively to the war indemnities. The gap of the reparations for the Holocaust was closed by the Luxembourg Agreement, the "reparations Agreement between Israel and West Germany" of 10 September 195. The ratification of the two agreements was seen as a prerequisite of Allied powers to grant the sovereignty to Germany. Already during the war, various Jewish organisations had demanded restitution and collective redress for the Jewish population and founded the *International Jewish Reconstruction Commission*, which demanded the inheritance of Jewish property for the rebuilding of European Jewish communities.

[159]See Military Government, Germany, United States Area of Control, Law N. 59, Restitution of Identifiable Property, https://www.dfs.ny.gov/consumer/holocaust/present_day_restitution/US%20Military%20Law%2059.pdf, last visited on 15 January 2019.

[160]See Bundesentschädigungsgesetz (BEG) 29 June 1956.

been persecuted because of their race, their belief or their ideology and where they had suffered damage to life, body, health, freedom and/or property (Regulation 1 *Bundesentschädigungsgesetz* (BEG)).

One of the important satisfactory reparations was the criminal prosecutions of Nazi perpetrators. This is what the IMT was for. Besides international prosecution, the controlling governments organised their own trials for the perpetrators, e.g. the Nuremberg Military Tribunal's Trials under U.S. control, known as the Nuremberg Subsequent Trials, the British War Crimes Trials, such as the Belsen Trial,[161] the Soviet Military Tribunal's Trials, such as the Sachsenhausen Trial[162] and the French Military Tribunal's Trials, such as the Röchling Trial.[163] What was significant in nature was the satisfactory reparation which was received by the act of German Chancellor Willy Brandt with his Warsaw genuflection, known as the "*Kniefall*". Similar reparations were also forced onto other members of the Axis powers, such as Austria,[164] Italy[165] and Japan.[166] To date, parallel to the ongoing individual compensation payments, there are still reparation issues between the members of Axis and Allied Powers. Recently the Greek and Polish governments raised the issue that they had not received reparations stemming from the Nazi occupation.[167]

4.1.4.3 Case Study

It is true that after each conflict there follows a process of reparation, redress and reconciliation. The main issue is that of time and the efficiency of the steps considered by the process. There were dozens of reparation proceedings conducted after World War II and each of them was unique regarding the features of the specific case. On an individual basis, every kind of method and mechanism can be employed for reparation proceedings. On the one hand there is an involvement of the

---

[161]Bloxham (2003), p. 91.

[162]Friedman (2008), p. 160.

[163]Lauterpacht and Lauterpacht (1975), pp. 3–6.

[164]Despite of the fact, that Austria does not consider itself as perpetrator, rather victim Klinkhammer and Späti (2006), p. 525.

[165]Pursuant to Article 74 Treaty of Peace with Italy, 1947 the Italian Government was obligated to pay reparations to Soviet Union US $ 100 million, Yugoslavia US$ 125 million, Greece US $ 105 million, Ethiopia US $ 25 million, Albania US $ 5 million.

[166]Pursuant to Article 14 Peace Treaty with Japan (San Francisco Treaty 1951) recognised the insufficient resources of Japan to pay the reparations however it established provisions for the members of Allied Powers to seize, liquidate or otherwise dispose of all property, rights and interests of Japanese nationals, according to Article 11 Peace Treaty with Japan, Japan was bound to recognize the judgment of the International Military Tribunal for Far East.

[167]Deutsche Welle, Poland, Greece team up on Nazi-era war reparations demands, see https://www.dw.com/en/poland-greece-team-up-on-nazi-era-war-reparations-demands/a-45836168, last visited on 18 December 2020, Neoskosmos, Germany shuts down talks on reparations to Greece and Poland, https://neoskosmos.com/en/122476/germany-shuts-down-talks-on-reparations-to-greece-and-poland/, last visited on 18 December 2020.

international institutions, such as the UN, in order to allocate and regulate the reparation proceedings, whilst on the other hand the national political willingness establishes a national platform for reconciliation and reparation. Accordingly, it is possible to divide the reparation process into two important levels. First, on the political level, the subjects have to agree upon the legal standards, points, principles, rules and the amount of reparations. Secondly, the implementation of the reparation in practice does not always correspond to the agreed topics. In order to make an appropriate analysis of reparation proceedings, it is furthermore necessary to subsume them into three different categories. The first category involves those instruments which are considered internationally for the enabling of the reparation process in the specific case. The second category may consider interstate or mixed reparation practices, which might be implemented differently. The third category includes national instruments for providing reparations within its domestic boundaries and jurisdiction.

4.1.4.3.1 International Reparation

Taking into account the liability of Iraq under international law for any direct loss and damage as a result of the unlawful invasion and occupation of Kuwait,[168] the Security Council of the United Nations decided, under Resolution 692, to establish a fund and a subsidiary organ, the United Nations Compensation Commission (UNCC) to the Security Council based on Article 29 UN Charter. In this way, the government of Iraq was made responsible for its financial contribution from the recovery of damages from Iraqi oil revenues.[169] The main task of the Commission was to determine the amount of contribution to the Fund, considering the oil export revenue of Iraq. The UNCC distinguished itself as a political organ which had fact-finding, verifying and evaluating functions. However, it still has a quasi-judicial function when it comes to the decision of assessing payments and resolving the disputed claims.[170] Distinguishing the high level of victimisation due to the war, the Commission categorised the claims into six different groups based on the type of damage suffered by various groups of subjects, including individuals, corporations and governments.

- A: Claims from individuals who suffered injuries or death as a result of the invasion.
- B: Claims from individuals for business losses, pain and anguish, property damage etc. under $100,000.
- C: Claims from individuals for business losses, pain and anguish, property damage etc. exceeding $100,000.

[168] UNSC, Resolution 687 (1991), 3 April 1991, para. 16.

[169] UNSC, Resolution 692 (1991), 20 May 1991, paras. 3–8.

[170] Rattalma and Treves (1999), p. 78, Eichhorst (2011), pp. 47–50.

- D: Claims from corporations and other entities for business (including oil sector) losses.
- E: Governmental claims for the cost of resettling and providing relief to citizens, claims for damage to government property and to the environment.
- F: International agency claims for the cost of resettling and providing relief to citizens, claims for damage to government property and to the environment.

Since the establishment of the Commission in 1991, this subsidiary organ has received 2.7 million claims submitted by governments.[171] In 2005, the Commission evaluated $52.4 billion in compensation awards to approximately 1.5 million successful claimants. To date, $48.1 billion worth of compensation awards have been paid to the victims.[172] At the same time, the Commission is not in a position to be able to compensate the victims directly; it initially establishes the amount of compensation[173] and the Fund subsequently remits the amount established to the government which is, in turn, obligated to distribute the compensation to the victims.[174]

4.1.4.3.2 Inter-State or Mixed Reparations

In distinguishing the inter-state practice of reparations, it is still possible to subcategorise this type of reparation. This is due to the fact that either the states have come to bilateral agreement on reparations, or that the domestic jurisdiction enables or creates a platform for foreign nationals to be awarded compensation for violations. A striking example of the first subcategory is the Eritrean-Ethiopian Claims Commission (EECC). The War between Eritrea and Ethiopia ended with the Algiers Peace Agreement of 18 June 2008. Article 5 of the Peace Agreement established a neutral Claims Commission with the mandate to determine the loss and damage caused by both governments as a consequence of the war and in relation to the violations of international humanitarian law.[175] Compared to the UNCC, the claims brought before the EECC were not raised on behalf of individuals, but were rather inter-state claims and it lay at the discretion of each claiming state to ensure

[171] The individuals were not able to submit a direct claim before the UNCC, the governments were issued to raise the compensation claims on behalf of individuals and corporations, Taylor (2009), p. 202.

[172] See UNCC, Press Release, PR/2019/1, United Nations Compensation Commission Pays US $100 Million, 18 January 2019, Klee (2011), pp. 29–66, see narrow in Taylor (2009), pp. 199–200.

[173] See UNCC, Priority of Payment and Payment Mechanism, S/AC.26/Dec.17, Decision taken by the Governing Council of the United Nations Compensation Commission at its 41st meeting, held in Geneva on 23 March 1994, 24 March 1994, para. 2.

[174] Cf. Gattini (2002), p. 170, Salvador-Crespo (2015), pp. 221–241.

[175] See Article 5(1) Agreement Between the Government of the Federal Democratic Republic of Ethiopia And the Government of the State of Eritrea, Giorgis (2014), p. 568.

the rehabilitation of the victims of the war.[176] Despite proposals for collective reparations of the parties,[177] the Commission decided on monetary awards, namely compensation awards rising from *jus ad bellum* and *jus in bello* damages. The compensation claims for moral damage were dismissed[178] and, as a result, the Commission established an award of $163 million to Eritrea and $174 million to Ethiopia.

Compensation to Eritrea		Compensation to Ethiopia	
Award in mio	Damage *jus in bello*	Award in mio	Damage *jus in bello*
$13	Losses of residential and business property	$11	Death, physical injury, disappearance, forced labor and conscription of Ethiopian civilians
$36	Damage to and destruction of building	$2	Failure to prevent rape of known and unknown women
$1.5	Injuries to civilians due to loss of access to health care	$13.9	Looting and destruction, damage to houses
$4	Mistreatment of PoWs	$28.5	Looting and destruction of property
$2	Failure to prevent rape of known and unknown women	$3.2	Seizure and looting of company
$1,5	Forcible expulsion of the population	$7.5	Mistreatment of PoWs
$15	Wrongful expulsion of an unknown, but considerable, number of dual nationals	$2	Failure to protect Ethiopian civilians in Eritrea from threats and violence
$11	Receiving, caring for and resettling rural Ethiopian nationals	$1.5	Failure to ensure Ethiopian civilians in Eritrea access to employment
$2	Failure to provide humane and safe treatment	$2	Wrongful detention and abusive treatment
$46	Expellees' losses of property	$1.5	Harsh treatment in detention camp
$25	Ethiopia's failure to return or provide compensation after the war for vehicles	$10	Detention of Ethiopians under harsh conditions
$1.5	Property losses of non-residents	$4	Failure to protect property of detained Ethiopians and repatriation
$2.6	Imprisoning Eritrean civilians		Damage *jus ad bellum*
$2	Compensation for individuals	$45	Human suffering and lost income because of displacement
		$8.5	Civilian death
		$18	Damage to property

(continued)

[176]Cf. EECC, Ethiopia's Damages Claims between The Federal Democratic Republic of Ethiopia and The State of Eritrea, Final Award (17 August 2009) para. 82, however in case of Eritrea, the government of Eritrea filed claims on behalf of several individuals, see also paras. 396–436.

[177]Cf. Matheson (2009).

[178]Cf. EECC, Ethiopia's Damages Claims between The Federal Democratic Republic of Ethiopia and The State of Eritrea, Final Award (17 August 2009) para. 65.

Compensation to Eritrea		Compensation to Ethiopia	
Award in mio	Damage *jus in bello*	Award in mio	Damage *jus in bello*
		\$1.5	Deaths and injuries caused by landmines
		\$6.5	Further damages

In this case, the beneficiaries are, once again, the governments, the same as in UNCC cases. The victims or affected population do not receive the compensation directly, but rather through the government's established mechanisms, funds or other indirect methods. It is, once again, left to the discretion of the state to decide the implementation of compensation in practice based upon the final award of arbitration. Another example of inter-state reparation is the Iran-United States Claims Tribunal (IUSCT). The Arbitral Tribunal was established as a result of the Hostage Crisis in Iran,[179] created through the bilateral agreement between U.S. and Iran. Pursuant to Article II of the Algiers Accords 1981, the purpose of the Tribunal is to decide on the claims arising from contracts, transactions, etc. of Iranian nationals against the U.S. and of U.S. nationals against Iran.[180] Since its establishment, the Tribunal has ruled on 3900 cases.[181] However, unlike the EECC, the awards were delivered directly to the beneficiaries and not merely to the governments.

The second subcategory includes such mechanisms which allow foreign nationals to be granted reparation for a violation of rights. This may be decided either on a political or judicial level. The High Court in London established in 2012 that the British government may be held liable for the torture and the brutal colonial regime in Kenya on the basis of five Kenyan claimants' allegations against the Foreign and Commonwealth Office of UK (FCO).[182] Shortly afterwards, the British Government recognised that the Kenyans' had been subjected to torture during the Mau Mau uprising in the 1950s and determined an almost £20 million compensation award for 5228 living survivors, £3000 per victim.[183] However, in 2018 the High Court of Justice in London dismissed the case brought against FCO on behalf of 40,000 victims of brutal colonial regime in Kenya as they were statute barred pursuant to Section 33 of the Limitation Act 1980.[184] Another out-of-court settlement was reached in the case of Cypriot victims of torture under British rule in the 1950s.[185]

[179]See ICJ, *U.S.A. v. Iran, Case concerning U.S. Diplomatic and Consular Staff in Teheran*, Judgemnet (24 May 1980) para. 90, Schweigman (2001), see also Houghton (2001), p. 46.

[180]Brower and Brueschke (1998), pp. 288–291.

[181]Cf. College (2017), pp. 17–18.

[182]Cobain, Richard Norton-Taylor, and Clar Ni Chonghaile, Mau Mau veterans win right to sue British government, The Guardian, 5 October 2012.

[183]BBC News, Mau Mau torture victims to receive compensation—Hague, 6 June 2013.

[184]High Court of Justice, Queens's Bench Division, Kimanthi, Ors and The Foreign and Commonwealth Office, [2018] EWHC 2066 (QB), Judgment, 2 August 2018, paras. 423–464.

[185]See Smith, Cypriot fighters seek damages over torture under British rule, The Guardian, 28 November 2017, see also the claims of Malawians for the damages of British rule in 1950s in

Similar to the Kenyan case, the British Government agreed to pay compensation amounting to £1 million for the alleged human rights abuses of 33 victims of torture. However, this did not constitute an admission of liability on the part of the British government.[186]

In 2017, the representative of the Herero and Nama people issued a lawsuit against government of Germany before the New York District Court under the Alien Tort Statute 1789,[187] demanding reparations for the massacres carried out by the German colonial regime in South-West Africa (Namibia) between 1904 and 1908.[188] The case was dismissed.[189] Even if the Court granted an award in this case, the judgment would not be binding upon the German jurisdiction on the grounds of Section 328 (1), 722 and 723 German Code of Civil Procedure (*Zivilprozessordnung*; ZPO).

In most cases, the judicial settlement in court for the reparation of human rights violations and abuses is unsuccessful for various reasons including the absence of political will and the fear that it may open for the floodgates to thousands of similar claims. In contrast, governments attempt to settle reparation issues in out-of-court proceedings, with no admission of liability.

Malawi, Godfrey Mapondera, Malawians seek compensation for Nyasaland massacre during British rule, The Guardian, 20 April 2015.

[186]See Adam Smith, UK Government agrees to pay £1,000,000 to 33 'torture victims from Cyprus', Metro, 23 January 2019.

[187]The Act enables to lodge a civil claim by a foreigner for a tort committed in violation of international law or international treaty in relation to the U.S, see Stephan 2018, Dören and Wentke (2018), cf. South Korean judiciary found in several cases the ruling for compensation for the forced labor during the colonial regime by the Japanese companies, such as Mistubishi Heavy Industries Ldt., Nippon Steel & Sumitomo Metal Corporation despite the international agreement between the South Korea and Japan, which the Constitution Court of South Korea found not admissible in the case of forced labor, Agreement on the Settlement of Problems Concerning Property and Claims and on Economic Cooperation between Japan and the Republic of Korea 1965, see South Korean court upholds ruling against Mitsubishi Heavy over forced wartime labor in Japan, the Japan Times, 5 December 2018, under https://www.japantimes.co.jp/news/2018/12/05/national/crime-legal/south-korean-court-upholds-ruling-japan-firm-forced-labor/#.XFAkVM1CeM8 visited on 18 December 2020, Choe Sang-Hun and Rick Gladstone, How a World War II-Era Reparations Case Is Roiling Asia, New York Times, 30 October 2018, see also Sayuri Umeda, South Korea: Constitutional Court Decides Long-Running Case on Compensation for Forced Labor During Colonial Rule, Global Legal Monitor, 6 January 2016, http://www.loc.gov/law/foreign-news/Article/south-korea-constitutional-court-decides-long-running-case-on-compensation-for-forced-labor-during-colonial-rule/, visited on 18 December 2020.

[188]The case District Court, S.D. New York, *Rukoro v. Federal Republic of Germany* dismissed because of lack of jurisdiction, the case under https://www.courtlistener.com/docket/6280874/rukoro-v-federal-republic-of-germany/.

[189]See Talmon (2020).

4.1.4.3.3 National Reparation System

The national practice for reparation programs within a state's boundaries is common. The result of long negotiations brought about the end of apartheid rule in South Africa and with it the establishment and creation of the unique system of restorative justice known as the Truth and Reconciliation Commission (TRC) introduced by the Promotion of National Unity and Reconciliation Act 1995 in South Africa. The functions of the TRC include facilitation, initiation or coordination of: inquiries concerning human rights violations; the identification of the victims; the granting of amnesty in respect to political objectives; the preparation of reports; and making recommendations pursuant to Section 4 of the Act. The institution consists of three committees: the Committee on Human Rights Violations (CHRV) under Section 12 of the Act, the Committee for Amnesty (AC) under Section 16 of the Act and the Committee for Reparation and Rehabilitation (CRR) under Section 23 of the Act. The functions of the CHRV are, first and foremost, to complete the investigation and determine whether a gross violation of human rights has occurred in the specific case. Furthermore, it is responsible for the identification of the victims. As soon as the CHRV identifies violations and the victims thereof, it refers the case to the CRR for reparation and rehabilitation pursuant to Section 15 in conjunction with Section 26 of the Act. In close cooperation with the CRR, the CHRV distributes all the necessary evidence and information about the gross violation and victimisation of the person. The third committee on amnesty engages with the process of granting amnesties if the act, omission or offence relates to political objective in the course of the conflicts and the past (Section 20 of the Act). The CRR's main objective was to write a report for and make recommendations regarding reparation methods to the president of the state and to parliament, both of which are, pursuant to Section 27 of the Act, in a position to be able to decide about the implementation of the report and any recommendations. Those victims who were recognised by the Commission as victims pursuant to Section 1 of the Act have the possibility of being granted interim reparation, individual reparation grants (IRG), symbolic reparations, reparations through community rehabilitation programs and reparations through institutional reforms.[190] The TRC considered the fact that the victims, who might be in urgent need of money in order to pay for services, might be entitled to the interim reparations in accordance with Section 27 (4) of the Act. The IRG includes elements to ease access to services and facilities and daily living costs for the victim and the victims' dependents.[191] Symbolic reparation consists of remembrance and commemoration for the pain and suffering by conducting exhumations, erecting tombstones, memorials or monuments and renaming streets and

---

[190]See TRC, Policy Framework For Urgent Interim Reparation Measures.

[191]See TRC, A Summary of Reparation and Rehabilitation Policy, Including Proposals to be Considered by the President, see also Buford and van der Merwem (2004), pp. 274–275, Villa-Vincecio (2006) pp. 74–75.

public facilities.[192] Community programs were aimed at improving and promoting the social activity of the individuals and remedying the pain of society. Parallel to this, there are institutional reforms aimed at making administrative, legal and institutional developments for the establishment of state-society trust.

However, from practical perspectives, even though the recommendations and the final report of the Commission were made to parliament and to the president two decades ago (29 October 1998)[193] and the President Fund was established by the government in 2003 to compensate almost 17,000 victims,[194] to date less is being done to fully implement redress for the victims due to a lack of recourses.[195] Pursuant to the reparation plan, the victims should receive redress on the following basis:[196]

- Individual reparation grant - each R30,000/R5 million[197]
- Assistance for reburial R35 million
- Education assistance—R350 million
- Health care—R270 million
- Housing assistance—R110 million
- Community rehabilitation—R500 million

Similar methods of national transitional and restorative justice were practiced in Latin American states after their transition to democracy. In 1983, an investigative organization called the National Commission on the Disappearance of Persons (CONADEP) was created in Argentina with the main aim of identifying the victims of enforced disappearance. In its report, the organisation was able to identify two groups of victims. The first group of victims consisted of 8960 disappeared victims. The second group contained 1300 victims who were still missing, but had been seen in secret detention facilities.[198] Even though CONADEP did not possess the competence to set reparation and compensation for the victims who had been identified, it still recommended that the Argentinean government assist the victims economically.[199] The newly established government followed CONADEP's

[192]TRC, Report of the Reparation & Rehabilitation Committee, vol. 6, sec.2 chapter 8, p. 95.

[193]See TRC, Final Report.

[194]Established by the TRC process from 21,676 victims' applications, see the list of victims under.

[195]Lwando Xaso, Financial reparations: a moral debt, IOL online, 24 May 2015, https://www.iol.co.za/sundayindependent/financial-reparations-a-moral-debt-1862390 visited 19 December 2020, Chris Makhaye and Nce Mkhize, Thousands of apartheid-era victims still waiting for compensation, Business Day, 14 December 2018, https://www.businesslive.co.za/bd/national/2018-12-14-thousands-of-apartheid-era-victims-still-waiting-for-compensation/ last visited 18 December 2020, Krzan 2016, p. 277.

[196]Farren Collins, R1.5-billion for apartheid victims but thousands still waiting for money, Times Live, 28 August 2017, https://www.timeslive.co.za/politics/2017-08-28-r15-billion-for-apartheid-victims-but-thousands-still-waiting-for-money/ last visited on 20 December 2020.

[197]South African Rand Currency.

[198]See CONADEP, Report 1984, Part II.

[199]CONADEP, Report 1984, Part IV, Recommendations, see Gualde and Luterstein (2009), pp. 417–420.

recommendations and adopted several laws which created a place for the compensation of victims being illegally detained.[200]

Almost the same scenario of a transition to democracy occurred after political change in Chile. The establishment of the National Truth and Reconciliation Commission (NTRC) was aimed at identifying human rights violations which had occurred in Chile during the dictatorship. The Commission identified 2298 people who had died for political reasons.[201] As a result, the Chilean government initiated legal reforms in order to provide compensation to the victims of the brutal regime.[202] This illustrates the fact that although various instruments are used for the reparations, victims do not have the possibility in all cases to be beneficiaries of those reparations when it comes to material compensation. It is one thing to agree upon reparations, it is another thing to implement them.

4.1.5 Practice of International Courts

The participation of victims during international criminal proceedings, as already mentioned, is a unique procedure which often is followed by reparation procedures. Bearing in mind the special procedural system at the ICC, other tribunals are considering redress practice for the victims who have suffered harm as a consequence of a crime. The main binding principle here is the connection or otherwise the causality between the convicted person and his or her charges and the victims and their suffering. Each international criminal institution to date practices its own reparation procedure for victims. The STL does not consider any compensation for victims, however, the conviction of the accused opens a door at the national level for the victim to be able to claim compensation through the Lebanese domestic courts. Pursuant to Article 25(2) STL Statute, the Tribunal may assist victims in seeking and gaining compensation at the national level, bearing in mind that the judgment is final.[203] To date, there has not been a single conviction by the STL. Hence, there have been no reparation proceedings considered for the victims.

With regard to Kosovo, Article 22 (8) of the Law on Specialist Chambers and Specialist Prosecutor's Office establishes a possibility for the victims to be granted a collective or an individual reparation order by the Court as soon as the accused has been convicted. However, it is still in a position to refer the victims to civil litigation in the other courts of Kosovo. The Court is statutorily in a position to assist the

---

[200]See Sveaass and Sønneland (2015), p. 226, Wilson (2004) p. 796, Duffy (2018), p. 184, Guembe (2006), pp. 27–31.

[201]Lira (2006), p. 56–57.

[202]Lira (2006), pp. 59–66, NTRC, Report of the Chilean National Commission on Truth and Reconciliation, under https://www.usip.org/sites/default/files/resources/collections/truth_commissions/Chile90-Report/Chile90-Report.pdf, last visited 18 December 2020.

[203]See also Morisson Pountney (2014), p. 170.

victims in seeking damages by serving a certified copy of the judgment and its decision upon the victims. However, there are no resources for the Court to be able to compensate the victims financially.[204] To date, there has been no judgment or reparation order.

Another unique reparation mechanism is in place at the ECCC. The Hybrid Tribunal does not have the power to grant victims monetary compensation, but rather it is in the position to determine collective and moral reparation for the victims pursuant to Rule 23 (1) (b) IRR.[205] The victims at the ECCC may still refer to Cambodian domestic courts in order to seek financial reparations. Under collective and moral reparation, the Hybrid Court considers an acknowledgment of the harm of victims and the provision of benefits to the victims pursuant to 23qui IRR. Accordingly, dissipating the judgment through the official channels, establishing victims' health centers or support sections,[206] providing documentation and educational projects[207] and setting up remembrance and memorialisation projects[208] may still be considered under collective and moral reparation.[209] In its first judgment, the ECCC clearly made a distinction between the hybrid Tribunal and regional human rights courts by stating that the Tribunal does not have jurisdiction over Cambodian or other national authorities or international bodies, with regard to directing them to grant the victims reparations.[210] It furthermore noted that in the event of there being no resources available for the convicted person, there is currently no mechanism allowing the ECCC to substitute or supplement awards against them with any funds.[211] However, the ECCC may encourage any institution to display solidarity with the victims. In the recent Judgment of the ECCC, the Tribunal sought the judicial recognition of 14 projects, from a total of 18. Those projects included forms of education as a guarantee of non-repetition, documentation highlighting the experience of specific groups, the commemoration of the suffering of civil parties, whilst also making them available to society at large, and healthcare components for the victims.[212]

[204]See also Garcia (2018), p. 19.

[205]See Cohen (2020a), p. 68.

[206]See ECCC, *Case of Nuon Chea, Khieu Samphan*, (Case 002/01), 002/19-09-2007/ECCC/TC, Judgment (7 August 2014) paras. 1154–1155.

[207]ECCC, *Case of Nuon Chea, Khieu Samphan*, (Case 002/01), 002/19-09-2007/ECCC/TC, Judgment (7 August 2014) paras. 1156–1160.

[208]ECCC, *Case of Nuon Chea, Khieu Samphan*, (Case 002/01), 002/19-09-2007/ECCC/TC, Judgment (7 August 2014) para. 1152.

[209]Cf. Evans (2012), p. 116.

[210]ECCC, *Case of Kamg Guek Eav (Case 001)*, 001/18-07-2007-ECCC/SC, Appeal Judgement (3 February 2012) para. 663.

[211]ECCC, *Case of Kamg Guek Eav (Case 001)*, 001/18-07-2007-ECCC/SC, Appeal Judgement (3 February 2012) para. 664.

[212]See ECCC, *Case of Nuon Chea, Khieu Samphan* (Case 002/02), 002/19-09-2007/ECCC/TC, Summary of Judgment (16 November 2018) paras. 63–68, See ECCC, *Case of Nuon Chea, Khieu*

4.2 Reparation at the ICC

As previously mentioned, the ICC is the only international institution which considers direct individual financial compensation for the victims of crimes. If, in the case of regional human rights courts, the compensation occurs via a payment to the state, the ICC, in contrast, grants victims awards directly, bearing in mind that the Trust Fund is an organ of the Court. It is important to note that compared to the practice of the ad hoc tribunals, the involvement of the victims at international criminal proceedings and the broad mechanism of redress for the victims is a success for the international criminal justice system. How efficient the practical implementation of this political decision[213] to include reparation mechanism into the procedural order actually is, remains a challenge for the Court.

Article 75 RS sets the basic principle of reparation for the victims, while Rules 95-99 RPE guide the victims through the reparation procedure. Nevertheless, the codified provisions do not provide the full picture of the reparation procedure, and it is rather left to the Chambers to determine how the reparations will function. In the three reparation orders which have been issued since the establishment of the Court, it is still not possible to identify a common methodology and a set of principles used by the Court in delivering these orders.[214] Compared to the regional human rights courts,[215] the ICC uses a specific process of reparation which is, as such, unprecedented. The judgments at the regional human rights courts include not only the merits but also the decision on reparations, as was discussed above. The ICC, however, usually uses a separate decision in cooperation with the Trust Fund, which firstly drafts an implementation plan and, after the adaptation by the Court, is entitled to implement the decision.[216] If, in the other stages of the proceedings before the ICC, the victims had a role as participants, their role changes as soon as the Court enters the reparation procedure. Bearing in mind that the victims gain more rights in the reparation procedure, they are assigned the role of party before the ICC at this stage.[217] The outcome of this stage must reflect the context from which it arises, namely the reparation should be the result of the individual criminal

Samphan (Case 002/02), 002/19-09-2007/ECCC/TC Judgement (16 November 2018) paras. 4419 et seq.

[213]Cf. Donat-Cattin (2000), p. 251.

[214]See the concerns on each reparation order in Tigroudja (2017), pp. 7–11.

[215]Slight difference by the Inter-American Court for Human Rights, where often the reparation order follows the judgment and is not included in the judgment.

[216]Article 76(3) of the Rome Statute consider a separate proceedings for the reparations, see Baumgartner (2008), p. 431, Regulation 56 RoC consider the reparation at the same time as for the purposes of trial, see Schabas and Ambos (2016), Rn. 10, p. 1875.

[217]See ICC, *Prosecutor v. Lubanga*, ICC-01/04-01/06-2953, Decision on the admissibility of the appeals against Trial Chamber I's Decision establishing the principles and procedures to be applied to reparations" and directions on the further conduct of proceedings (14 December 2012) para. 67.

responsibility for the offences for which the person was convicted.[218] Before it is possible to distinguish the process from the point of view of the victims, it is initially important to understand and to analyse the legal background of the reparation procedure at the ICC.

4.2.1 Principles of Reparation

As soon as the accused is convicted, the Court enters the reparation stage which is bound by the charges for which the accused was convicted. Statutorily, the Court is entitled to create general principles relating to reparations.[219] However, the Statute does not allocate whether the principles should be established for each case individually, or whether the general principles of reparation should be attributable to all further cases. Taking into account that since the establishment of the ICC only three reparation orders have been issued, it is fair to state that the first reparation order was used as a guideline for future reparations. However, pursuant to Article 21(3) RS, it is at the discretion of the Court as to whether it shall be bound by its own previous decisions, and whether to employ the reparation principles established in previous decisions as guidelines. Even though the Trial Chamber in *Lubanga* decided that the principles established by the Court were bound to the specific circumstances of the case, the Appeals Chamber made a distinction by stating that the principles include general concepts which might be adapted, expanded upon, added or applied in future cases.[220]

A further question which arose at the Appeals Chamber was whether establishing the principles of reparations should include both types of reparations, namely individual and collective redress. The Appeals Chamber decided that the established principles must also be attributable to the individual awards. It mostly relied on the fact that the award is made by the Trial Chamber pursuant to individual request or to a *proprio motu* decision. At the same time, the award is based on the principle set by the Court in accordance with Article 75 (1) RS and Rules 98 (2) and (3) RPE.[221] In cases of collective reparation and their connection to the principles established by the Court, the Appeals Chamber considered the fact that reparation includes such

[218]See also Cohen (2020b), p. 83, McCarthy (2014), pp. 130–135, Dwertmann (2010), pp. 45–50, ICC, *Prosecutor v. Lubanga*, ICC-01/04-01/06-3129, Judgment on the appeals against the "Decision establishing the principles and procedures to be applied to reparations" of 7 August 2012 with Amended order for reparations (Annex A) and public annexes (3 March 2015) paras. 65–67.

[219]ICC, *Prosecutor v. Lubanga*, ICC-01/04-01/06-3129, Judgment on the appeals against the "Decision establishing the principles and procedures to be applied to reparations" of 7 August 2012 with Amended order for reparations (Annex A) and public annexes (3 March 2015) para. 52.

[220]ICC, *Prosecutor v. Lubanga*, ICC-01/04-01/06-3129, Judgment on the appeals against the "Decision establishing the principles and procedures to be applied to reparations" of 7 August 2012 with Amended order for reparations (Annex A) and public annexes (3 March 2015) para. 55.

[221]Safferling, Petrossian (2020), p. 23 et seq.

modalities as restitution, compensation and rehabilitation, as stated in Article 75 (1) RS and, in cases of collective forms, the reparations may, pursuant to Rule 98 (3) RPE, be more appropriate, in which case collective reparation should also be formed on the principles set by the Court.[222]

4.2.1.1 General Principles of the Reparation Procedure

In the first reparation procedure at the ICC, the Court clarified what reparation at the ICC stands for. The Trial Chamber established the following principles which a reparation order should be based upon and which are to be applied.

- While deciding on the method of reparation, the Court is free to apply and to consider further international norms pursuant to Article 21 RS.
- The principle of dignity, non-stigmatisation and non-discrimination presumed that all victims should be treated equally and fairly. The Court should bear in mind the different backgrounds of the victims depending on their political, cultural, racial or gender grounds while implementing the Rules 87 and 88 RPE and while involving the victims in the reparation procedure. Reparations should secure reconciliation between the convicted person, the victims of the crimes and the affected communities.[223]
- The principles of establishing the beneficiaries of reparations determined those victims who might be taken into account for the reparation awards, recalling the definition of the victims pursuant to Rule 85 RPE.[224]
- The principle of accessibility and consultation with the victim considered a special approach to the victims, in order to make the reparation procedure as accessible as possible. Furthermore, according to this principle the Court should consult with the victims on issues relating to their priorities and obstacles.[225]
- The principle of special measures for the special group of victims, such as victims of sexual violence and child victims, considered a special approach to these victims, in order to enable their equal participation in the reparation proceedings, especially in the rehabilitation programs.[226]
- The principle of identification of the scope and modalities of the reparations. Accordingly, the Court is bound to identify the type of reparation that should be implemented in the specific matter. At the same time, the Court has found that

[222]Balta et al. (2018), p. 225.

[223]See ICC, *Prosecutor v. Lubanga*, ICC-01/04-01/06-2904, Decision establishing the principles and procedures to be applied to reparations (7 August 2012) paras. 187–193.

[224]ICC, *Prosecutor v. Lubanga*, ICC-01/04-01/06-2904, Decision establishing the principles and procedures to be applied to reparations (7 August 2012) paras. 194–201.

[225]ICC, *Prosecutor v. Lubanga*, ICC-01/04-01/06-2904, Decision establishing the principles and procedures to be applied to reparations (7 August 2012) paras. 202–206.

[226]ICC, *Prosecutor v. Lubanga*, ICC-01/04-01/06-2904, Decision establishing the principles and procedures to be applied to reparations (7 August 2012) paras. 207–216.

besides statutorily established modalities of reparations, the Court may also order other types of reparations, such as those of a symbolic, preventative or transformative value.[227]

- The principle of proportionality and adequate reparations presumes that the victims have to be entitled to receive prompt, proportional and adequate reparations.[228]
- The principle of causality considers a tight connection between the crimes committed, the harm suffered and the reparation claims.[229]
- The burden of proof rests with the victims who have to prove the harm suffered by adducing evidence and documentation. However, those drafting the Rome Statute agreed that the standard should be lower than that required for a guilty verdict.[230]
- The principle of a fair and impartial trial considers that during the reparation process the established principles and reparation modalities will not prejudice and may not be inconsistent with the rights of the defense.[231]
- The principle of cooperation and publicity of the reparations determines, firstly, that the states or other institutions have the obligation not to prevent the implementation of the reparations and should rather cooperate and assist in the implementation process. Furthermore, the Court is responsible for the wide range of accessibility of the reparations order. It has to take all possible measures to deliver the principles of reparation to the national authorities and the affected communities.[232]

On the basis of Rule 153 (1) RPE, the Appeals Chamber amended the principles for the reparations which had been laid down by the Trial Chamber. It mostly determined that even in cases of the indigence of the convicted person, the principle of reparation is bound by the accountability of the convicted person in all circumstances, bearing in mind that the reparations are made through the Trust Fund pursuant to Article 75(2) RS.[233] This principle was enshrined during the drafting

---

[227]ICC, *Prosecutor v. Lubanga*, ICC-01/04-01/06-2904, Decision establishing the principles and procedures to be applied to reparations (7 August 2012) paras. 217–241.

[228]ICC, *Prosecutor v. Lubanga*, ICC-01/04-01/06-2904, Decision establishing the principles and procedures to be applied to reparations (7 August 2012) paras. 242–446.

[229]ICC, *Prosecutor v. Lubanga*, ICC-01/04-01/06-2904, Decision establishing the principles and procedures to be applied to reparations (7 August 2012) paras. 247–250.

[230]ICC, *Prosecutor v. Lubanga*, ICC-01/04-01/06-2904, Decision establishing the principles and procedures to be applied to reparations (7 August 2012) paras. 251–254.

[231]ICC, *Prosecutor v. Lubanga*, ICC-01/04-01/06-2904, Decision establishing the principles and procedures to be applied to reparations (7 August 2012) para. 255.

[232]ICC, *Prosecutor v. Lubanga*, ICC-01/04-01/06-2904, Decision establishing the principles and procedures to be applied to reparations (7 August 2012) paras. 256–259.

[233]ICC, *Prosecutor v. Lubanga*, ICC-01/04-01/06-3129, Judgment on the appeals against the "Decision establishing the principles and procedures to be applied to reparations" of 7 August 2012 with Amended order for reparations (Annex A) and public annexes (3 March 2015) paras. 69–73, Stahn (2015), Musiał-Budnicka (2016), pp. 110, 121.

process and during the negotiations for the Rome Statue, determining that the Court's aim does not lie in the establishment of the state's responsibility and the reparations provided by the state, but rather in establishing the liability of the individual for the crimes committed, followed by the concept of justice for victims.[234] Furthermore, the Appeals Chamber noted that besides the fact that the reparation order should be directed against the convicted person, reparation itself should be proportionate to the harm caused and to the perpetrator's participation in the commission of the crimes for which they were convicted.[235] The Appeals Chamber stressed in its judgment that the Trial Chamber failed to establish the liability of the convicted person for the reparation awarded and that, because of the indigence of the convicted person, the Trial Chamber stated that the reparation award should be paid out of other sources from within the Trust Fund.[236] The Appeals Chamber was not of the opinion that the principle of liability to remedy can be presumed from indigence or lack of funds and possibilities and from the fact that the reparations will be then paid from other sources of Trust Fund. On this matter the Appeals Chamber employed Article 75 (4) RS and mentioned the narrow cooperation with the Member States aiming at exercising the reparation order, namely identifying, tracing or freezing the proceeds and property of the convicted person. Furthermore, the Appeals Chamber cited Regulation 117 RoC stating that the indigence of the convicted person at the time of judgment does not impose the liability of the said person, and since their financial situation may change, the perpetrator will furthermore be liable for the remedies.[237] In respect of the "other sources", the Appeals Chamber referred to Rule 98 (5) RPE in order to provide victims reparations without establishing any liability on the part of the convicted person to pay for that award. The Appeals Chamber distinguished a dual mandate of the Trust Fund which is, firstly, the assistance to the victims within the Court's jurisdiction and, secondly, the implementation of the reparation orders. The Court strictly separated these two mandates from each other and mentioned that the use of the other sources for the benefit of the victims lies within the discretion of Trust Fund itself and not of the Court. Consequently, the Court does not have control over the

[234]Moffett (2017), pp. 1204–1222, this provision was then again confirmed by the ASP Resolution, see ASP, Resolution ICC-ASP/10/Res.3, Adopted at the 7th plenary meeting, on 20 December 2011, by consensus, ICC-ASP/10/Res.3, Reparations, para. 2.

[235]ICC, *Prosecutor v. Lubanga*, ICC-01/04-01/06-3129, Judgment on the appeals against the "Decision establishing the principles and procedures to be applied to reparations" of 7 August 2012 with Amended order for reparations (Annex A) and public annexes (3 March 2015) Annex A, para. 5.

[236]ICC, *Prosecutor v. Lubanga*, ICC-01/04-01/06-3129, Judgment on the appeals against the "Decision establishing the principles and procedures to be applied to reparations" of 7 August 2012 with Amended order for reparations (Annex A) and public annexes (3 March 2015) Annex A para. 101.

[237]ICC, *Prosecutor v. Lubanga*, ICC-01/04-01/06-3129, Judgment on the appeals against the "Decision establishing the principles and procedures to be applied to reparations" of 7 August 2012 with Amended order for reparations (Annex A) and public annexes (3 March 2015) Annex A paras. 102–105.

'other sources' which comprise contributions which are not from the convicted person.[238]

As the third essential element for the principles of reparations, the Appeals Chamber stated that these should include the fact that the reparation itself must specify and provide reasons for the type of reparations ordered, either collectively or individually or both. In this regard, the Appeals Chamber assumed a victim-centric position stating that even if the Trial Chamber correctly considered the reparations to be voluntary, it made the participation in such restorative programs dependent upon the Trust Fund, pointing to Rule 98 (3) RPE.[239] Therefore, the Appeals Chamber noted that the victims first should give their consent when a collective award is being made.[240]

At the same time, the Appeals Chamber had made the distinction that the reparation order must define the harm caused to direct and indirect victims as a result of the crimes for which the person was convicted as well as identify the appropriate modalities of reparations based on the circumstances of the case. On this matter, the Appeals Chamber highlighted the fact that the Court may not distinguish other types of harm for which the accused was not convicted. However, it lies within the discretion of the Trust Fund to consider other victims during the assistance activities.[241]

The order must identify the victims eligible to benefit from the awards for reparations or set out the criteria of eligibility based upon the link between the harm suffered by the victims and the crimes for which the person was convicted. The Appeals Chamber directed the Trial Chamber that it failed to identify the victims by compiling a list of victims eligible for the reparations. It stressed the fact that the Trial Chamber referred to the affected communities as beneficiaries of the reparations, without making any distinction between which member of the community had suffered harm pursuant to Rule 85 RPE. Furthermore, it stated that the community approach may be distinguished by the Trust Fund in its assistance activities pursuant to Regulation 50 of the Regulations for the Trust Fund for Victims.[242]

---

[238]ICC, *Prosecutor v. Lubanga*, ICC-01/04-01/06-3129, Judgment on the appeals against the "Decision establishing the principles and procedures to be applied to reparations" of 7 August 2012 with Amended order for reparations (Annex A) and public annexes (3 March 2015) Annex A paras. 111–117.

[239]See ICC, *Prosecutor v. Lubanga*, ICC-01/04-01/06-2904, Decision establishing the principles and procedures to be applied to reparations (7 August 2012) para. 204.

[240]ICC, *Prosecutor v. Lubanga*, ICC-01/04-01/06-3129, Judgment on the appeals against the "Decision establishing the principles and procedures to be applied to reparations" of 7 August 2012 with Amended order for reparations (Annex A) and public annexes (3 March 2015) paras. 160.

[241]ICC, *Prosecutor v. Lubanga*, ICC-01/04-01/06-3129, Judgment on the appeals against the "Decision establishing the principles and procedures to be applied to reparations" of 7 August 2012 with Amended order for reparations (Annex A) and public annexes (3 March 2015) para. 199.

[242]ICC, *Prosecutor v. Lubanga*, ICC-01/04-01/06-3129, Judgment on the appeals against the "Decision establishing the principles and procedures to be applied to reparations" of 7 August

Summarising the principles, it is possible to maintain that the Appeals Chamber amended the principles established by the Trial Chamber in the case of *Lubanga* with the following essential elements:[243]

- The order for reparation must be made against the convicted person
- The order for reparation must establish and inform the convicted person of his or her liability
- The order for reparation must specify the type of reparation
- The order for reparation must define the harm suffered
- The order for reparation must identify the victims.

The Trial Chambers in the cases of *Katanga*[244] and *Al Mahdi*[245] decided not to deviate from these established and amended provisions and the principles set by the Appeals Chamber in the *Lubanga* case.

4.2.1.2 Beneficiaries of the Reparation Awards

Another statutorily important provision can be found in Article 75 (1) RS relating to reparation awards which have to be granted "to the victims" and "in respect of the victims". Such wording provides a wide range of space for the inclusion of different victims within the reparation procedure. If the notion "to the victims" means the direct restorative or remedial award to individuals defined by Rule 85 RPE, then the notion "in respect of the victims" still may incur a dual interpretation of victimhood. On the one hand, it may include the reparations to the indirect victims or their family members or successors, defined by Rule 85 RPE.[246] On the other hand, however, "in respect of the victims" may be interpreted abstractly and include the communities and groups of unidentified victims affected by the convicted person's crimes. The Appeals Chamber in the *Lubanga* case did not generally disagree with the point that the community, including unidentified victims, may still be deemed a beneficiary of collective reparations. The Chamber noted that certain crimes may have an effect on a community as a whole and in cases demonstrating a sufficient causal link between the harm and the crime, collective reparation may still be considered for that group of victims. However, at the same time the remedial collective awards for the

2012 with Amended order for reparations (Annex A) and public annexes (3 March 2015) paras. 210–215.

[243]See also Redress, Ending Torture, Seeking Justice for Survivors, Moving Reparations Forward at the ICC: Recommendations, November 2016, pp. 6–7.

[244]ICC, *Prosecutor v. Katanga*, ICC-01/04-01/07-3728-tENG, Order for Reparations pursuant to Article 75 of the Statute (24 March 2017) para. 30.

[245]ICC, *Prosecutor v. Al Mahdi* ICC-01/12-01/15-236, Reparations Order (17 August 2017) para. 26.

[246]See Donat-Cattin (2016), Rn. 10, p. 1857.

community have to be specified.[247] The Trial Chamber in the *Lubanga* case took a very broad victim-centric approach, when it held that the victims who did not participate or apply for the reparations may still benefit from the reparation awards.[248] This approach was approved by the Appeals Chamber, which also stated that the reparation procedure is a distinct process and does not require any participation on the part of the victim in the criminal proceedings.[249]

4.2.1.3 Modalities of the Reparations

Although Article 75 (1) RS considers the forms of reparation as restitution, compensation and rehabilitation, the Court stressed that this list is not exhaustive.[250] The Court has the discretion to imply other modalities of reparations with regard to the specific circumstances of a given case. The Court is free to adopt paragraphs 18–23 of the Basic Principles and Guidelines on the Right to a Remedy and Reparation for Victims of Gross Violations of International Human Rights Law and Serious Violations of International Humanitarian Law,[251] known as the *Van-Boven-Principles*.[252] These reparations may be of either symbolic, preventive or transformative value.[253] However, the selected form should be the most appropriate mechanism at hand for the specific issue. Under this broad interpretation of the non-exhaustive list of reparations, the participation of the victims at the criminal proceedings, for example, may still be viewed as some form of rehabilitation, where the victims are given a voice to articulate issues which concern them or to express the harm they have suffered. The statutory uncertainty and the freedom of action of the Court in cases of reparations opens all the boundaries for the victims, although it also gives the Court the power to limit the victims' claims.

Distinguishing between the practice of mass violations and the ensuing restorative justice observed above, it is possible to determine that, in many cases, a form of

[247] ICC, *Prosecutor v. Lubanga*, ICC-01/04-01/06-2904, Decision establishing the principles and procedures to be applied to reparations (7 August 2012) para. 212, see also de Brouwer and Heikkilä (2013), p. 1359.

[248] See ICC, *Prosecutor v. Lubanga*, ICC-01/04-01/06-2904, Decision establishing the principles and procedures to be applied to reparations (7 August 2012) paras. 8, 219.

[249] ICC, *Prosecutor v. Lubanga*, ICC-01/04-01/06-2953, Decision on the admissibility of the appeals against Trial Chamber I's Decision establishing the principles and procedures to be applied to reparations" and directions on the further conduct of proceedings (14 December 2012) paras. 69–72, Friman (2017), Article 75(1).

[250] See ICC, *Prosecutor v. Lubanga*, ICC-01/04-01/06-2904, Decision establishing the principles and procedures to be applied to reparations (7 August 2012) para. 222.

[251] UN, GA, Basic Principles and Guidelines on the Right to a Remedy and Reparation for Victims of Gross Violations of International Human Rights Law and Serious Violations of International Humanitarian Law, Adopted and proclaimed by GA resolution 60/147 of 16 December 2005

[252] See Bock (2010), p. 559.

[253] See ICC, *Prosecutor v. Lubanga*, ICC-01/04-01/06-2904, Decision establishing the principles and procedures to be applied to reparations (7 August 2012) paras. 222–239.

non-pecuniary reparation is very often more appropriate for society than individual monetary compensation. These individual compensation payments may not cover the harm suffered due to the mass violations, however, they are aimed at "building bridges" between the affected societies and are more effective. At the same time, it is important to consider moral aspects of the compensation provided by the Court through the Trust Fund. This is bound to the fact that despite the lack of legal connection between the Court's administrative tasks and reparations to the victims, monetary compensation will never be on the same level as, say, the salary of the Court's employees.

Parallel to the modalities of the reparations, an essential role of reparation is also how these modalities will be implemented, either individually, collectively or both. Rules 94 and 95 RPE consider individual reparation, whilst Rules 97 (1) and 98 (3) RPE enable the Court to provide a collective award. In order to make a distinction between individual and collective reparation, the Appeals Chamber drew upon the conflicting opinions during the Rome Conference, highlighting that some delegates raised the issue of the quantity of the victims and the consequences arising from this quantity. Mostly, they were of the opinion that if there are only a few victims, the Court is in a position to make findings concerning their damages rather easily. In contrast, in cases involving large numbers of victims, it is not necessary to identify the victims and their claims separately and because of this, the Court may decide upon collective reparations.[254] Individual reparations are, however, based upon the request of the victims.[255] In contrast, the Appeals Chamber is not bound by the merits of the individual request of the victims for reparations when deciding upon collective reparations, but rather by the determination that it is more appropriate to award collective reparations.[256] At the same time, the Appeals Chamber stated that a decision not to award reparations to individuals does not restrict them from participating in the collective reparation programs. This is, according to the Appeals Chamber, not inconsistent with the internationally recognised human rights pursuant to Article 21 (3) RS.[257] Hence, individual and collective reparations are not mutually exclusive and may also be awarded concurrently.[258] In cases of individual

[254]Friman and Lewis (2001), p. 478, see also ICC, *Prosecutor v. Lubanga*, ICC-01/04-01/06-3129, Judgment on the appeals against the "Decision establishing the principles and procedures to be applied to reparations" of 7 August 2012 with Amended order for reparations (Annex A) and public annexes (3 March 2015) para. 150.

[255]See Schabas (2017), p. 1143.

[256]ICC, *Prosecutor v. Lubanga*, ICC-01/04-01/06-3129, Judgment on the appeals against the "Decision establishing the principles and procedures to be applied to reparations" of 7 August 2012 with Amended order for reparations (Annex A) and public annexes (3 March 2015) para. 151.

[257]ICC, *Prosecutor v. Lubanga*, ICC-01/04-01/06-3129, Judgment on the appeals against the "Decision establishing the principles and procedures to be applied to reparations" of 7 August 2012 with Amended order for reparations (Annex A) and public annexes (3 March 2015) para. 155, Ferstman (2017), p. 401, Schabas (2017), p. 1143.

[258]ICC, *Prosecutor v. Lubanga*, ICC-01/04-01/06-3129-AnxA, Order for Reparations (3 March 2015) para. 33.

reparation, the harm to a specific person is assumed to have been repaired/recovered by the ensuing benefits. Accordingly, individual reparations confer a benefit on a victim to which the person is exclusively entitled.[259] These awards do not have to create tensions and divisions within the affected societies.[260] In cases of collective reparation, group harm is targeted before repair.[261] The Trial Chamber in the case of *Katanga* encoded the definition of collective reparation stating that, on the whole, a group has to be bound by a collective and shared harm and suffering as a consequence of the crimes committed by the convicted person. Accordingly, the collective award can only be granted where the victims perceive themselves as having been victimised by the shared harm of the group.[262] This, however, assumes that even individuals who were not directly harmed could still benefit from the collective reparations. Accordingly, collective reparations may have two aims: on the one hand, to include all members of the community, irrespective of the fact of victimisation and, on the other hand, only those members of the group who were targeted as victims.[263] With collective awards, not only one victim will benefit from the reparations, but also all the members of the group or the community. The Appeal Chamber stressed in the case of *Lubanga* that the harm of victims under collective reparation should be identified and specified on both an individual and a collective basis.[264]

4.2.1.4 Reparation Decision

In order to make a decision on reparation, the victim must make a request for reparation for the harm suffered. However, as explored above, the reparation procedure is a voluntary process and prior to any remedial reward the Court is bound to the consent of each victim, a notion which was established by the Trial Chamber[265] and afterwards approved by the Appeals Chamber.[266] At the same time, the Rome

[259]See ICC, *Prosecutor v. Katanga*, ICC-01/04-01/07-3728-tENG, Order for Reparations pursuant to Article 75 of the Statute (24 March 2017) para. 271.

[260]ICC, *Prosecutor v. Lubanga*, ICC-01/04-01/06-3129-AnxA, Order for Reparations (3 March 2015) para para. 33.

[261]Cf. Rosenfeld (2010), pp. 732–733, both types of reparations are undefined by the regulations and rules of the Court.

[262]See ICC, *Prosecutor v. Katanga*, ICC-01/04-01/07-3728-tENG, Order for Reparations pursuant to Article 75 of the Statute (24 March 2017) paras. 272–275.

[263]Cf. ICC, *Prosecutor v. Katanga*, ICC-01/04-01/07-3728-tENG, Order for Reparations pursuant to Article 75 of the Statute (24 March 2017) paras. 278–280.

[264]ICC, *Prosecutor v. Lubanga*, ICC-01/04-01/06-3129-AnxA, Order for Reparations (3 March 2015) para. 33.

[265]See ICC, *Prosecutor v. Lubanga*, ICC-01/04-01/06-2904, Decision establishing the principles and procedures to be applied to reparations (7 August 2012) para. 204.

[266]ICC, *Prosecutor v. Lubanga*, ICC-01/04-01/06-3129, Judgment on the appeals against the "Decision establishing the principles and procedures to be applied to reparations" of 7 August

Statute enables the Court, in exceptional circumstances, to consider reparations on its own motion, too. It lies within the discretion of the Court to identify the exceptional circumstances of the specific case.

4.2.1.5 Reparation for Harm

Another important point with regard to the reparation procedure is the identification of the harm of the victims. The Court may invite experts who will be able to assess the damage suffered by the victims. The Trial Chamber established that the standard of proof should be lower and where it concerns the causality link between the crime for which the accused has been found guilty beyond reasonable doubt, and the harm suffered by the victim is to be on the balance of probabilities.[267] The Appeals Chamber has generally accepted the approach of the Trial Chamber, however, it held it that the victim has to provide sufficient proof of the causal link between the crime and the harm suffered, based upon the specific circumstances of the case.[268] In the case of *Katanga*, the Trial Chamber emphasised that, at the time of the reparation order, 14 years had elapsed since the crimes had been committed against the victims. As a result, the victims were likely to face difficulties in obtaining evidence to support their claim. Therefore, the Trial Chamber accepted the same standard of proof—"*the balance of probabilities*"[269]—as had previously been established by the Appeal Chamber in the *Lubanga* case.[270] While implementing the standard within the balance of probabilities, the Trial Chamber in *Katanga* did not find sufficient evidence for the material harm resulting from the destruction of a building,[271] even though this was supported by a residence certificate signed by a person acting in an official capacity who stated that the immoveable property belonged to the applicant. Nevertheless, it lacked precise information about the property as to whether it was made of straw, rammed earth or fired/unfired bricks.[272] However, at the same time,

2012 with Amended order for reparations (Annex A) and public annexes (3 March 2015) paras. 159–160, Friman (2017).

[267]Donat-Cattin (2016), Rn. 18, p. 1863, ICC, *Prosecutor v. Lubanga*, ICC-01/04-01/06-2904, Decision establishing the principles and procedures to be applied to reparations (7 August 2012) para, 226.

[268]ICC, *Prosecutor v. Lubanga*, ICC-01/04-01/06-3129, Judgment on the appeals against the "Decision establishing the principles and procedures to be applied to reparations" of 7 August 2012 with Amended order for reparations (Annex A) and public annexes (3 March 2015) para. 81.

[269]The applicant must show that it is more probable than not that he or she suffered harm as a consequence of one of the crimes of the convicted person.

[270]See ICC, *Prosecutor v. Katanga*, ICC-01/04-01/07-3728-tENG, Order for Reparations pursuant to Article 75 of the Statute (24 March 2017) paras. 47–51, see also ICC, *Prosecutor v. Al Mahdi*, ICC-01/12-01/15, Reparation Order (17 August 2017) para. 58.

[271]Under Article 8(2)(e)(xii) of the Rome Statute.

[272]ICC, *Prosecutor v. Katanga*, ICC-01/04-01/07-3728-tENG, Order for Reparations pursuant to Article 75 of the Statute (24 March 2017) para. 85.

the Chamber was satisfied with the fact that if the applicant is in position to prove the destruction of immovable property, the Chamber will presume—in the absence of any specific piece of evidence—the destruction or pillaging of other property of the applicants which pertains to daily life,[273] and precisely this was confirmed by the Appeals Chamber in the *Katanga* case. However, it advised the Trial Chamber to indicate to the parties and participants that it was intending to draw the impugned presumption, including, but not limited to, inviting submissions on its formulation. Accordingly, this could have benefited from further reference.[274] On the other matter, the Trial Chamber was satisfied by the signatures of two credible witnesses who testified the loss of ownership as a result of the crime.[275]

In order to establish reparation for the physical harm, the Trial Chamber has taken into account the medical certificates and reports from non-governmental institutions and hospital records which were provided by the applicants in order to prove the wounds occasioned by the crimes committed by the convicted person. Notwithstanding, the Court was not satisfied with the establishment of the nexus to the crime. The certificates did not allocate and specify that the wounds were sustained as a result of the attacks of the convicted person.[276]

For the establishment of reparation for psychological harm, the Trial Chamber considered several important aspects. Firstly, it highlighted the fact that if the applicant claims for reparation because of the death of a relative, it is necessary to establish the nexus of the death of the direct victim to the crime committed by the convicted person and, furthermore, to prove the close personal relationship between the direct victim and the applicant.[277] In regard to psychological harm sustained as a consequence of the experience of the attack, namely seeing or fleeing the atrocities, the Trial Chamber stated that the applicants who were physically or materially affected by the attacks were also in a position to claim for the psychological harm sustained.[278] For the first time, the Trial Chamber in the case of *Katanga* dealt with such a question—known as transgenerational psychological harm—which assumes that the persons born after the commission of the crimes suffer psychological harm because their parents experienced the atrocities.[279] However, due to a lack of

[273] ICC, *Prosecutor v. Katanga*, ICC-01/04-01/07-3728-tENG, Order for Reparations pursuant to Article 75 of the Statute (24 March 2017) paras. 90–93.

[274] ICC, *Prosecutor v. Katanga*, ICC-01/04-01/07-3778-Red, Public redacted Judgment on the appeals against the order of Trial Chamber II of 24 March 2017 entitled "Order for Reparations pursuant to Article 75 of the Statute" (9 March 2018) paras. 91–92.

[275] ICC, *Prosecutor v. Katanga*, ICC-01/04-01/07-3728-tENG, Order for Reparations pursuant to Article 75 of the Statute (24 March 2017) paras. 102–104.

[276] ICC, *Prosecutor v. Katanga*, ICC-01/04-01/07-3728-tENG, Order for Reparations pursuant to Article 75 of the Statute (24 March 2017) para. 111.

[277] ICC, *Prosecutor v. Katanga*, ICC-01/04-01/07-3728-tENG, Order for Reparations pursuant to Article 75 of the Statute (24 March 2017) paras. 113–122.

[278] ICC, *Prosecutor v. Katanga*, ICC-01/04-01/07-3728-tENG, Order for Reparations pursuant to Article 75 of the Statute (24 March 2017) para. 129.

[279] See also Cohen (2020b), p. 93.

evidence proving the nexus between the trauma and the attack and due to the hypothetical nature of the suffering, the Court did not consider reparation for the harm mentioned. At the same time, the Trial Chamber highlighted that the children in question would have to be given special attention within the Trust Fund assistance programs.[280] The Appeals Chamber in *Katanga* reversed the decision of the Trial Chamber ruling that the grounds for not establishing the nexus between the harm suffered and the crime were not sufficiently reasoned by the Trial Chamber, and therefore it was directed to carry out a new assessment regarding those victims.[281] However, the Trial Chamber was still not able to establish the nexus between the victims' harm and the crimes committed by the convicted person and dismissed reparations for the applicants.[282] The Trial Chamber in the case of *Al Mahdi* did approve the psychological harm. This comprised, in particular, the emotional distress suffered by the victims due to the destruction of cultural and religious buildings and the shattering the community's collective faith.[283] In the case of *Lubanga*, the Trial Chamber estimated that the fact of enlisting children into armed groups alone causes not only psychological but also physical and material damage to children as direct victims, as well as to the parents and close relatives as indirect victims.[284] Therefore, the Chamber found it fit to apply a presumption of harm to each direct and indirect victim, as soon as the child-soldier status had been established.[285]

Another important element of the establishment of the reparation for the harm caused, as can be seen in the examples mentioned, is causation, namely the nexus between the harm and the crime. As correctly mentioned by the Appeals Chamber, the standard of causation is not a principle, but rather a determination on a specific standard used by the Court, taking into account the competing interests and rights of the victims and the convicted person.[286] The Appeals Chamber approved the determination of the Trial Chamber that the standard of causation for reparations is

[280]See ICC, *Prosecutor v. Katanga*, ICC-01/04-01/07-3728-tENG, Order for Reparations pursuant to Article 75 of the Statute (24 March 2017) paras. 132–135.

[281]ICC, *Prosecutor v. Katanga*, ICC-01/04-01/07-3778-Red, Public redacted Judgment on the appeals against the order of Trial Chamber II of 24 March 2017 entitled "Order for Reparations pursuant to Article 75 of the Statute" (9 March 2018) paras. 237–239.

[282]ICC, *Prosecutor v. Katanga*, ICC-01/04-01/07-3804-Red-tENG, Decision on the Matter of the Transgenerational Harm Alleged by Some Applicants for Reparations Remanded by the Appeals Chamber in its Judgment of 8 March 2018 (19 July 2018) paras. 30–31, 142.

[283]ICC, *Prosecutor v. Al Mahdi*, ICC-01/12-01/15, Reparation Order (17 August 2017) paras. 84–88.

[284]ICC, *Prosecutor v. Lubanga*, ICC-01/04-01/06-3379-Red-Corr-tENG, Corrected version of the"Decision Setting the Size of the Reparations Award for which Thomas Lubanga Dyilo is Liable (21 December 2017) para. 180.

[285]ICC, *Prosecutor v. Lubanga*, ICC-01/04-01/06-3379-Red-Corr-tENG, Corrected version of the"Decision Setting the Size of the Reparations Award for which Thomas Lubanga Dyilo is Liable (21 December 2017) para. 185.

[286]See ICC, *Prosecutor v. Lubanga*, ICC-01/04-01/06-2904, Decision establishing the principles and procedures to be applied to reparations (7 August 2012) para. 250, ICC, *Prosecutor v. Lubanga*, ICC-01/04-01/06-3129, Judgment on the appeals against the "Decision establishing the principles

based upon a 'but-for' relationship[287] between the harm and the crime, with the further requirement of proximate cause.[288] The burden of proof for demonstrating the causality between the harm and the crime lies with the applicant so that the Court is in a position to be able to evaluate the nexus with regard to the characteristics of the case under consideration.[289]

4.2.1.6 Communication with Stakeholders

Article 75(3) RS creates a space not only for the victims and convicted persons, but also for other subjects to be involved in the reparation procedure. However, the question arises as to whether the involvement of other subjects or stakeholders and *bona fide* third parties is mandatory in character. The difference exists due to the fact that it lies within the Court's discretion to decide when to invite, or, indeed, whether it is generally necessary to invite interested stakeholders, either interested persons or states, to make representations pursuant to Rules 97 (2) and 143 RPE[290] and Regulation 56 RoC.[291] Hence, as soon as representations regarding specific matters of the case at hand are delivered to the Court by the interested stakeholders, the Court must take them into account before any reparation order is made.[292] The applicants' interests for representation may be very broad and may depend on the matters of the case. Therefore, different scenarios may be developed, in order to involve other subjects in the process. Besides the involvement of states in the proceedings,[293] there is also the possibility for interested individuals, such as property owners or those who might be interested in the case of reparations or institutions or experts, to make

and procedures to be applied to reparations" of 7 August 2012 with Amended order for reparations (Annex A) and public annexes (3 March 2015) para. 81.

[287] Actual Causation.

[288] See ICC, *Prosecutor v. Lubanga*, ICC-01/04-01/06-2904, Decision establishing the principles and procedures to be applied to reparations (7 August 2012) para. 250, ICC, *Prosecutor v. Lubanga*, ICC-01/04-01/06-3129, Judgment on the appeals against the "Decision establishing the principles and procedures to be applied to reparations" of 7 August 2012 with Amended order for reparations (Annex A) and public annexes (3 March 2015) paras. 120–127.

[289] ICC, *Prosecutor v. Katanga*, ICC-01/04-01/07-3728-tENG, Order for Reparations pursuant to Article 75 of the Statute (24 March 2017) paras. 163.-167, see also ICC, *Prosecutor v. Lubanga*, ICC-01/04-01/06-3379-Red-Corr-tENG, Corrected version of the"Decision Setting the Size of the Reparations Award for which Thomas Lubanga Dyilo is Liable (21 December 2017) para. 45.

[290] Cf. Submissions made according to Rule 103 RPE (amicus curiae).

[291] In parallel reading of Article 76 (3) of the Rome Statute.

[292] ICC, *Prosecutor v. Lubanga*, ICC-01/04-01/06-2870, Decision which Thomas Lubanga Dyilo is Liable on granting leave to make representations in the reparations proceedings (20 April 2012) paras. 19–20, see Donat-Cattin (2016), Rn. 10, p. 1865, see also ICC, *Prosecutor v. Lubanga*, ICC-01/04-01/06-3129-AnxA, Order for Reparations (3 March 2015) para. 79.

[293] Cf. ICC, *Prosecutor v. Al Mahdi*, ICC-01/12-01/15, Reparation Order (17 August 2017) para. 4, states may also participate in the proceedings, if the it is a bona fide third party, or the convicted person was acting in a public capacity, see narrower in Donat-Cattin (2016), Rn. 10, p. 1866.

representations with regard to the case at hand. In the case of *Katanaga*, the Trial Chamber found that the involvement of several NGO's who had significant and extensive practical experience of the reparations procedure was indeed in the interests of justice.[294]

4.2.1.7 Cooperation

In order to enforce the reparation order against the convicted person, it is assumed that firstly the reparation awards have been served from the assets and the property of the convicted person, which had been seized or frozen as a safeguard for the reparation proceedings. However, before seizing or freezing the assets, this property must first be identified. The ICC is not able to do this alone for reasons already known. As a result, it required close collaboration with the national authorities, on the one hand, and cooperation with the Member States of the Rome Statue on the other. Even during the pre-trial proceedings, the Court is in a position to seek the cooperation of states in order to take protective measures for the purpose of forfeiture,[295] namely for the benefit of the victims pursuant to Article 57(3)(e) RS, as soon as the arrest warrant has been issued. If this provision is not considered by the PTC, the Trial Chamber is, pursuant to Article 75(4) RS and pursuant to the Regulation 117 RoC, still in a position to seek cooperation regarding protective measures even after the conviction of the person. These protective measures mostly refer to the identification, tracing and freezing or seizure of proceeds, property and assets and instrumentalities of crimes in accordance with Article 93(1)(k) RS.[296] The Appeals Chamber in the case of *Lubanga* was of the view that indigence is not an obstacle for the imposition of a liability for reparations; as a result the Trial Chamber may seek assistance from State Parties in order to give effect to the reparation order.[297] The cooperation proceedings take place pursuant to the provisions of Article 87 RS. When issuing the request for cooperation, in accordance with Article

[294]ICC, *Prosecutor v. Katanga*, ICC-01/04-01/07-3533-tENG, Order granting leave to file representations pursuant to Article 75(3)of the Statute (1 April 2015) paras. 14–16 see e.g. ICC, *Prosecutor v. Al Mahdi*, Queen's University Belfast Human Rights Centre and the Redress Trust observations pursuant to Article 75(3) of the Statute and Rule 103 of the Rules (2 December 2016) see also Carter et al. (2016), p. 272.

[295]The Court interpreted forfeiture as a broad meaning, as an award for reparations and as a divestiture of property without compensation, see ICC, *Prosecutor v. Kenyatta*, ICC-01/09-02/11-931, Decision on the implementation of the request to freeze assets (8 July 2014) paras. 7–8, see also Ferstman (2017), pp. 389–391.

[296]See Ferstman (2016), pp. 233–234, Kreß and Prost (2016), Rd. 36, p. 2089, e.g. ICC, *Prosecutor v. Bemba*, ICC-01/05-01/08-8, Decision Et Demande En Vue D'obtenir L'identification, La Localisation, Le Gel Et La Saisie Des Biens Et Avoirs Adressées A La Republique Portugaise (28 May 2008).

[297]ICC, *Prosecutor v. Lubanga*, ICC-01/04-01/06-3129, Judgment on the appeals against the "Decision establishing the principles and procedures to be applied to reparations" of 7 August 2012 with Amended order for reparations (Annex A) and public annexes (3 March 2015) para. 103.

87 RS, the Court expects full cooperation from the State Parties, reminding them of their duty to cooperate pursuant to Articles 86–111 RS.[298]

4.2.2 *Victim Participation in the Reparation Proceedings*

The reparation procedure is a distinct process and differs from the penal proceedings,[299] however, it is nevertheless a judicial process.[300] Its purpose is to oblige those responsible for serious crimes to repair the harm they have caused to the victims and to enable the Court to ensure the offenders are made accountable for their acts.[301] As mentioned above, the victims' role during the reparation procedure is that of a party to the proceedings, in contrast to Article 68 (3) RS[302] where the victims' role was predominantly as a participant in the proceedings. Participation in the reparation proceedings does not exclude those who did not take part in the other stages of the proceedings. The victims who did not manage to, or did not want to, be involved in the main proceedings are still given the opportunity of applying for participation in the reparation proceedings.[303] This is bound either to the individual request to the Court pursuant to Rule 94 RPE or to the Court's own motion pursuant to the Rule 95 RPE.[304] The scope of the rights of the victims at this stage slightly differs from their legal standing in the main proceedings.

---

[298] Cf. ICC, *Prosecutor v. Katanga*, ICC-01/04-01/07-7-tENG, Urgent request to the Democratic Republic of the Congo for the purpose of obtaining the identification, tracing, freezing and seizure of the property and assets of Germain Katanga (6 July 2007), see also ASP, Resolution ICC-ASP/10/Res.3, Adopted at the 7th plenary meeting, on 20 December 2011, by consensus, "*Underlines that as the freezing and identification of any assets of the convicted person, which are indispensable for reparations, is of paramount importance the Court should seek to take all measures to that end, including effective communication with relevant States so that they are in a position to provide timely and effective assistance pursuant to Article 93, paragraph 1 (k), where possible, in all cases and at as early a stage of the proceedings as possible, irrespective of the declaration of indigence for the purpose of legal aid which bears no relevance to the ability of the accused to provide reparations*";

[299] ICC, *Prosecutor v. Katanga*, ICC-01/04-01/07-3728-tENG, Order for Reparations pursuant to Article 75 of the Statute (24 March 2017) para. 16.

[300] ICC, *Prosecutor v. Lubanga*, ICC-01/04-01/06-3129, Judgment on the appeals against the "Decision establishing the principles and procedures to be applied to reparations" of 7 August 2012 with Amended order for reparations (Annex A) and public annexes (3 March 2015) para. 237.

[301] ICC, *Prosecutor v. Lubanga*, ICC-01/04-01/06-3129-AnxA, Order for Reparations (3 March 2015) para. 2.

[302] ICC, *Prosecutor v. Lubanga*, ICC-01/04-01/06-2953, Decision on the admissibility of the appeals against Trial Chamber I's Decision establishing the principles and procedures to be applied to reparations" and directions on the further conduct of proceedings (14 December 2012) para. 67.

[303] See Dwertmann (2010), p. 196.

[304] The Article 75 of the Rome Statute creates a potential rights to reparations for the victims, see Ambos (2016), p. 198.

4.2.2.1 Victims' Request for Reparation

Rule 94 (1) RPE considers that any victim willing to request reparation and consequently to participate in this stage, should make a written application to the Registrar using the standard form designed by Regulation 88 RoC. The application contains three important points; descriptive information, claims for reparations and evidentiary materials. At the same time, the Registrar is obligated to assist the victims in completing the request and to present the reparation requests as a report to the Chamber pursuant to the Regulation 110 RoR. In its recent reparation orders, the Court decided not to deviate from its own jurisprudence at the reparation phase and applied the same standards of identification and recognition of victimhood, bearing only in mind the different standards of proof for those applying for reparations.[305] Another important feature is that the applicants who are claiming that they have suffered harm have to point to the exact harm and identify the casual link to the crimes committed by the convicted person and for which he or she was convicted.[306] In the case of *Lubanga*, the Appeals Chamber estimated the harm caused by the convicted person to the direct and indirect victims who could be granted reparation. This list contained harm, damage and injury or loss such as physical injury and trauma, the development of psychological disorders, interruption and loss of schooling, separation from families, difficulties socialising within families for the direct victims as well as psychological suffering due to the sudden loss of a family member, material deprivation that accompanied the loss of the family members contributions etc. for the indirect victims.[307] Accordingly, the victims who can prove, on the balance of probabilities, that they have suffered specific harm due to the crimes of the convicted person and, if other elements of the victimhood were met pursuant to Rule 85 RPE, could be eligible for reparations.

4.2.2.2 Proprio Motu Reparation

Taking into account the lack of information regarding the Court's proceedings or the mechanism of reparation under the ICC amongst the victims, the drafters also

---

[305] ICC, *Prosecutor v. Al Mahdi*, ICC-01/12-01/15, Reparation Order (17 August 2017) paras. 39–41, ICC, *Prosecutor v. Lubanga*, ICC-01/04-01/06-3379-Red-Corr-tENG, Corrected version of the"Decision Setting the Size of the Reparations Award for which Thomas Lubanga Dyilo is Liable (21 December 2017) paras. 40–43.

[306] ICC, *Prosecutor v. Katanga*, ICC-01/04-01/07-3728-tENG, Order for Reparations pursuant to Article 75 of the Statute (24 March 2017) para. 37, ICC, ICC, *Prosecutor v. Lubanga*, ICC-01/04-01/06-3379-Red-Corr-tENG, Corrected version of the"Decision Setting the Size of the Reparations Award for which Thomas Lubanga Dyilo is Liable (21 December 2017) paras. 136–137, the Court stressed that potentially eligible victim cannot attribute the same enlistment or conscription to both *Lubanga* and *Katanga*, who were members of different militias, McCarthy (2014), p. 184.

[307] ICC, *Prosecutor v. Lubanga*, ICC-01/04-01/06-3129, Judgment on the appeals against the "Decision establishing the principles and procedures to be applied to reparations" of 7 August 2012 with Amended order for reparations (Annex A) and public annexes (3 March 2015) para. 191.

considered reparation procedures initiated by the Court on its own motion and on behalf of the victims of crimes of a convicted person.[308] Rule 95 RPE allows the Court to start a reparation process independently of whether the Court receives individual requests for reparation from victims. As soon as the Court decides to initiate the reparation process it has to instruct the Registrar to notify any interested subjects about the upcoming remedial proceedings pursuant to Rule 95 (1) RPE and under "the exceptional circumstances" of Article 75 (1) RS. In the event of the victims making a request to be involved in the proceedings, they must apply pursuant to Rule 94 RPE. At the same time, if the victim makes a clear request not to be granted any reparation after being notified, the Court should bear in mind not to make individual reparation in respect of such a victim pursuant to Rule 95 (2) RPE.

4.2.2.3 Scope of Rights of Victims in the Reparation Proceedings

The legal standing of the victims in the reparation proceedings is much "better" and the scope of the rights of victims at this stage is much broader than in the penal proceedings before the ICC. However, the rights of the victims at the reparation stage are not strictly statutorily enshrined. Similar to Article 68(3) RS, Article 75 of the Rome Statue mentions the participation of the victims in general at this stage.[309] Analysing Article 75 RS, it is possible to determine that the victims have a general right to participate in the reparation stage. This was stressed by the Trial Chamber in the case of *Lubanga* recalling that the victims and their families have to be granted all necessary possibilities to participate throughout the reparation process.[310] Parallel to this, the Chamber highlighted that the victims have the right to be supported by the Registry.[311] Similar to the representations of the interested persons with regard to the reparations in accordance with Article 75(3) RS, the victims also have the right to make their own representations, which at the same time have to be taken into account by the Court. Unlike the preceding penal proceedings, the victims are entitled through their legal representatives, if permitted by the Court, to question the witnesses and experts and other persons involved without any limitations in accordance with Rule 91 (4) RPE.

---

[308] See ICC, *Prosecutor v. Lubanga*, ICC-01/04-01/06-2953, Decision on the admissibility of the appeals against Trial Chamber I's Decision establishing the principles and procedures to be applied to reparations" and directions on the further conduct of proceedings (14 December 2012) para. 187, Ferstman (2017), p. 400.

[309] ICC, *Prosecutor v. Lubanga*, ICC-01/04-01/06-2953, Decision on the admissibility of the appeals against Trial Chamber I's Decision establishing the principles and procedures to be applied to reparations" and directions on the further conduct of proceedings (14 December 2012) para. 181.

[310] ICC, *Prosecutor v. Lubanga*, ICC-01/04-01/06-2953, Decision on the admissibility of the appeals against Trial Chamber I's Decision establishing the principles and procedures to be applied to reparations" and directions on the further conduct of proceedings (14 December 2012) para. 203.

[311] See e.g. Regulation 110 RoR.

Pursuant to Article 75 (6) RS, decisions on reparations by the Court may not operate to prejudice the rights of the victims under national and international law, at the same time the decisions by other bodies do not affect the rights of victims to receive reparations pursuant to Article 75 RS. However, the Court may take into account any other awards or benefits given by other bodies. This should help the Court to guarantee that reparations are not applied unfairly or in a discriminatory manner.[312] Even if victims received reparations from the Court, the states are not hampered from awarding reparations in accordance with the other treaties or national regulations.[313]

Furthermore, the victims have the right to withdraw from the reparation order pursuant to the Rule 95 (2) (b) RPE, in which case the Court is obligated not to proceed to make an individual order in respect of that victim. The Court is, at the same time, bound to the fact that before making a decision or taking any action on its own motion it must respect the rights of the victims pursuant to the Rule 97 (3) RPE.

The important element which makes the victims in the reparation proceedings incomparably stronger is the right to appeal the reparation orders pursuant to Article 82 (4) RS.[314] The Appeals Chamber noted in the case of *Lubanga* that the right to appeal lies with the victims and not with the Legal Representatives of the Victims. Furthermore, the appeal could be brought only with the assistance of LRVs.[315]

In relation to Rule 153 RPE, Article 82 (4) RS enables not only the victims participating in the penal proceedings to lodge the appeal against the reparation order, but also those individuals who claimed reparations in this distinct stage or were affected adversely by the reparation order.[316] The latter also includes those victims who participated in the penal proceedings but who did not claim reparations in the reparation proceedings. This uncertainty is bound to the term "victims" at the

---

[312]ICC, *Prosecutor v. Lubanga*, ICC-01/04-01/06-2953, Decision on the admissibility of the appeals against Trial Chamber I's Decision establishing the principles and procedures to be applied to reparations" and directions on the further conduct of proceedings (14 December 2012) para. 201, see in this regard Donat-Cattin (2016) Rn. 28, p. 1868.

[313]In relation to Article 25(4) of the Rome Statute, ICC, *Prosecutor v. Katanga*, ICC-01/04-01/07-3728-tENG, Order for Reparations pursuant to Article 75 of the Statute (24 March 2017) para. 323.

[314]This way the victims get the standing of the party in the reparation order, see ICC, *Prosecutor v. Lubanga*, ICC-01/04-01/06-2953, Decision on the admissibility of the appeals against Trial Chamber I's Decision establishing the principles and procedures to be applied to reparations" and directions on the further conduct of proceedings (14 December 2012) para. 67.

[315]ICC, *Prosecutor v. Lubanga*, ICC-01/04-01/06-2953, Decision on the admissibility of the appeals against Trial Chamber I's Decision establishing the principles and procedures to be applied to reparations" and directions on the further conduct of proceedings (14 December 2012) para. 67.

[316]The Prosecutor is not a party to the reparation proceedings; therefore the prosecutor is not in position to bring an appeal against the reparation order, ICC, *Prosecutor v. Lubanga*, ICC-01/04-01/06-2953, Decision on the admissibility of the appeals against Trial Chamber I's Decision establishing the principles and procedures to be applied to reparations" and directions on the further conduct of proceedings (14 December 2012) para. 74.

reparation stage which is not strictly defined statutorily.[317] In response to the OPCV's view that it also represents those unidentified victims who will benefit from the collective reparation, the Appeals Chamber determined that it is not possible to consider unidentified victims for the right to appeal because the Appeals Chamber cannot discern who will belong to that group due to a lack of criteria.[318]

4.2.3 Determination of Award and Liability

Neither the Rome Statute nor the Rules of the Court give any guidance to the Court for the determination of specified individual and collective reparations other than in the case of sentencing.[319] Since the establishment of the Court, only three reparation orders have been issued to date:

- *Katanga*, from 24 March 2017 by the Trial Chamber II and amended by the Judgment on Appeal from 8 March 2018,
- *Al Mahdi* from 17 August 2017 by the Trial Chamber VIII and amended by the Judgment on Appeal form 8 March 2018,
- *Lubanga* from 3 March 2015 and amended by the decision from 15 December 2017 by the Trial Chamber II and confirmed by the Judgment on Appeal from 18 July 2019.

Although the Appeals Chamber in the *Lubanga* case also tried to establish guidance for the upcoming reparation orders, it is difficult to standardise the concept of the remedy and the determination of the awards in the above-mentioned orders. In some respect, these awaited orders disappointed the victims who had been participating in the proceedings from the first case before the ICC. Nevertheless, taking into account the individual circumstances of each case and the damage caused to the victims, and analyzing the concepts of reparation orders against *Lubanga* and *Katanga*, which generally have similar elements, it is not possible to determine the grounds for the reparation awards to the victims in the reparation order against *Al Mahdi*. All three convicted persons where recognised by the Court as being

[317] ICC, *Prosecutor v. Lubanga*, ICC-01/04-01/06-2953, Decision on the admissibility of the appeals against Trial Chamber I's Decision establishing the principles and procedures to be applied to reparations" and directions on the further conduct of proceedings (14 December 2012) paras. 68–71.

[318] ICC, *Prosecutor v. Lubanga*, ICC-01/04-01/06-2953, Decision on the admissibility of the appeals against Trial Chamber I's Decision establishing the principles and procedures to be applied to reparations" and directions on the further conduct of proceedings (14 December 2012) para. 72, see also Nerlich (2016), Rn. 26, p. 1963, cf. ICC, *Prosecutor v. Lubanga*, ICC-01/04-01/06-3129, Judgment on the appeals against the "Decision establishing the principles and procedures to be applied to reparations" of 7 August 2012 with Amended order for reparations (Annex A) and public annexes (3 March 2015) para. 68.

[319] Cf. Article 77 of the Rome Statute.

indigent.[320] All three Chambers have held the position that the indigence may not reflect upon the reparation order as such, recalling the Appeals Chamber's determination that the financial situation of the convicted person is not an obstacle to the imposition of financial liability for proportionate[321] reparations to that person.[322] Rule 97 (1) RPE provides that the Chamber has to take into account the scope and extent of any damage, but not the personal financial situation of the convicted person.[323]

4.2.3.1 Order Against Al Mahdi

The determination of reparation in the *Al Mahdi* case is relatively obvious compared to the other cases before the ICC, as it does not deal with the physical damage to persons, but rather to the economic loss of the residents of the cultural city. 139 victims participated in the reparation procedure.

4.2.3.1.1 Order and Conviction

Al Mahdi was convicted as a co-perpetrator pursuant to Article 25 (3) (a) RS for the organisation of the attack on the ten Protected Buildings (monuments and one mosque) and for the direct participation in the attacks on five of the Protected Buildings pursuant to Article 8 (2)(e)(iv) RS. Therefore, the reparation order is bound only to the damage caused by the attacks on the Protected Buildings.[324] Other harm done during the occupation to the other cultural heritage of the city may not be taken into account within the reparation order against Al Mahdi.

---

[320]ICC, *Prosecutor v. Katanga*, ICC-01/04-01/07-3728-tENG, Order for Reparations pursuant to Article 75 of the Statute (24 March 2017) para. 246, ICC, *Prosecutor v. Al Mahdi*, ICC-01/12-01/15, Reparation Order (17 August 2017) para. 138, ICC, *Prosecutor v. Lubanga*, ICC-01/04-01/06-3379-Red-Corr-tENG, Corrected version of the"Decision Setting the Size of the Reparations Award for which Thomas Lubanga Dyilo is Liable (21 December 2017) para. 283.

[321]E.g. ICC, *Prosecutor v. Katanga*, ICC-01/04-01/07-3728-tENG, Order for Reparations pursuant to Article 75 of the Statute (24 March 2017) para. 264.

[322]ICC, *Prosecutor v. Lubanga*, ICC-01/04-01/06-3129, Judgment on the appeals against the "Decision establishing the principles and procedures to be applied to reparations" of 7 August 2012 with Amended order for reparations (Annex A) and public annexes (3 March 2015) para. 103.

[323]ICC, *Prosecutor v. Al Mahdi*, ICC-01/12-01/15, Reparation Order (17 August 2017) para. 114.

[324]The mausoleum Sidi Mahmoud Ben Omar Mohamed Aquit, the mausoleum Sheikh Mohamed Mahmoud Al Arawani, the mausoleum Sheikh Sidi Mokhtar Ben Sidi Muhammad Ben Sheikh Alkabir, the mausoleum Alpha Moya, the mausoleum Sheikh Sidi Ahmed Ben Amar Arragadi, the mausoleum Sheikh Muhammad El Micky, the mausoleum Cheick Abdoul Kassim Attouaty, the mausoleum Ahamed Fulane, the mausoleum Bahaber Babadié, and Sidi Yahia mosque.

4.2.3.1.2 Reparation Type

In determining the type of reparations, the Court distinguished the fact that the Protected Buildings damaged by Al Mahdi belonged to the entire community of the cultural city and their loss was felt by the community as a whole. Therefore, the Chamber considered collective reparations as the most appropriate way to address the damage.[325]

The Trial Chamber did not consider a further apology to certain victims necessary, as it deemed the general and collective apology of the convicted person for the property damage to be genuine, categorical and empathetic.[326] However, the Chamber stressed that the reparation order and the judgments should be widely accessible for the other victims pursuant to Rule 96 RPE.[327]

In order to determine the reparation modality for the consequential loss of the victims of the cultural city, the Court considered that the harm caused by the convicted person was primarily collective in character. This was much larger and of a different nature than the harm suffered by the 139 applicants/victims who claimed for individual compensation for the loss of economic income. In this regard, the Chamber found it more equitable to use individual reparations to compensate the victims on the basis of the extent of the harm suffered, rather than solely on whether a victim had applied for reparations.[328] However, distinguishing the fact that the whole community was economically affected, the individual reparations for the applicants before the Court may have caused frustration among the other community members who did not apply for compensation. Accordingly, the Court found it appropriate to compensate only those whose livelihoods exclusively depended upon the Protected Buildings. As the scope of the direct beneficiaries was not determined, the Appeals Chamber stressed that the applicants for individual reparations should be able to contest before the Trial Chamber the decision taken by the Trust Fund for

---

[325] ICC, *Prosecutor v. Al Mahdi*, ICC-01/12-01/15, Reparation Order (17 August 2017) para. 67.

[326] ICC, *Prosecutor v. Al Mahdi*, ICC-01/12-01/15, Reparation Order (17 August 2017) para. 70, "*I am really sorry, I am really remorseful and I regret all the damage that my actions have caused. I regret what I have caused to my family, my community in Timbuktu, what I have caused my home nation, Mali, and I'm really remorseful about what I had caused the international community as a whole*", see ICC, *Prosecutor v. Al Mahdi*, ICC-01/12-01/15, Judgement and Sentence (27 September 2016) paras. 103–105, ICC, *Prosecutor v. Al Mahdi*, Transcript of Hearing (22 August 2016) p. 8, Cohen (2020b), p. 146.

[327] ICC, *Prosecutor v. Al Mahdi*, ICC-01/12-01/15, Reparation Order (17 August 2017) para. 71, cf. Balta and Banteka (2017).

[328] ICC, *Prosecutor v. Al Mahdi*, ICC-01/12-01/15, Reparation Order (17 August 2017) para. 79, cf. ICC, *Prosecutor v. Al Mahdi*, ICC-01/12-01/15-190-Conf, Public redacted version of "Submissions of the Legal Representative of Victims on the principles and forms of the right to reparation" dated 2 December 2016 (3 January 2017) paras. 38–43.

Victims on their eligibility for individual reparations and the Trial Chamber was in a position to make a final determination in that respect.[329]

At the same time, the Trial Chamber also considered collective reparation for the community of the cultural city as a whole aiming at rehabilitating the community. This included such activities as educational and awareness-raising programs, resettlement programs and microcredit systems assisting the community in generating income.[330]

The Trial Chamber recognised that the destruction and damage of the Protected Buildings caused emotional distress among the community members. Therefore, it found that the crime committed by the convicted person was both the actual and proximate cause of the moral harm, arguing that it was reasonably foreseeable that attacking the property would cause emotional distress among community members.[331] The Court considered, at this stage, to implement again both individualised and collective reparations for the moral harm, particularly, in determining the award of individual reparations to those victims whose ancestors' burial sites were damaged in the attack, as they had a different emotional connection to the destroyed sites than the rest of the cultural city.[332] In order to address the emotional distress suffered as a result of the attack on the Protected Buildings, the building of memorials and the organising commemoration or forgiveness ceremonies was considered.[333]

4.2.3.1.3 Restoration to the Protected Buildings

With the support of the experts, the Court determined that the restoration of the Protected Buildings damaged by *Al Mahdi* amounted to 97,000 EUR[334] and set the liability for that harm at 97,000 EUR.

[329]ICC, *Prosecutor v. Al Mahdi*, ICC-01/12-01/15-190-Conf, Public redacted version of "Submissions of the Legal Representative of Victims on the principles and forms of the right to reparation" dated 2 December 2016 (3 January 2017) para. 70.

[330]ICC, *Prosecutor v. Al Mahdi*, ICC-01/12-01/15, Reparation Order (17 August 2017) paras. 80–83.

[331]ICC, *Prosecutor v. Al Mahdi*, ICC-01/12-01/15, Reparation Order (17 August 2017) paras. 86–87.

[332]ICC, *Prosecutor v. Al Mahdi*, ICC-01/12-01/15, Reparation Order (17 August 2017) paras. 89–90.

[333]ICC, *Prosecutor v. Al Mahdi*, ICC-01/12-01/15, Reparation Order (17 August 2017) paras 90.

[334]UNESCO have spent over 2.53 million euros in rebuilding the cultural city's mausoleums and rehabilitation of the mosques and libraries, however the amount included not only the mentioned ten buildings, which were damaged by *Al Mahdi*, the experts could determine the exact amount of the restoration of only those ten Buildings, see ICC, *Prosecutor v. Al Mahdi*, ICC-01/12-01/15, Reparation Order (17 August 2017) paras. 116–118.

4.2.3.1.4 Economic Loss of the Victims

In order to determine the amount of economic loss, the Chamber appointed experts who arrived at a total amount of economic harm of over 44.6 million EUR from the time of the attack until the reconstruction efforts were completed in 2015. The experts also mentioned that there are further interlinked causes for the economic losses, such as the loss of tourism, transportation difficulties and security concerns. The Court, however, did not find that this amount was the exact amount for which the convicted person may be held liable. First, it determined that the amount included not only the losses of the cultural city of Timbuktu, but also the city of Bamako, for which the convicted person was not responsible. Second, it excluded the costs and expenses for the work during the reconstruction as it had already been considered by the reparation for the damage to the Protected Buildings and also the transportation and tourists costs.[335] Taking into account these reductions, the Court established the liability of the convicted person for consequential economic loss at 2.12 million EUR.[336]

4.2.3.1.5 Moral Harm

Bearing in mind the similar case in the Eritrea Ethiopia Claims Commission, where an award of 23,000 USD was considered for the mental harm reflected to the damage of the Stela of Matara,[337] the Court applied the aforementioned methodology to the case at hand, taking into account inflation, the conversion into euros and the number of damaged buildings. Accordingly, it concluded that the liability of the convicted person for the mental harm was 483,000 EUR.

4.2.3.1.6 Total Liability

The total liability for Al Mahdi for the harm caused amounted to 2.7 million EUR.[338] The convicted person is, however, not liable for the administrative implementation costs.

[335]See ICC, *Prosecutor v. Al Mahdi*, ICC-01/12-01/15, Reparation Order (17 August 2017) paras. 121–127.

[336]See ICC, *Prosecutor v. Al Mahdi*, ICC-01/12-01/15, Reparation Order (17 August 2017) para. 128.

[337]Cf. Reports Of International arbitral Awards, Eritrea-Ethiopia Claims Commission - Partial Award: Central Front - Eritrea's Claims 2,4,6, 7,8, & 22, 28 April 2004, p. 150, para. 114, Crawford (2017), p. 210, Starrenburg (2017).

[338]ICC, *Prosecutor v. Al Mahdi*, ICC-01/12-01/15-190-Conf, Public redacted version of "Submissions of the Legal Representative of Victims on the principles and forms of the right to reparation" dated 2 December 2016 (3 January 2017) paras. 130–132.

4.2.3.2 Order Against Katanga

The order against *Katanga* was the first ever reparation order issued by the ICC since its establishment. 341 victims applied for participation in the reparation procedure against *Katanga*, however, only 297 victims were able to demonstrate "*on the balance of probabilities*" that they were victims of the crimes for which *Katanga* had been convicted.

4.2.3.2.1 Order and Conviction

Katanga was convicted as an accessory pursuant to Article 25(3)(d) RS to the crimes committed on 24 February 2003 of murder as a crime against humanity under Article 7(1)(a) RS, murder as a war crime under Article 8 (2) (c) (i) RS, an attack against civilian population as such or against individual civilians not taking direct part in hostilities, as a war crime under Article 8 (2) (e) (i) RS, destruction of enemy property as a war crime under Article 8 (2) (e) (xii) RS and pillaging as a war crime under Article 8 (2) (e) (v) RS. The charges of rape and sexual violence, as well as using of children under the age of 15 years in hostilities, were not confirmed. Accordingly, the reparations are granted only for the offences of which Katanga was convicted.

4.2.3.2.2 Reparation Type

In determination of the type reparation, the Court highlighted and agreed with the submissions of the LRVs and the Defense that individual reparations ensure that the victim does not feel excluded, marginalised or further stigmatised, as each victims suffered individually as a result of the attack.[339] The individual reparations will allow the victims to regain their economic self-sufficiency and to make decisions for themselves on the basis of their needs. Although the parties agreed to grant the victims a symbolic one euro compensation amount,[340] the Trial Chamber considered it appropriate to increase the amount of symbolic damages, which is not aimed at being compensation for the harm entirely, but to create a space for the victim to purchase tools or livestock or to set up a small business.[341]

With regard to collective reparations, the Trial Chamber stressed that the majority of the victims lived in Bogoro, where the crimes were perpetrated, and even though

[339] ICC, *Prosecutor v. Katanga*, ICC-01/04-01/07-3728-tENG, Order for Reparations pursuant to Article 75 of the Statute (24 March 2017) paras. 282–285.

[340] ICC, *Prosecutor v. Katanga*, Victims' Proposals (8 December 2016) paras. 10–19, ICC, *Prosecutor v. Katanga*, Defence Response (30 December 2016) paras. 4–6.

[341] ICC, *Prosecutor v. Katanga*, ICC-01/04-01/07-3728-tENG, Order for Reparations pursuant to Article 75 of the Statute (24 March 2017) para. 300.

each individual did not suffer the same harm, all the residents of Bogora perceived themselves as a part of a group subjected to the attack. Accordingly, the Trial Chamber considered them under collective reparations.[342] The Trial Chamber determined that it is appropriate to award collective reparations which are designed to benefit each victim so as to provide a meaningful remedy.[343] The victims rejected any collective symbolic reparations, such as commemoration, or broadcast of the trials or other similar measures, arguing that they are useless or may cause fresh trauma or exacerbate social unrest. In contrast, they mainly focused on the financial and development programs which would provide an efficacious remedy for the harm suffered. This included support in housing, in income-generating activities, education and psychological assistance. This was confirmed by the Trial Chamber highlighting that these reparations designed to benefit each victim must include clear and sufficient explanations to inform victims of and foster their trust in the measures.[344]

4.2.3.2.3 Material Harm

In consultation with the domestic organisations, the Trial Chamber concluded by considering a minimum figure for the economic damage:[345]

Destruction or pillaging of	Value
House	600 USD
Outbuildings	100 USD
Furniture	500 USD per house
Personal effects	75 USD per person
Business premises (restaurant)	800 USD
Business premises (hotel)	3000 USD
Wares of a business premises	100 USD
Cow	400 USD
Goat	50 USD
Hen	8 USD
Livestock	524 USD
Fields and harvests	150 USD per applicant

[342] ICC, *Prosecutor v. Katanga*, ICC-01/04-01/07-3728-tENG, Order for Reparations pursuant to Article 75 of the Statute (24 March 2017) para. 288.

[343] ICC, *Prosecutor v. Katanga*, ICC-01/04-01/07-3728-tENG, Order for Reparations pursuant to Article 75 of the Statute (24 March 2017) para. 289.

[344] ICC, *Prosecutor v. Katanga*, ICC-01/04-01/07-3728-tENG, Order for Reparations pursuant to Article 75 of the Statute (24 March 2017) paras. 301–306.

[345] ICC, *Prosecutor v. Katanga*, ICC-01/04-01/07-3728-tENG, Order for Reparations pursuant to Article 75 of the Statute (24 March 2017) paras. 193–222.

4.2.3.2.4 Physical Harm

Two applicants were claiming reparation for the physical harm caused by bullet wounds, however, as the Trial Chamber was not in a position to be able to determine the precise figure for that harm, it set an award *ex aequo et bono* at 250 USD.[346]

4.2.3.2.5 Mental Harm

Examining the international practice of compensation for psychological harm, the Court distinguished between two types of harm arising from psychological distress. On the one hand, there is the mental harm bound to the personal experience of the attack and, on the other hand, the harm arising from the death of close and distant relatives. Under close relatives, the Court considered the spouse, parents, children, grandparents and grandchildren.[347]

Psychological harm because of death of or	Reparation award
Close relative	8000 USD
Other relative	4000 USD
Own experience of the attack	2000 USD

4.2.3.2.6 Total Liability

Although the Court assessed the total monetary value of the harm suffered by the 297 victims to be 3,752,620 USD, it held Katanga liable for 1,000,000 USD. The decision of the Court was bound to the principle set out by the Appeals Chamber that the liability for reparation of the convicted person must be proportionate to the harm caused and their participation in the commission of the crimes for which they were found guilty in the specific circumstances of the case.[348] Bearing in mind that Katanga was found guilty as an accessory for his contribution pursuant to Article 25(3)(d) RS,[349] the Trial Chamber noted that the liability of Katanga should be

[346]ICC, *Prosecutor v. Katanga*, ICC-01/04-01/07-3728-tENG, Order for Reparations pursuant to Article 75 of the Statute (24 March 2017) para. 226.

[347]ICC, *Prosecutor v. Katanga*, ICC-01/04-01/07-3728-tENG, Order for Reparations pursuant to Article 75 of the Statute (24 March 2017) paras. 227–239, see also ICC, *Prosecutor v. Katanga*, ICC-01/04-01/07-3778-Red, Public redacted Judgment on the appeals against the order of Trial Chamber II of 24 March 2017 entitled "Order for Reparations pursuant to Article 75 of the Statute" (9 March 2018) para. 126.

[348]ICC, *Prosecutor v. Lubanga*, ICC-01/04-01/06-3129, Judgment on the appeals against the "Decision establishing the principles and procedures to be applied to reparations" of 7 August 2012 with Amended order for reparations (Annex A) and public annexes (3 March 2015) para.118.

[349]ICC, *Prosecutor v. Katanga,* ICC-01/04-01/07, Judgment pursuant to article 74 of the Statute (7 March 2014) paras. 658–659.

considered under his contribution in the context of a criminal purpose harbored by many other persons.[350] Therefore, there is an assumption that a plurality of persons potentially bears responsibility for having contributed to the commission of crimes which caused harm to the victims.[351]

4.2.3.3 Order against Lubanga

Although the case of *Lubanga* is the first case before the ICC since its establishment, and although since 2012 the Court has established jurisprudence on this matter and on the entire reparation procedure of the Court, the reparation order against Lubanga of 21 December 2017 was confirmed by the appeal judgment of 18 July 2019. 425 victims from 473 potentially eligible victims have shown on the balance of probabilities that they are direct or indirect victims of the crimes for which Lubanga was convicted.

4.2.3.3.1 Order and Conviction

Lubanga was found guilty for co-perpetration pursuant to Article 25 (3) (a) RS of war crimes, of conscripting and enlisting children under 15 years old into the military units and of using them to participate actively in hostilities from 1 September 2002 to 13 August 2003, punishable under Article 8 (2) (e) (vii) RS. Accordingly, the reparations may be directed only to those child victims who were enrolled in the military activities within the aforementioned time frame. Despite the fact that some child soldiers were enlisted before this time frame does not obviously mean that they cannot be considered under the reparations, as the main point is the participation or usage of child soldiers under 15 years of age in the military activities during this time frame.[352]

[350]ICC, *Prosecutor v. Katanga*, ICC-01/04-01/07-3728-tENG, Order for Reparations pursuant to Article 75 of the Statute (24 March 2017) paras. 251–263.

[351]ICC, *Prosecutor v. Katanga*, ICC-01/04-01/07-3728-tENG, Order for Reparations pursuant to Article 75 of the Statute (24 March 2017) para. 263, see also ICC, *Prosecutor v. Katanga*, ICC-01/04-01/07-3778-Red, Public redacted Judgment on the appeals against the order of Trial Chamber II of 24 March 2017 entitled "Order for Reparations pursuant to Article 75 of the Statute" paras. 181–186.

[352]See ICC, *Prosecutor v. Lubanga*, ICC-01/04-01/06-3379-Red-Corr-tENG, Corrected version of the"Decision Setting the Size of the Reparations Award for which Thomas Lubanga Dyilo is Liable (21 December 2017) paras. 92–94.

4.2.3.3.2 Reparation Type

Compared to the cases of *Katanga* and *Al Mahdi*, the Trial Chamber found it appropriate to consider only collective reparations for the victims, recalling the determination approved by the Trial Chamber in the case of *Katanga* that the beneficiaries of collective reparations may not only be a group of persons bound by ethnicity, race, political or religious beliefs, but also be bound to the collective harm and shared experience of suffering. Therefore, the Trial Chamber identified the similar characteristics of the group of 425 victims participating in the reparations in *Lubanga* as a collective beneficiary of the reparations.[353] At the same time, the Trial Chamber highlighted the fact that the number of victims of the crimes for which Lubanga was convicted far exceeded the 425 persons. The Chamber found that it was also difficult to determine the exact number of all victims, but presumed the existence of approximately 2451 potential victims of the crimes committed by Lubanga.[354] The Trial Chamber stated that further potential victims may be identified at the implementation stage.[355]

4.2.3.3.3 Harm

Although the Trial Chamber stated that each victim suffered individually, it did not determine the specific harm of every single victim, but rather it applied a presumption of existing harm as soon as the status of child soldier or the close relationship to the direct victim was able to be established.[356] Bearing in mind that many other victims of the crimes mentioned were still eligible for reparations at the implementation stage, the Chamber did not proceed to assess the separate monetary value of

[353] ICC, *Prosecutor v. Katanga*, ICC-01/04-01/07, Judgment pursuant to article 74 of the Statute (7 March 2014) para. 274, see ICC, *Prosecutor v. Lubanga*, ICC-01/04-01/06-3379-Red-Corr-tENG, Corrected version of the"Decision Setting the Size of the Reparations Award for which Thomas Lubanga Dyilo is Liable (21 December 2017) paras. 193–194.

[354] ICC, *Prosecutor v. Lubanga*, ICC-01/04-01/06-3379-Red-Corr-tENG, Corrected version of the"Decision Setting the Size of the Reparations Award for which Thomas Lubanga Dyilo is Liable (21 December 2017) paras. 211–212, 229. The Trial Chamber estimated a calculation in order to find out how many children could be possibly be involved in the hostilities. Another calculation resulted of the possible existence of 5938 potential victims of crimes of Lubanga.

[355] The Appeals Chamber ruled that the victims who were denied participation at the reparation stage may still seek for reparations in the course of implementation stage, see ICC, *Prosecutor v. Lubanga*, Judgment on the appeals against Trial Chamber II's 'Decision Setting the Size of the Reparations Award for which Thomas Lubanga Dyilo is Liable' (18 July 2019) paras 170–174.

[356] ICC, *Prosecutor v. Lubanga*, Judgment on the appeals against Trial Chamber II's 'Decision Setting the Size of the Reparations Award for which Thomas Lubanga Dyilo is Liable' (18 July 2019) para. 247.

the individual harm suffered by each victim.[357] Analyzing the established national practice on reparations and the practice in the case of *Katanga,* the Trial Chamber considered *ex æquo et bono* harm suffered by direct or indirect victim to be 8000 USD.[358]

4.2.3.3.4 Total Liability

The Trial Chamber has set the total reparation award for which Lubanga is liable at 10,000,000 USD. In its determination, the Trial Chamber addressed the important role of the convicted person in the organisation and the gravity of his co-perpetration of enlisting and using boys and girls under the age of 15 in different military activities. It determined that 3,400,000 USD from the total amount are directed to reparations of the victims participating in the case at hand, the rest of the award (6,600,000 USD) is to be directed to the other potential victims, who are still, at this stage, not identified and might be identified during the implementation stage of reparations.[359]

4.2.3.4 Conclusion

These are the first cases in which the ICC has dealt with the reparation procedure. Since the establishment of the Court, the reparation process has been periodically discussed amongst scholars. Different theoretical scenarios have been designed to add color to a process which was never practiced before. Even if the awards for reparations are difficult to determine, it is even more difficult to implement them in practice. This has been shown by the practice of the national courts as well as international regional human rights courts.

Reparation award			
	Al Mahdi	Katanga	Lubanga
Crime	Destruction of cultural and religious property	Murder and destruction of property	Enlisting child soldiers and using them in the hostilities

(continued)

[357] ICC, *Prosecutor v. Lubanga*, Judgment on the appeals against Trial Chamber II's 'Decision Setting the Size of the Reparations Award for which Thomas Lubanga Dyilo is Liable' (18 July 2019) paras. 248–250.

[358] ICC, *Prosecutor v. Lubanga*, Judgment on the appeals against Trial Chamber II's 'Decision Setting the Size of the Reparations Award for which Thomas Lubanga Dyilo is Liable' (18 July 2019) para. 259.

[359] ICC, *Prosecutor v. Lubanga*, Judgment on the appeals against Trial Chamber II's 'Decision Setting the Size of the Reparations Award for which Thomas Lubanga Dyilo is Liable' (18 July 2019) paras. 277–280.

Reparation award			
	Al Mahdi	Katanga	Lubanga
Monetary value	2,700,000 EUR	1,000,000 USD	10,000,000 USD
Victims	139	297	425

4.2.4 Trust Fund for Victims

The Trust Fund for Victims completes the essential part of the reparation proceedings at the ICC. The first question to raise is whether the activities mentioned could be considered as part of the prosecutorial activity. Article 42 RS describes the functions of the OTP and excludes any further activity besides receiving referrals and any substantiated information on crimes within the jurisdiction of the Court, for examining them and for conducting investigations and prosecutions before the Court. It was also mentioned by the Trial Chamber that the OTP is not a part of the reparation proceedings. Therefore, the Trust Fund for Victims enters the proceedings within the meaning of the Article 79 RS. Although the Rome Statute mentions the Trust Fund, its establishment was as a result of the decision of the Assembly of States Parties pursuant to the Article 79 (1) RS. Two months later, after entering into force on 1 July 2002, the ASP established by resolution a fund for the benefit of victims of crimes within the jurisdiction of the Court, and of the families of such victims.[360] Accordingly, the newly established partly independent institution within the Court received two mandates. On the one hand, the implementation of the Court-ordered reparation in relation to the Article 75 (2) and Article 76 RS. On the other hand, the assistance mandate, which is considered for the rehabilitation of the victims and their families for matters such as physical, psychological and material support, independent of the court proceedings. This leads to the question of when precisely, i.e. in which stage of the proceedings, the Trust Fund for the Victims comes into consideration. This is bound to the similar question of when precisely the victims may benefit from the reparations, considering the fact that in accordance with Article 75 (2) (3) RS and Rule 98 RPE, reparation orders may only be made after a conviction.[361] Therefore, as soon as the accused is convicted of the charges, the Trust Fund enters the proceedings in order to implement the reparation order afterwards. However, in order to practice its second mandate, namely the assistance mandate, the Trust Fund for Victims may be separately involved from the beginning of the proceedings.

[360]ASP-ICC, Resolution ICC-ASP/1/Res.6, Adopted at the 3rd plenary meeting, on 9 September 2002, by consensus.

[361]See Khan (2016), p. 1905, Rd. 7, the Article 79 of the Rome Statute does not explicitly mention the stage of involvement of the Trust Fund for Victims in the proceedings.

In their resolution, the State Parties determined that the funding of the TFV will be based on four main sources:[362]

- Voluntary contributions from any subject;
- Money and other property collected through the fines and forfeiture in accordance with the Article 79 (2) of the Rome Statue;
- Resources collected through awards for reparations in accordance with Rule 98 RPE; and
- Resources or other contributions decided upon by the ASP.

In the first years its existence, the Trust Fund within the Court was mainly busy with the organisation, management and structuring of its own institution as well as with drafting the regulations. Not until 2007 did it begin to practice its mandates. On 3 December 2005, the ASP, by approving the Regulations for the Trust Fund for Victims (RoTFV), agreed pursuant to Article 79 (3) RS on the criteria of management and structure of the institution, on receipt of funds and on its activities, projects and functions.

4.2.4.1 Structure

In its establishing resolution in 2002, the ASP appointed the Board of Directors (BoD) of the TFV which consisted of five members for a term of 3 years and which served in an individual capacity on a *pro bono* basis pursuant to Regulation 16 RoTFV.[363] The members of the BoD are elected by the ASP by consensus[364] and in consideration of the equitable geographical, gender and national representation. Another key criterion requires that members of the BoD "be of high moral character, impartiality and integrity and shall have competence in the assistance of victims of serious crimes."[365] The BoD, coordinated by the Chair and elected by the absolute majority of the members of the BoD according to Regulation 1 RoTVF, is directed by the ASP to meet at least once a year to establish and to direct the

[362]ICC-ASP, Resolution ICC-ASP/1/Res.6, Establishment of a fund for the benefit of victims of crimes within the jurisdiction of the Court, and of the families of such victims, Adopted at the 3rd plenary meeting, on 9 September 2002, by consensus, para. 2, codified by the Regulation 21 RoTVF.

[363]ICC-ASP, Resolution ICC-ASP/1/Res.6, Establishment of a fund for the benefit of victims of crimes within the jurisdiction of the Court, and of the families of such victims Adopted at the 3rd plenary meeting, on 9 September 2002, by consensus, Annex to Resolution, paras. 1–2.

[364]See ICC-ASP, Resolution ICC-ASP/1/Res.7, Procedure for the nomination and election of members of the Board of Directors of the Trust Fund for the benefit of victims, Adopted at the 3rd plenary meeting, on 9 September 2002, by consensus, one seat from: African States, Asian States, Eastern Europe, Group of Latin American and Caribbean States, Western European and Other States.

[365]ICC-ASP, Resolution ICC-ASP/1/Res.6, Establishment of a fund for the benefit of victims of crimes within the jurisdiction of the Court, and of the families of such victims, Adopted at the 3rd plenary meeting, on 9 September 2002, by consensus, Annex to Resolution, para. 3.

activities and projects of the Trust Fund and the allocations of the property and money available to it.[366] The BoD is assisted by the Secretariat established by the ASP on 10 September 2004 attached to the Registry of the Court.[367] Along with the supportive function of the Secretariat for the proper functioning of the BoD, it still has a duty to provide periodic reports on the activities of the BoD in accordance with Regulations 17–19 RoTFV. Both the BoD and the Secretariat are independent organs. In its relationship with the ICC, the Trust Fund for Victims is considered as a partner covering three different dimensions, as an independent expert body during judicial proceedings and as the implementing and funding agency.[368]

4.2.4.2 Funding Sources

The funding sources of the Fund are the voluntarily contributions, money and property collected from fines or forfeiture pursuant to Article 79 (2) RS, resources collected pursuant to the Rule 98 RPE and other resources.

4.2.4.2.1 Voluntarily Contributions

The fund is open to receive any amount of contributions from governments, international organisations, individuals, corporations and other entities. The BoD, with the support of the Secretariat, establishes contact with donors and designs the guidelines on how to solicit financial contributions. However, the sources of funding have to be verified and approved by the BoD.[369] In the event of the contributions contradicting the goals and the activities of the Trust Fund, the BoD is in position to refuse them. At the same time, the BoD also has to refuse those contributions which would result in a manifestly inequitable distribution of available funds and property among the different groups of victims.[370] Another reason why the BoD has to take negative decisions in response to voluntary contributions relates to those

---

[366] ICC-ASP, Resolution ICC-ASP/1/Res.6, Establishment of a fund for the benefit of victims of crimes within the jurisdiction of the Court, and of the families of such victims, Adopted at the 3rd plenary meeting, on 9 September 2002, by consensus, Annex to Resolution, para. 7, see Regulation Regulation 3–11 RoTFV.

[367] ICC-ASP, Resolution ICC-ASP/3/Res.7, Establishment of the Secretariat of the Trust Fund for Victims, Adopted at the 6th plenary meeting, on 10 September 2004, by consensus, para. 1, see also ICC-ASP, ICC-ASP/3/14/Rev.1, Report to the Assembly of States Parties on the activities and projects of the Board of Directors of the Trust Fund for Victims, 2003–2004, p. 15.

[368] ICC, *Prosecutor v. Lubanga,* ICC-01/04-01/06-3430, Observations pursuant to rule 103 of the Rules of Procedure and Evidence (15 November 2018) para. 19.

[369] See Regulation Regulation 22–26 RoTVF.

[370] See ICC-ASP, Resolution ICC-ASP/1/Res.6, Establishment of a fund for the benefit of victims of crimes within the jurisdiction of the Court, and of the families of such victims, Adopted at the 3rd plenary meeting, on 9 September 2002, by consensus, Annex to the Resolution, paras. 9–10.

contributions which would jeopardise the institution's independence and would make it in any way in dependent. The BoD does not accept contributions which would breach Regulation 27 RoTFV, namely if the contribution were to result in discrimination on any ground.[371]

Even in the early stages of its establishment (2003), the Trust Fund received over 20,000 USD in voluntary contributions from the Republic of Namibia[372] as a state and from various individuals (799) and organisations (5).[373] From March 2003 to July 2020, 46 states made voluntary contributions to the Trust Fund for Victims. However, only a few governments from Asia[374] Latin America[375] and Africa[376] donated to the Fund. At the same time, it is important to note that the contributions to the Fund are not bound to the membership of the ASP, however, it still may have a political effect. In 2019, 29 states contributed 2,611,648 EUR to the Trust Fund for Victims,[377] which is the most active year of donating in 17 years. However, in 2013 the Trust Fund for Victims received 6,241,521 EUR in donations only from 20 contributing governments, predominantly from Sweden, the UK, the Netherlands and Germany.[378]

---

[371]See Regulation 30 RoTVF.

[372]First state contribution 500 USD, ICC itself contributed to the Trust Fund over 4.000 EUR.

[373]ICC-ASP, ICC-ASP/3/14/Rev.1, Report to the Assembly of States Parties on the activities and projects of the Board of Directors of the Trust Fund for Victims, 2003–2004, p. 27, contributions from 18 May 2003 to 15 July 2004.

[374]South Korea 365.909 EUR, Japan 853.452 EUR, Bangladesh 4.613 EUR, Philippines 4.049 EUR.

[375]Columbia 31.746 EUR, Uruguay 7.647 EUR.

[376]DRC, 2.223 EUR, Senegal 76.156 EUR, South Africa 45.000 EUR, Nigeria 16.909 EUR, Mali 17.062 EUR, Sierra Leone 2991 EUR.

[377]See ICC-ASP, ICC-ASP/19/14, Report to the Assembly of States Parties on the projects and the activities of the Board of Directors of the Trust Fund for Victims for the period 1 July 2019 to 30 June 2020, 16 September 2020.

[378]ICC-ASP, ICC-ASP/13/14, Report to the Assembly of States Parties on the projects and the activities of the Board of Directors of the Trust Fund for Victims for the period 1 July 2013 to 30 June 2014, 21 August 2014.

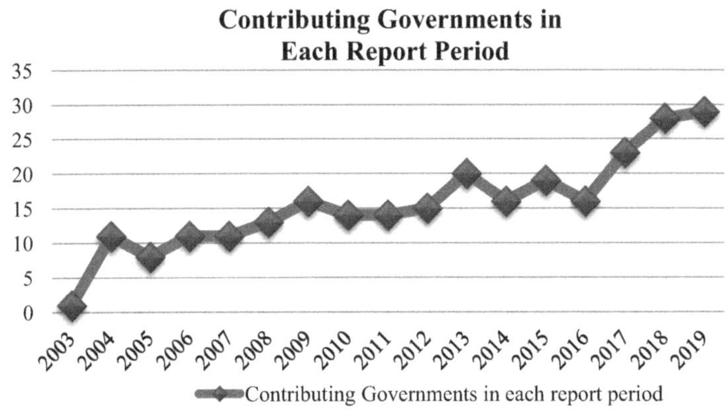

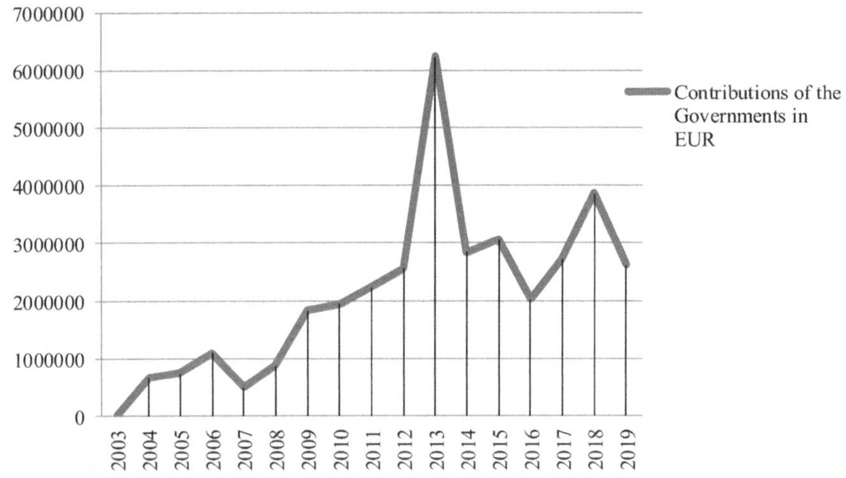

Over 17 years, the states contributing the most are Sweden, with over 9 million EUR, the UK and Germany with over 4 million EUR. Accordingly, the Trust Fund for Victims was able to collect over 35 million EUR in donations from governments in 17 years.

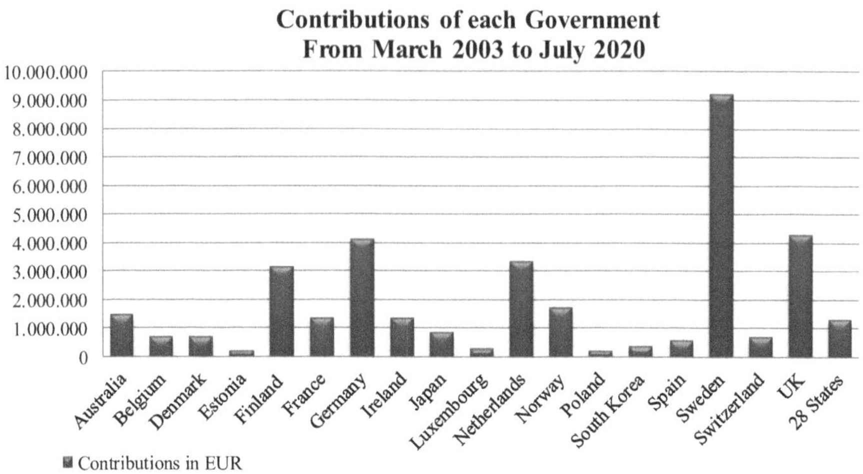

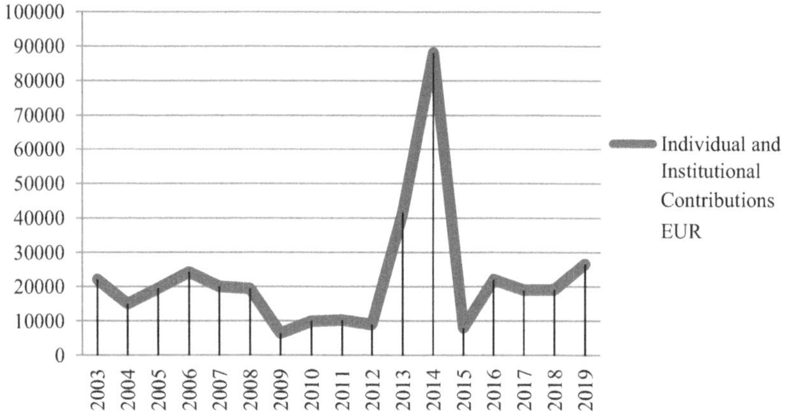

The individual and institutional contributions to the Trust Fund are, however, less than the contributions made by governments. In 17 years, the Secretariat was able to collect over 350,000 EUR in donations from individuals and organisations and it is true that the staff of the Court, both the judges as well as the employees of the Court, periodically participate in the donation campaign to the Trust Fund. Furthermore, the average individual and institutional contributions to the Court is approximately 20,000 EUR per year.[379]

[379]In 2014 because of the transfer from the PayPal account the amount of contributions were doubled, see the report ICC-ASP, ICC-ASP/12/14, Report to the Assembly of States Parties on the projects and the activities of the Board of Directors of the Trust Fund for Victims for the period 1 July 2012 to 30 June 2013, 31 July 2013.

4.2.4.2.2 Money and Property Collected from Fines or Forfeiture

Pursuant to Article 77 (2) (a) and (b) RS, the Court may order fines and the forfeiture of proceeds, property and assets in addition to imprisonment. This is, however, an optional penalty set by the Court in appropriate circumstances. During the drafting of the Rome Statute, there were still a number of uncertainties as to how the determination of a fine should be set by the Court.[380] In this regard, the delegates of the Rome Conference agreed upon Rule 146 RPE. In order to set the level of the fine, the Court should take into account several factors. First and foremost, it has to determine whether imprisonment is a sufficient penalty and to consider the financial situation of the convicted person. Furthermore, it has to take into account the damage and injuries caused by the convicted person. In order to avoid impossibly high fines, it was agreed to set a maximum possible amount in accordance with Rule 146 (2) RPE. This stipulates that the total amount of a fine imposed upon the convicted person may not exceed 75% of the value of the convicted person's identifiable property or other assets after the deduction of an appropriate amount that would satisfy the financial needs of that person. The convicted person is also given a reasonable period of time in which to pay the fines. In the event of the convicted person not paying the fine, the Presidency is allowed to extend the term of imprisonment in accordance with the provisions set out by Rule 146 (5)–(7) RPE.[381]

Another source of funding comes from Court-ordered forfeitures pursuant to Rule 147 RPE. In contrast to the fines, the order of forfeiture may be considered by the Court at any stage of the proceedings. The Court is also obligated to hear any evidence locating and identifying specific proceeds, property or assets which were derived directly or indirectly from the crime. As soon as an order of forfeiture is issued, the State Party must act in accordance with Article 109 RS. If the State Party is unable to give effect to the order, it is furthermore obliged to recover the value of the property, assets or proceeds ordered to be forfeited without prejudice to the rights of *bona fide* third parties.[382] Before transferring any money and property to the Trust Fund which has been collected through fines and forfeitures pursuant to Article 79 (2) RS, the Court may request the representatives of the Fund to submit observations in accordance with Rule 148 RPE and Regulation 31 RoTFV. In the cases of *Lubanga*, *Katanga* and *Al Mahdi*, no fines or forfeiture were ordered.[383]

---

[380] Fife 2016, Rd. 25–26, p. 1887.

[381] Cf. FIDH, Victims' Rights before the ICC, Reparations and the Trust Fund for Victims, 2007, p. 23.

[382] See also Abtahi and Koh (2012), p. 20.

[383] Guariglia et al. (2018), cf. ICC, *Prosecutor v. Kenyatta*, ICC-01/09-02/11-931, Decision on the implementation of the request to freeze assets (8 July 2014), ICC, *Prosecutor v. Bemba*, Decision on the Second Defence's Application for Lifting the Seizure of Assets and Request for Cooperation to the Competent Authorities of the Republic of Portugal (14 November 2008), ICC, *Prosecutor v. Bemba* et al. Decision on Mr. Kilolo's 'Notice of appeal against the decision of the Single Judge ICC-01/05-01/13-743-Conf-Exp' dated 10 November 2014 and on the urgent request for the partial lifting of the seizure on Mr. Kilolo's assets dated 24 November 2014 (1 December 2014).

4.2.4.2.3 Resources Collected Through Award of Reparations

Another source of funding for the Trust Fund for Victims is the award of reparation against the convicted person. Accordingly, a strict distinction must be made between the fines and the awards issued by the Court. The fine is optional and is an additional penalty imposed upon the convicted person whereas the award of reparation is, pursuant to the Rule 98 RPE, for the damage or injury caused by the convicted person. Pursuant to Regulation 34 RoTFV, the Trust Fund shall separate awards received from the remaining resources.

4.2.4.2.4 Other Sources

The Assembly of States Parties may allocate financial or other contributions to the Trust Fund if suggested by the BoD. However, where no such stipulation has been made by the ASP as to the uses of the financial or other contributions, the Trust Fund may, pursuant to the Regulation 35–36 RoTFV, allocate these contributions to its General Account for the benefit of victims. These sources, however, are unlikely to be all that significant in view of the limited resources.[384]

4.2.4.3 Activities and Projects

It is true that the functions, projects and activities in relation to the beneficiaries of the Trust Fund are bound to the sources of the funding. As previously mentioned, the beneficiaries of the resources of the Trust Fund are the victims of crimes within the jurisdiction of the Court in accordance with the Rule 85 RPE and Regulation 42 RoTFV. Accordingly, such resources which were collected through the fines or forfeiture and awards for reparations have to be directed towards the reparation of those victims who were affected as a consequence of the crimes for which the person was convicted. The use of other sources, such as voluntary governmental contributions pursuant to the Rule 98 (5) RPE, may be used for the reparations should the BoD, pursuant to Regulation 56 RoTFV, find it appropriate to do so. Thus, the Trust Fund for Victims has a dual mandate. Firstly, it has its reparation mandate and, secondly, the assistance mandate.

[384]See, FIDH, Victims' Rights before the ICC, Reparations and the Trust Fund for Victims, 2007, p. 24.

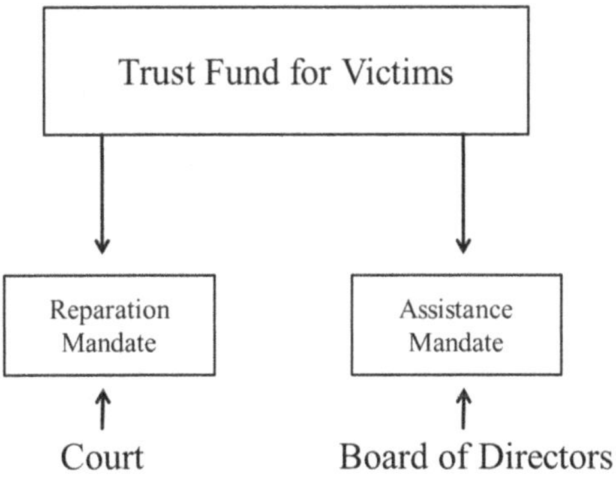

When providing its mandate, the Trust Fund for Victims is bound to the programmatic principles, such as:

- Supporting the advancement of women's human rights; increasing the participation of women and incorporating gender perspectives including addressing disparities; and the impact of sexual and gender-based violence in line with the Convention on the Elimination of All Forms of Discrimination against Women (CEDAW) and UNSC Resolutions on women, peace and security.
- Restoring dignity and promoting peace-building, community reconciliation, acceptance and social inclusion through conflict-prevention, the rebuilding of community safety nets, and the mitigation of stigma, discrimination and trauma.
- Supporting the rights of children affected by armed conflict by supporting intergenerational responses for integrating and rehabilitating former child soldiers and other war-affected youth in line with the UN Convention on the Rights of the Child (CRC).
- Developing and implementing communications and outreach initiatives for cultivating relationships, enhancing visibility, mobilising communities, changing attitudes, managing crisis, generating support and encouraging financial contributions.
- Based upon best practices and evidence-based programming, linking grant-making to technical and organisational capacity-building to strengthen quality and sustainability.
- Working with implementing partners to assess, mitigate and evaluate the likely environmental impact of a proposed project, taking into account interrelated socio-economic, cultural and human-health impacts, both beneficial and adverse.
- Facilitating action-learning through participatory planning, research, programming, monitoring and evaluation by safeguarding a dynamic, interactional, and transformative process between people, groups, and institutions that enables

victims both individually and collectively, to realise their full potential and to be engaged in their own redress.[385]

The fundamental implementation principle of the Trust Fund is the "do no harm" principle, which is aimed at not causing subsequent harm by assisting or repairing the damage caused by the crimes within the jurisdiction of the Court.

4.2.4.3.1 Assistance Mandate

Rule 98 (5) RPE enables the Trust Fund to provide field assistance activities if there are other resources available and approved by the BoD. Under such mandates, the Trust Fund for Victims may initiate activities, independent of the case pending before the ICC, to assist the victims affected by the crimes committed within the jurisdiction of the Court pursuant to Regulation 50 RoTVF. Accordingly, the assistance of the Trust Fund is directed to those situations at the ICC where investigations are ongoing and enables the victims and their families to receive support separately from and prior to a conviction by the Court.[386] These activities may include:

- Physical rehabilitation, aiming at supporting victims who have suffered physical injuries in order to recover and resume their roles as productive and contributive members of society. These activities include surgeries, the implementation of orthopedic and medical devices and implants, further medical assistance.[387]
- Psychological rehabilitation aimed at offering cost-effective health benefits. This also involves educating the population about the needs of victims and the resources available to assist in their recovery. The rehabilitation includes individual, family and group trauma counseling, psychological group workshops and community meetings.[388]
- Material support responds to the destruction of the property and the consequences of displacement and the loss of income-earning family members, which diminish the sources of livelihood and subsistence.[389] The projects include livelihood activities, income generation and training opportunities on economic activities.[390]

---

[385] ICC, TFV, Strategic Plan 2014–2017, 2014, pp. 20–25, cf. REDRESS, Comments to the Trust Fund for Victims on its Draft Strategic Plan 2014–2017, 2014.

[386] REDRESS, No Time to Wait, 2019, p. 30.

[387] ICC, TFV, Strategic Plan 2014–2017, 2014, p. 19.

[388] ICC, ASP, Report to the Assembly of States of Parties on the Projects and the Activities of the Board of Directors of the Trust Fund for Victims for the Period 1 July 2017 to 30 June 2018, paras. 58–77.

[389] ICC, TFV, Strategic Plan 2014–2017, 2014, p. 19.

[390] See Peschke (2013), p. 320, REDRESS, No Time to Wait, 2019, p. 30, Koller (2015), p. 86, ICC, TFV, Assistance and Reparations, Achievements, Lessons Learned and Transitioning, 2015 p. 9.

Bearing in mind the various groups of victims with different types of injuries, in its assistance mandate the Trust Fund has generally targeted those vulnerable victims who suffered sexual violence, whose partners were killed, children, orphans, those who suffered physical and psychological trauma and family and other members of the directs victims.[391] Another important role of the Trust Fund for Victims besides the assistance provided is the identification of the beneficiaries, namely the victims of the crimes within the jurisdiction of the Court. For that reason, the stakeholders who are involved in the identification of the victims are trained appropriately.[392]

Currently, the Trust Fund for the Victims is providing assistance in four Countries: the DRC,[393] Uganda,[394] Côte d'Ivoire[395] after the acquittal of Bemba, in the CAR,[396] Mali, Kenya and Georgia.[397] Since 2008, the Trust Fund for Victims has been providing its assistance mandate in the DRC and Uganda. In the notification to the Court, the BoD approved three categories of projects in both cases—physical, psychological and material - relying upon the activities of the intermediaries for 10 years.[398] Further assistance activities were approved by the BoD and

[391] See ICC, TFV, Assistance and Reparations, Achievements, Lessons Learned and Transitioning, 2015, p. 12.

[392] During the conduction one on one interviews the stakeholders have to inquire about the nature and circumstances of the individual injury, when the injury occurred, location of the incident, how it occur and what treatment the victims may receive. This will enable the stakeholders to analyse if the mentioned person could be fall under the eligibility of the victims pursuant to the Rule 85 RPE, cf. see ICC, TFV, Assistance and Reparations, Achievements, Lessons Learned and Transitioning, 2015 pp. 13–15.

[393] ICC, *Situation in DRC*, Notification of the Board of Directors of the Trust Fund for Victims in accordance with Regulation 50 of the Regulations of the Trust Fund for Victims with Confidential Annex, (24 January 2008).

[394] ICC, *Situation in Uganda*, Notification of the Board of Directors of the Trust Fund for Victims in accordance with Regulation 50 of the Regulations of the Trust Fund for Victims with Confidential Annex (25 January 2008).

[395] The assistance project will start in 2019, see M. Noguchi, Report of the Board of Directors of the Trust Fund for Victims, Seventh Session of Assembly of States Parties, 5 December 2018.

[396] ICC, *Situation in CAR*, Notification from the Board of Directors of the Trust Fund for Victims in accordance with Regulation 50 of the Regulations of the Trust Fund for Victims (30 October 2009), ICC, Situation in CAR, Notification by the Board of Directors in accordance with Regulation 50 a) of the Regulations of the Trust Fund for Victims to undertake activities in the Central African Republic (11 October 2012).

[397] ASP-ICC, ICC-ASP/19/14* Report to the Assembly of States Parties on the projects and the activities of the Board of Directors of the Trust Fund for Victims for the period 1 July 2019 to 30 June 2020 (16 September 2020) para. 65.

[398] ICC, *Situation in DRC*, Notification of the Board of Directors of the Trust Fund for Victims in accordance with Regulation 50 of the Regulations of the Trust Fund for Victims with Confidential Annex (24 January 2008) paras. 53–58, cf., ICC, TFV, Assistance and Reparations, Achievements, Lessons Learned and Transitioning, 2015 pp. 16–19, over 400.000 victims have benefited from the rehabilitation programs, see M. Noguchi, Report of the Board of Directors of the Trust Fund for Victims, Seventh Session of Assembly of States Parties, 5 December 2018.

appropriately notified to the Court in December 2018.[399] Although the assistance to the victims in the CAR has been provided since 2009, especially to victims who suffered sexual violence, the Trust Fund decided to relaunch the assistance program after the acquittal of Bemba, prioritising the victims who had been participating in the *Bemba* case.[400]

4.2.4.3.2 Reparation Mandate

The reparation mandate is linked to the convicted person and the victims who suffered as a result of the crimes for which the perpetrator was convicted and the Court's order against the convicted person. As soon as the reparation order against the convicted person is issued, it triggers the Trust Fund for Victims into entering the preparation of the Draft Implementation Plan (DIP) of the reparation order pursuant to Regulation 57 RoTFV. In order to implement the DIP, the Court has to approve it and it still has the possibility to reject or to modify the DIP. In cases where the reparation order cannot be afforded, in accordance with the Rule 98 (3) (4) RPE, the BoD may, pursuant to the Regulation 56 and 50(a) RoTFV, complement the resources collected by the contributions. Entering the DIP stage, the benefits for the victims depend solely on the quick activities and the sufficient draft plans of the Trust Fund.[401] The Court has already been dissatisfied with the DIPs of the Trust Fund for Victims on two occasions, highlighting the fact that it had not completed its functions appropriately thus causing the victims to suffer more.[402]

As was discussed above, there are two possibilities for how the beneficiaries of reparations in the case of a reparation order may receive their reparations. The reparations may be received individually or collectively. As far as the Court identifies each victim who is entitled to receive the reparation, the Trust Fund for the Victims will specifically name the beneficiaries in the DIP, pursuant to Regulation 59 RoTFV, and if the details of the person are missing, the Trust Fund must indicate how it is going to locate and gather the missing information about the victim. If the Court does not identify the victims in its order, the Trust Fund has to set out all relevant demographic and statistical data in order to allocate the groups of victims as

[399] ICC, *Situation in Uganda*, Notification by the Board of Directors in accordance with Regulation 50(a) of the Regulations of the Trust Fund for Victims of its conclusion to undertake further activities in Uganda (19 December 2018), ICC, *Situation in Uganda*, Decision on the "Notification by the Board of Directors in accordance with Regulation 50(a) of the Regulations of the Trust Fund for Victims of its conclusions to undertake further activities in Uganda" (4 February 2019).

[400] ICC, ASP, Report to the Assembly of States of Parties on the Projects and the Activities of the Board of Directors of the Trust Fund for Victims for the Period 1 July 2017 to 30 June 2018, para. 57.

[401] ICC, *Prosecutor v. Al Mahdi*, ICC-01/12-01/15-273-Red, Public redacted version of 'Decision on Trust Fund for Victims' Draft Implementation Plan for Reparations' (12 July 2018) paras. 9–10.

[402] ICC, *Prosecutor v. Al Mahdi*, ICC-01/12-01/15-273-Red, Public redacted version of 'Decision on Trust Fund for Victims' Draft Implementation Plan for Reparations' (12 July 2018) paras. 9–10

defined in the order of the Court, in accordance with the guidance set out by Regulation 61 RoTFV. A final list of beneficiaries must then be approved by the BoD. In the cases of collective reparations, the DIP shall include the precise nature of the collective award as well as the methods for its implementation, which should be approved by the Court, pursuant to Regulation 69 RoTFV.

4.2.5 Enforcement and Implementation Plan

As soon as the reparation order is issued, the states are entitled to enforce the decisions of the Court in accordance with Article 75 (5) RS, bearing in mind the tight cooperation relationships between the Court and the Member States.[403] Under this provision, the states are obligated not to prevent the enforcement of reparation orders or the implementation of awards.

Although the DIPs are still pending in some cases, the TFV has already experienced a lack of success in drafting the DIPs. the Court has, on a number of occasions, been unsatisfied with the drafts provided by the Trust Fund.[404] The failure of the DIPs is, however, unlikely to be linked to a lack of guidance for the implementation plans. In its functions, the BoD encountered during the reparations implementation phase a number of practical difficulties such as a significant increase in its workload, induced by new and unfamiliar activities to deliver reparations awards, complexity induced by legal proceedings, an intense collaborative working relationship with various stakeholders and the need for resource mobilisation.[405] With the decision of March 4, 2019, the Court set criteria for approving the proposed projects. It considers the project as approved if the proposed action from the Trust Fund[406]

(1) falls within the scope of the Chamber's prior rulings
(2) is justified
(3) puts forward a reasonable time frame for its execution
(4) is proportionate, in that the estimated costs for the measure must be commersurate with the estimated benefits.

[403] See ICC, *Prosecutor v. Lubanga*, ICC-01/04-01/06-2953, Decision on the admissibility of the appeals against Trial Chamber I's Decision establishing the principles and procedures to be applied to reparations" and directions on the further conduct of proceedings (14 December 2012) para. 256.

[404] ICC, *Prosecutor v. Al Mahdi*, ICC-01/12-01/15–273-Red, Public redacted version of 'Decision on Trust Fund for Victims' Draft Implementation Plan for Reparations' (12 July 2018) paras. 11–13, 30.

[405] M. Noguchi, Report of the Board of Directors of the Trust Fund for Victims, Seventh Session of Assembly of States Parties, 5 December 2018.

[406] ICC, *Prosecutor v. Al Mahdi*, ICC-01/12-01/15-324-Red 04-03-2019, Decision on the Updated Implementation Plan from the Trust Fund for Victims (4 March 2019) para. 16.

4.2.5.1 Lubanga

On 21 October 2016, the Court approved the DIP for the collective symbolic reparations in the case of *Lubanga* which had been submitted by the TFV on 19 September 2016 and ordered a start to its implementation.[407] The TFV set as its goal the reintegration and rehabilitation of former child soldiers. The plan included the construction of symbolic commemoration centres where the interactive symbolic activities have to be hosted, such as the organisation of exhibitions and artwork created by former child soldiers, or the organisation of music, dance and other cultural events. This will help to reduce the stigmatisation of the former child soldiers and the affected communities.[408] The second part of the plan consists of a mobile memoralisation component which also helps to reduce the stigma in the affected communities by spreading awareness and sensitisation of the harm. Accordingly, the plan considers training for local leaders regarding memoralisation and reconciliation activities. This also includes radio transmissions, programmes and flash messages about the activities. Those activities should help the community to openly discuss the traumatising events with the aim of improving, understanding and reducing conflicts.[409]

4.2.5.2 Al Mahdi

On 12 July 2018 the Court was not satisfied with the work of the Trust Fund. In general, it accepted the DIP but ordered the Trust Fund to update it on 22 November 2018.[410] The BoD decided on its intention to complement the payment of the reparations awards amounting to 1,350,000 EUR.[411] However, there is still a gap in the finances in order to be able to accomplish the total liability of 2.7 million EUR.

[407] ICC, *Proseuctor v. Lubanga*, Order approving the proposed plan of the Trust Fund for Victims in relation to symbolic collective reparations (21 October 2016).

[408] ICC, *Prosecutor v. Lubanga*, Filing regarding symbolic collective reparations projects with Confidential Annex: Draft Request for Proposals, ICC-01/04-01/06-3223-Con (19 September 2016) paras. 31–37.

[409] ICC, *Prosecutor v. Lubanga*, Filing regarding symbolic collective reparations projects with Confidential Annex: Draft Request for Proposals, ICC-01/04-01/06-3223-Con (19 September 2016) paras. 38–43, In its report to the ASP in 2020, the BoD announced that up to 3 million EUR has been completed, see ASP-ICC, ICC-ASP/19/14* Report to the Assembly of States Parties on the projects and the activities of the Board of Directors of the Trust Fund for Victims for the period 1 July 2019to 30 June 2020 (16 September 2020) paras 30–32.

[410] The new plan was adopted on 4 March 2019, see ICC, *Prosecutor v. Al Mahdi*, ICC-01/12-01/15-324-Red 04-03-2019, Decision on the Updated Implementation Plan from the Trust Fund for Victims (4 March 2019).

[411] ICC, ASP, Report to the Assembly of States of Parties on the Projects and the Activities of the Board of Directors of the Trust Fund for Victims for the Period 1 July 2017 to 30 June 2018, 23 July 2018, para. 54, ASP-ICC, ICC-ASP/19/14* Report to the Assembly of States Parties on the projects

4.2.5.2.1 Individual Reparations

Taking into account the fact that the Trial Chamber awarded the individuals reparations for moral harm which met the direct descendant requirement, provable by historical genealogy records and according to local experts,[412] the Trust Fund was not able to identify all the possible victims eligible for the reparations of moral harm. This was based upon the finding of the Trust Fund that the inclusion of female-based lineage may lead to an increased number of qualifying victims recalling the principle of fair and equal treatment of the victims.[413] Similarly, the Court awarded the victims individual reparation for economic harm, pointing to their livelihood dependence on the Protected Buildings.[414] However, in the DIP, the Trust Fund mentioned that it would still remain within the limit of 2.7 million EUR reflecting the totality sum of the liability.

4.2.5.2.2 Collective Reparations

Taking into account the fact that the Court ordered that collective reparations have to address the damage caused to the Protected Buildings, consequential economic harm and the moral harm inflicted onto the population of the cultural city in general, the Trust Fund proposed improving the protection and maintenance of Protected Buildings, which was subsequently approved by the Court.[415] Furthermore, in order to address the reparation of the collective economic harm upon the direction of the

---

and the activities of the Board of Directors of the Trust Fund for Victims for the period 1 July 2019 to 30 June 2020 (16 September 2020) para. 41.

[412] ICC, *Prosecutor v. Al Mahdi*, ICC-01/12-01/15-289-Red, Public redacted version of "Trust Fund for Victims' submission of draft application form" ICC-01/12-01/15-289-Conf submitted on 26 October 2018 (30 October 2018) para. 42

[413] ICC, *Prosecutor v. Al Mahdi*, ICC-01/12-01/15-291-Red2, Public redacted version of "Updated Implementation Plan", submitted on 2 November 2018, ICC-01/12-01/15-291-Conf-Exp (22 November 2018) paras. 54–55.

[414] ICC, *Prosecutor v. Al Mahdi*, ICC-01/12-01/15-289-Red, Public redacted version of "Trust Fund for Victims' submission of draft application form" ICC-01/12-01/15-289-Conf submitted on 26 October 2018 (30 October 2018) para. 18, see also screening procedure of individual applications approved by the Court, ICC, *Prosecutor v. Al Mahdi*, ICC-01/12-01/15-324-Red 04-03-2019, Decision on the Updated Implementation Plan from the Trust Fund for Victims (4 March 2019) para. 61.

[415] ICC, *Prosecutor v. Al Mahdi*, ICC-01/12-01/15-273-Red, Public redacted version of 'Decision on Trust Fund for Victims' Draft Implementation Plan for Reparations' (12 July 2018) para. 107, it includes rehabilitation of doors, windows and enclosures, cementery walls, planting of trees and living hedge, improving lighting, surveillance and new proposed project was estimated by the updated implementation plan supporting the maintenance of the Protected Buildings, ICC, *Prosecutor v. Al Mahdi*, ICC-01/12-01/15-291-Red2, Public redacted version of "Updated Implementation Plan", submitted on 2 November 2018, ICC-01/12-01/15-291-Conf-Exp (22 November 2018) paras. 54–55 para. 109.

Court,[416] the Trust Fund proposed a new project to assist the return of victims to the cultural city Timbuktu, by awarding them transportation costs.[417] Another project regarding collective economic harm which was approved by the Court was dedicated to the activities to improve the economic resilience of the community.[418] In addressing the reparations for the collective moral harm, the Trust Fund suggested psychological support, the creation of women and girls' safe spaces[419] and community therapy through sermons broadcast on the radio, which involved a discussion in scheduled radio broadcasts. However, the Trust Fund came to the conclusion that community therapy through radio was not feasible.[420] To address the symbolic collective reparations, the Trust Fund suggested that the community itself should decide whether, what and how the attack should be memorialised, and accordingly it proposed that the memorialisation projects should be transmitted to the Trust Fund by December 2019.[421]

4.2.5.3 Katanga

On 25 July 2017, the Trust Fund submitted the DIP to the Court In December 2020, the BoD stated that the Trust Fund had complemented the totality of the award.[422]

---

[416] ICC, *Prosecutor v. Al Mahdi*, ICC-01/12-01/15-273-Red, Public redacted version of 'Decision on Trust Fund for Victims' Draft Implementation Plan for Reparations' (12 July 2018) para. 100.

[417] ICC, *Prosecutor v. Al Mahdi*, ICC-01/12-01/15-291-Red2, Public redacted version of "Updated Implementation Plan", submitted on 2 November 2018, ICC-01/12-01/15-291-Conf-Exp (22 November 2018) paras. 118–119.

[418] ICC, *Prosecutor v. Al Mahdi*, ICC-01/12-01/15-291-Red2, Public redacted version of "Updated Implementation Plan", submitted on 2 November 2018, ICC-01/12-01/15-291-Conf-Exp (22 November 2018) paras. 120–137.

[419] ICC, *Prosecutor v. Al Mahdi*, ICC-01/12-01/15-291-Red2, Public redacted version of "Updated Implementation Plan", submitted on 2 November 2018, ICC-01/12-01/15-291-Conf-Exp (22 November 2018) paras. 142–155.

[420] ICC, *Prosecutor v. Al Mahdi*, ICC-01/12-01/15-291-Red2, Public redacted version of "Updated Implementation Plan", submitted on 2 November 2018, ICC-01/12-01/15-291-Conf-Exp (22 November 2018) paras. 141.

[421] ICC, *Prosecutor v. Al Mahdi*, ICC-01/12-01/15-291-Red2, Public redacted version of "Updated Implementation Plan", submitted on 2 November 2018, ICC-01/12-01/15-291-Conf-Exp (22 November 2018) paras. 161–164, see also ICC, *Prosecutor v. Al Mahdi*, ICC-01/12-01/15-324-Red 04-03-2019, Decision on the Updated Implementation Plan from the Trust Fund for Victims (4 March 2019) para. 88.

[422] M. Noguchi, Report of the Board of Directors of the Trust Fund for Victims, Seventh Session of Assembly of States Parties, 5 December 2018, ASP-ICC, ICC-ASP/19/14* Report to the Assembly of States Parties on the projects and the activities of the Board of Directors of the Trust Fund for Victims for the period 1 July 2019 to 30 June 2020 (16 September 2020) para. 33.

4.2.5.3.1 Individual Compensation Award

The Trust Fund ensured that the financial advisor was responsible for the payment of the symbolic compensation to the victims and it concluded in 2017.[423]

4.2.5.3.2 Collective Reparations

Under collective reparations, the Trust Fund proposed housing assistance, educational assistance, income-generating activities and psychological rehabilitation. Under housing assistance, the Trust Fund included the construction of a home with basic household furnishings, the renovation of current homes, assistance in purchasing a plot of land or a home outside the region of Bogoro or assistance with rent payments.[424] Under educational activities, the Trust Fund considered the payment of primary or secondary school fees and related costs.[425] The payment of higher-educational enrolment and fees had already considered been by the Trust Fund as a part of the income-generating activity such as vocational training in small business enterprises, training people on how to develop business plans and budgets and provisions for a small business kit.[426] Under psychological rehabilitation, the Trust Fund proposed individual trauma-based counselling sessions and group counselling.[427]

[423]ASP-ICC, ICC-ASP/19/14* Report to the Assembly of States Parties on the projects and the activities of the Board of Directors of the Trust Fund for Victims for the period 1 July 2019 to 30 June 2020 (16 September 2020) para. 35, ICC, *Prosecutor v. Katanga*, ICC-01/04-01/07-3751-red, Public redacted document Draft implementation plan relevant to Trial Chamber II's order for reparations of 24 March 2017 (25 July 2017) para. 118.

[424]ICC, *Prosecutor v. Katanga*, ICC-01/04-01/07-3751-red, Public redacted document Draft implementation plan relevant to Trial Chamber II's order for reparations of 24 March 2017 (25 July 2017) para. 124.

[425]ICC, *Prosecutor v. Katanga*, ICC-01/04-01/07-3751-red, Public redacted document Draft implementation plan relevant to Trial Chamber II's order for reparations of 24 March 2017 (25 July 2017) para. 127.

[426]ICC, *Prosecutor v. Katanga*, ICC-01/04-01/07-3751-red, Public redacted document Draft implementation plan relevant to Trial Chamber II's order for reparations of 24 March 2017 (25 July 2017) para. 128.

[427]ICC, *Prosecutor v. Katanga*, ICC-01/04-01/07-3751-red, Public redacted document Draft implementation plan relevant to Trial Chamber II's order for reparations of 24 March 2017 (25 July 2017) para. 130.

References

Abtahi H, Koh SA (2012) The emerging enforcement practice of the International Criminal Court. Cornell Int Law J 45(1):1–25

Altwicker TH, Altwicker AP, Peters A (2016) Measuring violations of human rights: an empirical analysis of awards in respect of non-pecuniary damage under the European convention on human rights. Heidelberg J Int Law ZaöRV 76:1–51

Ambos K (2016) Treatise on international criminal law. Oxford University Press, Oxford

Ashworth A (2010) Sentencing and criminal justice. Law in context, 5th edn. Cambridge University Press, Cambridge

Aust A (2010) Handbook of international law, 2nd edn. Cambridge University Press

Aust H (2014) Circumstances precluding wrongfulness. In: Nollkaemper A, Plakokefalos I, Schechinger J (eds) Principles of shared responsibility in international law: an appraisal of the state of the art. Studies on shared responsibility in international law, First paperback edition. Cambridge University Press, Cambridge, pp 169–207

Aust H (2016) Circumstances precluding wrongfulness. In: Nollkaemper A, Plakokefalos I, Schechinger JNM (eds) Principles of shared responsibility in international law: an appraisal of the state of the art. Cambridge University Press, Cambridge, pp 169–207

Balta A, Banteka N (2017) The Al-Mahdi reparations order at the ICC: a step towards justice for victims of crimes against cultural heritage. Opinio Juris

Balta A, Bax M, Letschert R (2018) Trial and (potential) error: conflicting visions on reparations within the ICC system. Int Crim Just Rev 29:221–248

Baumgartner E (2008) Aspects of victim participation in the proceedings of the international criminal court. Int Rev Red Cross 90(870):409–440

Biela A, Tomson Ch (2017) Kraftverkehrs-Haftpflicht-Schäden. Handbuch für die Praxis, 26th edn. Verlagsgruppe Hüthig Jehle Rehm

Bloxham D (2003) British war crimes trial policy in Germany, 1945–1957: implementation and collapse. J Br Stud 42(1):91–118

Bock S (2010) Das Opfer vor dem Internationalen Strafgerichtshof. Beiträge zum Internationalen und Europäischen Strafrecht vol 7. Duncker & Humblot, Berlin

Boczek BA (2005) International law: a dictionary. Dictionaries of international law, vol 2. Scarecrow Press

Bonafè IB (2009) The relationship between state and individual responsibility for international crimes. Martinus Nijhoff, Leiden

Borchard ME, Wynne HW (2000) State insolvency and foreign bondholders, vol 2, Reprinted. Beard Books

Boujong K (1989) Section 844. In: Boujong K (ed) Das Bürgerliche Gesetzbuch. 12. neubearb. Aufl. Walter de Gruyter

Brower NC, Brueschke JD (1998) The Iran-United States claims tribunal. Nijhoff, Leiden

Buford W, van der Merwem H (2004) Reparations in Southern Africa. Cahiers d'études africaines 44:263–322

Burgorgue-Larsen L, Úbeda de Torres A, Greenstein R (2011) The inter-American court of human rights: case law and commentary. Oxford University Press, Oxford

Büyüksagis E (2009) The calculation of damages according to Article 41 of the European Convention on Human Rights

Cançado Trindade AA (2018) Reflections on the 2015 Strasbourg conference. In: van Aaken A (ed) Motoc I European convention on human rights and general international law. Oxford University Press, Oxford, pp 285–303

Cane P (1997) The anatomy of tort law. Hart

Cane P, Goudkamp J (2018) Atiyah's accidents, compensation and the law. The law in context series, 9th edn. Cambridge University Press, Cambridge

Carrillo A (2006) Justice in context: the relevance of inter-American human rights law and practice to repairing the past. In: de Greiff P (ed) The handbook of reparations. Oxford University Press, Oxford

Carter L, Ellis SM, Jalloh C (2016) The international criminal court in an effective global justice system. Edward Elgar Publishing
Christenson G (1991) Attributing acts of omission to the state. Mich J Int Law 12:312–370
Cohen M (2020a) Realizing reparative justice for international crimes: from theory to practicevon. Cambridge University Press, Cambridge
Cohen IA (2020b) Apologies and moral repair: rights, duties, and corrective justice. Routledge studies in ethics and moral theory. Routledge, New York
College JC (2017) The Iran-United States claims tribunal: the effect of future awards on international terrorism. Arbitr Law Rev 9:1–19
Condry R (2010) Secondary victims, secondary victimisation. In: Shoham SG, Knepper P, Kett M (eds) International handbook of victimology. CRC Press, Taylor & Francis Group, pp 219–250
Cottrell LP (2013) Austrian reconstuction 1920–1921: a matter for private business or the league of nations. In: Berghoff H, Kocka J, Ziegler D (eds) Business in the age of extremes: essays in modern German and Austrian economic history. Publication of the German Historical Institute, Cambridge University Press, Cambridge
Crawford J (2017) The international legal order: essays in honour of Djamchid Momtaz. BRILL, Leiden
de Brouwer A-M, Heikkilä M (2013) Victim issues: participation, protection, reparation and assistance. In: Sluiter G (ed) International criminal procedure: principles and rules. Oxford Univ. Press, Oxford
Devaney M (2009) A comparative assessment of personal injuries compensation schemes: lessons for tort reform? Electr J Comp Law 19:1–9
Dinah S (2015) Remedies in international human rights law. Oxford University Press, Oxford
Donat-Cattin D (2000) The role of victims in ICC proceedings. In: Lattanzi F (ed) Essays on the Rome statute of the international criminal court. Il Sirente
Donat-Cattin D (2016) Article 68. In: Triffterer O, Ambos K (eds) Rome Statute of the International Criminal Court: a commentary. Beck, Munich
Dören R, Wentke A (2018) Jurisdictional immunities in the New York Southern District Court?: The case of Rukoro et al. v. Federal Republic of Germany. EJIL: Talk!
Drees J-D (1994) Schadensberechnung bei Unfällen mit Todesfolge. 2. aktualisierte und erg. Aufl. VVW
Duffy H (2018) Strategic human rights litigation: understanding and maximising impact. Hart
Dwertmann E (2010) The reparation system of the international criminal court: its implementation, possibilities and limitations. Martinus Nijhoff Publishers, Leiden
Eichhorst M (2011) Rechtsprobleme der United Nations Compensation Commission. Veröffentlichungen des Walther-Schücking-Instituts für Internationales Recht an der Universität Kiel, vol 141. Duncker & Humblot, Berlin
El Zeidy M (2008) The principle of complementarity in international criminal law: origin, development, and practice. Martinus Nijhoff Publishers, Leiden
Emmerich V (2012) BGB-Schuldrecht, besonderer Teil. Schwerpunkte Pflichtfach, 13. neu bearb. Aufl. C. F. Müller, München
Erdal U, Bakirci H (2006) Article 3 of the European convention on human rights: a practitioner's handbook OMCT handbook series vol 1. OMCT
Evans C (2012) The right to reparation in international law for victims of armed conflict. Cambridge studies in international and comparative law, vol 91. Cambridge University Press, Cambridge
Ferstman C (2016) Cooperation and international criminal court: the freezing, seising and transfer of assets for the purpose of reparations. In: Bekou O, Birkett D (eds) Cooperation and the international criminal court: perspectives from theory and practice, Nottingham studies on human rights. BRILL, pp 227–247
Ferstman C (2017) Reparations, assistance and support. In: Tibori-Szabó K, Hirst M (eds) Victim participation in international criminal justice: practitioners' guide. International criminal justice series v. 11. T.M.C. Asser Press, The Hague, pp 413–431

Findlay M, Chuah Hui Ying J (2018) Principled international criminal justice: lessons from tort law. International and Comparative Criminal Justice Ser. Routledge
Fleischmann M, von Liszt F (1925) Das Völkerrecht. Zwölfte Auflage, Springer, Berlin
Friedman J (2008) Occupation zone and in West and East Germany. In: Heberer P, Matthäus J (eds) Atrocities on trial: historical perspectives on the politics of prosecuting war crimes. Nebraska University Press, Lincoln, pp 159–186
Friman H (2017) Article 75 (1). In: Klamberg M (ed) Commentary on the law of the international criminal court. FICHL publication series N. 29. Torkel Opsahl Academic E-Publisher 2017
Friman H, Lewis P (2001) Reparations to victims. In: Lee SR (ed) The international criminal court: elements of crimes and rules of procedure and evidence. Transnational Publishers
Fuchs M (2003) Deliktsrecht. Springer-Lehrbuch, Vierte, aktualisierte und überarbeitete Auflage. Springer, Heidelberg
Garcia MA (2018) An analysis of victims' participation in the Kosovo specialist chambers from a restorative justice perspective: a comparison with the international criminal court. University of Amsterdam
Gardner J (2011) Offences and defences: selected essays in the philosophy of criminal law. Oxford University Press, Oxford
Gattini A (2002) The UN compensation commission: old rules, new procedures on war reparations. Eur J Int Law 13(1):161–181
Giorgis AW (2014) Eritrea at a crossroads: a narrative of triumph, betrayal and hope. Strategic Book Publishing and Rights Co
Goldberg CPJ, Zipursky B (2010) The Oxford introductions to U.S. law: the Oxford introductions to U.S. law. Oxford University Press, Oxford
Goldberg J, Sebok A, Zipursky B (2016) Tort law: responsibilities and redress. Wolters Kluwer Law and Business, New York
González-Salzberg D (2010) The American states compliance with the judgments of the inter-American court of human rights. Revista Colombiana de Derecho Internacional 16:115–142
González-Salzberg D (2014) Do states comply with the compulsory judgments of the inter-American court of human rights?: an empirical study of the compliance with 330 measures of reparation. Revista do Instituto Brasileiro de Direitos Humanos 13:93–114
Grenville J, Wasserstein B (2013) The major international treaties of the twentieth century: a history and guide with texts. Taylor and Francis, London
Grey C (2010) Restitution. In: Crawford J et al (eds) The law of international responsibility. Oxford University Press, Oxdord, pp 589–599
Grotius H, Tuck R (2005) The rights of war and peace book II, XXVI. Natural law and enlightenment classics. Liberty Fund
Gschnitzer F (1963) Schuldrecht Besonderer Teil und Schadenersatz. Springer, Berlin
Gualde A, Luterstein N (2009) The Argentinean reparations programme for grave violations of human rights perpetrated during the last military dictatorship (1976–1983). In: Ferstman C, Goetz M, Stephens A (eds) Reparations for victims of genocide, war crimes and crimes against humanity: systems in place and systems in the making. Martinus Nijhoff Publishers, Leiden, pp 415–435
Guariglia F et al (2018) The appeals chamber of the International Criminal Court: commentary and digest of jurisprudence. Cambridge University Press, Cambridge
Guembe JM (2006) Economic reparations for grave human rights violations. In: de Greiff P (ed) The handbook of reparations. Oxford University Press, Oxford, pp 21–55
Günther K (2016) Responsibility to protect and preventive justice. In: Ashworth A, Zedner L, Tomlin P (eds) Prevention and the limits of the criminal law. Oxford University Press, pp 69–90
Harke DJ (2010) Allgemeines Schuldrecht. Enzyklopädie der Rechts- und Staatswissenschaft: Abteilung Rechtswissenschaft, Spinger, Heidelberg
Haupt H, Weber U, Bürner S (2003) Handbuch Opferschutz und Opferhilfe. 2. Aufl. Nomos
Horne J, Kramer A (2001) German atrocities, 1914: a history of denial. Yale Univ. Press, London
Houghton PD (2001) US foreign policy and the Iran hostage crisis. Cambridge studies in international relations, vol 75. Cambridge University Press, Cambridge

Hulsebosch D, Bernstein ER (2013) Making legal history: essays in Honor of William E. Nelson. NYU Press, New York

Ichim O (2015) Just satisfaction under the European convention on human rights. Cambridge University Press, Cambridge

Ireland T (2016) Damage standards for wrongful death/survival actions: loss to survivors, loss to the estate, loss of accumulations to an estate and investment accumulations. J Leg Econ 22:5–23

Issaeva M, Sergeeva I, Suchkova M (2011) Enforcement of the judgments of the European court of human rights in Russia: recent developments and current challenges. Int J Human Rights 12:67–83

Jahnke J (2018a) Section 249. In: Burmann M et al (eds) Straßenverkehrsrecht: Kommentar: mit StVO nebst CsgG, dem StVG, den wichtigsten Vorschriften der StVZO und der FeV, dem Vcrkchrsstraf- und Ordnungswidrigkeitenrecht, dem Schadensersatzrecht des BGB, Zivilprozessrecht und Versicherungsrecht, der Bußgeldkatalog-Verordnung sowie Verwaltungsvorschriften. 25. neu bearbeitete Auflage. C.H. Beck, München

Jahnke J (2018b) Section 844. In: Burmann M et al (eds) Straßenverkehrsrecht: Kommentar: mit StVO nebst CsgG, dem StVG, den wichtigsten Vorschriften der StVZO und der FeV, dem Verkehrsstraf- und Ordnungswidrigkeitenrecht, dem Schadensersatzrecht des BGB, Zivilprozessrecht und Versicherungsrecht, der Bußgeldkatalog-Verordnung sowie Verwaltungsvorschriften. 25. neu bearbeitete Auflage. C.H. Beck, München

Kelsen H (2004) Principles of international law. 5. printing. Nachdr. d. Ausg. New York, Rinehart, 1952, Lawbook Exchange Ltd

Khan K (2016) Article 34. In: Triffterer O, Ambos K (eds) Rome Statute of the International Criminal Court: a commentary. Beck, Munich

Kelsen H (2009) Pure theory of law. The Lawbook Exchange

Klee J (2011) The process. In: Payne RC, Sand HP (eds) Gulf war reparations and the UN compensation commission: environmental liability. Oxford University Press, Oxford, pp 29–66

Klein E (1981) Beihilfe zum Völkerrectsdelikt. In: v Münch I (ed) Staatsrecht - Völkerrecht – Europarecht. Festschrift für Hans-Jürgen Schlochauer zum 75. Geburtstag am 28. März 1981. De Gruyter

Kleinlein T (2017) Jus Cogens re-examined: value formalism in international law. Eur J Int Law 28 (1):295–315

Klinkert W (2017) Espionage is practiced here on a vest scale, The Netherlands, 1914–1940. In: Baudet F et al (eds) Perspectives on military intelligence from the first world war to Mali. T.M.C. Asser Press, The Hague, pp 23–54

Klinkhammer A, Späti C (2006) Neutralität statt Moralität: Die Entschädigung der Opfer des Nationalsozialismus in der Schweiz. In: Hockerts GH (ed) Grenzen der Wiedergutmachung: Die Entschädigung für NS-Verfolgte in West- und Osteuropa 1945–2000. Wallstein-Verl

Koller D (2015) The global as local: the limits and possibilities of integrating international and transitional justice. In: de Vos C, Kendall S, Stahn C (eds) Contested justice: the politics and practice of the International Criminal Court interventions. Cambridge University Press, Cambridge, pp 85–105

Korn A, Sethi M (2011) Employment tribunal remedies, 4th edn. Oxford University Press, Oxford

Krajewski M (2017) Völkerrecht. 1. Auflage, Nomos

Kreß C, Prost K (2016) Article 93. In: Triffterer O, Ambos K (eds) Rome statute of the international criminal court: a commentary. Beck, München

Kunz R (2020) Richter über internationale Gerichte? Springer, Berlin

Lambert-Abdelgawad E (2008) The Execution of Judgments of the European Court of Human Rights. Dossiers sur les droits de l'homme vol 19, 2. éd, Éd. du Conseil de l'Europe

Lange H, Schiemann G, Joachim G (2003) Schadensersatz. Handbuch des Schuldrechts in Einzeldarstellungen/neubearb. Aufl. Mohr Siebeck

Lanovoy V (2016) Complicity and its limits in the law of international responsibility. Bloomsbury Publishing, New York

Lauterpacht H (2012) The function of law in the international community. Reprinted with corr. first publ. 1933, Oxford University Press, Oxford

Lauterpacht H, Lauterpacht E (1975) International law. Being the collected papers of Hersch Lauterpacht. Cambridge University Press, Cambridge

Lira E (2006) The reparations policy for human rights violations in Chile. In: de Greiff P (ed) The handbook of reparations. Oxford University Press, Oxford, pp 56–101

Lojkó M (2006) Meddling in middle Europe: Britain and the 'Lands Between' 1919–1925. Central European University Press

Maddrell P (2005) Operation matchbox and scientific containment of the USSR. In: Jackson JP, Siegel LJ (eds) Intelligence and statecraft: the use and limits of intelligence in international society. Praeger

Marboe I (2010) State responsibility and comparative state liability for administrative and legislative harm to economic interests. In: Schill SW (ed) International investment law and comparative public law. Oxford University Press, Oxford, pp 377–412

Marfn RR, Sandoval C (2011) Engendering the reparations jurisprudence of the inter-American court of human rights: the promise of the Cottonfield judgment. Hum Rights Q 33:1062–1091

Marks S (2003) The illusion of peace: international relations in Europe, 1918–1933. The making of the 20th century. Macmillan Education, London

Marschik A (1997) Subsysteme im Völkerrecht: Ist die Europäische Union ein "Self-Contained Regime"? Schriften zum europäischen Recht vol 44. Duncker & Humblot, Berlin

Matheson JM (2009) Eritrea-Ethiopia Claims Commission: damage awards. Am Soc Int Law 13

McBride JN, Bagshaw R (2018) Tort law. Longman law series, 6th edn. Pearson Education Limited, London

McCarthy C (2014) Reparations and victim support in the international criminal court. Cambridge studies in international and comparative law. Cambridge University Press, Cambridge

McGinn T (2013) Obligations in Roman law. University of Michigan Press, Ann Arbor

Mierzejewski CA (2000) The most valuable asset of the Reich. History of the German National Railway Volume 2, 1933–1945. The University of North Carolina Press

Moffett L (2017) Reparations for victims at the international criminal court: a new way forward? Int J Human Rights 21(9):1204–1222

Morisson H, Pountney E (2014) Victim participation at the special tribunal for Lebanon. In: Alamuddin A (ed) The special tribunal for Lebanon: law and practice (Oxford monographs in international humanitarian and criminal law). Oxford University Press, Oxford, pp 153–176

Mühl J (2015) Strafrecht ohne Freiheitsstrafen - absurde Utopie oder logische Konsequenz?: Die Laufzeitleistungsstrafe als alternative Sanktion. Studien und Beiträge zum Strafrecht vol 1, Mohr Siebeck

Musiał-Budnicka J (2016) ICC court decision on reparation for victims of the post-election violence: no reparation without conviction prosecutor v. William Samoei Ruto and Joshua Arap sang, decision on the request regarding reparations, 1 July 2016. Wroclaw Rev Law Adm Econ 11(6):110–126

Nerlich V (2016) Article 82. In: Triffterer O, Ambos K (eds) Rome statute of the international criminal court: a commentary. Beck, München

Nollkaemper A (2003) Concurrence between individual responsibility and state responsibility in international law. Int Comp Law Q 3:613–640

Owen R (2003) Essential tort law, 3rd edn. Taylor & Francis

Pasqualucci MJ (1996) Victim reparations: inter-American human rights: a critical assessment of current practice and procedure. Mich J Int Law 18:1–59

Paulsson J (2005) Denial of Justice in International Law. Hersch Lauterpacht memorial lectures vol 17. Cambridge University Press, Cambridge

Pérez-León-Acevedo P J (2016) The situation of reparations in the Inter-American Human Rights System: analysis and comparative considerations. Am Soc Int Law 20

Peschke K (2013) The role and mandates of the ICC trust fund for victims. In: Bonacker T, Safferling S (eds) Victims of international crimes: an interdisciplinary discourse. T. M. C. Asser Press, Amsterdam, pp 317–327

Peters A (2018) Rights to Reparation as a Consequence of Direct Rights under International Humanitarian Law Zeitschrift für ausländisches öffentliches Recht und Völkerrecht, pp 545–549

Petrossian G (2019) Staatenverantwortlichkeit für Völkermord. Duncker und Humblot, Berlin

Pfeffer R (2012) Das Verhältnis von Völkerrecht und Landesrecht: Eine kritische Betrachtung alter und neuer Lehren unter besonderer Berücksichtigung der Europäischen Menschenrechtskonvention. Mohr Siebeck

Posner R, Landes MW (1980) The positive economic theory of tort law. Georgia Law Rev 15:851–924

Rattalma MDF, Treves T (1999) The United Nations compensation commission: a handbook. Kluwer Law International

Roberts MP (2019) The Cold War: interpreting conflict through primary documents. ABC-CLIO, LLC

Rombeck-Jaschinski U (2011) Das Londoner Schuldenabkommen: Die Regelung der deutschen Auslandsschulden nach dem Zweiten Weltkrieg. Veröffentlichungen des Deutschen Historischen Instituts London Band 58, Oldenbourg Wissenschaftsverlag

Rosenfeld F (2010) Collective reparation for victims of armed conflict. Int Rev Red Cross 92:731–756

Safferling C (2011) Internationales Strafrecht, Strafanwendungsrecht - Völkerstrafrecht - Europäisches Strafrecht. Springer, Berlin

Safferling C, Petrossian G (2020) Wiedergutmachung für Opfer von Makroverbrechen. Die Praxis des Internationalen Strafgerichtshofes im Überblick. MRM– MenschenRechtsMagazin Heft 1 / 2020:20–31

Salvador-Crespo I (2015) Making good for forced exodus. In: Feighery JT, Gibson SC, Rajah MT (eds) War reparations and the UN compensation commission: designing compensation after conflict. Oxford University Press, Oxford, pp 221–243

Sandoval C (2020) International human rights adjudication, subsidiarity and reparation for victims of armed conflict. In: Correa C, Furuya Sh, Sandoval C (eds) Reparation for victims of armed conflict von. Cambridge University Press, Cambridge, pp 179–264

Sandoval-Villalba C (2009) The concepts of 'Injured party' and 'Victim' of gross human rights violations in the jurisprudence of the inter-American court of human rights: a commentary on their implications for reparations'. In: Ferstman C, Goetz M, Stephens A (eds) Reparations for victims of genocide, war crimes and crimes against humanity: systems in place and systems in the making. Martinus Nijhoff Publishers, Leiden, pp 243–282

Saul B (2003) Compensation for unlawful death in international law: a focus on the inter-American court of human right. Am Univ Int Law Rev 19:523–585

Schabas W (2017) An introduction to the international criminal court. Cambridge University Press, Cambridge

Schabas W (2018) The trial of the Kaiser. Oxford University Press, Oxford

Schabas W, Ambos K (2016) Article 76. In: Triffterer O, Ambos K (eds) Rome statute of the international criminal court: a commentary. Beck, München

Schneider J (2015) Reparation and enforcement of judgments: a comparative analysis of the European and inter-American human rights systems. Epubli GmbH, Berlin

Schramm A (2010) Haftung für Tötung: Eine vergleichende Untersuchung des englischen, französischen und deutschen Rechts zur Fortentwicklung des deutschen Haftungsrechts in Tötungsfällen. Mohr Siebeck, Göttingen

Schroth K, Schroth M (2018) Die Rechte des Opfers im Strafprozess. Praxis der Strafverteidigung, vol. 26. C.F. Müller, Heidelberg

Seegers M (2005) Das Individualrecht auf Wiedergutmachung: Theorie, Struktur und Erscheinungsformen der völkerrechtlichen Staatenverantwortlichkeit gegenüber dem Individuum. Kölner Schriften zum internationalen und europäischen Recht vol 14. LIT

Seifert H (1971) Die Reparationen Japans: Ein Beitrag zum Wandel des Reparationsproblems und zur wirtschaftlichen Entwicklung Japans nach 1945. Vol 6. VS Verlag für Sozialwissenschaften

Shaw M (2014) International law, 7th edn. Cambridge University Press, Cambridge

Shelton D (1996) The jurisprudence of the inter-American court of human rights. Am Univ Int Law Rev 10:333–372

Shelton D (1998) Remedies in the inter-American system: the challenge of non-state actors. Am Soc Int Law 92:202–206

Shelton D (2015) Remedies in international human rights law. Oxford University Press, Oxford

Soto BM, Velásquez GA (2015) An approach to the state responsibility by an omission in the inter–american court of human rights jurisprudence. Rev CES Derecho:3–17

Spinedi M (1989) International crimes of states. In: Cassese A, Weiler J, Spinedi M (eds) International crimes of state: a critical analysis of the ILC's Draft Article 19 on state responsibility. Series A-Law vol 10, De Gruyter, Berlin, pp 7–140

Stahn C (2015) Reparative Justice after the Lubanga appeals judgment on principles and procedures of reparation. EJIL!, Talk

Starrenburg S (2017) Who is the victim of cultural heritage destruction? The reparations order in the case of the prosecutor v Ahmad Al Faqi Al Mahdi. EJIL: Talk

Sugarman S (2005) Comparative law look at pain and suffering awards. DePaul Law Rev 55:399–434

Sveaass N, Sønneland MA (2015) Dealing with the past: survivors' perspectives on economic reparations in Argentina. Int Persp Psychol Res, Pract Consult 4:223–238

Talmon S (2020) Germany not answerable in U.S. courts for alleged colonial genocide. GPIL

Taylor AL (2009) The United Nations compensation commission. In: Ferstman C, Goetz M, Stephens A (eds) Reparations for victims of genocide, war crimes and crimes against humanity: systems in place and systems in the making. Martinus Nijhoff Publishers, Leiden

Tigroudja H (2017) Reparation before the international criminal court. Aix-Marseille University

Trapp NK (2011) State responsibility for international terrorism: problems and prospects. Oxford monographs in international law. Oxford University Press, Oxford

Underwood T, Palmer N (2003) Ecological perspective of victimisation. In: Edmunds Ch, Underwood LT (eds) Victim assistance: exploring individual practice, organisational policy, and societal response. Springer series on family violence, New York, pp 21–40

Verdross A (1926) Die Verfassung der Völkergemeinschaft. Springer, Berlin

Vesper T (2010) Death and legal blame: wrongful death. In: Bryant DC (ed) Handbook of death & dying. Gale virtual reference library. Sage Publications, pp 950–968

Villa-Vincecio C (2006) A difficult justice. In: Doxtader E, Villa-Vicencio C (eds) To repair the irreparable: reparation and reconstruction in South Africa. New Africa Books, pp 66–87

von Arnauld A (2012) Völkerrecht. C.F. Müller, München

Wagner G (2019a) Section 823. In: Bamberger GH et al (eds) Bürgerliches Gesetzbuch: Kommentar. 4. Auflage. Beck München

Wagner G (2019b) Section 844. In: Bamberger GH et al. Bürgerliches Gesetzbuch: Kommentar. 4. Auflage. Beck München

Ward J (2015) Economic damages and tort reform. In: Okrent JC, Buckley RW (eds) Torts and personal injury law, 5th edn. Cengage Learning

Wengler W (2014) Völkerrecht. Springer, München

White R (2000) Remedies in a multi-level legal order: the Strasbourg court and the UK. In: Kilpatrick C, Novitz T, Skidmore P (eds) The future of remedies in Europe. Hart, Oxford, pp 191–204

Wilson MC (2004) Argentina's reparations bonds: an analysis of continuing obligations. Fordham Int Law J 28:786–826

Zimmermann R (1996) The law of obligations: Roman foundations of the civilian tradition. Clarendon Paperbacks, Oxford University Press, Oxford

Zwißler F (2016) Schmerzensgeld Katalog Ausgabe, Die aktuelle Entscheidungshilfe; Mit Schmerzensgeldtabellen und Fachwortverzeichnis, Walhalla und Praeto

Chapter 5
Summary: Victims of International Crimes

The aim of this book was to provide a detailed overview of the different mechanisms that exist in offering modes of participation in criminal prosecution to the victims of mass atrocities at an international level. The book has outlined the victims' system enshrined in the Rome Statute and compared it to the existing practice of victim participation in several other national and international circumstances. It has now been almost two decades since victims of international crimes were first granted access to courts and tribunals allowing them to participate and express their suffering, concerns and interests in key international criminal trials. Victim-oriented movements throughout the world in the mid-1980s began to challenge the original purely perpetrator-oriented approach of modern enlightened thinking in criminal procedure. New forms of involvement for the victims of crime in criminal procedures have allowed them to take part in the criminal process separately and actively. The role of victims has been politically tightened inside and outside of the criminal justice system. However, despite national developments aimed at strengthening the role of the victim, the *ad hoc* tribunals for Rwanda and the former Yugoslavia did not take into account the distinction between victims and the witnesses. Accordingly, victims of crimes in these conflicts have never been given the opportunity to participate actively in an international trial or to voice their concerns before a trial chamber. This was changed with the "*new era*" of international criminal mechanisms, including the ICC, the ECCC, the STL and the Kosovo Chambers, in which the victims were taken into account as genuine subjects in the proceedings.

The consideration of the interests of victims of macro-crimes plays an important role in the resolution of conflicts. The victims' wishes, views and concerns must be taken into account as they help to understand the political conflict and also serve to achieve justice. On the one hand, the chances in the truth-finding process are enhanced by consulting with the victims, on the other hand, the link to the victims' suffering can help in the fine-tuning of objectivity and balance between the accuser and the accused.

© The Author(s), under exclusive license to Springer Nature Switzerland AG 2021

C. Safferling, G. Petrossian, *Victims Before the International Criminal Court*,
https://doi.org/10.1007/978-3-030-80177-9_5

In contrast, the victims themselves wish to be heard, to be informed and to be compensated for the harm suffered as any injury, harm or suffering that is not recognised simply leads to further frustration. As such, these victims will always remain in search of recognition and justice. The urge and struggle for recognition might even become a part of the cultural life of the victims and their society and the pain will never end. Recognition of the harm, in contrast, is a definitive first means of reparation and contributes to reconciliation and to peace and non-recognition of the violation is based upon a lack of respect towards the victims of crime. Furthermore, the external perception of the victims' group is affected by such a failure to recognize. For this, a decisive function lies in the factual and legal background of the victimisation. The victim of a simple theft or a violent robbery must be distinguished from a victim of deportation as a crime against humanity.

Even legally, it is not possible to compare the quality of harm of the victims of crimes, but acknowledging a certain crime leads to different consequences. Providing victims with the opportunity to actively participate in the justice system is another form of recognition of the damage suffered. The expectations and frustrations of those who have suffered as a result of the crime are an indicator of the effectiveness of justice.

However, the involvement of victims in the justice system does have to be symbolic. The wishes of the victims should seriously be taken into account. The involvement of the victims should be effective and meaningful and not lead to further frustration and discrimination.

However, how effective and meaningful this involvement has been to date, or how it should be dealt with in future international criminal cases, remains open to debate.

In order to answer the question of how effective the involvement of crime victims might be considered in international criminal prosecution, the problems arising for the victims of crimes such as genocide, crimes against humanity, war crimes and the crime of aggression have been considered from three perspectives in this book: (1) who exactly are the victims? (2) how do the victims participate in international criminal proceedings? and (3) how are the victims of international crimes being compensated?

5.1 Definition

In order to analyse the legal definition of the victim of international crimes under the rules of the ICC, a comprehensive overview of the different definitions of international law was drawn up. This made it possible to illustrate the different legal views on the definition of victims both under international and domestic law.

The UN Declaration of Basic Principles of Justice for Victims of Crime and Abuse of Power remains the *magna carta* of victims' rights, and although this instrument is not binding, it offers guidelines for national and international instruments to identify the victims of crimes. On that basis, each international instrument has developed its own framework to allocate the victims of the specific crimes. The number of multilateral conventions in international law which provide a definition of 'victim' pursuant to the elements of the respective crimes, and which establish the relevance of the victims' rights and, accordingly, their participation and compensation. The existence of victimhood with a view to a specific crime is, therefore, related to the elements of that crime. If the elements of the crime are not fulfilled, it is likewise not possible to identify the victim of that crime. Correspondingly, the connections between the definitions of the crime and the victim are very closely tied. However, another question which arises is whether it is possible to identify victims of that crime at all without a judgment that confirms that the alleged crime has been committed. In contrast, the existence of the victims would counter the presumption of innocence of the accused. At the same time, it is difficult to confirm that the victims are not victims, but alleged or presumed victims, as this would secondarily victimise persons already injured, considering the fact that victims may be victims regardless of whether the perpetrator is identified, apprehended, prosecuted or convicted.

The debate on victimhood varies depending upon whether it is addressed from a human rights' law perspective or from a criminal law perspective. This makes the victims' identification both at national and international level still generally questionable.

Another difficult problem arises from the nature of the crimes under the jurisdiction of the ICC. As described in the third chapter of this book, crimes under the Rome Statute are mostly collective crimes, such as the crime of genocide, crimes against humanity and the crime of aggression. The crime of genocide primarily defends protected groups, crimes against humanity foresee a systematic or widespread attack on several people, and the crime of aggression even presupposes an attack on a state. Purely individual victimisation may arise under specific circumstances with regard to crimes against humanity and, in particular, with regard to war crimes, aiming mostly at the protection of the individual combatant or the individual civilian. Accordingly, the elements of victims' definition pursuant to Rule 85 RPE offer a wide range of possibilities to involve individual victims in an international criminal trial. To date, the Court has not dealt with the crime of genocide or crimes against humanity (e.g.[1] extermination or deportation) that require collective victimisation. Even in cases involving only individual victimisation, a large number of victims were able to register and were recognised under the provisions of Rule 85 RPE.

Dealing with the cases at hand, it is possible to presume the Court's tendency to continue to distinguish the victims of mass crimes on an individual basis.

In order to distinguish the definition from the perspectives of the procedural problems, it is important to note that due to the broad definition of victim status under Rule 85 RPE, there is a need for the categorisation of victims according to the

[1]Exception the case of *Ntaganda*, the persecution of one victim on ethnic grounds.

procedural stages, such as the victims of a situation, the victims of a case or the victims of specific charges.

The ICC should assume a definite position concerning victims. Until now, the practice of the Court has focused merely on the victims of the specific charges brought against the accused. Consequently, this approach has led to fewer victims who had the chance to be recognised as victims before the Court. Nevertheless, this tactic has still created a high number of applications and a multitude of victim recognitions. However, despite recognition, not every victim has had the opportunity to voice their concerns personally in court. Thus, if the victims do not have the possibility of speaking out and expressing their views personally, why can the victims of the situation not claim for victimhood pursuant to Rule 85 of the Court? Unwarranted discrimination between the victims is the consequence of this limited application policy. If the prosecutor of the ICC was unable to gather sufficient evidence on other perpetrators, why should the victims be excluded simply because other perpetrators identifiable within the situation are, for whatever reason, not prosecuted by the ICC? Furthermore, in the cases where the accused is acquitted, the victims lose their victim' status, which discriminates and victimises them within their societies a second time.

One of the possible solutions might be the registration or recognition of the situation victims as victims by the Registry and not by a Judge with a view to an individual case. This would also significantly reduce the workload of the judges. The victims' groups might then be represented by common legal representatives for victims' in the further proceedings.

It seems to be that after two decades, there is still a place for discussion about the fundamental questions pertaining to victim participation, starting with the very definition of who counts as a victim pursuant to Rule 85 RPE.

5.2 Participation

As shown in the third chapter of this book, the victims go through an extremely long process to achieve their goals in the various stages of the criminal process. Considering that the objective of victim participation is that the victims are in a position to express their views and concerns about various procedural issues that infringe upon their interests pursuant to Article 68 RS, it can be seen that this is not always the case. The involvement of victims is, in part, an abstract topic where legal representatives take more action and consider appropriate participation in consultation with the victims. If the victims' goal is redress, then the victims will have to wait much longer to claim monetary reparation for the damage caused by the crime. It took almost thirteen years in the case of *Lubanga* for the Court to decide on the reparation issues after the arrest warrant had been issued in in 2006, and almost ten years in the case of *Katanga* which started with an arrest warrant in 2007.

Victims, or legal representatives of victims, do not enjoy party status in the ICC proceedings; they are mere participants in the criminal proceedings. Accordingly, they do not have absolute rights to intervene in the proceedings. The national comparison carried out in the first chapter of this book shows that numerous states (29 European states) are interested in including victims as civil party in national criminal justice, rather than granting them the status of subsidiary prosecutor's status *(Nebenklage)*. The same practice was carried out by the ECCC.

It is also important to mention that each bench designs its own rules for the practical participation of victims in the proceedings adopted by the respective Chamber. Here it is important to bear in mind the different legal backgrounds and preconceptions of each individual judge with regard to the victims' participation. Whereas one bench may grant the victims a wide range of participatory rights, another may exclude some of the victims' participatory rights or legal representatives for the victims.

Given that there are many technical and logistical difficulties arising within the Court due to the victims' applications, this, however, has no impact on the legal representatives' work. The reason is simple; theoretically, there is no difference as to whether there are more than a thousand victims or ten victims who are represented by legal counsel. The question arises as to why the task of the legal representative should not be simplified into a manner of representation of the affected victim communities disregarding the fact of whether they are registered as victims at the Court or not. If the Court is able to recognise all members of a particular territory as victims under the definition of a situation under the Rome Statute or all the members of a particular group of persons, the legal representatives then have the right not to represent a group of individual victims but rather the communities and groups of people affected as a consequence of macro-crimes. Returning to the starting point, the broad definition, pursuant to Rule 85 RPE, enables the recognition of collective victim groups.

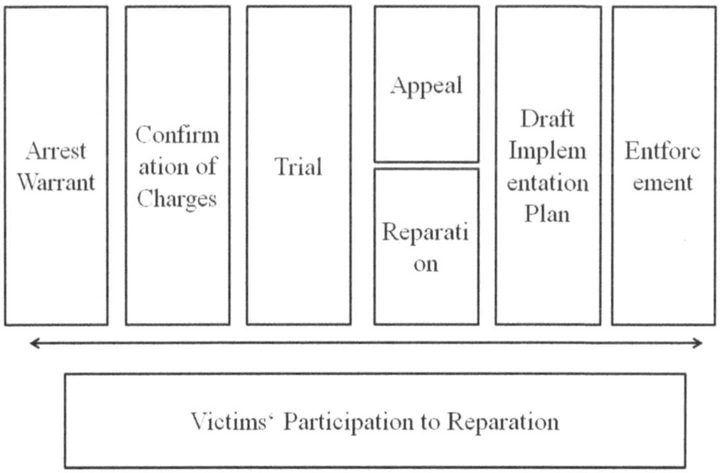

5.3 Reparation

The fourth chapter of this book dealt with redress from the perspectives of civil law, international law and criminal law. This helps to distinguish between the legal differences and to categorise the different types of reparations. From a civil or tort law point of view, the comparison between the German and the British compensation tables provide a good overview of the compensation for bodily injuries. This could be seen as a guideline for compensation at an international level, but it is doubtful whether the compensation rates set by the European countries will be practically applicable. The same refers to the other financial, economic and psychological damages. The perpetrators will never be able to financially compensate for the damage caused by their criminal acts. This has already been approved by the third reparation case before the ICC, in which the convicted persons were recognised as being incapacitated.

From an international law perspective, there is a question of state responsibility, too. As described above, it can go in different directions, either in international law or in national law. However, this scenario does not seem to be the best solution for the cases before the ICC. The reason for this is that states confronted with international crimes are, for various reasons, unable to demonstrate their willingness to compensate for the damage caused by those crimes.

The ICC, with its Trust Fund, aims at compensating the victims of international crimes. However, as a result of lengthy proceedings before the ICC, the victims' hopes rest on the assistance mandate of the Trust Fund for Victims. In the framework of its mandate, the Trust Fund organises various projects in the situation territories, in order to work with the affected regions and the victims. Moreover, the reparation mandate that is bound to the conviction and to the individual judgment does not seem to be all that effective. The damage caused by the convicted person is almost irreparable. Bearing in mind the objective reality that in Cambodia financial reparation will not be possible, the ECCC stated that it would focus only on satisfaction and symbolic reparations. The reparation process according to the ICC-structure takes an exceedingly long time and produces exhausted victims who have long been waiting for redress and are, once again, given false hopes of receiving possible reparations. The Trust Fund for Victims should operate independently from the Court. It should collect the resources from the donations of the voluntary contributions and carry out projects in the affected regions and situation countries. The Court may still make a quick reparation order against the convicted person, who should then contribute directly to the Trust Fund for Victims.

In conclusion, the entire system of victim participation in the ICC has been created in good faith and with good goals, respecting established human rights. However, it appears that the Court has ended up in the dead end of the effectiveness and meaningfulness of the mechanism.

Chapter 6
Annex: Victim-Related Relevant Decisions

6.1 Situation in the CAR and in the CAR II

6.1.1 Prosecutor v. Jean-Pierre Bemba Gombo

Prosecutor v. Jean-Pierre Bemba Gombo			
Date	Stage	Decision	Description
11 November 2010	Pre-Trial	Decision on Victims' Participation in Proceedings Related to the Situation in the Central African Republic	Application of the framework for the possible participation of victim set forth in the "Decision on Victim's Participation in Proceedings Related to the Situation in the Republic of Kenya" (ICC-01/09-24) in the context of the situation in the Central African Republic
12 September 2008	Pre-Trial	Decision on Victim Participation	Submission of complete applications
23 October 2008	Pre-Trial	Second Decision on the question of victims' participation requesting observations from the parties	Setting time limit for submission of the observations by the parties
4 November 2008	Pre-Trial	Decision Designating a Single Judge on Victims' Issues	Designating a Single Judge
17 November 2008	Pre-Trial	Third decision on the question of victim's participation requesting observations from the parties	Submission of observations of the parties
2 December 2008	Pre-Trial	Decision Concerning the Time Limit for the Submission of New Victim Applications	No more effect of the time limit for the submission of new victim applications
12 December 2008	Pre-Trial	Fourth Decision on Victims' Participation	Recognition of the victims and granting procedural status

(continued)

© The Author(s), under exclusive license to Springer Nature Switzerland AG 2021
C. Safferling, G. Petrossian, *Victims Before the International Criminal Court*,
https://doi.org/10.1007/978-3-030-80177-9_6

Prosecutor v. Jean-Pierre Bemba Gombo			
Date	Stage	Decision	Description
16 December 2008	Pre-Trial	Fifth Decision on Victims' Issues Concerning Common Legal Representation of Victims	Request to choose CLRV
8 January 2009	Pre-Trial	Sixth Decision on Victims' Participation Relating to Certain Questions Raised by the Office of Public Counsel for Victims	Rejection of the requests of OPCV
22 April 2009	Pre-Trial	Decision concerning the Application by the Legal Representative of Victims a/0278/08, a/0279/08, a/0291/08 to a/0293/08, a/0296/08 to a/0298/08, a/0455/08 and a/0457/08 to a/0467/08 filed on 20 April 2009	Rejection of the Application by the LRV
26 August 2009	Appeal	Order on the filing of responses to the "Observation of the Legal Representatives of the Victims on the Participation of the Victims in the Interlocutory Appeal Filed by the Office of the Prosecutor under Article 81(2)(b) of the Rome Statute" and the Prosecutor's request for suspensive effect	Allowance to file a response to the Victims' Filing
3 September 2009	Appeal	"Decision on the Participation of Victims in the Appeal against the Decision on the Interim Release of Jean-Pierre Bemba Gombo and Convening Hearings with the Kingdom of Belgium, the Republic of Portugal, the Republic of France, the Federal Republic of Germany, the Italian Republic, and the Republic of South Africa"	Allowance to present submissions by the victims
20 October 2009	Appeal	Reasons for the "Decision on the Participation of Victims in the Appeal against the Decision on the Interim Release of Jean-Pierre Bemba Gombo and Convening Hearings with the Kingdom of Belgium, the Republic of Portugal, the Republic of France, the Federal Republic of Germany, the Italian Republic, and the Republic of South Africa"	Reasons for the Decision
22 February 2010	Trial	Decision defining the status of 54 victims who participated at the pre-trial stage, and inviting the parties' observations on applications for participation by 86 applicants	Continuation of participation of Pre-Trial victims

(continued)

Prosecutor v. Jean-Pierre Bemba Gombo			
Date	Stage	Decision	Description
14 July 2010	Trial	Corrigendum to Decision on the participation of victims in the trial and on 86 applications by victims to participate in the proceedings	Granting 86 victims procedural status
16 July 2010	Trial	Order inviting the parties' observations on 192 victims' applications	Ordering the parties to file responses
11 August 2010	Appeal	Order on the filing of a response to the application by victims for participation in the appeal against the "Decision on the review of the detention of Mr Jean-Pierre Bemba Gombo pursuant to Rule 118(2) of the Rules of Procedure and Evidence" of Trial Chamber III	Allowance to file a response to the victims' application
18 August 2010	Appeal	Decision on the Participation of Victims in the Appeal against the "Decision on the review of the detention of Mr Jean-Pierre Bemba Gombo pursuant to Rule118(2) of the Rules of Procedure and Evidence" of Trial Chamber III	Granting the right to participate in the appeal
6 September 2010	Trial	Decision on three issues related to victims' applications for participation in the proceedings	Instructing the Defense to submit observations
7 September 2010	Trial	Decision setting a time-limit for the submission of new victims' applications for participation	Setting a time limit for submission of new applications
12 November 2010	Trial	Decision on common legal representation of victims for the purpose of trial	Granting two CLRV the right to represent the victims
18 November 2010	Trial	Decision on 772 applications by victims to participate in the proceedings	Granting 624 victims procedural status
19 November 2010	Trial	Decision on the legal representation of victim applicants at trial	Granting OPCV to represent applicants at the trial
23 December 2010	Trial	Decision on 653 applications by victims to participate in the proceedings	Granting 553 victims procedural status
14 July 2011	Appeal	Decision on the Participation of Victims in the Appeal against the "Decision on Applications for Provisional Release" of Trial Chamber III	Granting the right to participate in the appeal

(continued)

Prosecutor v. Jean-Pierre Bemba Gombo			
Date	Stage	Decision	Description
17 July 2011	Trial	Decision on the OPCV's application concerning the inquiry into victims' applications completed with the assistance of Intermediary 1	Granting OPCV to provide additional information on 75 individuals
21 July 2011	Trial	Corrigendum to the Decision on 401 applications by victims to participate in the proceedings and setting a final deadline for the submission of new victims' applications to the Registry	Granting 307 victims procedural status
6 September 2011	Appeal	Order on the filing of submission by victims and by Mr Bemba Gombo and the Prosecutor	Granting the right to victims to file their views and concerns
9 September 2011	Trial	Decision setting a timeline for the filing of observations on pending victims' applications	Setting a time-limit for submission of observations
11 September 2011	Appeal	Order on the filing of a response to the application by victims for participation in the appeal against the "Decision on the accused's application for provisional release in the light of the Appeals Chamber's judgement of 19 August 2011" of Trial Chamber III	Granting the right to file a response
3 October 2011	Trial	Decision on the request of the legal representative of victims to question Witness 65	Partly granting the LRV to ask the questions
26 October 2011	Trial	Decision on 270 applications by victims to participate in the proceedings	Granting 264 victims procedural status
21 November 2011	Trial	Order regarding applications by victims to present their views and concerns or to present evidence	Establishing the procedure to be followed by the Legal Representative for seeking leave to present evidence
15 December 2011	Trial	Decision on 418 applications by victims to participate in the proceedings	Granting 404 victims procedural status
21 December 2011	Trial	Second order regarding the application of the legal representatives of victims to present evidence and the views and concerns of victims	Setting a time limit for submission of a supplemented Application or applications containing additional information
1 February 2012	Trial	Third order regarding the applications of the legal representatives of victims to present evidence and the views and concerns of victims	Deciding on the extension of time limits for the submission of written statements

(continued)

Prosecutor v. Jean-Pierre Bemba Gombo			
Date	Stage	Decision	Description
1 February 2012	Appeal	Decision on "Application of Legal Representative of Victims Mr Zarambaud Assingambi for leave to participate in the appeals proceedings following the Defence appeal of 9 January 2012 and addendum of 10 January 2012"	Rejection of participation in appeal
22 February 2012	Trial	Decision on the supplemented applications by the legal representatives of victims to present evidence and the views and concerns of victims	Authorisation of victims to present evidence, express their views and concerns
6 March 2012	Trial	Order on the implementation of Decision on the supplemented applications by the legal representatives of victims to present evidence and the views and concerns of victims	Ordering the VPRS to provide the parties with less redacted versions of some application forms
11 March 2012	Trial	Decision on 471 applications by victims to participate in the proceedings	Granting 457 victims procedural status
28 March 2012	Trial	Decision postponing the commencement of the presentation of evidence by the legal representatives of victims	Postponement of the date of the commencement of the presentation of evidence by the legal representative of victims
21 May 2012	Trial	Decision on 1400 applications by victims to participate in the proceedings	Granting 1377 victims procedural status
24 May 2012	Trial	Decision on the presentation of views and concerns by victims a/0542/08,a/0394/08 and a/0511/08	Authorises victims to present views and concerns via video-link technology
19 July 2012	Trial	Public redacted version of "Decision on the tenth and seventeenth transmissions of applications by victims to participate in the proceedings"	Granting 331 applicants procedural status
5 November 2012	Trial	Decision on 799 applications by victims to participate in the proceedings	Granting 777 victims procedural status
21 August 2013	Trial	Decision on the Defence Motion on the Questioning of Defence Witnesses by the Legal Representatives of Victims	Rejection of the motion

(continued)

Prosecutor v. Jean-Pierre Bemba Gombo			
Date	Stage	Decision	Description
29 January 2014	Trial	Decision on Maître Douzima's Requête de la Représentante légale de victims en vue de soumettre des documents en tant qu'éléments de prevue selon l'article 64(9) du Statut de Rome	Admission and rejection of certain items of evidence
07 February 2014	Trial	Order on the legal representation of victims previously represented by Me Assingambi Zarambaud	Authorising the Registry to assign victims
21 May 2014	Trial	Decision on "Requête de la Représentante légale des victimes relative à l'augmentation du nombre de pages autorisé et à la prorogation du délai dedépôt des conclusions écrites"	Closing brief may not exceed 200 pages
8 September 2014	Trial	Decision on "Requête de la Représentante légale des victims relative à l'augmentation du nombre de pages autorisés afin de répondre aux 'Closing Brief of Mr. Jean-Pierre Bemba Gombo' (ICC-01/05-01/08-3121-Conf)"	Extension of the page limit to 45 pages
24 December 2014	Trial	Decision on "Requête de la Représentante légale des victimes sollicitant l'accès à la requête non expurgée de 'Defence Request for Relief for Abuse of Process' Conf-Exp + Conf-Exp-Anxs I, II, III & X + Conf-Anxs IV, V, VI, VII, VIII & IX ainsi qu'aux annexes I, II, III et X"	Rejection of the request to access information
15 July 2015	Trial	Decision on "Demande d'autorisation de répliquer à la Réponse de la Défense concernant la «Requête relative à la reprise des actions introduites devant la Cour par des victimes décédées»"	Grant of the request for Leave to Reply
15 September 2015	Trial	Decision on "Demande d'autorisation de répliquer aux «Soumissions supplémentaires de la Défense concernant la 'Requête relative à la reprise des actions introduites devant la Cour par les victimes décédées'» (ICC-01/05-01/08-3293-Conf)"	Grant of the request for Leave to Reply

(continued)

Prosecutor v. Jean-Pierre Bemba Gombo			
Date	Stage	Decision	Description
8 January 2016	Trial	Redacted Version of "Decision on the legal representatives of victims' applications to question Witness D04-19"	Granting LRV to question the witness
24 March 2016	Trial	Decision on "Requête relative à la reprise des actions introduites devant la Cour par des victimes décédées"	Authorising the Successors to resume the actions initiated before the Court by the respective Deceased Victims
15 April 2016	Appeal	Decision on the participation of victims in the appeal against Trial Chamber III's "Judgment pursuant to Article 74 of the Statute"	Granting 5229 victims to participate in the appeal
1 September 2016	Appeal	Decision on the participation of victims in the appeals against Trial Chamber III's "Decision on Sentence pursuant to Article 76 of the Statute"	Granting 5229 victims to participate in the appeal
04 October 2016	Appeal	Order Shortening Time Limit for Responses to the Request of Legal Representative of Victims	Setting a time limit for the responses
17 October 2016	Appeal	Decision on the Request of Legal Representative of Victims for Access to Documents	Order to file the documents requested
03 February 2017	Appeal	Order shortening time limit for response to Mr Bemba's request to strike the Prosecutor's reply to victims' observations on the additional evidence request	Setting a time limit for the response
07 February 2017	Appeal	Decision on Mr Bemba's request regarding the Prosecutor's reply to victims' observation	Order to the Prosecutor to refrain from unnecessary and repetitive submissions
29 August 2017	Trial	Second decision on applications for resumption of actions initiated by deceased victims	Authorising the applicants to resume the actions initiated before the Court by the respective Deceased Victims
14 December 2017	Trial	Decision on the Legal Representative of the Victims request for extension of time	Amendment of the deadline to file the Final Submissions

6.1.2 *Prosecutor v. Alfred Yekatom and Patrice-Edouard Ngaïssona*

Case: Alfred Yekatom and Patrice-Edouard Ngaïssona			
Date	Stage	Decision	Description
5 March 2019	Pre-Trial	Decision Establishing the Principles Applicable to Victims' Applications for Participation	Deciding on application process
23 May 2019	Pre-Trial	Decision on the Legal Representation of Victims	Decision on legal representation appointing OPCV to represent former child soldiers
21 June 2019	Pre-Trial	Decision regarding the Registry's First Assessment Report on Applications for Victim Participation, the Registry's First Transmission of Group C Applications, the appointment of counsel for Victims of Other Crimes, and the victims' procedural position	Allowing 15 victims to participate, appointing legal representation for other crimes and clarifying the procedural position of the victims
13 September 2019	Pre-Trial	Decision regarding the Registry's Outstanding Transmissions of Applications for Victim Participation	Allowing 1070 victims to participate and rejecting 14 applications
23 November 2020	Trial Chamber	Decision on Victims' Participation in Trial Proceedings	Allowing 1 victim to participate and rejecting 12 applications
11 December 2020	Trial Chamber	Second Decision on Victims' Participation in Trial Proceedings (Group A)	Allowing 100 applicants to participate

6.2 Prosecutor v. Laurent Gbagbo and Ble Goude

Case: Laurent Gbagbo and Charles Blé Goudé			
Date	Stage	Decision	Description
6 February 2012	Pre-Trial	Decision on issues related to the victims' application process	Mapping of victims' applications and identification of potential victims
20 February 2012	Pre-Trial	Decision on OPCV's "Request to appear before the Chamber pursuant to Regulation 81(4)(b) of the Regulations of the Court on the specific issue of victims' application process"	Rejection of request of OPCV for appearance before the Chamber

(continued)

Case: Laurent Gbagbo and Charles Blé Goudé			
Date	Stage	Decision	Description
2 March 2012	Pre-Trial	Decision inviting observations from the parties in relation to the victims' application process	Inviting parties to present their observations about partly collective application form
13 March 2012	Pre-Trial	Decision on the OPCV's "Second Request to appear before the Chamber pursuant to Regulation 81(4)(b) of the Regulations of the Court on issues related to the victims' application process"	Granting the OPCV to submit observations
5 April 2012	Pre-Trial	Second decision on issues related to the victims' application process	Ordering the Registry to modify the collective application form
4 June 2012	Pre-Trial	Decision on Victims' Participation and Victims' Common Legal Representation at the Confirmation of Charges Hearing and in the Related Proceedings	Granting victims procedural status and appointing OPCV as CLRV in the case Gbagbo
5 October 2012	Appeal	Decision on Observations submitted by OPCV on behalf of victims	Grating victims to submit observation in Appeal
11 October 2012	Pre-Trial	Decision on the «Demande d'autorisation d'interjeter appel de la décision de la Juge unique portant sur la question de la participation des victimes à la procedure relative à l'état de santé du Président Gbagbo et à son aptitude à être jugé (ICC-02/11-01/11-211)	Rejection of the request for Leave to Appeal
23 January 2013	Pre-Trial	Decision on the "Demande aux fins de prorogation du délai fixé pour le dépôt par la défense d'observations concernant les demandes de participation des victimes transmises par le Greffe le 18 janvier 2013"	Granting the Defence time to submit observations on victims' applications for participation
6 February 2013	Pre-Trial	Corrigendum to the Second decision on victims' participation at the confirmation of charges hearing and in the related proceedings	Grating victims procedural status in the case Gbagbo
13 February 2013	Pre-Trial	Decision on the OPCV's "Requests to receive information and access documents for the effective participation of victims at the confirmation of charges hearing"	Granting OPCV to access confidential documents
27 August 2013	Appeal	Decision on the application by victims for participation in the appeal	Authorising Pre-Trial victims (199) to participate in Appeal

(continued)

Case: Laurent Gbagbo and Charles Blé Goudé			
Date	Stage	Decision	Description
29 August 2013	Appeal	Decision on the participation of victims in the Prosecutor's appeal against the "Decision adjourning the hearing on the confirmation of charges pursuant to article 61(7)(c)(i) of the Rome Statute"	Granting victims to present their views and concerns
23 November 2012	Appeal	Decision on the Presiding Judge of the Appeals Chamber in relation to the filing of the Office of Public Counsel for victims entitled "Requests in relation to the 'Decision on the review of Laurent Gbagbo's detention pursuant to article 60(3) of the Rome Statute'"	Designation of the Presiding Judge
11 June 2014	Pre-Trial	Decision on victims' participation in the pre-trial proceedings and related issues	Granting victims procedural status and appointing OPCV as CLRV in the case Ble Goude
1 August 2014	Pre-Trial	Second Decision on victims' participation in the pre-trial proceedings and related issues	Granting victims procedural status in the case Ble Goude
19 January 2015	Trial	Decision on the Legal Representative of Victims' access to certain confidential filings and to the case record	Granting LRV access to confidential records
6 March 2015	Trial	Decision on victim participation	Authorising applicants granted victim status at the confirmation stage to participate in the trial proceedings
22 July 2015	Appeal	Decision on the "Request for the recognition of the right of victims authorised to participate in the case to automatically participate in any interlocutory appeal arising from the case and, in the alternative, application to participate in the interlocutory appeal against the ninth decision on Mr Gbagbo's detention (ICC-02/11-01/15-134-Red3)"	Authorising that victims authorised to participate in the case have an automatic right to participate in the appeal
31 July 2015	Appeal	Reason for the "Decision on the 'Request for the recognition of the right of victims authorised to participate in the case to automatically participate in any interlocutory appeal arising from the case and, in the alternative, application to participate in the interlocutory appeal against the ninth decision on Mr Gbagbo's detention (ICC-02/11-01/15-134-Red3)'"	Reasons for the decision

(continued)

Case: Laurent Gbagbo and Charles Blé Goudé			
Date	Stage	Decision	Description
10 August 2015	Appeal	Decision on the "Requête de la Défense aux fins de voir constater son droit automatique de pouvoir répondre à toute intervention du Représentant des victimes et, à titre subisidiare, demande de la Défense à être autorisée à répliquer à la réponse du Représentant des victimes «to the Defence's document in support of the appeal against the ninth decision on the review of Mr. Gbagbo's detention (ICC-02/11-01/15-161-Conf-ExpAnx2)» (ICC-02/11-01/15-168-Conf-Exp)"	Rejection of the requests
2 September 2015	Trial	Decision on the Legal Representative of Victims' requests to maintain redactions to information relating to certain intermediaries	Granting the request to maintain redaction to information relating to certain intermediaries
7 October 2015	Trial	Decision setting time limits for submissions on Victims' Applications	Transmission to defence and prosecutor supporting documents
7 January 2016	Trial	Decision on victims' participation status	Granting victims procedural right and appointing LRV
09 May 2016	Trial	Decision on Prosecutor's request for lifting of certain redactions in victim application forms (ICC-02/11-01/15-465 and ICC-02/11-01/15-493)	Rejection and grant of requests
19 June 2018	Trial	Decision on the common legal representative of victims' application to submit one item of documentary evidence	Authorising to submit evidence

6.3 Situation in the DRC

Situation in the DRC			
Date	Stage	Decision	Description
18 August 2007	Pre-Trial	Decision on the Requests of the Legal Representative of Applicants on application process for victims' participation and legal representation	Rejecting the requests of LRV

(continued)

Situation in the DRC			
Date	Stage	Decision	Description
22 August 2007	Pre-Trial	Decision on the time limit to submit observations on applications a/0163/06 to a/0187/06 for participation as victims	Setting time limit for observation on applications
26 September 2007	Pre-Trial	Decision on the requests of the Legal Representative for victims VPRS1 to VPRS 6 regarding "Prosecutor's information on further investigation"	Rejecting the requests of victims
10 December 2007	Pre-Trial	Decision on the Request of the OPCV	Rejecting the requests of the OPCV
18 January 2008	Pre-Trial	Decision on the Application for Leave to Appeal the Decision on the Requests of the OPCV	Rejecting the request for Leave to Appeal
1 February 2008	Pre-Trial	Corrigendum to the "Decision on the Applications for Participation Filed in Connection with the Investigation in the Democratic Republic of the Congo by a/0004/06 to a/0009/06, a/0016/06 to a/0063/06, a/0071/06 to a/0080/06 and a/0105/06 to a/0110/06..."	Granting victims procedural status at the stage of investigation
7 February 2008	Pre-Trial	Decision on the Prosecution, OPCD and OPCV Requests for Leave to Appeal the Decision on the Applications for Participation of Victims in the Proceedings in the Situation	Rejecting request of the OPCV for leave to appeal
13 February 2008	Appeal	Decision of the Appeals Chamber on the OPCV's request for clarification and the legal representatives' request for extension of time and Order of the Appeals Chamber on the date of filing of applications for participation and on the time of the filing of the responses thereto by the OPCD and the Prosecutor	Rejection of the request of the OPCV
19 February 2008	Pre-Trial	Decision on the "Demande des représentants légaux de VPRS1, VPRS2, VPRS3, VPRS4, VPRS5, VPRS6 et a/0071/06 aux fins d'accéder au document confidentiel depose par le Conseil de direction du Fonds d'affectation spéciale au profit des victimes le 7 février 2008"	Rejection of the request of the Legal Representatives
26 February 2008	Pre-Trial	Decision on the "Demande de prorogation de délai suite à l'enregistrement tardif des 'Obsverations des représentants légaux de VPRS 1 à 6 et de a/0071/06 sur la "Notification by the board of Directors of the trust Fund for victims"''"	Granting the Request of the Legal Representatives

(continued)

Situation in the DRC			
Date	Stage	Decision	Description
11 April 2008	Pre-Trial	Decision designating a Single Judge Responsible for Issues Related to Victims' Applications for Participation at the Investigation Stage of the Situation in the DRC	Designation of a single judge
30 June 2008	Appeal	Decision on Victim Participation in the appeal of the Office of Public Counsel for the Defence against PTC I's Decision of 7 December 2007 and in the appeals of the Prosecutor and the Office of Public Counsel for the Defence against PTC I's Decision of 24 December 2007	Granting the applications for participation by victims
19 December 2008	Appeal	Judgment on victim participation in the investigation stage of the proceedings in the appeal of the OPCD against the decision of PTC I of 7 December 2007 and in the appeals of the OPCD and the Prosecutor against the decision of PTC I of 24 December 2007	Reversing the previous decision from 1 February 2008
25 October 2010	Pre-Trial	Decision on the request of the legal representative of victims VPRS 3 and VPRS 6 to review an alleged decision of the Prosecutor not to proceed	Rejecting requests of victims
11 April 2011	Pre-Trial	Decision on victims' participation in proceedings relating to the situation in the Democratic Republic of the Congo	Retaining the Chamber's previous findings
18 August 2011	Pre-Trial	Redacted version of the Decision on 13 applications for victims' participation in proceedings relating to the situation in the Democratic Republic of the Congo	Granting applicants victim status

6.3.1 *Prosecutor v. Thomas Lubanga Dylio*

Case: Thomas Lubanga Dylio			
Date	Stage	Decision	Description
24 July 2006	Pre-Trial	Decision Inviting The Democratic Republic Of The Congo And The Victims In The Case To Comment On The Proceedings Pursuant To Article 19 Of The Statute	Inviting victims to make submissions
8 August 2006	Pre-Trial	Decision Establishing a Time Limit for the Prosecution and the Victims to submit their responses to the Request for Leave to Appeal by the Defence	Setting a time limit

(continued)

Case: Thomas Lubanga Dylio			
Date	Stage	Decision	Description
9 August 2006	Pre-Trial	Decision Rectifying the Time Limit for the Prosecution and the Victims to submit their responses to the Request for Leave to Appeal by the Defence	Rectifying the time limit
10 August 2006	Pre-Trial	Decision Authorising the Prosecutor and the Defence to Respond to the Observations of the Legal Representatives of the Victims regarding the Manner in which Victims a/0001/06, a/0002/06 and a/0003/06 are to Participate in the Confirmation Hearing	Inviting the parties to respond to the observations
17 August 2006	Pre-Trial	Decision on the Application for Participation of Victims a/0001/06 to a/0003/06 in the Status Conference of 24 August 2006	Rejecting to grant victims procedural status
4 September 2006	Pre-Trial	Decision on the application for participation of victims a/0001/06 to a/0003/06 in the status conference of 5 September 2006	Rejecting to grant victims procedural status
22 September 2006	Pre-Trial	Decision on the Arrangements for Participation of Victims a/0001/06, a/0002/06 and a/0003/06 at the Confirmation Hearing	Rejecting the victims to access to the whole record of the situation and to participate in ex parte hearing, deciding the modalities of participation
6 November 2006	Pre-Trial	Decision on the Defence request for leave to appeal regarding the transmission of applications for victim participation	Rejecting the request of the Defence
13 June 2007	Appeal	Decision of the Appeals Chamber on the Joint Application of Victims a/0001/06 to a/0003/06 and a/0105/06 concerning the "Directions and Decisions of the Appeals Chamber" of 2 February 2007	Dismissal of the victims' application
5 October 2007	Trial	Decision on the request of the legal representatives of victims for an extension of time to file submissions on the e-court protocol	Granting the extension of the time limit
25 October 2007	Trial	Decision on "Demande de déposition du représentant légal des demandeurs de victimes"	Rejecting the application

(continued)

Case: Thomas Lubanga Dylio			
Date	Stage	Decision	Description
8 November 2007	Trial	Order on the Office of Public Counsel for Victims' request for extension of time limit	Rejecting the request for extension of the time limit
27 November 2007	Trial	Order on the Office of Public Counsel for Victim's request filed on 21 November 2007	Partial grant of OPCVs request to submit observations
21 January 2008	Trial	Decision on victims' participation	Deciding on modalities of participation
27 February 2008	Trial	Decision on the Defence and Prosecution Request for Leave to Appeal the Decision on Victims' Participation of 18 January 2008	Granting Leave to appeal on certain issues
6 March 2008	Trial	Decision on the role of the Office of Public Counsel for Victims and its request for access to documents	Defining the role of OPCV
16 May 2008	Trial	Decision on the request of the OPCV and on the prosecution's filing which concern the Trial Chamber's decision inviting the parties' observations on applications for participation of victims issued on 6 May 2008	Modifying a previous decision concerning disclosure of certain personal information of victims
18 May 2008	Appeal	Decision, in limine, on Victim Participation in the appeals of the Prosecutor and the Defence against Trial Chamber I's Decision entitled "Decision on Victims's Participation"	Granting of the application of certain victims
22 May 2008	Appeal	"Decision on the request of the Prosecutor and the Defence for suspensive effect of the appeals against Trail Chamber I's Decision on Victim's Participation of 18 January 2008"	Ordering the suspension of the impugned decision, to the extent that is affected by the issues on appeal
2 June 2008	Trial	Decision on the legal representative's request for clarification of the Trial Chamber's 18 January 2008 "Decision on victims' participation"	Clarifying the previous decision
5 June 2008	Trial	Decision on certain practicalities regarding individuals who have the dual status of witness and victim	Guidance on dual status
9 July 2008	Appeal	Scheduling Order for Judgement on the appeals of the Prosecutor and the Defence against Trail Chamber I's Decision on Victim's Participation of January 2008	Setting the date for the delivery of the judgement

(continued)

Case: Thomas Lubanga Dylio			
Date	Stage	Decision	Description
11 July 2008	Appeal	Judgement on the appeals of the Prosecutor and the Defence against Trail Chamber I's Decision on Victims' Participation of 18 January 2008	Confirming and reversing the findings of the Trial Chamber
15 July 2008	Appeal	Order on the filing of responses to the applications by victims for participation in the appeal	Granting the right to respond to the applications for participation
28 July 2008	Appeal	Order on the filing of responses to the application by victims for participation in the appeal	Granting the right to respond to the applications for participation
6 August 2008	Appeal	Decision on the participation of victims in the appeal	Granting victims procedural right in the appeal
18 December 2008	Trial	Decision on the applications by 3 victims to participate in the proceedings	Granting victim procedural rights
19 December 2008	Trial	Order issuing Annexes to the "Decision on the applications by victims to participate in the proceedings" of 15 December 2008	Issuing different versions of annexes
13 January 2009	Trial	Corrigendum to the Decision on the applications by victims to participate in the proceedings	Granting victims procedural status
21 January 2009	Trial	Decision on the defence application for disclosure of victims applications	Establishing principles for the disclosure of victims applications
8 April 2009	Trial	Redacted version of "Decision on 'indirect victims'"	Defining indirect victims in relation to child soldiers
8 May 2009	Trial	Order issuing public redacted annexes to the Decisions on the applications by victims to participate in the proceedings of 15 and 18 December 2008	Issuing public redacted versions of annexes
26 June 2009	Trial	Decision on the request by victims a/0225/06, a/0229/06 and a/0270/07 to express their views and concerns in person and to present evidence during the trial	Allowing three victims to present views and concerns
9 July 2009	Trial	Order issuing public redacted version of the "Decision on the request by victims a/0225/06, a/0229/06 and a/0270/07 to express their views and concerns in person and to present evidence during the trial"	Issuing a public redacted version of the Decision

(continued)

Case: Thomas Lubanga Dylio			
Date	Stage	Decision	Description
10 July 2009	Trial	Decision on the applications by 7 victims to participate in the proceedings	Granting victims procedural status
21 July 2009	Trial	Decision on the supplementary information relevant to the applications of 21 victims	Granting victims procedural status
23 July 2009	Trial	Order issuing confidential and public redacted versions of Annex A to the "Decision on the applications by 7 victims to participate in the proceedings" of 10 July 2009 (ICC-01/04-01/06-2035)	Issuing different versions of annexes
8 September 2009	Trial	Decision on the defence application for leave to appeal the Trial Chamber's "Decision on the request by victims a/0225/06, a/0229/06 and a/0270/07 to express their views and concerns in person and to present evidence during the trial"	Refusal of leave to appeal
10 September 2009	Trial	Decision on the applications by 2 victims to participate in the proceedings	Granting victims procedural status
16 September 2009	Trial	Decision on the Manner of Questioning Witnesses by the Legal Representatives of Victims	Establishing a presumption in favour of a neutral form of questioning
22 September 2009	Trial	Decision on the request by the legal representative of victims 0001/06, a/0002/06, a/0003/06, a/0049/06, a/0007/08, a/0149/08, a/0155/07, a/0156/07, a/0404/08, a/0405/08, a/0406/08, a/0407/08, a/0409/08, a0149/07 and a/0162/07 for admission of the final report of the Panel of Experts on the illegal exploitation of natural resources and other forms of wealth of the Democratic Republic of the Congo as evidence	Refusal of the application of the legal representative of victims
14 October 2009	Appeal	Order on the filing of a clarification in relation to the "Demande de participation du représentant légal des victimes a/0051/06, a/0078/06, a/0232/06 et a/0246/08 à la procédure	Demand for clarification

(continued)

Case: Thomas Lubanga Dylio

Date	Stage	Decision	Description
		d'appel interjetés par la Défense et l'Accusation à l'encontre de la 'Decision giving notice to the parties and participants that the legal characterisation of the facts may be subject to change in accordance with regulation 55 (2) of the Regulations of the Court' rendue le 14 juillet 2009"	
20 October 2009	Appeal	Decision on the participation of victims in the appeals	Granting victims procedural status in the appeal
27 October 2009	Trial	Order issuing public and confidential redacted annex to the Decision on the applications by 2 victims to participate in the proceedings of 10 September 2009 (ICC-01/04-01/06-2115)	Issuing different versions of annexes
10 December 2009	Trial	Decision on Supplementary Information concerning victims' applications a/0609/08 and a/0053/09	Decision on a status of a victims
3 August 2010	Appeal	Order on the Filing of a Response to Victims Applications for Participation in the Appeal of the Prosecutor against Trial Chamber I's decision of 15 July 2010 to release Thomas Lubanga Dyilo	Granting the right to file a response
13 August 2010	Appeal	Order on the Filing of a Response by Mr Lubanga Dyilo to Applications for Victim Participation	Granting the right to file a respone
17 August 2010	Appeal	Decision on the Participation of Victims in the Appeal against Trial Chamber I's Oral Decision of 15 July 2010 to Release Thomas Lubanga Dyilo	Granting victims procedural status in the appeal
18 August 2010	Appeal	Decision on the Participation of Victims in the Appeal against Trial Chamber I's Decision to Stay the Proceedings	Granting victims procedural status in the appeal
29 September 2010	Appeal	Order on the filing of observations as to the confidential status of victim's observations dated 23 August 2010 (ICC-01/04-01/06-2559-Conf)	Ordering to submit observations

(continued)

Case: Thomas Lubanga Dylio			
Date	Stage	Decision	Description
4 February 2011	Trial	Redacted Decision on the disclosure of information from victims' application forms (a/0225/06, a/0229/06 and a/0270/07)	Ordering disclosure of information
8 February 2011	Trial	Redacted version of the Corrigendum of Decision on the applications by 15 victims to participate in the proceedings	Granting victims procedural status
8 March 2011	Trial	Order on the transmission of 7 new victims' applications and the submission of observations	Order to transmit the applications and to submit observations
25 July 2011	Trial	Redacted version of the Decision on the applications by 7 victims to participate in the proceedings	Granting victims procedural status
27 January 2012	Reparation	Order on the applications by victims to participate and for reparations	Ordering on applications for reparations
5 April 2012	Reparation	Decision on the OPCV's request to participate in the reparations proceedings	Allowing OPCV to represent unrepresented victims at the reparation proceedings
7 August 2012	Reparation	Decision establishing the principles and procedures to be applied to reparations	Deciding on the principles of reparations for victims
13 December 2012	Appeal	Decision on the participation of victims in the appeals against Trial Chamber I's conviction and sentencing decisions	Granting victims procedural status in the appeal
5 February 2013	Appeal	Order relevant to the request for an extension of time filed by the Legal Representatives of Victims V02	Granting the right to file a response
7 February 2013	Appeal	Decision on the request for an extension of time filed by the Legal Representative of Victims V02	Granting the request for extension of time
14 February 2013	Appeal	Order on the filing of submissions on new applications to participate as victims in the proceedings	Ordering the Public Counsel for victims to represent applicants
27 August 2013	Appeal	Decision on 32 applications to participate in the proceedings	Granting victims to participate in the proceedings
26 May 2014	Appeal	Order on "Prosecution's request for transmission by VPRS of the application for reparation of victim a/0078/06"	Order to file an unredacted version of an application for reparations by a certain victim

(continued)

Case: Thomas Lubanga Dylio			
Date	Stage	Decision	Description
3 March 2015	Reparation	Judgment on the appeals against the "Decision establishing the principles and procedures to be applied to reparations" of 7 August 2012 with AMENDED order for reparations (Annex A) and public annexes 1 and 2	Reparations for Victims
12 November 2015	Reparation	Order fixing the schedule for the submission of observations on the draft implementation plan submitted by the Trust Fund for Victims	Instructing the Prosecution and interested persons or States to submit observations
13 January 2016	Reparation	Decision on the request of the Office of Public Counsel for Victims and the request of the Legal Representatives of Victims V02	Considering the request for access to be moot and granting in par the request for extension of time
9 February 2016	Reparation	Order instructing the Trust Fund for Victims to supplement the draft implementation plan	Instructing the Trust Fund for Victims to continue developing and transmitting information
4 March 2016	Reparation	Decision on the request of the Trust Fund for Victims for leave to appeal against the order of 9 February 2016	Dismissing the request
29 March 2016	Reparation	Decision on the request of the Trust Fund for Victims for an extension of the time limit for the submission of the first batch of files of potential victims	Granting an extension of the time limit
14 June 2016	Reparation	Order setting the time limit for observations on the latest documents filed by the Trust Fund for Victims	Granting an extension of the time limit
15 July 2016	Reparation	Order instructing the Registry to provide aid and assistance to the Legal Representatives and the Trust Fund for Victims to identify victims potentially eligible for reparations	Instructing the Registry to support the Legal Representatives of victim and Trust Fund for Victims
20 September 2016	Reparation	Order setting time limits for observations on the motion of the Office of Public Counsel for Victims of 16 September 2016	Setting a time limit to file observations
23 September 2016	Trial	Decision granting an extension of time limit to submit observations on the request of the Office of Public Counsel for Victims of 16 September 2016	Granting an extension of the time limit

(continued)

Case: Thomas Lubanga Dylio			
Date	Stage	Decision	Description
21 October 2016	Reparation	Order approving the proposed plan of the Trust Fund for Victims in relation to symbolic collective reparations	Approving the plan of the Trust Fund for Victims
21 October 2016	Reparation	Order relating to the request of the Office of Public Counsel for Victims of 16 September 2016	Instructing to continue the identification process and to begin outreach missions
8 December 2016	Reparation	Order instructing the Trust Fund for Victims to Submit Information regarding Collective Reparations	Instructing to submit the relevant information
8 December 2016	Reparation	Decision rejecting the application for leave to appeal of the Legal Representatives of the 01 Group of Victims	Rejection of the application for leave to appeal
21 December 2016	Reparation	Order to complete the process of identifying victims potentially eligible to benefit from reparations	Extending the deadline to complete the Identification Process
22 February 2017	Reparation	Order for the Transmission of the Application Files of Victims who may be Eligible for Reparations to The Defence Team of Thomas Lubanga Dyilo	Instructing the VPRS to transmit the applications to the Defence
6 April 2017	Reparation	Order approving the proposed programmatic framework for collective service- based reparations submitted by the Trust Fund for Victims	Approving the first stage of the programmatic framework for collective service-based reparations
6 April 2017	Reparation	Decision on Requests for the Extension of Time submitted by the Office of Public Counsel for Victims, the Registry and the Legal Representatives of V02 Victims	Granting the Registry's Request
5 June 2017	Reparation	Decision on the Application of the Defence for Thomas Lubanga Dyilo of 24 April 2017 concerning Redactions in some of the Files of Potentially Eligible Victims	Rejecting the application of the Defence
16 June 2017	Reparation	Decision on the Applications of the Office of Public Counsel for Victims and the Legal Representatives of the V02 Group of Victims for Leave to Reply to the Observations of the Defence Team of Thomas Lubanga Dyilo of 22, 30 and 31 May 2017	Authorisation to reply to the Defence

(continued)

Case: Thomas Lubanga Dylio			
Date	Stage	Decision	Description
13 July 2017	Reparation	Decision on the Motion of the Office of Public Counsel for Victims for Reconsideration of the Decision of 6 April 2017	Rejecting the Motion for Reconsideration
20 July 2017	Reparation	Decision on the Application of the Office of Public Counsel for Victims seeking leave to reply to the Observations of the Defence for Thomas Lubanga Dyilo of 11 July 2017	Granting the OPCV's application in part
21 July 2017	Reparation	Decision on the Application of the Office of Public Counsel for Victims for an extension of the time limit set by the Order of 13 July 2017	Granting in part the application
6 September 2017	Reparation	Decision Granting the Request of the Office of Public Counsel for Victims for Extension of Page Limit	Granting the request
8 September 2017	Reparation	Decision on the Request by the Legal Representative of the V01 Group of Victims of 7 September 2017	Finding the request to be moot
7 November 2017	Reparation	Order Instructing the Trust Fund for Victims to Inform the Chamber of the Progress Made in the Implementation of Reparations	Instructing the Trust Fund for Victims to report on the progress made in the implementation of collective reparations
25 January 2018	Reparation	Order Directing Further Information from the Trust Fund for Victims on the Procedure for Determining Victim Status at the Implementation Stage of Reparations	Directing from the Trust Fund for Victims further information on the Procedure for determining the status of victim for the purposes of reparations
16 March 2018	Reparation	Order Instructing the Trust Fund for Victims to File the Documents Requested by the Chamber on the Process of Screening New Victims, the Progress of Discussions with the Stakeholders Involved in Locating and Identifying New Victims, the Possibility of Earmarking an Additional Amount for Reparations and the Progress of the Implementation of Reparations	Instructing the Trust Fund for Victims to file the information on the procedure for determining at the implementation stage of reparations the status of victim for the purpose of reparations

(continued)

Case: *Thomas Lubanga Dylio*			
Date	Stage	Decision	Description
26 July 2018	Appeal	Order on the reclassification of documents and on the filing of a public version of the legal representatives of the V02 group of victims' consolidated response	Ordering the Registry to reclassify certain documents as public
21 September 2018	Appeal	Scheduling order for a hearing before the Appeals Chamber and invitation to the Trust Fund for Victims to submit observations	Ordering a hearing before the Appeals Chamber in order to hear submissions and observations
10 October 2018	Appeal	Decision on Trust Fund for Victims' request for time extension	Granting an extension of the time limit
4 March 2019	Reparation	Decision Approving the Proposals of the Trust Fund for Victims on the Process for Locating New Applicants and Determining their Eligibility for Reparations	Approving the proposals submitted by the Trust Fund
12 July 2019	Appeal	Order on reclassification of documents filed by the V02 group of victims	Directing the Registrar to reclassify documents

6.3.2 *Prosecutor v. Germain Katanga*

Case: *Germain Katanga and Mathieu Ngudjolo Chui*			
Date	Stage	Decision	Description
2 April 2008	Pre-Trial	Decision on the Applications for Participation in the Proceedings of Applicants a/0327/07 to a/0337/07 and a/0001/08	Granting procedural status and deciding to make their observations on the set of procedural rights
23 April 2008	Pre-Trial	Decision on the Request of the Legal Representative of Victim a/0333/07 for Leave to Reply the Prosecution and the Defence's Observations on the Anonymity and Modalities of Participation in the Proceedings	Granting the request for leave to reply
15 May 2008	Pre-Trial	Decision on the Set of Procedural Rights Attached to Procedural Status of Victim at the Pre-Trial Stage of the Case	Granting victims procedural status

(continued)

Case: Germain Katanga and Mathieu Ngudjolo Chui			
Date	Stage	Decision	Description
21 May 2008	Pre-Trial	Decision regarding Responses to the Requests for Limitations on Access to Confidential Materials by Non Anonymous Victims of the Case	Granting the Defence and the Prosecution the right to file responses
29 May 2008	Pre-Trial	Decision on Request of Mathieu Ngudjolo Chui for Leave to Appeal the 'Decision on the Set of Procedural Rights Attached to Procedural Status of Victim at the Pre-Trial Stage of the Case'	Rejecting the request of the Defence
30 May 2008	Pre-Trial	Decision on Limitations of Set of Procedural Rights for Non-Anonymous Victims	Granting LRV to have access to confidential records,
10 June 2008	Pre-Trial	Public Redacted Version of the "Decision on the 97 Applications for Participation at the Pre-Trial Stage of the Case"	Granting victims procedural status
13 June 2008	Pre-Trial	Decision rectifying errors in the "Decision on the 97 Applications for Participation at the Pre-Trial Stage of the Case"	Rectifying two victims' statuses
23 June 2008	Pre-Trial	Decision on Victims' Requests for Anonymity at the Pre-Trial Stage of the Case	Granting victims the request not to disclose their identities
27 June 2008	Pre-Trial	Decision on "Victims and Witnesses Unit's considerations on the system of witness protection and the practice of 'preventive relocation'" and "Prosecution's request for leave to file a response to 'Victims and Witnesses Unit's considerations on the system of witness protection and the practice of 'preventive relocation''"	Authorising the Registrar to submit a document
3 July 2008	Pre-Trail	Decision on the provisional separation of Legal Representative of Victims a/0015/08, a/0022/08, a/0024/08, a/0025/08, a/0027/08, a/0028/08, a/0029/08, a/0032/08, a/0033/08, a/0034/08 and a/0035/08	Separating the Legal Representative of Victims from his functions
8 July 2008	Pre-Trial	Decision authorising the filing of observations on the "Report of the Registry on the apparent conflict of interest in relation to the Legal Representative of	Authorising the Prosecution and the Defence to file observations

(continued)

Case: *Germain Katanga and Mathieu Ngudjolo Chui*			
Date	Stage	Decision	Description
		Victims a/0015/06, a/0022/08, a/0024/08, a/0025/08, a/0027/08, a/0028/08, a/0029/08, a/0032/08, a/0033/08, a/0034/08 and a/0035/08"	
11 July 2008	Appeal	Reasons for the "Decision on 'Victims and Witnesses Unit's considerations on the system of witness protection and the practice of 'preventive relocation''' and "Prosecution's request for leave to file a response to 'Victims and Witnesses Unit's considerations on the system of witness protection and the practice of 'preventive relocation''"	Giving reasons for a previous decision
16 July 2008	Pre-Trial	Decision on the Apparent Conflict of Interest in relation to the Legal Representative of Victims a/0015/08, a/0022/08, a/0024/08, a/0025/08, a/0027/08, a/0028/08, a/0029/08, a/0032/08, a/0033/08, a/0034/08 and a/0035/08	Refusal to identify the existence of a conflict of interest
18 December 2008	Trial	Order Instructing the Registry to File Documents on the Influence that the Accused may have Retained in the DRC and on the Pressure that they Might Currently Exert on Victims and Witnesses	Requesting the Registry to file certain documents
26 February 2009	Trial	Decision on the treatment of applications for participation	Allowing pre-trial victims to participate in the trial
22 July 2009	Trial	Order on the organisation of common legal representation of victims	Setting out rules concerning the organisation of the common legal representation of victims
31 July 2009	Trial	Dispositif de la décision relative aux 345 demandes de participationde victimes à la procédure	Granting victims procedural status
5 August 2009	Trial	Corrigendum of Operative part of the Decision on the 345 applications for participation as victim in the proceedings	Granting victims procedural status
23 September 2009	Trial	Grounds for the Decision on the 345 Applications for Participation in the Proceedings Submitted by Victims	Giving reasons for a previous decision

(continued)

Case: Germain Katanga and Mathieu Ngudjolo Chui			
Date	Stage	Decision	Description
28 October 2009	Trial	Decision Inviting the Prosecutor and the Defence to Submit their Observations on Certain Applications for Participation from Victims (Rule 89(1) of the Rules of Procedure and Evidence)	Inviting the Prosecutor and the Defence teams to make observations
6 November 2009	Trial	Décision relative à la divulgation de l'identité des victimes aux parties	Ordering the Registry to disclose to the parties the identities of 189 victims
12 November 2009	Trial	Corrigendum to the "Decision on the Disclosure to the Parties of the Identities of the Victims" (ICC-01/04-01/07-1607)	Ordering the Registry to disclose to the parties the identities of 190 victims
18 November 2009	Trial	Second Decision on the Disclosure to the Parties of the Identities of the Victims	Ordering the Registry to disclose to the parties the identities of certain victims
23 November 2009	Trial	Operative Part of the Second Decision on the Applications by Victims for Participation in the Proceedings	Granting victims procedural status and ordering LRV to contact with new victims
17 December 2009	Trial	Third Decision on the Disclosure of the Identities of Victims to the Parties	Ordering the Registry to disclose to the parties the identity of 36 victims
22 December 2009	Trial	Motifs de la deuxième décision relative aux demandes de participation de victimes à la procedure	Giving reasons for a previous decision and granting victims procedural status
22 January 2010	Trial	Decision on the Modalities of Victim Participation at Trial	Deciding the procedural rights of the victims
16 March 2010	Trial	Motifs de la troisième décision relative à 8 demandes de participation de victimes à la procedure	Granting 3 victims procedural status
19 April 2010	Trial	Decision on the "Defence Application for Leave to Appeal the Trial Chamber's *Décision relative aux modalités de participation des victimes au stade des débats sur le fond*"	Partially granting leave to appeal
19 May 2010	Appeal	Decision on the Presiding Judge of the Appeals Chamber in the Appeal of Germain Katanga Against the Decision of Trial Chamber II Entitled "Decision on the Modalities of Victim Participation at Trial"	Appointing the Presiding Judge in the appeal

(continued)

Case: *Germain Katanga and Mathieu Ngudjolo Chui*			
Date	Stage	Decision	Description
24 May 2010	Appeal	Decision on the Participation of Victims in the Appeal of Mr Katanga Against the "Decision on the Modalities of Victim Participation at Trial"	Granting the right to victims to participate in the appeal for the purpose of presenting their views and concerns with respect to their personal interest in the issues raised on appeal
26 May 2010	Trial	Decision inviting the Prosecutor and the Defence to submit their observations on an application for participation by a victim (rule 89(1) of the Rules of Procedure and Evidence)	Ordering the Prosecutor and two Defence teams to submit their observations as to whether or not the status of victim participating in the proceedings should be granted
8 November 2010	Trial	Fourth decision on two applications for victims' participation in the proceedings	Granting victims procedural status
9 November 2010	Trial	Decision authorising the appearance of Victims a/0381/09, a/0018/09, a/0191/08, and pan/0263/09 acting on behalf of a/0363/09	Authorising victims to appear and to act via representative and on her own
23 November 2010	Trial	Decision on the arrangements for contact between represented victims and the parties	Deciding on the arrangements
10 January 2011	Trial	Decision inviting the Prosecutor and the Defence to submit observations on two victims' applications for participation (rule 89(1) of the Rules of Procedure and Evidence)	Ordering the Prosecutor and both Defence teams to submit their observations as to whether or not the status of victim participating in the proceedings should be granted
31 January 2011	Trial	Decision on the notification of the removal of Victim a/0381/09 from the Legal Representative's list of witnesses	Noting the removal of a victim from the list of victims whom the Chamber authorised to appear
9 February 2011	Trial	Cinquième décision relative à 2 demandes de participation de victimes à la procedure	Granting victims procedural status
11 February 2011	Trial	Décision relative à la Notification du retrait de la victime a/0363/09 de la liste des témoins du représentant légal	Noting the removal of a victim from the list of victims whom the Chamber authorised to appear
22 February 2011	Trial	Decision on the application for the institution of protective measures for Witnesses a/0381/09, a/0018/09, a/0191/08, pan/0363/09 and Victim a/0363/09, issued on 27 January 2011	Granting the application

(continued)

Case: Germain Katanga and Mathieu Ngudjolo Chui			
Date	Stage	Decision	Description
10 March 2011	Trial	Public redacted version of the Order to Consult the Victims and Witnesses Unit Regarding the Situation of Witnesses 219, 267 and 353 (ICC-01/04-01/07-1037-Conf-Exp, 7 April 2009)	Ordering the Prosecution to disclose the Applications to the Victims and Witnesses Unit
11 April 2011	Trial	Decision on the disclosure of the identity of victims to the parties and order to the Prosecutor and the Defence to submit additional observations in respect of certain deceased victims	Ordering the Registry to provide the Prosecutor and the Defence with a redacted version of the additional documents related to certain deceased victims
14 June 2011	Trial	Decision on the applications to resume action submitted by the family members of deceased Victims a/0025/08, a/0051/08, a/0197/08 and a/0311/09	Authorising the persons mandated respectively by the families of certain deceased victims to participate in the proceedings on behalf of said victims
7 July 2011	Trial	Decision on the maintenance of participating victim status of Victims a/0381/09 and a/0363/09 and on Mr Nsita Luvengika's request for leave to terminate his mandate as said victims' Legal Representative	Revoking the victim status of certain victims
21 October 2011	Trial	Décision relative aux demandes de reprise d'instance formées par les proches des victimes décédées a/0025/08 et a/0311/09	Authorising the persons mandated respectively by the families of certain deceased victims to participate in the proceedings on behalf of said victims
24 October 2011	Trial	Corrigendum of the decision on the applications to resume action submitted by the family members of deceased Victims a/0025/08 and a/0311/09	Authorising the persons mandated respectively by the families of certain deceased victims to participate in the proceedings on behalf of said victims
8 February 2012	Trial	Decision on the Prosecutor's request seeking leave to meet Witness P-219 in the presence of the Victims and Witnesses Unit	Declaring the Prosecutor's request null and void
15 February 2012	Trial	Decision on the request for an extension of the time limit for the submission of written conclusions by the Common Legal Representative of the main group of victims	Dismissing the Legal Representative's request

(continued)

Case: Germain Katanga and Mathieu Ngudjolo Chui			
Date	Stage	Decision	Description
5 March 2012	Trial	Decision on the application for an extension of time for the filing of the final submissions of the common legal representative of the main group of victims	Granting the application
23 April 2012	Trial	Decision on the Urgent Requests by the Legal Representative of Victims for Review of Registrar's Decision of 3 April 2012 regarding Legal Aid	Rejecting the request
17 January 2013	Appeal	Decision on the application of victims to participate in the appeal against Trial Chamber II's decision on the implementation of regulation 55 of the Regulations of the Court	Granting 364 victims the right to participate for the purpose of presenting their views and concerns with respect to their personal interests in the issues raised on appeal
10 June 2013	Trial	Decision on the application to resume action, submitted by a family member of deceased Victim a/0253/09	Authorising the person mandated by the family of the deceased victims to participate in the proceedings on behalf of that victims
11 March 2014	Trial	Décision relative à la requête du Représentant légal commun du groupe principal des victimes aux fins de prorogation du délai de dépôt des observations sur l'application de la règle 145 du Règlement	Rejecting the request for an extension of the time limit
24 July 2014	Appeal	Decision on the victims' requests to participate in the appeal proceedings	Rejecting victims to participate at the appeal because of the discontinuance of the appeal
24 April 2015	Reparation	Decision on the "Request by the Board of Directors for extension of time to submit Observations on Reparations Procedure"	Granting the request
11 May 2015	Reparation	Decision on the applications for resumption of action submitted by the family members of deceased victims a/0170/08 and a/0294/09	Authorising the persons mandated by the families of certain deceased victims to continue the action initiated in the Court on behalf of those victims
22 June 2015	Reparation	Decision on the "Defence Request Relating to the Trust Fund for Victims"	Rejecting the request to the Chamber to order the Fund to disclose the amount of money to be made available for reparations

(continued)

Case: Germain Katanga and Mathieu Ngudjolo Chui			
Date	Stage	Decision	Description
1 September 2015	Reparation	Decision on the "Defence Request for the Disclosure of Unredacted or Less Redacted Victim Applications"	Granting the request in part
21 September 2015	Reparation	Decision on the requests of the Common Legal Representative of Victims and the Registry for an extension of time limit for transmitting and filing applications for reparations	Granting the extension of the time limit
9 October 2015	Reparation	Decision on the request of the common legal representative of victims for assistance from the Victims and Witnesses Unit	Rejecting the request
8 December 2015	Reparation	Decision granting a further extension of time to the Common Legal Representative of Victims for submitting applications for reparations	Granting the extension of the time limit
16 February 2016	Reparation	Corrigendum to the "Order relating to the submission of the Legal Representative of Victims"	Ordering the Registry to apply the instructions provided in a previous decision
20 May 2016	Trial	Decision on the applications for resumption of action lodged by the family members of deceased victims a/0015/09, a/0032/08, a/0057/08, a/0166/09, a/0192/08, a/0225/09, a/0281/08, a/0282/09, a/0286/09, a/0298/09, a/0354/09, a/0361/09, a/0391/09, a/2743/10 and a/30490/15	Authorising the persons appointed by the families of certain deceased applicants to resume the action brought before the Court on their behalf
15 July 2016	Trial	Order instructing the parties and the Trust Fund for Victims to file observations on the monetary value of the alleged harm	Instructing the parties to file additional observations on the monetary value they consider fair for each type of harm alleged by the requesters
23 August 2016	Reparation	Ordonnance relative a la requête du Fonds au profit des victimes sollicitant accès au document ICC-01/04-01/07-3681-Conf et relative aux observations concernant la valeur monétaire des prejudices allégués	Ordering the Registry to reclassify documents as "confidential ex-parte"
30 September 2016	Reparation	Decision on the urgent request by the Common Legal Representative of Victims for an extension of the page limit for observations on the monetary value of the harm alleged	Granting the request for extension of the page limit

(continued)

Case: Germain Katanga and Mathieu Ngudjolo Chui			
Date	Stage	Decision	Description
12 December 2016	Reparation	Decision on the Application for Resumption of Action Submitted by a Relative of Deceased Victim a/0265/09 and the Appointment of a New Representative for Victim A/0071/08	Authorising the person designated by the family of the deceased victim to continue, on behalf of the victim, the action initiated before the Court
22 February 2017	Reparation	Decision on the Request by the Common Legal Representative of Victims for a Hearing to be Convened	Dismissing the request
3 March 2017	Reparation	Order Setting a Deadline for the Submission of Observations on the Application by the Common Legal Representative of Victims of 2 March 2017	Instructing the Defence to submit observation on the Application for Resumption of Action
15 March 2017	Reparation	Decision on the Application made by the Common Legal Representative of Victims on 2 March 2017	Deciding on several matters
24 March 2017	Reparation	Ordonnance de réparation en vertu de l'article 75 du Statut	Reparations for victims
24 March 2017	Reparation	Order Instructing the Parties to Propose Redactions and the Victims to Consent to Disclosure of their Contact Information to the Trust Fund for Victims	Instructing the Legal Representative and the OPCV to seek consent of the victims they each represent to the disclosure of their contact details to the Trust Fund
13 April 2017	Reparation	Decision rejecting the Request from the Legal Representative of Victims of 5 April 2017	Rejecting the request for an extension of the time limit
22 June 2017	Reparation	Decision granting the Trust Fund for Victims an extension of time for submission of the Draft Implementation Plan	Granting the request
11 July 2017	Reparation	Decision granting the Trust Fund for Victims an extension of time for submission of the Draft Implementation Plan	Extending the time limit for the Trust Fund for Victims
8 September 2017	Reparation	Decision Granting the Request by the Legal Representative of Victims for a Page Limit Extension	Granting the request
16 March 2018	Reparation	Order Instructing the Legal Representative of Victims and the Defence Team for Germain Katanga to File Submissions Further to the Appeals Chamber Judgment on Reparations of 8 March 2018	Instructing the Legal Representative and the Defence to file submissions

(continued)

Case: Germain Katanga and Mathieu Ngudjolo Chui			
Date	Stage	Decision	Description
8 May 2018	Reparation	Order Instructing the Defence Team for Germain Katanga to File Observations on the Application of the Office of Public Counsel for Victims of 19 April 2018, and for the Office of Public Counsel for Victims to File a Public Redacted Version of its Application	Instructing the Defence to file observations and the OPCV to file a public redacted version of its Application
12 July 2018	Reparation	Décision relative à la requête du Bureau du conseil public pour les victimes aux fins de modification partielle de l'Ordonnance de réparation rendue en vertu de l'article 75 du Statut de Rome	Rejecting the request of the OPCV
7 December 2018	Reparation	Decision on the Application by the Legal Representative for Victims regarding Compliance with Ethical Rules by the Parties and the Trust Fund for Victims in the Reparations Proceedings	Deciding that the ethical rules of the Code of Conduct shall apply mutatis mutandis to the Trust Fund

6.3.3 Prosecutor v. Bosco Ntaganda

Case: Bosco Bosco Ntaganda			
Date	Stage	Decision	Description
26 April 2013	Pre-Trial	Decision Requesting the Victims Participation and Reparations Section to Submit Observations	Ordering the VPRS to submit observations
28 May 2013	Pre-Trial	Decision Establishing Principles on the Victims' Application Process	Deciding on application process
26 June 2013	Pre-Trial	Decision on the "Demande de participation de neuf victimes admises dans le procès de M. Thomas Lubanga Dyilo"	Granting in part the application
21 August 2013	Pre-Trial	Decision Ordering the Parties to Provide Risk Assessment with Respect of Witnesses and the Victims and Witnesses Unit to Submit Observations Thereupon	Ordering the parties to provide a risk assessment

(continued)

Case: Bosco Bosco Ntaganda			
Date	Stage	Decision	Description
20 November 2013	Pre-Trial	Decision Requesting the VPRS and the OPCV to take steps with regard to the legal representation of victims in the confirmation of charges hearing and in the related proceedings	Requesting the OPCV to provide its observations
2 December 2013	Pre-Trial	Decision Concerning the Organisation of Common Legal Representation of Victims	Deciding on the modalities of the organisation of the Common Legal Representation of Victims
15 January 2014	Pre-Trial	Decision on Victims' Participation at the Confirmation of Charges Hearing and in the Related Proceedings	Granting victims procedural status
7 February 2014	Pre-Trial	Second Decision on Victims' Participation at the Confirmation of Charges Hearing and in the Related Proceedings	Granting victims procedural status
30 January 2015	Trial	Decision on Prosecution requests relating to victims applications	Granting the Prosecution request to disclose lesser redacted versions of the Applications
6 February 2015	Trial	Decision on victims' participation in trial proceedings	Setting out the admission system for victims to participate in the trial proceedings
9 February 2015	Trial	Decision on Prosecution request for an extension of time for disclosure of victim applications	Declaring the request moot
12 March 2015	Trial	Order requesting submissions on the conduct of proceedings pursuant to Rule 140 of the Rules and on modalities of victims' participation at trial	Instructing the parties, the LRVs and the Registry to submit observations
13 April 2015	Trial	Decision on the request of the Legal Representatives of Victims regarding joint instruction of experts	Rejecting the request
16 June 2015	Trial	Second decision on victims' participation in trial proceedings	Granting and rejecting victims procedural status
2 July 2015	Trial	Third decision on victims' participation in trial proceedings	Granting and rejecting victims procedural status
1 September 2015	Trial	Fourth decision on victims' participation in trial proceedings	Granting victims procedural status
16 November 2015	Trial	Fifth decision on victims' participation in trial proceedings	Granting victims procedural status
17 December 2015	Trial	Sixth decision on victims' participation in trial proceedings	Deciding to uphold the status of one person as a victim in the present proceedings

(continued)

Case: Bosco Bosco Ntaganda			
Date	Stage	Decision	Description
17 December 2015	Trial	Order on the provision of victim application forms of dual status witnesses	Directing the VPRS to provide the full length application forms, including supporting documents, of all dual status witnesses in the Ntaganda case to the Prosecution
1 July 2016	Trial	Seventh decision on victims' participation in trial proceedings	Authorising family members of victims to resume the action initiated before the Court
27 October 2016	Trial	Eighth decision on victims' participation in trial proceedings	Authorising applicants in respect of certain victims to resume the action initiated before the Court
11 January 2017	Trial	Order relating to the deadline for any requests by the Legal Representatives of Victims to present evidence or views and concerns of victims	Ordering the LRVs to proceed in accordance with the directions set out in the decision
15 February 2017	Trial	Public redacted version of 'Decision on the request by the Legal Representative of the Victims of the Attacks for leave to present evidence and victims' views and concerns' (10 February 2017, ICC-01/04-02/06-1780-Conf)	Authorising certain victims to present evidence, views and concerns
22 February 2017	Trial	Order amending the schedule for the presentation of victims' views and concerns	Setting a date for the hearing for the presentation of views and concerns by the Victims
28 February 2017	Trial	Public redacted version of 'Decision on request for Measures pursuant to Rules 87 and 88 for victims a/01635/13, a/20018/14 and a/30286/15'	Granting the request for use of a pseudonym and voice and face distortion
24 March 2017	Trial	Decision on Defence request for lifting of redactions in documents related to victims authorised to present evidence	Granting the request in part
20 June 2017	Trial	Decision on withdrawal of a victim's application for participation	Terminating the status of the victim
23 November 2017	Trial	Ninth decision on victims' participation in trial proceedings	Authorising applicants in respect of certain victims to resume the action initiated before the Court by the respective deceased victims
12 February 2018	Trial	Tenth decision on victims' participation in trial proceedings	Authorising applicants in respect of certain victims to resume the action initiated before the Court by the respective deceased victims

(continued)

Case: *Bosco Bosco Ntaganda*			
Date	Stage	Decision	Description
26 April 2018	Trial	Eleventh decision on victims' participation in trial proceedings	Authorising applicants in respect of certain victims to resume the action initiated before the Court by the respective deceased victims
8 October 2019	Appeal	Decision on victim participation	Allowing the victims to participate
13 February 2020	Appeal	Decision on victim participation	Allowing the victims to participate

6.3.4 *Prosecutor v. Callixte Mbarushimana*

Case: *Callixte Mbarushimana*			
Date	Stage	Decision	Description
15 March 2011	Pre-Trial	Order setting a deadline for the transmission of applications for victims' participation	Setting a deadline for the transmission of applications for victim's participation
24 May 2011	Pre-Trial	Decision requesting the Parties to submit observations on 14 applications for victims' participation in the proceedings	Requesting the parties to submit their observations
10 June 2011	Pre-Trial	Decision on the "Proposal on victim participation in the confirmation hearing"	Rejecting the proposal of registry
4 July 2011	Pre-Trial	Decision requesting the Parties to submit observations on 124 applications for victims' participation in the proceedings	Requesting the Defence and the Prosecution to submit their observations on the applications
11 August 2011	Pre-Trial	Decision on the 138 applications for victims' participation in the proceedings	Granting victims procedural rights
23 August 2011	Pre-Trial	Decision on the "Defence request for disclosure of information related to the alleged victims of sexual violence"	Rejecting and granting partially the request of the Defence
9 September 2011	Pre-Trial	Decision on the representation of participating victims formerly represented by Mr Hervé Diakiese	Appointing a different legal representative for 30 participating victims
23 September 2011	Pre-Trial	Decision on the applications for participation of victim applicants a/2176/11 and a/2195/11	Granting victims procedural rights

(continued)

Case: Callixte Mbarushimana			
Date	Stage	Decision	Description
27 September 2011	Pre-Trial	Decision on the "Defence Application for leave to appeal the 'Decision on the Defence request for disclosure of information related to the alleged victims of sexual violence'"	Rejecting the application of the Defence
8 May 2012	Appeal	Order on the filing of a public redacted version of the "Observations des victimes autorisées à participer à la procédure sur l'appel du Procureur contre la 'Décision relative à la confirmation des charges' (ICC-01/04-01/10-465-Conf-tFRA)"	Ordering to file a public redacted version of a document

6.4 Situation in the Republic of Kenya

Situation in the Republic of Kenya			
Date	Stage	Decision	Description
10 December 2009	Pre-Trial	Order to the Victims Participation and Reparations Section Concerning Victims' Representations Pursuant to Article 15(3) of the Statute	Ordering the VPRS to implement the procedure outlined in the order
3 November 2010	Pre-Trial	Decision on Victims' Participation in Proceedings Related to the Situation in the Republic of Kenya	Deciding that victims may participate in the proceedings related to the situation in the Republic of Kenya in accordance with the framework established in the decision
10 November 2010	Pre-Trial	Decision on Victims' Participation in Proceedings Related to the Situation in the Republic of Kenya	Granting victims procedural status
5 November 2015	Pre-Trial	Decision on the "Victims' request for review of Prosecution's decision to cease active investigation"	Rejecting victims' request to participating at the appeal

6.4.1 Prosecutor v. William Samoei Ruto and Joshua Arap Sang

Case: William Samoei Ruto and Joshua Arap Sang			
Date	Stage	Decision	Description
30 March 2011	Pre-Trial	Decision on the Motion by Legal Representative of Victim Applicants to Participate in Initial Appearance Proceedings	Rejecting the motion
30 March 2011	Pre-Trial	First Decision on Victims' Participation in the Case	Setting the framework for victims' participation
6 April 2011	Pre-Trial	Second Decision on the Motion of Legal Representative of Victim Applicants to Participate in Initial Appearance Proceedings and Article 19 Admissibility Proceedings	Rejecting the motion to participate by the victim applicants
3 June 2011	Pre-Trial	Decision Requesting the Victims and Witnesses Unit to Submit Observations	Ordering the VWU to submit its observation on the Prosecutor's risk assessment
28 June 2011	Pre-Trial	Decision on the Registrar's "Request for instructions on the processing of victim's applications"	Ordering the VPRS to submit only complete applications for participation
8 July 2011	Pre-Trial	Decision on the Defence Requests in Relation to the Victims' Applications for Participation in the Present Case	Rejecting request of the Defence
5 August 2011	Pre-Trial	Decision on Victims' Participation at the Confirmation of Charges Hearing and in the Related Proceedings	Granting victims procedural status
19 August 2011	Pre-Trial	Decision on the "Request by the Victims' Representative for authorisation by the Chamber to make written submissions on specific issues of law and/or fact"	Rejecting the request
9 September 2011	Pre-Trial	Decision on the "Motion from Victims a/0041/10, a/0045/10, a/0051/10 and a/0056/10 requesting the PTC to Reconsider the Appointment of Common Legal Representative Sureta Chana for All Victims"	Rejecting the request for reconsideration
21 September 2011	Pre-Trial	Decision on the "Request by the Victims' Representative for access to confidential materials" and Requesting Observations from the Prosecutor	Rejecting the request

(continued)

Case: William Samoei Ruto and Joshua Arap Sang			
Date	Stage	Decision	Description
22 September 2011	Pre-Trial	Decision on the "Renewed Request by the Victims' Representative for authorisation by the Chamber to make submissions on specific issues of law and/or fact"	Granting the request
23 September 2011	Pre-Trial	Second Decision on the "Request by the Victims' Representative for access to confidential materials"	Ordering the Registrar to notify the legal representative of victims a specific document
3 October 2011	Pre-Trial	Decision on the "Request by the Victims' Representative for authorisation to respond to the 'Defence Request Regarding Prejudicial Comments Made by Victims' Legal Representative Sureta Chana during Closing Statements"	Granting the VLR the right to file a written response to the request
9 December 2011	Pre-Trial	Decision on the "Request by the Victims' Representative for authorisation to make a further written submission on the views and concerns of the victims"	Rejecting one of the requests and deciding to address the other one in the Chamber's decision pursuant to article 61(7) of the Statute
9 March 2012	Pre-Trial	Decision on the "Urgent Request by the Victims' Representative for an order from the Chamber requiring the Registrar to provide appropriate resources for the current mission in Kenya"	Dismissing in limine the VLR request and her application for leave to reply to the Registrar's observations
27 March 2012	Appeal	Order on the submission of observations by the Registrar on the "Application of the Victims' Representative pursuant to Article 83 of the Regulations"	Ordering the Registrar to submit observations in relation to the "Application of the Victims' Representative pursuant to Article 83 of the Regulations"
23 April 2012	Appeal	Decision on the "Application of the Victims' Representative pursuant to Article 83 of the Regulations"	Rejecting the application of the Victims' Representative
3 October 2012	Trial	Decision on victims' representation and participation	Deciding on modalities of participation
9 November 2012	Trial	Decision on the supplementary protocol concerning the handling of confidential information concerning victims and contacts of a party with victims	Deciding that the parties and common legal representative of victims shall apply the Supplementary Protocol set out in the decision
23 November 2012	Trial	Decision appointing a common legal representative of victims	Deciding on CLRV
13 December 2012	Trial	Decision on the request to present views and concerns of victims on their legal representation at the trial phase	Rejecting the request

(continued)

Case: William Samoei Ruto and Joshua Arap Sang			
Date	Stage	Decision	Description
13 February 2013	Trial	Order regarding the Victims and Witnesses Unit's assessment of the security situation and protection status of Witnesses 495,534 and 536	Ordering the VWU to file an updated report on three witnesses
20 February 2013	Trial	Order regarding the Victims and Witnesses Unit's request for an extension of time to submit a report on the security situation and protection status of Witnesses 495, 534 and 536	Granting the VWU's request for an extension of time to submit the report
24 July 2013	Trial	Order authorising disclosure of lesser redacted versions of victims' applications	Authorising the Prosecution to disclose lesser redacted versions of the victim's applications related to certain witnesses
1 August 2013	Trial	Order authorising disclosure of a lesser redacted victim application of Witness 128	Authorising the Prosecution to disclose the lesser redacted version of the victim application related to a certain witness
6 September 2013	Trial	Order shortening time limit to respond to the 'Common Legal Representative for Victims' Comprehensive Report on the Withdrawal of Victims from the Turbo area by Letter dated 5 June 2013'	Directing the parties to file any response to the LRV Report no later than the date set out in the order
9 September 2013	Trial	Order authorising disclosure of victims' applications	Directing the LRV to transmit to the parties the application forms of certain dual status victims
27 September 2013	Appeal	Order on the filing of a response to the request by the Common Legal Representative for victims to participate in the appeal against PTC II's decision of 16 August 2013	Ordering the parties to file a response to the above-mentioned application until a date set out in the order
14 November 2013	Trial	Decision on the Legal Representative's Report on the Withdrawal of Victims	Directing the Registry to withdraw certain victims from the database
20 November 2013	Trial	Decision on Common Legal Representative for Victims' Request to Participate in Hearings and Examine Witnesses	Rejecting the Legal Representative's request to attend a certain session
31 October 2014	Trial	Decision on Victims and Witnesses Unit's Submission Pursuant to Regulation 41 of the Regulations of the Court on Witness KEN-RDW-P-0072	Directing the VWU to provide the information contained in its submission

(continued)

Case: William Samoei Ruto and Joshua Arap Sang			
Date	Stage	Decision	Description
27 November 2014	Trial	Decision on the Application by the Legal Representative of Victims requesting Leave to Appear in Court and Question Witness 658	Granting the Legal Representative's request to attend the hearing throughout a witness' testimony
20 July 2015	Trial	Decision on the Common Legal Representative for Victims' Request for viva voce Presentation of Views and Concerns by the Victims	Ordering the VWU to submit a report to the Chamber pursuant to the requirements set out in the decision
7 September 2015	Trial	Order on the Timing of the Victims' Views and Concerns	Granting partially the request and authorising the Legal Representative to present his clients' views

6.4.2 Prosecutor v. Francis Kirimi Muthaura, Uhuru Muigai Kenyatta and Mohammed Hussein Ali

Case: Francis Kirimi Muthaura, Uhuru Muigai Kenyatta and Mohammed Hussein Ali			
Date	Stage	Decision	Description
30 March 2011	Pre-Trial	First Decision on Victims' Participation in the Case	Ordering VPRS to submit applications for participation and to comply with the requirements set forth in the decision
6 June 2011	Pre-Trial	Decision Ordering the Victims and Witnesses Unit to Submit Observations	Ordering the VWU to submit its observations on the Prosecutor's risk assessment
28 June 2011	Pre-Trial	Decision on the Registrar's "Request for instructions on the processing of victims' applications"	Ordering VPRS to submit only complete applications
1 July 2011	Pre-Trial	Decision on the "OPCV's Request for Leave to Respond to 'Defence Observations on 4 Applications for Victim Participation in the Proceedings'"	Rejecting requests
8 July 2011	Pre-Trial	Decision on the Defence Requests in Relation to the Victims' Applications for Participation in the Present Case	Ordering the Registry to transmit to the Prosecutor the unredacted version of all the victims' application for participation received in the present case

(continued)

Case: Francis Kirimi Muthaura, Uhuru Muigai Kenyatta and Mohammed Hussein Ali			
Date	Stage	Decision	Description
12 August 2011	Pre-Trial	Decision on the Extension of Time Limit to File Observations on Victims' Applications for Participation in the Proceedings	Granting the Defence the opportunity to file its observations after the confirmation hearing and before the issuance of the confirmation decision
26 August 2011	Pre-Trial	Decision on Victims' Participation at the Confirmation of Charges Hearing and in the Related Proceedings	Granting victims procedural status
14 September 2011	Pre-Trial	Decision on the Request for Access to Confidential *Inter Partes* Material	Rejecting request of CLRV
27 March 2012	Appeal	Order on the submission of observations by the Registrar on the "Notification regarding the Legal Representation of Participating Victims in these Appeals Proceedings"	Ordering the registrar to submit observations in relation to the "Notification regarding the Legal Representation of Participating Victims in these Appeals Proceedings"
23 April 2012	Appeal	Decision on the "Notification regarding the Legal Representation of Participating Victims in the Appeal Proceedings"	Rejecting the request and alternative request made in the "Notification regarding the Legal Representation of Participating Victims in the Appeal Proceedings"
3 October 2012	Trial	Decision on victims' representation and participation	Deciding on modalities of participation
9 November 2012	Trial	Decision on the supplementary protocol concerning the handling of confidential information concerning victims and contacts of a party with victims	Deciding that the parties and common legal representative of victims shall apply the Supplementary Protocol set out in the present decision
20 November 2012	Trial	Decision appointing a common legal representative of victims	Appointing a new common legal representative of victims
2 April 2013	Trial	Order authorising disclosure of lesser redacted versions of victims' applications	Authorising the Prosecution to disclose lesser redacted versions of the victims' applications related to certain witnesses
18 September 2013	Trial	Decision on disclosure of lesser redacted version of victim's application relating to Witness 232	Authorising the Prosecution to disclose the lesser redacted version of the victim's application related to certain witnesses
30 September 2013	Trial	Redacted version of Decision concerning 'Victims' application relating to possible disclosure of confidential information'	Dismissing the relief sought in the Application
26 November	Trial	Decision on request of the Legal Representative of Victims for leave to reply	Granting the request for Leave to Reply in relation to certain issued outlined in the decision

(continued)

Case: Francis Kirimi Muthaura, Uhuru Muigai Kenyatta and Mohammed Hussein Ali			
Date	Stage	Decision	Description
11 December 2014	Trial	Decision on request of the Legal Representative of Victims for a public redacted version of the pre-trial brief	Granting in part the portion of the request relating to the filing of a public redacted version of the Prosecution's second updated pre-trial brief
24 April 2015	Appeal	Decision on the victims' request to participate in the appeal proceedings	Granting victims procedural status

6.5 Prosecutor v. Ahmad Al Faqi Al Mahdi

Case: Ahmad Al Faqi Al Mahdi			
Date	Stage	Decision	Description
8 June 2016	Trial	Public redacted version of 'Decision on Victim Participation at Trial and on Common Legal Representation of Victims'	Granting victims procedural status
20 June 2016	Trial	Decision on Prosecution Request for an Extension of Time to Conduct the Review of the Case Record to be Made Available to the Legal Representative of Victims	Granting the request
22 July 2016	Trial	Decision on Legal Representative of Victims' access to the case record	Directing Registry to maintain ex parte filings
12 August 2016	Trial	Public redacted version of 'Second Decision on Victim Participation at Trial', 12 August 2016	Granting victims procedural status
19 August 2016	Trial	Decision on LRV Request for Redacted Victim Applications and Additional Information	Granting the request of LRV
31 May 2017	Reparation	Decision on LRV's request for clarification of procedure applicable to newly collected reparations applications	Rejecting the request
2 June 2017	Reparation	Decision on LRV Request for Resumption of Action for Deceased Victim a/35084/16	Granting the request of LRV
17 August 2017	Reparation	Reparations Order	Reparations for victims
24 November 2017	Appeal	Decision on the Trust Fund for Victims' request for time extension	Granting the request for extension of time
14 February 2018	Reparation	Public redacted version of 'Decision on Trust Fund for Victims' Request for Extension of Time' dated 12 February 2018 (ICC-01/12-01/15-257	Granting in part the request for extension of time

(continued)

Case: Ahmad Al Faqi Al Mahdi			
Date	Stage	Decision	Description
8 March 2018	Appeal	Judgment on the appeal of the victims against the "Reparations Order"	Reparations for victims
5 April 2018	Reparation	Public redacted version of 'Decision on Second Trust Fund for Victims' Request for Extension of Time', 5 April 2018	Granting the request for extension of time
24 May 2018	Reparation	Decision on Legal Representative of Victims' Request for Extension of Time to Respond to Draft Implementation Plan	Granting the request for extension of time
12 July 2018	Reparation	Public redacted version of 'Decision on Trust Fund for Victims' Draft Implementation Plan for Reparations', 12 July 2018	Approving draft implementation plan
31 August 2018	Reparation	Decision on TFV Request for Clarification Regarding Individual Reparations for Economic Harm	Rejecting the relief sought in the Request
5 November 2018	Reparation	Decision inviting Malian authorities to submit observations on the Trust Fund for Victims' Updated Implementation Plan	Inviting Malian authorities to submit observations
21 November 2018	Reparation	Decision on TFV Submission of Draft Application Form	Adopting new application form
4 March 2019	Reparation	Decision on the Updated Implementation Plan from the Trust Fund for Victims	Approving selected projects

6.6 Prosecutor v. Al Hassan Ag Abdoul Aziz Ag Mohamed Ag Mahmoud

Case: Al Hassan Ag Abdoul Aziz Ag Mohamed Ag Mahmoud			
Date	Stage	Decision	Description
24 May 2018	Pre-Trial	Decision Establishing the Principles Applicable to Victims' Applications for Participation	Instructions on application system
11 September 2018	Pre-Trial	Public Redacted Version of Decision on the Registry's Reports concerning Victim Participation	Authorising registry to obtain additional information
8 October 2018	Pre-Trial	Second Decision on the Principles Applicable to Victims' Applications for Participation	Instructions on application system
20 March 2019	Pre-Trial	Decision on Principles Applicable to Victims' Applications for Participation, to Legal Representation of Victims, and to the Manner of Victim Participation in the Proceedings	Deciding not to adopt a collective application form in the instant case
1 July 2019	Pre-Trial	Décision relative à la participation des victimes à la procedure	Granting 882 victims procedural status

(continued)

Case: Al Hassan Ag Abdoul Aziz Ag Mohamed Ag Mahmoud			
Date	Stage	Decision	Description
20 December 2019	Trial Chamber	Decision on the Prosecution request for access to the identity and applications of participating victims and inviting report and submissions on victim application procedure	Decision on dual status victims
12 March 2020	Trial Chamber	Decision on the procedure for the admission of victims to participate in proceedings for the purposes of trial	Decision on modalities
12 June 2020	Trial Chamber	Decision on request for extension of deadlines for the final transmission of victim applications for participation at trial	Setting deadlines
17 June 2020	Trial Chamber	Public redacted version of 'Second decision on the admission of victims to participate in trial proceedings'	Admissions of 4 group victims and rejected 1
10 August 2020	Trial Chamber	Third decision on the admission of victims to participate in trial proceedings	Allowing 1097 victims to participate and rejected 47 applications
14 December 2020	Trial Chamber	Fourth decision on the admission of victims to participate in trial proceedings	Allowing 183 victims to participate

6.7 Situation in Sudan

Situation in Sudan			
Date	Stage	Decision	Description
23 May 2007	Pre-Trial	Decision authorising the filing of observations on applications for participation in the proceedings a/0011/06 to a/0015/06	Authorising the parties to submit observations
23 July 2007	Pre-Trial	Decision authorising the filing of observations on applications a/0021/07, a/0023/07to a/0033/07 and a/0035/07 to a/0038/07 for participation in the proceedings	Authorising the parties to submit observations
22 August 2007	Pre-Trial	Decision on the time limit to submit observations on applications for participation as victims a/0021/07, a/0023/07 to a/0033/07 and a/0035/07 to a/0038/07 and on the extension of page limit	Rejecting the request for an extension of the page limit
6 December 2007	Pre-Trial	Decision on the Applications for Participation in the Proceedings of Applicants 000000000000000000000000000000a/0011/06 to a/0015/06, a/0021/07, a/0023/07 to a/0033/07 and a/0035/07 to a/0038/07	Granting victims procedural status

(continued)

Situation in Sudan

Date	Stage	Decision	Description
6 February 2008	Pre-Trial	Decision on the Request for Leave to appeal the Decision on the Application for Participation of Victims in the Proceedings in the Situations	Granting in part the request for leave to appeal
29 February 2008	Appeal	Decision of the Appeals Chamber on the OPCV's request for clarification and Order of the Appeals Chamber on the date of filing of applications for participation and on the time of the filing of the responses thereto by the OPCV and the Prosecutor	Dismissing the request for clarifications by the OPCV
18 June 2008	Appeal	Decision on Victim Participation in the appeal of the Office of Public Counsel for the Defence against PTC I's Decision of 3 December 2007 and in the appeals of the Prosecutor and the Office of Public Counsel for the Defence against PTC I's Decision of 6 December 2007	Granting victims procedural status
19 June 2008	Appeal	Directions to the Prosecutor and the OPCD on the request of Legal Representatives of Victims a/0011/06 to a/0015/06, a/0021/07, a/0023/07 to a/0033/07 and a/0035/07 to a/0038/07 for an extension of the page limit	Deciding that the Prosecutor and the OPCD may file a response to the request of the legal representative
24 June 2008	Appeal	Order on the request of Legal Representatives of Victims a/0011/06, a/0012/06, a/0013/06, a/0015/06, a/0023/07, a/0024/07, a/0026/07, a/0029/07, a/0036/07, a/0037/07 and a/0038/07 for an extension of the page limit	Granting the request of the legal representatives for an extension of the page limit
8 September 2008	Pre-Trial	Decision on the Indigence of Victims a/0015/06, a/0029/07, a/0036/07, a/0037/07 and a/0038/07	Deciding to consider the victims indigent
29 February 2009	Appeal	Scheduling Order for the judgment on victim participation in the investigation stage of the proceedings in the appeal of the OPCD against the decision of PTC I of 3 December 2007 and in the appeals of the OPCD and the Prosecutor against the decision of PTC I of 6 December 2007	Scheduling the date for the judgement on victim participation
2 February 2009	Appeal	Judgment on victim participation in the investigation stage of the proceedings in the appeal of the OPCD against the decision of PTC I of 3 December 2007and in the appeals of the OPCD and the Prosecutor against the decision of PTC I of 6 December 2007	Reversing the decision on participation of the victims at the investigation stage

6.7.1 Prosecutor v. Harun and Abd-Al-Rahman

Case: Ahmad Muhammad Harun and Ali Muhammad Ali Abd-Al-Rahman			
Date	Stage	Decision	Description
19 August 2009	Pre-Trial	Decision on the Designation of a Single Judge on Victims' Issues	Appointing a Single Judge responsible for all issues related to victims' applications
26 April 2010	Pre-Trial	Decision Setting a Time Limit for the Parties' Replies to 6 Applications for Victims' Participation in the Proceedings	Granting the parties time to reply to the applications
17 June 2010	Pre-Trial	Decision on 6 Applications for Victims' Participation in the Proceedings	Granting victims procedural status

6.7.2 Prosecutor v. Al Bashir

Case: Omar Al Bashir			
Date	Stage	Decision	Description
19 August 2009	Pre-Trial	Decision on the Designation of a Single Judge on Victims' Issues	Appointing a Single Judge responsible for all issues related to victims' applications
27 August 2009	Pre-Trial	Decision on the 'Legal Representative's Request to Expedite the Consideration of Applications for Victim Status'	Ordering Registry to transmit the applications to the parties
1 September 2009	Pre-Trial	Decision Ordering the Parties to Submit their Observations on the Applications for Victims' Participation in the Proceedings	Ordering the Registry to transmit the applications to the parties
23 October 2009	Appeal	Decision on the Applications by Victims a/0443/09 to a/0450/09 to Participate in the Appeal against the "Decision on the Prosecution's Application for a Warrant of Arrest against Omar Hassan Ahmad Al Bashir" and on the Request for an Extension of Time	Rejecting the request for an extension of time
6 November 2009	Pre-Trial	Decision Ordering the Parties to Submit their Observations on Applications a/0443/09 to a/0450/09 for Participation as Victims in the Proceedings	Ordering the parties to submit their observations on the applications for participation

(continued)

Case: Omar Al Bashir			
Date	Stage	Decision	Description
10 December 2009	Pre-Trial	Decision on Applications a/0011/06 to a/0013/06, a/0015/06 and a/0443/09 to a/0450/09 for Participation in the Proceedings at the Pre-Trial Stage of the Case	Granting procedural status
17 December 2009	Pre-Trial	Decision on the ad hoc Counsel for the Defence Request Regarding Victims' Participation in the Case	Granting an extension of the time limit for the submission of observations by the *ad hoc* Counsel
28 January 2010	Appeal	Decision on the Second Application by Victims a/0443/09 to a/0450/09 to Participate in the Appeal against the "Decision on the Prosecution's Application for a Warrant of Arrest against Omar Hassan Ahmad Al Bashir"	Granting victims procedural status at the appeal
26 May 2010	Pre-Trial	Decision Setting a Time Limit for the Parties' Replies to 8 Applications for Victims' Participation in the Proceedings	Granting the parties time to reply to the applications
9 July 2010	Pre-Trial	Decision on 8 Applications for Victims' Participation in the Proceedings	Denying certain applicants the authorisation to participate as victims in the proceedings at the pre-trial stage

6.7.3 *Prosecutor v. Abu Garda*

Case: Bahar Idriss Abu Garda			
Date	Stage	Decision	Description
12 June 2009	Pre-Trial	Decision on issues relating to victims' applications in the Case	Ordering the VPRS to take all steps which might be necessary and appropriate for the applications to be completed and transmitted to the Chamber
19 August 2009	Pre-Trial	Decision on the Designation of a Single Judge on Victims' Issues and on the Deadline for the Filing of Applications for Participation	Appointing a Single Judge responsible for all issues related to victims' applications to be authorised to participate as victims in the proceedings
27 August 2009	Pre-Trial	Decision Ordering the Parties to Submit their Observations on the Applications for Victims' Participation in the Proceedings	Ordering the parties to file observations on the applications for participation

(continued)

Case: Bahar Idriss Abu Garda			
Date	Stage	Decision	Description
16 September 2009	Pre-Trial	Decision Ordering the Parties to Submit their Observations on the 52 Applications for Victims' Participation in the Proceedings	Ordering the parties to file their observations on the applications for participation
25 September 2009	Pre-Trial	Decision on the 34 Applications for Participation at the Pre-Trial Stage of the Case	Granting victims procedural status
6 October 2009	Pre-Trial	Decision on victims' modalities of participation at the Pre-Trial Stage of the Case	Deciding on modalities of participation
7 October 2009	Pre-Trial	Decision on the "Response to Defence Observations on Applications for Victim Participation in the Proceedings"	Dismissing in limine the response to defence observations
9 October 2009	Pre-Trial	Public Redacted Version of "Decision on the 52 Applications for Participation at the Pre-Trial Stage of the Case"	Granting victims procedural status
14 October 2009	Pre-Trial	Decision on the "Request in respect of Information relevant to Victim Participation on the basis of the Decision on 52 Applications for Participation at the Pre-Trial Stage of the Case"	Rejecting in limine the Legal Representatives' Request
14 October 2009	Pre-Trial	Decision setting a deadline for request to lift anonymity of victims	Setting a deadline for requests to lift anonymity of victims
19 October 2009	Pre-Trial	Decision Amending the "Decision Lifting Anonymity of Victims"'	Ordering the Registry to provide the Defence only with the names of certain victims
13 November 2009	Pre-Trial	Decision on the Legal Representatives of Victims' Request	Granting the LRV time to submit their final written observations
20 November 2009	Pre-Trial	Decision on the Legal Representative of Victims' Request	Rejecting the request
29 January 2010	Pre-Trial	Decision Setting a Time Limit for the Parties' Replies to 20 Applications for Victims' Participation in the Proceedings	Granting the parties time to reply to the applications
19 March 2010	Pre-Trial	Decision on Applications a/0655/09, a/0656/09, a/0736/09 to a/0747/09,and a/0750/09 to a/0755/09 for Participation in the Proceedings at the Pre-Trial Stage of the Case	Granting victims procedural status
24 March 2010	Pre-Trial	Decision requesting clarification on submission of Response by Legal Representative of Victims	Ordering the Registrar and the LRV to submit a report recounting and explaining the circumstances surrounding the submission of the Response by the Legal Representative

(continued)

Case: *Bahar Idriss Abu Garda*			
Date	Stage	Decision	Description
8 April 2010	Pre-Trial	Decision on the Legal Representative of Victims' Application for extension of time limit	Rejecting the LRVs' application for extension of time for filing his response to the prosecutor's application for Leave to Appeal

6.7.4 *Prosecutor v. Abdallah Banda Abakaer Nourain*

Case: *Abdallah Banda Abakaer Nourain*			
Date	Stage	Decision	Description
27 July 2010	Pre-Trial	Decision Setting a Time Limit for the Parties' Replies to 87 Applications for Victims' Participation in the Proceedings and a Deadline for the Filing of Applications for Participation	Granting the parties time to reply to the applications
24 August 2010	Pre-Trial	Decision Setting a Time Limit for the Parties' Replies to 8 Victims' Applications for Participation	Setting the parties a time limit to reply to the applications
29 October 2010	Pre-Trial	Decision on Victims' Participation at the Hearing on the Confirmation of the Charges	Granting victims procedural status
6 December 2010	Pre-Trial	Order to the Defence and the Legal Representatives of Victims a/1646/10 and a/1647/10 to file a response to the "Prosecution Objection to the Continued Representation of Victims a/1646/10 and a/1647/10 by Messrs Geoffrey Nice and Rodney Dixon"	Ordering the Defence and the Legal Representatives of certain victims to file a response to the Prosecutor's filing
17 October 2011	Trial	Decision on the Registry Report on six applications to participate in the proceedings	Authorising pre-trial victims to participate at trial
31 October 2011	Trial	Order on the application on behalf of victims a/1646/10 and a/1647/10 for leave to reply	Granting the victims' application
6 May 2013	Appeal	Decision on the participation of victims in the appeal	Dismissing application, because of lack of personal interests of victims
20 March 2014	Trial	Decision on the participation of victims in the trial proceedings	Deciding on modalities of participation

6.8 Situation in Uganda

Situation in Uganda			
Date	Stage	Decision	Description
17 June 2005	Pre-Trial	Decision to hold a hearing on the protection of victims and witnesses in connection with the Prosecutor's application for warrants of arrest and the Prosecutor's application dated 13 June 2005	Deciding to hold a hearing regarding the protection of victims and witnesses
10 August 2007	Pre-Trial	Decision on victims' applications for participation a/0010/06, a/0064/06 to a/0070/06,a/0081/06 to a/0104/06 and a/0111/06 to a/0127/06	Granting victims procedural status
28 August 2007	Pre-Trial	Decision on legal representation of Victims a/0101/06 and a/0119/06	Appointing the Principal Counsel of the OPCV as legal representative of victims
3 September 2007	Pre-Trial	Decision Designating a Single Judge on Victim's Issues for the Period of 6 September to 15 October 2007	Designating a Single Judge responsible for all victims' related issues in the proceedings
19 December 2007	Pre-Trial	Decision on the Prosecution's Application for Leave to Appeal the Decision on Victims' Applications for Participation a/0010/06, a/0064/06 to a/0070/06, a/0081/06 to a/0104/06 and a/0111/06 to a/0127/06	Rejecting the Prosecutor's Application
15 February 2008	Pre-Trial	Decision on legal representation of Victims a/0090/06, a/0098/06, a/0101/06 a/0112/06, a/0118/06, a/0119/06 and a/0122/06	Appointing a Legal Representative of Victims
14 March 2008	Pre-Trial	Decision on victims' applications for participation a/0010/06, a/0064/06 to a/0070/06,a/0081/06, a/0082/06, a/0084/06 to a/0089/06, a/0091/06 to a/0097/06, a/0099/06,a/0100/06, a/0102/06 to a/0104/06, a/0111/06, a/0113/06 to a/0117/06, a/0120/06,a/0121/06 and a/0123/06 to a/0127/06	Granting victims procedural status
2 June 2008	Pre-Trial	Decision on the Defence Application for Leave to Appeal the 14 March 2008 Decision on Victims' Application for Participation	Granting the Defense in part Leave to Appeal
19 June 2008	Appeal	Decision on the Presiding Judge of the Appeals Chamber in the appeal of the Defence against the "Decision on victims' applications for	Appointing the Presiding Judge

(continued)

Situation in Uganda

Date	Stage	Decision	Description
		participation a/0010/06, a/0064/06 to a/0070/06, a/0081/06, a/0082/06, a/0084/06 to a/0089/06, a/0091/06 to a/0097/06,n a/0099/06, a/0100/06, a/0102/06 to a/0104/06, a/0111/06, a/0113/06 to a/0117/06, a/0120/06, a/0121/06 and a/0123/06 to a/0127/06" of PTC II	
22 July 2008	Appeal	Order on the filing of responses by the Prosecutor and the ad hoc Counsel for the Defence to the request of victims a/0101/06 and a/0119/06 for participation in the appeal	Ordering the Prosecutor and the ad hoc Counsel for the Defense to file a response to the application for participation
4 September 2008	Appeal	Decision on the Presiding Judge of the Appeals Chamber in the appeal of the Defence against the "Decision on victims' applications for participation a/0010/06, a/0064/06 to a/0070/06, a/0081/06, a/0082/06, a/0084/06 to a/0089/06, a/0091/06 to a/0097/06, a/0099/06, a/0100/06, a/0102/06 to a/0104/06, a/0111/06, a/0113/06 to a/0117/06, a/0120/06, a/0121/06 and a/0123/06 to a/0127/06" of PTC II	Appointing the Presiding Judge
27 October 2008	Pre-Trial	Decision on the participation of victims in the appeal	Granting victim procedural status
17 November 2008	Pre-Trial	Decision on victims' applications for participation a/0066/06, a/0067/06, a/0069/06,a/0070/06, a/0083/06, a/0088/06, a/0091/06, a/0092/06, a/0102/06, a/0114/06, a/0115/06,a/0125/06 and a/0126/06	Rejecting victims procedural status and appointing LRV to victims
21 November 2008	Pre-Trial	Decision on victims' applications for participation a/0014/07 to a/0020/07 and a/0076/07 to a/0125/07	Granting victims procedural status
9 February 2009	Pre-Trial	Decision on legal representation of Victims a/0065/06, a/0066/06, a/0068/06,a/0088/06, a/0090/06 to a/0096/06, a/0098/06, a/0102/06, a/0103/06, a/0112/06, a/0115/06,a/0117/06, a/0118/06, a/0120/06 to a/0126/06, a/0076/07 to a/0078/07, a/0081/07,a/0082/07, a/0084/07, a/0085/07, a/0090/07 to a/0103/07, a/105/07 to a/0108/07,a/0112/07, a/0115/07, a/0117/07, a/0118/07 and a/0123/07	Appointing the Principal Counsel in the OPCV as LRV

(continued)

Situation in Uganda			
Date	Stage	Decision	Description
16 February 2009	Appeal	Scheduling Order for the judgment on the appeals of the Defence against the decisions entitled "Decision on victims' applications for participation a/0010/06, a/0064/06 to a/0070/06, a/0081/06, a/0082/06, a/0084/06 to a/0089/06, a/0091/06 to a/0097/06, a/0099/06, a/0100/06, a/0102/06 to a/0104/06, a/0111/06, a/0113/06 to a/0117/06, a/0120/06, a/0121/06 and a/0123/06 to a/0127/06" of PTC II	Scheduling the date for the judgement of the appeals of the Defense
10 March 2009	Pre-Trial	Decision on victims' applications for participation a/0192/07 to a/0194/07, a/0196/07,a/0200/07, a/0204/07, a/0206/07, a/0209/07, a/0212/07, a/0216/07, a/0217/07, a/0219/07 to a/0221/07, a/02228/07 to a/0230/07, a/0234/07, a/0235/07, a/0237/07, a/0324/07 and a/0326/07 under rule 89	Rejecting victims procedural status
23 March 2009	Pre-Trial	Decision Designating a Single Judge on Victims' Issues	Designating a Single Judge on Victims' Issues
9 March 2012	Pre-Trial	Decision on Victim's Participation in Proceedings Related to the Situation in Uganda	Granting victims to participate in accordance with established framework
4 February 2019	Pre-Trial	Decision on the "Notification by the Board of Directors in accordance with Regulation 50(a) of the Regulations of the Trust Fund for Victims of its conclusions to undertake further activities in Uganda"	Deciding to approve the proposed projects and specified activities

6.8.1 *Prosecutor v. Ongwen*

Case: Dominic Ongwen			
Date	Stage	Decision	Description
22 November 2006	Pre-Trial	Decision designating a single judge on victims' issues	Designating a Single Judge responsible for all issues arising in connection with victims' applications for participation
23 March 2009	Pre-Trial	Decision Designating a Single Judge on Victims' Issues	Designating a Single Judge responsible for all issues

(continued)

Case: Dominic Ongwen			
Date	Stage	Decision	Description
4 March 2015	Pre-Trial	Decision Establishing Principles on the Victims' Application Process	Establishing the principles on the victims' application process
15 April 2015	Pre-Trial	Decision on an application by the Uganda Victims Foundation to submit amicus curiae observations	Rejecting the application
29 July 2015	Pre-Trial	Decision on the "Prosecution's Request to be Provided with Unredacted Copies of Victims' Applications Submitted in the Situation in Uganda and the Case of the Prosecutor v. Joseph Kony et al."	Granting the Prosecutor's request
3 September 2015	Pre-Trial	Decision concerning the procedure for admission of victims to participate in the proceedings in the present case	Admitting victims who were not objected by the parties
28 October 2015	Pre-Trial	Order to the Registrar in relation to the legal representation of victims participating in the proceedings	Ordering the Registrar to verify and acknowledge the powers of attorney issued by victims currently admitted to participate in the proceedings
25 November 2015	Pre-Trial	Decision on requests to extend the time limit for observations on the victims' application transmitted on 18 and 19 November 2015	Granting the extension of the time limit
27 November 2015	Pre-Trial	Decision on contested victims' applications for participation, legal representation of victims and their procedural rights	Granting victims procedural status and appointing OPCV as CLRV
15 December 2015	Pre-Trial	Decision on issues concerning victims' participation	Revoking the appointment as common legal representative
24 December 2015	Pre-Trial	Second decision on contested victims' applications for participation and legal representation of victims	Appointing OPCV as CLRV and rejecting victims procedural status
26 May 2016	Trial	Decision on the "Request for a determination concerning legal aid' submitted by the legal representatives of victims"	Rejecting the request
17 June 2016	Trial	Decision on Disclosure of Victims' Identities	Granting the Legal Representative of Victims' Request
17 June 2016	Trial	Decision on Request Concerning Organisation of Victim Representation	Deciding that the participating victim shall have the procedural rights set out in the decision
26 September 2016	Trial	Decision concerning 300 Victim Applications and the Deadline for Submitting Further Applications	Appointing OPCV and granting victims procedural status

(continued)

Case: Dominic Ongwen			
Date	Stage	Decision	Description
4 November 2016	Trial	Decision Concerning 610 Victim Applications (Registry Report ICC-02/04-01/15-544) and 1183 Victim Applications (Registry Report ICC-02/04-01/15-556)	Appointing OPCV and granting victims procedural status
14 November 2016	Trial	Decision on Registry's Request for Clarification on the Issue of Legal Assistance Paid by the Court for the Legal Representatives of Victims	Deciding that no further guidance is warranted
16 December 2016	Trial	Order Concerning Four Victim Applications	Ordering the Registry to file an updated consolidated list of victims admitted to participate in the present case which reflects the information contained in this order
6 July 2017	Trial	Decision on Prosecution's Request to Disclose Lesser redacted Versions of 43 Victims' Applications	Ordering the Registry to file lesser redacted versions of the applications identified in the Request in the case record following the Prosecution's disclosure to the Defence
30 August 2017	Trial	Decision on LRV Request Concerning the Deaths of Participating Victims	Directing parties for resumption
22 December 2017	Trial	Decision on Defence Request for the Identities of Potential Witnesses on the Legal Representatives of Victims' Preliminary Lists of Witnesses	Instructing the CLRV to disclose the name of its four expert witnesses to the Chamber and the parties
26 January 2018	Trial	Decision on Defence Request for Reconsideration of Decision ICC-02/04-01/15-1147 and Objections to Victim Participation	Rejecting the Reconsideration Request
6 March 2018	Trial	Decision on the Legal Representatives for Victims Requests to Present Evidence and Views and Concerns and related requests	Authorising victims to present the views and concerns
26 March 2018	Trial	Decision on the Legal Representative Request for Reconsideration of the Decision on Witnesses to be Called by the Victims Representatives	Rejecting the request
13 April 2018	Trial	Decision on Victims' Application for Protective and Special Measures	Granting the request

(continued)

Case: Dominic Ongwen			
Date	Stage	Decision	Description
31 May 2019	Appeal	Decision on the Victims' request for time extension	Extending the time limit for filing of further submissions
4 November 2019	Trial	Decision on Legal Representatives of Victims Request to Present Views and Concerns in Person	Rejecting the request to present views and concerns

6.8.2 *Prosecutor v. Kony*

Case: Joseph Kony			
Date	Stage	Decision	Description
22 November 2006	Pre-Trial	Decision designating a Single Judge on Victims' issues	Appointing a Single Judge
20 February 2007	Pre-Trial	Decision on Prosecutor's "Application to lift redactions from applications for Victims' Participation to be provided to the OTP" and on the Prosecution's further submissions supplementing such Application, and request for extension of time	Rejecting the requests
9 March 2007	Pre-Trial	Decision on the "Prosecution's Request for Leave to Appeal the Decision Denying the 'Application to Lift Redactions From Applications for Victims' Participation to be Provided to the OTP'"	Rejecting the request for Leave to Appeal
16 March 2007	Pre-Trial	Decision on the OPCV's 'Request to access documents and material'	Deciding to make the transcripts of the hearing public to some extent
4 April 2007	Pre-Trial	Decision on the Prosecution's Applications dated 22 March 2007 and on the OPCV's Requests dated 29 March 2007	Dismissing the Prosecution's Applications
16 April 2007	Pre-Trial	Decision on the OPCV's observations on victims' applications and on the Prosecution's objections thereto	Dismissing the OPCV's Observations as inadmissible
12 July 2007	Pre-Trial	Order to the Prosecutor and the Victims and Witnesses Unit to submit observations on the unsealing of certain documents in the record both of the situation and of the case	Ordering the Prosecutor to submit a proposal detailing the treatment of a number of documents filed in the record of the situation and of the case

(continued)

Case: Joseph Kony			
Date	Stage	Decision	Description
11 August 2007	Pre-Trial	Decision on victims' applications for participation a/0010/06, a/0064/06 to a/0070/06, a/0081/06 to a/0104/06 and a/0111/06 to a/0127/06	Granting victims procedural status
3 September 2007	Pre-Trial	Decision Designating a Single Judge on Victim's Issues for the Period of 6 September to 15 October 2007	Designating a Single Judge
15 February 2008	Pre-Trial	Decision on legal representation of Victims a/0090/06, a/0098/06, a/0101/06a/0112/06, a/0118/06, a/0119/06 and a/0122/06	Appointing LRVs
14 March 2008	Pre-Trial	Decision on victims' applications for participation a/0010/06, a/0064/06 to a/0070/06,a/0081/06, a/0082/06, a/0084/06 to a/0089/06, a/0091/06 to a/0097/06, a/0099/06,a/0100/06, a/0102/06 to a/0104/06, a/0111/06, a/0113/06 to a/0117/06, a/0120/06,a/0121/06 and a/0123/06 to a/0127/06	Granting victims procedural status
2 June 2008	Pre-Trial	Decision on the Defence Application for Leave to Appeal the 14 March 2008 Decision on Victims' Applications for Participation	Granting in part the Defence Leave to Appeal
19 June 2008	Appeal	Decision on the Presiding Judge of the Appeals Chamber in the appeal of the Defence against the "Decision on victims' applications for participation a/0010/06, a/0064/06 to a/0070/06, a/0081/06, a/0082/06, a/0084/06 to a/0089/06, a/0091/06 to a/0097/06, a/0099/06, a/0100/06, a/0102/06 to a/0104/06, a/0111/06, a/0113/06 to a/0117/06, a/0120/06, a/0121/06 and a/0123/06 to a/0127/06" of PTC II	Appointing the Presiding Judge
22 July 2008	Appeal	Order on the filing of responses by the Prosecutor and the ad hoc Counsel for the Defence to the request of victims a/0090/06, a/0098/06, a/0112/06, a/0118/06, a/0119/06 and a/0122/06 for participation in the appeal	Ordering the Prosecution and the ad hoc Counsel for the Defence to respond to the application for participation

(continued)

Case: Joseph Kony			
Date	Stage	Decision	Description
4 September 2008	Appeal	Decision on the Presiding Judge of the Appeals Chamber in the appeal of the Defence against the "Decision on victims' applications for participation a/0010/06, a/0064/06 to a/0070/06, a/0081/06, a/0082/06, a/0084/06 to a/0089/06, a/0091/06 to a/0097/06, a/0099/06, a/0100/06, a/0102/06 to a/0104/06, a/0111/06, a/0113/06 to a/0117/06, a/0120/06, a/0121/06 and a/0123/06 to a/0127/06" of PTC II	Appointing the Presiding Judge
23 October 2008	Pre-Trial	Decision on the request by the Office of Public Counsel for Victims dated 21 October 2008	Rejecting the OPCV's request
28 October 2008	Appeal	Decision on the participation of victims in the appeal	Grantng victims procedural status
11 November 2008	Pre-Trial	Decision on request by the Office of Public Counsel for Victims for extension of time limit in proceedings under article 19(1)	Rejecting the request
9 February 2009	Pre-Trial	Decision on legal representation of Victims a/0065/06, a/0066/06, a/0068/06, a/0088/06, a/0090/06 to a/0096/06, a/0098/06, a/0102/06, a/0103/06, a/0112/06, a/0115/06, a/0117/06, a/0118/06, a/0120/06 to a/0126/06, a/0076/07 to a/0078/07, a/0081/07, a/0082/07, a/0084/07, a/0085/07, a/0090/07 to a/0103/07, a/105/07 to a/0108/07, a/0112/07, a/0115/07, a/0117/07, a/0118/07 and a/0123/07	Appointing Legal Representative of Victims
13 February 2009	Appeal	Scheduling Order for the judgment on the appeals of the Defence against the decisions entitled "Decision on victims' applications for participation a/0010/06, a/0064/06 to a/0070/06, a/0081/06, a/0082/06, a/0084/06 to a/0089/06, a/0091/06 to a/0097/06, a/0099/06, a/0100/06, a/0102/06 to a/0104/06, a/0111/06, a/0113/06 to a/0117/06, a/0120/06, a/0121/06 and a/0123/06 to a/0127/06" of PTC II	Scheduling the date of the judgement in the appeal

(continued)

Case: Joseph Kony

Date	Stage	Decision	Description
25 February 2009	Appeal	Judgment on the appeals of the Defence against the decisions entitled "Decision on victims' applications for participation a/0010/06, a/0064/06 to a/0070/06, a/0081/06, a/0082/06, a/0084/06 to a/0089/06, a/0091/06 to a/0097/06, a/0099/06, a/0100/06, a/0102/06 to a/0104/06, a/0111/06, a/0113/06 to a/0117/06, a/0120/06, a/0121/06 and a/0123/06 to a/0127/06" of PTC II	The decisions recognising the applicants as victims are confirmed
10 March 2009	Pre-Trial	Decision on victims' applications for participation a/0192/07 to a/0194/07, a/0196/07,a/0200/07, a/0204/07, a/0206/07, a/0209/07, a/0212/07, a/0216/07, a/0217/07, a/0219/07 toa/0221/07, a/02228/07 to a/0230/07, a/0234/07, a/0235/07, a/0237/07, a/0324/07 and a/0326/07 under rule 89	Rejecting applicants as victims
23 March 2009	Pre-Trial	Decision Designating a Single Judge on Victims' Issues	Designating a Single Judge

Judgments and Decisions

- ECCC, *Case of Kamg Guek Eav (Case 001),* 001118-07-2007/ECCC/TC, Decision of the Trial Chamber Concerning Proof of Identity for Civil Party Applications (26 February 2009).
- ECCC, *Case of Kamg Guek Eav (Case 001),* 001/18-07-2007/ECCCffC, Decision on Motion Regarding Deceased Civil Party, E2/5/3 (13 March 2009).
- ECCC, *Case of Kamg Guek Eav (Case 001),* 001/18-07-2007/ECCC/TC, Judgment (26 July 2010).
- ECCC, *Case of Nuon Chea (Case 002),* 002119-09-2007-ECCC-OCIJ, Order On Admissibility of Civil Party Applicants From Current Residents Of Kratie Province (9 September 2010).
- ECCC, *Case of Kamg Guek Eav (Case 001),* 001/18-07-2007-ECCC/SC, Appeal Judgment, Supreme Court Chamber (3 February 2012).
- ECCC, *Case of Kamg Guek Eav (Case 001),* 001/18-07-2007-ECCC/SC, Appeal Judgement (3 February 2012).
- ECCC, *Case of Nuon Chea, Khieu Samphan (Case 002/01),* 002/19-09-2007/ECCC/TC, Judgment (7 August 2014).
- ECCC, *Case of Nuon Chea, Khieu Samphan (Case 002/02),* 002/19-09-2007/ECCC/TC, Summary of Judgment (16 November 2018).
- ECHR, *De Wilde, Ooms and Versyp v. Belgium,* 2832/66 2835/66 2899/66, Decision (Article 50) (10 March 1972).
- ECHR, *Klass and Others v. Germany,* 5029/71, Judgment (6 September 1978).
- ECHR, *Marckx v. Belgium,* 6833/74, Judgment (13 June 1979).
- ECHR, *Guzzardi v. Italy,* 7367/76, Judgment (6 November 1980).
- ECHR, *Sunday Times v. the United Kingdom,* 6538/74, Judgment (6 November 1989).
- ECHR, *Vijayanathan and Pusparajah v. France,* 17550/90 17825/91, Judgment (27 August 1992).
- ECHR, *Open Door and Dublin Well Woman v. Ireland,* 14234/88 14235/88, Judgement (29 October 1992).

© The Author(s), under exclusive license to Springer Nature Switzerland AG 2021

C. Safferling, G. Petrossian, *Victims Before the International Criminal Court*,
https://doi.org/10.1007/978-3-030-80177-9

- ECHR, *Van Geyseghem v. Belgium,* 26103/95, Judgment (21 January 1999).
- ECHR, *Selmouni v. France,* 25803/94, Judgment (28 July 1999).
- ECHR, *Lustig-Prean and Beckett v. the United Kingdom,* 31417/96 32377/96, Judgment (27 December 1999).
- ECHR, *Podkolzina v. Latvia,* 46726/99, Judgment (9 July 2002).
- ECHR, *Aktaş V. Turkey,* 24351/94, Judgment (24 April 2003).
- ECHR, *Ayder and Others v. Turkey,* 23656/94, Judgment (8 January 2004).
- ECHR, *Dizman v. Turkey,* 27309/95, Judgment (20 September 2005).
- ECHR, *Kadikis v. Latvia,* 62393/00, Judgment (4 August 2006).
- ECHR, *Nikolova and Verlichkova v. Bulgaria,* 7888/03, Judgment (20 December 2007).
- ECHR, *Burden v. U.K.* GC, Judgment (29 April 2008).
- ECHR, *Butolen v. Slovenia,* 41356/08, Judgement (9 January 2009).
- ECHR, *Andrejeva v. Latvia,* 55707/00, Judgment (18 February 2009).
- ECHR, *Ernewein v. Germany,* 14849/08, Decision (12 May 2009).
- ECHR, *Tanase v. Moldova,* 7/08, GC, Judgment (27 April 2010).
- ECHR, *Shesti Mai Engineering OOD and Others v. Bulgaria,* 17854/04, Judgment (20 September 2011).
- ECHR, *Remetin v. Croatia (2),* 7446/12, Judgement (24 July 2014).
- ECHR, *M.S. v. Croatia 2,* 75450/12, Judgment (19 February 2015).
- ECJ, *Ian William Cowan v Trésor public,* Case 186/87, Judgment (2 February 1989).
- ECJ, *Emil Eredics and Mária Vassné Sápi,* Case C-205/09, Judgment (21 October 2010).
- IACHR, *Velásquez-Rodríguez v. Guatemala,* Judgment, Merits (29 July 1988).
- IACHR, *Godínez Cruz v. Honduras,* Judgment, Compensatory Damages (20 January 1989).
- IACHR, *Aloeboetoe et al. v. Suriname,* Judgment (10 September 1993).
- IACHR, *El Amparo v. Venezuela,* Judgment, Reparation and Costs (14 September 1996).
- IACHR, *Neira Alegria v. Peru,* Judgment, Reparations (19 September 1996).
- IACHR, *Case of Garrido and Baigoma v Argentina,* Judgement (27 August 1998).
- IACHR, *Castillo-Páezv.Peru,* Judgement, Reparation and Costs (27 November 1998).
- IACHR, *Loayza Tamayo v. Peru,* Judgment, Reparations and Costs (27 November 1998).
- IACHR, *Ivcher-Bronstein v. Peru,* Judgment (6 February 2001).
- IACHR, *Villagrán Morales et al. v. Guatemala,* Judgment (26 May 2001).
- IACHR, *Cantoral-Benavides v. Peru,* Judgment, Reparation and Costs (3 December 2001).
- IACHR, *Durand and Ugarte v. Peru,* Judgment, Reparation and Costs (3 December 2001).
- IACHR, *Bámaca-Velásquez v. Guatemala,* Judgment, Reparation and Costs (22 February 2002).

- IACHR, *Myrna Mack Chang v. Guatemala,* Judgment (25 November 2003).
- IACHR, *Merchants v. Colombia,* Judgment, Reparation (5 July 2004).
- IACHR, *Gomez-Paquiyauri Brothers v. Peru,* Judgment (8 July 2004).
- IACHR, *Case of Plan de Sánchez Massacre,* Judgment, Reparations (19 November 2004).
- IACHR, *Plan de Sánchez Massacre v. Guatemala,* Judgment, Reparation (19 November 2004).
- IACHR, *Case of the Moiwana Community,* Judgment (15 June 2005).
- IACHR, *Indigenous Community Yakye Axa v. Paraguay,* Judgment (17 June 2005).
- IACHR, *Case of the "Mapiripán Massacre" v. Colombia,* Judgment (15 September 2005).
- IACHR, *Pueblo Bello v. Colombia,* Judgment (31 January 2006).
- IACHR, *Heliodoro Portugal v. Panama,* Judgment (12 August 2008).
- IACHR, *Radilla-Pacheco v. Mexico,* Judgment, Merits, Reparation and Costs (23 November 2009).
- IACHR, *Salvador Chiriboga v. Ecuador,* Judgment, Reparation and Costs (3 March 2011).
- IACHR, *Caracazo v. Venezuela,* Judgment, Reparations and Costs (29 August 2002).
- IACoHR, *Mevopal S.A. v. Argentina,* Report 39/99 (11 March 1999).
- IACoHR, *Bendeck-Cohdinsa v. Honduras,* Report N 106/99 (27 September 1999).
- IACoHR, *Janet Espinoza Feria et al. v. Peru,* Annual Report (10 October 2002).
- IACoHR, *Metropolitan Nature Reserve v. Panama,* Report 88/03 (22 October 2003).
- ICJ, *Certain German Interests in Polish Upper Silesia Case (*1926).
- ICJ, *Treatment of Polish Nationals and other Persons of Polish Origins in the Danzig Territory Case (*1932).
- ICJ, *Phosphates in Marocco Case (*1938).
- ICJ, *Corfu Channel Case Great Britain and Northern Ireland v. Albania,* Judgment (9 April 1949).
- ICJ, *Barcelona Traction Case,* Judgment (5 February 1970).
- ICJ, *U.S.A. v. Iran, Case concerning U.S. Diplomatic and Consular Staff in Teheran,* Judgement (24 May 1980).
- ICJ, *Nicaragua v. U.S.A. Case concerning Military and Paramilitary Activities in and against Nicaragua,* Judgment (27 June 1986).
- ICJ, *Portugal vs. Australia, Case Concerning East Timor,* Judgment (30 June 1995).
- ICJ, *Hungary/Slovakia, Case concerning the Gabcikovo-Nagymaros Project,* Judgment (25 September, 1997).
- ICJ, *LeGrand Brothers Case,* Judgment (27 June 2001).
- ICJ, *Case Concerning Armed Activities on The Territory Of The Congo (Democratic Republic Of The Congo v. Uganda),* Judgment (19 December 2005).

- ICJ, *Bosnia and Herzogowina v. Yugoslavia (Serbia and Montenegro) Application for Revision,* Judgment (26 February 2007).
- ICTR, *Prosecutor v. Akayesu,* ICTR-96-4, Judgment (2 September 1998).
- ICTR, *Prosecutor v. Kayishema and Ruzindana,* ICTR-95-1, Judgment (21 May 1999).
- ICTR, *Prosecutor v. Rutanganda,* ICTR-96-3, Judgment (6 December 1999).
- ICTR, *Prosecutor v. Musema,* ICTR-96-13-T, Judgement and Sentence (27 January 2000).
- ICTR, *Prosecutor v. Semanza,* ICTR-97-20-T, Judgment (15 May 2003).
- ICTR, *Prosecutor v. Niyitegeka,* ICTR-96-14, Judgment (16 May 2003).
- ICTR, *Prosecutor v. Kajelijeli,* ICTR-98-44A, Judgment (1 December 2003).
- ICTR, *Prosecutor v. Niyitegeka,* ICTR-96-14, Appeal Judgment (9 July 2004).
- ICTR, *Prosecutor v. Niyitegeka,* ICTR-96-14, Appeal Judgement (9 July 2004).
- ICTR, *Prosecutor v. Baglishema,* ICTR-95-lA-T, Judgment (7 June 2001).
- ICTY, *Prosecutor v. Msksic, Radic, Sljivancanin,* IT-95-13/1, Review of the Indictment Pursuant to Rule 61 of the Rules of Procedure and Evidence (3 April 1996).
- ICTY, *Prosecutor v. Tadic,* IT-94-1, Appeal Judgment (15 July 1999).
- ICTY, *Prosecutor v. Jelisić,* IT-95-10, Appeals Judgement (14 December 1999).
- ICTY, *Prosecutor v. Blaskic,* IT-95-14, Judgement (3 March 2000).
- ICTY, *Prosecutor v. Kordic and Cerkez,* IT-95-14/2-T, Judgment (26 February 2001).
- ICTY, *Prosecutor v. Kunarac et al,* IT-96-23 & 23/1, Appeal Judgement (12 June 2002).
- ICTY, *Prosecutor v. Vasiljevic,* IT-98-32, Judgement (29 November 2002).
- ICTY, *Prosecutor v. Stakić,* IT-97-24, Judgement (31 July 2003).
- ICTY, *Prosecutor v. Krstić,* IT-98-33-A, Appeal Judgment (19 April 2004).
- ICTY, *Prosecutor v Brđanin,* IT-99-36, Judgment (1 September 2004).
- ICTY, *Prosecutor v. Kordic and Cerkez,* IT-95-14/2-T, Appeal Judgment (26 January 2005).
- ICTY, *Prosecutor v. Strugar,* IT-01-42-T, Judgement (31 January 2005).
- US Supreme Court, *Ex Parte Milburn,* 34 U.S. (9 Pet.) 704 (1835).
- US Supreme Court, *Duncan v. Louisiana,* 391 U.S. 145 (1968).
- US Supreme Court, *Linda R.S. v. Richard,* D. 410 U.S. 614 (1973).
- US Supreme Court, *Booth v. Maryland,* 107 US 2529 (1987).
- US Supreme Court, *Caroline v. Gathers,* 490 US 805 (1989).
- US Supreme Court, *Hughey v. U.S.,* 495 U.S. 411 (1990).
- US Supreme Court, *Payne v. Tennessee,* 501 SC 808 (1991).
- US Supreme Court, *Littlefield v. Williams,* 540 S.E. 2d 81 (2000).

The manufacturer's authorised representative in the EU is Springer Nature Customer Service Centre GmbH, Europaplatz 3, 69115 Heidelberg, Germany. If you have any concerns regarding our products, please contact ProductSafety@springernature.com

Printed and bound by CPI Group (UK) Ltd, Croydon, CR0 4YY
30/09/2026
02225704-0012